PAPER EMPERORS

SALLY YOUNG is professor of political science at the University of Melbourne. She is the author of four previous books on Australian media and politics, including works on political journalism (*How Australia Decides*, 2011), press photography (*Shooting the Picture*, with Fay Anderson, 2016) and political advertising (*The Persuaders*, 2004).

To Jay, Abi and Megan.
Like the very best newspapers, you illuminate,
entertain and inspire me every day.

And with my love and thanks to Kathy, Harold, Frances and Joe.

PAPER EMPERORS

THE RISE OF AUSTRALIA'S NEWSPAPER EMPIRES

SALLY YOUNG

UNSW PRESS

A UNSW Press book

Published by
NewSouth Publishing
University of New South Wales Press Ltd
University of New South Wales
Sydney NSW 2052
AUSTRALIA
newsouthpublishing.com

ISBN   9781742234984 (paperback)
           9781742244471 (ebook)
           9781742248936 (ePDF)

A catalogue record for this book is available from the National Library of Australia

Design Josephine Pajor-Markus
Cover design Hugh Ford
Cover images News stand in a railway station showing billboards publicising the opening of Parliament House in Canberra and an advertisement for Lustre Silktex stockings, Melbourne, 1927. National Library of Australia

Australian Government
Australian Research Council

This research was supported under the Australian Research Council's Future Fellowship scheme (project number FT130100315). A Future Fellowships Establishment Grant and a Faculty of Arts Publication Subsidy Scheme were provided by the University of Melbourne.

CONTENTS

List of figures   vii

List of tables   x

Acknowledgments   xi

Abbreviations   xiv

Introduction   1

PART ONE: THE FOUNDATIONS   **9**

1   The first days of the Australian 'fourth estate'   10

2   The rise of newspapers   51

3   The age of press empire building   87

PART TWO: THE OWNERS   **127**

4   Hugh Denison: Australia's first newspaper emperor   128

5   'Who owns the owners of the *Herald*?': The kingdom of Collins House   170

6   The real story of the birth of News Limited   209

7   Keith Murdoch: Journalist, kingmaker, empire builder, puppet?   240

8   Keith Murdoch: Newspaper owner   278

9   'Never trust Sydney newspaper proprietors'   311

PART THREE: THE BATTLES   **353**

10   The press, Joe Lyons and the Depression   354

11   A friend in office and a falling out   380

12   Capturing the airwaves: Newspapers, radio
      and the ABC   406

13   Emperors of air   432

14   Paper and cable cartels   453

15   'Killing me': Menzies and the press   494

16   Menzies' downfall   517

Postscript   542

Appendix: Biographies of key newspapers   545

Notes   554

Bibliography   601

Index   621

LIST OF FIGURES

1.1   The *Australian* protests Governor Darling's changes to libel laws, 1830   17

1.2   Reading rooms like this one, at the Ballarat Mechanics' Institute, 1881, encouraged the habit of reading newspapers; note the two women at the back of the room (in the 'Ladies only' section) reading newspapers   24

1.3   The *Sydney Morning Herald* occupied this prominent site at the apex of Hunter, Pitt and O'Connell streets in Sydney from 1856 to 1956; this was its first building on the site, a three-storey stone building constructed in 1856, shown here in 1870   28

1.4   The *Worker*'s representation of the ghoulish 'capitalistic press' sheltering a monstrous, blood-thirsty mine owner, 1905   47

2.1   The front pages of the Sydney *Sun* and the *Sydney Morning Herald* at the outbreak of World War I, 1914   58–59

2.2   A fleet of *Herald* newspaper delivery vehicles lined up in Russell Street outside the old Herald and Weekly Times building, corner of Flinders Street, Melbourne, circa 1915–20   62

2.3   State Governor Sir Reginald Talbot turns the switch to convert the gas engine rotary press to electricity in the machine room of the Herald and Weekly Times building, 1901   66–67

3.1   The flapper *Daily Guardian* scandalises the respectable and staid Sydney newspapers   96–97

3.2   The *Sydney Morning Herald*'s new building, constructed between 1922 and 1929 on its Hunter Street site, shown circa 1930   100

3.3   The powerful men of the newspaper industry at the Australian Newspapers' Conference dinner in 1932   107

4.1   Hugh Denison as a younger and older man   131

4.2   The first edition of the ground-breaking, and much imitated, *Sun News-Pictorial*, 11 September 1922   141

4.3   The exterior and interior of the *Sun*'s Elizabeth Street building in Sydney, with its famous roof-top globe, 1929; today, the building houses shops on the ground floor and the globe is painted grey, but it is still visible looking up from the corner of Martin Place   148–49

4.4   The 'greatest duel in newspaper history' according to *Newspaper News*' dramatic report of the 12 June 1931 shareholders' meeting   156

5.1   The man behind the *Herald*: Australia's most powerful industrialist, William Lawrence Baillieu, circa 1909–11   174

5.2   Theodore Fink, circa 1939; he was a director of the HWT from 1889 to 1942, and chair of its board from 1906 to 1942   174

5.3   The famous Collins House, 360 Collins Street, Melbourne, circa 1918   191

6.1   James Edward Davidson, managing director and editor-in-chief of the *News* with his original staff, circa 1923; Davidson is seated at the centre of the front row   212–13

7.1   Australia's most powerful newspaper executive, Sir Keith Murdoch, 1936   243

7.2   The *Herald*'s sensational coverage of the trial of Colin Ross shares the front page with reports of a boxing match, 1922   255

7.3   The 'Colin Ross Memorial'; the *Herald*'s grand new building, corner of Flinders and Exhibition streets, Melbourne, 1925   264

8.1   A rare photograph of the publicity-shy John Wren, showing a photographer pursuing him outside the City Court, Melbourne, 1950 295

9.1   The dreamy aristocrat and custodian of the *Sydney Morning Herald*, Warwick Oswald Fairfax, circa 1941 317

9.2   The 'brains' behind Fairfax & Sons, RAG Henderson, in his early seventies, outside his home in Point Piper, Sydney 323

9.3   Frank Packer's beloved mother, Ethel Maud Packer, and his mentor and partner, EG Theodore, start the presses for the launch of the *Sunday Telegraph* in 1939 346

9.4   Advertisement for the 'young feller' *Sunday Telegraph* in the industry publication *Newspaper News*, 1940 348

10.1   *Smith's Weekly* cartoonist, Stan Cross, shows Keith Murdoch manipulating Lyons and other ministers over radio station ownership limits in 1935 357

10.2   How the commercial dailies represented EG Theodore's economic policies, 1931 365

12.1   A family in their living room listen to a radio broadcast in New South Wales circa 1930; note that the newspaper is still prominent and has not been usurped 420

14.1   Imported newsprint reels are loaded onto the presses at the Sydney *Sun*, circa 1930 456

14.2   The complicated race to make newsprint in Australia, 1920s to 1941 464–65

14.3   Australian Newsprint Mills, Boyer, Tasmania, circa 1950s 480

15.1   RG Menzies with Otto Olsen, the Canberra representative for the *Sun*, 1939 510

16.1   The first edition of the *Sun*'s worst nightmare, the *Daily Mirror*, 12 May 1941 530

16.2   *Truth* lampoons Frank Packer's military service, 1941 533

LIST OF TABLES

2.1 The modernisation of Australian newspapers: News on the front page 53

2.2 Penny newspapers in Australia 72

2.3 The shrinking newspaper: From broadsheet to tabloid 83

3.1 The partisan preferences of major newspapers, 1922–1943 118–19

3.2 The partisan preferences of major newspapers, 1946–1969 122–23

13.1 Regulations for B-class radio station ownership limits, 1935 437

13.2 Newspaper ownership of radio stations under the Lyons government, 1932–39 450

ACKNOWLEDGMENTS

Over several years, five wonderful research assistants helped with different aspects of the research for this book – Maria Rae, Amanda McKittrick, Jessica Megarry, Rodney Kirkpatrick and Tom Roberts. I am very grateful for their excellent work. Maria Rae found material and summarised the secondary literature in a very helpful way that kick-started the project. Amanda McKittrick and Jessica Megarry patiently collected election editorials from newspapers. Rodney Kirkpatrick gave me the benefit of his incredible knowledge of newspaper history, including by reading and commenting upon drafts of all chapters, and also made valuable editorial suggestions. Tom Roberts read the two main chapters on Keith Murdoch and generously shared his knowledge of 'KM'. In addition, James Curran kindly read the first chapter and provided information on British newspaper history. Any errors or omissions that remain in the book despite all of this excellent support are my responsibility alone.

I also wish to thank Phillipa McGuinness at UNSW Press/ NewSouth Publishing for her unflagging enthusiasm and patience, even as this project became larger than expected, Emma Hutchinson and Fiona Sim for their project and editorial support, and an anonymous reviewer who provided important feedback and suggestions.

This book could not have been written without the incredible TROVE digitised newspaper service from the National Library of Australia (NLA). Both are national treasures. The *Australian Dictionary of Biography* was another crucial resource. I have drawn information and inspiration from the work of pioneers in Australian newspaper and media history, as indicated in the bibliography. The largest gap in scholarship and primary material in Australian newspapers relates to the Herald and Weekly Times (HWT) – arguably the most important media company in our history. I sought access to the HWT's records, but permission was not granted. It is regrettable that an organisation that writes the first draft of history is not more open to later drafts, and I hope this might be rectified in the future. In the meantime, RM Younger's unpublished manuscript, and private correspondence in archives, tells part of the company's story.

Many people helped me in one way or another for this book, including providing information, source material, or relating their experiences in interviews, and I wish to thank: John Bednall, Eric Beecher, Margaret Boothman (ASIC), Carl Bridge, Moss Cass, Stan Correy, James Curran, John Dahlsen, William L (Bill) Denison, David Dunstan, Geoff Gallop, Peter Gardener, Dorothy Gollner, Murray Goot, Bridget Griffen-Foley, Peter Kennedy, Stuart Macintyre, Robyn McClelland (Clerk Assistant (Committees), House of Representatives), Ranald Macdonald, Andrew Male, Patrick Martin (Port Pirie *Recorder*), Nicholas Miller (State Records of South Australia), Lyndon Moore, National Library of Australia Manuscripts and Oral History staff, Joan Newman, Janette Pelosi (State Records Authority of NSW), Natasha Petrovic (Office of the Clerk Assistant, Department of the House of Representatives), Chris Read (State Library of South Australia), Debra Reeves (Parliamentary Library, Parliament of Victoria), Tom Reynolds (State Records Office of Western Australia), Beryl Schahinger (South Australian Genealogy & Heraldry Society Inc.), Gavin Souter, Shannon Sutton (National Library of Australia), Julie Sweeten (Mitchell Library), Rodney Tiffen, Edward Vesterberg (State Library of NSW), Georgina Ward (University of Melbourne Archives), Peter Yule and others who wished to remain anonymous.

Estimates of historical currency into present day equivalents were calculated using the website 'Measuring Worth': https://www.measuringworth.com/australiacompare/.

ABBREVIATIONS

AANA	Australian Association of National Advertisers
AAP	Australian Associated Press
ABC	Australian Broadcasting Commission
ACP	Australian Consolidated Press
AIF	Australian Imperial Force
AIS	Australian Iron and Steel Ltd
AMP	Australian Mutual Provident Society
ANA	Australian Natives Association
ANC	Australian Newspapers' Conference (not to be confused with the later Australian Newspapers Council, which is not abbreviated in this book to distinguish between them)
ANM	Australian Newsprint Mills Ltd
ANPA	Australian Newspaper Proprietors' Association
ANPA (US)	American Newspaper Publishers Association
AP	Associated Press (US)
APA	Australian Press Association (also known as the United Cable Association)
APM	Australian Paper Manufacturers
APPM	Associated Pulp and Paper Mills Ltd
AWA	Amalgamated Wireless (Australasia) Ltd
AWU	Australian Workers' Union
AZ	Amalgamated Zinc (De Bavay's) Ltd
BACAL	British Australian Cotton Association Ltd
BALM	British Australian Lead Manufacturers Ltd

BBC	British Broadcasting Corporation (originally called the British Broadcasting Company until 1 January 1927)
BHAS	Broken Hill Associated Smelters Pty Ltd
BHP	Broken Hill Proprietary Ltd
CSIR	Council for Scientific and Industrial Research
CSIRO	Commonwealth Scientific and Industrial Research Organisation
CSR	Colonial Sugar Refining Company
CUB	Carlton and United Breweries Ltd
ES&A	English, Scottish & Australian Bank Ltd
EZ	Electrolytic Zinc Co. of Australia Ltd
FCC	Federal Communications Commission (US)
HWT	Herald and Weekly Times Ltd
ICI	Imperial Chemical Industries of Australia Ltd
MP	Member of Parliament
NAB	National Australia Bank
NMLA	National Mutual Life Association of Australasia
PIEU	Printing Industry Employees Union
PMG	the Postmaster-General's Department
UAP	United Australia Party
UCS	United Cable Service (it had many aliases and was also known as the Australian Newspapers Cable Service, the United Service, and the *Sun-Herald* Cable Service)
UP	United Press (US) (in 1958, it became United Press International (UPI))
WAN	West Australian Newspapers Limited
WIU	Workers Industrial Union
WMC	Western Mining Corporation

INTRODUCTION

Newspapers have found it very difficult to tell the truth about themselves. David Bowman, the former editor of two Australian newspapers, observed that 'Newspapers will expose many things but seldom each other'.[1] Academic scholar James Carey noted along similar lines that: 'The newspaper does not, perhaps it cannot, turn upon itself the factual scrutiny, the critical acumen, the descriptive language, that it regularly devotes to other institutions'.[2] Media economist Robert G Picard also pointed out that 'journalists have never covered their own industry with the same interest and vigor that they have covered other industries'.[3]

For a journalist to criticise their own proprietor, or apply the techniques of investigative journalism to their owner's business affairs, is still a career-limiting move today. But the phenomenon is broader than that. An evocative phrase in a letter captures the approach of 'respectable' newspapers (some of the wilder Sydney papers were exceptions). The letter was written in 1945, by John Butters, the chair of Associated Newspapers Ltd (publisher of the Sydney *Sun* newspaper), to the general manager of the HWT. Butters complained that the HWT's newspapers – the *Herald* and the *Sun News-Pictorial* – had been reporting on his whereabouts. In the past, he said, the HWT's papers had 'been good enough not to mention my arrival in or departure from Melbourne', but 'something slipped on the occasion of my last visit ... and my presence was mentioned'. Butters asked, 'On the general principle that "dog does not eat dog"', '[w]ould you be so kind as to have a word with the two Editors and ask them if they would let me off?'[4]

Although Butters was from a separate media company, the HWT directed its reporters to never mention his Melbourne visits, and this was even written into the company's all-important style guide (that reporters had to follow and which usually focused on matters of spelling and writing style).[5] It is impossible to imagine that an ordinary citizen would have such success if they asked a newspaper to respect their privacy.

Because newspapers have done such a poor job at reporting on themselves ('dog does not eat dog'), there is a big gap in our knowledge about who owned newspapers and why. Publicly, newspapers were usually silent about the machinations of their owners, while privately, some newspaper owners were prone to overestimate their influence. Lord Northcliffe, the pioneer of popular newspapers in the United Kingdom, and a mentor to Keith Murdoch, once said that his newspapers were so powerful 'we can cause the whole country to think with us overnight whenever we say the word'.[6] That was obviously an exaggeration, but one of the more interesting aspects of press power is how widely assumed it was, and especially within the political class. In Australia, this was not an uninformed view. An unusually high number of national leaders had experience of how press power worked from the inside. Among the prime ministers who had worked for, or been an owner or part owner of, a newspaper, were Alfred Deakin, Chris Watson, Andrew Fisher, Billy Hughes, Joe Lyons (very briefly), John Curtin and Ben Chifley.

Politicians were keenly aware that, even if newspaper industry dogs did not eat each other, they *did* regularly bite their political opponents, and there was a long history of anxiety about that. Napoleon Bonaparte once said he feared 'four hostile newspapers' more 'than a thousand bayonets'. It was even worse for politicians who had to contest elections and were constantly fearful about the consequences of negative publicity. In the United States, a well-known political saying (often wrongly attributed to Mark Twain) warned: 'Never pick a fight with those who buy ink by the barrel'. Australian politicians had more to fear than most in this regard, because Australia's press proprietors were unusually powerful. In no other western democracy did such a small number of newspaper owners build up such dominant media companies.[7]

Only a few maverick politicians dared to pick a fight with Australia's powerful press barons. Archdale Parkhill and Eric Harrison were two, and both feature in this book. Later, there was Arthur Calwell, Moss Cass and Stephen Conroy. But this was unusual behaviour. Most politicians instead viewed self-preservation and the good will of the press as synonymous. Robert Menzies summed up this mindset in the mid-1930s when the future prime minister was then the attorney-general. By then, it was obvious that the country's largest and most powerful newspaper groups were also becoming dominant in radio broadcasting. Menzies was asked in private if his government was ever going to do something to curtail them. He replied frankly: 'We haven't the guts'.[8]

This book charts the rise of the most powerful newspaper empires in Australia up to 1941, the five companies that had the power to truly frighten Australian politicians:

Associated Newspapers was the first, and most promising, newspaper empire. It did not last long, so it has now been largely forgotten, but this needs to be remedied because its story is one of the most dramatic accounts of industry ambition, overreach and betrayal.

The **Herald and Weekly Times (HWT)** was a giant. It grew so large and powerful under Keith Murdoch's hand that it became the undisputed media titan of the period. The story of Australian newspapers cannot be told without significant reference to the HWT, a pioneer in popular journalism and newspaper empire building.

John Fairfax & Sons (also called John Fairfax Ltd during the 20th century) is the oldest group, but a late blooming empire. It remained essentially a single daily newspaper company – focused on the *Sydney Morning Herald* – until the early 1950s, then it embarked upon a frenzy of acquisitions that saw its share of the Australian newspaper market double.[9] By 1941, the point at which this book ends, Fairfax & Sons was beginning to flex its political and industrial muscle.

News Limited (later known as News Corporation) – whose secret origins are disclosed in this book – was the surprise story of the 20th century. Founded in the early 1920s, it moved from hidden backers and Depression-era difficulties, to being propped up by Keith Murdoch in the 1930s. It was the key piece of his son's inheritance in the 1950s. Rupert Murdoch then gradually built News Limited into a global media empire, and expanded the Australian section by taking over the mighty HWT in 1987.

Consolidated Press was the outsider. A lesser player in newspapers compared to several of the other groups, but a vocal one that could not be ignored. It began as a publishing company and developed a wildly successful women's newspaper (that became a magazine, the *Australian Women's Weekly*), and also owned the Sydney *Daily Telegraph* (from 1936 to 1972). In 1941, it was beginning to play politics more ruthlessly but its real power and profits would come later, when it entered television in the mid-1950s.

Originally, the power of these empires was built upon an object – the printed newspaper – that is now in its twilight years, but in its heyday, was considered exciting and essential. Until the arrival of radio in the 1920s, newspapers were the only mass medium available for news and entertainment. Even after radio broadcasting began, newspapers remained the pre-eminent source of mass communicated news for decades. It is difficult now to appreciate just how eagerly people awaited the arrival of their morning paper and how reliant upon it they were. Or to picture the thousands of people who, during their lunch hour, and after work, sought out afternoon papers from newspaper vendors strategically positioned across their cities.

The printed newspaper was the end product. This book also peels back the complicated layers of ownership around the five companies to reveal that, behind the major newspapers were mining companies, sugar refiners, tobacco manufacturers, breweries, banks and insurance companies, including many of the largest and most well-known companies in Australian corporate history, such as Colonial Sugar Refining Company (CSR), Carlton and United Breweries Ltd (CUB), British Tobacco, Broken Hill Proprietary Ltd (BHP), Australian Mutual Provident Society (AMP), the Bank of New South Wales and the National Bank.

Many books on newspapers focus on journalists, but this book turns the spotlight onto newspaper owners, their corporate connections and political interests. This perspective reveals the corporate contexts in which journalism was produced. To point out this context, and to note that owners often had strong political views and preferences, is not meant to suggest that all of the journalists who worked for them were acting as their mouthpieces, or that those journalists did not honestly attempt to report different sides of issues and events. But it is to suggest that there was significant pressure on journalists. And we know this is still the case, as recent studies of journalism workplaces have documented.

Despite the perception of creativity and independence surrounding journalism – of reporters following their 'nose' for news wherever it might take them – newspapers are very hierarchical workplaces in which conformity is valued. In the days of anonymous journalism, when there were no by-lines and only in-house training, most journalists were considered easily replaceable. The most dangerous topics they had to navigate related to their proprietors' commercial and political interests. One journalist who worked during the 1930s later said that newspaper owners 'exercised rigid censorship over everything that affected their own interests, especially politics'.[10]

Whether owners and executives dictated policy coarsely – as in the case of Frank Packer – or more smoothly and subtly, through mentoring and with greater respect for their employees' intelligence – as with Keith Murdoch – it is not surprising that journalists felt significant pressure to report politics in a way that fitted with their paper's 'house style' and its previously expressed editorial views. Sometimes, bold journalists and editors bucked the group-think conformity of their outlets, and even the direct editorial instructions of their proprietors, but this was a risky path and it led to dismissal for some.

Newsrooms are one of the main settings of this book, along with boardrooms, parliaments, mining towns and exclusive gentlemen's clubs – all male-dominated environments. Family newspaper dynasties passed over women in the family (and often still do). Only the sons were considered capable of inheriting and running a newspaper empire. In newsrooms and newspaper offices, women were making important contributions from the mid-1800s, but until the 1970s female journalists were mostly confined to the 'women's pages', and rarely accorded authority at major mastheads. The first female editor of a daily metropolitan newspaper in Australia, Ita Buttrose, was not appointed until 1981.

The newspaper industry between 1803 and 1941 was considered a world of 'chairmen', 'newspapermen', and even 'newsboys' and 'copy boys'. The language is dated and problematic, but I have erred on the side of historical context and clarity so have kept it in cases where it would be inaccurate to change it (for example, to change Keith Murdoch's title of 'chairman of the HWT' to 'chairperson of the HWT'), and also where it would be confusing to substitute a gender-neutral term if it does not capture the full meaning (for example, the term 'paper deliverer' or 'paper seller' does not adequately capture the phenomenon of the 'newsboys').

I should also point out an important qualifier about the scope of this book. It is focused on the commercial press, but more specifically, the daily metropolitan press – otherwise known as the capital city dailies. Other types of publications are only touched upon lightly, and only if they were relevant to the fortunes of the major newspaper companies. This means that labour newspapers, weekly newspapers, the local, regional and country press, and magazines, are briefly discussed, but other types of publications – such as independent newspapers, the ethnic press and Indigenous publications – are not.

The book tries to take a national approach to the newspaper industry, but there is an emphasis on Sydney and Melbourne that was difficult to avoid because the newspaper empires grew out of those two cities. They developed in the rough world of Sydney newspapers – where guns, bodyguards and brawls were not unknown – and in Melbourne – where outwardly things were more genteel but a ruthless corporate approach still underpinned the rise of the most formidable empire of all, the HWT.

The foundations for Australia's major newspaper empires began many decades earlier, with the country's first newspapers, and the commercial and political ambitions of their owners. This is where the book begins. The first part charts how newspapers developed in Australia from the early 1800s, through to the rise of popular journalism, and into the ruthless 1920s. The second part of the book introduces the major newspaper owners of the 20th century – the empire builders, and in some cases, destroyers. It outlines the most important individuals, corporate manoeuvres and early political interventions on issues such as conscription, and William Morris (Billy) Hughes' defection from the Labor Party.

The final part of the book shows how press power was employed during a crucial period in Australian press (and political) history – the decade between 1931 and 1941.

The major newspaper groups did more than simply write about politics in a way that was designed to influence public opinion and politicians' activities. Some of them were actively involved in internal party politics, in financing and organising conservative political parties, and in promoting – and then attacking – individual politicians such as Billy Hughes, Joe Lyons and Robert Menzies. Newspaper groups tried to direct public policies to support their interests – sometimes successfully – including on economic issues, radio broadcasting, and commercial ventures such as paper production. By the time of Menzies' downfall, he was not alone in believing that Australia's powerful newspapers could build up and tear down leaders, split parties, and make and break governments.

PART ONE

THE FOUNDATIONS

CHAPTER 1

THE FIRST DAYS OF THE AUSTRALIAN 'FOURTH ESTATE'

CONVICTS AND BANKERS

The owners of Australia's first newspapers were a motley group of convicts, bankers, lawyers and politicians. Newspapers later told a romantic story about how these early publishers, their pre-decessors, had struggled valiantly to achieve press freedom in the 1820s–30s. But the development of Australian newspapers was neither as straightforward nor as glorious as the press history told by newspapers would have us believe. Partly, the problem was one of appropriation. In the early 1900s, when Australian newspapers were forging a creation story about their origins, they were greatly inspired by the already well-known history of the British press breaking free from state control in the mid-19th century. Since the Victorian era, newspapers around the world had been reciting the rousing story of brave British newspaper publishers forging a democratically essen-tial role for an independent press. It was a touchstone for Australian newspapers then, and is still a major influence upon how they view themselves today.

The celebrated version of British press history that made such an impact on Australian newspapers goes like this ... In the early to mid-1800s, British authorities ruthlessly imposed onerous taxes on newspapers as a way of controlling information and repressing political dissent. Newspapers had to pay for a stamp that indicated their legality, plus a tax on each advertisement in the paper, and a duty on paper. As a result, newspaper prices had to be set so high that ordinary people could not afford to buy them. In the 'war of the unstamped' from 1830, many brave British newspaper owners flouted the law, refused to pay the taxes, published their papers illegally, and sold them cheaply to a working-class audience. Almost 800 publishers and vendors of illegal, unstamped papers were imprisoned in England between 1830 and 1836. As a result of their resistance, and popular support for their cause, the 'taxes on knowledge' were gradually repealed, signalling a victory for a free press by the mid-1850s.

This conventional version of British press history has been masterfully critiqued by media historian James Curran and others who have pointed out that those flouting the law were part of a radical working-class press that had arisen from the 1810s. These cheap, working-class papers had shown little concern for commercial considerations. They were instead designed to educate and rouse the working classes and, in the 1830s, to secure universal suffrage, and the repeal of the hated stamp duty taxes on the press. Because these unstamped 'pauper press' newspapers were outselling the 'respectable' press, and helping to energise the working-class movement, they came to be seen as a threat to the social order and the state.[1] Parliamentary opponents realised that the best way to stop the pauper press was to give them what they wanted.

Abolishing the stamp duty and other press taxes made a new type of cheap press possible. All newspapers became dependent upon advertising, which was a problem for the left press. The capital costs of publishing also increased, and the climate of opinion changed.[2] Commercially oriented publishers flooded the market with a raft of cheap, capitalist owned newspapers. Confronted by falling sales, the unstamped radical press began to make their papers 'less austerely political', more 'cheerful', and to include miscellany and general, non-political, features.[3]

The British reformers had both hoped and anticipated that this would happen – that anti-authority outlets would become less radical and depoliticised once a larger scale, mass production, cheap press emerged.[4] Even from as far away as Sydney, and as early as 1852, the conservative newspaper, the *Sydney Morning Herald*, believed this shift was taking place. It argued with approval that lowering the stamp duty from four pence to a penny in 1836 had led British newspapers of 'moderate opinions' to thrive in the sixteen years since, while 'the organs of extreme radicalism' and class feeling had declined.[5] The *Sydney Morning Herald* was celebrating a little prematurely though. The key change occurred in 1855, when the last penny of the stamp duty was removed.

Curran has documented how the parliamentary reformers behind that move wanted to actively encourage 'a cheap press that was in the hands of men of … respectability, and of capital' who would support the social order.[6] They expected 'that cheap newspapers, owned by business people, would become a crucial weapon in the fight against trade unionism' and generally help 'secure the loyalty of the working class to the social order …'.[7] They also expected that journalists would be a part of this process because journalists came from what the conservative lawyer JF Stephens in 1862 called 'the comfortable part of society' and would 'err rather on the side of making too much of their interests than on that of neglecting them'.[8]

In Australia, because newspapers have told Australian press history through the lens of the conventional British version, they have focused upon several outspoken, anti-authority Australian newspaper owners in the 1820s–30s. Oppressed by colonial governors, these brave publishers also went to gaol in defence of their right to publish. As a broad sketch, this crafts the same message of press heroism and independence as British press history, but a closer look at the details reveals a different story. From its earliest days, the Australian press was characterised by deference to authority and commercial ambition rather than radical politics.

The 'struggle' for a free press in Australia

Because Australia was established as a British penal colony in the late 18th century, the Australian press evolved under unusual circumstances, and quite abruptly, more than a century and a half after the British press had begun developing. In the unique environment of a penal settlement with only a small population of literate citizens, Australia's first publishers of 'news' were not commercial publishers, let alone politically oriented radicals – they were the governors of the early colonies who used convict labour to publish official government gazettes of printed orders and proclamations. One of those convict government printers, George Howe, applied to Governor Philip Gidley King for permission to publish Australia's first newspaper in 1803. King granted permission because he felt the newspaper would be useful to the administration.[9]

It *was* useful because Howe's *Sydney Gazette and New South Wales Advertiser* was essentially a government mouthpiece, published under government supervision at Government House. Printed 'on a government press with government ink on government paper', the *Sydney Gazette* communicated government-sanctioned information to Sydney's 7000 colonists, of whom less than 1000 were free persons.[10] This met the governor's needs, but Howe also had his own commercial aims, which he made clear by inserting the word '*Advertiser*' in his paper's title. In its first edition, he called for advertisements and set out his advertising rates.

As Howe was a ticket-of-leave convict publishing under government supervision, it is not surprising that his paper was 'filled with deference to all authority'.[11] Critics described it as 'moral to the point of priggishness, patriotic to the point of servility …'.[12] In the *Sydney Gazette*'s early years especially, publishing it was not an easy way to make money. Paper, type and ink were in short supply, and Howe had to undertake other work to make ends meet. But publishing the government's messages, with accompanying commercial advertisements, eventually proved to be a profitable business, even if subscribers were notorious for not paying.

Fully emancipated in 1806, and married to a shop-owning widow in 1812, Howe became a wealthy man and invested in other commercial enterprises. In 1817, he became one of the fourteen foundation shareholders of Australia's first bank, the Bank of New South Wales (today known as Westpac).[13] Howe acted as the bank's unofficial publicist, reporting its meetings with zeal. He gave full rein to his enthusiasm when the bank was founded by publishing a rapturous report that described it as the 'most distinguished …' advancement in the colony, which would now 'progressively advance to perfection'.[14]

In Van Diemen's Land (Tasmania), Andrew Bent, the convict publisher of the *Hobart Town Gazette*, was also subject to restraint and censorship. In 1824, Bent took a step towards independence when he challenged the position of the government-appointed editor of his paper by withholding its proofs from that editor's oversight. When the autocratic Governor George Arthur took the side of his appointed editor and disputed Bent's ownership of the paper, Bent appealed to a higher authority, the more benign Governor-in-Chief of New South Wales, Governor Thomas Brisbane. Brisbane decided there were no legal grounds for censorship of the colony's newspapers. When this decision seemed to affirm press independence, two ambitious Sydney barristers, William Charles Wentworth and Robert Wardell, recognised the opportunity. Only a month later, Wentworth and Wardell (who had been editor of the London newspaper, the *Statesman*, before he arrived in Sydney), launched the fiercely independent *Australian* up against the government-sanctioned *Sydney Gazette*.

By this time, the number of free inhabitants had grown and so had their distaste for the subservient, officially sanctioned news of papers like the *Gazette*, still filled with its 'fulsome flattery of Government officials ...'.[15] When Wentworth and Wardell launched the *Australian*, they did not seek permission to publish it. Recognising that there was probably no legal requirement for them to do so, Governor Brisbane allowed the paper to continue. He also seemed optimistic that there was little to fear from trying 'the experiment of full latitude of freedom of the Press'.[16] In this environment of authority-sanctioned freedom, George Howe's son Robert, in 1824, also went through official channels and requested that all government restraint be lifted off the *Sydney Gazette*. Brisbane again agreed.

At this point, under Brisbane in the mid-1820s, there was more freedom of the press in Australia than in the United Kingdom. There was no registration, and no stamp or advertisement duties in Australia. Unburdened by such taxes, the Australian newspapers were able to offer advertising that was cheap, plentiful and profitable. This meant that, from their earliest days, Australian newspapers developed with a dependence on advertising that British newspapers did not have until decades later. Heavy taxation stymied the commercial development of the British press, but in Australia, the commercial aspects of newspaper publishing were allowed to develop comparatively unencumbered – to the extent that a convict newspaper publisher like Howe could become proprietor of a bank and the owner of property worth £4000 at his death (about $7 million in today's money).[17]

The outspoken *Australian* was also proving profitable for Wardell and Wentworth by attracting audiences for columns of advertisements, including for cheese, locks, hats, lamps, pipes, rum and china plates. The commercial possibilities caught the eye of Edward Smith Hall, son of a British bank manager, who had been given an enormous and valuable land grant in New South Wales. Hall was Australia's first banker. He was the first secretary and cashier of the Bank of New South Wales (the bank of which George Howe was a proprietor). But the restless Hall found banking administration, land management, and then a position as Coroner in New South Wales (that his father pulled strings to obtain for him), unsatisfying. He became one of the bank's proprietors from 1818, and turned to newspaper publishing in 1826, when he began the *Monitor*.

While George's son, Robert Howe, remained content to publish government flattery, Hall, Wardell and Wentworth published reports and editorials that antagonised Brisbane's replacement, Governor Sir Ralph Darling. And in Van Diemen's Land, Bent was also proving an irritation to Governor Arthur. Where Brisbane had taken a laissez faire approach to freedom of the press, Darling and Arthur were less disposed to freedom of expression. Darling made several attempts to suppress newspapers through the British means of taxation, and also through licensing and registration. Higher authorities eventually thwarted these attempts, but there was a very brief period (only a fortnight) in 1827 when stamp duty taxes were applied. The Sydney newspaper owners complained vehemently, but three of the four publishers paid up, rather than take the British radical path of illegal resistance. The only publisher who did not pay the tax was Wardell who, as a skilled lawyer with high-up legal contacts, correctly believed the requirement to be legally invalid.

When Darling's *Stamp Duty Act* was disallowed, he turned instead to criminal libel laws to control the press. Darling's nemesis, Hall, made himself an easy target by publishing fierce criticisms that sometimes contained factual inaccuracies. Hall was

FIGURE 1.1 The *Australian* protests Governor Darling's changes to libel laws, 1830
SOURCE The *Australian*, 24 February 1830, p. 2.

prosecuted six times for libel, and sentenced to three years' imprisonment for criminal libel against Darling. But Hall kept publishing, even from prison. In Tasmania, Governor Arthur was using similar tactics to 'relentlessly hound' Bent. Prosecuted for criminal libel, Bent was fined 'the ruinous sum of £500', and imprisoned.[18] When Arthur imposed his own version of a stamp duty, and put newspapers under a licence, Bent was already in gaol but, like Hall, was still publishing. As he had no licence, Bent chose to publish only commercial advertisements – no editorials – for fourteen months in order to stay within the bounds of the law. Again, there was no attempt to publish illegally. Only once Arthur's legislation was disallowed by the home authorities in January 1829, did Bent return to publishing opinion, commentary and criticism.

Back in New South Wales, in 1830, Darling was still determined to stop Hall's continued 'libels' against him from Parramatta Gaol. Darling induced the Legislative Council to pass a new law making it mandatory for the court to impose a sentence of banishment on any person who was convicted twice for seditious libel. Again, all of the rebellious newspaper publishers acquiesced. The *Australian* deleted its editorials lest it fall foul of the new law and published an image of a printing press in chains and with the publisher strung up on it (Figure 1.1). Similarly intimidated, Hall left a blank space where his editorials usually went and inserted an image of a coffin. The publishers visually let their readers know they were in mourning for the death of freedom of the press, but they complied nonetheless with oppressive law lest they be banished from the colony.

The clauses relating to banishment were also disallowed, this time because parliament in England was repealing that section of its own law and the colonial Act could not be inconsistent with English law. Darling and Arthur had tried a variety of means to silence the press. While the owners of the *Australian* had been able to use their legal brilliance to ward off challenges, Hall, and especially Bent, had suffered the most extreme forms of government harassment of newspapers. But once the two autocratic governors were recalled – Darling in 1831 and Arthur in 1836 – the unique powers they tried to exercise do not appear to have been attempted again. After their departure, the press developed relatively unencumbered, although there continued to be examples of governments using government advertising and printing contracts to reward friends and punish enemies, and of libel suits used to tame recalcitrant publishers. Sydney especially developed an early reputation as the 'libel capital of the world'.[19] Newspaper publishers were not just the victims of this litigious tendency, they were also contributors to it. From the 1830s, Sydney publishers who would loudly proclaim the importance of freedom of speech, simultaneously tried to silence rivals through libel actions.[20]

The men behind Australia's struggle for a free press

Subservience to authority was not just a feature of the original papers in Sydney and Hobart. As newspaper historian Rod Kirkpatrick has explained, other early newspaper owners in Perth and Adelaide were also government employees, including Charles Macfaull who published the *Perth Gazette and Western Australian Journal* from 1833, a paper that was also considered a 'Government mouthpiece'.[21] Adelaide's first newspaper, the *South Australian Gazette and Colonial Register*, was printed initially in London in 1836, before the colony of South Australia was even proclaimed. It was then sent out on the ship that carried the first official European settlers of South Australia. Edited by the private secretary to the governor, it too was criticised for being the 'voice of government', and its editor used the paper to wage war against enemies of the governor.[22]

Because the first papers were associated with grovelling deference to authority, the next generation of commercially minded, politically strident owners sought a wider audience by publishing anti-authority content. They used clashes with government as publicity to prove their independence, and some faced harsh retaliation from offended authorities. Offended governors considered them dangerous 'radicals', but the Australian newspaper owners were not 'radical' in the sense of the British radical publishers – who had non-commercial aims, were focused on rousing the working class, advocated for universal suffrage, and opposed capitalism and monarchy. Hall was a banker and bank proprietor. Wardell and Wentworth were barristers, and, remarkably, were also owners of the Bank of New South Wales. (In their case, their shareholdings were large enough that they were directors of the bank.[23])

All three of the 'radical' Sydney newspaper owners were bank proprietors and landowners. They were part of a commercial-legal middle class that was seeking greater authority in a military-controlled penal settlement. Up against the often autocratic military rulers of their day, they wanted the sort of citizen rights – and accompanying political, commercial and social opportunities – that their English counterparts enjoyed, such as civil juries and an elected assembly. They wanted reform of the harsh social conditions created by military rule, and to be free to pursue their aspirations, including commercial aspirations. As a group, Australia's first newspaper owners were a commercially oriented bunch, several of whom also held an ambition to obtain personal political power. These two elements set a tone for the Australian press from the beginning.

While Bent is considered the 'martyr' of press freedom in Australia, the convict publisher and official government printer was said to be barely literate and came to Arthur's attention for publishing letters that were violently critical of Arthur's administration but were written by another man.[24] There is evidence that Bent was 'used' by a faction in Hobart.[25] According to Bent's biographer, even Governor Arthur believed that Bent was 'the stupid tool of a group of Hobart businessmen, traders and farmers'.[26] Bent's 'libels' were more in the category of allegations of corrupt or inept conduct by officials, made on behalf of rivals with an axe to grind, rather than any grand political agitation on behalf of convicts, servants or the working class. Like Howe, Bent was said to have amassed 'a fortune' through his government printing contracts and his newspaper.[27] Unlike Howe, he lost that fortune after his struggles with Arthur. After his imprisonment, Bent ended his days in poverty.

In the Sydney *Monitor*, the deeply religious Hall sympathised with the poor, and abhorred the oppression of convicts and convict servants. He printed examples of ill treatment and socially discriminatory laws. But the *Monitor* was a commercial concern. Hall's biographer noted that he 'always had an eye to the commercial and material aspects of daily life'.[28] (While in gaol, Hall initiated five

actions for damages against his critics and won four of them.) Hall's
paper cost a shilling per copy in 1828 (about $92 in today's money).
Rivals accused Hall of publishing content that was aimed at convicts
(for Hall's commercial gain, they claimed, not for the advancement
of the convicts). But it seems the *Monitor* was read predominantly
by small property owners, tradespeople, shopkeepers and other
small business owners such as bakers, innkeepers and brewers. It
was this group of middle-class traders and land owners, politically
unrepresented but economically burdened by duties and other forms
of taxation, on which the *Monitor*'s main advocacy was focused.
It regularly attacked the colonial administration – 'the drones of
Sydney', 'fatten[ing] on the people's labour' through invisible, indirect taxation on everyday essentials.[29]

However, Hall's advocacy on behalf of the poor only went so far.
He was against universal suffrage, believing that the lower classes in
society were 'too drunken and ignorant' to vote.[30] While the *Monitor* called for a representative assembly and trial by common jury,
Hall was opposed to emancipists in the jury box. He despaired of
the conditions endured by convict labourers, but was the beneficiary
of his own assigned convict labourers who helped him produce the
paper. By 1833, Hall had retreated from his earlier sympathy for
the oppressed and was writing in support of conservative causes,
including changing the policy of his paper to represent the interests
of wealthy Hunter Valley landowners who had given him financial
aid. When Hall sold the newspaper in 1838, he tried to return to
banking, unsuccessfully lobbying to be made a managing director.
He later began work in the Colonial Office, a figure of the colonial
authority that he used to abhor.

Another of the 'radical' owners was Wentworth, an owner of
the *Australian*. He was a barrister, the illegitimate son of a surgeon
father and convict mother. Wentworth wanted to break down bar-
riers between the ruling aristocrats and the emancipists and off-

spring of convicts, and to further the cause of those, like himself, who were 'Australian-born'. He too advocated for civil juries, but, as his biographer notes, Wentworth was 'no democrat' – he believed landed property was an essential precondition for voting rights – and 'Like his father he was a monopolist at heart'.[31] Wentworth's father was another founder of the Bank of New South Wales, one of its original directors and largest shareholders. At the meetings in 1816 that established the bank, Howe, Hall and Wentworth Senior were all present, connecting the Australian press with banks from the beginning.[32]

Both Wardell and Wentworth became wealthy men. Wentworth became one of the wealthiest in the colony, with a stately mansion and fifteen properties. He gave up his shares in the *Australian* around 1828–29, and like Hall, became more conservative as he aged. He advocated for high property qualifications for voting, and wanted to establish an unelected hereditary upper house (an idea ridiculed by his opponents as a 'bunyip aristocracy'). Like many other newspaper owners after him, he went on to become a Member of Parliament (MP) in 1843, where he led conservatives in Opposition to a widening of the franchise, and called for the resumption of convict transportation so that he and other landowners could access cheap labour.

Australia's rebellious colonial owners were individuals with strong views, publishing during an era of crusading 'personal' journalism. By the standards of journalism today, their papers were remarkably abusive and sometimes vicious. Personal squabbles, vendettas and insults were as much a part of their content as high-minded appeals for increased political and civil rights. They were seeking the political and economic emancipation of a middle class that was restrained within a military system. Unlike British radical newspapers, they were not calling for universal suffrage, nor were they agitating against royalty, religion or private property.[33]

The commercial and middle class that these newspapers represented advanced rapidly and was soon integrated with the sources of wealth and power in the colony (as evidenced by Hall becoming a colonial official, Wardell a large property owner, and Wentworth a mansion-owning landowner and MP). Following in Wentworth's footsteps, once elections were being held, ambitious men were using newspapers as launching pads to office. In 1838, the *Australian* was purchased by yet another lawyer, George Nichols, who also became a politician after responsible government was introduced. The paper that had been known for its hostility to authority began 'placing a new emphasis on law, order and respect for property'.[34] That same year, in Adelaide, two lawyers/public officials, who had been viciously criticised by the government-aligned *South Australian Register,* founded their own paper, the *Southern Australian*, and ran it in direct competition with the *Register*. One became Adelaide's first mayor and then a member of the Legislative Council.[35]

From liberal to conservative

Rich in land, livestock and minerals, Australia was rapidly developing. According to the landowners' *Atlas*, between 1826 and 1841, the colony witnessed a growth in revenue, commerce and population 'probably without parallel in the history of the world'.[36] Convict transportation declined significantly in the 1840s, and halted altogether in 1868. There was greater immigration by middle-class British, especially after discoveries of gold in the 1850s. The gold rushes in New South Wales, and especially Victoria, fostered mass immigration, an economic boom and the seeds of a radical liberal tradition that led to democratic political reforms and extensions of voting rights that were making Australia a leading democracy worldwide.

Australia had transformed in the space of thirty years from two convict colonies, ruled by governors, to an advanced democracy.

READING-ROOM, BALLARAT MECHANICS' INSTITUTE.

FIGURE 1.2 Reading rooms like this one, at the Ballarat Mechanics' Institute, 1881, encouraged the habit of reading newspapers; note the two women at the back of the room (in the 'Ladies only' section) reading newspapers
SOURCE *Australasian Sketcher with Pen and Pencil*, 8 October 1881, p. 325.

Compared to the United Kingdom, Australia was also a more socially fluid country, with a high standard of living. Newspapers were promoted as an essential way for colonists in an isolated country to be connected with one another, and to receive news from 'home' (that is, the United Kingdom). Pubs and taverns provided their patrons with newspapers, which were often shared and read aloud. The rise of over-the-counter sales, reading rooms and Mechanics' Institutes, also helped spread newspapers more widely. The development of rail, with train lines opening in Melbourne, Sydney and Adelaide in the 1850s, was also crucial to the spread of newspapers.

Liberal newspapers had contributed to a climate of popular

support for democratic reforms, but it was also becoming evident by the 1840s that newspapers which started out as liberal organs had a habit of becoming conservative, and allied with authority, once they were established and profitable. Even taking into account that Australian politics was more progressive than in the United Kingdom at the time, and also that politics is fluid (what was once considered radical can become conservative and vice versa), the trend towards conservatism in newspapers was striking. One important newspaper that made the shift began as the *Sydney Herald* in 1831, and changed its title to the *Sydney Morning Herald* in 1842.

When it began, the *Sydney Herald* had a low price compared to the other papers, and quickly found a solid audience. Within six months of its commencement, its circulation was higher than the other three Sydney papers (the *Sydney Gazette*, Hall's *Monitor* and Wardell's *Australian*) combined.[37] The *Sydney Herald* considered itself the progressive successor to Wardell's *Australian* and Hall's *Monitor*. It said it wanted to uphold their policies of reform.[38] At first, the *Sydney Herald* welcomed the liberal administration of Sir Richard Bourke, was concerned about inequality, and critical of 'opulent landholders'.[39] But within only a few years, it was representing the views of wealthy landowners and those with mercantile interests, and campaigning against Bourke, elected assemblies and emancipist rights. As a later chapter explains, the paper's owner, John Fairfax, and his sons, became wealthy investors with interests across the sugar, shipping, gas, banking and insurance industries.

When economic depression hit Sydney in the 1840s, the now *Sydney Morning Herald* saw the downturn as 'a fine opportunity' for 'capitalists' to pick up 'bargains' in land and livestock.[40] But among the poor, the depression hit hard and caused a rise in class consciousness that was reflected in a range of short-lived democratic papers aimed at urban workers. RB Walker argued that there were more of these papers in the 1840s than at any time since in Australia.[41]

Among them was the first penny newspaper, the weekly *Star and Working Man's Guardian* (1844–45). But the *Guardian* lasted for only eighty-three issues and eighteen months. The paper that endured was the *Sydney Morning Herald*. It had responded to the *Guardian's* complaints about an 'up start aristocracy' by saying: 'In young colonies who are not working men? ... We have no peerage, no aristocracy: we are all working men ... the interests of employers and employed are in this country so closely identified with each other ... [that] ... Injure the capitalist and you injure the labourer.'[42]

By the 1840s, the *Sydney Morning Herald's* low price and strong advertising basis had helped it become the dominant newspaper in the colony. It had seen off the *Monitor* (closed 1841), the *Australian* (closed 1848) and several other papers. New papers kept cropping up with the stated aim of representing the working classes of New South Wales – such as the popular *People's Advocate and New South Wales Vindicator* (1848–56) – but they too failed up against the Tory *Sydney Morning Herald*. Its most successful challenger was the *Empire*, launched by Henry Parkes in 1850 with financial help from wealthy businessmen. Parkes was a skilled journalist and politician, but he was often in financial difficulty. The *Empire* failed in 1858 due to his debts, but while it existed, was considered the 'voice of liberalism' and the main competitor to the *Sydney Morning Herald* (run by Parkes' friend John Fairfax).[43]

The *Empire* promoted the interests of the free immigrant middle and working classes, and Parkes' strong support for universal male suffrage and land reform gave the paper a radical edge. Parkes was another who used his newspaper as a springboard to office. Only four years after starting the paper, Parkes entered the Legislative Council. From that time, he increasingly used the *Empire* to promote his own political career, and devoted less attention to the financially struggling paper than it needed. Never as popular with advertisers as the *Sydney Morning Herald*, the *Empire* was in trouble by 1857. Fairfax saw an opportunity to finish it off by cutting the price of his *Sydney Morning Herald*, forcing the *Empire* to follow suit with a price reduction it could not afford. It closed in August 1858.

Throughout the *Empire*'s liberal reign, the *Sydney Morning Herald* had remained implacably opposed to universal male suffrage. It argued the legislature should represent property and 'interests' and supported a plan for nominees to be appointed to the Legislative Council instead of elected.[44] The paper despaired when liberals won in elections in 1860. By then, it faced a re-launched *Empire*, that between 1859 and 1875 was owned by Samuel Bennett, once a printer at the *Sydney Morning Herald*. The revived *Empire* began with a promise to carry on the 'radical' and liberal traditions of Parkes, but also stressed its belief in 'rigid observance of law and order ... and the rights of property ... and affectionate and loyal devotion to the Crown'.[45] By the 1860s, it too had become more conservative and similar to the *Sydney Morning Herald* in its politics.

In 1867, Bennett declared that the *Empire* would henceforth be less political.[46] This announcement came at a time when the costs of steam-powered printing, and the use of the telegraph for newsgathering, had added greatly to the expenses of running a daily paper. Newspapers were increasingly aiming for popularity to attract advertising revenue to pay their bills. (In Melbourne, the *Herald* also declared in 1869 that it too would now be less focused on political content.[47]) In 1867, Bennett had also launched a new paper, the *Evening News*, and it became his major concern. It was a pioneer among afternoon papers, focusing on luring large audiences with stories on crime and popular news topics. In 1868, Bennett cut the price of the *Empire* to one penny, but its content was not much altered. In 1875, Bennett shut it down during a compositors' strike, suggesting it was probably unprofitable by then.

In other cities, the same trends towards political conservatism and more depoliticised content were playing out. In Melbourne,

FIGURE 1.3 The *Sydney Morning Herald* occupied this prominent site at the apex of Hunter, Pitt and O'Connell streets in Sydney from 1856 to 1956; this was its first building on the site, a three-storey stone building constructed in 1856, shown here in 1870

SOURCE The *Sydney Mail*, 23 March 1872, p. 360.

the *Argus* performed the most abrupt about-face. It had begun as a radical journal in 1846 under its first owner, William Kerr. In 1848, Kerr having been bankrupted by libel damages, Edward Wilson bought into the *Argus*. Wilson continued the outspoken stance of the paper and used it to virulently, and sometimes libellously, oppose the government of Charles La Trobe and the Colonial Office. Under the slogan 'Unlock the Lands', Wilson sought to break the powerful squatters' 'ruinous monopoly' over land. His *Argus* 'columns were open to any radical group or charitable movement'.[48]

The paper's sympathy for gold miners (which was so strong it sometimes exaggerated abuses of power by goldfield officials), and its preaching of social and political reforms during the heady gold rush days, saw the *Argus'* circulation skyrocket from 3200 copies a day in 1852, to around 15 000 only two years later.[49] The *Argus* claimed to have 'twice the circulation of any London journal [except] *The Times*'.[50] But when the miners took action and rebelled during the Eureka Stockade in 1854, the paper that had encouraged them suddenly turned away. The *Argus* toned down and veered away from its radicalism. Wilson, regretting his own earlier radicalism, now advocated 'multiple electorates to prevent manual workers from gaining a majority vote, and special representation of property interests'.[51] But his co-owner from 1852, pastoralist and MP Lauchlan Mackinnon, seems to have been the main driver behind the paper's conservative transformation. By the 1870s, the *Argus* was conveying such a 'militant and offensively expressed ultra-conservative policy', that even Wilson (who had lost editorial control by then) despaired of the paper's 'old-womanish Toryism'.[52] The once radical paper was now considered almost comically conservative – 'the organ of the [exclusive] Melbourne Club … large wool-growers … [and] the importers of Flinders Lane'.[53]

Australia's first owners

Romantic accounts of the struggle for a 'free press' overlook the fact that Australia has a long history of deferential papers with commercial motives. Although a product of significant ingenuity, Australia's first newspaper was essentially a government mouthpiece. Australia's first newspaper owner was a convict, but also a proprietor of the country's first bank. Hall, dubbed the 'father of the Australian free press', was another proprietor of the same bank.[54] The 'struggle' for a free press was actually a rather tame, surprisingly administrative affair in Australia. The publishers operating under government censorship applied for independence by asking permission, and writing letters to authorities. When briefly faced with controlling devices initiated by autocratic governors, such as taxes, stamp duty and registration, publishers complied with stamp duties (with the exception of two skilled lawyers who were able to challenge the legality of the rules), and they also complied with censorship compelled by banishment laws.

The publishers who went to gaol in the 1820s ran afoul of libel laws (a matter that continues to be an issue even for the far more careful journalists of today). They *were* terribly persecuted, and some were known for their advocacy of liberal initiatives, and for standing up for the poor and for emancipists, but they were not 'radical' publishers in the sense of the British working-class radical publishers. The Australian publishers were commercially minded men, most of whom did not want universal suffrage, and who recognised the advantages of controlling a key organ of public opinion that had strong commercial prospects. With no stamp duty, no advertising taxes, and then a range of government subsidies, newspapers presented unique opportunities for both commercial and political gain. As the next part of this chapter shows, share ownership and the involvement of businessmen came early, and it was not uncommon for newspapers to be owned by politicians.

AUSTRALIA'S 'APOLITICAL' PRESS

In Australia, as in the United Kingdom, the development of untaxed, advertising-dependent, cheap newspapers, run by men of capital, was encouraging papers that gravitated to the political mainstream and supported the existing social order. There was one important sign that Australian authorities were happy with this. It is often overlooked that, when the British newspapers paid stamp duty, they received something for their payment. They were, literally, embossed with a stamp, which granted them free delivery by the post office. By the mid-19th century, copies of stamped newspapers were being widely circulated, posted on from one address to another by thrifty middle-class readers in a way that boosted the spread of 'respectable' papers, especially *The Times*. In Australia, it says a great deal about the early lobbying power of newspapers, and the authorities' general satisfaction with their content, that newspapers did not have to pay for a stamp but still received free postage nonetheless.

Government subsidies underwrite the press

In 1825, legislation in New South Wales enabled newspapers to be delivered by post at a heavily discounted rate and, from 1835, to be posted for free. Other colonies followed, including Van Diemen's Land, Victoria and Western Australia. In South Australia, news-paper postage was free until 1881. In New South Wales, newspapers were transported for free for fifty-four of the sixty-seven years between 1835 and 1902.[55]

At a time when British and American newspapers were paying for their own postage (albeit at a discounted rate in the United States), free postage was an enormous advantage to Australian newspapers in building up their circulations. Newspapers were expensive to sort and transport by post, and Australian taxpayers were paying hundreds of thousands of pounds for their postage. That public expenditure coincided with a boom in the circulation and popularity of newspapers. For example, in New South Wales, in 1848, 1.3 million papers were distributed free by post. By 1890, that had increased to 31 million a year, and was costing taxpayers £40 000 a year ($4.5 million in today's money).[56] Sometimes, the post office was being run almost entirely in service of newspapers. In 1849, newspapers constituted around 90 per cent of all mail in New South Wales. Walker calculated that, in relation to population, 'four times as many newspapers were posted in the colony as in the United Kingdom'.[57]

Newspaper owners argued that free postage was for the benefit of the public in a young colony of vast geographic distances, and that newspapers helped enlighten the uneducated. But when free postage began, a high proportion of newspaper content was advertising, not editorial, so taxpayers were mostly paying to transport ads around the country. And unlike in the United States, where postal subsidies advantaged the local press and country newspapers, in Australia, it was the powerful city daily papers and their weeklies, such as the *Sydney Morning Herald* and its weekly *Sydney Mail* that benefited the most. The *Sydney Mail* was a weekly resume edition of the *Sydney Morning Herald* that included woodcut illustrations from 1871, and photographs from 1888.[58] The *Sydney Mail* proved very popular among country readers to whom the daily papers could not be delivered in time, and also among workers who could not afford a daily *Sydney Morning Herald*. Its success, boosted by free postage, exceeded all expectations and contributed to the *Sydney Morning Herald*'s financial strength.

When Federation saw new postage rates brought in during 1901, newspapers complained bitterly. Again drawing upon the spectre of British press history, they argued that charging them postage (like every other customer of the post office) was the equivalent of imposing a 'tax on knowledge'. Suitably intimidated, the government set cheap rates for newspapers that were a third of the standard price for post customers, and only a half or a third that charged for newspapers in England.[59]

Newspaper lobbying for special treatment was unabashed and filled with hyperbole. The *Register* argued that paying postage would amount to a 'gag' on the 'voice of public opinion' that would 'crush the liberty of the press'.[60] In Sydney, newspaper owners even pressured the government into setting up special early paper-trains that carried their morning newspapers for free from 1874. (In the United Kingdom, *The Times* was paying to charter its own specially equipped trains.) In Melbourne, the owners of *The Age* and the *Argus* contributed £2410 each towards the special newspaper trains that delivered their papers to Ballarat and Bendigo, but taxpayers contributed the other £50 000. By 1899, there was political debate about how much revenue the special newspaper trains were costing, with estimates of up to £100 000 annually.[61]

Papers like the *Sydney Morning Herald*, the *Argus* and the *Register* saw no contradiction between their vehement support for free trade and the state aid they received. Among the newspapers, there were many free traders who did not want free trade in news-papers. The *Register* addressed the obvious hypocrisy by arguing that 'Free Trade is a good, but the immortal mind – unshackled [by newspapers] – is a better thing'.[62] Newspapers jealously guarded their commercial advantages bestowed by government. After Fed-eration, they lobbied the postmaster-general to make sure that other competing publications – such as monthly magazines – could not take advantage of their special low postage rates.

Governments also gave newspapers reduced duties on ink and paper. From the mid-1800s, they allowed newspapers to use publicly financed telecommunications infrastructure as tele-graph cables were developed. The government, along with some private entrepreneurs, paid for the laying of telegraph cables, first within Australia and then overseas. The newspapers were among the largest users of these services, and again the federal govern-ment charged the press a special and exceptionally low rate for conducting its business by telegraph, and later by telephone.

Government subsidies went on for decades, and still occur today in various forms (including taxation rebates, unpursued tax avoidance and various special subsidies).[63] In 1931, when the postmaster-general was faced with falling revenue from the telegraphic service his department had built up at considerable expense, he decided to abolish the telephone concession rates for newspaper proprietors. He was met by a storm of protest from the industry as two deputations of newspaper heavyweights, including Keith Murdoch, descended upon his office to protest and try to change his mind. As with free postage, the newspaper industry portrayed the subsidy as something approaching a divine 'right'.[64] The intimidated postmaster-general put the matter to Cabinet, which decided the press could receive a 66 per cent concession on daytime telephone rates compared to ordinary users.[65]

When he was feeling stung by what he considered unfair reporting of parliament in 1933, the conservative politician Robert Archdale Parkhill, then postmaster-general, said the newspapers of Australia had to be considered 'semi-public institutions' despite their 'bowel-less commercialism' because 'taxpayers contribute £1 million a year to them in concessions', including £500 000 in federal concessions for 'postal, telephonic and telegraphic rates', and £500 000 from state governments for concessions in rail freights and other subsidies.[66] In today's money, this is equivalent to around $83 million per year. In the 1950s, postage concessions were still costing taxpayers £2.4 million per year (around $72 million).[67]

Newspapers have never really acknowledged that their success was underwritten by decades of government subsidies that other commercial businesses could only dream of. Despite their criticism of government handouts for others, and their steadfast advocacy of free market principles, with nearly every new technological innovation, newspapers sought – and usually won – special treatment from government. The original intention of all this government assistance was that newspapers would encourage literacy and the dissemination of news and information, but subsidies lingered for longer than was necessary to achieve those goals, and long after newspapers were making enormous profits. By the 1980s, the post office had been complaining for over a century about losses in revenue caused by postal subsidies for newspapers. Subsidies of between 50 and 70 per cent for posting metropolitan newspapers were still in force in 1982–83, and still costing taxpayers about $4.2 million.[68] A conservative estimate suggests that hundreds of millions of dollars was provided by Australian taxpayers to subsidise newspapers between 1890 and 1970.

The 'fourth estate' concept

By the Victorian era, newspapers were an observably powerful institution and they justified their power by fostering the notion of the press as a 'fourth estate' that used its power in service of the public, as a vital part of democracy. The 'fourth estate' role situated the press as separate from, and keeping watch on the other branches of power – including parliament, government and the courts. Central to this role was the premise that newspapers, because they had no formal links with political parties, were truly independent, non-partisan, neutral spectators in the political process. When the *Sydney Morning Herald* began in 1831, it declared itself innocent of the pro- and anti-government propaganda evident in other papers and adopted the motto: 'Sworn to no Master, of no sect am I'. In the 1840s, the *Sydney Morning Herald* placed another motto on its front page: 'In moderation placing all my glory, while Tories call me Whig – and Whigs a Tory'. In 1854, the Hobart *Mercury* told its readers that it was founded on the principle that it was 'the servant of one master ... the public'.[69] Best of all though, for its sheer simplicity, was the Queensland *Evening Telegraph*'s 1907 motto: 'We have no friends'.[70]

These papers – and many others – were trying to separate themselves from a history of strident partisanship in newspapers. Most London newspapers in the late 18th and early 19th centuries had been owned, financed or managed by a political party. (*The Times*, for example, began life as a journal paid £300 a year from Treasury to champion ministerial policy.[71]) In the United States, political factions had their own newspapers. The early newspapers in the Australian colonies had also been known for strong associations with particular individuals and causes. Claiming political independence was an important way to break free of a taint that clung to the press – that newspapers were handmaidens of political parties, propagandists for hire, and hacks in search of patronage.

Independence built credibility, but it also made sense economically after the industrialisation and mechanisation of the press. Once newspapers had become large investments, and were reliant upon attracting the widest possible audience to secure advertising revenue, owners wanted to avoid narrowing their potential readership by being too closely associated with one side of politics. But most newspapers still had political 'friends' and solid political preferences.

Despite the *Sydney Morning Herald*'s motto, it was far more regularly being called a Tory by Whigs, than the other way around. And once Australian politics firmed up into a contest between Labor and non-Labor parties, the *Sydney Morning Herald* was a mainstay of the anti-Labor side. In the first ninety-two years that the Labor Party contested elections, from 1891 to 1983, the *Sydney Morning Herald* endorsed Labor only once, in 1961 – and this was a bizarre aberration that was widely regarded as having been due perhaps as much to personal factors as political ones. At the state level, the *Sydney Morning Herald* was even more conservative. It did not support

Labor for 112 years, not until 2003.[72] During those years, if Labor was popular and won large election victories, the *Sydney Morning Herald* did not mind running against public opinion. It developed a unique style of reporting politics that drew upon factual, comprehensive accounts in 'objective' language, while simultaneously representing viewpoints that made it a bastion of the conservative political, social and economic establishment in Sydney for over a century.

Likewise, the Hobart *Mercury*, which declared it had no political master, strongly supported conservative parties for over a century. Until 2007, the *Mercury* never advocated a vote for Labor federally. From 1901 to 2016, across forty-five federal elections held over 115 years, it only advocated a vote for Labor twice (in 2007 and 2010). In 1925, the *Mercury* said that it regarded Labor as controlled by Communists, and considered a Labor government a 'terrible thing'.[73] In an editorial on the eve of the 1910 election, the *Mercury* argued there was 'no distinction in classes' in Australia, but rather that 'many of those who are called the non-workers are those who work the hardest', while 'the aim of most of the so-called workers is to do as little work as possible. They are constantly demanding shorter hours...'.[74]

Even when their content suggested otherwise, newspapers vehemently insisted that they were neutral because the 'fourth estate' concept was so powerful. It helped newspapers to establish the press as a legitimate, but separate, part of the political system; outside of it but just as vital. It also raised the status of journalism (which had previously been considered a disreputable occupation), and allowed newspapers to cast any attempts by government to regulate the press – including attempts to prevent monopolies, or even to remove government subsidies – as deeply undemocratic. This was a line of defence that newspapers would use consistently from the Victorian era onwards.

In 1855, the *Adelaide Times* foreshadowed how far the concept could be stretched when it argued that *any* 'insult' towards the press had to be viewed as an attack on the public.[75] But *The Age* exhibited a far more nuanced understanding in 1854, when it described the press as 'the safeguard of liberty against the excesses of power, and the support of government against the caprices of popular excitement'.[76] *The Age* was acknowledging that the press' role was as much about protecting government from the public as it was about protecting the public from governments.

In Australia, the 'fourth estate' concept was explicitly promoted by newspapers from the 1830s. In an 1844 article headed 'The Fourth Estate', the *Sydney Morning Chronicle* said, 'The Press has long been considered the guardian of public liberty, and shield of the weak against the strong'. But in the same article the newspaper neatly highlighted one of the main problems with the fourth estate – the tensions between the commercial and public functions of the press. The *Chronicle* accused an unnamed rival paper of being unworthy of the fourth estate mantle. It claimed the unnamed paper was publishing negative stories against an industrial campaign by drapers and shop workers who wanted to reduce their working hours and shut their shops at 6 pm or 7 pm in the evening instead of 10 pm, because the paper was in 'secret sympathy' with a gas company that profited from shops being open later because they had to use more gas for lighting.[77]

The *Chronicle* was almost certainly talking about the *Sydney Morning Herald* which had a strong association with the monopoly Australian Gas Light Company (today known as AGL, and still one of Australia's largest energy providers), which had started lighting up Sydney with gas from 1841. The *Sydney Morning Herald*'s owners, John Fairfax and Charles Kemp, were both directors of the company, and Fairfax became its deputy chair. The *Sydney Morning Herald*'s influential editor, Ralph Mansfield, acted concurrently as the director and secretary of the Australian Gas Light Company. He was associated with both companies for over forty years.[78]

In Adelaide, the early owners of the *Register* had also found there were commercial limits to the fourth estate role. James Allen, owner from 1842, had been a vigorous critic of the governor. This had cost him government contracts and government advertising but had also frightened off commercial advertisers. When Allen sold the *Register* only three years later he remarked that 'freedom of speech does not pay'.[79] The paper's next owner, John Stephens, was also outspoken and took on directors of the Burra mines who mounted nine libel cases simultaneously in an effort to silence the paper. After Stephens' premature death, the *Register* was turned into a joint stock company in 1853 and purchased by wealthy shop owners and merchants with political ambitions. The *Register* then became another paper that transformed from maverick to conservative. It became known for its 'ferociously anti-socialist and anti-Labour [sic]' stance.[80]

In 1858, a second group of wealthy Adelaide businessmen and politicians funded an opposition morning newspaper, the *South Australian Advertiser*. They too used the method of a joint stock company to raise enough capital. At elections for the first fully elected South Australian parliament in 1857, several owners and directors of both rival papers were elected, including the editor and joint owner of the *Register*, along with a shareholder, Alexander Hay. *Advertiser* owner, John Henry Barrow, was elected in 1858, only weeks after starting the paper. Its company director, Thomas King, was elected in 1876. The *Advertiser* was considered the 'liberal' paper of the two, but by the 1920s, it was firmly in the conservative camp. In 1893, its editor, John Langdon Bonython, drew on his successful investments in mining shares to become the paper's sole proprietor – a role he held for the next thirty-five years. In 1898, Bonython was knighted on the same day as John Fairfax's son, James Reading Fairfax. The two were Australia's first newspaper knights. In 1901, Bonython was elected to the House of Representatives. The combination of newspaper proprietor/mining investor/politician/knight had begun.

Newspaper ownership and politics entwined

Aside from newspaper content, the biggest hint that the press was not as politically independent or depoliticised as it claimed was the fact that so many newspaper owners *were* politicians. Since the 1840s, men like Parkes and Nichols had combined the roles of politician/newspaper owner in New South Wales. With self-government in other colonies from the 1850s, other politician/owners included John Pascoe Fawkner in Victoria (Fawkner was yet another who began as a liberal but ended up voicing conservative views, including opposing universal male suffrage). In 1853, in Adelaide, several businessmen established the *Adelaide Examiner* with the specific purpose of promoting their political views ahead of an election in which several of them were standing as candidates. They were the investors who ended up buying the Adelaide *Register*, and several of them became MPs in 1857.

The *Sydney Morning Herald*'s John Fairfax unsuccessfully ran for office in 1856, and in 1874 accepted nomination to the Legislative Council. The other early owner of the *Sydney Morning Herald*, Charles Kemp, left the paper to run for office in 1854. In Tasmania, the *Mercury*'s owner, John Davies, became an MP in 1861, seven years after entering into newspaper publishing. Two of his sons who took over the paper also became MPs. One, Charles Davies, was dubbed the 'uncrowned King' of Tasmania.[81]

Combining politics with newspaper ownership was not at all unusual. Most of the owners of the major daily newspapers in Australia in the late 19th and early 20th century were politicians at some point, including: Hugh Denison (*Sun*), Theodore Fink (*Herald*), WL Baillieu (*Herald*), TM Shakespeare (*Canberra Times*), John Norton (*Truth*), James Joynton Smith (*Smith's Weekly* and *Daily Guardian*), Lauchlan Mackinnon (*Argus*), John Winthrop Hackett (*West Australian*), James Casey, Angus Mackay and

James Francis (*Daily Telegraph*), and John Langdon Bonython (*Advertiser*). Frank Packer was not an MP but his co-owner, Edward Granville (EG) Theodore, was a former Labor federal treasurer and Queensland premier turned businessman and mining company owner.

Even into the mid-20th century, and in stark contravention of their 'non-partisan' claims, some newspaper owners provided election candidates with funding, the services of their newspaper staff, and the inestimable value of positive publicity. One of the most egregious examples occurred in 1903, when the *Argus* secretly ran its own field of 'anti-socialistic' candidates during the federal election. It chose four elderly, conservative businessmen (critics described them as 'fine, old crusted Tories'),[82] to continue the *Argus'* campaign against compulsory arbitration, and put them forward for the Senate under the title of 'The Victorian Four'.[83] The *Argus* promoted the four as 'the only candidates opposed to labour domination'.[84] This furtive intervention in the election was about as far from independent as it was possible to be.

One important exception to the politician-newspaper owner was David Syme, owner of *The Age*. Syme never held public office but, through his paper, exercised a high degree of informal political influence in Victoria where he was known as 'King David'. CE Sayers, one of Syme's biographers, wrote that Syme 'used *The Age*'s power for fearless and ruthless prosecution of his public policies', and 'for thirty-five years before Federation, Victoria had a high protection wall that was at Syme's bidding if not wholly of his making. This was his greatest newspaper achievement.'[85] In 1901, Syme's rival, George Reid, told federal parliament that *The Age* 'rules Victoria' and that Syme was 'the virtual dictator of Victoria, who has all those Victorian politicians in the hollow of his hand'.[86]

For decades, *The Age* was the standout exception to the trend of newspapers abandoning their liberal origins. *The Age* had begun only six weeks before the Eureka rebellion, and when the *Argus* turned conservative in the mid-1850s, *The Age* filled that gap in the market. It was founded on the principle of being 'an efficient, independent organ of Progressive Opinions'.[87] Under its founding owners, John and Henry Cooke, *The Age* vigorously supported the Eureka miners against the authorities. This caused the first of many advertising boycotts by government and business opponents, which *The Age* managed to withstand by building up a strong classified advertising section filled with ads from small advertisers.

After its purchase by Ebenezer Syme in 1856, *The Age* vigorously supported the progressive causes of its day, including universal adult male suffrage; compulsory, free and secular education; the eight-hour working day; reform of land laws to open up public estates for use by small farmers; the growth of mechanics institutes; 'fair wages and decent working conditions, and for laws to abolish child labour and factory sweatshops'.[88] As mentioned, Ebenezer's brother, David Syme, who took over as manager and editor in 1860, was best known for his 'zeal for tariff protection against cheap imports to nurture local manufacturing and full employment'.[89] His was the outspoken voice of Australian manufacturers seeking customs protection.

With its lucrative classified advertising base, and Syme's fusion of political and commercial interests, competitors in 1879 noted of *The Age* that: 'it has always been a [political] compromise – sway-ing between the working classes, the auctioneers and the stock agents'.[90] La Nauze argued that Syme's version of liberalism had spoken 'simultaneously ... for the ex-miners and immigrants with-out property, for the small farmer and for the industrialist-groups whose interests ... were largely identical [at this time]; and the common factor was nationalism'.[91] Syme's protégé, Alfred Deakin, came to embody liberalism during the early Commonwealth years and became prime minister three times in the first decade of Federation.

Under Syme, *The Age* had been antagonistic towards the Labor Party.[92] But after his death in 1908, and with the meaning of 'liberalism' changing, *The Age* suggested in 1910 that protectionists might need to vote Labor.[93] Under Syme's fourth son, Geoffrey Syme, who was managing editor from 1908 to 1942, *The Age* gradually shifted to the right, supporting Geoffrey Syme's friend, Robert Menzies, the leader of the non-Labor side of politics, despite some tensions over political issues. During World War I, *The Age* joined with conservative press owners to support the two failed plebiscites on conscription for overseas service. In the 1920s and 1930s, *The Age* remained more likely than other daily papers to support Labor because protectionism remained its grand theme – and Labor was the party most allied with that goal as a way of protecting Australia's manufacturers so they could provide employment and a living wage for Australian workers. But the paper became far more conservative after 1945, and remained reliably conservative into the 1960s (Tables 3.1, pages 118–19 and 3.2, pages 122–23).

Corporate ownership

Many of Australia's late 19th and early 20th century daily newspaper owners were either politicians or would-be politicians (including several who liked to exercise power without the irksome responsibilities and accountability of formal office). But, by the mid- to late-19th century, owners needed more than just political skill or ambition, as the running costs of newspapers were rising exponentially. From the 1860s, there was a continued move away from single proprietors, family-run fiefdoms and small partnerships, towards joint stock companies which saw newspapers as a commercial venture.[94] In Australia, this transition to share ownership seems to have begun decades earlier than in the United Kingdom.[95] The new investor/owners had large amounts of capital at stake and were more likely to be cautious, conservative businessmen than maverick 'fire-eaters and reformers' like Allen and Stephens.[96]

Before the 1860s, newspaper owners had been a mixture of printers, artisans, clerks, clergymen, journalists and merchants. Allen had been a trained Baptist minister, and Stephens was formerly an apprentice in the book trade, and a journalist and author. Samuel Bennett was a printer. John Pascoe Fawkner was a prisoner, builder, baker and hotelkeeper before he founded the *Launceston Advertiser*, and later a bookseller, when he founded the *Melbourne Advertiser* and the *Port Phillip Patriot*. John and Henry Cooke, founders of *The Age*, were merchants. George Kavanagh, founder of the *Port Phillip Herald* (later the *Herald*) was a clerk and a dairy owner. Parkes had been a labourer and ivory turner. Of the three original founders of the *Sydney Morning Herald*, two were clerks and the other was a bookseller.

From the 1870s, newspapers were more regularly being purchased, or launched, by groups of businessmen. The Brisbane *Telegraph* was launched in 1872 by a coalition of businessmen (including an MP), and so was the *Daily Telegraph* in Sydney, in 1879. The *Herald* in Melbourne received new owners in 1871, which included two printers (who both owned successful businesses in printing and publishing), and another businessman, John Halfey, who had made his fortune from gold mining at Bendigo. Halfey was a shareholder (and later a director) of the Colonial Bank. He was also a politician, albeit a fairly unsuccessful one, who his biographer said 'was active in parliament only on mining questions ...'.[97] With his background ranging across mining, banking and politics, Halfey was indicative of the next breed of owners to come.

With profitable newspapers increasingly in the hands of wealthy businessmen, there was a narrowing in the spectrum of political views they represented. Most daily papers were advocating free trade (exceptions included the protectionist *Star* in Sydney, and

The Age in Melbourne). And most were very concerned about the impact of organised labour upon business. The British reformers who repealed newspaper taxes in the 1850s felt they needed cheap capitalist-owned newspapers to suppress trade unions, but in Australia, industrialists must have felt that need even more acutely. In the 1850s, Australian trade unions had won important industrial reforms, including the eight-hour day (a milestone achieved by Victorian stonemasons in 1856, but not effectively achieved in the United States or United Kingdom until decades later). By the late 19th century, Australia was developing a reputation for being a 'working man's paradise'. Australia's conservative newspaper owners were concerned about the effects of demands for improved working conditions on the profitability of industries that many were now heavily invested in – including mining, retail, production, agriculture and, of course, the newspaper industry.

Industrial action was not common at newspaper offices though. Journalists did not strike until the 1910s (the founder of the Australian Journalists' Association (AJA)) described his fellow journalists as 'a spineless, downtrodden crew')[98] but there had been strikes by mechanical staff at the *Sydney Morning Herald* in 1840, and by compositors working on Melbourne papers in the 1850s. As noted, the *Empire* was shut down by its owner in 1875, during a compositors' strike. Compositors paid by the piece also walked off the job at the *Mercury* in 1879 – an event the paper described to its readers as 'terrorism'.[99] In the 1880s, there were printers' strikes at newspapers in Adelaide, Brisbane and Sydney. A larger canvas for industrial demands began to surface after a period of severe depression and a rise in industrial action in the 1890s helped the Labor Party to establish itself as a political force.

Newspaper reactions to the rise of the Labor Party

On the formation of the Labor Party, the *Sydney Morning Herald* described 'the intrusion … of the labour struggle into the field of politics' as the nation's 'greatest peril'.[100] With remarkable speed, only thirteen years after the Labor Party was formed, and three years after Federation, Australia gained its first national Labor government, headed by Chris Watson, in 1904. For conservative newspaper owners, it must have been particularly unsettling that Watson had risen from within their own industry. He had been a compositor on the *Daily Telegraph* and the *Sydney Morning Herald* and was 'father of the chapel' (equivalent to a shop steward) at the protectionist *Australian Star*.

As Ross McMullin has noted, when Watson's government was sworn in, it became the first national labour government in the world, and 'curious visitors crossed the globe to [Australia] to scrutinise this advanced social laboratory for themselves'.[101] It would be another two decades before there was a Labour government in the United Kingdom, and three decades in New Zealand. For conservative businessmen, the untried experiment of a national Labor government with socialistic aims was alarming. They held fears of confiscation, nationalisation of industries, the end of free enterprise, and even French Revolution-style bloodshed.[102]

McMullin argued that the Watson government was met with a 'barrage of sledging … from the conservative press …' before it was even sworn in. He gave several examples. The *Argus* said '[the new government] will exist entirely on sufferance' and 'has no claim on an extended life'. The Adelaide *Register* asserted that 'a year of unrestrained socialist government would be to Australia – and particularly to the working classes – a greater disaster than half a dozen droughts'.[103] The *Sydney Morning Herald* wanted the new government to be removed as soon as possible, and later described

FIGURE 1.4 The *Worker*'s representation of the ghoulish 'capitalistic press' sheltering a monstrous, blood-thirsty mine owner, 1905

SOURCE The *Worker* (Wagga NSW), 28 January 1905, p. 5.

the Watson government as a 'scratch team of untried extremists'. The *Daily Telegraph* dismissed the Watson government as a 'curious political freak … which avowedly holds the interests of one section of the people paramount over those of all other sections … [and] goes too far beyond a joke'.[104]

Not surprisingly given this reception, many Labor politicians saw themselves as up against the commercial press from their party's beginning. Many believed that Labor would never get a fair hearing from a 'capitalist daily press' that was an organ of advertisers and capitalist propaganda. This led to a Labor plan – never completely fulfilled – of starting up a Labor daily newspaper in every capital city as an antidote. In 1890, the *Worker* was established by labour unions in Queensland. The *Hummer* began in NSW in 1891 (later called the *Worker* and then the *Australian Worker*). From 1898, there was the *Barrier Truth* in the mining town of Broken Hill, which was renamed the *Barrier Daily Truth* and became the first fully-fledged labour daily newspaper in Australia in 1908.[105] The Adelaide *Daily Herald* (1910–24), the Brisbane *Daily Standard* (1912–36), and Australian Workers' Union (AWU)–controlled *World* of Hobart (1918–24) were others.

The AWU controlled Labor Papers Ltd, directors of the *World* newspaper, which had started a campaign for a daily paper in Sydney in 1910, and secured enough money from union levies and other sources to have authorised capital of £250 000, to build Macdonell House, and install an up-to-date printing plant. But then the venture stalled until 1921. By that point, costs had risen extensively, and a fresh campaign for more funds was launched. Fed up with waiting for Labor Papers Ltd to actually launch a paper, in 1922, the Miners' Federation began publishing the morning *Labor Daily* in Sydney.

The *Labor Daily* was a vehement supporter of one of its major creditors, Labor's John Thomas (Jack) Lang, who became New

South Wales premier in 1925. Meanwhile, the anti-Lang AWU was finally motivated to launch the *World* as an afternoon paper in 1931. It appointed the highly experienced Montague Grover as editor. But even Grover could not make the paper successful. Its fateful take-over and closure is described in Chapter 4. In 1938, Lang and his allies lost control and withdrew their capital from the *Labor Daily*. It tried a new name (the *Daily News*) and a less political formula that included astrology, comic strips and other 'lighter matter', but was still financially unviable and in 1941, it was taken over by Frank Packer's *Daily Telegraph* and closed.[106]

At times, Labor had enjoyed the support of several important weekly newspapers, especially in their early years, including the *Bulletin*, as well as *Truth* and *Smith's Weekly*. The influential *Bulletin*, dubbed the 'Bushman's Bible', contributed to Labor's electoral success before World War I, with its bush nationalism and wide reach, but it became markedly more conservative after 1907, and especially after 1914. As for the official Labor papers, for a time, they provided a point of view that was deliberately slanted towards Labor to contrast with the anti-Labor daily press. But most Labor papers were short-lived.

The Labor papers faced a range of obstacles, including a lack of advertising from politically hostile commercial advertisers, and difficulties in accessing cable news that was controlled by commercial papers. Their openly partisan content was also out of step with the professed depoliticisation of popular newspapers, and the creed of journalistic objectivity that other newspapers claimed they followed. It did not help matters when Labor papers became caught up in the in-fighting of different Labor factions, and corruption and inept management were also alleged of some outlets. The 'capitalist' papers provided them with strong competition; they were usually larger and tended to have more features. By 1936, there was only one capital city Labor paper left – the *Labor Daily* in Sydney. When it closed in July 1941, all of the Labor daily papers had expired, except for the *Barrier Daily Truth*. The commercial nature of Australian newspaper publishing was so strong that, unlike in other countries, even Australia's Labor papers were usually registered as businesses, with allotted share capital, boards of directors and limited liability.

The 'apolitical' press

Although the fourth estate notion continues to inspire, and to be a noble aim of journalism, the press was never the disinterested outsider it claimed to be. Newspapers were deeply entwined with both politics and commerce from the start, and faced strong disincentives to act as a true watchdog on such power. For the fourth estate concept to work, it had to have diversity and variety, with newspapers encompassing all types of viewpoints and ideas. But diversity would become thin on the ground, in terms of daily newspapers having either a variety of views or owners. The habit that newspapers demonstrated early, of tending towards conservatism, grew even more pronounced in the 20th century as ownership consolidated among a handful of owners. But the concept of political independence that underpinned the 'fourth estate' was so central to the identity of newspapers that it had to be vehemently proclaimed even when there was much evidence to the contrary. This has continued through to the present day. The *Mercury*, for example, was one of the most resolutely conservative daily papers of the 20th century, but in 2014, when its editor surveyed the paper's 160 years, he declared that its legacy was 'unashamedly apolitical'.[107] Newspapers would not admit to being active and interested participants in the political system.

CHAPTER 2

THE RISE OF NEWSPAPERS

In 1883, author Richard Twopenny described Australia as 'essentially the land of newspapers'.[1] It had only been eighty years since the country's first newspaper, but growth in population and public demand for papers were strong, and so were the commercial prospects in an industry that was benefitting from generous government subsidies. By 1888, over sixty daily newspapers had been launched in Australia. Many of these were short-lived, but about twenty-one titles were being published at the same time in the early 1890s.[2] By 1909, Australia had three times as many separate daily newspapers as the United Kingdom (in relation to population).[3] A state librarian noted wistfully that Australians were great readers – but only of newspapers, not books.[4] One newspaper claimed in 1901 that Australians were 'the greatest newspaper reading people in the world'.[5] Later, sales and circulation figures would confirm that Australians were indeed among the highest per capita consumers of newspapers.[6]

Australians were an appreciative audience despite the fact that, when World War I broke out in 1914, the typical daily newspaper still looked much the same as it had for decades. It was a large broadsheet with a masthead in old English type. Its front pages were covered with long columns of dense, text-heavy advertisements. News was tucked away on the inside pages, and also presented in long, traditional, 'pack-it-in' single columns. At best, there might be some plain single-column headings to help the reader navigate through the paper. But two brash afternoon newspapers had been bucking this conventional format and were achieving enviable success. From these two newspapers, the first two Australian newspaper empires developed. They were drawing upon important shifts in technology, journalism practice and social change.

MELBOURNE'S *HERALD* AND SYDNEY'S *SUN*

The first of the two trailblazing newspapers was the Melbourne afternoon *Herald*. Twenty-five years earlier, in 1889, it had taken the radical step of putting news on its front page. This was well ahead of its time. Other established newspapers did not follow suit until forty or fifty years later (Table 2.1). The 'serious' morning papers, including *The Age, Advertiser, Sydney Morning Herald* and the *West Australian*, stuck to their traditional format of advertisements on the front page until the 1940s. While Australian newspapers usually took their inspiration from British newspaper practice, the *Herald* had even beaten the British by eleven years. The British press was on the cusp of a revolution, and Alfred Harmsworth – better known as the legendary press baron Lord Northcliffe – would soon change Fleet Street forever with his brand of popular daily newspapers. But front-page news was introduced to England only in 1900 – and by a rival to Northcliffe, Arthur Pearson's *Daily Express*. Northcliffe's own famous, mass circulation newspaper, the *Daily Mail* (launched in 1896), only moved to front-page news in 1939. And the 'serious' British papers took even longer than Australia's. (The British *Guardian* moved news to the front page in 1952, and *The Times* in 1966.) It was American practice, not British, that the *Herald* was following. News had started gravitating to the front page of American newspapers from the 1860s.[7]

The *Herald*'s shift to front-page news had been a gradual process but the major change came on 17 October 1889. Its front page that day was brash, not only because it contained news, but also

TABLE 2.1 The modernisation of Australian newspapers:
News on the front page

Newspaper	First placed news on its front page
Herald (Melbourne)	1889*
Australian Star	1904
Sydney *Sun*	1910 – from its inception
Sun News-Pictorial (Melbourne)	1922 – from its inception
Adelaide *News*	1923 – from its inception
Daily Telegraph (Sydney)	1924
Canberra Times	1926 – from its inception
Argus (Melbourne)	1937
Brisbane *Courier-Mail*	1938
Hobart *Mercury*	1939
Age (Melbourne)	1941
Sydney *Daily Mirror* (1941)	1941 – from its inception
Adelaide *Advertiser*	1942
Sydney Morning Herald	1944
West Australian	1949

* The transition was a gradual process but the main changes occurred on this date.
Multiple sources including: Victor Isaacs, 'Front page news' in *Australian Newspaper History Group Newsletter*, no. 3, January 2000, pp. 4–5; and Rod Kirkpatrick, 'Press timeline: Select chronology of significant Australian press events to 2011', compiled for the Australian Newspaper History Group, reproduced by the NLA, <https://www.nla.gov.au/australian-newspaper-plan/for-researchers/newspaper-chronology>.

because it focused on crime news reported in a sensational manner under bold headings. A column of snappy news item summaries, later sub-headed 'The Busy Man's Column', helped harried readers quickly scan the top stories of the day from the front page. The *Herald* had developed a reputation for experimenting with cheap, popular news formats. In the 1840s, it was using a style of illustrations and crisp presentation that other papers did not adopt until much later. In the 1860s, it was one of the first major daily papers to drop its price to a penny. In the 1870s, it astutely boosted its sports coverage to capitalise on the success of the early-closing movement and the eight-hour day, which had increased leisure time and driven a burgeoning interest in community activities and outdoor sports.[8]

When sports coverage became extremely popular, the *Herald* also had a natural advantage. As an afternoon paper, it was able to publish fast-breaking news of what had happened during the day, including late sports results gleaned from the telegraph, and later the telephone. This 'same-day' model of sports coverage was well ahead of other daily papers, and by the late 1880s, the *Herald* was publishing third and fourth editions to keep up with demand for reports of afternoon horseracing, football and other sports. The *Herald*'s sports and broad news coverage – including a focus on crime, divorce and scandal that led a rival to call it 'the literature of the gutter' in 1889 – won it a large audience of up to 50 000 readers by 1900.[9] From 1907, the *Herald* was being pushed forward by its talented and energetic editor, the journalist James Edward (JE) Davidson, who was fresh from studying American-style 'new journalism', including working on the *Detroit Free Press*. Davidson demanded an even 'crisper', 'brighter' style for the *Herald*.

In Sydney, another popularly focused afternoon newspaper emerged two decades after the *Herald* began putting news on its front page. In 1910, the *Australian Star*'s new owner Hugh Denison relaunched it as the *Sun*. The *Sun* became the first Australian daily paper to have news on the front page from its inception, and also pioneered other aspects of style and design. Compared to its rivals, the *Sun* looked fresher, with large headlines, illustrated advertisements, more use of white space, and a bold illustrated logo showing a horse-drawn chariot riding out of a vibrant sun. In its first week, the *Sun*'s headline stories included 'A LEGISLATOR'S TRAGIC END: DROPS DEAD WHILE SPEAKING', 'A HUMAN EAR IN A BOTTLE',

'A Traitor's Doom', and one of the *Sun*'s reporters asked a pioneering suffragette what he judged to be an all-important question: 'Has She Ever Been Kissed?'[10]

An upcoming world boxing championship was reported prominently, and the *Sun* boasted that it was sending its own correspondent to Reno City to report on the match. Taking advantage of its afternoon deadlines, the *Sun* promised that its cable service and later publication time would deliver the fight result to readers while rival morning papers were still 'marking time on the doormat'.[11] On 5 July 1910, the *Sun*'s front page was dominated by a vivid photograph of the losing boxer prone on the canvas, the victor standing over him. To get that photograph through so quickly, and to print it so clearly and prominently, the *Sun* was drawing upon all of the latest developments in printing technology, photography and cable news.

It was no coincidence that the two innovators in popular news were both afternoon papers. Their publication time gave the *Herald* and the *Sun* strong motivation to lead the way towards a lighter news style and a more eye-catching format. Unlike morning papers, which could rely upon subscribers who had their paper delivered to their home, the afternoon papers had to depend upon street sales. They were sold at newsstands and on street corners, usually near transport hubs, by a small army of mostly poor, young 'newsboys' who were known for guarding their territory with their fists. In order to get commuters to part with their pennies on their way home from work, the afternoon papers needed attractive front pages, and novel, sensational content that could be condensed into strong headlines, which the newsboys would shout out to lure buyers.

Because morning papers were generally read at home over breakfast, and then throughout the day, they could have longer and more complex content. But the afternoon newspaper reader was usually reading it on the way home, in crowded trains, trams and buses. Even though they were broadsheets, the afternoon papers aimed to deliver an easily digestible news service for busy readers who wanted to grasp the facts quickly through short, lively stories. Because they lacked a subscription model, they were heavily reliant on advertising revenue. Their need to capture large audiences for advertisers was at the heart of their efforts to popularise content. But the afternoon papers were also leading the industry in terms of managerial and organisational change because they had to be printed and distributed very quickly in order to maximise afternoon sales.

The *Herald* and the *Sun* were at the forefront of both responding to, and encouraging, changes in audience taste. They were contributing to a redefinition of news as information that was accessible, up to date, visual, and focused on the everyday and human-interest stories. Even traditional papers that prided themselves on maintaining their focus on 'serious' news, as opposed to 'soft' human interest news, soon felt the need to respond with a more lively presentation of news or else risk being viewed as too wordy, sober and dull by comparison. For example, by 1912, even the *Sydney Morning Herald* – which was as conservative in matters of style and format as it was in politics – had a summary column of news on its front page (albeit still alongside seven columns of ads), and its inside news pages included a women's page on Wednesdays, and increased sports coverage. The notoriously turgid *Sydney Morning Herald* even curtailed its long verbatim reports of parliament and its famously verbose editorials. The revamped paper had more illustrations, larger headings (some decorated with art nouveau flourishes), maps showing national weather, and even some small photographs.

Newspapers were responding to the fact that readers wanted to *see* the news, as well as read it. In the 1890s, the *Herald* published sketches of people, events and places to illustrate news. In the 1880s and 1890s, photography became easier to incorporate into newspapers with half-tone printing, and then linotype machines (which mechanically set type). The major illustrated magazines and weeklies, with their smooth paper and offset printers, began publishing photographs in the late 1880s, including the *Sydney Morning Herald*'s own weekly, the *Sydney Mail*. But traditional daily papers, such as the *Sydney Morning Herald* and *The Age*, did not begin publishing photographs until twenty years later, in 1908. Technical difficulties were one reason. The half-tone process did not work as well on the rougher paper and faster rotary machines used by the daily papers. But it was also about attitudes to imagery. The more 'serious' traditional papers were resistant to photography at first because they viewed it as being associated with 'lowbrow', sensational journalism. Impervious to such concerns, the *Herald* had been regularly publishing photographs from 1899.

THE SALES BOOM OF WORLD WAR I

When World War I created a sudden demand for news in 1914, the Melbourne *Herald* and the Sydney *Sun* were well placed to capitalise. Compared to other papers, their format was fresher and more modern. Their popularity with audiences and advertisers meant they were in good financial shape to withstand wartime costs, including a steep rise in the cost of paper and labour. Importantly, they also had a major organisational advantage because they were the two papers with the strongest international news, provided by a jointly operated cable service. As the two papers were publishing in different cities, and not direct rivals, they were working together to boost their news-gathering capacity.

Denison's *Sun* had pioneered a service of news cables supplied by the authoritative and prestigious *The Times* of London in 1912, and the *Herald* had joined as a partner in 1913, just in time for the coming war. *Herald* and *Sun* readers were promised 'the cream' of

ABOVE ALL FOR AUSTRALIA

THE SUN

SUNDAY EDITION

CIRCULATION LARGER THAN THAT OF ANY OTHER SUNDAY PAPER IN AUSTRALIA.

NO. 592.   SYDNEY: SUNDAY, AUGUST 2, 1914.   24 PAGES—ONE PENNY.

LATEST WAR NEWS.

War Cables from London and Berlin received up to 7.30 last night appear on Page 3.
Later Messages will be found on Page 4

ACCIDENT TO GUILLAUX AT ASCOT.

The photograph shows the wrecked aeroplane a few seconds after it fell. In the inset Guillaux is snapped as he was being assisted to the motor car which took him to hospital.

DUBLIN RIOTS.

OFFICERS' EVIDENCE.

(Published in the Times.)

BURNT TO ASHES.

DEATH OF FOUR MEN.

(Published in the Times.)

BIRTHS AND DEATHS.

SATISFACTORY FIGURES FOR JULY.

TO-DAY'S WEATHER.

FINE DAY, COLD NIGHT.

GOVERNOR-GENERAL

NO BANQUET IN WOLLONGONG

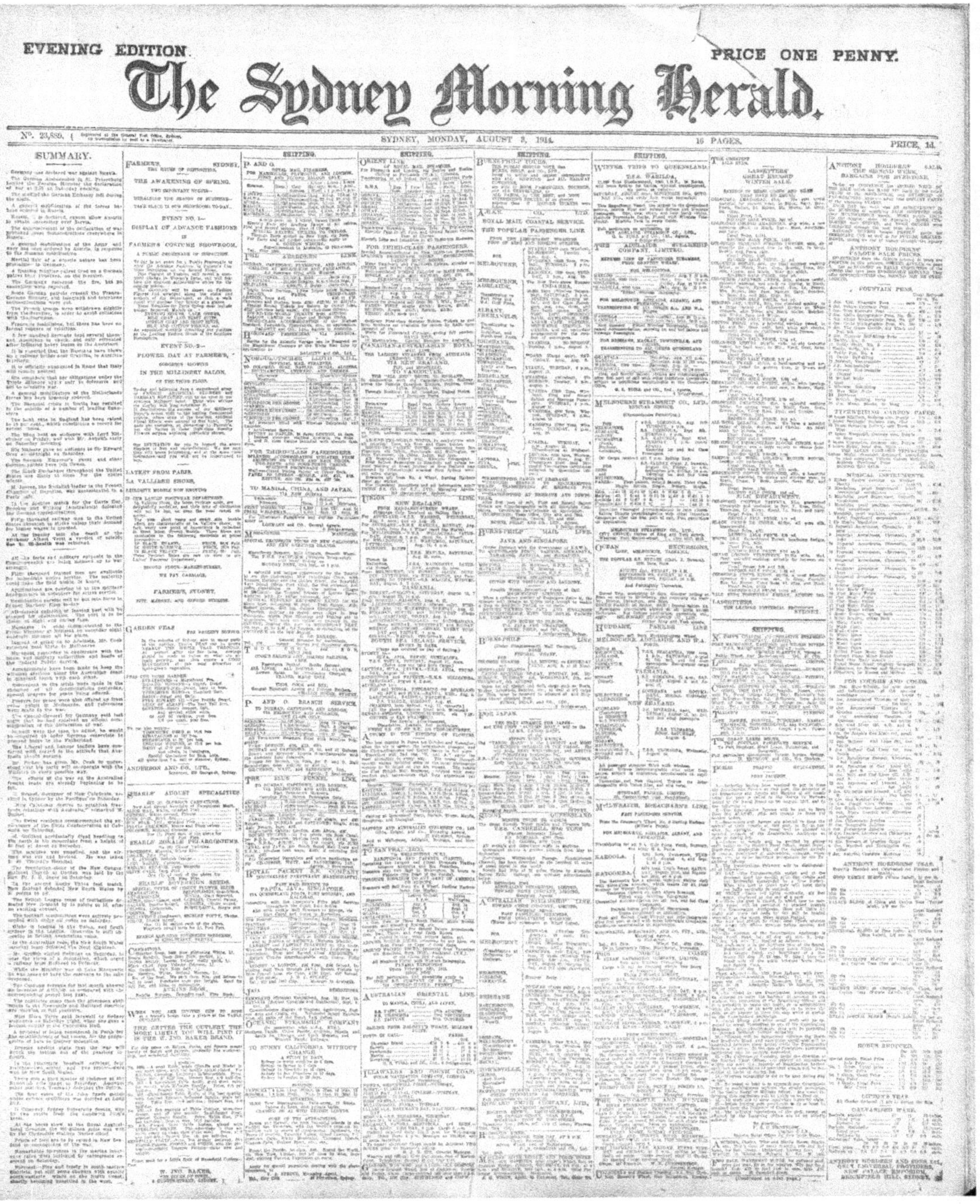
EVENING EDITION. PRICE ONE PENNY.

The Sydney Morning Herald.

SYDNEY, MONDAY, AUGUST 3, 1914. 16 PAGES. PRICE, 1d.

SUMMARY.

SHIPPING.

FIGURE 2.1 The front pages of the Sydney *Sun* and the *Sydney Morning Herald* at the outbreak of World War I, 1914

SOURCE The *Sun*, 2 August 1914, p. 1; the *Sydney Morning Herald*, 3 August 1914, p. 1.

international and war news, including 'early and exclusive cables' from the front. Making the most of their temporal advantage as afternoon papers, they claimed their reports were 'later and more complete' than their morning rivals'.[12]

From the war's outset, the public was encouraged to feel that its fervour for war and for newspapers were synonymous, and newspaper sales surged. When the war began, the *Sun*'s circulation trebled in three days. It sold 696 950 copies in seventy-two hours, a feat it described as 'without parallel in the history of Australian journalism'.[13] Before World War I, newspapers had covered conflict, but they had never covered it so extensively, or for such large audiences, and with such great influence on its conduct. Over at the *Herald*, the chair of the HWT's directors, Theodore Fink, was worried about how newspapers would cope once the war was over. How would they be able to 'continue to interest the public with ordinary fare, after the highly spiced dishes we have been used to'?[14]

Wartime reporting also changed journalistic style. Human-interest stories about heroism and tragedy were run alongside big picture stories about international politics. More prominent, bold headlines were used, and audiences wanted visual information to make sense of events in unfamiliar, far-off locations. Both popular and traditional papers began to publish photographs far more regularly, along with maps and illustrations.

Although a serious shortage of newsprint limited the number of pages available, newspapers also accommodated the shift towards larger, bolder ads as commercial advertisers used the war to sell products and services. There were advertisements for engagement and wedding rings for soldiers' sweethearts, household items for the thrifty housewife making do, brain and nerve tonics to soothe war-addled tension, and dentistry services for men looking to enlist. Advertisers were paying more attention to the psychology of sales and to graphic art and copywriting – and newspapers were paying more attention to advertisers and the crucial revenue that they provided. Sun Newspapers saw its profits quadruple from 1913 to 1914. It made £2293 in 1913, and then £9569 in 1914.[15]

When World War I ended, newspapers were on the verge of a new era. They had already benefitted from decades of development in the crucial infrastructure that carried news and delivered newspapers – particularly the railroads, telegraph lines, postal services, and overland and submarine cables. Cable communication had allowed daily war news to be provided to Australian newspaper readers, stimulating a sense of being close to the action, and encouraging a demand for news as it broke. It had taken over half a century of development to get to this point, through milestones that included the introduction of the electric telegraph, which began connecting the capital cities from 1858, the first cable messages from England being received and published in 1872, and the first use of wireless telegraphy in 1903.

Before the telegraph, newspaper offices had been dependent upon slow, irregular mail from around the country, and upon ships bringing news from London. Rival reporters would rush out in rowboats to meet arriving ships and take possession of stale, four-month-old news from overseas. With the telegraph, once the overseas cable service was extended in the 1870s – from London (via Singapore) through to Darwin, and with Darwin then linked to Adelaide, and Adelaide to the east-coast telegraph services – the time in which news could be received from England reduced from a matter of months to only hours. Newspapers proudly published 'telegraphic despatches'. Some new papers even called themselves the *Telegraph* (Adelaide, 1862, and Brisbane, 1872), or the *Daily Telegraph* (Melbourne, 1869, and Sydney, 1879).

At first, cable news was very expensive, but rates had reduced between the 1870s and 1910s. By the beginning of World War I, newspaper offices were also using telephones for gathering and

FIGURE 2.2 A fleet of *Herald* newspaper delivery vehicles lined up in Russell Street outside the old Herald and Weekly Times building, corner of Flinders Street, Melbourne, circa 1915–20
SOURCE Newspix (NPX1258100).

distributing news, and building fleets of automobiles that allowed faster delivery of papers to newsagents, vendors and subscribers. Among all of these important developments, was the single, biggest technological leap: revolutionary printing technology.

THE PRINTING REVOLUTION

When World War I began, the major daily newspapers were being printed on machines that could print, cut and fold over 30 000 copies of a sixteen-page newspaper every hour. This technology made mass-produced newspapers possible, paving the way for the popularisation of news and the expansion of newspapers. Historical accounts have tended to glorify the machinery – the 'magnificent creation of man's genius' – as one Australian newspaper described the rotary press.[16] But newspaper sales did not grow simply because machines made it possible to collect news more efficiently (by telegraph), to print newspapers faster and in greater quantities (on steam-powered and then rotary presses), and to distribute them faster and more widely (by train and then automobile). The expansion of newspapers also required an expansion of readers – people who *could* read, had the leisure time to do so, and wanted to know about the world around them.

At the same time that printing technology was advancing, so too were public health, housing, education, literacy and working conditions, as well as democratic reforms and voting rights. In Australia, the best way to explore how printing technology changed newspapers and their audiences is to examine the *Sydney Morning Herald*. This is not only because, as Australia's oldest surviving newspaper, its history coincides with the main shifts, but also because the *Sydney Morning Herald* was renowned for being an early adopter of new printing technology and had a reputation for having the best printing machinery in the country.

When the *Sydney Morning Herald* (then called the *Sydney Herald*) was founded in 1831, it was a four-page paper printed on a small hand press called a Columbian. It had 750 subscribers in a city of 15 000 inhabitants. Like other newspapers at that time, its audience consisted of literate political, business and mercantile elites. The *Sydney Morning Herald* provided them with essential notices for commerce and trade in their city, including shipping intelligence; trade advertisements; commercial and banking news; and reports of parliament, councils and courts, including details of new laws and regulations. But there was also a social and 'human interest' element, because papers gave notice of events on the social calendar, and the shipping notices on the front page were sought by those anxiously awaiting the arrival of friends and family in the colony, and the all-important mail from 'home' (the United Kingdom).

Although only four pages long, the *Sydney Morning Herald* cost six pence for a single copy, or 15 shillings a quarter for a subscription. In today's money, that equates to $31 per copy or $942 for a quarterly subscription (and the *Sydney Morning Herald* was cheaper than competitors). Newspapers were expensive, and only affordable to a small number of affluent subscribers because they were a scarce and labour-intensive product. In theory, the *Sydney Morning Herald*'s Columbian could turn out 125 four-page papers in an hour, but it seldom achieved that because hand operating a press was slow, backbreaking labour. To print enough copies for the paper's 750 subscribers, it took printers up to ten hours a night, working by candlelight. And they faced a rising workload. Only a few months after it began, the *Sydney Morning Herald*'s circulation went up to 1000 subscribers. The growing demand saw the paper move from being published weekly, to bi-weekly, tri-weekly and then, in 1840, it became a daily paper.

To try to keep up with demand, the *Sydney Morning Herald*'s co-owner, John Fairfax, had a new printing press built locally by a German engineer in 1848, but this was still operated by hand, and was such heavy labour that operators could only work in half-hour stretches. It was exhausting and dangerous work that often resulted in crushed fingers and dislocated shoulders. (Experienced printers often developed a lopsided gait from uneven muscle development caused by pulling heavy levers.) In England, this type of intense human labour had already been supplanted at the biggest London newspapers over the previous three decades. *The Times* in London developed the first steam-powered press in 1814. Its owners had the paper secretly produced off-site by a steam-powered machine that could turn out papers five times faster than by hand, and then surprised its printers with the machines in order to stop them resorting to industrial action because their jobs were threatened by the machinery.

It took thirty-nine years for the technology to reach Australia. In 1853, the *Sydney Morning Herald* became the first Australian paper to be printed by steam. John Fairfax had visited England the previous year and purchased a new printing press. It took many months for it to be delivered in pieces, and then installed at the *Sydney Morning Herald* office. It was a two-feeder steam-powered Cowper press that could print 2000 copies of the paper in an hour, equating to a sixteen-fold increase in the printing capacity of the paper. This shift from manual printing to steam-powered printing changed the economic basis for newspapers. Rather than having to rely upon a subscription model of charging elite subscribers a high price for a limited number of newspapers produced by labour-intensive methods, publishers could now mass-produce a newspaper and sell many copies of it for an affordable price to a much larger middle-class audience.

Other Australian newspapers soon updated to steam power, including the *Herald* that same year, and the *Register* in Adelaide the year after. But printing technology was developing so rapidly that, only three years later, when the *Sydney Morning Herald* moved into new premises in Hunter Street, it installed new equipment, powered by engine and boiler, that was capable of printing 4000 copies per hour. Only another three years later, the *Sydney Morning Herald* updated again, proudly installing a state-of-the-art Hoe six cylinder type-revolving printing press in 1859, the first of its kind in the Southern Hemisphere. The cost of the machine underlined the fact that newspaper publishing would henceforth require large amounts of capital. It cost about £6000 (half a million dollars in today's money). It could turn out 8000 copies of the paper in an hour, but still had its limitations. It could only print on one side of

FIGURE 2.3 State Governor Sir Reginald Talbot turns the switch to convert the gas engine rotary press to electricity in the machine room of the Herald and Weekly Times building, 1901

SOURCE Newspix (NPX1258114).

the paper, and required six workers to continually feed it with paper, while others had to collect the pages and run them back through the machine to print the other side. Then, more machines and workers were needed to fold the printed papers.

In ten years, the *Sydney Morning Herald*'s owners purchased ten different machines to try to keep up with changes in printing technology. But all of these machines relied upon workers to feed the paper through, and it was becoming physically impossible to do that job fast enough to meet demand for the paper. In 1875, only two years before his death, John Fairfax installed a revolutionary new type of press in the *Sydney Morning Herald* office. It was a 'Bullock-Hoe rotary stereotype web-perfecting printing press'. American Richard Hoe had created the high-speed rotary press thirty years earlier, and William Bullock had improved it.

The rotary press had curved stereo plates clamped onto cylinders, and it printed rapidly on a 'web' of continuous reels of printing paper that eliminated laborious hand feeding. It printed on both sides of the paper, a sharp knife then cut off each page automatically, before the papers were run through an apparatus that folded them. Complete newspapers – printed, folded and ready for distribution – emerged from the machines as quickly as the eye could follow them. The rotary press purchased by the *Sydney Morning Herald* could run with just one machinist and an assistant to work it, and it could produce 14 000 papers an hour.

Major American newspapers had used the rotary press since the late 1840s, and London papers had used it since the mid-1850s. In Australia, the *Sydney Morning Herald* had been beaten to the new technology by *The Age* in Victoria, which had installed a rotary press in 1872, three years before the *Sydney Morning Herald*. *The Age*'s owner, David Syme, had been to England in 1870, and purchased two Duncan and Wilson Victory Printing and Folding Machines. But Syme's were among the first machines that the patent holders had made and were beset by serious mechanical problems that took years to resolve. The *Sydney Morning Herald*'s rotary press was far more reliable and successful, and *The Age* later updated to Hoe machines. Other papers with sufficient capital soon acquired their own rotary presses in the 1870s, although it took another twenty years for papers in Western Australia and Tasmania. The wealthy *Sydney Morning Herald* continued to update its printing equipment, making big investments in 1912, 1922 and 1941. But these machines were all rotary presses of increasing size and sophistication. The industry's greatest advance in newspaper production technology was over until the development of web offset printing and photo-composition in the 1960s.

THE PENNY PRESS

Steam-powered and rotary printing enabled faster, cheaper, mass-produced newspapers at the same time as increasing literacy provided larger markets of readers to buy them. In the 1830s, enter-prising American newspaper publishers had used steam-powered printing presses to produce and sell affordable newspapers. Most papers then cost six cents, but these publishers priced their 'penny papers' at one cent per copy in order to attract a larger audience of middle-class American readers. The New York *Sun*, launched in 1833, is generally considered the first successful penny daily news-paper in the world. In the United Kingdom, after the removal of government taxes on newspapers, penny newspapers sprouted from the 1850s, including the pioneering *Daily Telegraph*, which was con-sidered the world's largest circulation paper by the mid-1870s.

Penny newspapers were building upon a long tradition of public interest in topics such as crime and scandal, as expressed in oral culture, including songs and ballads, and in early popular literature, such as broadsides and chapbooks. The enormous interest in Sunday newspapers among working-class British readers who could only afford a newspaper once a week – including *Lloyd's Weekly* (launched 1842), the *News of the World* (from 1843) and *Reynolds's Weekly Newspaper* (launched 1850) – had confirmed there were profits to be made in publishing human interest stories to a wide audience. The penny papers continued with this process of broadening out the definition of 'news' to include reports on daily life, ordinary people and personal events. These papers used more accessible language, and some used humour and sharp opinions. Some penny papers remained serious and respectable but ran reports on crime, sports and entertainment alongside traditional topics such as public policy, commerce and literature. Others were known for their more sensational and scandalous coverage of tragedy, death, divorce and gossip.

Australian newspaper owners were very aware of these trends, especially in British newspapers, because they imported copies of overseas papers, and several owners visited England in the mid-19th century. The *Sydney Morning Herald*, in an 1858 editorial, despaired that London penny papers were seeking circulation in a manner it judged to be offensive to morals and propriety.[17] This was a common response among the older and more expensive newspapers to the popularisation of papers. But the *Sydney Morning Herald* would soon come to adopt some of the features of the popular journalism that it was lambasting. One feature that could not be ignored was cheaper pricing.

Every time it had purchased new printing presses, or new buildings to house them, the *Sydney Morning Herald* had spent enormous sums of money. The costs involved drove less well resourced newspapers to closure. While the *Sydney Morning Herald* was a wealthy paper crammed with pages of classified advertisements, and its owner was well connected into the wealthiest enterprises of his day, it too felt the pinch. Over time, the *Sydney Morning Herald*'s owners had to balance their desire to recoup the costs of new equipment by charging a higher cover price against the need to generate more advertising revenue by making the paper more affordable and thereby increasing its circulation and attractiveness to advertisers.

Between 1849 and 1868, the *Sydney Morning Herald* vacillated between wanting to be an elite newspaper with a high price, and seeking to be a more affordable, and therefore more popular, newspaper. In 1849, striving for popularity, it dramatically halved its price to three pence per copy. But in 1854, it put its cover price back up to six pence to pay for rising costs, including the new steam-powered press. In an increasingly competitive market, this price was unsustainable, and only three years later, the cover price went down to four pence, and then three pence two years later. In 1868, the *Sydney Morning Herald* settled on a compromise position of two pence and remained at that price for nearly thirty years.

From the 1860s, the *Sydney Morning Herald*, and other older papers, were under pressure from the emergence of new, cheap, afternoon penny papers in Australia. After the connection of Melbourne and Adelaide via telegraph, the new *Telegraph* in Adelaide began in 1862, and it is believed to be the first penny daily evening paper in Australia. It was followed by the *Adelaide Express* in 1863, another penny afternoon paper, published by the *Advertiser*. In 1867, penny pricing arrived in Sydney when New South Wales' first penny daily, Bennett's *Evening News*, began. The *Herald* in Melbourne was again trailblazing when it reduced its price to a penny in 1863 because, at this time, the *Herald* was not yet an afternoon paper. It was still a morning paper, and most of the other established morning papers did not lower their prices to a penny until the 1880s and 1890s (Table 2.2).

The *Herald*'s price drop put such pressure on rival David Syme's *Age* that, in 1867, Syme purchased the *Herald*. He concealed

TABLE 2.2 Penny newspapers in Australia

Newspaper	Price dropped to a penny
Telegraph (Adelaide)	1862 – from its inception
Adelaide Express (owned by the *Advertiser*)	1863 – from its inception
Herald (Melbourne)	1863
Evening News (Sydney)	1867 – from its inception
Empire (Sydney)	1868
Age (Melbourne)	1868
Afternoon Telegram (owned by the *SMH*)	1870 – from its inception
Echo (owned by the *SMH*)	1875 – from its inception
Daily Telegraph (Sydney)	1879 – from its inception
Adelaide *Advertiser*	1884
West Australian	1887
Register (Adelaide)	1892
Brisbane *Courier*	1893
Argus (Melbourne)	1893
Sydney Morning Herald	1893
Hobart *Mercury*	1893
Sydney *Sun*	1910 – from its inception

Multiple sources including: Rod Kirkpatrick, 'Press timeline: Select chronology of significant Australian press events to 2011', compiled for the Australian Newspaper History Group, reproduced by the NLA, <https://www.nla.gov.au/australian-newspaper-plan/for-researchers/newspaper-chronology>; and Rod Kirkpatrick, *Dailies in the Colonial Capitals: A Short History*, 2016.

the acquisition by registering the purchase in the names of his associates and employees (a technique that powerful newspaper owners continued to use into the 20th century). Syme then turned the *Herald* into an afternoon paper to eliminate its competition from the morning market where his *Age* was already battling the *Argus*, and the newcomer *Daily Telegraph*. The *Herald* remained a penny paper when it shifted to the afternoon market in 1869, after which Syme sold it. He also took the step of reducing *The Age*'s own price to one penny (in 1868), saying the 'cheap press' in England had been a success and that following suit would make *The Age* 'within the means of the humblest individual in the colony'.[18] Other, more conservative, morning papers felt their wealthier audiences could afford to pay higher prices for a few more years to come (Table 2.2).

By 1893, most papers accepted that they would have to cut their price in order to stay competitive. It had become common wisdom among newspaper executives that dropping from a two penny paper to a penny paper would triple circulation.[19] In March, even the *Argus* with its wealthy audience and determinedly old-fashioned format became a penny paper. For years, the *Argus* had resisted lowering its price. While it held out, the penny *Age*'s circulation grew from 15 000 in 1868 to 101 000 in 1892, overwhelming the *Argus*, which only had a circulation of under 30 000 before it finally dropped its price to a penny.[20] The *Argus*' owners had been reluctant, but once they made the price reduction, they boasted a month later that its circulation had increased so 'far beyond the expectation of the proprietors' that they had to obtain an emergency stock of paper.[21] Other papers followed: in June, the *Sydney Morning Herald*, and in October, the *Mercury*.

The *Sydney Morning Herald* was also under pressure. Its morning rival, the *Daily Telegraph*, priced at a penny, was using a lighter, brighter style, and its circulation had overtaken the *Sydney Morning Herald*'s by the end of the 1880s. The *Sydney Morning Herald* was known for its comprehensive treatment of topics. A single report on parliament could occupy nearly a whole broadsheet page, while a ponderous editorial on political matters, such as tenders for iron pipes or the Vine Disease Bill, could take up many columns.[22] When the *Sydney Morning Herald* became a penny paper in 1893, it solemnly promised readers that: 'Care will be taken to maintain the character' of the paper.[23] Overall, the *Sydney Morning Herald* did retain its 'serious' and traditional style. The front page remained sacred to advertisements and notices, and the paper maintained its fondness for high culture and encyclopaedic tone. It was teasingly said that the *Sydney Morning Herald* could not report a story on Sydney's water supply without recounting the history of Roman aqueducts.

The *Sydney Morning Herald*'s owners could dare to be dull because the paper was sustained by a different economic model than papers like the *Herald* and the *Sun*. While the *Sydney Morning Herald* had to modernise in certain respects, particularly design and pricing, as a 'quality', 'serious' morning paper with an elite subscription base, and run by a family-owned company, it did not have to dive headlong into a downmarket spiral of 'human interest' news in order to chase popular audiences. It could continue to express faith in older definitions of news that placed a high priority on public affairs. Its lucrative classified advertising gave it the latitude to stick to its traditions. With its small type, long columns and lengthy, detailed reports, the *Sydney Morning Herald* was aimed at an elite and educated audience. It had a moral tone and there was a moral dimension to reading it. Seen as 'respectable', educational and 'mature', people took a certain pride in reading such a paper, and because this style attracted the wealthy, and those who aspired to wealth and status, the *Sydney Morning Herald* could charge advertisers a higher rate. For the paper to have leapt into full-blown populism would have been economically foolish as that would have diluted its more elite audience with working-class readers. Instead, the paper sought a balance between lower price/wider market, with a maintenance of its more elite news style and content.

The *Sydney Morning Herald*'s owners wanted to keep their respected flagship paper high-toned, serious and sacrosanct, but they had been experimenting on the side with 'down-market' penny papers for over twenty years. In 1870, the *Sydney Morning Herald* had debuted a penny evening paper, the *Afternoon Telegram*, but did so rather half-heartedly. The public and advertiser responses were similarly lacklustre, and the paper closed four months later. In 1875, the *Sydney Morning Herald* tried again and published another smaller, lighter, evening penny paper, the *Echo*. It found more success and lasted nearly twenty years.

The *Sydney Morning Herald*'s experiment with cheap afternoon papers was similar to that undertaken by the *Advertiser* with its *Adelaide Express*. These established papers wanted to capitalise on the popularity of cheaper, lighter fare, while insulating their main product from being downgraded by populism. When the *Mercury* dropped its price in 1893, its editorial was noticeably defensive on this point, arguing that the owners had come to the conclusion that there was nothing wrong with papers being 'cheap' so long as they remained 'wholesome'. Like the *Sydney Morning Herald*, the *Mercury* promised that its content would not shift down-market along with its price, but it also acknowledged that a lower price would mean wider access to the paper. And the *Mercury* could not resist a condescending boast that its lower price would allow it to help the working class, a class 'full of lofty aspirations, vague hopes … and need[ing] the help of enlightened criticism to save them … from themselves'.[24]

By 1893, all of the main capital city daily newspapers were penny papers, at least in price, if not in full-blown populist content. This shift highlighted an important issue for newspapers that would continue to dog them for another century, and well into the digital era. The strong public demand for newspapers was highly conditional upon price. In the 1890s, around the English-speaking world, the reading public seemed determined not to pay more than a penny for a newspaper. While journalists and editors hoped that a newspaper's success depended upon the quality of its content, many reluctantly came to the conclusion that, because newspapers tended to aim at the same middle market with similar content, it was often simply a matter of price that led one to succeed while another failed.[25]

THE 'NEW JOURNALISM'

In their push to convince Australians to hand over their pennies, the *Herald* and *Sun* had been enthusiastic adopters of what had been dubbed 'new journalism'. This was the term coined to describe a style of journalism developing in the 1880s that aimed to make newspapers more topical, readable, and focused on people and daily life. This style obviously had many antecedents, including the American penny press of the 1830s, and British weekly newspapers from the 1840s, but 'new journalism' occurred in a more intense fashion and in tandem with the industrialisation of the press between the 1880s and 1920s. There were cultural variations in different locations, and some newspapers took the style much further than others, but in essence, 'new journalism' advocates called for news to be reported with more brevity, clarity and simplicity, to be better organised, with a stronger narrative, snappy headlines, and a more attractive layout. 'People-oriented news' was paramount, including news of the bizarre and unusual, as well as trivia, gossip and speculation. 'Scoops' and 'exclusives' were highly valued.

Arthur Christiansen, editor of the British *Daily Express* in the 1930s, described the aim of 'new journalism' as: to 'make the news exciting even when it [is] dull ... Make the unreadable readable.'[26] News was to be presented in a modern layout, made possible by technical innovations including improved newsprint, linotype, photoengraving and photographs. The curved stereotype plates of rotary printing had allowed the breaking of columns to incorporate larger headlines and pictures, more advertising and syndicated features. Illustrations, comics and photographs became important elements of the visual nature of 'new journalism'.

In Australia, 'people oriented' news, that sought to amuse and entertain, also had a long trajectory. In 1832, a printer named Alfred Hill had launched a cheap Sunday paper filled with sports news, including boxing and racing, that was modelled on an English weekly. Although short-lived, *Hill's Life* used entertaining matter, humour and direct language, and seems to have found an audience among convicts and ticket-of-leave holders.[27] Some other short-lived early periodicals were known for their salacious content, including *The Currency Lad* (1832–33) with its focus on crime as entertainment, and the *Satirist* (1843), which printed ribald gossip as news. The *Satirist* only thinly disguised its targets' identities. For example, 'F – b – s you libidinous old goat, if you do not reform we shall expose you – fornication at your age is ridiculous, give it up man, your day is gone by. It is marvellous to us how Emily contrives to get up the steam ...' and 'If Mr C – – y is not a little less flash with the odious strumpet he has attached himself to, since his brutal conduct drove his unfortunate wife to the Lunatic Asylum, we shall give him a place in the *Satirist*'.[28]

The naughty *Satirist* lasted less than three months, but other scandal sheets took up the cause, including an early *Truth* and the *Innocents of Sydney*, before John Norton's own infamous weekly *Truth* (founded 1890). In the daily newspapers, there were also elements of 'new journalism' since at least the 1860s. The *Evening News* from 1867 had, as Henry Mayer pointed out, 'bold type, short stories ...' and reports of 'rapes and garrottings'.[29] The *Herald* had its crisper presentation style and focus on court proceedings, including crime and divorce by the 1870s. In Sydney, the *Daily Telegraph* had reinvented itself, and like the *Herald*, was accused of sensationalism.

But it is telling that Australian newspapers in the 1890s used the term 'American-style journalism' as a synonym for personality-focused 'new journalism'.[30] In the decade before the *Herald* started putting news on its front page, a nascent transformation had begun in American journalism. Hungarian immigrant Joseph Pulitzer, who had been experimenting with popular journalism since the late 1870s, had purchased the New York paper, the *World*, in 1883. He then began an aggressive circulation-building campaign by building upon the techniques of earlier penny papers such as the New York *Sun*, which had relied on local news, crime, scandals and high society gossip. Pulitzer's *World* used accessible language to build a wide audience that included immigrants and the working class, many of whom had limited formal education and only developing literacy. Pulitzer's papers relied on sensational banner headlines to entice readers: 'Who Murdered Mrs Bush?', 'Blood on a Mother's Lips', 'Did She Steal the Diamonds? A Hotel Maid Accused of Stealing Jewels', 'A Brother on the War-Path – He Attacks his Sister's Dentist and Then Tries to Shoot Him'.[31] It was also known for its vibrant illustrations and cartoons.

William Randolph Hearst, son of a millionaire politician and mine owner, imitated Pulitzer's style when he took over the *San Francisco Examiner* in 1887. In 1895, he made his move into New York, purchasing the *Morning Journal* (later named the *New York American*). Hearst started a circulation war in New York when he reduced the cost of his *Morning Journal* to one cent. In 1896, Pulitzer responded by cutting the price of the *World* to one cent. (This was three years after even the more conservative Australian dailies had dropped their prices to a penny, an indication of how competitive the Australian newspaper industry was at the time.) In London, Harmsworth (ennobled as Lord Northcliffe in 1905) launched the halfpenny *Daily Mail* in 1896, undercutting its rivals. The trends in content that these overseas owners were driving – especially Hearst and Pulitzer – would give the righteous *Mercury* (whose owners were actually the sons of a convict, and the grandsons of another convict) some vivid examples of just how 'unwholesome' 'cheap' journalism could be.

The intense competition between Pulitzer's and Hearst's giant newspapers in New York led their papers to be described as 'yellow journalism'. This term's origin is debated but it may have derived from a yellow-coloured comic strip originally featured in Hearst's paper and bitterly fought over by Pulitzer and Hearst. Established papers that were scandalised by the new popular approach, and infuriated by the success of more popular papers, used the term to describe journalism that was prone to exaggeration, scandal-mongering and stories based on speculation and lies. Showing more than just a touch of exaggeration itself, the *Sydney Morning Herald* called the American 'yellow press' 'the most horrible thing on earth'.[32]

Speed was an important element of Hearst's and Pulitzer's competition and they pushed their journalists to rush news onto the page in order to scoop each other. Some of those reporters did not bother to wait for verification and, especially under Hearst (whose demands were relentless), reporters sometimes turned to their imagination to fill in gaps in newsgathering. Sensationalism, exaggeration, unsubstantiated claims and sometimes outright falsehoods, were certainly part of what Pulitzer and Hearst unleashed but, especially in their early years, they also used their newspapers to reach audiences neglected by the traditional newspapers, to advocate for important social reforms, and to investigate government corruption and negligence by public institutions.

Pulitzer believed his papers had to have 'sympathy for the oppressed' and be devoted to public welfare.[33] His *World* campaigned for social reforms, including investigating and exposing mistreatment of immigrants, labourers and the poor. His papers 'called for

curbs on the great commercial monopolies, defended the right to
unionize, supported income tax and death duties …'.[34] Pulitzer
hired female journalists and gave them key assignments, not just
confining them to the 'women's pages' as so many other outlets did
for decades to come. Hearst's politics were less consistent. Despite
his privileged background, when he began in newspapers it was as
a crusader for liberal causes, who fought hard to 'combat economic
and social injustices'.[35] Hearst's papers advocated for the eight-hour
day, female suffrage and anti-trust legislation. Later in life, Hearst
became politically conservative, while Pulitzer came to regret the
downward spiral his competition with Hearst had initiated. Pulitzer
shifted the *World* back to its progressive roots and its social reform
campaigning. The 'yellow' papers' social reforming stance was not
lost on the more conservative Australian papers: in 1904, the *Sydney
Morning Herald* condemned Hearst for preaching 'socialism'.[36]

'Yellow journalism' encouraged a debate about popularisation
that continues today in relation to the tabloid press. Should popular journalism be applauded for making news more accessible to
general readers from the oppressed classes, and advocating on their
behalf? Or should it be condemned for its crass commercial motives,
for promoting only a veneer of radical politics, and for misleading
and turning readers into 'consumers of excitement, sensation, pity
and fear'?[37] For established papers, there was little doubt: the new
breed of papers was vulgar, their readers unsophisticated, and they
represented a threat to decency. In 1898, the *Mercury* published an
article that called the *World* and *Journal*'s ground-breaking colour
printing 'gaudy', saying their pages looked 'like a fried egg'. It sniffed
that such papers were aimed at 'shop girls, store porters, errand boys,
counter-jumpers and bar room loungers, who get their daily education out of this sort of pabulum'.[38]

The established papers griped but it would not be long before
they too adopted bolder headings, more concise reporting, more

human interest news, specialised sections, increased sports coverage, illustrations and photographs. The popularity and impact of new styles of journalism were simply too big to ignore. Only two years after Pulitzer cut the price of the *World*, it was reaching a mammoth circulation of over 1.5 million. Even the respectable *New York Times* reduced its price from three cents to one cent in 1898 in order to compete. Like the *Sydney Morning Herald*, the redoubtable *New York Times* set out to prove that not all of the penny papers were sensationalist. It tried to make its news more concise and attractive, while still retaining its authority and claims to objectivity.

One man who had been watching this American transformation avidly was Harmsworth (Northcliffe). The British journalist had been to New York to learn from the sensational and highly illustrated journalism of Pulitzer and other popular papers. Returning to the United Kingdom, Northcliffe became the major pioneer of popular journalism in daily papers in Britain, drawing on elements from popular British Sunday papers (which pre-dated Northcliffe's populism by fifty years), and from American 'new journalism'. Northcliffe believed that commuters travelling to and from work in cities wanted light entertainment to brighten their bleak, industrialised lives. He began by launching periodicals in the late 1880s and early 1890s, then launched the instantly successful halfpenny *Daily Mail* in 1896.

The *Daily Mail* had bold headlines, lively and concise writing, plenty of competitions, human interest stories, and serials designed to entice the reader to return. Techniques from the American popular press were made culturally appropriate for British readers, so although the *Daily Mail* had its fair share of crime, it was still designed to be respectable reading – nothing that would embarrass a commuter reading it in public – and its serials were designed to be read to the whole family at night. Northcliffe repeatedly told his staff that 'people are so much more interesting than things' and called for stories that would feed the curiosity of readers about their fellow citizens. Crime and court reporting were awarded considerable prominence, but the *Daily Mail* also tried to keep up to date with modern interests, such as motoring, cinema and sport. In a pre-radio era, Northcliffe instructed his editors to have 'something for everyone', including women's pages for female readers, sports for men and boys, fashion for teenage girls, and comics for kids. Northcliffe also spent lavishly on sensational scoops, prize competitions, publicity stunts, and special campaigns to build up the *Daily Mail*'s circulation. Circulation hit more than one million in 1902, and a world-beating 1.7 million by 1924.[39]

In Australia, some of these circulation-building techniques were already in evidence in the 1890s and early 1900s, including in the *Herald*. But in 1915, an ambitious Australian journalist named Keith Murdoch went to London and closely studied Northcliffe's methods. When Murdoch returned to Australia in 1921, as the new editor of the *Herald*, he was armed with a set of the British newspaper baron's notes, which Murdoch referred to as his 'bible' (Chapter 7). Through the 1920s he set about adapting Northcliffe's methods to the *Herald*, building upon the work of earlier editors who had already been popularising the paper for decades.

In 1903, Northcliffe had launched the tabloid-size *Daily Mirror* as a women's newspaper but then changed it to a pictorial newspaper with a broader focus. Consisting mainly of half-tone photographs, it became the world's first successful pictorial tabloid newspaper. The smaller tabloid page size was judged easier for commuters to carry, read and unfold on public transport. American versions of pictorial tabloids followed in 1919 and 1924.[40] As a later chapter explains, Hugh Denison, owner of the Sydney *Sun*, launched Australia's first pictorial tabloid, the remarkably successful *Sun News-Pictorial*, in Melbourne in 1922. The success of that paper inspired much imitation in the Australian newspaper industry.

TABLE 2.3 The shrinking newspaper: From broadsheet to tabloid

Newspaper	Changed from a broadsheet to a tabloid size
Sun News-Pictorial (Melbourne)	1922 – tabloid from its inception
Daily Telegraph (Sydney)	1927–31 – then went back to broadsheet size from 1931 to 1942
Daily Mirror (Sydney)	1941 – tabloid from its inception
Daily Telegraph (Sydney)	1942 – converted to a tabloid again
Mercury (Hobart)	1942–57 – then reverted to broadsheet size from 1957 to 1993
Sydney *Sun*	1947
Adelaide *News*	1948
Brisbane *Telegraph*	1948
West Australian	1949
Argus (Melbourne)	1950
Canberra Times	1956–64 – then reverted to broadsheet size from 1964 to 2016
Herald-Sun (Melbourne)	In 1990, the *Herald* and *Sun News-Pictorial* were merged and published as the tabloid *Herald-Sun*.
Mercury (Hobart)	1993 – converted to a tabloid again
Adelaide *Advertiser*	1997
Brisbane *Courier-Mail*	2006
Age (Melbourne)	2013
Sydney Morning Herald	2013
Canberra Times	2016

Multiple sources, including: Rod Kirkpatrick, 'Press timeline: Select chronology of significant Australian press events to 2011', <www.nla.gov.au/anplan/heritage/1901-1950. html>; articles in the *Courier-Mail*, 20 June 2016; *Mercury*, 2 October 1942, 5 July 1944, 18 November 1947; *Telegraph* (Brisbane), 27 December 1947; and *SMH*, 20 October 1941.

Northcliffe had been interested in smaller page sizes for news-papers since 1901. He believed the tabloid size – 'small, portable (and) neatly indexed' – was destined to become the 'newspaper [format] of the 20th century'.[41] His prediction was mostly correct: in Australia, only a handful of papers held out from shifting to a tabloid size until the early 21st century (Table 2.3). (At the time of writing, the *Australian* is the only remaining broadsheet daily paper.) Many dailies converted to tabloid size in the 1940s, spurred by news-print rationing during World War II, and newsprint shortages in the post-war period. The more venerable broadsheets – *The Age*, *Sydney Morning Herald* and the *Canberra Times* – took longer, until the second decade of the 21st century, to move to what they called a 'compact' size (to avoid negative connotations associated with the term 'tabloid'). In the United Kingdom, Northcliffe's own *Daily Mail* had become a 'compact' in 1971, the prestigious *The Times* switched to tabloid format in 2004, and the *Guardian* moved to a smaller 'Berliner' size in 2005, and an even smaller tabloid size in 2018.

POPULARISATION AND AUDIENCES

Like front-page news and photography, the tabloid page size proved to be part of an unstoppable wave of popularisation. By the 1940s, even the most conservative Australian newspapers had both front-page news and comic strips. Popularisation reflected changing attitudes about the needs and desires of newspaper audiences. At the 'serious' papers, owners and executives tended towards a pater-nalistic view of their readers, believing they were in need of moral, political, and even spiritual, guidance. These papers were happy to lecture and lead. At the popular papers, assessments of readers were unflattering in a different way. When he was angling for influence

with Theodore Fink of the HWT in 1918, Keith Murdoch counselled that the *Herald* should not make its content too upmarket
because it needed to hold on to readers from what he called 'the
uneducated unthinking class'.[42]

In public, newspaper executives presented the popularisation
of news as a democratisation of knowledge; that by making news
more accessible, they were responding to audience tastes, and performing a public service by reaching those who had been neglected
by elitist newspapers. In private, the concept was often expressed in
a way that showed contempt for audiences, including an ingrained
sexism that inhibited newspapers' attempts to build large female
audiences with just token women's pages. Hearst said 'crime and
underwear' were the primary ingredients for popular newspapers.
Another American journalist characterised the news formula as
'blood, money and broads'.[43] But the Australian version was cruder
still. The cynical chief of staff of the *Herald*, the unflappable Frank
Murphy (said to be the one person on staff who was not afraid of
Keith Murdoch), said newspapers' hunt for circulation was about
the three C's – 'crime, cunt and comics'.[44]

Reporters who wrote for newspapers in the 1930s said they were
taught that the public were 'morons' and nothing was too simple
for readers.[45] A later chairman of the HWT, John Williams, was a
former journalist and famous among his reporters for dispensing
strong advice about audiences. Longstanding HWT columnist
Keith Dunstan recalled that Williams often told journalists that the
typical Australian newspaper reader had a 'mental age of 14', was
married, had two kids, was struggling with a mortgage, and was
'conservative and easily shocked'.[46] Reporters were told 'never use
a sentence longer than 12 words. You never use a word that a child
could not understand.'[47]

From the mid-19th century, developments in technology,
allied with social and economic change, had spurred newspapers

to experiment with mass-produced penny papers, 'new journal-ism' and popular news formats. They were trying to achieve a mix of price, format and journalistic style that would attract large and profitable audiences. These mass audiences were the bases for advertising revenue and economic success, but also for public influ-ence and political power. For the most ambitious and successful newspaper owners, mass audiences laid the foundation for a period of empire building in the 1920s that would change the shape of Australia's newspaper industry, and its politics.

CHAPTER 3
THE AGE OF PRESS EMPIRE BUILDING

Equally as important as the changes in journalism style that American and British newspaper barons were driving in the late 19th and early 20th centuries, were the transformations they were making in newspaper organisation and management. American popular newspapers were known for their emphasis on speed, and for paying large sums of money to obtain news from cables and investigations in order to 'scoop' competitors. The largest newspaper groups established extensive newsgathering operations, with large costs and infrastructures, and owned chains of newspaper titles. Some also branched out into radio, film and other media. In the United Kingdom, Northcliffe similarly built up a stable of newspapers, but he also developed control over the production of paper – the most expensive raw material of newspapers. Australian newspaper owners were watching all of these transatlantic trends with interest.

In the United States, the owner who organised the first major chain of newspapers was Edward Willis (Wyllis) Scripps. Between 1878 and 1917, his company founded twenty-seven papers, and he eventually owned thirty-four newspapers in fifteen states. Scripps' organisation pioneered the use of syndication by reproducing the same content across different papers to reduce costs. But Scripps was an unusual businessman whose motto was 'always opposing the rich, always supporting the working man'. His newspapers were aimed at a working- and middle-class audience that

he referred to as the '95 per cent' of society who were neither powerful nor privileged.

Scripps' papers vigorously supported the right to organise in
unions (something that mainstream American newspapers usually
opposed at the time), and they campaigned against corrupt monopolies, unfair wages, excessive streetcar fares, unsafe working conditions and private ownership of utilities. Denounced by business
rivals as a radical, socialist and anarchist, Scripps experimented
with profit-sharing schemes, employee ownership in his companies,
ad-less newspapers (that made money out of circulation only), and
reportedly paid his employees above award wages. In 1907, the year
before he retired, Scripps formed an independent press association
to produce cable news – United Press (UP) – in order to oppose
the much larger Associated Press (AP), because he felt AP was
monopolistic and too close to the establishment.

Ten years after Scripps retired, Hearst was building his own
nation-spanning chain of newspapers, magazines, radio stations
and a movie studio. Between 1918 and 1928, Hearst's organisation
embarked upon a newspaper buying spree that included closing sixteen newspapers. Buying a competitor and closing it down, or merging it with a stronger paper, was a business strategy used to eliminate
competition – and one that Australian newspaper empires would
imitate. By the early 1930s, the Hearst organisation was at its peak
and was a publishing empire with twenty-six daily papers and eighteen Sunday papers across nineteen cities. Hearst's papers accounted
for 13.6 per cent of total daily circulation in the United States, and
24.2 per cent of Sunday circulation.[1]

But Northcliffe was the press baron held in greatest awe by
Australian newspaper owners and executives. The bullying proprietor, who insisted on being called 'the Chief' by his often grovelling staff, led an economic reorganisation of the British newspaper industry that transformed Fleet Street in the 1900s to 1910s.

His stable of papers had an immense audience reach, but he also came to exert significant control over the management of paper production, printing, distribution, retailing and advertising content. In 1909, Northcliffe opened one of the largest paper mills in the world, in Newfoundland (Canada), so he could by-pass sellers and produce his own newsprint. In Australia, the companies associated with the *Sydney Morning Herald*, the *Herald* and the *Sun* began to imitate this strategy in the 1920s (Chapter 14).

Before Northcliffe, newspapers in England had usually been family-owned, and run on a fairly small and inexpensive scale; few 'ever offered their shares for sale'.[2] But in 1905, Northcliffe had three of his papers – the *Daily Mail*, the *Evening News* and the *Weekly Dispatch* – incorporated as a public company. Shares for Associated Newspapers Limited sold rapidly. Australian joint stock newspaper companies had been in existence since at least the 1860s, and as with Northcliffe's experience, share ownership provided capital to invest in staff, facilities and the latest expensive equipment, but it also had the effect of incorporating the profit motive more firmly into newspaper companies. Once they were public companies, they were under constant pressure to pay strong dividends to investors. This meant even greater focus on advertising revenue and on maximising circulation.

In 1905, Northcliffe rescued the financially struggling *Observer*, and he took over the prestigious *The Times* in 1908. In London, he controlled 39 per cent of the morning daily newspaper market, 31 per cent of the evening market, and nearly 12 per cent of Sunday papers.[3] By the beginning of the 1920s, Northcliffe and his brother Harold (Viscount Rothermere) controlled newspapers that had a total circulation of six million.[4] After Northcliffe's death in 1922, the financially savvy (and fascist-supporting) Rothermere carried on the empire building by moving into the field of provincial newspaper publishing.

Inspired by the business practices of overseas chains – and boosted by their World War I increases in audiences, advertising and profits – three Australian newspaper companies shifted into empire-building mode in the 1920s. All three companies developed not from the old, sober, morning papers, but from three populist afternoon papers – the Sydney *Sun* (Associated Newspapers), the *Herald* (the HWT) and the Adelaide *News* (News Limited). But among the proprietors of these daily papers, there was no Scripps, Pulitzer or early Hearst – men who had combined commercial ownership with a reforming zeal, and created papers that declared a social conscience and claimed to reveal corruption, injustices, hardships and oversights in American society. The Australian owners were more like Northcliffe. They saw no need to go searching for social problems. Their motivation was to meet the tastes of a new public that was better educated, more affluent, and more open to buying the latest consumer goods.

NEWSPAPERS IN THE ROARING 1920S

As the 1920s dawned, the conditions were right for newspapers to expand in Australia. The population was growing and highly literate. Sydney had one million people by the end of 1924, and Melbourne by 1929. Decades of free education policies dating from the 1870s meant that there was a very high rate of literacy among even the working class.[5] Reduced working hours and increases in salary meant that Australians had more disposable income and more leisure time and, after World War I, their social attitudes and consumption practices had changed.

As historian Robert Murray explained, a post-war housing boom had also seen the development of new suburbs by the 1920s, and more people than ever before were commuting to and from work using public transport. Electric trains were running regularly in Melbourne by the mid-1920s, and in Sydney by the end of the 1920s. There were also buses and, in major cities, electric trams. Reading newspapers had become a popular way for commuters to pass the time.[6] Although the advent of radio broadcasting in the 1920s had caused much excitement, and radio grew rapidly in terms of popularity and affordability, it was not portable for decades, and its programming, at first, focused on music and entertainment. As Chapter 12 explains, newspaper owners afraid of the competition successfully sought to limit radio broadcasting of news. But even once news bulletins became more regular and prominent, the anecdotal and sales evidence suggested that radio (and cinema news reels as well), helped to stimulate greater interest in news and this encouraged more people to buy newspapers, not less.

As business owners started pursuing the opportunities, new titles sprang up to compete with old 19th century newspapers. The newcomers included, in Sydney, the official Labor organ, the *Labor Daily* (1922) and the brazen *Daily Guardian* (1923). Melbourne saw the launch of Australia's first pictorial daily, the *Sun News-Pictorial* (1922), and the short-lived *Evening Sun* (1923). The *News* launched in Adelaide (1923) and, briefly, in Hobart (1924). The *Canberra Times* began in the new capital in 1926. Born in the jazz era of journalism, these papers were more willing to adopt the principles of 'new journalism', including front-page news, crisp presentation, more visual journalism, and dashes of humour and strong opinion.

It was a sign of things to come that several of these new papers were owned by existing newspaper companies, rather than by new or independent entrants. But, in 1923, chain ownership was not yet common. There were still twenty-one different owners publishing twenty-six daily capital city newspapers.[7] This was more competition than Australia would ever see again among daily newspapers.

The pioneering media scholar Henry Mayer described the 1920s as 'by far the toughest and most ruthless period in Australian journalism'.[8] Daily newspapers were vigorously trying to entice readers from their rivals by offering free insurance, prizes, competitions, serials, new features and comic strips (including the hugely popular comics Ginger Meggs (in the *Sunday Sun*), and Fatty Finn (in the *Evening News*' Sunday edition), both created in the early 1920s). But one area where rivals were unwilling to compete was on price.

On the contrary, major newspaper companies tended to engage in price fixing, a business strategy with a long history, dating back to the 1850s in Sydney and Melbourne. In 1919, the *Sydney Morning Herald* raised its penny price to 1½d, and then put it up again, to two pence, in 1920. But when the paper's executives heard rumours in 1922, that *Smith's Weekly* was going to launch a new penny paper (this turned out to be the *Daily Guardian*), the *Sydney Morning Herald* pre-emptively dropped back to a penny price. On the very same day, the three other Sydney daily papers also dropped to a penny. By 1930, even the once independently minded, but now cash-strapped, *Daily Guardian* joined the price cartel. That year, all the Sydney papers again moved as one to a 1½d price: the *Sydney Morning Herald*, the *Telegraph Pictorial* (as the *Daily Telegraph* was known during one of its many makeovers), the *Daily Guardian*, the *Sun* and the *Evening News*. Even the 'worker's friend', the *Labor Daily*, put up its price, although it was a period of high unemployment when their readers could least afford it. Archival papers show that Associated Newspapers had cut a secret deal with one of the *Labor Daily*'s directors, JT Lang (leader of the NSW Labor Party), to pay his paper £3000 if it would increase its cover price along with the other papers.[9]

The Melbourne papers also cooperated to avoid competition on price. *The Age* and the *Argus* both moved up to a 1½d price on the same day in 1920. When word came through in 1921 that Hugh

Denison, owner of the Sydney *Sun*, was about to launch the *Sun News-Pictorial* in Melbourne, it was rumoured that he was planning to price it at one penny. All of Melbourne's major papers held a meeting and the *Herald*, *The Age* and the *Argus* made a joint decision to hold their cover price to 1½d.[10] Lo and behold, when the *Sun News-Pictorial* launched in 1922, it was not a penny paper at all but priced at 1½d, ensuring there would be no competition on price in Melbourne either.

Newspaper owners were very anxious about price because newspapers had expanded so greatly in size and production costs that a 1½d selling price for a daily newspaper did not even cover the cost of the newsprint it was printed on. But to raise the cover price was risky because, even decades after the move to penny pricing, and despite all of the new features that had been added into newspapers since then, readers still did not want to pay much more than a penny for their paper. In the 1920s, the owners knew that Australians were not willing to pay for a newspaper even half as much as they were paying for a pint of milk or a loaf of bread. No daring Australian newspaper owner stepped forward though, in the footsteps of Northcliffe and Hearst, to break the price cartels and boldly undercut their rivals. Instead, the Sydney and Melbourne daily newspapers all held at 1½d for another decade. (When Sydney newspapers next raised their price, to two pence in 1940, they all did so on the same day again, while the Melbourne papers moved up to two pence within months of each other in 1941.)

Because the cover price did not cover their costs, the papers were heavily reliant on advertising revenue to make profits. This provided a powerful incentive for them to keep pursuing middle-market mass circulations with popular content, because extra readers made each inch of space more expensive for advertisers. Department stores, clothing and drapery retailers had become the lifeblood of papers, especially the afternoon papers. In Sydney, it was not just the crucial David Jones, but also Horderns', Grace Bros and Mark Foy's. In Melbourne, Myer was king, but GJ Coles and Co was important, and so were other big drapery stores selling towels, sheets, curtains, fabrics and clothes, such as Snow's in Glenferrie and The Colosseum in Windsor. Thursday evening and Saturday papers were saturated with drapery store ads. They took up to 90 per cent of advertising in the *Herald* on Thursdays.[11] And even at the height of the Depression, drapery announcements took up more than half of the total display advertising in Melbourne and Sydney newspapers.[12]

Newspaper executives believed that these advertisements were more attractive than the news content to many readers – especially women.[13] Since newspapers had begun, people had, at least in part, tended to buy them for the advertisements and classifieds, and not just purely for the journalism. This is why ads were originally placed on the front page, and why some papers were given titles like 'the *Advertiser*'. (This fact tends to be forgotten by those who value journalism, but it was exposed anew in the 21st century when digital classified websites such as eBay, Seek, Gumtree, Carsales.com and Domain stripped advertising from newspapers. This uncoupled the advertising from the journalism with disastrous results for newspaper journalism – both in print and online.)

In the 1920s, newspapers were investing more time and effort into attracting large advertisers, including experimenting with colour advertisements. Newspapers were increasingly visual, especially after the stunning success of the *Sun News-Pictorial* from 1922; and photography was also becoming far more prominent because improvements in camera technology meant that a wider range of events could be photographed. Larger, more sensational photographs appeared in the popular and tabloid-style press on themes such as violence, crime, accidents and society scandals. Photographs of sport were especially important for Australian newspapers.

Beauty contests based on photographs of women were also used as circulation-boosting devices by some papers, including the *Herald*, the *News* and the *Daily Guardian*.

But, even in the competitive 1920s, the tone and content of the Australian daily newspapers never turned as 'yellow' as Hearst's and Pulitzer's at the height of their New York circulation war. In Australia, most papers were middle-of-the-road. At one end of the spectrum were the *Sydney Morning Herald* and the *Argus*, which considered themselves the 'gentlemen' of the press: quality, respectable journals of record. At the other end was the *Daily Guardian*, which extended the sort of 'larrikin journalism' and pseudo-muck-raking popularised by its stablemate *Smith's Weekly*. With its manufactured, sensational exposés on white slavery and cocaine buying, and its unethical practices (including stealing and publishing a letter from a murder-suicide crime scene), the *Daily Guardian* was the closest the Australian daily press got to 'yellow' journalism. Its photographs of women in bathing suits led critics to refer to it as 'The Flapper's Daily' and the 'Daily Girlie'. *Smith's Weekly* played up the criticism, portraying its stablemate as a scandalous flapper, addicted to cigarettes and cocktails, who scandalised the old maids of the Sydney press, including 'old granny' *Sydney Morning Herald* and sedate aunt *Daily Telegraph* (Figure 3.1).

In between these two ends of the spectrum were the majority of middle-of-the-road papers that aimed to be family reading, even if they were pushing the boundaries of popular journalism. The *Herald*, for example, rode a line between the sensational and serious, but always considered itself decent. It prided itself on its strong news coverage and was considered a more serious afternoon paper than its interstate counterparts. This was part of Keith Murdoch's skill in leading the paper in the 1920s – his ability to know just how far he could push the novel and sensational in prim, conservative Melbourne. This was the same balancing act that Northcliffe's

October 3, 1931   Smith's Week

CONCERNING THE BAD, BAD

SKITTISH NEWSPAPER FLAPPER
COCKTAIL INTO THE WOR

Once There Was One "Daily Gua
Now There Are Three

*THIS is the story of a Highly Respectable Family which
It was the most decorous family in the world—the fam
in Sydney City.
And all the dreadful things happened, because in a u
Family adopted a strange niece, a skittish little modern
cigarettes and cocktails; and her name was the "Daily G
At length the Family threw the flapper out; but not be
deadly work had been done.   All the rest of the Fami
taken to bad ways—absinthe and night clubs and cocaine.
Granny "Herald" herself did not wholly escape the dar
influence.*

S Y D. MILLER

WHEN that bad little hussy, the "Daily Guardian," first came into the doors of the Sydney family, with her vanity-bag, her lip-stick, and her cheeky smile, it was the primmest and most strait-laced family you ever saw, Grandma "Herald" was nearly a hundred years old, and if her past ever contained any indiscretions, they had been wholly forgotten. She was an indulgent old thing, who seldom lost her temper; and people liked her, even though they thought her rather dull and prosy.

Grandma's sister, whom the family called Auntie, was the "Evening News."   There was a rather awkward mystery about Auntie. She was strangely fond of an obscure member of the family named the "Sunday News." Among neighbors the "Sunday News" was generally referred to as Auntie's Little Miss one, and the poor little thing never looked as though it would live very long.

There were two brothers in the family; the elder was named the "Sunday Sun," and the younger was called the "Daily Sun." They were regarded as fine young fellows; both of them being in steady jobs, and earning good money.

The sons, however, were not the oldest of the new generation; their sister, the "Daily Telegraph," was their senior. During her girlhood and young womanhood she had been something of a prig and blue-stocking; she wore spectacles, and she always pretended to know an awful lot about Culture and Economics. As she came to Middle Age she appeared to become a trifle sillier, which is a natural event; but

she remained essentially a Priscilla.

It was a portentous risk, to take a frisky damsel like the "Daily Guardian" into that orderly home.

Whereas they had been accustomed to breakfast on rather soggy toast and eggs with a remote suggestion of staleness, she would jump out of bed in her kimono (or even less than that) and run round the house offering everybody a caviar biscuit and a cocktail.

She smoked a cigarette during family Bible readings. She taught Auntie "Evening News" to wear jazz garters; and she persuaded her old-maid cousin "Telegraph" to introduce a few drops of metho into her Peppermint Cure.

As for the two sons, Mr. "Sunday Sun" and Mr. "Sun," they began to knock round with little Miss "Daily Guardian" in a manner which was simply disgraceful. Auntie shook her head and said that no good could come of such goings-on.

"Horrid Hussy"

The two young men broke an engagement which they had made to go with their sister, Miss "Telegraph," to a lecture before the English-Speaking Union; and, arm in arm with fluffy Miss "Guardian" they attended a cocktail party in King's Cross Road, which ended in a police inquiry.

"She is a horrid little hussy," said Miss "Telegraph."

"I'm sure I don't know what will be the end of it all," sighed Auntie "News," who was visibly growing thinner and more miserable every day. "That awful child will worrit me to my death, I know she will." Auntie added pathetically.

"Don't take on so 'ard, I mean hard," said Granny to Auntie. "In some ways I rather like the child. You see, sister, she's so different to us, I mean from us. Somehow, when I look at her I feel that perhaps I've missed a lot in life. And she really is pretty, sister, and she does look strong and healthy."

But Auntie "News" refused to be comforted, and at length she became really ill.

Meantime, gay Miss "Daily Guardian" jazzed through her bright career.

But the whole Family was outraged when she brought along her Boy Friend, and introduced him as Mr. "Sunday Guardian."

REPAIRS

THE SHOEMAKER'S LAST!

DAILY SUN

Poor little Master "Sunday N depressed by Auntie's continued ness, suddenly gasped and died, all believed that Miss "Guardian the Boy Friend had given him much to drink, or something; and collapsed.

FIGURE 3.1 The flapper *Daily Guardian* scandalises the respectable and staid Sydney newspapers

SOURCE *Smith's Weekly*, 3 October 1931, p. 7.

Daily Mail performed – it too reflected 'middle class morality and prejudices', while investing events 'with an emotional intensity … to capture the public imagination'.[14]

As the 1920s was an era of exciting new technologies, newspapers were keen to associate themselves with aviation, radio, cinema, the gramophone and motor cars, along with advances in home technology, science and medicine. Popular newspapers heavily promoted cars and the latest Hollywood films, and drew upon the glamour of aviation. Imitating his mentor, Northcliffe, Keith Murdoch's *Herald* sponsored aviation feats, tracked flight attempts, and promoted aviators as celebrities. The *Sun* and the *Herald* cooperated to secure the rights to a story about a flight competition between the Smith brothers and Captain Douglas. The two papers arranged for the air crews to cable an exclusive story from each stopping place so that only their readers could exclusively follow the adventure. Soon, the wealthier newspapers were showing off their own planes, with the *Sun* claiming to be the first to have its own plane as part of its regular equipment.

THE RISE OF PRESS CHAINS

By the 1920s, the most successful newspaper companies were making record profits and moving up the list of the wealthiest companies in the country. The HWT jumped up nineteen places between 1910 and 1930, to become the fifty-first wealthiest company in Australia.[15] The Sydney *Sun*'s parent company, Sun Newspapers, made a reported profit of £150 000 in 1927; while the HWT reported a profit of £265 000 in 1929.[16] When Denison merged his Sun Newspapers with Samuel Bennett Ltd (owner of the *Evening News*) in 1929, he christened his newly enlarged company 'Associated Newspapers' – the same name Northcliffe called his epic newspaper group – and so an indication of where Denison's ambitions lay. By 1930, Associated

Newspapers was ranked in the top twenty-five wealthiest companies in Australia.[17]

All of this rapid growth meant that several companies had to move to new premises to accommodate increasingly large printing presses, staff and equipment. Their large, grand, new buildings were an outward display of their post-war profit-making, and their growing power and prestige.

In 1923, the *Herald* moved into a monumental, five-storey, neo-classical facade building on the corner of Flinders and Exhibition streets, considered one of the most impressive buildings in Melbourne (Figure 7.3). In Sydney, the *Sun*'s new double building, in skyscraper-gothic style, on Elizabeth Street was finished in 1929 (Figure 4.3). It was reportedly the tallest building in Sydney at the time, with ornate marble-lined interiors, seven elevators, and a golden dome on the roof that caught the sun's rays and could be seen for miles. The *Sydney Morning Herald* also ended the 1920s in new premises – a twelve-storey Palazzo-style building on its triangular site at the apex of Hunter, Pitt and O'Connell streets (Figure 3.2). Finished in sandstone, and complete with polished Tuscan columns and marble stairways, it housed the paper's latest printing equipment, sixteen electric-motorised Scott multi-unit rotary web presses that were so advanced they fulfilled the *Sydney Morning Herald*'s printing needs until 1941.

The value of the *Sydney Morning Herald*'s properties and printing equipment had trebled between 1921 and 1929, to £920 956 (or $65 million in today's money).[18] Any newcomer bold enough to want to challenge it would now need enormous sums of capital, and not just for equipment and premises. Newspapers were also facing much higher production costs in technology, newsprint, foreign news cables, wages, and the editorial costs involved in producing a more elaborate product. (In 1920, the *Sydney Morning Herald* was only twelve pages long, but by 1929, it was up to twenty

FIGURE 3.2 The *Sydney Morning Herald*'s new building, constructed between 1922 and 1929 on its Hunter Street site, shown circa 1930

SOURCE Fairfax syndication (FXT280292).

pages, and had specialist sections and columns. The *Sun*, which had also been only twelve pages in 1920, was a mammoth thirty-two pages on ad-filled Thursdays by 1929.)

Costs in the newspaper industry had risen with abnormal speed. The Sydney *Daily Telegraph*'s annual production costs had increased tenfold in its first twenty-four years, from 1879 to 1903.[19] The cost of newsprint jumped by 120 per cent in the ten years after World War I.[20] It had been possible to start a new paper in Sydney in 1893 for about £50 000 (about $6 million in today's money).[21] But when JE Davidson launched the *News* in Adelaide thirty years later, he needed capital of £175 000 ($13 million in today's money).[22] With this level of investment at stake, the newspaper market became much more competitive and cut-throat.

New owners entering the industry had to be able to sustain big losses for years in order to make any profit at all. When Sir James Joynton Smith, Claude McKay and RC Packer launched the *Daily Guardian* in 1923, the paper suffered losses of £103 000 ($7.5 million today) in its first year. Joynton Smith footed the bills and said he accepted that it would take five years for the paper to become profitable.[23] But only seven years after he launched the *Daily Guardian*, he wanted out because its profits were still small, despite a circulation of 182 000 (Chapter 4).[24]

Newspapers needed larger audiences and more advertising to survive but Australia's population was small: there were only so many readers, pennies and advertisers to go around. Intense competition, along with high capital and production costs, depleted weaker newspapers, and then the Depression, beginning in 1929, finished off the financially shaky ones. With almost one in three adult men unemployed, shops empty, factories idle and families living in poverty, newspaper audiences and advertising fell. The result was a series of closures, mergers and takeovers, with larger groups preying on smaller ones to survive. Only twenty daily newspapers survived the 1920s, and companies associated with Keith Murdoch of the HWT and Hugh Denison of Associated Newspapers owned ten of those twenty papers.[25]

By 1933, many papers were gone. The victims included short-lived papers: the *Daily Guardian*, *Evening Sun*, the *News* (Hobart) and the tabloid *Daily Pictorial*; as well as much older papers: the *Register*, the *Evening News* (and the distinct *Brisbane Courier* and the *Daily Mail* which merged into one paper, the *Courier-Mail*). The industry was being driven away from small-scale, independent ventures towards large-scale, integrated players who could aim for continuous growth. Of these, the HWT was the dominant force. By 1925, it had taken over the most promising paper of Associated Newspapers (the *Sun News-Pictorial*). In 1931, it formally took over the nascent empire of News Limited (owner of the Adelaide *News*).

At the end of the 1930s, the HWT controlled the Melbourne *Herald*, the Melbourne *Sun News-Pictorial*, the Adelaide *Advertiser*, the Adelaide *News*, and had been linked with the Perth *West Australian* and *Daily News*.[26] In addition to its newspapers, the HWT owned several radio stations (including 3DB in Melbourne, and its interests in two stations in Queensland and four stations in South Australia (Table 13.2)), as well as various magazines (including *Sporting Globe*, *Listener In*, *Aircraft*, *Home Beautiful*, *Wild Life* and *Table Talk*). The HWT's managing director, Keith Murdoch, oversaw the company's many newspapers, but also had a personal stake in the *Courier-Mail*, which he directed, and his own personal interests in three metropolitan radio stations.

THE REACTION TO PRESS CHAINS

In the United States and the United Kingdom, the Depression and fierce circulation battles had also caused a period of amalgamations and closures by the 1930s. By 1931, even the famous *World* had been closed, and by 1937, Hearst's *American* and *Evening Journal* had to be merged. But consolidation in these two countries was still spread among a larger number of players. In the United States, by 1935, 26 per cent of the nation's newspaper circulation was spread between *six* newspaper chains, which included Hearst's and Scripps-Howard's (the later name of EW Scripps' company).[27] In the United Kingdom, in 1937, half of national newspaper circulation was controlled by *three* owners: Rothermere, Beaverbrook and Cadbury.[28] But, in Australia, in that same year, *one* owner – the HWT – already controlled over 40 per cent of daily metropolitan newspaper circulation, and two owners – the HWT and Associated Newspapers – controlled over 60 per cent.[29] By 1969, the HWT published more than half of the metropolitan daily papers sold in Australia.[30] Even at their peak, individual press chains like Hearst's in the United States, and Northcliffe's in the United Kingdom, never achieved levels of concentration of ownership like this.[31]

Because newspaper groups were also expanding into radio from the 1920s, the issue of press influence became even more urgent. In the United States, since the 1890s, there had been vocal concern about the dominance of American newspaper chains and the way their commercialism was distorting their coverage. Several critical books about 'press lords' were published in the 1920s and 1930s and stimulated debate further, as did investigations by the Federal Trade Commission (FTC) that revealed power companies had been buying up American newspapers and planting stories to ward off public regulation.[32]

Public concern intensified when major American newspaper companies – including the now conservative Hearst – crusaded blatantly against President Franklin Delano Roosevelt's 'New Deal' because of its impact on business, even though Roosevelt's policies were in the interests of many of their Depression-affected readers.

Criticism of the press chains was not just about their size, but also about their political bias, especially after key owners threw their financial and publicity weight behind Roosevelt's opponents in the 1936 and 1940 elections (which Roosevelt won regardless, including a landslide victory in 1936). The Roosevelt administration felt under siege from hostile newspapers. A confidential memorandum sent to Roosevelt's trust-busting assistant attorney-general, Thurman Arnold, in 1938, warned Arnold that: 'As a businessman, the [newspaper] publisher reflects the prejudices of his kind. Anything which increases his costs or curtails his profits – the wages and hours bill, the NLRB [National Labor Relations Board], a tightening up of taxation – is anathema …'.[33]

By the 1940s, Victor Pickard says the American press faced a 'rising chorus of criticism – from Congress, the Roosevelt administration, the courts, and the public …'.[34] Encouraged by rising calls for government intervention, the Roosevelt administration began to use more aggressive tactics. There were multiple Congressional inquiries, reports into monopolistic practices, the scholarly Hutchins Commission reports, Federal Communications Commission (FCC) scrutiny of newspaper chains, and Supreme Court action that upheld an important anti-trust provision against the Associated Press (AP). There was also greater scrutiny and regulation of broadcasting, with FCC inquiries aimed at protecting the public interest from major newspaper groups dominating radio as well. Under the spotlight, large newspaper companies moved away from national empires and began to focus on local and regional dominance. This caused the growth of local monopolies, which led to the problem of one-newspaper towns, but unlike in Australia, the large companies' percentage of *total* newspaper circulation decreased from the 1930s.[35]

In the United Kingdom, there was also 'widespread public concern over the excessive power of the press' in the 1930s and 1940s.[36]

This resulted in a Royal Commission on the Press in 1947–49. This commission displayed little concern about monopoly ownership though, and was ineffectual in challenging it, so chain ownership of national newspapers continued to increase. By 1961, three companies controlled 89 per cent of national daily circulation.[37] Another Royal Commission in 1961–62 recommended greater oversight of press ownership, and from 1965, significant mergers were referred to the Monopolies and Mergers Commission. This did not stop controversial mergers from going ahead, nor did it stop regional newspaper chains from growing, but it did, as in the United States, slow the growth of media empires seeking national dominance. The proportion of national daily and Sunday newspapers owned by the three largest corporations in the United Kingdom fell between 1961 and 1989.[38]

Not all of the state interventions used in the United States and the United Kingdom to stop press chains were effective. And by the 1950s, the nature of press criticism had shifted dramatically in the United States, and the FCC had backed away from trying to prevent media monopolies.[39] Nonetheless, it is striking that, at the time when public concern about press chains was at its height in the United States and the United Kingdom – between the 1920s and 1940s – mainstream debate about press chains in Australia was very subdued. There was no comparative attempt at state intervention to halt their growth. In Australia, no formal, federal parliamentary inquiry into the press was held until 1992. This was more than four decades after the major inquiries by the United States Congress and the United Kingdom's first Royal Commission. In Australia, newspaper empire building went ahead from the 1920s largely unchecked. The major newspaper groups expanded without significant challenge, and for decades flouted even minor government restrictions that were placed on group ownership.

BUSINESS, ADVERTISING AND THE POLITICS OF CONSUMPTION

The expansion of newspapers into major businesses created a managerial class within newspaper organisations. Mechanical improvements brought specialisation and larger workforces for them to manage, including negotiating with more organised national unions. In 1915, the Printing Industry Employees Union of Australia (PIEUA) was formed out of the Australian Typographical Union (a confederation of state typographical unions that had begun in 1880). The Australian Journalists' Association (AJA) had formed in 1910.

The AJA was a 'moderate and discreet white-collar' union.[40] Its members tended to see themselves as upwardly mobile professionals whose fates were entwined with those of their employers. For example, Bert Cook, who founded the AJA, was no firebrand union leader. He began as a poorly paid young journalist at the *Herald*, but went on to do publicity work for Prime Minister William Morris Hughes and powerful businessmen associated with the HWT and News Limited, before finishing his career as the financial and commercial editor of the conservative *Argus*. Both the AJA and the PIEUA preferred conciliation with employers to industrial action, and strikes at daily papers remained uncommon. From the first known journalists' strike in 1912, until the end of the 1960s, the only other major strikes at commercial dailies were in 1922, 1944, 1955 and 1967. It is notable that the longest period of industrial quiet – between 1922 and 1944 – coincided with a period when many papers were closed, merged or changed hands, putting a large number of journalists out of work.

Although far from militant, the AJA helped improve the status, conditions and pay of journalists. It began during the blatantly exploitative 'penny-a-liner' era of the early 1900s, when journalists (including Keith Murdoch and Bert Cook) were 'sweated', working

AUSTRALIAN NEWSPAPERS' CONFERENCE IN SESSION.
Left to Right: Messrs. Thorold Fink (Herald, Melbourne), Lavington Bonython (Advertiser, Adelaide), C. H. Briggs (Brisbane Courier), H. R. Maughan (Daily Mail, Brisbane), F. Usher (Mercury, Hobart), W. H. Cummins (Telegraph, Brisbane), A. C. C. Holtz, Chairman (Argus, Melbourne), E. J. K. Thompson, secretary, C. P. Smith (West Australian, Perth), Keith Murdoch (Herald, Melbourne), H. Pacini (Sun News-Pictorial, Melbourne), R. E. Denison (Sun and Daily Telegraph, Sydney), H. Burston (News, Adelaide, and Daily News, Perth).
—Photo exclusive to Newspaper News.

FIGURE 3.3 The powerful men of the newspaper industry at the Australian Newspapers' Conference dinner in 1932

SOURCE *Newspaper News*, 1 December 1932, p. 1.

long hours for very low pay. By the 1920s, journalism was considered a solid, white-collar, desirable job, and the pay was good by the standards of the times.[41] It remained a fundamentally insecure occupation though, because job opportunities were limited, especially with consolidated ownership and decreasing outlets from the 1930s onwards. Workplace structures were hierarchical, conformity was valued, and journalists could be fired at whim by proprietors and quite easily replaced.

As newspaper owners and managers dealt with the business problems of the day, including labour and industrial laws, newsprint supply, government postage and telegraph rates, they came to recognise the advantages of working together on matters of common interest. In 1925, the major papers organised themselves into a body called the Australian Newspapers' Conference (ANC) that soon became a who's who of the key players in the industry, and a powerful lobbyist of governments and politicians (Figure 3.3).[42]

The ANC was not only a way of dealing collectively with government, but also with advertisers, another group that was increasingly conscious of its collective power. Advertisers formed the Australian Association of National Advertisers (AANA) in 1928. Fed up with the exaggerated circulation figures reported by individual newspapers, the AANA wanted newspapers to measure their audiences in a way that was standardised across outlets, and could be independently verified. It called on the newspaper industry to establish an audit bureau of circulation modelled on the one that had been established in the United States in 1914. In 1931, the AANA managed to persuade the reluctant ANC owners to set up an Audit Bureau of Circulations, although the haughtily independent *Sydney Morning Herald* refused to participate, insisting that its system of independently audited figures 'required no further evidence of accuracy'.[43]

Reliance on advertising was leading newspapers to view their audience more and more as consumers, rather than as readers or citizens. The target audience for popular papers like the *Sun* and the *Herald* was people who would spend large sums of money in shops and department stores. Associated Newspapers called its readers 'Mr and Mrs Buyer' when it described them to advertisers.[44] Newspapers were using their modern design to try to attract readers in the younger age brackets who 'spend the most money on clothes, food, getting married, furnishing homes, rearing families, taking holidays [and] enjoying themselves'.[45] In 1929, the *Daily Telegraph* told advertisers that women under forty years, the 'younger, faster-spending housewives are your market – and they're your readers in the *Daily Telegraph* ...'.[46] The launch of the *Australian Women's Weekly* in the 1930s, and radio (with its focus on sponsors and products), boosted consumerism further.

An important part of the 'new journalism' formula was to give more space to news on daily life, as opposed to the traditional press' heavy focus on political and commercial news. The advertising posters promoting the first issue of Northcliffe's *Daily Mail* in 1896 had promised: 'Four leading articles, a page of Parliament and columns of speeches will NOT be found in the *Daily Mail* on 4 May'.[47] In the popular papers, political events were reported not just for educated elites who had a strong interest in detailed political news, but for the average reader who, it was presumed, did not. The papers were also actively shaping their readers' preferences in this direction by passing over the complexities of public policy in favour of intriguing material from everyday life.

Although the popular papers did not want to appear dominated by verbose reports on weighty matters of public affairs, nor lecture or bore their readers, they *did* report on politics. They also had a habit of becoming more political once their audiences – and influence on public opinion – grew, and as their owners became more invested in politics.[48] Northcliffe, for example, may have kept his promise to avoid pages of parliamentary proceedings in the *Daily Mail*, but he still managed to infuse the paper with his strong political opinions. The paper strongly supported capitalism, the Boer War, World War I, conscription, patriotism and Empire. It strongly opposed the *National Insurance Act*, taxation increases to provide social security and the leadership of HH Asquith. Widely known for its jingoism, the paper was considered the 'trumpet ... of British Imperialism'.[49]

As with the Australian owners of the late 19th and early 20th centuries, the key 'new journalism' owners were politically involved. Pulitzer had been active in politics, first as a Republican and then a Democrat. Hearst was a politician and presidential aspirant who directed the editorial positions and coverage of political news in his newspapers. Northcliffe used his mass circulation papers to exercise considerable political influence that delivered him a reputation for being 'a maker and breaker of governments'.[50] In the final years of World War I, Northcliffe took up official positions, including Director of Propaganda in Enemy Countries.

The popular papers reported politics differently to the traditional papers. They reported it through the lens of daily life, expanding the scope from an overwhelming focus on parliament to a much broader sense of power, justice and social issues. Some popular papers – like Pulitzer's, Scripps' and Hearst's – were activist and ran campaigns on various political and social issues, including living standards. Other papers appeared much more focused on entertainment, including cheesecake beauty contests and sports results. But even the seemingly depoliticised papers communicated strong viewpoints on issues around gender, race, immigration, labour relations, war, and other political and social topics. They did this in a particular way though. Instead of having a designated 'politics' section in the paper, written in long-winded, hectoring prose, the popular papers integrated political views within other content in a way that was lively, but also made the views appear to be 'common sense'.

Retail and department store advertisers had all but insisted that popular newspapers expand their reach, and be less partisan. The papers took up this sentiment enthusiastically and mirrored it back to advertisers. In a 1933 promotion to advertisers, Hugh Denison's Associated Newspapers called its readers: 'the middle classes – the spenders of the community ...'.[51] Taking a swipe at traditional papers like the conservative *Sydney Morning Herald*, Associated Newspapers said its papers attracted readers who were open-minded 'with receptive minds and responsive purses', as opposed to those of 'conservative, fixed minds' upon whom 'advertising makes little impression'.[52] The *Daily Telegraph* in 1933 said similarly of its audience: 'They have ... flexible, young minds which respond to advertising suggestions'.[53]

Newspaper owners throughout the 20th century would be ever vigilant against any government interference with the 'freedom of the press'. But their dependency upon advertising revenue meant that large advertisers exerted a different form of control over them. It was very difficult for a newspaper owner to 'oppose the political or commercial interests of his advertising customers ...'.[54] More broadly, newspapers had to create a mood that would keep their readers open to all of their 'advertising suggestions'. Patriotism was linked with this goal. In 1931, Associated Newspapers told advertisers that readers of its *Sun* and *Daily Telegraph* were 'people with money to spend; with optimism in their hearts; with a belief in Australia and themselves. The worthwhile section of the popu-lation which is interested in life ... interested in advertising that sells ideas'.[55] To keep these middle-class 'spenders' interested and optimistic, newspapers had to be respectable and their content could not be too radical, off-putting, strident or negative. But while the popular papers were at pains to appear open-minded, modern and non-partisan, underneath all of their focus on lighter fare, their political preferences were often just as 'fixed' and 'conservative' as those of their older rivals.

POLITICS AND THE POPULAR PAPERS

Newspapers had been making vehement proclamations of non-partisanship since the mid-1800s, but with such large investments to protect by the 1910s, they were especially wary of narrowing their audience. Owners and managers understood that newspaper readers did not want party-political propaganda delivered to their breakfast tables, and that being seen as too close to politicians would harm their credibility and prestige. Some of the popular papers, including the *Sun*, liked to flaunt that they existed primarily for commercial rather than political reasons.

When the *Sun* was launched in 1910, it rose from the ashes of an earlier paper, the *Australian Star*, that had begun with political intentions in 1887. The *Star* had many workers as shareholders, strongly supported the 'rights of labour', and advocated for protectionism to shield domestic industry (all four of the other Sydney daily papers were staunch free trade advocates). According to the *Sun*'s own account of its history, when industrialist Hugh Denison acquired the paper in 1910, the directors of his new board spent four hours debating which political party the new paper should tie up with. One section of the board (probably the two directors who had been associated with the *Star*) believed commercial success would come if the new paper filled a gap in the market for a Labor-supporting paper in Sydney. Another faction, which undoubtedly included Denison, was 'strongly opposed' to that.[56] After vigorous debate, they decided, on a commercial basis, that to reach the broadest possible market of readers, the *Sun* should be non-partisan and independent of any political organisation.[57] The *Sun* made this a selling point, promising readers on the front page of its first edition that it was going to be 'unique in its freedom from party ties and its exemption from political entanglements'.[58]

The 1913 election was the first time the rebranded *Sun* could try out its non-partisan stance on a federal election. Its election eve editorial took a 'pox on both your houses' approach. The paper refused to endorse any particular candidate. Voicing suspicion of all political parties, it declared that both major parties were run by 'machines' and not representative of the people. But this tone of non-partisan cynicism lasted only for this one election. When the next federal election was held, only fifteen months later, the *Sun*'s election editorial continued to declare: 'This paper hates a party vote', but then told readers to vote for the anti-Labor, Commonwealth Liberals.[59] For the next forty-seven years, across seventeen federal elections, the *Sun* continued to recommend that readers vote for non-Labor parties.[60]

Despite its original stated intention, the *Sun* had quickly become conservative in its outlook, joining the majority of the daily press, including the other pioneering popular paper, the Melbourne *Herald*. When the *Herald* advocated a vote for Bob Hawke's pro-business Labor Party in 1984, it confessed that: 'The *Herald* has never before advocated a vote for Labor'.[61] And it never did so again before it closed in 1990. In its 150-year history, the *Herald* advocated a vote for Labor only that one time.

Even the popular newspaper which, on face value, should have been most likely to be pro-Labor in the 1920s, was not. The *Daily Guardian* targeted a working class audience, its editor, Voltaire Molesworth, was the son of two socialists. He was an official in the AJA, a former Labor MP, and had been Labor politician Jack Lang's 'right hand man'. But, for the three federal elections that the *Daily Guardian* covered before the paper closed, it did not advocate a vote for federal Labor. In 1928, it told its readers that workers were better off under a 'capitalist' conservative government than under Labor.[62] The paper did not approve of what it saw as an extremist/communist element in Labor. Like its editor, it had also become caught up in the internecine battles of NSW Labor. Molesworth had fallen out bitterly with Lang in 1924, and the *Daily Guardian*, which had often been critical of Lang, thereafter became stridently so. In turn, Lang's *Labor Daily* derided Molesworth as a member of the anti-Labor 'capitalist press' and a 'lingerie editor' (for his paper's frivolous beauty competitions).[63] Molesworth ended up joining the conservative Nationalists and their successors, the United Australia Party (UAP), as a publicity director, and ran for election as a UAP candidate in 1932.

Another of the new breed of papers that were established in the 1920s was the Adelaide *News*. Its editor and ostensible owner (Chapter 6 calls this into question) was JE Davidson, an advocate of American-style 'new journalism' and former editor of the Melbourne *Herald*. Davidson had been pushed out of the *Herald* by HWT chairman Theodore Fink, partly because Fink did not approve of Davidson's attempts to move away from partisan editorials. At the *News*, Davidson was able to give free rein to his instincts that readers should not be brow beaten. The *News'* first federal election editorial said that: 'to dictate a line of action to voters is … wrong … this paper, being non-party, has not taken sides … A modern newspaper [should] … allow electors to form their own judgments. To do anything else is to attempt to turn a newspaper into a political machine …'.[64]

However, this strong declaration of non-partisanship did not stop the paper from voicing opinions elsewhere in its pages. For example, other editorials and articles argued that coal miners were 'lazy' and took too many holidays, that labourers earned too much, and that unions were the cause of 'trouble' at Broken Hill (Chapters 5 and 6 explore what may have been behind such views).[65] Nonetheless, the *News* did stick to its non-directive election editorials for the next two federal elections, while Davidson remained at the helm. But after his death in 1930, the *News* came under the control of the HWT and Keith Murdoch, a man who had no reservations about directing readers. Like the other papers under Murdoch's control, the *News* strongly promoted Murdoch's confidant Joe Lyons' UAP in 1931 (Chapter 11).

PARTISANSHIP AND POLITICAL PREFERENCES

The political economy of newspapers was transformed in the 1920s and 1930s by the rise of newspaper chains, newspapers' greater dependency on advertising revenue, a sharp decline in the number of daily papers, and the growth of monopoly newspaper cities (such as Adelaide, where the HWT owned the only daily morning paper *and* the only daily afternoon paper from 1931 to 1948). This

commercial transformation created a more politically homoge-
nous news media. Australia's commercial daily newspapers were
now owned by men of immense wealth, their boards of directors
filled with men of industry and commerce, and run by ambitious
executives.

These owners and executives generally felt their interests
coincided with conservative policies, and their editors and newspapers tended to reflect this view. The major commercial daily papers
were strongly pro-business, antagonistic to organised labour (particularly militant unionism), and to socialism and Marxism, which
they viewed as great threats to prosperity. They supported the British
Empire, free enterprise, balanced state budgets, minimum public
spending, the White Australia policy, the monarchy and traditional
family values. As Robert Murray noted, they were against 'inter-
nationalism', 'government intervention in the economy ...' and any
reforms deemed too radical and that would threaten established
institutions or undermine capitalism.[66] The *Sydney Morning Herald*
summarised the business community's opposition to Labor in 1919
when it interpreted Labor's aim as 'the elimination of the capitalist
and the private employer ... the nationalisation of everything ...
[and] to drive the private employer out of business ...'.[67]

It is not unexpected that wealthy newspaper owners would have
conservative political views, and studies of editorial support in the
United States and the United Kingdom have shown newspapers in
those countries were also more likely to be conservative – but not
with the level of uniformity seen in Australia. Even when Roosevelt
felt himself up against a pro-business press that was overwhelmingly against him, studies found he still had the editorial support of
37 per cent of daily newspapers (in 1936).[68] Two later snapshots of
American newspapers, taken in 1940 and 1960, found that a quarter
of the large daily newspapers supported Democratic candidates. In
the United Kingdom, a study by Colin Seymour-Ure of nine British

daily papers between 1945 and 1970 found that four papers were consistently Conservative, two consistently Labour, one consistently Liberal, and two varied between parties.[69] These figures, and those from the United States, show a level of variety that was not evident in Australia during the same period.

Later chapters discuss specific elections in more detail, but Tables 3.1 and 3.2 summarise the editorial stance of key newspapers during federal elections over fifty years from 1920 to 1970. These tables are based upon the papers' election-eve editorials. During election campaigns, Australian newspapers traditionally publish an editorial, usually on the day before polling day, that sums up the paper's views about the election, and tells readers who they should vote for. Editorials are the principal means by which a paper articulates its identity. They speak as the institutional 'voice' of the paper because the editorials are considered to be an authorised representation of the views of the owner or investors. Election-eve editorials are particularly useful because, traditionally, they were the means by which the paper explicitly articulated its *political* identity.

Newspapers used to stubbornly maintain that opinionated editorials were a distinct genre that had no bearing upon their news coverage which, they insisted, was always kept rigorously 'straight' and impartial. But this claim tends to be less accepted now because it is usually observable that papers which have strong and consistent partisan preferences tend to give prominence to that side of politics in their news and commentary as well. Interestingly, British newspapers call editorials 'leaders'. According to one theory, this was because they were traditionally seen as a way for the newspaper to 'lead' its readers. But most ordinary newspaper readers probably do not read the editorials, and nor do they have to because the paper's editorial stance on major issues usually permeates its news coverage. Instead, editorials send their strongest and most direct messages to political elites and journalists (including journalists who work on the paper).

This book concludes in 1941, with Menzies' resignation, but the political stances of the newspapers need to be viewed in a longer context to see how determinedly conservative the mainstream daily press was, and would remain for decades. From 1922 until 1969, the majority of daily newspapers were conservative (Tables 3.1 and 3.2) – especially in the 1920s–40s, when 85–90 per cent of commercial dailies supported the conservative parties. Even up to the 1960s, Labor never received the support of a quarter of the Australian daily press. Instead, for five decades, the conservative parties could count on the backing of a core group of papers that *always* directed their readers to vote conservative. This group included: the *Mercury*, the *Herald*, the *Sun News-Pictorial*, the *Advertiser*, the *West Australian*, and from its formation in 1933, the *Courier-Mail*.

To this group of core conservative papers can also be added the *Daily Telegraph*, which never advocated a vote for Labor during this period (although in 1940, under a younger Frank Packer, it was critical of the Menzies government's war effort and individual ministers (Chapter 16)).[70] The *Sydney Morning Herald* must also be included because it opposed Labor at every election except one – 1961. Likewise, the *Sun* only supported Labor once, also in 1961, and that was because it was the *Sydney Morning Herald*'s stablemate by then, so it was ensnared in the Fairfax group's anti-Menzies campaign that year.[71]

Table 3.1 focuses on the period before the Liberal Party of Australia was formed in 1944–45. It shows that newspaper opposition to Labor was especially strong between 1922 and 1943. Even if Labor was popular and electorally ascendant in this period, conservative papers did not mind being out of step with public opinion. The 1929 and 1943 elections are a case in point. In those years, Labor won federal elections in landslide results even though many voters were reading newspapers that counselled against a vote for Labor. Only two papers out of the seventeen shown in Table 3.1, advocated a

TABLE 3.1 The partisan preferences of major newspapers, 1922–1943

Newspaper	1922	1925	1928	1929	1931	1934	1937	1940	1943
Victor (Labor in **bold** type)	Hughes Nationalist	SM Bruce Nationalist/Country Party	SM Bruce Nationalist/Country Party	Scullin **Labor**	Lyons UAP	Lyons UAP/Country Party	Lyons UAP/Country Party	Menzies UAP/Country Party	Curtin **Labor**
Sydney Morning Herald	Con. (Nationalist)	Con.	Con.	Con.	Con.	Con.	Con.	Con. but wanted a national govt with ALP involved	Critical of both parties. Advocated a vote for new parties or independents
Sun	Con. (Nationalist)	Con.	Con.	Con.	Con.	Con.	Con.	Con.	Con.
Daily Telegraph	Con.	Con.	Con.	Con.	Con.	Con.	Con.	Con. but critical and wanted 'new men' brought into the govt	Con.
Daily Guardian		Con.	Con.	Con.					
Daily Mirror									Con.
Age	Con. (Liberal-Country Party)	Con.	Con.	Lab.	Lab.	Con.	Lab.	Con.	Advocated a vote for new parties/independents
Argus	Con.	Con.	Con.	Con.	Con.	Con.	Con.	Con.	Con.
Sun News-Pictorial	Con. (Nationalist)	Con.	Con.	Con.	Con.	Con.	Con.	Con.	Con.

Newspaper	1922	1925	1928	1929	1931	1934	1937	1940	1943
Herald	Con. (Liberal-Country Party)	Con.	Con.	Con.	Con.	Con.	Con.	Con.	Con.
Courier-Mail						Con.	Con.	Con.	Con.
Brisbane Telegraph	No clear support	Con.	Con.	Con.	Con.	Con.	Con.	Con.	Con.
Advertiser	Con. (Nationalist)	Con.	Con.	Con.	Con.	Con.	Con.	Con.	Con.
News		Policy of not directing readers	Policy of not directing readers	Policy of not directing readers	Con.	Con.	No clear support	Con.	Con.
West Australian	Con.	Con.	Con.	Con.	Con.	Con.	Con.	Con.	Con.
Daily News	Con.	Con.	Con.	Con.	Con.	Con.	Con.	Con.	Con.
Mercury	Con. (Nationalist)	Con.	Con.	Con.	Con.	Con.	Con.	Con.	Con.
Canberra Times			Con.	Lab.	Con.	Con.	No clear support	Con.	No clear support

SOURCES Election-eve editorials between 1922 and 1943.

NOTE Where an election-eve editorial was unclear, the previous week's editorials were also analysed to provide a broader sense of the paper's stance. 'Conservative' refers to the non-Labor parties, which were variously named before 1949 (including the United Liberal Party, the Nationalists, the United Australia Party and then the Liberal Party from 1945 (usually in coalition with the Country Party)).

vote for Labor between 1922 and 1943. They were *The Age* (three times) and the *Canberra Times* (once). In this period, as historian Sybil Nolan has noted, '*The Age*'s ... intermittent support for the Labor Party ... can only be properly understood as part of [Geoffrey] Syme's post-Deakinite agenda'.[72] Deakinism had long since been eclipsed, but *The Age* was sticking with Deakinite protectionist policies, and elements of these policies were advocated by Labor.

Table 3.1 also reflects how rival newspapers were jostling to shape internal conservative party politics during two periods of leadership turmoil on that side of politics: in 1922 and 1940–43. The 1922 election saw a split in the conservative Nationalist party with the Melbourne *Herald* and *The Age* advocating for the mainly Victorian- and South Australian-based Liberal-Country Party, while the *Sydney Morning Herald* and other conservative papers backed WM Hughes' Nationalists. During another period of leadership tumult, between 1940 and 1943, several papers delivered Menzies a public dressing down in their editorials. But once Menzies re-grouped and formed the Liberal Party in 1944–45, support for the conservatives became reliable among the conservative papers. Even *The Age*, despite its more radical and dissenting past, lent dependable support to the conservatives between 1949 and 1969 (Table 3.2).

The *Daily Telegraph* was another paper that became more conservative. When Frank Packer began his involvement as a partner in the *Daily Telegraph* in 1936, he took on a paper that had once made space for radical, feminist and pro-Labor views. Although it had been formed by a syndicate of businessmen and politicians, the *Daily Telegraph*'s editor, LJ Brient, was supportive of female suffrage and his paper gave the movement sympathetic coverage in the 1890s. Between 1907 and 1911, the paper had published a popular weekly column by WM Hughes that gave him invaluable access to put Labor's case before the paper's large, middle-class audience. One of his biographers said Hughes' columns 'did much to disarm middle-class hostility and prepare the way for the party to win office'.[73] Although this was a paper known for its conservative views (it advocated a vote against 'Labor-Socialism' in the 1910 federal election, and criticised Hughes severely even while he was writing for the paper), the *Daily Telegraph* of the early 20th century still made space for opposing views.

By the 1950s, Packer was an active supporter of the conservatives and in firm control of the paper. David McNicoll worked for the Packer family for fifty years as a journalist, columnist and editor, including nearly twenty years as editor-in-chief of Australian Consolidated Press (ACP). McNicoll pointed out that, under Packer, one of the paper's major aims was to persuade a working-class audience not to vote for the Labor Party. In 1997, McNicoll said that: 'The [*Daily*] *Telegraph*, like all tabloids was aimed principally at C and D class [lower income, usually manual workers'] homes. We believe, and so do the pollsters, that our influence, our right wing influence of the *Telegraph* on all those near metropolitan seats around Sydney, they would all have gone Labor long before but for the *Telegraph*. I think there's no doubt about that at all.'[74]

Packer joined a long list of newspaper owners who began with more fluid, or open, views, but converted firmly to conservatism, their earlier liberalism, and even radicalism, dimmed by age and wealth. This list included Edward Smith Hall, WC Wentworth and Edward Wilson (and one could also add JE Davidson, as well as Keith Murdoch and his son Rupert – both Murdochs flirted with left-wing politics before becoming staunch conservatives). In the United States, Hearst also famously made the shift from liberal crusader to political conservative. Even Scripps self-deprecatingly quipped in his later years that 'I am just a conservative old millionaire. You can't be rich and be a radical.'[75]

TABLE 3.2 The partisan preferences of major newspapers, 1946–1969

Newspaper	1946	1949	1951	1954	1955	1958	1961	1963	1966	1969
Victor (Labor in **bold** type)	Chifley **Labor**	Menzies Coalition	Menzies Coalition	Menzies Coalition	Menzies Coalition	Menzies Coalition	Menzies Coalition	Menzies Coalition	Holt Coalition	Gorton Coalition
Sydney Morning Herald	Con.	Con.	Con.	Con.	Con.	Con.	Lab.	Con.	Con.	Con.
Sun	Con.	Con.	Con.	Con.	Con.	Con.	Lab.	Con.	Con.	No editorial
Daily Telegraph	Con.	Con.	Con.	Con.	Con.	Con.	Con.	Con.	Con.	Con.
Daily Mirror	Lab.	No clear support	Con.	Lab.	Con.	Lab.	Con.	Lab.	Con.	Con.
Age	Moderate support Con.	Con.	Con.	Con.	Con.	Con.	Con.	Con.	Con.	Con. (with some criticism)
Argus	Con.	No endorsement	No endorsement	Lab.	Against anti-Communist Labor (DLP)					
Sun News-Pictorial	Con.	Con.	Con.	Con.	Con.	Con.	Con.	Con.	Con.	Con.
Herald	Con.	Con.	Con.	Con.	Con.	Con.	Con.	Con.	Con.	Con.
Courier-Mail	Con.	Con.	Con.	Con.	Con.	Con.	Con.	Con.	Con.	Con.
Brisbane Telegraph	Con.	Con.	Con.	Con.	Con.	Con.	Con.	No clear support	No clear support	No editorial

Newspaper	1946	1949	1951	1954	1955	1958	1961	1963	1966	1969
Advertiser	Con.	Con.	Con.	Con.	Con.	Con.	Con.	Con.	Con.	Con.
News	Con.	Con.	Con.	Critical of both major parties	No clear support	No clear support	Con.	No clear support	Con.	Con.
West Australian	Con.	Con.	Con.	Con.	Con.	Con.	Con.	Con.	Con.	Con.
Daily News	No editorial	Con.	No clear support	No editorial	No editorial	No editorial	No editorial	No editorial	No clear support. Critical of both	No editorial
Mercury	Con.	Con.	Con.	Con.	Con.	Con.	Con.	Con.	Con.	Con.
Canberra Times	Moderate support for Con.	Con.	Con.	Con.	Con.	No clear support	No clear support	Con.	Con.	No clear support (critical of both)
Australian Financial Review				Con.	Con.	Con.	Lab.	Con.	No clear support (critical of both)	No clear support
The Australian									Con.	Con.

NOTE The *Australian Financial Review* became a daily newspaper in 1963.
'Conservative' refers to the Liberal Party of Australia (usually in coalition with the Country Party).

POLITICS AND THE PAPERS FROM THE 1920S

The daily press in Australia between the 1920s and 1960s was unusually politically conservative, but it had long been so. When author Richard Twopenny, who had observed papers in England and Europe, made his survey of Australian newspapers in 1883, he said: 'It is curious … that all the leading organs of public opinion in Australia are strongly Conservative and Imperialistic …'.[76] He noted only one exception – *The Age* in Melbourne. If Twopenny had been able to return a century later, he would have found that *The Age* (back to supporting Labor after decades of conservatism) was still the only daily paper to endorse Labor in 1983. And that was during an election that Labor won in a record result.

Even in the very competitive years of the 1920s, when rival daily papers in Australia offered new forms of journalism to attract audiences, they did not offer political diversity. The owners of popular daily papers wanted the pennies of the working class but they did not use their papers to advocate politically on behalf of those readers. It was the style and design of Pulitzer's newspapers that the Australian popular press wanted to imitate, not their campaigns for social and political reform. In the United States, Pulitzer, Scripps, and originally, Hearst, had used their populist papers to advocate for social and political reforms that would benefit their working-class audiences. In Australia, even the ground-breaking popular daily papers – such as the *Herald*, the *Sun News-Pictorial* and the Sydney *Sun* – did not adopt the reforming, union-supporting politics of Pulitzer. They did not take on Scripps' goal of 'opposing the rich', nor reproduce the pro-labour, pro-immigrant and anti-conservative stance of Hearst in his early years.

What impact did Australia's remarkable press homogeneity have on its political life? In the fifty years between January 1920

and December 1969, conservative parties were in office at the
federal level for forty years and nine months, while Labor was in
government for nine years and three months. Conservative parties
won sixteen of the nineteen elections held over that time. Defenders
of the press would probably view these facts simply as proof that the
press acts as a mirror. If newspapers were unusually conservative,
they would argue, it was only because they were reflecting public
opinion. But others would ask whether the relationship could have
worked the other way around. Did conservatives win so many elections because conservative newspapers (and their radio and television stations) successfully put forward assumptions that tilted
public opinion towards a conservative view of economics, industrial
relations, foreign policy and a host of other issues?

Untangling cause and effect with any precision, especially from
this historical distance, is impossible. But there are examples in this
book that show that, rather than acting as a 'mirror', newspapers
sometimes deliberately set out to shape public opinion and influence party politics as a way of dictating the course of events. Even
outside of those specific examples, the daily newspapers in Australia
were so unusually politically homogeneous that it would be naïve
to believe that this did not have a major impact upon the nature of
political debate, and on the behaviour of its political elites.

PART TWO

....

THE OWNERS

CHAPTER 4

HUGH DENISON: AUSTRALIA'S FIRST NEWSPAPER EMPEROR

Tobacco industrialist Hugh Denison was the owner who transformed the Sydney *Sun* and created Australia's first newspaper empire. A pioneer in radio, cable news and paper manufacturing, Denison was ahead of his rivals in the cutting-edge technologies of the day. At its peak, his media company was a colossus, the largest in the Southern Hemisphere. It controlled a stable of newspaper titles, including the ground-breaking *Sun* and the much-imitated Melbourne *Sun News-Pictorial*. In the early 1930s, it owned four of the six daily papers in Sydney. With such a strong base, the Denisons should have been secure in newspapers for generations, and their family name as well known as Fairfax, Murdoch and Packer. But Denison's empire burned out almost as quickly as it flared, and he never achieved the dynasties forged by three men who had all worked for him at one point – Keith Murdoch, RC Packer and Frank Packer. Denison's descendants were out of newspapers by 1953, and today, Denison's significant impact on the Australian media has been largely forgotten. This chapter tells the story of his doomed empire and how other newspaper owners learned from Denison's grand ambitions and exploited his mistakes.

THE 'RAG, NAG AND FAG KING'

Born in 1865, the son of a tobacco industrialist, Hugh Denison completed his expensive private schooling in Melbourne, Adelaide and London before he took up his inheritance in the family business after the death of his father, Robert Dixson, in 1891. Distinguished looking, with a waxed and curled moustache, Denison was known as a persuasive and gifted speaker with a wide range of interests. Over the next decade, he set about merging several competing tobacco companies and, by 1904, had achieved a near total monopoly in British Tobacco (Australia) Ltd, which became the second largest company in Australia.[1] This made him very wealthy, but Denison was also a man of strong political opinions who always had his finger in many pies, and he had also gone into politics while expanding his business. From 1888 to 1905, he was firstly an Adelaide City councillor (a seat he won when he was only twenty-three years old), then a member of the South Australian legislature. Denison's political views were conservative and, according to his family, it was his fear of a Labor government leading to socialism that had inspired him to go into politics: he loved the British Empire, disliked taxation and feared socialism.[2] But his stint as a politician was short-lived as Denison chose to pursue his commercial ambitions.

In 1905, Denison moved to Sydney. He was involved in horseracing and his famous horse Poseidon won the Australian Jockey Club (AJC) and Victoria Racing Club (VRC) Derbies plus the Melbourne and Caulfield Cups all in one season in 1906. It was his involvement in horseracing that led Denison to change his surname from Dixson to Denison in 1907 in order to avoid embarrassing his namesake uncle, Sir Hugh Dixson, a strict Baptist. Denison was also a radio pioneer. In 1909, he founded a wireless company as part of his dream to establish an empire-wide radio service. But the medium was new and expensive. Neither Denison's company nor the famous Marconi Wireless Telegraph Company were making money in Australia. Denison went to London and Berlin to try to arrange a merger between Marconi and the German Telefunken company (to which Denison held the local rights in Australia). As with tobacco, Denison's strategy was to aim for monopoly and try to eliminate or absorb competition. He brokered a deal to form a powerful alliance of joint operations registered as Amalgamated Wireless (Australasia) Ltd (AWA) in 1913. Like his tobacco mergers, the anti-competitive radio deal was only possible because of Australia's weak anti-trust laws: in countries with stronger laws it would likely have been outlawed.[3]

In 1910, the year after Denison went into radio, he also went into newspapers – and almost by accident according to his company's account of its own history.[4] The ailing *Australian Star* newspaper needed money for a new plant and its chairman approached Denison to ask if his tobacco company would give the newspaper company a loan of £10 000 on debenture security over the existing plant, which was already the subject of a bank overdraft. When the newspaper company went into liquidation soon after, Denison acquired its assets. Instead of winding it up, Denison was convinced by one of the newspaper's directors to keep the paper going on the basis that there was room for an evening newspaper in the Sydney market if it could be revitalised.

Denison formed a new board with several Sydney businessmen and two of the remaining directors from the previous company.[5] Rather than try to 'revive a corpse', as Denison put it, they decided to relaunch the paper with a new name and identity.[6] The protectionist, labour-supporting *Star* was re-born as the commercially oriented and allegedly non-partisan *Sun* in 1910. Among its shareholders were major retailers, including from the Hordern family and Charles Lloyd Jones (of David Jones), plus theatrical entrepreneurs JC Williamson and George Tallis.[7]

FIGURE 4.1 Hugh Denison as a younger and older man

SOURCES National Library of Australia, JJ Pascoe, *History of Adelaide and Vicinity*, Hussey & Gillingham, Adelaide, 1901; and Sun Newspapers, *Sun Newspapers Ltd 1920–1929*, Sun Newspapers, Sydney, 1929, p. 11.

The new company was called the 'Sun Newspaper Company Limited'. With interests now across newspapers, racing and tobacco, Denison was dubbed the 'rag, nag and fag king of Australia'.

THE RISE OF THE *SUN*

Denison wisely recognised that he had no experience with newspapers so shrewdly hired talented staff and left the *Sun*'s journalism and administration to them. One of his key appointments was journalist Montague (Monty) Grover, already considered a brilliant and original journalist, who had been an *Argus* journalist and a *Sydney Morning Herald* subeditor. Grover drove the paper's design and news style. A savvy and formidable journalist named Herbert Campbell Jones also came across from the *Argus*, and later became the paper's managing editor. Albert Fordyce Wheeler managed the paper's advertising and is credited with inventing 'display' advertising by combining art and sales techniques. Later, the *Sun* grew bloated with lucrative advertising, and Fordyce Wheeler became extremely wealthy and very influential within the company.

But it was Grover who did most to shape the new *Sun*. Following the principles of 'new journalism', he called for a crisp, fresh and bright presentation of news, including news on the front page, and the bold use of photographs and visual material. He wanted the public to be able to get 'something different' from the paper and instructed his reporters to look for human interest as well as news stories.[8] When the new-look sixteen-page *Sun* rolled off the presses in July 1910, its first edition was issued at 12.45 pm, in time for the lunch-hour rush, and it quickly found its market with workers and shoppers. The ailing *Star* had a circulation of only 15 000. The *Sun*'s first day's sales doubled that and it held on to many of those first readers, averaging 26 000 copies a day in its first month.[9]

The *Sun* had only eight publishing staff, and was still being taken out for distribution by horse-drawn carriages, but Denison's talented team rapidly built up the paper. One gap in the market they pursued was international news. In the first decade of Federation, the Australian public had lacked overseas news. Local news was widely available, and much the same across different newspapers, but foreign news was something special and exclusive. Several old morning papers – the *Argus*, the *Sydney Morning Herald* and the Adelaide *Register* – had set up an anti-competitive news cable combine in the 1870s. The Fisher Labor government had tried to break it by subsidising an Independent Cable Service for three years from 1910. Denison lobbied for the expansion of this service and paid extra so that the *Sun* could take more than the usual amount of words in cables.[10] He benefitted from the Independent Cable Service for two years but then, in 1912, scored a major coup when he secured access to news cables from Lord Northcliffe's famous British paper, *The Times*.

Australian newspapers considered *The Times* to be the 'world's greatest newspaper'.[11] It was at the 'very centre of world newsgathering',[12] and so authoritative a source it was considered almost the official voice of the British Empire. When in London in 1912, an audacious Denison had visited Northcliffe and boldly asked for *The Times* to supply a news service to his *Sun*. Northclifffe was reluctant but the smooth-talking Denison convinced him that distributing *The Times'* news in far-flung parts of the Empire would be as beneficial for *The Times* as it would be for Denison's Sydney paper. When the agreement was formalised under the name the Australian Newspapers Cable Service (later also called the United Cable Service (UCS)), it was the first time the prestigious *The Times* allowed another publication access to its editorial proofs and news. Denison immediately sent Herbert Campbell Jones to London to start picking out choice items of *The Times'* world news. Campbell Jones would then supplement these items and send them back to the *Sun*. To replace him as the *Sun*'s Melbourne correspondent, Denison hired the stammering but hard-working young *Age* reporter Keith Murdoch.

The *Sun* now had unique foreign news delivered with authority, speed and reliability. Its net sales doubled in three months, and it soon had to publish more editions in order to meet demand. It published an issue before noon, and then four other editions during the day, with its printing plates continually updated. This put the *Sun* at the forefront of the 'breaking' news model of the day. It was the most up-to-date evening newspaper in the country, and by 1913, its circulation was over 50 000.[13]

The *Sun*'s success did not go unnoticed in Melbourne where the board of the HWT was concerned that Denison would next try to move into the Melbourne newspaper market. Their *Herald* was vulnerable to competition in its afternoon market where it was used to having a monopoly, and especially because its own cable news (supplied through the *Argus/Sydney Morning Herald/Register* combine), was so inferior. But in 1913, a deal was suddenly struck for the *Herald* to become a partner with the *Sun* in its *The Times* cable service operating out of London. This enterprise, in which the two papers jointly managed the service, was now known as the United Cable Service (UCS) or the *Sun-Herald* Cable Service (UCS had several aliases, and was sometimes still referred to as the Australian Newspapers Cable Service).

Why did the *Sun* suddenly agree to share its precious cable news with a potential rival? The *Herald*'s editor, JE Davidson, was apparently the 'driving force' behind an initial partnership that began in 1911,[14] but the HWT chairman Theodore Fink later claimed that he travelled to Sydney in 1913, when Denison was away in England, and persuaded the unsupervised *Sun* staff to enter into a partnership with the HWT to run the cable service together. Fink said that 'if Denison and Campbell Jones had been there they would not have agreed to the equal partnership' and would only have taken on the HWT as a subscriber. As Fink's biographer Don Garden noted, 'This may be true, but it seems rather strange that those in Sydney did not clear the arrangement with their boss'.[15] Fink also insisted upon a clause in the agreement stating that the new partners would not move into each other's city during the period of the contract.[16] So the HWT now had joint access to the most valuable news cables in the country, and an agreement that minimised the threat of Denison moving into Melbourne.

According to Fink's account, Denison was exploited by a more cunning newspaper rival, and this would become something of a theme. Denison was not in the mould of other newspaper owners who, as a group, tended to be unusually absorbed with their work. Keith Murdoch and JE Davidson, for example, were renowned for being workaholics who were unwaveringly focused on newspapers, and worked long hours under stress that took its toll on their health. Denison was instead involved in a range of businesses, not just newspapers, and he wore his ambitions far more lightly than other owners. During at least one crucial business negotiation, he was out on the golf course. Denison pursued a wide range of interests outside of his work. He was a fine baritone and keen sportsman, involved in horseracing, rowing, cricket, football, bowls and golf. He was known for being approachable and courteous, and also seems to have been a fairly amiable boss whose company initiated an unusually generous profit-sharing scheme with its staff.[17] And although Denison was wealthy and lived an opulent lifestyle, with a chauffeur and his wife in mink coats, unlike several other newspaper moguls, he was also a generous philanthropist who gave to local hospitals, charities, the Royal Empire Society and other causes. Denison lived in better health and to a longer age than several of his competitors. But, up against more ruthless rivals, his more laid-back style of newspaper management may have cost him his empire.

THE POLITICS OF THE *SUN*

By 1917, the *Sun* had given up any pretence of non-partisanship and was fervently backing the conservatively aligned Nationalists, a new party led by William Morris 'Billy' Hughes. Hughes had become Labor prime minister in October 1915, but had been expelled from the Labor Party in 1916 over his support for conscription (the role that Melbourne newspaper owners played in that split is described in the next chapter). Hughes had then formed the Nationalist Party, a merger between the conservative Liberal Party and other pro-conscription defectors who had followed him out of the Labor Party.

Hughes' attempt to have Australians forced into military service for World War I to defend the Empire was a highly divisive issue in Australia. Hughes was convinced that only compulsory reinforcements of troops overseas could win the war, and ended up holding two unsuccessful referendums on the issue. Denison had previously had stoushes with Hughes, when Hughes was Labor leader, over business matters including patents, the wireless mergers and Denison's German business connections. But, as a passionate loyalist of the British Empire, Denison came to admire Hughes' conscription stance. This was not unusual. Wealthy, conservative businessmen were among the strongest supporters of conscription, and pro-conscription calls were ringing out loudly in commercial newspapers across the country.

One of Denison's employees was making sure that the pro-conscription case was prominent in the foreign news cables that were being reproduced in the *Sun*, the *Herald*, and many provincial newspapers throughout Australia. In 1915, Denison had recalled Campbell Jones from London to become managing editor of the *Sun* and sent Keith Murdoch to replace him as head of the UCS. This was an important posting and Murdoch made the most of it, including prodigiously networking with influential people in London. One of Murdoch's powerful friends from his political reporting days was Hughes. When Hughes arrived in London in 1916, Murdoch worked tirelessly as an unofficial publicist for him, at the same time as fulfilling his official job responsibilities for Denison and Fink. The news cables that Murdoch was sending from London were so heavily supportive of Hughes and his conscription campaign that they were more propaganda than news. Even the pro-Hughes Campbell Jones complained that 'it is not the personal views of Keith Murdoch which we and our [cable] clients are buying'.[18]

Notwithstanding their concerns about the overblown nature of Murdoch's cables, Denison and Campbell Jones decided in 1916 that the *Sun* should back Hughes' conscription campaign to the hilt. The *Sun* was so supportive that Campbell Jones later claimed the Nationalist party was 'called into being by the *Sun*'.[19] The paper that had promised to be free of 'political entanglements' had taken sides on the most divisive issue of the day. An account produced by the Sun Newspaper company said that the *Sun*'s owners knew that 'a very large number of [the paper's] friends and subscribers were vehemently opposed to [conscription]' but decided nonetheless that 'the *Sun* should support [Hughes] with every ounce of its strength … [and that] cost many friendships'.[20]

One internal friend who was appalled was Grover. He strongly disapproved of Hughes' campaign, and so did a large segment of the *Sun*'s Labor-voting audience. The paper's pro-conscription stance reportedly saw its sales fall 'by 40,000 in two months'.[21] But the reader backlash subsided and did not impede the paper's progress. The war had created a hunger for news, especially overseas news, that the *Sun* had a natural advantage in providing. Between 1913 and 1918, the paper's circulation more than doubled. By 1920, it was selling 148 000 copies.[22] In ten years, the *Sun* had increased its audience nine-fold. It had also increased its capital twelve-fold and its profits thirty-fold (from £3109 in 1912 to £103 386 in 1922).[23] Denison saw a solid base for expansion.

DENISON'S ASSAULT ON MELBOURNE

In tobacco and wireless, Denison's business strategy had revolved around creating a monopoly, and once the war was over, he set about trying to apply that strategy to newspapers as well. He started off by purchasing the *Northern Times*, a small evening newspaper in Newcastle, in 1918, which was re-named the *Newcastle Sun*. At fifty-five years of age, Denison then continued to look for other opportunities in Sydney and further afield. After years of nervous anticipation at the HWT, in 1921 Denison finally moved to start up an afternoon paper in Melbourne to compete directly with the *Herald*. His former employee Keith Murdoch was now at the helm of the *Herald*. After his five years in London, Murdoch had returned to Australia a very different man; urbane, confident and well connected. Denison had wanted Murdoch to become editor of the *Sun*, but Murdoch had instead accepted an offer from his co-employer, Fink and the HWT.

As editor at the *Herald*, Murdoch was on a mission to modernise the paper and fortify it against the looming competition. While Grover was busy designing Denison's new Melbourne paper, Murdoch dashed to Sydney and started buying up shares in the *Evening News*. He threatened Denison that the HWT would buy the staid afternoon paper and turn it into real competition for Denison's *Sun*. This did not eventuate as planned (Chapter 7), but Fink and Murdoch had another card to play.

Murdoch recounted what happened in a letter to Northcliffe in December 1921:

> I asked our lawyers – [Fink's company] – for a ruling on a
> cable matter. This led to the production of a dusty pile of
> agreements with the *Sun*. And lo! black with dust and forgotten
> by everyone was found a letter written [in December 1915] by
> Denison extending [the Sun Newspapers-HWT] partnership
> agreement until September 1923 and thus pledging the *Sun*
> not to start in Melbourne before that date. This meant that
> all their preparations were illegal, and our counsel even
> advised that they could be cast in damages. They had bought
> buildings and plant and engaged staff, intending to start next
> September. Denison was dumbfounded and at once proposed
> amalgamation of the two companies. Baillieu and Fink looked
> into this. It amounted to a pretty big swindle of the public and
> I was strongly against it. Fink came round to my view.[24]

In December 1921, Sun Newspapers and the HWT discussed merging their interests. Murdoch believed that it was only his strong opposition that stopped the merger going ahead. But his statement that it would have amounted to 'a pretty big swindle of the public' is intriguing. Could it be that the two companies were considering secretly amalgamating while pretending to compete against each other? Throughout the coming years, outsiders would often speculate about the puzzling relationship between these two companies that, even when they appeared to be competing, had strong links between them.

Because Denison had, as he later admitted, 'forgotten' about the addition to the agreement, his new Melbourne paper could not start publishing until April 1923.[25] Grover was 'aghast' because his plans were so advanced.[26] He and Denison decided that instead of waiting passively, they would side-step the territorial agreement and make use of their idle Melbourne plant by publishing a morning paper instead. And it would not be just any morning paper. Denison had remembered that Northcliffe once asked him why there was 'no pictorial paper in Sydney or Melbourne or both' when pictorial papers had been such a success in England.[27]

Denison's new paper would be Australia's first pictorial daily newspaper. It would have to compete against two well-established morning competitors, *The Age* and the *Argus*, but both had grown quite stale and were vulnerable to competition. Grover designed the morning pictorial to be in a tabloid size that, like the London ones he modelled it on, was easier for morning commuters to handle. When the *Sun News-Pictorial* launched on 11 September 1922, it was lively, good humoured, and contained many photographs. Although some critics derided it as frivolous and aimed at 'flappers', the paper quickly found a market with its handy size and light-hearted, pictorial approach. It especially appealed to young readers, who found *The Age* and the *Argus* too sombre, and it immediately began snatching circulation from them.

Once the territorial agreement expired, the success of the *Sun*

News-Pictorial convinced Denison that his team could now beat Keith Murdoch in the Melbourne afternoon market, where the *Herald* had held sway since 1869. But it was a serious mistake. Murdoch had used the delay to rejuvenate the *Herald* and had managed to transform it into what Monty Grover's grandson, journalist and author Michael Cannon, described as 'an excellent broadsheet, full of "human interest" stories as well as hard news, yet with a mildly conservative outlook which suited Melbourne's middle-class commuters and advertisers'.[28] When Denison launched his competing afternoon paper, called the *Evening Sun*, in April 1923, he spared no expense and recruited the best staff, but the paper misjudged the Melbourne market. Printed on startling pink paper, it was too flashy and cheeky for the Melbourne afternoon paper reader. The *Evening Sun* looked 'lightweight, even erratic, beside the revitalised *Herald*' and never overtook the popularity of the *Herald*, with its deep community roots.[29]

Soon, the heavy financial losses from the failing *Evening Sun* began to drag down the far more successful *Sun News-Pictorial*. Denison was overseas when his staff tried reducing pages in both papers and cutting costs to stem the losses, but it was soon being whispered that Denison's company, which had invested £500 000 on the Melbourne venture, had lost at least a quarter of a million pounds.[30] Denison's timing with the *Evening Sun* had been amiss, especially once Murdoch was in charge at the *Herald*, but by his own admission, Denison's overseas travel and lack of supervision were other factors. He said that mistakes at the *Evening Sun* were 'partly owing to certain mistakes which had been made in my absence by the Editorial Department and which had a serious affect [sic] on the circulation of the evening paper, with the result that when I got back here they were losing about £1200 per week'.[31] In 1925, Denison sold his two Melbourne papers to the HWT for a reported £150 000.[32] The HWT closed the *Evening Sun* but

FIGURE 4.2 The first edition of the ground-breaking, and much imitated, *Sun News-Pictorial*, 11 September 1922

SOURCE *Sun News-Pictorial*, 11 September 1922, p. 1.

continued to publish the *Sun News-Pictorial*, guiding it to continued success.

In his post-mortem to shareholders explaining what had gone
wrong, Denison conceded that the late start had hurt the *Evening
Sun* because the *Herald* had become so 'strongly entrenched in every
possible way', but he also said that it had been a big mistake to try
to put out 'two papers in the one day, under the same name [of the
"Sun" in the one city] ... that was our undoing. It has never been
a success in any other part of the world.' Explaining why the board
had 'risk[ed] it knowing that', Denison gave the underwhelm-
ing response that, 'Gentlemen, we are only human'. But the mis-
judgement had meant the papers' advertising departments found it
difficult 'getting advertisements for two papers of the same name
published on the same day'. Denison claimed the newspapers had
also been painted as a Sydney venture, arousing Melburnians' geo-
graphical prejudice.[33]

Denison blamed other factors as well, including high commissions to selling agents in Melbourne and the 'interference of the
unions'. But he also revealed that the HWT backed him into a corner
by threatening to align with the *Sun*'s competitors in cable news in a
way that would increase the *Sun*'s costs and 'cut us off from certain
sources of supply and certain sources of revenue'. Denison said he
ultimately complied with the HWT's demand to close the *Evening
Sun* and sell it the *Sun News-Pictorial*, because the HWT agreed
to 'halve the whole cost of [the *Sun*'s] cable service', re-sign to the
joint UCS for another ten years, and provide a 'fair price' for the
Sun News-Pictorial. Putting a very positive spin on events, Denison
argued his company had got 'out of Melbourne with our flags flying
[and] our capital intact'.[34]

While Denison's Melbourne foray has tended to be viewed as
an all-out assault on a rival owner, Denison had several important
links with the HWT. The cable news service was one, but he was

also linked to industrialist WL Baillieu, the HWT's most powerful director and shareholder (Chapter 5). Denison and Baillieu were among the richest men in Australia, they shared similar world views, and had some connections through social circles. In December 1922, only three months after Denison started competing with the HWT in Melbourne, Baillieu installed Denison as chairman of one of his many other companies, a textile company called the British Australian Cotton Association Ltd (BACAL), in which Denison acquired 68 000 shares.[35] If Baillieu appointed Denison for his business acumen, he must have been disappointed as BACAL continued to be beset by problems and to lose money. Baillieu was looking to get out of it by August 1924, but Denison was still travelling around on behalf of the ailing company. Denison was away in October 1924, when the *Evening Sun* was dying, because he was in England on BACAL company business. Whether that was Baillieu's intention, to distract Denison from his Melbourne papers, is not known, but the BACAL chairmanship certainly added to Denison's already over-committed schedule.

After losing to the HWT, Denison returned to Sydney and his press empire was thereafter confined to New South Wales. Knighted in 1923 for services to the Empire, Denison was Commissioner for Australia in the United States from 1926 to 1928. Once he returned from the United States, Denison turned his attention back to newspapers and embarked upon a sudden splurge of acquisitions. In 1928, there were six daily and five Sunday newspapers in Sydney, and Denison's company bought up one Sydney daily a year for the next three years. Denison ended up running two competing morning dailies, two competing afternoon dailies, and three Sunday newspapers. Two of these papers were purchased from a partnership that included RC Packer, a former employee of Denison's, who would go on to outmanoeuvre his former employer in a series of controversial business decisions that helped seal the fate of Denison's newspaper empire.

ROBERT CLYDE PACKER: FRIEND AND ENEMY

RC Packer was born in Tasmania in 1879, and worked as a journalist, at first in Hobart, then in Dubbo, Townsville and Sydney. He joined Denison's *Sunday Sun* as a subeditor in 1916 and, within months, was promoted to chief subeditor and then editor. He was energetic, canny, and a hard man who was prone to bursts of temper and notorious bullying of his employees. Historian Bridget Griffen-Foley has described RC as 'tough, uncompromising, suspicious and secretive'.[36] He was considered a highly skilled subeditor and newspaper manager – 'a newspaperman to the tip of his pen' – who had a talent for building up newspaper circulation through an instinctive feel for tabloid journalism, a flair for design, and his shrewdness as an executive.[37]

In 1919, RC Packer left Denison's company to help found a new weekly paper called *Smith's Weekly* with his journalist friend Claude McKay and the wealthy, flamboyant politician James Joynton Smith, who had served as a Labor-backed Sydney lord mayor and also as an Independent in state and local politics. Like Denison, Joynton Smith owned horses, but he also managed and promoted pony racing at Brighton and Epping racecourses. He owned the Victoria Park racecourse. Horseracing was a prominent topic in popular newspapers, including the ones that Joynton Smith and Denison pioneered, providing valuable cross-promotion opportunities. But there were also political motivations. Through his campaigning to raise war loans during World War I, Smith had 'discovered the thrill of [political mobilisation and was now more specifically interested in] conservative mobilisation ... [he] set out consciously to use his paper to mobilise a "League of Citizens"'.[38] Smith wanted to launch a newspaper that would present his views. He generously financed *Smith's Weekly*, cheerfully putting in extra money and patiently waiting for it to become profitable. Packer managed it, and Claude McKay edited it.

Smith's Weekly was aimed at the middle classes and flamboy-antly took up the cause of the 'common man', the 'underdog' and returned diggers. Compared to the other Sydney papers, *Smith's* was witty and cheeky, with lively cartoons, lots of illustrations and vivid artwork contributed by well-paid artists. By the standards of today, it was also shockingly racist and sexist. Like the *Sun*, *Smith's* also proclaimed itself to be anti–party politics, but it too admired Hughes and hated communism.[39] (Joynton Smith donated money to at least one of Hughes' election campaigns.[40]) *Smith's Weekly* was a success, and by 1922, was selling 150 000 copies a week.[41] As soon as it became profitable in 1921, Joynton Smith generously gave a one-third share of ownership of the paper to each of his co-founders, making Packer and McKay wealthy men.

Encouraged by their success, the partners soon launched another paper, the *Daily Guardian*, in July 1923. It was a morn-ing tabloid pictorial, a format inspired by the launch of the *Sun News-Pictorial* the previous year. The *Daily Guardian* also car-ried all the hallmarks of the bright, brief news style pioneered by the *Herald* in Melbourne and the *Sun* in Sydney. But it had its own distinctive character, combining brash populism, humour, sensational reporting, and a crusading style of reporting politics, sometimes harping on the pet causes of its owners, reporters and editors. But where *Smith's Weekly* had enjoyed rapid success, the *Daily Guardian* was up against the well-established *Sydney Morn-ing Herald* and *Daily Telegraph* in the morning market, and it immediately struggled. It lost £20 000 per month for its first three months, and over £100 000 in its first year.[42] RC Packer took over the day-to-day running. His son Frank, who had proved an indif-ferent student, left school early to join the paper. But the losses continued and Frank Packer's second-rate journalism skills were no remedy, so he was laid off and went to work as a jackaroo in western New South Wales.

In 1925, RC Packer hit upon the circulation-boosting idea of launching the first Miss Australia contest after seeing American dailies' photographs of women in bathing suits. After nine months of publishing photographs of entrants, West Australian Beryl Mills was crowned the winner in June 1926 and the *Daily Guardian* sold 275 000 copies that day.[43] Frank re-joined the paper in November 1926 and watched as his father continued to push up circulation by subduing the paper's cranky tone, and increasing its sensational crime reporting – including trying to track down a missing body in a trunk, and sending a reporter to buy cocaine from a chemist who was then charged by police.[44] The *Daily Guardian*'s free insurance and prize competitions also helped to boost its circulation to 180 000 by 1929.[45] This put it within close reach of the once formidable *Sydney Morning Herald*, which reported a circulation of 190 000.[46]

ASSOCIATED NEWSPAPERS AS BRIEF COLOSSUS

The *Daily Guardian* gave Denison an opportunity for another acquisition because its success was hurting the moribund *Daily Telegraph*, a paper which had failed to keep up with changing audience tastes. In April 1927, there had been an attempt by the *Daily Telegraph*'s directors (reportedly businessmen with little journalistic flair) to transform it into a pictorial tabloid, including a Sunday version that was called the *Daily Telegraph Sunday News Pictorial* – 'a name no reader could possibly remember'.[47] But the new pictorial format was proving difficult and the directors were struggling with debt on a new building. In 1927, they approached Denison about merging their interests. When Denison's Sun Newspapers bought a controlling interest in the *Daily Telegraph*, it shortened the unwieldy paper titles, changed page sizes, improved the ink and paper, put in more art and photographs, and made other editorial changes to try to make the paper 'brighter and more attractive to a newer generation'.[48]

Meanwhile, Denison's original paper, the *Sun*, had continued to rise steadily in the 1920s with its circulation swelling from 147 000 in 1920, to 212 000 by the end of 1928.[49] But the *Sun*'s competitor, the *Evening News*, was also now doing well. The *Evening News* was backed by directors from financial and commercial interests, including advertisers who wanted to prevent a monopoly in evening newspapers that they knew would lead to higher advertising rates. After journalist Errol Knox had been promoted to managing director, the paper critics dubbed the 'Evening Snooze' was revitalised with larger headings, more pictures, a larger women's section, twice-weekly turf guides, radio features, competitions and more sensational news coverage. It pioneered the use of crossword puzzles in Australia and by 1924, its circulation had doubled in less than a year.[50] But in the expensive world of newspaper publishing the *Evening News*' owners needed more capital to pay for new land and a new building. Assured by the smooth-talking Denison that their advertising rates would not increase if the two companies joined forces, the retailers behind the *Evening News* agreed to a merger.

On 1 October 1929, Samuel Bennett Ltd, owner of the *Evening News*, merged with Sun Newspapers to form a new company called Associated Newspapers Ltd. Bennett's company contributed the *Evening News*, *Sunday News*, *Woman's Budget* (later re-named *Woman* and later still, *Woman's Day*) and *Sporting and Dramatic News*. Sun Newspapers contributed the *Sun*, *Sunday Sun*, *Daily Telegraph*, *Sunday Pictorial*, *Newcastle Sun*, *Wireless Weekly* and *World's News*. On its formation, Associated Newspapers became the largest newspaper company in the Southern Hemisphere. It had paid-up capital of £3.5 million (over $265 million in today's money), and valued its nominal capital as £5 million in 1931.[51] After

THE HOME OF SUN NEWSPAPERS LTD., 60-66 ELIZABETH STREET.

FIGURE 4.3 The exterior and interior of the *Sun*'s Elizabeth Street building in Sydney, with its famous roof-top globe, 1929; today, the building houses shops on the ground floor and the globe is painted grey, but it is still visible looking up from the corner of Martin Place

SOURCE Sun Newspapers, *Sun Newspapers Ltd 1920–1929*, pp. 10, 58.

THE SUN

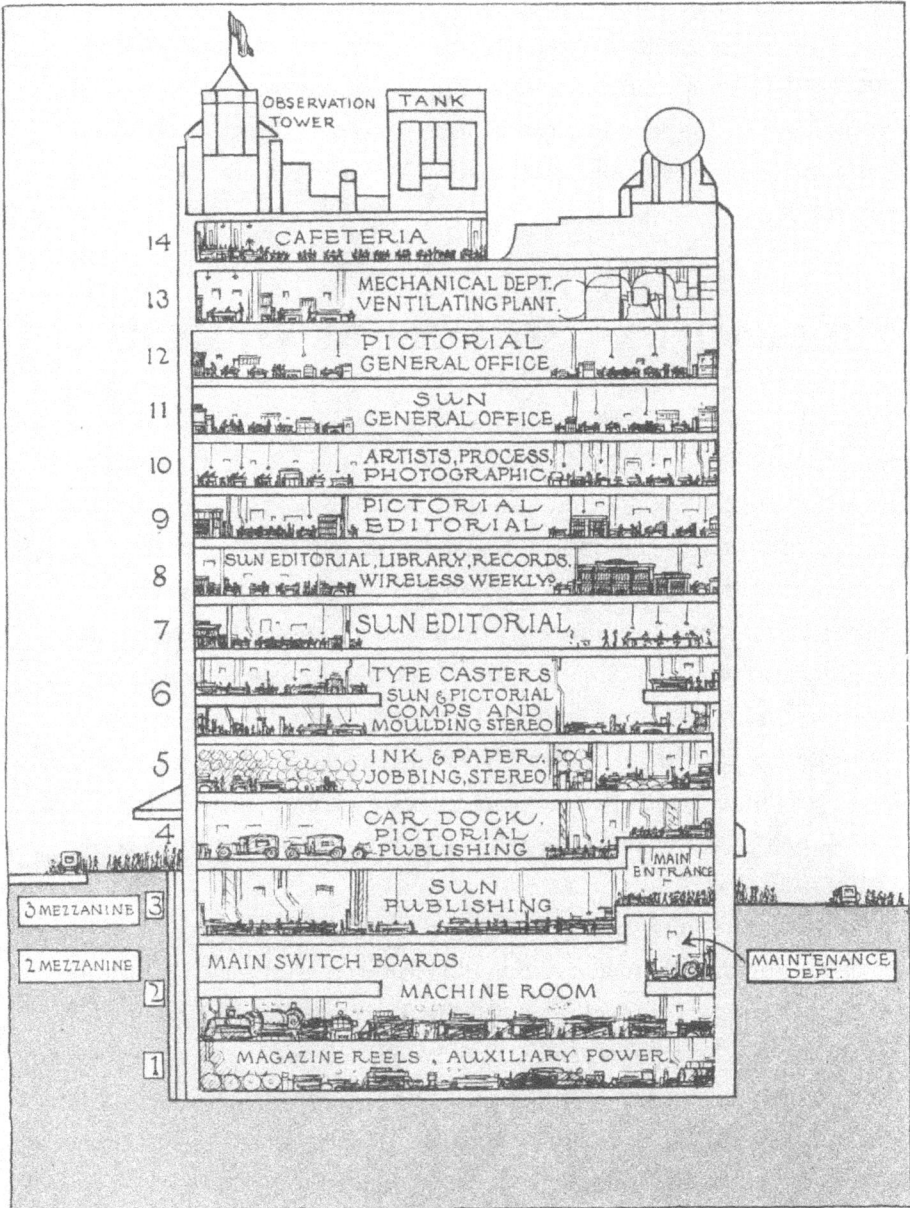

	OBSERVATION TOWER
	TANK
14	CAFETERIA
13	MECHANICAL DEPT. VENTILATING PLANT.
12	PICTORIAL GENERAL OFFICE
11	SUN GENERAL OFFICE
10	ARTISTS, PROCESS, PHOTOGRAPHIC
9	PICTORIAL EDITORIAL
8	SUN EDITORIAL, LIBRARY, RECORDS, WIRELESS WEEKLY
7	SUN EDITORIAL
6	TYPE CASTERS SUN & PICTORIAL COMPS AND MOULDING STEREO
5	INK & PAPER, JOBBING, STEREO
4	CAR DOCK. PICTORIAL PUBLISHING
	MAIN ENTRANCE
3 MEZZANINE / 3	SUN PUBLISHING
2 MEZZANINE	MAIN SWITCH BOARDS
2	MACHINE ROOM
	MAINTENANCE DEPT.
1	MAGAZINE REELS, AUXILIARY POWER

PHILLIP STREET.   SECTIONAL PLAN.   ELIZABETH STREET.

58

the merger, Associated Newspapers was publishing two evening papers and three Sunday papers in direct competition with each other in the same Sydney market. This was an unusual business strategy, even for the time. Denison probably counted on being able to increase his papers' low cover price from one penny to 1½d, the usual price in other cities by this time.[52] But when the Depression hit, it put a stop to that strategy.

THE CRASH OF ASSOCIATED NEWSPAPERS

Hugh Denison was still determined to expand, and in 1930, he bought yet another Sydney paper when Joynton Smith decided that he wanted to sell his seven-year-old *Daily Guardian* (which had been one of the bitterest critics of Denison's *Sun*). In September 1929, Joynton Smith and Denison were negotiating about the sale when Smith and his partners shrewdly launched a new paper, the *Sunday Guardian*, as a direct competitor to Denison's cherished *Sunday Sun*. Joynton Smith was in no financial position to run the new paper as an ongoing concern so it seems very likely that it was a calculated bluff, designed to put pressure on Denison. Denison took the bait and offered a better price for what was now ostensibly two papers rather than one.

Associated Newspapers valued the two *Guardian*s as worth £575 000 and gave its rival company £175 000 cash (about $12 million in today's money) as well as 400 000 £1 preference shares in itself in return for the two papers.[53] The Associated Newspapers shares were divided among ordinary shareholders in Smith's Newspapers, mainly Joynton Smith, Packer and McKay – neglecting the preference shareholders. The Packers received about 173 000 of the Associated Newspapers shares, which meant that they now had a significant stake in Denison's company. A separate part of the deal was that Smith's Newspapers agreed not to publish a morning, afternoon or Sunday newspaper for twenty-one years. Scandal sheet *Truth* argued that a 'panic-stricken' Denison 'had it put over him in the merger negotiations'.[54] He had paid more than the *Guardian*s were worth – a fact that even the Packers later admitted – and all for the sake of owning two more newspapers that were just going to compete with his existing morning paper, the *Daily Telegraph Pictorial* (as it was then called) and his *Sunday Sun*.

By 1930, the Depression was biting. Many readers had stopped buying newspapers, and advertisers were cutting their ads. With its large, unwieldy stable of papers, Associated Newspapers was feeling the effects of Depression-era contraction far worse than the leaner, more economically sound HWT in Melbourne. But Denison went away to England for ten months, from February to December 1930, leaving his board and staff to deal with the consequences of his acquisitions. The *Evening News* was already losing money when he left. It was soon joined by the yet again retitled *Daily Telegraph* (now called the *Daily Pictorial*).

Associated Newspapers' board decided to raise the cover price of its flagship evening newspapers to 1½d. But when that change took effect on 7 April 1930, sales plunged 40 per cent in a few days (a result the directors attributed to 'a definite boycott by the Labour Unions' [sic]).[55] Associated Newspapers lost its nerve. It revoked the price rise on 12 April without much explanation to confused readers, only to put the price back up again just four months later when all Sydney newspapers went up to 1½d. Denison wrote from England to his acting chairman, retailer Sydney Snow (one of the *Sun*'s largest advertisers), that it was a 'terrible shock to me' that the price rise was only trialled for less than a week, but he said he trusted his board to make the right decisions in his absence.[56]

THE 'GREATEST DUEL IN NEWSPAPER HISTORY'

Despite the reports of how poorly his new acquisitions were faring, Denison was still so keen on expansion that when Geoffrey Fairfax, a director and owner of the *Sydney Morning Herald*, died in late April 1930, Denison wrote to Snow saying that this was their chance to 'acquire the *Sydney Morning Herald*', and 'I believe I can raise the necessary funds'.[57] Denison said that no one need know Associated Newspapers was behind any takeover, and it would solve their price problem (because the *Sydney Morning Herald* had refused to raise its price when the *Sun* had attempted it in early April). But Australia's oldest and most prestigious newspaper was an expensive proposition, firmly held within the Fairfax family, and Associated Newspapers was having trouble managing the newspapers it already had. Snow seems to have judiciously ignored Denison's wild suggestion. (And the price problem was soon resolved when the *Sydney Morning Herald* agreed to lift its price, along with the other Sydney dailies – including the *Labor Daily*, which Associated Newspapers had paid off.)

In July, Campbell Jones wrote to tell Denison that the *Daily Guardian* was deteriorating because 'it is no longer the saucy, cheeky paper that Smith's produced'. Under Associated Newspapers, it had lost 'its original character ... its naughtiness and nastiness', while the *Daily Pictorial* (which would revert to the title of *Daily Telegraph* in February 1931) was also suffering because it had been 'drained of ads' by advertising manager Fordyce Wheeler. Campbell Jones warned that they might be 'knocked to our knees' by losses from these two papers.[58] He wanted to take charge of all of the papers in Associated Newspapers' crowded stable and try to turn the under-performers around.

For fifteen years, Campbell Jones had been 'King of the *Sun*'.[59] Commonly known as 'CJ', he had first arrived at the paper in 1910, working with fellow *Argus* alumni Monty Grover, Adam McCay and George Redmond, to make the *Sun* a phenomenal success. Where Grover disdained boards and personal ambition, Campbell Jones was ambitious and after being called back from the UCS in London, he had leapfrogged over Grover and become managing editor of the *Sun* from 1916. Campbell Jones was widely credited, including by Denison, with driving the success of the *Sun* since then, but even so, Denison did not want all of the company's papers under 'one man's control'.[60]

Denison had not allowed Campbell Jones to get involved in the management of the *Guardian*s since the papers had been acquired because of the deep animosity between the *Guardian* staff and Campbell Jones. Denison was worried that some of the best *Guardian* staff would leave if Campbell Jones was put in charge of them, and this would leave Associated Newspapers 'at the absolute mercy' of 'one man without any understudy or alternate [sic]'.[61] Denison had been urging Campbell Jones to appoint an understudy for five years, but none had emerged and Denison felt this was deliberate, so that 'we could not do without him'.[62]

The other problem was Campbell Jones' 'political leanings'. Denison had specifically told editors Errol Knox (*Evening News*) and FW Tonkin (*Daily Guardian*) that they should maintain the political stances of those papers as they had been before Associated Newspapers had acquired them. He did not want the *Sun* editor's pro-Hughes stance reflected across all of the company's papers. Hughes had been expelled from the Nationalists in August 1929 for his role in bringing down the Bruce–Page coalition government that year. He had launched a new party as a vehicle for his personal ambitions, the Australian Party. The *Sun* had been the only major paper to promote it.

Denison told Snow that Campbell Jones' 'attacks on Bruce' and his promotion of Hughes 'who of course is [now] anathema to the

154   **THE OWNERS**

big body of Nationalists, has antagonised most National supporters and especially those who are well to do and see in this attitude a continuance of Labour Party [sic] domination in the Commonwealth parliament'.[63] Denison's 'well to do' friends were firmly against the Scullin Labor government (Chapter 10). But Denison also feared something more specific. He was worried that wealthy Nationalist supporters, including some of Associated Newspapers' shareholders, were so 'offended' by Campbell Jones' political stance that they would start up a rival newspaper.[64]

Despite all of these fears, in September 1930, Denison agreed to appoint Campbell Jones as managing director of Associated Newspapers, and let him take control of all the papers, including the *Guardian*s. Snow had warned Denison that Campbell Jones would leave otherwise, and shareholders 'would not approve of our letting go the driving force of the only money spinner we have (the *Sun*)'.[65] Campbell Jones also seemed to be the only person up to managing the increasingly desperate situation. The public had 'strongly resented' the August price rise when the stable's papers had daily been preaching economy and sacrifice to readers as a way out of the Depression.[66] Then, when free insurance was dropped for three of the papers, this reduced their sales even further. Circulation had dropped by 25 per cent for the *Sun*, 45 per cent for the *Evening News*, 35 per cent for the *Daily Guardian*, and 20 per cent for the *Daily Pictorial*.[67] A lack of advertising meant that profits from the *Sun* were no longer enough to cover losses from the other papers. For the first time, the company was losing money on a weekly basis.[68]

Under the stress of the Depression, it was becoming very clear that Denison's strategy of running multiple newspapers in competition with each other was not working. At the 10 February 1931 board meeting, criticism was made of the excessive price paid for the two *Guardian*s and the board resolved to combine the *Daily Guardian* and the *Daily Pictorial* into a new *Daily Telegraph*, and also to merge the *Sunday Pictorial* into the *Sunday Guardian*. A later vote by shareholders confirmed the *Evening News* was also to be closed and it died on 21 March 1931. Boardroom tensions were mounting, and in May 1931, Denison barely survived a board resolution asking him to take a leave of absence. Those who had wanted Denison to go – Campbell Jones, Sydney Snow and two other directors – all resigned, stating they had lost confidence in him.

By June 1931, the value of Associated Newspapers shares had fallen disastrously, with £1 shares dropping to only two shillings. With shareholder anger rising, on 12 June 1931, 600 of Associated Newspapers' shareholders crowded into King's Hall, while hundreds waited outside when they could not get in. The fiery meeting heard from the two different factions, each claiming the other group was responsible for the company's woes. One faction supported Denison, while the other was grouped around Snow, Campbell Jones and the resigned directors. Snow claimed that Denison had tried to mislead banks over the company's financial position, while Campbell Jones argued that the source of the company's problems was the price paid for the *Guardians*, 'a price no sane person would have paid'.[69] Campbell Jones warned that the preference shareholders, including Joynton Smith and RC Packer, were trying to take control of Associated Newspapers.

RB Walker says that, after the estranged directors had put their case, Sir Hugh 'rose and spoke so convincingly that the meeting passed an overwhelming vote of confidence in him'.[70] But it was not only Denison's famed silver-tongue that ensured his survival on the night. Griffen-Foley has revealed that RC Packer stacked the meeting with friendly shareholders and proxies, and arranged for them to lambast the resigned directors rather than Denison.[71] One of those proxies who 'viciously attacked' Campbell Jones was Packer's ally Voltaire Molesworth, who had been Packer's managing editor at the *Daily Guardian*.[72] Ahead of the meeting, *Smith's Weekly*

NEWSPAPER NEWS, WEDNESDAY, JULY 1, 1931   Page Eleven

DRAMA OF ASSOCIATED NEWS

**1,000 Shareholders Take
Part in Greatest Duel
in Newspaper History**

**DIRECTORS REVEAL
WHY THEY RETIRED**

*Urgent, Bitter, Intriguing
Uproarious Denunciations*

HUNDREDS OF THE OVERFLOW HAMMERED AT THE DOORS
FOR ADMISSION.

SIR HUGH DENISON WINS OVERWHELMING VOTE OF CONFIDENCE

A SSOCIATED Newspapers Ltd., Sydney, a publishing house capitalised at £3,800,000 and owned by 3,000 shareholders, has endured...

SIR HUGH DENISON OPENS.
The Chairman (Sir Hugh Denison)...

FIGURE 4.4 The 'greatest duel in newspaper history' according to *Newspaper News*' dramatic report of the 12 June 1931 shareholders' meeting
SOURCE *Newspaper News*, 31 July 1931, p. 11.

had also been publishing articles blaming Campbell Jones for the company's woes. A copy of one particularly vicious article had been sent to shareholders before the meeting.

New directors were recruited to the board in an attempt to resuscitate it, but none had experience in running newspapers. Some were Nationalist-aligned businessmen who Denison suspected were interested in starting up a rival evening paper, including industrialist FH Stewart, and later, lawyer Graham Waddell.[73] Others were closely linked to banks and pastoral finance, including Frederick Tout who was a director of the Bank of New South Wales and the AMP Society. These two companies had strong views on economic policies during the Depression and interests that they wanted to protect (Chapter 10). The Bank of New South Wales and AMP were also strongly linked to the Fairfaxes, owners of the *Sydney Morning Herald*.

Another owner who was watching Associated Newspapers closely was RC Packer whose shareholding in the company was now rapidly losing value. With his reputation for being a circulation wizard and 'newspaper builder', Packer crossed the road from Smith's Newspapers to the giant building of Associated Newspapers in September 1931, as its managing editor, on a declared mission to turn the company around.[74] It was later claimed that Packer had been reluctant to make the shift because his health was not good, and he only went because Frank convinced him that he needed to safeguard their future and their shares. Others, like Campbell Jones and Snow, believed that RC Packer was intent on ultimately gaining control of Associated Newspapers.

Snow had warned Denison back in July 1930 that their experience of Packer had proved they needed to be wary of putting him in a leadership position.[75] But Denison overlooked Packer's tempestuous manner and accepted Packer's assurances that he just wanted to protect his large interest in the company.[76] Denison had not wanted Packer to be managing editor though, fearing it gave him too much power, but he again gave in and, on 17 August 1931, formally offered Packer the job. For two weeks, Packer used a lawyer to haggle over the terms of his contract before signing it. His unusual job pitch had reflected his characteristic bluntness. Packer had told Denison that his board members lacked ability, that Denison knew little about the scale of the task at hand, and had shown a 'pathetic fear of [competition] and a lack of confidence'.[77] Later, Packer would use that 'pathetic fear' of competition to his advantage.

AN INSIDE JOB: THE DEAL OF THE CENTURY

Two weeks after Packer took over, he merged the *Sunday Guardian* with the *Sunday Sun*. Between January 1930 and September 1931, Associated Newspapers had closed six of its papers and was now being lampooned as 'Assassinated Newspapers' – 'the graveyard of newspapers'.[78] The slimmed-down Associated Newspapers was now focused on just three papers: one each of a morning, afternoon and Sunday paper: the *Daily Telegraph*, the *Sun* and *Sunday Sun*. Packer freed up the display of these papers, increased their focus on news, and put in more photographs. He also stirred things up at the management level. On arrival, Packer had quickly fired off a memo to the board scolding the directors for incompetence and accusing Denison of mismanagement. Three months later, he launched another written attack accusing advertising manager Fordyce Wheeler of a conflict of interest and robbing shareholders of £15 000 a year. Management tension was so high that both Packer and Wheeler reportedly had bodyguards and carried revolvers.

Although one of his restructuring suggestions had been that Denison's son should be dismissed to save money, Packer then proceeded to install his own son, Frank, at the company, in January 1932. Denison and others on the board were concerned that RC was trying to gain a foothold in the company for his son, which would upset their own dynastic plans. Amid this escalating boardroom intrigue, Frank Packer was seen to be acting as the office spy. In February 1932, Denison confirmed that he and the board would not allow Frank to stay. It was a rejection that Frank Packer never forgot, and that RC Packer was also deeply offended by.

RC Packer was at Associated Newspapers for less than two years. He caused an incredible degree of internal animosity and turmoil, but he did manage to steady the company. Between 1931 and 1933, it had been unable to pay dividends on its ordinary shares. In 1933, it was able to pay a dividend of 5 per cent.[79] The consolidation of newspaper titles and RC's energetic cost-cutting and new vigour had helped, but so too had a reconstruction that had reduced share values and written down assets by a million pounds. RC Packer may have helped Associated Newspapers in the short term, but his more enduring legacy to the company was a damaging one.

In October 1932, Frank Packer received a telegram. He was twenty-five years old, and after his humiliating departure from Associated Newspapers, had gone away on a gold-finding mission. The telegram was from George Warnecke, a brilliant English journalist who RC Packer had brought to Australia in the mid-1920s. Warnecke had strong connections within the Australian Worker's Union (AWU) and the Labor Party, and was friends with EG Theodore, the former Labor premier of Queensland and former treasurer in the federal Scullin government. Warnecke told Frank that he had heard the *World* (an evening rival of the *Sun*'s that was owned by the AWU), was doing so badly that its directors were going to close it. Griffen-Foley says it was Warnecke who suggested taking advantage of Denison's well-known anxiety about competition: '[Warnecke] decided that a syndicate should acquire the *World* and announce that it intended to convert the title into a penny newspaper … [Hopefully,] Hugh Denison … would panic and offer to take over the new paper'.[80]

Warnecke put this cunning plan to RC Packer but, as an executive at Associated Newspapers, Packer senior knew that he would not be able to effect the deal. He decided that his son was better placed to broker it, and preferably with the financial backing of the wealthy Theodore. Theodore did agree to back Frank, going into business with the young man in a company called 'Sydney Newspapers Ltd'. In October 1932, RC Packer went to Denison and told him that his son had teamed up with Theodore but was refusing to tell his own father what the pair's intentions were. Frank and Theodore then purchased the financially struggling *World* from the AWU, in a deal cut 'over a few lubricating drinks' with AWU leaders, on 1 November 1932.[81] Theodore paid £100 for an option on a one-year lease. Packer and Theodore then started publicising their plans to re-launch the paper and let it be widely known that they would price it at a penny, undercutting the *Sun*'s price of 1½d.

On hearing this news, Denison reportedly went white. RC Packer disingenuously reassured Denison that he was doing everything he could to stop his son.

Denison was especially anxious about any new competition because the *Sun*'s position had only recently stabilised. He started negotiating directly with Theodore and offered a financial incentive for Packer and Theodore to either reduce the cover price, or not publish the *World* at all. But Theodore kept refusing Denison's rising offers so Denison authorised RC Packer to 'fix up the matter'. This now seems like extreme naïvety, as Packer's temperament was known, and he had an obvious conflict of interest. Packer duly cut a deal with his son and Theodore, but Denison was furious when he was called off the golf course and told that RC Packer's solution had been to commit Associated Newspapers to pay Frank and Theodore's new company (registered only two days before) £86 500 in return for an agreement that they would not compete with the *Sun* nor publish a daily or Sunday newspaper for three years. In less than ten days, Frank Packer and Theodore had effectively turned a £100 option into £86 500 (about $7 million in today's money).[82] They promptly took the cash and closed the *World*, throwing 280 employees out of work during the Depression. It seems unlikely they ever sincerely intended to re-launch the *World*. Its purchase was yet another calculated bluff and Denison's second major mistake in dealing with the Packers.

A WOMEN'S NEWSPAPER

Frank Packer and Theodore still had the *World*'s plant at AWU headquarters, Macdonell House, and they had plenty of capital. They saw an opportunity to use the plant because, while the non-competition agreement prevented them from starting a daily paper, it left the path open for other types of publications. Warnecke, who was still an employee of Associated Newspapers but already known to be in the Packer camp, came up with another brilliant idea. He and his wife, Nora, had spent weeks studying women's interests and shopping habits and developed a prototype of a women's newspaper, the *Australian Women's Weekly*. In one account, Warnecke developed this dummy edition when he was on sick leave and holiday leave from his position as editor of Associated Newspapers' *Sunday Sun*. But a former general manager of Associated Newspapers claimed that Warnecke developed the dummy edition *before* he went on leave and was supposed to submit it to his employer, but never did. After Warnecke's period of leave, he resigned, and took the dummy with him to Frank Packer and EG Theodore's Sydney Newspapers, leading the former manager of Associated Newspapers to believe that the '*Women's Weekly* [was] conceived in the same office that [unintentionally] provided Packer with the funds to launch it'.[83]

Warnecke designed the *Women's Weekly* to be distinctly Australian, to appeal across age groups, and to be topical. Unlike overseas women's magazines which went to press up to six weeks before publication, the *Women's Weekly* was designed to focus on news — but news about lifestyle, homes, cooking, fashion, beauty, parenting and current affairs that were judged as being of interest to women. With advertisers so keen to reach women, as the custodians of the family purse, the publication provided a unique opportunity to capture advertising revenue.

The first issue of the *Australian Women's Weekly* appeared in Sydney on 10 June 1933. It was a forty-four-page black and white newspaper (it later became a colour magazine). It was priced at two pence and boasted it was 'the biggest value in the world'. The front cover included stories on 'What smart Sydney women are wearing', 'equal social rights for sexes' and 'unique new jumpers'. There were ads for hats, insurance, gas fires, department stores, cleaning products, cars, biscuits and stout beer. Frank Packer had estimated the paper would sell 50 000 copies per week but neglected women readers bought up 121 162 copies. On its first day, it was sold out by lunchtime and the printing presses were pushed to their limit. The *Women's Weekly* was such an immediate and outstanding success that interstate editions quickly followed in Victoria and Queensland. Its average circulation grew from 260 000 in 1935, to 445 000 by 1939.[84] It became Australia's best-selling and most profitable magazine. Denison had unwittingly provided Frank Packer with the capital to establish what would become a major publishing business, and later still, a multi-media empire.

AFTER RC PACKER: DEALING WITH HIS SON

Frank's career was just beginning, but RC Packer's was ending. He was in poor health and resigned from Associated Newspapers in June 1933. He died a year later, aged fifty-five, on his return to Australia from a holiday in England. Frank's *Women's Weekly* memorialised his father in extravagant terms as a 'genius' who 'always used the power of his papers for the welfare of his country'.[85] The Packer family believed that RC had 'killed himself' through overwork, trying to save his family's shareholdings and resuscitate Associated Newspapers.[86] The Denisons' feelings about Packer's impact were more mixed. They did not attend his funeral.

Associated Newspapers continued trying to strengthen its remaining papers. In April 1934, its *Daily Telegraph* became the first Australian newspaper to publish a rotogravure pictorial supplement, with scenes of animals, beauty, sport and fashions. This boosted circulation by 25 000.[87] But the paper had gone through many changes already, it was a lower priority for the company than its cherished *Sun* and *Sunday Sun*, and it was up against the oldest newspaper in

Australia, the *Sydney Morning Herald*, which had been improving its pages to shore up its own position. The *Daily Telegraph* continued to struggle and, although Australia was emerging from the Depression, Denison's newspaper empire again found itself in trouble. In 1935, Associated Newspapers decided to protect its key assets and, in the process, starved the *Daily Telegraph* of funding, including cutting its expensive rotogravure supplement, its cartoons and Saturday magazine section. The *Daily Telegraph* became barely profitable and 'an industry joke'.[88]

Other troubles were also brewing in 1935. The three-year restrictive period of Packer and Theodore's 1933 agreement with Associated Newspapers was about to lapse and they were looking to expand off the success of the *Women's Weekly*. They considered launching a daily newspaper and, in January 1936, made an unsuccessful offer to buy Ezra Norton's *Truth*. Rumours then began to circulate that Frank Packer was planning to launch an afternoon newspaper. Associated Newspapers was freshly alarmed at the prospect of a new competitor to the *Sun*. Denison suggested to Packer and Theodore that, instead of starting a new afternoon paper, they should take over his ailing *Daily Telegraph*, along with the premises and plant of the defunct *Evening News*. Keen to avoid the risk and expense of starting a brand new paper, Packer and Theodore agreed.

In January 1936, Associated Newspapers therefore joined forces with Packer and Theodore's Sydney Newspapers. Associated Newspapers contributed its poorly performing *Daily Telegraph* while Sydney Newspapers provided its successful *Women's Weekly* to form a new company, Consolidated Press Limited. Keen as always to avoid competition, Denison ensured that the terms again included that Packer and Theodore would not establish an evening newspaper nor a Sunday paper for three years. He also cheerfully told shareholders that he had made 'friendly arrangements' with Packer so that the *Daily Telegraph* would not be priced less than Denison's

Sun.[89] Theodore was appointed chairman of Consolidated Press while Packer became managing director and deputy chairman. Associated Newspapers nominated an accountant to fill its one position on the board – a sign that it had very little understanding of what it had unleashed.

The partnership proved to be a colossal bargain for Packer and Theodore, with Denison yet again coming off second best in dealing with the Packers. Critical observers said that Associated Newspapers had been rendered 'a tame and copious milch cow for Theodore and Packer'.[90] Denison had opened the door for them to move into publishing a daily newspaper and, even if that newspaper was struggling and up against the formidable *Sydney Morning Herald*, a daily paper was a powerful political asset, and Packer and Theodore made the most of the opportunity. Where Associated had starved the *Daily Telegraph* of funds, they now threw money at it. They hired a new and expensive large staff to revitalise the paper, including Sydney (Syd) Deamer as editor, and Harry Cox as assistant editor. Both came across from the Melbourne *Herald*, and brought with them the *Herald*'s house style of large volumes of brief and diverse news items.[91]

In March 1936, the new *Daily Telegraph* appeared. Packer had brought Warnecke back from the *Women's Weekly* temporarily to redesign it, and Warnecke modelled it on the style of Lord Beaverbrook's London *Daily Express*, a paper that set records for newspaper sales in the 1930s. The revitalised *Daily Telegraph* declared itself unapologetically 'free and frank', and 'thoroughly modern – as modern as television, wireless and airmails'.[92] Frank also drew on some of his father's tried-and-tested circulation-boosting gimmicks, including free insurance for readers who had the newspaper delivered and competitions with large prizes, but also full-page comics and a racing supplement. When Consolidated Press took over the *Daily Telegraph* in December 1935, its circulation had been 96 246 and dropping, while its morning competitor, the *Sydney Morning Herald*, had a circulation of 222 903. After eighteen months of competition, the *Daily Telegraph*'s circulation had risen to 187 610, and the *Sydney Morning Herald*'s to only 226 413.[93] For the rest of the 1930s and into the 1940s, Packer continued transforming the *Daily Telegraph* into one of Australia's top-selling newspapers.

THE END OF AN EMPIRE

By the end of the 1930s, Denison's newspaper empire was much diminished and left with only the *Sun*, the *Sunday Sun* and a number of magazines. It never returned to the colossus status it once commanded. Although now in his seventies, Denison turned his attention to radio (Chapter 13), and in 1938, founded the Macquarie network. But Denison's time was running out and he died from cancer while on a business trip to Melbourne on 23 November 1940. He was seventy-five years old. Denison's newspaper-owning contemporaries Keith Murdoch and RC Packer were fixated on securing a dynasty in newspapers, and carefully arranged their assets and wills to ensure their sons would be the leading figures in their companies after their death. But Denison did not have the same dynastic drive.

After Denison's death, his son Reginald remained a director of Associated Newspapers, and another son, Leslie, was its production manager. But it was Denison's friend and longstanding executive, John Butters, who stepped in to become chair of Associated Newspapers. And where Murdoch's and Packer's wills left very specific bequests to their sons, Denison's will left his sons no assets at all. It stated that Denison had 'made adequate provision in his lifetime for Lady Denison, his sons, and other relatives'.[94] He instead bequeathed large sums of money to philanthropic and educational causes, and to his grandchildren. Denison's grandson William Leslie (Bill) Denison believes that his grandmother, Denison's wife Lady Sara Rachel Denison, was behind the unusual will; that she had encouraged Denison to be a philanthropist and not to spoil their sons.[95] Denison had certainly not cut them off entirely. Before his death, he had set up his sons in Denison Estates, the company that managed his assets. And through that proprietary company they stayed involved in radio until 1951, and newspapers until 1953. But, only thirteen years after Denison's death, his family was out of the newspaper industry.

By that time, Associated Newspapers was a shadow of what it had once been. Only two months after Denison's death, its future prospects took a dramatic dive when the Menzies government awarded a licence to Ezra Norton, owner of *Truth*, to start a new afternoon newspaper. For years, Norton had been wanting to start an evening paper to rival the *Sun*, and had used Campbell Jones' inside knowledge to help him develop a plan in the mid-1930s. Campbell Jones' career had come to an abrupt halt when he was still at the peak of his powers because he had backed Snow over Denison in 1931. He was still an energetic and first-rate newspaper administrator, but he also knew all of the secrets of the *Sun* and how to beat it.

Denison was so concerned about Campbell Jones starting up a rival newspaper that he solicited Keith Murdoch's help at the end of 1932 to get him out of harm's way. Murdoch agreed for Campbell Jones to be sent back to the UCS in London. At first, Denison reported that Murdoch was not 'particularly keen' on this idea because 'he thinks [Campbell Jones] has definitely passed his best, and has dropped so much in his appearance and manner that he does not think he would do us very much credit in *The Times* office'.[96] But Murdoch relented and told Denison that he was happy to find a 'minor position' for Campbell Jones because 'he is a capable man and, what any one of us might be some day, a journalist who has fallen on bad times'.[97] Campbell Jones became the UCS European correspondent in February 1933. But by October he was trying to get released from his four-year contract, and was back in Sydney by 1934.[98]

Before he had been spirited off to London, Campbell Jones had been working with Norton and, on his return, he became a director of Truth and Sportsman Ltd and editor-in-chief of *Truth*. But this position also did not last long. Campbell Jones resigned in June 1935. Associated Newspapers believed that Campbell Jones had also been working with Sydney Snow (who had become deputy president of the United Australia Party (UAP) in 1932), Alexander McLachlan (the UAP's postmaster-general), and several other conservative lawyers, politicians, businessmen and wealthy retailers.[99] In mid-1934, Associated Newspapers believed this group was planning to bring out a new evening paper 'in the interests of the [UAP]' that would sell advertising at half the rate the *Sun* charged, and with a cover price of one penny (Denison's worst fear).[100]

But Campbell Jones could not get financial backing for his intended new projects. A former colleague said that the ex-*Sun* King used to 'laugh at fate [for] he was a good loser'.[101] Early in his career, it had been said of Campbell Jones that he possessed the '"divine fire" of the journalist born' and an insatiable writing itch.[102] In the final years of his life, he still had it, but had been reduced to writing letters to the editor. He wrote prolifically to different newspapers on a wide range of random topics, a type of over-eager audience member that journalists usually consider something of a crank. But when he died in 1942, *Smith's Weekly* – which had dubbed Campbell Jones inept and overrated in the 1920s – noted that the *Sun* 'never shone as brightly' after he left.[103]

In 1941, Denison's worst fear of an afternoon rival in Sydney was finally realised. Norton's new, circulation snatching *Daily Mirror* drained the *Sun* and its parent company (Chapter 16). Associated Newspapers shrank further in 1948 when it sold its shares in Consolidated Press to Packer and Theodore, making them an independent force in newspapers. Its own fortunes then continued to decline. In 1953, the value of £1 shares in Associated dropped disastrously to ten shillings and six pence.[104] Fairfax moved in to acquire what was left of the company after a battle with Frank Packer, who had also wanted to scoop up the remnants of the former giant. The company had never really recovered from Denison's overreach. In 1934, its paid-up capital had been reduced to £2.5 million. Ten years later, it had not grown: it was still £2.5 million.[105] And when the *Sydney Morning Herald* took it over in 1953, Associated Newspapers' chairman, Butters, admitted that ever since the Depression, for a 'period of almost a quarter of a century, the Company has been short of liquid funds'.[106]

Hugh Denison, the man with the Midas touch across a range of industries, was the major casualty of the newspaper wars of the 1920s and 1930s, toppled by Depression-era economics and his own monopolising tendencies, but also by a softness when dealing with far more ruthless rivals who considered him a pushover, and a poor manager of his newspapers once times got tough. Denison made some disastrous mistakes – forgetting about the agreement with the *Herald* that fatally delayed the *Evening Sun* in Melbourne, paying too much for the *Guardian*s, going away for long periods at crucial times, and thinking that he could ever trust the Packers. But if Denison was not the most successful newspaper owner in Australia, he may well have been one of its nicest.

Denison's desire for cooperation and partnerships, his naïvety in not understanding the devious psychology of his opponents, and his wide range of interests, all played against him in the newspaper business. But, psychologically, he seems to have been far milder in temperament than the more successful – but obsessive and manipulative – newspaper owners. Denison's companies gave generously to charity. When Campbell Jones turned on him, Denison allowed his son, Alan Campbell Jones, to remain at the company (Alan later became general manager of radio station 2UE). Denison's family also seems to have been happier than some of the scandal-ridden newspaper dynasty families. Former employees often spoke well of the Denisons and when Frank Packer's biographer sought out Reginald Denison years later, he was surprised to find that Reg was dispassionate about the perceived betrayals of the 1930s and bore no hatred towards the Packers. On hearing this, Frank Packer was not surprised though, remarking that 'the Denisons are very reasonable people'.[107]

Hugh Denison's legacy was to set in motion a monopolising tendency in the newspaper industry. His frustrated ambition to create a chain of newspapers encouraged other proprietors to imitate his empire-building strategies, but they had the benefit of being able to learn from his mistakes. In Victoria, a rival newspaper empire soon emerged out of the ashes of Denison's unsuccessful foray into that state. Denison's *Sun News-Pictorial* gave the HWT a firm base to expand from, and it approached the task with a ruthlessness that Denison had lacked. Where Denison's instinct had been to form partnerships with rivals – first with Samuel Bennett Ltd in 1929 and then with Theodore and Packer in 1936 – the HWT gave no quarter to rivals, favouring full-blooded takeovers to mergers. Where Denison's talented team had taken the risk of creating new papers, the HWT preferred to gobble up or close existing ones. But as the HWT spread across the country, it was not well known that the newspaper company was, itself, part of a much larger empire. Known as Collins House, it was the most formidable industrial network in Australian history.

CHAPTER 5

'WHO OWNS THE OWNERS OF THE *HERALD*?': THE KINGDOM OF COLLINS HOUSE

When the HWT group outplayed Denison in Melbourne in 1925, it made the newspaper deal of the century. It closed his *Evening Sun* – putting the *Herald* back into monopoly position as the city's only afternoon daily, but now with an additional 30 000 subscribers who came across from its eliminated rival.[1] It also cheaply acquired Denison's popular morning tabloid, the *Sun News-Pictorial*, which already had a good circulation; but within ten years, was selling more copies than its two ageing rivals – the *Argus* and *The Age* – combined.[2] It would go on to break Australian sales records for decades, and at one time was said to be the most popular newspaper, per capita, in the English-speaking world.[3] In September 1925, one of the main players behind the HWT, William Lawrence (WL) Baillieu, accurately described the acquisition as 'one of the most advantageous transactions ever entered into by any [Australian] company'.[4]

The *Sun News-Pictorial* provided a solid foundation for the HWT to expand interstate under Keith Murdoch in the 1920s, and by the 1930s it had achieved Denison's thwarted dream and become a powerful national media empire. Denison had unwittingly helped, but behind the scenes, the HWT also had a formidable base of wealth and power that underwrote its expansion. In 1933, the eccentric and abrasive politician Archie Cameron wrote a marvellously rude letter to one of the HWT's most loyal editors, Lloyd Dumas of the Adelaide *Advertiser*. Complaining that Dumas' paper was covertly run from Melbourne by the HWT, Cameron jeeringly asked, 'Who owns the owners of the *Herald*?'[5]

Cameron was drawing attention to something that was not well known by either the general public or the thousands of readers of HWT newspapers. Behind the *Herald* and its parent company was Australia's wealthiest and most powerful industrial complex, a financial empire based in Melbourne and London that remains unique in Australian history.

Known as the Collins House group, after the name of the building it was housed in, it dominated the mining and manufacture of iron ore, silver-lead-zinc, copper and brass, at a time when those metals were vital and immensely profitable. Aside from newspapers, it also made plastic, rubber, paints, paper, glass and beer. It was involved in coal mining, steel, oil exploration, gas, aluminium, aircraft production, fertilisers, chemicals, medicines, shipping, gold mining, timber milling, banking, radio, cinemas, textiles, insurance, trustee funds, retail stores, real estate, agriculture and pastoral firms. Collins House developed some of Australia's most famous brands – including the Herald and Weekly Times, but also Consolidated Zinc (now Rio Tinto), Carlton and United Breweries (CUB), Dunlop Rubber, Dulux (originally British Australian Lead Manufacturers (BALM)), Broken Hill Associated Smelters (BHAS) and Associated Pulp and Paper Mills (APPM). It had strong connections with the banks that went on to become ANZ, NAB and Westpac, three of today's big four banks.

The many different companies that comprised Collins House were part of a sprawling labyrinth of assets held in a remarkable web of family and friendship networks that revolved around the Baillieu family. The Baillieus were involved with the *Herald* for eight decades, from 1889 to the 1960s. Over that period, the HWT group became a giant that dominated the Australian media. The story of how that media empire was forged begins in the boom and bust years of Melbourne in the 1880s and 1890s, winds through the mining town of Broken Hill, and into the boardrooms, stock exchanges and parliaments of the nation.

THE LAND BOOMERS

The *Herald* empire was driven forward by two men who had a secret. They wanted to conceal news, not break it. WL Baillieu and Theodore Fink were close friends and prominent Victorian identities who made a great deal of money in the frenzied 1880s land boom in Melbourne before they went bankrupt in the crash that followed. They had speculated during a period of extraordinary population growth in Melbourne that had seen land values soar as factories, houses and lavish city office buildings rose rapidly. Ordinary Victorians were encouraged by slick speculators and financiers, as well as speculative builders and estate companies, to borrow widely in order to buy into this boom. In the frenzy, many ended up investing more than their properties were worth, resulting in mass insolvencies, financial ruin for many, and a dramatic financial crash from which it took Melbourne decades to recover.

Tall, handsome and dynamic, Baillieu was one of the real estate auctioneers who contributed to, and profited from, the crazed atmosphere of the land boom. His firm of Munro and Baillieu was the busiest in Melbourne. It sold parcels of land on the fringes of Melbourne in new housing estates situated along rail and tramlines. The company would lure buyers to land auctions with slick promotional techniques that included advertisements in French, free railway tickets, marquees, brass bands, complimentary chicken, whiskey and champagne, and fanciful claims that buyers would 'quadruple' their purchase price in twelve months.[6] Baillieu was such a smooth boom-time auctioneer, he once managed to sell an allotment of land every minute for an hour.[7]

Baillieu's real estate firm was one of the *Herald*'s most important advertisers. Even before he went into ownership of the paper in the late 1880s, he could generally count on the *Herald* for favourable news reporting on his many ventures in real estate and land development. His business partner, Donald Munro, was the son of James Munro, a leading temperance advocate, financier, politician and Victorian premier (1890–92). This connection to political power was valuable. In 1893, the weekly magazine *Table Talk* called the Munro clan and its associates 'canny schemers' who displayed 'a wonderful foresight in buying up suburban paddocks just before railway lines were projected through their centre', and had a remarkable record of winning government contracts.[8] James Munro's banks, including the Federal Bank, were leading players in the speculative land boom. As notorious moneylenders and debt defaulters, they provided enormous sums of money on dubious security to Munro and his family and friends, including Donald Munro and Baillieu.

Baillieu was a leader and a risk-taker who could be brusque and ruthless, but was generally known as charismatic, friendly, optimistic, and extraordinarily loyal to his family. He was the second son born in a family of sixteen children. Their father had struggled financially but was politically ambitious and used his connections to become a councillor and mayor of Queenscliff, south-east of Geelong in Victoria. Baillieu's own extraordinary skill in cultivating political, family and friendship networks would become legendary. Baillieu built his immense wealth upon investments that derived from those associations, and one of his most important early connections, aside from the Munros, was his friendship with the Fink family.

FIGURE 5.1 The man behind the *Herald*: Australia's most powerful industrialist, William Lawrence Baillieu, circa 1909–11
SOURCE State Library of Victoria.

FIGURE 5.2 Theodore Fink, circa 1939; he was a director of the HWT from 1889 to 1942, and chair of its board from 1906 to 1942
SOURCE Photograph of a print, the Herald and Weekly Times portrait collection, State Library of Victoria.

Baillieu became involved in mining through his friendship with the one-time Victorian MP Benjamin Fink, who made a fortune in the 1880s by investing in an emporium, and then in coal mines, gold mines, and property. By the 1890s, Baillieu was a director of several mining companies and Benjamin's younger brothers, Theodore and Wolfe, were two of Baillieu's closest friends. It was Theodore Fink who encouraged Baillieu to become involved in the *Herald*. Fink was short, and wore glasses and elaborate hats. A solicitor by training, the cultured and sociable Fink also fancied himself as a writer and journalist. He enjoyed the opportunity of writing articles for his own newspaper after he bought shares in the Herald and Sportsman Newspapers Co. Ltd, publisher of the *Herald*, in 1889. The *Herald* had been an institution in Melbourne since 1840, when it began as the *Port Phillip Herald*. It was not as respected as the *Argus*, nor as influential as David Syme's *Age*, but the *Herald* had a solid circulation, it had already outlived several rivals, and it was a pioneering popular paper.

When Fink bought into the *Herald* it was as part of a syndicate that also included publisher Samuel Vincent (SV) Winter, printer Alfred Henry Massina (Fink was Massina's solicitor), Baillieu, Donald Munro and journalist George Walstab. Winter had been running the *Herald* with his long-time partner, John Halfey, since 1871, after they purchased it from David Syme. But when Halfey died suddenly in early 1889, Winter sought out new investors. It was an opportune time for Baillieu and Munro to become owners of a newspaper because they were concerned about publicity. After buying and selling real estate at inflated prices, their real estate company was encountering liquidity problems. It had also been accused of using 'dummy' vendors to mask land purchases, and had been named in newspapers in connection with several legal proceedings. The two estate agents had been firing off letters to various newspapers to defend themselves against the negative publicity.[9]

Baillieu was by now involved in real estate, banking, mining and beer brewing. The last activity was a result of his forging another valuable connection when he married into the wealthy Latham family in 1887. Baillieu's father-in-law, Edward Latham, was the leading shareholder in Melbourne's largest brewery, the Carlton Brewery. Latham personally guaranteed loans for Baillieu from James Munro's banks. Michael Cannon argued that Munro ran these banks 'as a convenient method of diverting huge amounts of the public's money into the pockets of himself, his family and their associates'.[10] Baillieu was among those associates. Personally, and as part of the Munro–Baillieu partnership, he had run up an overdraft of £230 000 (about $28 million in today's money).[11]

When the Federal Bank crashed in 1892, it took many Victorians' life savings with it. Aside from the dodgy banks, individual land boomers were also responsible for some of the worst speculations and unpaid debts. Among those who had 'caused an enormous amount of misery', was Baillieu's friend and business partner, Benjamin Fink.[12] Fink went bankrupt, owing £1.8 million ($200 million today), and then fled to London where he lived a life of luxury after successfully hiding his assets from creditors.[13] Other failed land boomers – including Baillieu – remained in Melbourne but paid their creditors only a small fraction of the sums they owed. When the time came for Baillieu to pay his creditors, in July 1892, he settled with them in private and agreed to pay back a measly six pence in the pound (equivalent to 2.5 cents in the dollar).[14]

Baillieu was able to make this arrangement because his friend and partner, Theodore Fink – who had also been caught up in the mania of the day and run up large debts – used his legal expertise in company and insolvency law to devise an ingenious method of keeping bankruptcies and debts quiet. Fink re-discovered a method of 'secret compositions', a little-used legal avenue for debtors to meet their creditors privately, and avoid public knowledge of their debts, by having financial arrangements worked out in secret and approved in the courts. Fink became a sought-after defender among the failed land boomers. He represented himself, his brothers, father-in-law and other prominent boomers, including Baillieu. One of Fink's skills, that he seems to have applied on behalf of Baillieu, was to round up amenable proxies (including friends, family and collapsing financial institutions) to act as creditors in order to obtain a good deal in secret compositions.

The secrecy of all of these arrangements was crucial because it allowed Baillieu and other boomers to escape the dishonour of bankruptcy. This meant they could still carry on operating other businesses that were hidden or otherwise protected in the secret compositions. They could also begin new business ventures, and still be advanced credit by unsuspecting banks and new partners. Baillieu made the most of the opportunity to simply carry on as if nothing had happened. He bounced back from his enormous debts very quickly, and in such spectacular fashion that no one has been able to adequately explain it.[15] By the late 1890s, he was again a wealthy man. His purchase of cheap bank shares may have been one factor. He was also still involved in mining, stockbroking and the *Herald*, and had launched a new real estate firm. He called the firm 'WL Baillieu & Co'. Munro's name was dirt, so he had been abandoned, but Baillieu's name was still good because his bankruptcy had been so successfully concealed.

It has been suggested that Baillieu's recovery was aided by his hiding of property during his bankruptcy proceedings and his failure to declare assets and money due. But this claim has been contentious. In a biography commissioned by the Baillieu family, historian Peter Yule mounted a defence of Baillieu. But other historians (including Michael Cannon, Don Garden and PD Gardner) argued that Fink and Baillieu acted dishonestly, did not declare all of their debts, kept important assets secret from investigators, and used family members as company liquidators to ensure a good deal on debts. It seems that Baillieu's and Fink's *Herald* shares were one of the key assets that they hid from creditors.[16]

As owners of the *Herald*, Baillieu and Fink were in a good position to suppress news of their financial troubles through their own paper, but other Melbourne newspapers were also curiously quiet. Michael Cannon says that 'Every newspaper ignored the financial crisis for as long as possible'.[17] The only publication to readily expose the land boomers and their tactics was not a newspaper but a weekly social magazine, *Table Talk*, run by Maurice Brodszky. A former *Herald* journalist who had married Theodore Fink's cousin, Brodszky had close knowledge of what was going on and, to his cost, he prioritised disclosure in the public interest over family relationships.[18] Only *Table Talk* tried to seriously pursue the speculators by reporting on what was happening behind the closed doors of the courts. *The Age*, run by Baillieu's and Fink's friend, David Syme, only briefly mentioned some of Baillieu's debts, and this was months after they had been reported in far more detail in *Table Talk*.[19]

THE MYSTERIOUS *HERALD* TAKEOVER

Protected from public knowledge of their debts, and able to keep their *Herald* shares, Baillieu went on to build a much larger fortune, while Fink's legal ingenuity made him a sought-after commercial lawyer. Both men would help steer the *Herald* from an insignificant Melbourne newspaper to the most powerful press organisation in the country, and one of the world's most successful. But first, they had to gain control of the paper. How they achieved this, in 1894, is a complex story of devious corporate manoeuvrings during the collapse of the boom, when many of those involved had much to hide, and when Baillieu and Fink were not the only land boomers circling the *Herald*.

In 1883, a group of teetotaller businessmen – Matthew Davies, James Balfour, John Robb, James McKinley and John Moodie – took over the Melbourne newspaper, the *Daily Telegraph* (1883–92), and set about making it into a virtuous Christian journal. But despite his religious views, Davies was another notorious land boomer who used his own bank, the Mercantile Bank, for his convenience. At the height of the boom years, he and his fellow *Daily Telegraph* directors were using recklessly borrowed money to prop up their failing morning paper. In 1890, several of them decided to also start up a new company called the City Newspaper Company Limited. They already owned the *Daily Telegraph* and the popular rural weekly, the *Weekly Times*. They now decided to go on a further buying spree, using other people's money. Through the City Newspaper Company, the directors bought into the *Herald*'s competitor, the *Evening Standard*, in October 1890. The next month, they bought the *Herald* (and its parent Herald and Sportsman company) from SV Winter and his fellow shareholders, including Baillieu and Fink.[20] In May 1892, the City Newspaper Company closed down the still-struggling *Daily Telegraph* to focus on the stronger papers in its stable.

Davies' scandalous banks and other companies were collapsing. He had lost £4 million of public money, and *Table Talk* claimed that the real reason that Davies and his family and friends bought up three of the five Melbourne daily papers was to 'silence … demand for their prosecution'.[21] While they controlled it, the *Herald* suppressed news of their misdeeds and flattered men of influence who could help keep them out of gaol. But Davies and his circle were running out of money, and they defaulted on their second payment to the old *Herald* shareholders (including Winter, Baillieu and Fink). In July 1892, with Davies having fled to the United Kingdom, it seems the former *Daily Telegraph* directors (now led by McKinley) tried to evade their debt by 'suddenly and secretly' starting up yet another company, the Victorian Newspaper Company, which had most of the same directors.[22]

Fink and Baillieu had been shareholders of City Newspapers since 1890, but Fink claimed later to have been ignorant of the under-handed sale of its assets to the new Victorian Newspaper Company. His biographer, Don Garden, believed Fink's ignorance was feigned, probably as part of his hiding of assets in his secret composition.[23] It is indeed remarkable timing that the Victorian Newspaper Company was established in the very same month that Baillieu's secret composition was held (and Fink's second composition), when complicated restructuring that helped obscure assets would have been most useful. Whether this was the original intention of the arrangement, or whether the *Daily Telegraph* faction tried to swindle the original Herald and Sportsman shareholders (as Fink claimed), the original agreement between the factions soured. Once their bankruptcy troubles were sorted out, the Baillieu–Massina–Fink group began trying to recover the *Herald* in late 1892, by forcing the rogue Victorian Newspaper Company into liquidation.[24] Fink's own dramatic (but vague) account of the recovery suggested that some legal, and even physical, intimidation convinced the dishonest directors to hand over control to the Baillieu–Fink faction 'without any election or legal steps' around late 1893.[25]

Conveniently, Baillieu's brother, Arthur, was appointed as the liquidator, and the Baillieu–Fink faction took over its assets. The *Herald*'s former proprietorship thus recovered not just the *Herald* but also gained the *Weekly Times*. More fortuitous outcomes were to come during this period of corporate chaos. In December 1893, Baillieu was appointed liquidator of the City Newspaper Company and then, in October 1894, of the Victorian Newspaper and Evening Standard companies. This last liquidation was a chance to acquire the *Evening Standard*, the *Herald*'s afternoon rival.

The *Evening Standard* (1889–94) was the most formidable rival the *Herald* had faced. Its directors included some of the wealthiest and most influential men in Australia, including the businessman, mining investor and former politician Thompson Moore. Despite this pedigree, and the fact that its journalism was so good that Fink considered it a 'better paper than the *Herald*', it was poorly managed and losing money.[26] On 31 October 1894, against the wishes of some of its shareholders, who claimed the liquidator was acting improperly, the *Evening Standard* ceased publication and was absorbed into the *Herald*.[27] When the two papers merged, the *Herald* called itself the *Herald and Standard*, a name it used until 1901.[28] Baillieu and Fink arranged for some of the *Standard*'s influential shareholders to be given three-tenths of the combined company. Fink considered this generosity 'a step ... to respectability', which was more valuable to the two former land boomers at this time than the cost of the shares.[29]

Out of all of these complex manoeuvres, the Baillieu–Fink group emerged in 1894, holding 95 per cent of the shares relating to the *Herald*.[30] They also owned the *Weekly Times*, had been able to close the *Evening Standard*, and Baillieu had become a powerful director of the newly formed Herald and Standard Newspaper Company. There is still an element of mystery about precisely how all of this was achieved, but the outcome was clear. A newly secure *Herald*, with a rival eliminated, and Baillieu injecting much-needed capital, soon began to prosper. In 1895, it moved into new premises on the corner of Flinders and Russell streets. The opening was attended by powerful friends who marvelled at its new linotype machines, its three Foster printing presses, and what it claimed was the largest composing room in the world.[31]

With the Victorian economy starting to recover, the *Herald* began paying good dividends from 1896. It had never troubled its readers during the crash by revealing that some of its owners were implicated among the despised land boomers. Instead, the *Herald* helped Baillieu to rehabilitate his reputation, and reliably promoted his business ventures. When Baillieu invested in the black-coal industry in the 1890s, the *Herald* campaigned strongly for government support for the industry and promoted its prospects. This helped it become the only Victorian coal mine to do well financially at that time.[32] The *Herald* also gave strong support to Baillieu's real estate ventures, and to the formation of the Society of Melbourne Brewers in 1903. This society was the precursor to Carlton and United Breweries, a cartel of brewers formed in 1907 so that they could raise prices in order to remain profitable at a difficult time for the beer market.

As he re-built his fortune, Baillieu was active at the *Herald* between 1894 and 1900. He was more active than Fink, who became a director only in 1900. But after 1902, when the company was reconstituted as the Herald and Weekly Times (HWT), their roles reversed. It was Fink who dedicated himself to the HWT thereafter. Baillieu was devoting more time to his other growing business interests, but he remained an imposing and influential figure on the HWT board, and was made its vice-chairman from 1906. Fink was appointed chairman the same year.[33] As the *Herald*'s chair, Fink would become one of the most powerful figures in Melbourne, and he enjoyed the status and influence the position attracted. Until Keith Murdoch was appointed the paper's chief editor in 1921, Fink was responsible for many of the changes that made the *Herald* more popular and financially successful. Garden noted that Fink 'was not, and never would be, more than a minor shareholder' in the public company that was HWT from 1902.[34] But the Fink family were important shareholders. Fink's sister-in-law, Catherine Fink (who was also his cousin), was the wife of Benjamin Fink. After the notorious land boomer fled to the United Kingdom, many of Benjamin's assets, including *Herald* shares, were transferred to Catherine, who lived to the age of ninety and died in 1943.[35]

Baillieu was a major investor who provided vital capital for the *Herald*'s modernisation and expansion. His fellow board members (including Fink) were either his friends, members of his socio-economic set, or reliant upon Baillieu's businesses and capital.[36] Some directors, including Fink, were also business partners with Baillieu in other ventures outside of the HWT.[37] This was all in keeping with how Baillieu's company boards were run. They tended to resemble 'gentlemen's clubs', with the Collins House figures in control and the non–Collins House directors chosen for their social standing and pliability rather than their business ability. When selecting a director to fill a vacancy on a Collins House mining company board, one of Baillieu's trusted staff told him approvingly that the selected candidate 'was useful to us on the political side in Adelaide being leader of the Upper House ... however, he has very little real ability, no knowledge of mining affairs and is altogether a weak, pliable reed'.[38] In other words, a perfect candidate.

FRIENDS IN HIGH PLACES

Baillieu used the *Herald* as a training ground for some of his numerous relatives, many of whom lived off his success. His brother, George Francis, became the *Herald*'s stock exchange reporter in 1890, followed by another brother, Edward Lloyd, into that post in 1895. Edward (also known as 'Prince') used the experience to start the well-known stockbroking firm EL & C Baillieu with his brother Clive ('Joe'). This firm provided WL Baillieu with valuable inside information to identify business opportunities, and helped connect him with the British finance that was essential to the rise of Collins House.

The ability to receive the first reports of important financial information from overseas news cables was another major advantage of being a financial reporter, along with the capacity to gather local information and contacts. And at this time there was no sense that financial reporters should be separate from what they were writing about. Over at *The Age*, a similar pathway to power – through the financial pages – was being forged by another journalist, who became Baillieu's loyal friend and business partner, a key part of Collins House and Australia's foremost mining financier.

William Sydney (WS) Robinson had joined Syme's *Age* in December 1896. Robinson's father had been commercial editor since 1876, and his family was well connected (an uncle was Edmund Barton, who became the nation's first prime minister). Robinson worked under his father before succeeding him as *The Age*'s commercial editor in 1900. This position gave Robinson some of his most important connections, including Baillieu. Although Baillieu was seventeen years his senior, the two men had a long, close friendship. Robinson claimed the two never had a dispute in their decades in business together.[39] Like Baillieu, Robinson was restless and dynamic, had a forceful personality, and the ear of Cabinet ministers and prime ministers.

By the mid-1890s, Baillieu was so well recovered financially, and so well connected politically, that he was able to persuade politicians to amend laws on his companies' behalf.[40] His power only increased into the 20th century, and was always magnified by his ownership of newspapers. Baillieu had observed the political impact that newspaper ownership could confer through his friendship with *Age* owner David Syme. Baillieu and Syme were friends, business partners and fellow investors in some ventures. The pair also had a mutual friend in the lawyer, journalist and rising political star, Alfred Deakin.

Like Baillieu, Deakin had been involved with James Munro, and had used the special bankruptcy laws to reach a deal with his creditors to avoid insolvency and hide debts. Burned by this experience,

Deakin turned his ambitions to politics. Syme and *The Age* enthusiastically backed him to become a Victorian MP (1879–1900), and Deakin's relationship with Syme – who had converted Deakin from free trade beliefs to protectionism – meant the politician was 'often taunted with being Syme's lapdog'.[41] But Deakin also had another newspaper connection – he was a secret shareholder in the *Herald*.

Garden believed that three of the six *Herald* shares that were listed as being held by Fink in 1889 were actually owned by his close friend Deakin.[42] When Deakin became Australia's second prime minister in 1903, he was still the secret owner of an interest in the HWT, and after Deakin's mental and physical breakdown in 1910, Fink believed the *Herald* shares kept Deakin and his family in comfort after his retirement.[43] Deakin's unusual notion of journalistic ethics saw him not only conceal his newspaper ownership but also, as prime minister, write anonymously for newspapers, and pass himself off as an independent (and sometimes surprisingly critical) observer of his own performance.

Deakin was at the centre of one of the sites that – along with the Freemasons and the exclusive 'gentlemen's club', the Athenaeum Club – were important networking spaces for influential men in politics, business and the media.[44] The Australian Natives' Association (ANA) was an influential pressure group for Australian-born, Deakin Liberal-affiliated businessmen, who used it to lobby for various causes, including Federation, World War I conscription, and the White Australia policy. There was a strong connection between the *Herald* and the ANA. SV Winter had been a keen founding member. James Moloney, a *Herald* director and Victorian MP, was another founding member. William Thomas Reay, the *Herald*'s managing editor (1904–07), was a senior member. Theodore Fink approved of the ANA, and Baillieu spoke at its meetings.

Another important political friend of Robinson's and Baillieu's, William Alexander (WA) Watt, was also a key figure in the ANA –

and later, in Collins House. Watt was premier of Victoria (1912–14), and became a leading federal politician (1914–29), including acting prime minister (1919) and treasurer (1918). From the 1920s, Watt formally worked out of Collins House. He was the director or chair of several Collins House companies, including Dunlop Rubber Company.

In the tradition of Australian newspaper owners of the late 19th and early 20th centuries, Fink and Baillieu also became politicians themselves. In 1894, five years after becoming a newspaper owner, Fink became a member of the Legislative Assembly, and served until 1904. The *Herald* ran some small puff pieces to help Fink's 1900 election campaign for the seat of Jolimont and West Richmond (never disclosing his connection to the paper).[45] One piece reported that a Fink campaign meeting had turned into a jolly 'surprise party' with more than 500 friends and supporters attending.[46]

Baillieu was elected to Victoria's Legislative Council the following year, and served for twenty-one years (1901–22), eight at ministerial rank (1909–17), where he helped shape public works and infrastructure. But when Baillieu first ran for office in 1901, it turned out that his boom-time exploits had not entirely escaped public attention, and that the Bendigo press was not as deferential as Melbourne's. The *Bendigo Independent* claimed Baillieu was 'morally' unfit for office because, although he had regained his fortune, Baillieu had failed to pay out his still-living creditors.[47] In response, Baillieu seems to have lied about the extent to which he had paid out his land boom debts.[48] He also encouraged electors to read positive testimonials about him in the Melbourne press (without mentioning that he was an owner and director of the *Herald* and that *The Age* was owned by his friend David Syme).[49] Just before polling day, newspapers reported that Baillieu had instructed his solicitor to serve a £10 000 writ for libel damages on the owner of the *Bendigo Independent*, but no mention was ever made of this again, and it seems not to have been served, nor resulted in any court case.[50]

At the time when Fink and Baillieu became members of parliament, many non-Labor MPs still ran as Independents by custom, rather than as members of a political party. They tended to form temporary coalitions and factions, and did not firm up into a stable, unified grouping until they later mobilised that way to counter the common threat of an organised Labor Party. When Baillieu first entered parliament he therefore began as an Independent, but became more affiliated with party politics from 1909 by serving as a minister in the Murray ministry, which was Liberal, and an honorary minister in both the Watt and Peacock ministries, which were also Liberal.

However, Baillieu was never a great orator or parliamentarian. He was far more effective at wielding power behind the scenes rather than out on the hustings, or in the glare of public view. As a result, his formal parliamentary positions were modest, but his informal political power was so immense that it led to a perception that conservative and non-Labor politicians performed his bidding. When Baillieu returned from an overseas trip, it was reported that the whole of the Victorian Cabinet waited on the train platform to greet him.[51] Labor leader Frank Tudor taunted in 1920 that there was a section of the government who 'meets at Collins House and rules the country from there instead of Spring Street'.[52]

Baillieu turned down an offer to be in Cabinet around 1918, and in early 1922, retired from the Council. He could afford to step back from parliament by then because Robinson's brother, Arthur Robinson, had become Victorian attorney-general and minister for public works. As Peter Yule notes, Baillieu could be content that Arthur Robinson 'would look out for the interests of Collins House' in state parliament.[53] Melbourne was the seat of federal government between 1901 and 1927, so there was also plenty of opportunity to influence federal politics in the *Herald*'s, and Collins House's, home town.

FROM THE WEALTH OF BROKEN HILL TO THE PAGES OF THE *HERALD*

By 1912, the *Herald*'s profits were strong and it was returning a handsome dividend of 22 per cent.[54] But it was mining – not newspapers – that was the foundation of Baillieu's wealth and political influence, and mining money that underwrote the expansion of the *Herald* group.

Baillieu was already an investor in gold, silver, base metal and coal mining when, in 1904, he went to Broken Hill, an isolated mining town located in the far west of New South Wales, on the border of South Australia. Herbert Hoover, the mining engineer, future US president, and fellow investor with Baillieu in Broken Hill, described it as 'one of the dreariest places in the world … It lay in the middle of the desert, was unbelievably hot in summer, had no fresh water [and] no vegetation.'[55] But beneath the surface of Broken Hill was a long, boomerang-shaped lode containing arguably the world's largest deposit of zinc-silver-lead ore.

Various mining companies already had a stake along the lode when Baillieu visited. The Broken Hill Proprietary Company Limited (BHP) had been incorporated in 1885, and operated a silver and lead mine. BHP's site was at the centre of the field, where deposits were closer to the surface, and BHP had been so efficient in removing the rich oxidised ore from its site that it was winding down its activities in Broken Hill. By 1911, BHP was turning its attention to iron mining at other locations, and then in 1915 moved into steel production in Newcastle.

To the north and south of BHP's site, the lode dipped deeper into the earth, and the companies that owned these sites had to go deep before finding ore. The difficulties associated with this meant the north and south mines regularly yielded losses and closed down. The old BHP directors considered the north end of the lode as doomed, while the south was 'the despised and neglected part' of the field.[56] But Baillieu took a risk and raised a loan for North Broken Hill in 1905 and, at the south end, went into a syndicate that bought half the shares in that mine at a cheap price. The gamble paid off in an extraordinary way. The north and south ends of the field proved so valuable that, as WS Robinson noted, the 'intruders' eventually controlled the field, taking over from where BHP had left off.[57]

Baillieu took another risk at this time that also paid off handsomely. He, WS Robinson, Herbert Hoover, William Clark and Francis Govett set up the Zinc Corporation in 1905. It started buying up vast heaps of mineral-rich tailings, the waste product of mining, that had been piled up in huge dumps around each mine at Broken Hill, and were considered of little value because nobody knew a process for separating the minerals contained in them. Baillieu and Montague Cohen (a fellow director of CUB) financed the work of AFJ de Bavay, the experimental chemist at Fosters Brewery, who developed a workable flotation process for separating zinc from the mine tailings. By employing this method, the Zinc Corporation prospered. Publicity had been a key to obtaining the necessary British finance to float the unorthodox company.

By 1913, there was enormous money pouring out of Broken Hill. Its companies had sold metals for more than £80 million – more money than all the savings held in Australian banks at the time.[58] In 1912, Baillieu had been able to move his expanding group into a new purpose-built building, Collins House, right near the Stock Exchange in exclusive Collins Street. The building is visible in John Brack's famous painting 'Collins St, 5 pm', where it is depicted to the right of the Bank of New South Wales (another company with a long and deep connection to newspapers). With its distinctive arched doorway, Collins House housed the offices of some fifty companies associated with the group – including mining companies, solicitors, accountants, insurance agencies, architects, stockbrokers, industrial chemists, engineers and CUB. These businesses often worked together, and were serviced by a central secretariat.

Collins House was made up of many loose and flexible alliances between these companies, alliances cemented through bonds of friendship and family. Aside from the many Baillieu relatives, the Baillieus intermarried with other wealthy and powerful families, including all-important retailers and newspaper advertisers: the Myers and Horderns. WL Baillieu's son Harry married Margaret, daughter of WS Robinson, cementing the long-term links between the two partners. As a *Financial Review* article noted, the dynastic tendencies of the Baillieu family 'certainly contributed a good deal of harmony at the top, even if only on the basis that one can't be too disagreeable to one's cousins'.[59] Under Baillieu and Robinson's leadership, the loose Collins House structure proved surprisingly strong for more than two decades.

But even as the many businesses settled into Collins House, a world war was on the horizon, and Australian politics and industry were undergoing rapid change. The 1910 election had seen Deakin defeated, and to the concern of industrialists like Baillieu, Andrew Fisher was leading the world's first national labour government. In 1913, Joseph Cook's team narrowly managed to win back office for the Liberals after Deakin's retirement, but then lost it again after a nationwide swing to Labor at a double dissolution that Cook called in 1914. Baillieu, who had long had the ear of sympathetic conservative governments, and had been acting as an adviser to the Cook federal government, now found himself cut off from power because many in the Fisher Labor government viewed him as a political enemy and exploitative industrialist.

FIGURE 5.3 The famous Collins House, 360 Collins Street, Melbourne, circa 1918
SOURCE Australian War Memorial.

SAVE AND SERVE BUY A WAR LOAN BOND

SAFE DEPOS
RE IN PET LBER

UALLY PROOF AGAINST FI
REALLY REPLANT SAFES

World War I also caused Baillieu another serious problem. Australia was the largest lead exporter in the world and, when war broke out, his companies were selling most of their Broken Hill lead concentrate to German smelters for treatment because there was no Australian smelter that could deal with their output. The rest of the British Empire was also weak in that area of metallurgy so a 'powerful German cartel' of metal groups had obtained a 'near-monopoly' on the treatment of Broken Hill's ore and zinc 'and nearly half [its] lead output'.[60] Once Australia was at war with Germany, the Collins House group was cut off from its main buyer and from the lucrative phase of treating its mining product. Without a smelter, its 'products were unsaleable'.[61] To the surprise of many, it would be a Labor leader who would furnish the solution to Baillieu's inability to sell metals to the Germans, and his difficulties in working with a Labor government.

BILLY HUGHES, FRIEND TO COLLINS HOUSE

William Morris 'Billy' Hughes was diminutive, loud, cantankerous, a gifted orator and talented politician. As noted in Chapter 3, he wrote for newspapers, notably for the *Daily Telegraph* (1907–11), which his biographer said was as much about publicising Hughes as his party.[62] Hughes adored publicity and was highly skilled in using the press. It turned out that the press was just as skilled at using him. Strongly backed by newspapers, including the *Herald*, Hughes left the Labor Party in 1916 to join with conservative politicians, his former enemies. Labor colleagues saw this as the treacherous act of a 'rat' who was lured away from Labor by Baillieu and other businessmen.

The seduction began with some fence-mending in 1915. The ferociously anti-German Hughes had accused the Broken Hill companies of supplying metal to the enemy, which Germany could use in the manufacture of weapons that would be used against Australian soldiers. As attorney-general, the firebrand Hughes had also authorised raids on the Broken Hill, Mount Lyell and Mount Morgan company offices in Melbourne in 1914, infuriating Baillieu. Gerald Mussen, a former *Daily Telegraph* federal politics reporter, and mutual friend of Hughes and WS Robinson, was brought in to broker a rapprochement between Hughes and Collins House. (Mussen reappears in the next chapter as a founder of News Limited.)

Mussen organised a meeting between Hughes and Robinson in July 1915 that was stunningly successful. Robinson left convinced that Hughes' fervent patriotism was compatible with the long-term interests of the Collins House mining companies, and Hughes left as a full-blooded supporter of the local mining industry. Robinson wrote to his brother not long after the meeting saying: 'The Metal Trade gave [Hughes] a dinner the other night and they all swear by him – three months ago they were all swearing at him!'[63] Even as he was still publicly lambasting the Collins House group, 'in private [Hughes] was meeting with them frequently and seeking their advice on restructuring the metals industry'.[64] When Andrew Fisher resigned as prime minister in October 1915, he was succeeded by Hughes, his intensely ambitious deputy.

Hughes was moving closer to Collins House. Around 1915, he recruited Robinson as his personal adviser on the lead and zinc industries, a position Robinson held until 1920. Robinson used his enormous influence in this position to design a new structure for the Australian metals industry. Robinson's plan centred around a cartel of zinc producers, to be run by Collins House, that could treat the entire output of the Broken Hill field to completion within Australia. Yule said of Baillieu and Robinson that: 'Their nightmare was nationalisation (a key plank of the Labor Party's platform) and they felt the best way to dissuade Hughes from taking that path was to work as closely as possible with him'.[65]

With Hughes' strong support, Baillieu and Robinson formed Broken Hill Associated Smelters (BHAS) in 1915 and, within twelve months of the outbreak of war, they had established a silver-lead-zinc cooperative monopoly at Broken Hill. BHAS bought out BHP's lead smelter at Port Pirie, South Australia, to process all of the lead and zinc ore from Broken Hill (400 kilometres away) and transport it via ship to global customers. Port Pirie became the world's largest lead smelting works. When it was formed, nearly three-quarters of BHAS was owned by Collins House companies, while the other 28 per cent was owned by BHP.[66] BHP retained its shareholding until 1926 so Collins House and BHP were closely linked until then, albeit as separate companies that were sometimes quietly at odds (including over industrial relations, with BHAS considered the 'gentler' employer compared to the notoriously harsh BHP).[67]

Hughes promoted the BHAS metals monopoly as a patriotic solution that wrestled control of metals manufacturing from the hated Germans. He was not particularly concerned about monopolies, which he regarded 'as a stage towards socialism' and more conducive to collective bargaining and regulation.[68] But some Labor MPs were furious. One accused Hughes of having 'placed the whole of the metal business, and a large amount of other industrial business, directly in the hands of WL Baillieu'.[69] Years before, when Hughes had been writing for the *Daily Telegraph*, he had been attacked by many newspapers for his views. At the time, he had told members of the Labor executive, 'Boys, when the capitalist press criticises me, you may rest assured that I am doing the work I have set out to do for the working classes of Australia. When they praise me you may begin to distrust me.'[70] Colleagues who recalled Hughes' words must have been feeling very distrustful by 1915, because the 'capitalist press' was now lauding Hughes as 'courageous', 'patriotic', 'a very great leader', with 'a career so distinguished and a mind so earnest'.[71]

Baillieu was openly admiring Hughes and gave the prime minister a glowing farewell speech when Hughes left for London in early 1916, accompanied by Robinson as his metals adviser. In the United Kingdom, Hughes emphasised the principle of imperial preference to convince the British government to purchase all of Broken Hill's lead output for the duration of the war, and its zinc concentrates until 1930. This spectacular coup secured the future of BHAS and Collins House. It bound the British government to purchase Australian zinc concentrates at wartime prices, so 'effectively resulted in the British taxpayer partially subsidising the profits of the Broken Hill mining industry'.[72] This allowed Collins House to expand the Zinc Corporation Limited (later called Consolidated Zinc) from initially focusing on the extraction of zinc from the mine tailings at Broken Hill, to branching into mining. Consolidated Zinc merged into the Rio Tinto group in the 1960s and is still one of the world's largest metals and mining corporations today.

Hughes' British lobbying paid off richly for Collins House and paved the way for the success of the Electrolytic Zinc (EZ) Company and its zinc refinery erected on the banks of the Derwent River at Risdon, Tasmania, in 1916. The Tasmanian government also helped by making cheap hydro-electric power available, reportedly at one-eighth the price charged to the public. As always, the *Herald* emphatically backed Baillieu's interstate adventures and promoted his companies.[73]

CONSCRIPTION, JOURNALISM AND POWER

By 1915–16, many in Hughes' Labor Party were despairing of his links with Collins House, but also his increasing support for military conscription. While he was away, opposition to conscription had been firming within the industrial and political wings of the labour movement, but Hughes' trip to England had convinced him of the need to pursue conscription. Emotional visits to Australian troops on the Western Front seemed to help shape his views, but Hughes later claimed that he was essentially 'talked into conscription by the British authorities and by powerful pressures in Australia'.[74] Collins House and the HWT were among those 'powerful pressures'. With metals prices soaring, Baillieu's companies were making huge profits from providing the metal for ammunition, shells and the machinery of war. Baillieu was a strong supporter of conscription, and so too was World War I hawk Theodore Fink.

Collins House and the HWT had close access to Hughes, and prime opportunities to influence him, when he was in England. Robinson, as his adviser, had become an important part of the state apparatus, with authority and prestige. Hughes was also working closely with the enthusiastic pro-conscriptionist Keith Murdoch in London, where Murdoch was head of the HWT's (and Sydney *Sun*'s) UCS. Murdoch was a friend of both Robinson and Hughes. He knew them from his stint as a reporter for *The Age* (but seems to have known Robinson even before he joined the paper in 1903).[75] As the main protectionist paper in Melbourne, *The Age* was important to Labor politicians, and Hughes was a master at cultivating and winning over young political reporters like Murdoch.

When Hughes visited England in 1916, Murdoch connected him with a circle of media and political elites who were clamouring for conscription (Chapter 7). Murdoch also acted as Hughes' unofficial, and largely unpaid, publicist and fixer. By helping

Hughes, Murdoch was also helping his co-employer, the pro-conscription HWT, and important friends. Murdoch had been a family friend of the Baillieus for over twenty years. As a school boy in the mid-1890s, Murdoch was friends with Baillieu's son Clive when the two went to Fairholme Preparatory School together. And the two boys' fathers, Baillieu and Reverend Patrick Murdoch, were friends within the circle that included Alfred Deakin and David Syme. Despite the age gap between Keith Murdoch and WL Baillieu, the two became close friends, playing golf and dining together.

In London, Hughes was therefore receiving ample encouragement from Collins House and its agents to pursue conscription, no matter what it cost his party. When Hughes returned to Australia in August 1916, he also found that almost all of the press, along with the Liberal Opposition, and many leading business and public figures, were also loudly clamouring for conscription. The ANA had started a campaign promoting conscription five months before Hughes returned from England, and the *Herald* had been vigorously promoting the cause (the *Herald* had actually been calling for compulsory military service since 1915). Baillieu's friend and business partner, WA Watt, was another leading pro-conscription voice in Hughes' ear.

When Hughes decided to fight for conscription, knowingly precipitating a Labor schism, Baillieu promised that he and the Victorian Ministry 'would work for the success of the vote with all their strength'.[76] In August 1916, Hughes announced a referendum on conscription (technically a plebiscite) to be held in October, causing an open split in the Labor Party. The bitter referendum campaign was characterised by propaganda on both sides of the debate but the commercial daily press had the loudest voice, and it campaigned with vigour for conscription, with the *Herald* at the vanguard as the most stridently pro-war and pro-conscription paper in Australia.

Garden argued that Fink used the *Herald* as 'a propaganda tool' for the conscription cause, aided at first by *Herald* editor JE Davidson.[77] From London, Murdoch was also intent on Australia sending fresh supplies of conscripted troops, and was applying his own considerable energy and propaganda-like cables, to the 'yes' campaign. Murdoch was thirty-one years old in 1916. He could have served in the war, but did not (Chapter 7). At fifty-seven years, Baillieu was not considered fit for active service, but three of his sons served in the war. All made it home.

Baillieu's son Clive served in largely administrative roles that kept him at a safe distance from battlefields. Another of Baillieu's sons was granted six months leave to come home to recuperate after being gassed, leading the *Bulletin* to suggest the unusually sympathetic treatment was only extended because he was a Baillieu.[78] Fink's eldest son was killed at Gallipoli, and another beloved son, Thorold, went off to war. Although he was pushing the *Herald*'s pro-conscription agenda with all his might, privately Fink was trying to pull every string he could – including through Murdoch in London – to get Thorold into officer training school to keep him out of harm's way. And when Thorold was injured, Fink again tried pulling strings to get him immediately discharged, although his injuries were judged not serious enough to warrant it.[79] To the anti-conscriptionists, these men were the worst sort of 'stay-at-home patriots' – newspaper owners, editors and journalists who beat the drum to send others to their deaths on the slaughterfields of Europe.

FROM THE ASHES OF DEFEAT: A NEW POLITICAL PARTY

Given the enormous support and one-sided reporting of major newspapers, the defeat of the 1916 plebiscite came as a surprise to most commentators. But the failure had a silver lining for Baillieu and other Liberals who had sought conscription so passionately. The bitter campaign had caused the Labor Party to 'tear itself apart', creating an opportunity to form a new non-Labor party.[80] In 1916, Baillieu, Watt, and ANA and Liberal member James Hume Cook, helped convince Hughes to leave the Labor Party and become leader of a coalition government. On 14 November 1916, Hughes and twenty-three supporters walked out of a meeting of the federal Labor Caucus and quit the party. Hughes was immediately recalled by the governor-general and, assured of the support of the Liberal Opposition, he was commissioned to form a new minority government. Hughes' group of supporters called themselves 'National Labor' and now governed with the support of his former opponents, the Liberals.

Baillieu's promise of funds to support the National Labor members was crucial to their decision to defect.[81] But conservatives could also offer much improved organisation and campaigning skills. Before the war, they had lagged behind Labor in these areas, but by leading patriotic organisations and running campaigns for war loans, and especially the conscription campaign, they had learned a great deal about how to mobilise a conservative base, including how to frame issues in terms of Empire and nation, and how to stress patriotism and development to mobilise conservative populism.[82] On the day Hughes walked out of Caucus, Watt chaired a meeting in Melbourne to discuss the formation of the new party, a merger between National Labor and the Commonwealth Liberal Party that would come to be called 'the Nationalists'.[83] Hughes' enemies alleged that he may also have personally received money to leave Labor.[84] This was never proven, but it is known that Hughes profited from shrewd investments which may have been made possible through his role in assisting industries like the Collins House metals cartel.[85] And Hughes' stockbroker was EL & C Baillieu.[86]

The *Herald* gave its full and enthusiastic support to Hughes' formation of the Nationalist Party. He left his mainly working-class electorate of West Sydney (which he had held from 1901), as he knew he could not win there once he was no longer a Labor member, and moved to Victoria. For the 1917 election, Hughes ran for the seat of Bendigo, 'on the edge of [Baillieu's] constituency'.[87] Baillieu campaigned for Hughes in the local area, and major newspapers around the country – but especially the *Herald* and the Sydney *Sun* – overwhelmingly supported him. The Nationalists won an emphatic victory in 1917.

Watt became a minister in the new government, and from 1918, treasurer. One of his first acts was to form a Federal Finance Council, which included Baillieu as a member. From facing the cold shoulder of the Fisher Labor governments, Collins House was now well situated to have its interests protected. The bitter split over conscription had removed Labor from office, and it would stay out for over a decade. Baillieu's biographer, Yule, noted that 'Fear of nationalisation and hopes for expanding their business were the sub-texts of [Baillieu's and Robinson's] support for efforts to separate Hughes from the Labor Party, even though the public fight appeared to be over conscription'.[88]

THE SECRET MONEY MEN AND THE 1922 ELECTION

Hughes went on to render 'sterling service to the anti-Labor cause' for three and a half decades, albeit in the guise of several different party formations.[89] Collins House's loyalty did not last nearly as long. By 1918, Baillieu, Fink and Murdoch were going cold on Hughes, along with others in business circles and within the conservatives. After another failed plebiscite on conscription in December

1917, Hughes' governing style became more erratic and dictatorial. Murdoch knew from long experience that Hughes was difficult to work with. By 1918, Murdoch was 'fed up' with him.[90] So too was Fink.[91] In 1919, Murdoch wrote to Fink criticising Hughes' performance at the Versailles Conference, saying 'There is no doubt that he has done badly … through [his] tactlessness and unscrupulousness'.[92] Murdoch threatened that he could spill all he knew on Hughes' 'doings during the war' in order to hurt him politically.[93]

At the 1919 election, Hughes' Nationalist Party lost seats and the Country Party was newly propelled into a pivotal position in Australian politics by the introduction of preferential voting. Hughes was an increasingly weakened figure, and by 1922 Collins House wanted to be rid of him. Hughes was not just less useful, but worse, they suspected his loyalties now lay in Sydney (Hughes had moved back there to contest the electorate of North Sydney). The 1922 election became a proxy battle between Melbourne and Sydney financial powers over the shape of the conservative side of politics, fought out through their respective newspapers.

Baillieu's friend (and Hughes' estranged former treasurer), Watt, had been attacking Hughes in parliament since mid-1922. By the time of the December election, Watt had revived the old Liberal Party so that the non-Labor side of politics was now split in two, based partly on urban/rural lines reflecting the increasing discontent in country areas with Hughes' government. Watt was most active in Victoria and support for him and the Liberal and Country parties came principally from the *Herald* and *The Age*. In the lead-up to the election, the *Herald* turned savagely against Hughes, calling him 'by temperament and practice an autocrat'.[94] Ironically, its main line of attack was a claim that shadowy businessmen were providing finance to Hughes and the Nationalist Party.

Just three weeks before polling day, the *Herald* accused Hughes of having personally pocketed a £25 000 cheque ($1.8 million in today's money) from secret 'admirers', including wealthy business-men in Australia and London.[95] These accusations were also pub-lished in *The Age*, which claimed 'moneyed interests' were behind Hughes.[96] *The Age*'s election editorial said that Hughes had brought 'nothing but disgust and disappointment' to the people of Aus-tralia.[97] The *Herald* was equally scathing and said Australia could not afford 'another term of sordid maladministration ... misused opportunities ... [and] sordid political intrigue'.[98] The *Herald* had previously recommended Hughes in the highest possible terms, but it did not direct its readers' attention to this dramatic change in editorial policy, nor take any responsibility for Hughes' 'sordid' government.

The infamous cheque was actually old news. Australian news-papers had been aware of it for two years and had reported on its presentation to Hughes in November 1920, allegedly in recog-nition of his service during the war.[99] The cheque was never meant to be made public but according to WS Robinson's private notes, Murdoch had 'blurted ... out' the 'hot news' of its existence before Hughes returned from London in 1920. This was an act that Hughes considered hostile.[100] Murdoch was still head of the cable service in London at the time and he was almost certainly the 'Special Rep-resentative' who published reports on the cheque from there.[101] At the time, little fuss was made about the presentation of such a large and compromising 'testimonial' to a sitting prime minister. But the *Herald* started re-publicising the matter during the 1922 election campaign as a weapon against Hughes.

Neither the *Herald* nor *The Age* named any of the shadowy financiers it claimed were behind Hughes. The *Herald* spoke only in opaque terms about 'the great organised forces behind the Nation-alist ... party's great fighting fund'.[102] Collins House was, of course, one of those 'organised forces' – a long-time, major contributor to the Nationalist party's finances – but in 1922 Collins House had withdrawn its financial support for Hughes. It was providing its money only to the Victorian branch of the Nationalists' fundraising body (the National Union),[103] which was not passing it on to New South Wales where Hughes faced a tough election campaign.

Sir Owen Cox, chairman of the New South Wales branch of the Nationalists' fundraising body (the Consultative Council Campaign), was a close friend of Hughes' and had written to BHAS managing director, Colin Fraser, asking for money from the 'Metal Interests' to 'keep the Anti-Labor forces in power'.[104] Cox threatened that if money was not provided directly to New South Wales by companies like BHAS, which had 'large financial interests' in the state, 'it will go hard with those interests'.[105] But Collins House was already playing 'hard', by refusing to send money to New South Wales, and by maligning Hughes in the *Herald*.

Several labour papers did, however, name one of the New South Wales 'forces' behind Hughes as GW Turner, general manager of Howard Smith Ltd, and claimed he was the main source of the funds for Hughes' 1920 cheque.[106] Howard Smith, one of the country's oldest shipping companies, had diversified into coal mining and steel production. It was one of multiple, competing firms making steel in the early 1920s, including the Hoskins family at Lithgow, as well as BHP (which had become a competitor to Hoskins when it opened its Newcastle steelworks in 1915).

The 1922 election was held during a period of transition and tension for the metals industry. Peace had caused demand and prices for metals to plummet. A shift was also starting to occur from iron to steel, and therefore from Collins House/BHAS to what would become Howard Smith/Hoskins/BHP. Five years after the 1922 election, Howard Smith went into partnership with the Hoskins' company and two famous British steel manufacturers. The merged group, called the Australian Iron and Steel company (AIS), was heavily involved in the building of the Port Kembla steelworks in 1928. In 1935, BHP bought out AIS, giving it an unassailable grip on the steel industry in Australia, which saw it emerge as a global force in mining and metals (Chapter 15). But in the early 1920s, BHP was not yet the major player. Howard Smith was making double its profits, and Hoskins was the Southern Hemisphere's largest steel producer.[107]

Aside from shipping and steel, the other major industrial issue of the election that concerned newspaper owners was sugar. The *Herald* said the Hughes government, having 'no principles', was trying to bribe sections of the community, including 'sugar growers'.[108] Hughes had extended wartime protections to the sugar industry (where the Colonial Sugar Refining Company (CSR) was the largest player) for years after the war had ended. Before the 1922 election, he had also tried to award it tariff protection, only to be thwarted by the Country Party and Labor.[109] The sugar industry described Hughes as a 'friend' six months before the election.[110]

The Sydney-based CSR was one of the richest companies in Australia.[111] As Chapter 9 explains, the Fairfax family, owners of the *Sydney Morning Herald*, had been shareholders in CSR since the 1850s.[112] The *Sydney Morning Herald* therefore saw the issues of the election very differently from the *Herald* and *The Age*. The *Sydney Morning Herald* said it was backing Hughes against 'Melbourne politicians' who were 'posing as Liberals' and wanted to pull down Hughes so they could 'strangle Canberra'.[113] This came close to revealing how the 1922 election had turned into a tug-of-war between Collins House and the Melbourne financial interests on one side, and the Sydney interests – including Howard Smith, CSR and the *Sydney Morning Herald* – on the other.[114] Hughes pointedly said that the Watt-led Victorian Liberals knew nothing outside of Collins Street – a clear dig at Collins House.[115]

When neither the incumbent Nationalists nor the Labor Party achieved the majority required to form government in its own right, the Country Party came to occupy a pivotal position in negotiations after the 1922 election. Its leader, Dr Earl Page, refused to work with Hughes, and the Country Party used its strong position to push Hughes out of the prime minister's office in February 1923, in favour of Treasurer Stanley Bruce. Hughes remained in parliament for another three decades (in his fifty-one years as a member of the House of Representatives, Hughes represented four different parties – three of which expelled him). With more free time available after being ousted from the prime minister's office, Hughes accepted an offer to rekindle his relationship with the *Daily Telegraph* from May 1923. It paid Hughes the 'princely' sum of £1000 a year retainer plus over £6 per article.[116] (As he wrote more than forty articles for it, the paper paid him over £1240 – $91 000 in today's money.) Back in Melbourne, although the relationship with Collins House had soured, there was one figure who never forgot Hughes' contribution. WS Robinson always acknowledged that Hughes was the man who had made the metals industry in Australia – and Collins House's fortune – possible.[117]

THE WEB OF COLLINS HOUSE

The war had been extremely profitable for Collins House, with astronomical prices for metals leading profits coming out of Broken Hill to increase by more than 100 per cent and, in the case of Broken Hill South, by more than 200 per cent.[118] As a result of Hughes' help, Collins House had become central to the Australian (and world) economy. By the end of World War I, it was in control of three of the four 'pillars of Australian heavy industry' – the lead smelter at Port Pirie in South Australia, a copper refinery at Port Kembla and the zinc works at Risdon in Tasmania.[119] The only pillar it did not control was steel.

The war had also dramatically boosted the *Herald*'s profits and popularity. Baillieu had been an attentive HWT director since 1894, but he became more keenly involved in the newspaper company after 1919, and remained an active director until 1931. Fink, who had been a director since 1900, and chairman of the board since 1906, remained its chair until his death in 1942. Fink hired creative editors such as JE Davidson (1907–18), and Guy Innes (1918–21), who helped push the *Herald* into a period of popularisation and expansion that Keith Murdoch continued with vigour from 1921.

Baillieu became more involved at the HWT just after the war ended, when metal prices plummeted, and Collins House needed to diversify into other industries. In the interwar period, Collins House diversified so extensively that it became the 'most prolific parent of industrial enterprises Australia has ever seen'.[120] By the 1930s, Collins House products and raw materials could be found in Australian homes, transport and businesses across the nation. It was in everything from felt hats to tin-plated kettles, paper, beer, house paint, car tyres, drinking glasses, carpet, telephone wires and fertilisers.

In its home base in Melbourne, Collins House had the *Herald* to advocate its interests, but it now also had vital interests stretched out across the country, especially in Broken Hill, Port Pirie, Adelaide, Hobart, Perth and western Queensland.

Adelaide was important because although Broken Hill is located in New South Wales, it is 1000 kilometres west of Sydney, but only 50 kilometres from the South Australian border. As historian Geoffrey Blainey noted, at its heyday, Broken Hill was considered 'part of South Australia to all but map-drawers and politicians'.[121] It was not linked by rail to Sydney until 1927. Most of its products were instead railed to Port Pirie in South Australia, where Collins House ran the lead smelter. Broken Hill's supplies mostly came from South Australia too, and the mining companies and their workers tended to spend their money or bank it in Adelaide. So entwined were South

Australia's wealthiest families with Collins House that communist critic, Len Fox, quipped in 1946 that 'Economically, Adelaide is a suburb of Melbourne'.[122]

Perth was also important because Collins House was involved in gold mining in Western Australia by 1914, and its interests grew in the 1920s and 1930s as Robinson began travelling there regularly and led the resuscitation of its gold mining industry. In 1933, Robinson established the Western Mining Corporation (WMC), which was controversially granted huge land reservations by the Western Australian government. In 1934, the directors of WMC – including Robinson, ML Baillieu (WL Baillieu's grandson) and Colin Fraser – brought a libel suit for damages that bankrupted two men who accused them of improperly attempting to obtain government contracts and subsidies in Western Australia.

In Tasmania, WL Baillieu had been involved in mining shares from the 1890s. He believed Tasmania was Australia's richest mineral area, with sources of largely untapped mineral resources.[123] Tasmania's other major attraction was its cheap hydro-electricity. By the 1930s, Collins House was a major force in Tasmania operating EZ, Associated Pulp and Paper Mills (APPM) and Mount Lyell. EZ became 'the industrial hub of Hobart', employing nearly 3000 workers, and using one-third of all of Tasmania's electricity.[124] Another Collins House critic taunted that the island state had become a province of Collins House.[125]

THE HWT BRANCHES OUT

It was two land boomers, keen to re-build their fortunes and reputations, who oversaw the growth of the *Herald* from Melbourne's third-ranked newspaper to Australia's largest and most enduring national media empire. Like Denison, Baillieu did not believe in free market competition as a stimulus to better profits; he too preferred monopolies and cartels.[126] Under Baillieu's leadership, the HWT's drive towards press empire building began in the 1920s, and when the HWT began to branch out, it focused on the cities of greatest strategic importance to Collins House – especially Perth and Adelaide. By the late 1920s, interstate expansion was going ahead with Fink's blessing and Keith Murdoch's skill. But, although attempts have been made to cover it up, there is evidence to suggest that Collins House had already made a separate, and more covert, attempt at expansion through another newspaper company, News Limited (later known as News Corporation). News Limited began in the dust of Broken Hill but went on to become a New York–based global media empire. Although it became one of the most important media companies in the world, News Limited's origins, and its connections with Collins House, have been hidden in plain sight for nearly a century.

CHAPTER 6

THE REAL STORY OF THE BIRTH OF NEWS LIMITED

On 1 June 1930, a fifty-nine-year-old Australian was found dead in his hotel room in London. A secret and chronic alcoholic, he died alone, surrounded by empty bottles. This man is recorded as News Limited's founder, JE Davidson, the brilliant journalist and hard-working former editor of the Melbourne *Herald*. Although Davidson was well known in journalism circles during his lifetime, he has since become a forgotten and mysterious figure. Unlike several other editors, Davidson did not leave any personal papers to libraries, and he has no direct descendants. His only surviving son, Norman, died childless in 1968, and although Norman was also a journalist, he left the profession after his father's death, and never seems to have written about his father nor been interviewed about him. As a result, what we know about Davidson's founding of News Limited has come almost entirely from the company's version of its own history.

According to News Limited, Davidson was the 'son of a Wimmera station hand' who rose to journalism's highest ranks but resigned from the *Herald* in 1918 because of Fink's editorial interference. Davidson then used the financial settlement he received from the HWT to buy two provincial newspapers: one in Broken Hill (the *Barrier Miner*) and one in Port Pirie (the *Recorder*). In 1921, having been a provincial newspaper owner for two years, Davidson was travelling on the Melbourne–Adelaide steam train when he sat next to an old friend, 'a miner' named Gerald Mussen. Over the noise of the 'rocking railway carriage', Davidson and Mussen hatched a plan for a new afternoon paper, the Adelaide *News*, to be owned by a company called News Limited. They drew up a prospectus on 7 June 1922 that is now considered the founding document of one of the world's most important media companies.[1]

If only this inspiring tale of rags-to-riches, individual endeavour by Davidson were true! 'IT ALL BEGAN WITH ONE MAN'S DREAM' is how the *News* headlined a story about Davidson when it was celebrating its fiftieth anniversary.[2] But for anyone familiar with Collins House and the background outlined in the previous chapter, all of the clues to unravel News Limited's real provenance are in the key words of the story – the *Herald*, Mussen, Broken Hill and Port Pirie.

FROM MINING TOWNS TO THE *HERALD*: THE RISE OF 'DAVY'

To journalists, Davidson was 'JED', to his friends 'Davy', and to his newspaper staff 'the Chief'. The fit former boxer was a 'deep thinker' and a man of strong, outspoken views. He was a 'forceful personality', tenacious and fearless. To some, he came across as a grumpy, opinionated workaholic; an autocrat and a 'hater'.[3] But others insisted that his gruff demeanour hid a generous heart, a tolerant disposition, and a 'genial and lovable personality'.[4] In an obituary for Davidson, his friend and former colleague, Monty Grover (another brilliant editor), tried to make sense of Davidson's manner. Grover described him as 'the most logical man I ever met', so fundamentally honest that he never hesitated to tell the truth no matter how unpleasant it was, including telling his friends off 'if they deserved it'.[5]

Davidson was such a committed 'newspaperman' that he was reputed to have no hobbies and take no leisure time. 'His work was his life', said Grover, and he 'never let his paper down'. Grover argued that Davidson 'wrote the truth as he saw it, and despite his perceived loyalty to the journal which employed him, he never made the mistake of distorting news in the hope that it would please the powers which paid his salary'.[6] It is interesting that Grover felt the need to say this.

For an editor, what company 'loyalty' usually means is that they share and uphold the views and methods of their newspaper. They would not be appointed to that position otherwise. For example, before his clash of wills with Fink, Davidson's pro-conscription stance had stood him in good stead at the pro-conscription *Herald*. Rather than distortion, a more important question may be about omission and disclosure. At a time when it was not encouraged for journalists to tell readers about their own role in events, to what extent did Davidson tell the reading public about the events he was witnessing, and participating in, at the top of the corporate and newspaper worlds? As Grover foreshadowed, Davidson's company loyalty versus his fundamental honesty is a big part of the puzzle that needs to be untangled in his story.

Davidson was born in 1870 at Pine Hills, Harrow, Victoria, but he lived with his family at Thackaringa Station, near Broken Hill, New South Wales from a young age. His father, James Johnstone Davidson, is described on Davidson's birth certificate as a twenty-three-year-old labourer. But Davidson senior was also involved in mining, albeit on a small scale, as a bushman and prospector on the hunt for precious metals. It is likely that he took his family to Thackaringa as one of the many prospectors who began working that area after hearing of metal finds there.

The Davidsons would continue their connection with mining. Davidson's brother Allan became a mine manager and a prominent international mining engineer and explorer. Davidson's father died in 1901 in West Africa because Allan was a mine manager there,

FIGURE 6.1 James Edward Davidson, managing director and editor-in-chief of the *News* with his original staff, circa 1923; Davidson is seated at the centre of the front row

SOURCE Adrian Savvas and Andrew Becker, *Sixty Nine Years of Events from the Pages of the News*, A Savvas, Adelaide, 1992, p. 3.

and father and son were making an exploration on behalf of a London-based syndicate. Allan had already mapped the central Australia region for the syndicate, searching for gold and other metals in incredibly harsh conditions.

While his father and brother were travelling around the country and the world, JE Davidson was also mobile. After working as a labourer in western New South Wales, he moved to South Australia and at seventeen, became a junior reporter on the *Port Augusta Dispatch*. He then moved to Perth where his excellent shorthand skills landed him a job as a shorthand writer in the Western Australian Treasury Department, and then secured him a position as official secretary to Western Australian Premier Lord Forest. Around 1892, Davidson decided to return to journalism and he worked for the *West Australian* for five years before moving to Melbourne.

Davidson worked as a political reporter for the *Argus* from 1897 to 1905. During the heady, early years of the new federal parliament when it was sitting in Melbourne, important friendships were made among a group of ambitious journalists and politicians. Davidson got to know Gerald Mussen who was the federal politics reporter for the *Daily Telegraph* from 1902. The two worked together on the Melbourne Press Bond, a forerunner of the Australian Journalists' Association (AJA).[7] The amiable Mussen also befriended Labor politician WM Hughes (who had joined the federal parliament in 1901) and *The Age*'s commercial editor (1900–06), WS Robinson.

In 1905, the talented Davidson was poached by the HWT to edit its *Weekly Times*, and in 1906, the HWT sent him to the United States to learn about ground-breaking techniques in evening newspaper production at the Detroit *Daily Free Press*. (The *Daily Free Press* was fighting a circulation war with the pioneering *Detroit News*, one of the first major American penny papers, founded by James E Scripps, the older half-brother of Edward W Scripps.) Davidson spent a year in Detroit and, on his return to Melbourne in 1907, possessed a much sought-after combination of editorial, technical and business skills. The HWT board appointed him assistant to the *Herald*'s editor, the lacklustre William Thomas Reay. Reay was so disengaged that Davidson was effectively editing the paper.

Davidson transformed the *Herald* into Australia's leading afternoon paper. He was officially promoted to editor-in-chief and general manager of the *Herald* in 1911. Considered a master practitioner of 'new journalism', he insisted that his staff follow his lead and only ever write in a style that was crisp and concise, with every fact included, every sentence clear, and never a wasted word. This was cutting-edge practice at the time, and Davidson was a pioneer of the new methods, and the modern school of editing in Australia. One journalist described Davidson as 'a force' in Australian journalism.[8] In recognition of his success in dramatically lifting the *Herald*'s news coverage and circulation, Davidson became a member of the board of directors of the HWT in 1916.

In his early years, Davidson had been a supporter of unionism and the Labor Party, and had tended towards socialist views, probably as a legacy of his days as a bush worker. In 1905, he had become president of the Melbourne Press Bond, and in 1910, helped to found its successor, the AJA. At a time when newspapers still exploited penny-a-liner reporters and did not want their workers unionising, a group of journalists met in secret on 10 December 1910, at a meeting advertised only by word-of-mouth, and held in the basement of a café in Flinders Street. This group drew up a secret list of members that contained 210 signatures. Keith Murdoch's name was among them. At the time, Murdoch was a junior reporter on *The Age*, which had a reputation for firing workers suspected of having union intentions, so he kept his involvement quiet. But Davidson had a senior position at the HWT, and bravely, he openly advocated improved working conditions for journalists.

Davidson reportedly stood up to other *Herald* directors and tried to convince them that their workers needed to be properly trained and adequately paid, and that moving in this direction did not represent a socialist revolution.[9] Davidson's advocacy helped pave the way for better working conditions for journalists. Even when he was a boss of journalists as a newspaper owner himself, twenty years later, the AJA said it considered Davidson a friend and pioneer who was sympathetic to his workers.[10]

Davidson's earlier socialistic views became more moderate as he grew older and settled into the position of editing the conservative *Herald*. By the time World War I broke out, Davidson and Fink, the HWT's chairman, were of like mind on the big issues. Both were 'bitterly anti-German' and pro-conscription. Davidson gave the *Herald* a hawkish and jingoistic tone that found public favour during the early years of the war. Its circulation, influence and profitability grew dramatically. Some accounts claim that, under his editorship, the *Herald*'s circulation increased by 80 per cent.[11] But Fink and Davidson were locked in a battle of wills over control of the paper.

Despite Davidson's incredible contribution, Fink grew dissatisfied with his editor. According to Fink, this was partly about Davidson's demotion of editorials. Davidson had dropped the 'leaders' at least two years before he was dismissed, but had apparently done so without consulting the HWT board. No great supporter of editorial independence, Fink remained unhappy about it, and also about Davidson's broader push to soften the paper's stance and lend it a less partisan tone after the second failed conscription referendum.

Fink, who had grown more conservative during the war, judged Davidson to be too left-leaning. Fink later claimed that, at a crucial point of 'crisis' during the war, Davidson had 'proceeded to color the paper something more pink than the worst radicalism ... and suddenly while the paper was supporting the National

Government, [came] out with [an editorial] that Mr Hughes, then Prime Minister, and his Government had to go'.[12] Fink could not deny Davidson's editorial skill but said he was unhappy with the editor's commercial ability (despite the huge increase in profits) and his autocratic nature. Perhaps alluding to Davidson's alcoholism, Fink concluded that Davidson had 'strong limitations and decided faults which grew worse with time, discounting his considerable ability'.[13]

'WHAT IS WRONG WITH BROKEN HILL?': AND THE SEARCH FOR A NEWSPAPER ANTIDOTE

Describing Mussen as a 'miner' is the most deliberately misleading part of the News Limited story. When Mussen and Davidson sat together on the train in 1921, Mussen was not a pick-in-hand, toiling-down-the-mines miner. He was Collins House's well-paid industrial consultant, and had worked for Baillieu for more than a decade. Back in 1908, through his friendship with Robinson, Mussen had landed a job superintending Baillieu's many investments. In 1915, Mussen had been crucial in bringing his two friends, Robinson and WM Hughes, together so they could jointly forge a path for the formation of BHAS. Good friends, Mussen and Robinson had also, remarkably, jointly drafted Commonwealth legislation for an iron and steel bounty to be paid to producers, which National Party minister Walter Massy-Greene then shepherded through parliament.[14] Since then, Mussen had been employed as BHAS' industrial consultant. Mussen had only ever briefly tried his hand at mining, during the 1897 gold rush at Coolgardie, Western Australia, a quarter of a century before the apocryphal train trip.

Even though he was a co-founder of News Limited, Mussen has been airbrushed from the company's history. He is either left out entirely, or misrepresented, probably to obscure his connections with Collins House. But Mussen is an important part of News Limited's story. When the company was formed, he – not Davidson – had the largest shareholding in it.

When BHAS took over the smelting works at Port Pirie, Robinson had sent Mussen there to help prevent industrial strife and solve the company's problems related to publicity and workers' welfare. Mussen focused on improving the poor housing, living and working conditions of BHAS workers, and on preventing strikes and industrial action. Under Mussen, the company introduced housing and industrial health and safety measures, including lunch and changing rooms, accident and sickness insurance, first-aid care, holiday accommodation access and a cooperative store.

Mussen had significant success in soothing industrial strife at Port Pirie, where BHAS was the sole manager. But the industrial situation at Broken Hill – where there were multiple companies working the field and multiple unions – was far more tense and difficult to resolve. During the war, industrial tension had escalated because the mining companies were obviously making enormous profits, but mine workers felt they were not sharing in the wealth that came from the lead and silver they were pulling out of the ground at great personal risk. In the arid, isolated town, the miners' living and working conditions were extremely poor. And when BHAS' managing director, Colin Fraser, returned in 1917 after two years in the United States, he judged the industrial situation at Broken Hill to be critical. One of the factors that had contributed to this was the bitter debate about conscription.

At first, there had been general support for the war in Broken Hill but as industrial relations historian, Sarah Gregson, has documented, this started to change as 'the hardship of the war ground

on, as mine managers pushed harder and harder for military contracts to be met while resisting wage increases [and] as news of
dead family [members] came from the front'.[15] At Broken Hill, the
anti-conscriptionists' campaign became so effective that the town
'went from being extremely jingoistic to voting "no" in both the 1916
and 1917 referenda'.[16] Representing the other side of the debate was
the local, pro-militarist newspaper, the *Barrier Miner*. Tension was
so high between the *Barrier Miner* and the anti-conscription activists
that the newspaper's office was bombed twice during the war.[17]

The *Barrier Miner* had once been a radical newspaper, which
had 'unequivocally sided with the men against the companies'
during the Big Strike of 1892.[18] But it had since developed a reputation for being on the side of the mining companies. (Unionists
called it an 'organ of vested interest' and the 'gramophone of the
profit-hunting mob'.[19]) Under John Smethurst as editor, the *Barrier
Miner* was strongly pro-conscription during the war, and Smethurst's
editorials 'pulled every possible heartstring to garner support for the
war effort', including a popular 'Sunday edition containing [sol-
diers'] letters [home] from the front'.[20]

The *Barrier Miner*'s staunch rival was Australia's first labour
daily, the union-owned *Barrier Daily Truth*. Launched in 1898, and
paid for by union members' dues, the *Barrier Daily Truth* had been
a major factor in the revival of union values in Broken Hill. The
town had developed a reputation for having Australia's strongest
trade union movement. During the war, the union newspaper 'had
become so subversive and unruly … that the Prime Minister sent a
military censor to Broken Hill to muzzle [it]'.[21]

On 29 June 1918, Fraser sat down to write a long document
called 'What is wrong with Broken Hill?' and then asked mine
managers and Collins House personnel to add their own comments.
Fraser's introduction cautioned that, without urgent remedy of the
industrial situation, there would be 'complete chaos' and a 'bleak'

future for the field.[22] The chief engineer at Broken Hill South mine, JC Cunningham, added that 'if things are allowed to drift from bad to worse' it could lead to 'nationalization'.[23] This was Collins House's worst fear.

One of Fraser's recommendations to fix industrial unrest was to 'Start a publicity campaign to combat the baneful effects of the "*Barrier Truth*", and to keep the [mining] Companies' case placed fairly before the Community'.[24] WE Wainwright, the general manager at Broken Hill South, also identified the union-owned newspaper as one of the main problems. He said its 'editorials are written with the object of encouraging class warfare, the worker is called the "Wage Slave"' and '"shorter hours and less work" is the cry'. Wainwright argued that, because there was no competing paper to counter *Barrier Daily Truth* 'a certain class of unionist is gradually educated up to believing absolutely the worst of his employer'.[25] This statement indicates that, for all the talk of the *Barrier Miner* as representing the mining companies, they did not believe it was an effective advocate. Wainwright concluded that the *Barrier Truth* 'is the worst sinner in fostering industrial unrest, and there should be some means of keeping it within bounds'.[26]

BACK TO MINING TOWNS: DAVIDSON AS NEWSPAPER OWNER

Just weeks after Collins House executives were writing about the need to stop the 'insidious' anti-employer 'propaganda' of the *Barrier Daily Truth*, at Fink's insistence, the HWT board demanded Davidson's resignation.[27] The official reason cited was 'profound differences' of opinion with the board on administration.[28] *Herald* news editor Guy Innes replaced Davidson as editor. Fraser continued searching for publicity solutions to combat the union-owned paper at Broken Hill. In late 1918, he seems to have suggested to WS Robinson that BHAS could buy the opposition *Barrier Miner* newspaper.[29] But the astute Robinson – knowing how it would look for a mining company to own a newspaper – wrote back in December 1918, telling Fraser, 'I note all your remarks about the press ... I am still unconvinced, however, that [BHAS] is the correct concern to buy the *Barrier Miner* – in fact I gravely doubt it, and live in hope of some other means having turned up'.[30]

Robinson did approve of another of Fraser's ideas though, for publicity in Port Pirie. Fraser's original letter to Robinson is missing from his personal papers, so we can only speculate about what this idea was, but Robinson's reply, which *is* in the BHAS archive, provides an important clue. Robinson wrote back to Fraser in mid-December 1918: 'I am glad to note that you are going to shake the Port Pirie *Recorder* up. There is great room for propaganda in Broken Hill and Port Pirie ... Let us try and educate our men, and the public too.'[31]

Nineteen days later, a new company was registered in Melbourne by a Collins Street solicitor, for the purpose of taking over the Port Pirie *Recorder*. Davidson was the key shareholder. Obviously, he was the means of 'shaking up' the Port Pirie *Recorder*. A month later, on 1 February 1919, Davidson bought *both* the Port Pirie *Recorder* and the *Barrier Miner*.[32] Robinson had wanted 'propaganda' at both ends of BHAS' supply chain, and had 'lived in hope' that someone suitable would turn up to buy the *Barrier Miner*. Now, here was Davidson, a brilliant journalist and editor, and a known entity.

Robinson had known Davidson since their reporting days, and WL Baillieu had sat with Davidson for two years on the HWT board, and observed him at the HWT for over a decade. Although Fink had clashed with Davidson, there is no evidence that Baillieu had lost confidence in him to the same degree. Through Fink, Baillieu would have been well aware of the editor's shortcomings, but he also appreciated Davidson's editorial skill,[33] and had seen him devote eleven years to modernising the *Herald*'s newsgathering capacity, and improving its quality and circulation to make it the leading afternoon paper in Australia. Davidson also had the advantage of a childhood connection to Broken Hill, and family connections to mining. His humble origins and known sympathy towards unions would also have been viewed favourably, as they had been for Mussen, because Collins House wanted publicists who 'understood and sympathised with the Australian worker'.[34]

Collins House's financial help explains how Davidson could afford to buy two newspapers. Even provincial newspapers were not cheap. The *Barrier Miner* was registered with a capital of £40 000 and the *Recorder* with £10 000.[35] Davidson's financial settlement when he left the HWT was reportedly £2500.[36] According to public records, he sank nearly all of this – £2250 – into the Port Pirie *Recorder* in early 1919.

When Davidson registered his new company to take over the *Recorder*, there were only two other shareholders: public accountants Harold Herbert Sherlock and Esmond Tuckett Daniell, of 53 Queen Street, near Collins House. Sherlock's firm of accountants and auditors had been 'professionally connected with several large mining companies' for over a decade.[37] It was a firm that Collins House used.[38] And surprisingly, Sherlock also had connections with Davidson's presumed enemy, Fink. Sherlock was a co-director with Fink of the moving pictures company, Amalgamated Pictures Ltd. (It produced what is recognised as the world's first full-length narrative feature film, *The Story of the Kelly Gang*. The company came to dominate Australia's film industry to the extent that it was investigated by a Royal Commission into the film industry in 1927.)

The accountants' combined share in the *Recorder* was very likely registered on behalf of Collins House. It was larger than Davidson's share at first, but perhaps as an agreed bonus, after Davidson had been in charge of the paper for one year, the accountants transferred 2140 of their shares to him, giving Davidson majority ownership of the *Recorder*.

The amount that Davidson put into the *Barrier Miner* could not be ascertained through archival sources, but he is likely to have had little more cash to contribute. When he met his new staff at the *Barrier Miner* after taking over the paper, Davidson told them that he had put all of his 'material interests' into the two papers.[39] This is likely to be true but he must have had other financial backers, especially for the *Barrier Miner*. Significantly, on arrival at its office, Davidson was introduced to the staff not as the new owner, but as 'the representative of the new owners'.[40]

When Davidson took over the papers in February 1919, Collins House was at a crossroads. World War I had ended only three months earlier. The group was facing plummeting demand and prices for metals, but also, as Baillieu had predicted, labour unrest because workers wanted to maintain their wartime wage rates while the companies wanted to lower wages as they were facing reduced profits.[41] BHAS' military contract with the British government for lead used in munitions expired in March, and it then had to pay a large tax bill on its wartime profits. Broken Hill South and North Broken Hill did not pay mid-year dividends in 1919 due to falling revenue. Collins House needed to find more investment income and to diversify into new industries. Not coincidently, this was the year that Baillieu began putting more effort into publicity, including by becoming more active at the HWT.

Almost as soon as Davidson arrived in Broken Hill in February 1919, the industrial unrest started to boil over. After his earlier success at Port Pirie, Mussen was despatched to soothe Broken Hill, and he arrived in March. But the more militant unionists there considered Mussen's policies for housing, living and working conditions as 'palliatives, sops, and doles to chloroform the worker' and the *Barrier Daily Truth* attacked him as 'the greatest menace Broken Hill unionists have ever had to fight'.[42]

Davidson's *Barrier Miner* would become known locally as the 'bosses' paper'.[43] It defended Mussen and promoted his welfare scheme for workers. It reported Mussen's views prominently, including his public lecture on 'happiness' and 'humanising' the mining industry. It published interviews with Mussen, and gave him space to reply when the company was criticised for proposing to peg workers' wages to fluctuating metal prices.[44] Fraser was pleased with the paper and wrote to Robinson to report that, after only a month under Davidson's guidance, the *Barrier Miner* was now minimising the impact of the *Barrier Daily Truth* by 'preaching ... sane economics, reform by constitutional methods [and] decent citizenship'.[45]

But despite Mussen's efforts, and the publicity support provided by Davidson's paper, the industrial turmoil did not cease. In May 1919, one of the longest strikes in Australian history began. It lasted eighteen months, ending in November 1920, when mine managers agreed to the first 35-hour working week in Australian history, and to improved health and safety conditions. The strike caused immense hardship among workers and their families in Broken Hill and in Port Pirie, which was also affected when the ore stopped arriving. It caused significant disruption to BHAS and the Collins House mining companies' operations. But Peter Yule revealed that Collins House secretly saw the strike as fortuitous. Because the commodities market had collapsed, they had more lead than they could sell, and were about to reduce production at Broken Hill anyway when the strike conveniently did it for them.[46]

That Collins House 'silently welcomed' the strike was not known at the time but helps explain its prolonged nature.[47] Outwardly, the mining companies expressed disappointment at a strike they claimed was caused by militant unionists. Mussen acted as a negotiator for the BHAS-aligned companies, while the *Barrier*

Miner called on workers to end the strike and go back to work. The paper said the militant 'strike makers' were intent on bringing about 'revolution'.[48] Davidson encouraged his reporters to focus attention on the strike leaders and expose any underhanded tactics or hypocrisy on their part. One union leader who was ridiculed, mounted a partly successful libel case against the paper.[49] The *Barrier Miner* was criticised for being 'silent' about one of the major causes of the strike, lead poisoning and other health risks from mining, but it editorialised that there was no firm 'evidence' that mining caused health problems.[50]

Davidson had kept on the *Barrier Miner*'s editor, John Smethurst, whose approach to journalism was laid bare several years later. Five years after Davidson's death, when Smethurst was put out of work, he sent a series of remarkable letters to Colin Fraser offering himself as a propagandist for hire and promising 'the kind of publicity' that could be 'very useful ... [to] the employing companies at Broken Hill'.[51] Smethurst reminisced how, as managing editor of the *Barrier Miner*, he had used 'subtle' tactics of publicity to combat the '*Barrier Truth*' and had it 'down to the very edge of extinction'. Smethurst said he was willing to 'enter the service of the mining companies as publicity and propaganda officer – either avowed *or otherwise*' (italics added).[52] Fraser wrote back that he was 'very interested', but confided to Robinson that he was not sure if Smethurst was the 'right man' for the job.[53]

Collins House was always acutely aware of the importance of publicity and willing to pay for it. Robinson had advised Colin Fraser two years before Davidson took over the papers that 'press men should be used to educate [workers]. Their views should be quietly moulded.'[54] That Davidson went to Broken Hill and Port Pirie in the service of Collins House to help fulfil that mission seems beyond doubt. Davidson's own paper described him as 'one of the most convinced unionists in Australia', but he promoted the mining companies' views so well, using his bright and sophisticated writing style, that he became an enemy to local union leaders.[55] George Dale called Davidson a 'sewer rat' and the paid mouthpiece of the mining companies. Dale said he believed that Mussen and Davidson were 'hand-in-hand', but he had no proof, only 'conjecture'.[56]

Union activists suspected that the mining companies had funded Davidson's purchase of the paper.[57] Davidson described these allegations as 'false reports' designed to damage him.[58] But the talk continued, and one union leader called Davidson 'the trusted servant of Collins House'.[59] Another, George Kerr, president of the Amalgamated Miners' Association of Broken Hill, told an open-air meeting of unemployed men in 1922 that Davidson was 'the worst thing ever known in the form of a human being'. As one newspaper coyly reported, Kerr also 'cast aspersions' upon Davidson's mother.[60] Davidson sued Kerr for slander, seeking £1000 compensation. He was awarded £750 damages.[61]

THE FOUNDING OF NEWS LIMITED

By the time the bitter and protracted strike ended in 1920, Collins House's attention had turned to influencing opinion in capital cities, especially Adelaide – Broken Hill's closest capital city, and where important decisions were made about transport, shipping, finance and industrial matters that affected both Broken Hill and Port Pirie. Davidson and Mussen began to plan the new paper in 1921. While details may have been sketched out during a train trip, it was not a rare or chance meeting. The two had seen each other regularly in Broken Hill over the years, where they socialised together at the Freemasons' Hotel, and Davidson's paper had regularly interviewed Mussen.[62]

After the prospectus for News Limited was drawn up in June 1922, Davidson stepped back from active management of the *Barrier Miner* to focus on establishing the new company and its flagship paper, the *News*, in Adelaide. News Limited was floated as a public company with a nominal capital of £250000. Mussen took up £16295 worth of shares, slightly more than Davidson. (Mussen listed his address as 'Collins House'.[63]) Davidson purchased £15300 worth of shares. This means both were supposedly putting in over $1 million each in today's money. Mussen's interest cost sixteen times his annual BHAS salary of £1000 (he had unsuccessfully sought £5000 per year, suggesting that he was not flush with cash). And Davidson's two tiny papers were only 'making peanuts'.[64] It is implausible that, through those papers, he had been able to turn his £2250 investment into a £15000 profit in just three years. Instead, it is highly likely that, at least initially, a portion of Mussen's News Limited shares were held on behalf of his employer, while Davidson's shares were provided to him by Collins House in return for arranging the start-up of News Limited and managing the company.[65] This is the same deal that Collins House extended to Keith Murdoch three years later for Murdoch's involvement in the *West Australian* (Chapter 7).

In 1922, Fink was not yet interested in expanding the HWT beyond Melbourne, but he seems to have allowed the HWT to help Baillieu's Adelaide project because the *Herald* 'sold' the *News* two Goss octuple printing presses (described as the 'greyhounds of the printing world').[66] The *Herald* also lent its works manager, one of the leading printing engineers in the country, to plan the layout of the plant at News Limited's new building. This was all remarkably generous of the HWT, a company not known for its charitable attitude to competitors, especially one that Fink had just had sacked.

The real owners behind the *News* gave it every opportunity to prosper, and money was no object. To clear its way in the field of evening papers, Davidson approached the owners of the *Advertiser* and the *Register* and offered to buy their two longstanding evening newspapers – the *Express and Telegraph*, and the *Journal*. These cost £10 000 each.[67] By purchasing the 'good will' of these papers, and then closing them down before the *News* began (the *Journal* closed the day before the *News* launched), News Limited eliminated competitors and gave the *News* a ready-made afternoon market.

But despite all of the support it was receiving, the *News* hit a 'sea of troubles' in its first year.[68] It was supposed to launch in April or May 1923, but the new building was not ready in time, its staff sat idle while British plant equipment was delayed. Then parts arrived broken, delaying the paper's launch until 24 July 1923. With no time to adequately prepare and test the machinery, everything went wrong on the paper's first day. The gas-jets on the linotype machines broke down, the power went out, and when Davidson pressed the button to start the printing press, paper breaks halted production, and spoiled almost as many copies as were printed. Mechanical workers worked around the clock to fix the problems but a plan to print four editions had to be abandoned; only two editions eventuated.

Technical issues aside, the paper was bright and brash, with big headlines, photographs and, new to conservative Adelaide, comic strips. The paper fully reflected Davidson's 'new journalism' commitment, and the Northcliffe practice of having something for everyone. It had news from overseas and country areas, news on industrial matters and trade unions, church news, sections on motoring, theatre, films and gardening, a column on 'keeping poultry for profit', women's sections, a children's story, an advice column, and a column of satire and jingle that promised to 'bring smiles to chase away the frowns'.[69] News Limited kept its sale price at a penny for its first twelve months so that the new paper could establish a foothold in the Adelaide market, but when it was judged that this was no longer sustainable, the cover price was raised to 1½d in August 1924.

Like other newspapers associated with Collins House, the *News* dutifully promoted Baillieu and his business ventures, reporting the successes of his established businesses, and talking up the prospects of new ones, including Electrolytic Zinc and the paper production venture.[70] It published optimistic interviews with Baillieu about the economic situation, and even found space to report the ugly, racist views of WL's son, Clive Baillieu, who remarked that something needed to be done to 'keep the black man under control' because 'the colored races were coming forward' and the world would otherwise soon be 'dominated by the black races'.[71]

CONTROL OF NEWS LIMITED

Tellingly, although Davidson was News Limited's managing director, and he had incorporated his two country papers into the business, he was never the chairman of its board. At the first annual general meeting of shareholders, the chair, AE Clarkson, described Davidson in a way that made him sound more like a contracted employee than the owner of the company. Clarkson told shareholders that the board wanted to recognise Davidson's service by offering him a 'limited option on 10 000 of the unissued shares' in return for Davidson agreeing 'to remain in his position for a further two years'.[72] As Davidson agreed to that condition, his contract was for seven years, or until around September 1930 (he died just short of that, in June 1930).

News Limited's board was stacked with Collins House's preferred combination of local men of high social status who had useful connections, and businessmen who made their living off Collins House. News Limited's first chairman, E Allnutt, was a director of the Executor Trustee and Agency Company of South Australia, which looked after trusts and estates. A lot of its business came from

Broken Hill, and like other trustee companies, it was a good way to mask ownership of shares in various businesses.[73] Allnutt was also chairman of the Freney Kimberley Oil Company which fruitlessly explored and drilled for oil in Western Australia from the 1920s to the 1940s, and was connected with Robinson. He was also a director of the South Australian Brewing Company, which had a branch at Broken Hill, and owned many hotels (allegedly more than thirty) in the mining town.

AE Clarkson became News Limited's chairman from 1925 until his death in 1936.[74] Clarkson's business, Clarkson Ltd, was a home decorating company that specialised in paints, glass, hardware and building materials. Since 1918, the paint manufacturing side of the business had been a subsidiary of Collins House's British Australian Lead Manufacturers Pty Ltd (BALM). BALM (which later changed its name to that of its best-known brand, Dulux) made lead paint from Broken Hill's metallic lead. BALM was an important business to Collins House. Arthur Robinson was its chairman, and WL Baillieu a director.

James Hay Gosse of the prominent Adelaide family (grandson of Alexander Hay, proprietor of the *South Australian Register*, and grandfather of the 1990s–2000s Liberal Party politician Alexander Downer) was managing director of George Wills & Co., one of Adelaide's oldest companies. It had a large soft goods and drapery warehouse in Broken Hill, and operated warehouses at other mining sites in Perth, Fremantle and Kalgoorlie. It was also a shipping company, and its ships were transporting Broken Hill's ore concentrates to England. Gosse was also a director of the even more vital Adelaide Steamship Company Ltd, Australia's largest shipping company, which dominated transport of passengers and cargo, including contracts with Broken Hill companies to carry its supplies and transport its metals. And Gosse was a director of the Collins House–aligned Bank of Adelaide, and of the already-mentioned important financial source for News Limited, the Executor Trustee and Agency Company Ltd.

The key board members of News Limited (Mussen was on the board for its first three years) had a vested interest in making sure that Collins House did well.[75] Their companies were carrying its ore concentrates from Broken Hill and Port Pirie; taking supplies and equipment between the field and other locations; selling soft goods and beer to its workers at Broken Hill; and making paint from its lead. But the story that a journalist had created News Limited, rather than a mining company, was important; and so too was the perception that it was a local venture. Although in reality, News Limited seems to have been run from Melbourne's financial heart, the company promoted itself as a 'South Australian enterprise, owned by South Australians'. One puff piece even falsely claimed that the company's shareholder list showed 'the great bulk of the capital is South Australian ... [with a] number of small shareholders'.[76]

The first lodged shareholder list, dated 31 March 1924, reveals that Collins House–aligned figures owned at least half of the ordinary shares in their own names. All of the key Collins House figures (except for Robinson who had a policy of not investing in ventures in which he was involved) were on that list: Baillieu, Fraser, Alexander Stewart, EH Shackell (Baillieu's brother-in-law), HL Shackell, WE Branson, George Klug, William Wainwright (the manager of Broken Hill South, who had advocated for a counter to the *Barrier Daily Truth*), along with other Collins House mine managers, superintendents and engineers.[77]

But Collins House figures are also likely to have held more shares under other names, including through trusts and private companies. The Baillieu family used companies for this purpose with names that ranged from the banal ('Pooled Assets Pty Ltd', 'Assets Pty Ltd', 'Securities Pty Ltd', 'Shares and Accounts Pty Ltd') to the picturesque ('Merrylands Pty Ltd') and the charming ('Mutual Trust Pty

Ltd' which reflected Baillieu's business philosophy of trust within his family and close circle of friends). Fraser's personal papers show that he was buying parcels of shares in News Limited and putting them into other names, including JD Campbell, a mysterious 'Miss White' and BALM. By 1931, the Baillieus' 31 000 shares in News Limited were held under the alias of 'AE Young and LL Ashton' (L Latham Ashton was a relative of Baillieu's through his wife's family). It was one of the legacies of the land boomer years that Baillieu (and Fink) were highly adept at corporate machinations, including hiding assets, masking ownership through complicated syndicates, using dummy shareholders and affiliated directors, and otherwise exercising covert control of a company. Control was always more important than ownership.

NEWS LIMITED EXPANDS

News Limited was in a hurry to expand right from its foundation. Only a year after its prospectus was drawn up, it had already bought – and closed – two afternoon papers to make way for the *News*. Then, before the *News* had even been launched – while its staff were still waiting for its equipment and building to be finished – the company bought the illustrated weekly paper, the *Mail*. It moved the sporting-focused Sunday newspaper to its North Terrace headquarters once the building was ready. Only thirteen months after the prospectus, it had already owned six papers, and had kept four – the *News*, the *Mail*, the *Recorder* (in South Australia), and the *Barrier Miner* (in New South Wales). Then, only two months after the chaotic launch of the *News*, the board announced that it would be expanding into Tasmania.

Collins House had established the Electrolytic Zinc (EZ) works in Risdon, a suburb of Hobart, in 1917, and Baillieu had invested a great deal of his personal money into the potentially risky project. By 1920, EZ had 1300 workers, but was not yet producing much zinc. In 1923, there was negative press about the plant's pollution, including from a Labor candidate who claimed the plant's poisonous fumes were sending its workers 'slowly to their graves'.[78]

That year, News Limited's chairman told shareholders that the directors had carefully surveyed the prospects of starting a paper in Hobart, and had 'firm expectations of success'.[79] The *News* (Hobart) began publishing in May 1924. This seemed somewhat rushed because, although the *Mail* was making money, the *News* (Adelaide) had not had time to establish itself, and still had a deficit of £17 471. But the optimistic chair advised shareholders that the Hobart paper should 'within reasonable time' begin making a profit.[80] It never did. A year later, in September 1925, the Hobart *News* recorded a loss of £15 000. The chair assured shareholders that it would soon 'show a big advance'.[81] But he was again wrong, and the board gave up on the Hobart edition and closed it in December 1925.

By then, it might well have been felt that a paper in Hobart was not strictly necessary. Risdon was not the industrial cauldron of Broken Hill. The EZ workforce was a lower paid and less unionised workforce than comparable ones on the mainland. The company had been able to avoid strikes, had convinced its workers to forgo a pay rise, and held off calls for a 44-hour week (the plant worked on a 48-hour week).[82] The well-established *Mercury* (which had been publishing in Hobart for seventy years) was already vigorously advocating politically conservative and pro-business views, and had been very supportive of EZ.[83]

Undeterred by the Hobart failure, News Limited's directors immediately steered the company towards Perth, where Collins House was involved in gold mining and oil exploration. On 19 January 1926, News Limited bought one of Perth's oldest newspapers, the *Daily News*. It was the only evening paper in the growing city, but Perth's morning paper, the *West Australian*, was more influential. Only six months later, a syndicate comprising WL Baillieu, WS Robinson and Keith Murdoch bought the *West Australian* on 1 July 1926 (Chapter 7). Perhaps Collins House was starting to lose confidence in Davidson after the Hobart failure, and the slow start to the *News*, and was now backing a different horse, Baillieu's friend and employee, Murdoch.

Murdoch had taken over Davidson's old job as *Herald* editor in 1921, established his credentials there, and would now be tailing Davidson around the country, following him from Melbourne to Perth, and then Adelaide. Like Davidson, Murdoch was a skilled editor, energetic, determined, and ambitious to be a newspaper owner. But Murdoch was fifteen years younger, and a man of more sober habits. Perhaps running the two Collins House–affiliated newspaper managers up against each other in Perth was a shrewd way to find out who was better equipped to lead Collins House's press empire–building project.

THE HWT AND KEITH MURDOCH SWOOP INTO ADELAIDE

When Fink was trying to push Davidson out of the HWT in 1918, he had been corresponding regularly with Murdoch in London. After Fink voiced some of his major criticisms of Davidson, Murdoch agreed that Davidson had an autocratic nature (and pointedly added that he could never work with Davidson as a result).[84] Aware of Fink's bitterness about the abandoned editorials, Murdoch suggested that Davidson had made the *Herald* 'curiously characterless' when it needed some 'sort of a fighting platform' and some 'push'.[85] Murdoch was no neutral sounding board on any of this; he was interested in Davidson's job.

We can safely presume that Davidson was no fan of Murdoch's either. In December 1923, the *News* published a gossip column that took a swipe at Keith Murdoch, the ageing thirty-eight-year-old bachelor. It described his scandalously young fiancée, eighteen-year-old Peggy Mills, as 'a reckless young thing' who had seriously injured herself in a motor accident while 'bubbling over with animal spirits'. It portrayed her as a vapid social climber (Murdoch's engagement to the injured Mills was later quietly abandoned).[86]

When News Limited was formed, Davidson had made sure that small amounts of its shares were spread around to journalists, including Smethurst and others working at his papers, but also friends, such as Bert Cook. (This means, in another sign of the uniquely corporatised nature of Australian newspapers, that the founder of the journalists' union was also a (minor) owner of News Limited. Cook also worked for Mussen in later years.) But in 1927, another journalist suddenly cropped up on the shareholder list – Keith Murdoch with 2700 shares in News Limited. Murdoch clearly had his eye on the *News* and on Adelaide. The next year, he went into another syndicate with Baillieu, but this one included the HWT and Fink.

In 1928, this syndicate bought the old and tired *Register* in Adelaide and used it to pressure the *Advertiser*'s owner into selling his better paper to the HWT in 1929 (Chapter 7). Murdoch and the HWT were now on Davidson's main patch, and Murdoch had succeeded where Davidson had failed. Davidson had reportedly made a previous, unsuccessful, offer for News Limited to buy the *Advertiser* for £1 million.[87] Murdoch was also slowly but surely adding to his small stake in News Limited.

In the year before Davidson's death, it was becoming obvious that Murdoch was the man for the job of empire building, not Davidson. The failed Tasmanian venture had left expensive debts, but News Limited's various papers were also suffering from the

Depression. In 1928–29, the company's income had reduced rather than grown. Financial strain had been added by investing in a new Hoe printing plant and expanding its North Terrace building, to almost double its size only six years after it was built. By contrast, Murdoch had been able to keep the *Herald*'s finances healthy even during the Depression.

News Limited was vulnerable, and Murdoch had a plan to get closer to it. According to his biographer, Desmond Zwar, in 1929 Murdoch went to News Limited's 'owners' and proposed a share swap between News Limited and the *Advertiser* as a sort of 'mutual protection' pact that would give 'both newspapers a better feeling of security against any potential attack' from a competitor.[88] Which owner did Murdoch go to – News Limited's titular owner, Davidson, or its real owner, Collins House? Certainly, Davidson did not seem to feel more secure after the swap was agreed. Given Collins House's involvement in both News Limited and the HWT, the deal might be more accurately viewed as a formalisation of joint ownership, a grouping of Collins House assets to be placed under Murdoch's stewardship, and confirmation of his ascendancy. News Limited was being sucked into the HWT.

In March 1929, News Limited's chairman asked shareholders at an extraordinary meeting to allow the directors to make a large increase in share capital. Clarkson said he could not disclose why but asked compliant shareholders to 'trust your directors' to distribute the shares as they saw fit.[89] The company's nominal capital was increased to £750000 by the creation of an additional 500000 shares of £1 each. In September, the directors revealed they had used this increased capital to negotiate a share swap as part of an agreement of cooperation between News Limited and the *Advertiser* (HWT) for twenty-one years. The *News* assigned a new issue of 150000 ordinary shares to the *Advertiser* and received the equivalent value of 91875 *Advertiser* shares in return. These exchanged shares would not provide voting power for ten years, and Clarkson assured shareholders that News Limited would still be independent with its 'control and public policy ... and its publications entirely unfettered'.[90] As the next chapter explains, this is not how things worked out. Within only two years, Murdoch demanded voting rights for the shares and took control of News Limited for the HWT.

Davidson agreed to the share swap, but died before it was activated. He may well have been depressed about what it heralded. His shareholding in what was ostensibly 'his' company had been reduced to an insignificant amount by the capital increase. He was being pushed out. And because Baillieu was acting chairman of the HWT for most of 1930 while Fink was overseas, Davidson must have known this was sanctioned by Baillieu. By early 1930, Davidson was in a deep slump. News Limited was in a bad way. Its profits had been reduced by 60 per cent from the previous year, and it was not able to pay a dividend on ordinary shares.[91] Davidson was drinking. He had separated from his wife. His brother Allan had died suddenly in January, before Davidson had had the chance to visit him in London. Davidson's youngest son Alan had died piloting a Qantas aeroplane in the company's first fatal air crash, three years earlier.

Davidson's contract at News Limited was likely drawing to an end, and he was not in favour with the board. He had been sent away, ostensibly to attend the Empire Press Conference, but it had been scheduled as a much longer, nine-month trip that was described as a 'much-needed holiday'.[92] Davidson was being removed from control of his papers for a long stretch, and it appears that Collins House was taking back its assets from the control of a man who was falling apart. His staff described how Davidson had badly needed a 'rest'. This was code for the deep strain, poor health and alcohol abuse that he was labouring under. Davidson's cause of death was noted as pneumonia. He had acquiesced to the share swap and his exile without making a fuss, but he knew that his company loyalty was now unreciprocated. Despite his 'fundamental honesty', he had never revealed to his readers what was really going on behind News Limited, and this is perhaps why, after Davidson's death, the word Murdoch chose to describe him was 'noble'.[93]

DAVIDSON'S LEGACY

Davidson had never been the real 'owner' behind News Limited, and when he died, he owned only 14 260 News Limited shares – less than 1 per cent of its capital. In the seven years since he had 'founded' the company, he had not increased his stake in it at all. And his will, signed only three months before he died, showed that Davidson was not as well off as one might expect for a business-man whose company owned multiple newspapers and was worth £750 000. He had £20 000 in assets, of which £18 762 were the News Limited shares that he had owned since 1923. He left the shares to his family, mostly to his oldest son, Norman.

The sons of other newspaper owners (including Frank Packer, Ezra Norton, Arthur Shakespeare, Warwick Fairfax and Rupert Murdoch) took over their father's newspapers upon their death. But, even though Norman had been a journalist on News Limited papers, and his father ostensibly owned several newspapers, Norman did not inherit or take over control of any of them. The stake he inherited was too small, and he left journalism and became an auto engineer. When he died in 1968, he was living in a small flat in the cheap accommodation, red-light district of St Kilda in Melbourne. As Norman did not have any children, there was to be no dynastic line in any form, newspapers or otherwise, for JE Davidson.

News Limited was the second major newspaper empire, but it was not the small, independent company that it purported to be, let alone the rags-to-riches story of a miner and a station hand's son. News Limited's true origins have been hidden for nearly a century but the company's history now needs to be rewritten. It was not the result of 'one man's dream'. Unpalatable though it may be for the company to acknowledge, News Limited was started by a mining and metals giant to put forward what it called 'propaganda'. This, of course, was a closely guarded secret because the *News'* reputation, like that of all commercial newspapers, depended upon its claim to be an 'independent' and 'impartial' newspaper. It had promised to be a 'wholesome, and thoroughly reliable mirror of the news of the day'.[94]

CHAPTER 7

KEITH MURDOCH: JOURNALIST, KINGMAKER, EMPIRE BUILDER, PUPPET?

Whereas News Limited's 'founder', JE Davidson, is the invisible man of Australian newspaper history, his nemesis, Keith Murdoch, is possibly Australia's most famous journalist – and certainly its most famous newspaper executive. Even in his lifetime, Murdoch was a well-known public figure, and since his death in 1952, has been the subject of four book-length biographies, several theses, and many other publications. Some of the early works were more hagiography than biography. And Keith's loyal son, Rupert Murdoch, has used his multinational news media and publishing organisations to present a glowing portrait of his father as a patriotic man of conviction and charm, a brilliant journalist, editor and businessman. But independent accounts, especially in recent times, have been more probing – and more critical.[1]

The ultra-flattering portraits of Murdoch now stand alongside meticulously researched, scholarly analyses, as well as poison-pen portraits written by Murdoch's adversaries in the 1930s to 1940s, and recollections written by sharp-eyed journalists who observed him closely over many years. This means that Murdoch has been viewed from a dizzying array of angles. He was the greatest 'newspaperman' in Australian history. Or an unimaginative imitator. He was a charming, meticulous and ethical 'working journalist'. Or a calculating, unscrupulous propagandist and ruthless power player. He was a patriot, kind mentor and generous employer. Or a greedy, humourless, status-driven rogue.

In this book, Murdoch's reputation as a political kingmaker and the master press empire builder of his age require the most attention. By the 1930s, there was a perception that Murdoch was running Australia's politics, and much of its newspaper industry, from his third-floor office in the HWT building. He was such a significant figure that several chapters in this book explore his influence, including Chapters 10 and 11, which describe Murdoch at the peak of his political powers, when he was widely credited with installing Joe Lyons as prime minister.

This chapter focuses on Murdoch's media empire building, the source of his power. This too was multi-faceted, for Murdoch was so associated with the *Herald* (which he oversaw for thirty-one years (1921–52)), that a misconception arose that he owned the paper and its company's assets. During his time at the helm, the HWT papers were often referred to, usually disparagingly, as 'the Murdoch press'. But Murdoch owned very few shares in the HWT. He expanded the company, and when he was its chairman of directors (1942–52), controlled the HWT's direction and its many newspaper titles. But he was never a major owner, and the larger he helped make the HWT, the smaller his stake in it became. Murdoch would later become a newspaper owner in his own right (Chapter 8), but when he began empire building in the 1920s, he was acting as an agent on behalf of Collins House, the HWT, or both. Collins House had selected an ambitious leader.

MURDOCH AND THE POWER OF THE PRESS

'Power' was a word that Murdoch used often in his correspondence with family and friends, and something he openly desired from a young age. When he was twenty-two years old, Murdoch wrote to his father that, if all went well in his career, he 'should become a power in Australia'.[2] For the stammering target of school bullies, who was driven out of at least one school by relentless teasing, power was an important goal, and for a young man who could not get his words out, journalism was the perfect vehicle for obtaining it by making his voice heard. Where most journalists talk about journalism in altruistic terms, as a way to make a contribution to informing the public, Murdoch wrote to Fink that his main goal in developing his journalism career was to achieve 'independence in the use of power'.[3] When he was looking forward to resuming a position at *The Age*, he wrote to his father, 'I think *The Age* can be made an even greater power than it is'.[4]

Murdoch understood, better than any other journalist of his generation, that political influence was at the heart of owning and running a newspaper. In private, he talked about 'training' the public through his journalism.[5] Murdoch was interested not just in reporting events, but in moulding public opinion. He sincerely believed in the power of the press, and there was no question in his mind that newspapers could influence the public and politicians. He saw it up close in London while studying at the foot of his idol and mentor, Northcliffe, the man who showed Murdoch how to 'govern by newspaper'.

Murdoch also understood that large audiences were the prerequisite for that type of power. In 1922, when he was transforming the *Herald*, he wrote to Northcliffe that: 'When we have built circulation, we will begin to make Australia talk. Great political influence and general influence will come in time. And part at least shall be

FIGURE 7.1 Australia's most powerful newspaper executive, Sir Keith Murdoch, 1936
SOURCE Fairfax Syndication (FXJ142853).

yours.'[6] Presumably, the other 'part' was for himself! One journalist who knew Murdoch well described him as having 'a keen love of power', while another said his power-lust was 'insatiable'.[7]

Driven by such intense ambition, Murdoch worked his way up from a lowly, penny-a-liner reporter to a millionaire executive and the most powerful national media figure in the country. This was an extraordinary achievement and it gained him immense admiration in newspaper circles, for Murdoch did not inherit great wealth nor a newspaper from his father – as Hugh Denison, Warwick Fairfax, Geoffrey Syme and the Davies brothers had. What Murdoch's father – the strict, Scottish and God-fearing Reverend Patrick Murdoch – *had* given him was an even temperament and valuable social connections.

Unlike the bullying and coarse Frank Packer, or the abusive and erratic Ezra Norton, Murdoch was supremely calm and self-controlled, a product of the Calvinistic discipline imposed by his father. He had a phenomenal memory, a prodigious work ethic, and exceptional journalism skills. But these qualities would have counted for much less under different circumstances. The key to Murdoch's extraordinary success was his close friendships with powerful men. Reverend Murdoch began this process by passing on to his son his own much-valued social connections to WL Baillieu, David Syme, Alfred Deakin and Andrew Fisher. As a political reporter and news-paper editor, Murdoch then cultivated many others.

When Murdoch set his heart on becoming a journalist, instead of following in the family calling (both Murdoch's grandfathers were also Presbyterian ministers), there was still a strong Scottish influence on the Australian newspaper world.[8] Through Reverend Murdoch's friendship with fellow Scot, *Age* proprietor David Syme, Murdoch landed his first journalism job. WS Robinson, who was then *The Age*'s commercial editor, later said that he recommended the paper to Murdoch as an appropriate starting place, suggesting the two were friends even before Murdoch started at *The Age* in 1903.[9]

Syme put Murdoch to work on the very bottom rung of journalism, as a penny-a-liner covering the sedate suburb of Malvern. Penny-a-liners were paid a set fee per line, but only if the words they wrote were published. This brutal payment system encouraged impoverished reporters to be creative. Journalist Colin Bednall recalled how one enterprising penny-a-liner constructed a fake shark fin, and on slow news days, would swim around the beaches between Portsea and St Kilda, creating enough commotion to result in a publishable story.[10] At *The Age*, Murdoch developed a reputation for being able to make news out of very little. He later admitted to 'scandal-ously' 'overwriting' stories, but others claimed that he also used to surreptitiously provoke fights among local councillors.[11] Famously, he also devised a longer method for reporting cricket scores in order to extract more pennies from his tight-fisted employer.

Murdoch was so good at manufacturing news from sleepy Malvern that he began to earn more than regular full-time reporters, and when he was promoted to a salaried position as a political reporter, at the uncommonly young age of nineteen, his pay dropped to about half. Murdoch scrupulously saved enough pennies to venture to London in 1908 to try to break into Fleet Street. But, after a disappointing and impoverished eighteen months that was a real low point in his life, Murdoch returned to Melbourne in 1910. After his father put in a word for him with the widowed Mrs Syme, Murdoch went back to *The Age* but found the paper stolid, and still slow to recognise his talent and pay him commensurately. In 1912, Murdoch took up Denison's better offer to become the Melbourne political correspondent for the more vibrant Sydney *Sun* and so Murdoch moved physically to the *Herald* building (because the *Herald* was a partner in the *Sun*'s cable news business, UCS).

Federal politicians went out of their way to cultivate Melbourne's parliamentary reporters, but Murdoch more than reciprocated their interest. He laid on lavish hospitality, hosting politicians and squiring them to his aunt's guest-house in the Dandenongs, leaving many politicians in the young reporter's debt. Murdoch also joined the right clubs and played the right sport – golf (at least in newspaper and business circles in Melbourne and London; in Sydney, it was also polo and sailing). Murdoch built up strong friendships with two Labor politicians in particular – the Scottish Andrew Fisher and the Welsh Billy Hughes. Possibly because it did not reflect well on the impartiality of his journalism, Murdoch did not want his 'sacred' friendship with Fisher to become known.[12]

Murdoch was mixing with Labor politicians, had been affected by his experience as a penny-a-liner, and had secretly joined the fledgling Australian Journalists' Association (AJA). The poverty he experienced in London, and his study of politics at the London School of Economics, also influenced his early political views. At this stage, Murdoch was left-wing enough to quit the *Sun* in order to join the planned, union-owned paper, the *World*, in 1914. When its launch was scrapped on the outbreak of World War I, Denison accepted him back.[13] Like Davidson, after Murdoch became editor of the *Herald*, he travelled sharply from the left to the right of the political spectrum. By the late 1920s, Murdoch was a strong advocate of conservative, anti-Labor politics. In 1942, he described Labor government as a form of 'proletarian dictatorship'.[14]

Murdoch's second, far more comfortable and successful, stay in London (1915–21) had contributed to his changing views. Denison had appointed Murdoch to the post of managing editor of the UCS in London. It was a coveted and powerful position. UCS cables were printed in up to 250 newspapers in Australia, including all of the largest mainland capital city papers.[15] Because cable news was scarce, the items that Murdoch cabled from London were sometimes the only source of foreign news published on a particular topic in Australia. Murdoch was now able to reach a very large Australian audience and exercise a strong influence on how events were viewed.

Even before he arrived at the UCS, Murdoch had begun that process. On his way across to London in 1915, he visited Egypt. This side trip, which Murdoch had suggested, was framed as an official request that Murdoch investigate mail arrangements on behalf of the government. Ostensibly it was needed because Murdoch's friend, Prime Minister Fisher, was concerned about the lack of information he was receiving on the progress of the war. Murdoch took it upon himself to expand this mission of investigating the unreliable postal service, and very briefly visited Gallipoli to check on the use of Australian troops. Concerned by what he saw there, but possibly also acting out of less altruistic motives, Murdoch wrote his famous 'Gallipoli letter' which helped establish a picture of the campaign as a military disaster.[16] When Murdoch's vivid, partisan letter (which contained some errors and exaggerated claims) was disseminated among London's media and political elites, it gave Murdoch admittance to the top press and political circles. Most significantly, it brought him to the favourable attention of Northcliffe, who had been looking for a way to influence the Dardanelles campaign.[17]

POWERFUL FRIENDS

Working as head of UCS from a corner of *The Times* office, Murdoch was now situated in the heart of Fleet Street and he made the most of his regular access to Northcliffe, who had acquired the prestigious paper in 1908. Murdoch cultivated a father-son-like relationship with the press baron that sharply boosted his career prospects by giving him valuable inside knowledge of the press baron's circulation-boosting techniques. Murdoch's grovelling to Northcliffe (he once addressed him in a letter as 'My dear Chief ... the Chief of All Journalists (of all ages))'[18] was fully in keeping with how Northcliffe expected his acolytes to act. His workplaces were said to be characterised by 'sickening' subservience that delighted or revolted Northcliffe depending upon his mood.[19]

Murdoch's role as Hughes' unpaid personal publicist during the conscription debate (as described in a previous chapter), was another example of his ability to ingratiate himself with men in power. Hughes said his heart ached for Murdoch's company, while Murdoch told Hughes that their friendship was one of his 'main inspirations and happinesses'.[20] When Hughes arrived in London in 1916, he dined at Murdoch's apartment with Murdoch's political-social set, which included Northcliffe, *The Times* editor Geoffrey Dawson, and British politicians Bonar Law, Lloyd George and Lord Alfred Milner.[21] All were committed to military conscription and Hughes and Murdoch took up the cause with enthusiasm.

Murdoch wanted other men to be forced to do what he had avoided. Although he was a fit, single man, Murdoch had not enlisted for military service himself. (*Smith's Weekly* would later quip that Murdoch only 'saw service (postal) in Gallipoli'.[22]) On one occasion he explained his lack of military service by saying that he felt his duty to Australia 'could be better done with a pen than a rifle'.[23] In service of the conscription cause, Murdoch used his pen as a propagandist, including publishing false claims to ruthlessly discredit opponents, and suppressing stories that were detrimental to the 'yes' campaign.[24] He wrote articles on the AIF that he hoped would stimulate recruitment. One, called 'The Slaughter in Daisy Wood', went too far in October 1917 when it described the 'moving sight' of exhausted and sick Australian troops weak from lack of reinforcements. Murdoch was accused of inaccuracy by Australian military commanders but explained his motivation had been to 'rouse Australia, to end forever the recruiting difficulties, to force another conscription campaign ... by an appeal to public feeling'.[25] Murdoch reportedly had a staff of twelve working for him trying to secure the outcome of the second (failed) referendum in 1917.[26]

Murdoch's vigorous efforts increased his standing with the Baillieus, and his co-employers – the ardently pro-conscription *Sun* and *Herald* – although Fink was more impressed than Denison (who felt that Murdoch was 'trying to run the Empire').[27] After the war, when Murdoch fell out with Hughes, he went from being Hughes' chief adviser and closest confidant to describing Hughes as an unscrupulous and 'dangerous man'.[28] WS Robinson described the ending of the friendship by saying that Murdoch 'was a great supporter of Billy Hughes while Billy was a great supporter of his'.[29]

By 1920, Murdoch was a man of some importance and influence in London in his own right, a sort of de facto Australian ambassador. Back in Australia, he was considered a brilliant journalist for his engaging and patriotic reports during the war, and was one of the few reporters whose articles carried a by-line (something that Murdoch had encouraged). The *Herald* especially had 'starred his name', whereas the Sydney *Sun* had tended to list him only as 'our correspondent'. This was because the *Sun*'s shrewd Campbell Jones was not one to help a potential rival. Of the more generous Davidson who, as editor of the *Herald*, had helped build up Murdoch's name, *Smith's Weekly* remarked that Murdoch repaid him by 'step[ping] over his head'.[30] With Davidson gone, Murdoch used his status to play his two employers off against each other before accepting Fink's better offer to become chief editor of the *Herald*.

Murdoch told Northcliffe that 'Denison is very vexed about my leaving him',[31] and 'is showing an extraordinarily mean spirit about [it, while] my old friend Campbell Jones is rubbing it in. It hurts a good deal after the whole-hearted service I gave Denison.'[32] Denison's reaction indicated how he felt he had been manipulated and deceived by Murdoch, but Denison did not seem to hold a grudge. It made sense that Murdoch would go home to Melbourne and specifically to the HWT, where his friend, WL Baillieu, was an influential owner and director. As noted in Chapter 5, Murdoch had known the Baillieus since his school days in the 1890s. Baillieu's family loyalty was legendary, and he had considered Murdoch 'a virtual son since childhood' and followed his career.[33] At one point, Murdoch had even been considered a prospect for marrying Baillieu's daughter.[34]

With Baillieu's advocacy cementing the deal, Murdoch joined the *Herald* and took up his position as editor-in-chief in September 1921. Conscious of what had happened to Davidson, Murdoch wangled job conditions that would help safeguard his autonomy from Fink's interference and, with Baillieu's support, had much greater success in exerting his authority. Early on, in 1922, Murdoch pushed out Arthur Wise, the *Herald*'s general manager, who had been resisting Murdoch's changes, and it seems was acting as a proxy for Fink.[35] Murdoch had successfully insisted that the board endorse his autonomy, and his victory in this first 'heavy fight' (as Murdoch described it) established his leadership credentials early.[36] Murdoch was confident that he had Baillieu's support if there were any more clashes between himself and Fink, and Baillieu's vote was worth more than one. As Murdoch explained in a letter to Northcliffe, there was a 'Baillieu party' on the HWT board.[37]

Over the next decade, Baillieu *did* back Murdoch over Fink when power struggles surfaced within the HWT. Baillieu also opened up profitable business opportunities for Murdoch, and he and his son Clive, and brother Maurice Howard Lawrence ('Jac'), helped Murdoch financially, including by selling him newspaper shares at cheap rates, and providing him with finance so that he could become a newspaper owner himself. Theodore Fink sniped that Murdoch 'made a good deal of money through his friendship' with the Baillieus.[38] But the relationship also worked the other way around. The Baillieus and other HWT investors (including Fink) profited greatly from Murdoch's expansion of the company. As another one of Murdoch's enemies, Labor MP Arthur Calwell, acknowledged, Murdoch 'made a fortune for the Baillieus and the others who backed him'.[39]

Murdoch's close relationship with the Baillieu family was even evident in his living arrangements. On a post–World War I visit to London, Murdoch had stayed with their mutual friend, WS Robinson, steadily filling his host's apartment with antiques.[40] In Melbourne, as the bachelor editor of the *Herald*, Murdoch lived in a luxurious apartment in the Baillieus' East Melbourne mansion Cliveden, a grand Italian Renaissance–style building where apartments had no kitchens because residents were served meals prepared by a French chef in a dining room with waiters. (When Murdoch imported his own British butler, 'complete with genuine side-whiskers and an icy-stare', his critics had a field day lampooning Murdoch's obvious desire for status and the trappings of wealth.[41]) Once he was a family man, Murdoch bought Baillieu's mansion, Heathfield, in Kooyong Road, Toorak. In 1929–30, Murdoch travelled with WL Baillieu and other Baillieu family members on a journey to and from the United Kingdom and the United States.[42]

Because the Baillieus played such a crucial role in Murdoch's advancement, and because the causes that he was best known for promoting during his career were causes that Collins House wanted pushed – including Hughes, conscription, the Nationalists, Joe Lyons, the UAP, and Australian newsprint – it can be difficult to untangle just how much Murdoch was acting on his own initiative, and how much he was acting on behalf of even more powerful men. Newspaper rivals and socialist critics put this in blunt terms in the 1930s, calling Murdoch a 'puppet' of the Baillieus, a 'reflex of what is decided by the Victorian money czars', and a skilled but unde-clared publicist for the Collins House group.[43]

MURDOCH AS *HERALD* EDITOR

Murdoch's most admiring biographers say that when he took over as editor of the *Herald*, the paper had grown 'stodgy' and complacent after long years without competition, and it was Murdoch's editorial and business skill that turned it into a leading newspaper.[44] Others argue that Murdoch inherited a pioneering popular newspaper that was already in good shape, even if his predecessor, Guy Innes, had not been as inspiring an editor as Davidson (Innes' predecessor).[45] Murdoch's main approach to transforming the paper was to apply

Northcliffe's brand of 'people-oriented news' as a way to lure new readers out in the suburbs that were emerging as part of Melbourne's postwar recovery housing boom. Murdoch told Northcliffe that he considered 'the Chief's' notes his 'bible' in this task, and laying on the obligatory flattery, told him that 'All the *Herald* success is due to them'.[46]

Murdoch continued the *Herald*'s direct language and short news reports, as well as its focus on nationalism, patriotism and support for the White Australia policy. But he put even more emphasis on human interest news, especially crime. He strengthened overseas news, called for deeper coverage of sport and local news, and added new fictional series. He hired more photographers and introduced more, and larger, photographs (especially after witnessing the success of Denison's *Sun News-Pictorial*). After Murdoch sent Northcliffe copies of the *Herald* so Northcliffe could provide specific advice, Murdoch added more feature articles and fictional series.

Murdoch also followed Northcliffe's advice to make changes gradually, but he stopped short of imitating the management style of the erratic, bullying British magnate. The respect of his staff was something that Murdoch valued and cultivated. He appreciated that journalism was the basis of his paper's success and he paid good salaries and provided good job conditions to attract the best staff. This had the effect of helping to lift the standard of working conditions across the industry. Unlike other executives, such as Fairfax's formidable Rupert Henderson (who avoided his staff by taking a private lift up to his office), Murdoch also made himself accessible. He prided himself on remembering his reporters' names, and even their wives' and children's names.

Michael Cannon (who had worked for Murdoch), remarked that he 'knew how to get the best out of his reporters, using their raw material to help build Australia's biggest newspaper empire'.[47] He was a hands-on editor-in-chief and manager, who would write long, detailed letters to his editors counselling them about their content, but also commenting on the size of a font they used, or telling them to get out a ruler and check a headline that seemed crooked.[48] As one reporter noted, Murdoch had risen among them, so 'knew his job, and could work at it alongside any one of us'.[49] But the respect was also tinged with fear of Murdoch's disapproval. It was rumoured that he made senior staff sign blank letters of resignation in case they were ever needed.[50] Murdoch ran a stiff and formal workplace, insisting upon formal attire and manners, even to the extent of having a policy against beards and facial hair.[51] One of his protégés, JA Alexander, said Murdoch was 'mostly kindly' to his staff and on 'excellent' terms with them, but he was also a 'despot with kid gloves … a law unto himself … [and] it didn't do to run foul of him or to differ sharply from him'.[52]

Where Northcliffe would 'suck' his best journalists' brains, one of Murdoch's most effective strategies was to cultivate the cream of young journalists into loyal protégés who craved his approval. The talented, chosen ones were known as Murdoch's 'young men'. He would invite them to grand dinners at his house, and treated them generously, including sending some overseas where they acted as an informal, international network for his influence.[53] Many were loyal to the end but some eventually grew weary of what they came to see as Murdoch's insincerity and manipulation. According to Colin Bednall, a Murdoch protégé who became one of his executives and closest confidants, Murdoch was a man who 'habitually' made promises that he had no intention of keeping.[54] John Hetherington, one of Murdoch's former 'young men' who grew disenchanted, said he came to feel that Murdoch collected young journalists in the same way he collected fine china, English glass and art. Bednall had separately come to the same conclusion. Many observers of Murdoch noted this aspect of his personality, that he was 'incurably' acquisitive. WS Robinson said Murdoch 'was a

great collector – of cash, news, antiques and pictures'.[55] He could
have added newspapers as well.

THE 'GUN ALLEY MYSTERY'

When he arrived at the *Herald*, Murdoch was in a hurry to boost
the paper's sales. Denison was on his way to Melbourne, and
Murdoch's contract offered substantial financial rewards for
increases in circulation.[56] But even though Murdoch had applied
his prodigious energy for months, the *Herald* still needed something
more. Northcliffe had advised him to be on the alert for a circulation-boosting story – 'a sensation'[57] – and Murdoch finally found
one on the last day of 1921. A twelve-year-old girl had been bru-
tally murdered in a city alleyway in Melbourne. Murdoch could not
believe his good fortune, telling Northcliffe that it 'was great luck
getting the murder story'.[58] Northcliffe, who used to instruct his staff
on the *Daily Mail* to find 'one murder a day', undoubtedly agreed.

The naked, strangled body of Alma Tirtschke had been found
in a dark city laneway off Gun Alley, near Little Collins Street. The
Herald published thirteen straight days of sensational front-page
stories on what it dubbed 'The Gun Alley Mystery'.[59] Demanding
that the police find the man responsible, it called on the government
to offer a substantial reward for discovery of the murderer. When
the government complied, the *Herald* matched the reward offer and
stirred up its audience, telling readers what to look for and how to
claim the reward, including playing into racist prejudices by suggesting the murderer might be 'oriental'.[60]

FIGURE 7.2 The *Herald*'s sensational coverage of the trial of Colin Ross shares
the front page with reports of a boxing match, 1922
SOURCE *Herald*, 13 January 1922, p. 1.

WEATHER FORECAST
Metropolitan. — Slight
showers in night. Fine
day.
State.—Rain in Gippsland
and along coast. W.
winds.

The Herald

MAGAZINE SECTION
Special Articles and
Sketches will be a feature
of Tomorrow's Magazine
Section.

Eighty-third Year

No. 14,300. [Registered at General Post Office, Melbourne, for transmission by post as a Newspaper; also Registered Under the British Post Act] MELBOURNE, FRIDAY EVENING, JANUARY 13, 1922. Price 1½d. (14 PAGES)

COLIN ROSS IN COURT

CHARGE OF MURDER

Bench Over-rules Objection to Remand

"A GREAT COUNTRY," SAYS ACCUSED

Colin Campbell Ross, 28, charged with the murder of Alma Tirtschke, was brought before the City Court this morning and remanded until January 21.

He strongly objected to the remand, and declared that he was able to call evidence to prove his whereabouts on the night of the murder.

THE ACCUSED MAN

Colin Ross, sketched in Court this morning

"Went to Arcade"

CROWD IN THE STREET

THOROUGHFARES CLEARED BY POLICE

Ross Objects to Remand

Story of Arrest

Weeps on Parting

AMNESTY TO IRISH

Political Offenders Freed at Once

KING'S HOPE FOR GOODWILL

LONDON, Jan. 12.

WOMEN SHOT AT THEIR DOORS

Belfast Desperadoes at Work

(Reuter)
LONDON, Jan. 12.

POPE CONGRATULATES KING

Contributed Effectually to Peace

(Reuter)
LONDON, Jan. 12.

RAND ORDERLY

Services Run Smoothly

DEMAND FOR MEDIATION

JOHANNESBURG, Jan. 12.

Will Railwaymen Join?

DEAD STATESMAN HONORED

Highest Rank Given to Marquis Okuma

("Herald" Special Representative)
TOKIO, Jan. 11.

CARPENTIER THE VICTOR

Cook Knocked Out in Fourth Round

FIERCE CONTEST FROM THE START

("Herald" Special Representative)

Georges Carpentier has just knocked out George Cook in the fourth round.

After boxing fiercely through the first three rounds, in which there was much in-fighting, Cook went down to a right which landed above his left ear.

Carpentier struck again, and the crowd yelled "Foul!" but Cook himself discounts that suggestion.

The referee ruled that there was no foul. Cook rolled over and rose groggily just after the count of ten had finished.

VANQUISHED THE AUSTRALIAN

GEORGES CARPENTIER

COOEES FOR COOK

Calm Frenchman and Grim Australian

"NO FOUL," SAYS THE REFEREE

("Herald" Special Representative)
LONDON, Jan. 12, 10.30 p.m.

Continued on Page 9

THE LOSER

GEORGE COOK

The Blow That Told

DRAMATIC SCENE IN THE CITY COURT

Sketch taken during the proceedings this morning. The accused is shown standing in the dock on the extreme right.

The *Herald* pressured the police for a quick arrest, and Colin Ross, licensee of a nearby wine bar, was soon arrested. The public mood was so intense that mounted police had to be called to disperse large crowds that had gathered around Ross' house. During his trial, the *Herald*'s circulation nearly doubled, from 120 000 sales a day to 230 000.[61] When the trial was over and its sales stabilised, the *Herald* had gained a 20 per cent boost in circulation. The paper's frenzied coverage was an early example of 'trial by media' in Australia. Despite a fairly solid alibi and his repeated pleas of innocence, Ross was found guilty and executed. Eighty-six years later, a forensic examination of the evidence found that Ross was an innocent man who had died a painful death by strangulation in a botched execution. He was officially pardoned in 2008.[62]

A PLACE FOR THE *SUN NEWS-PICTORIAL*

In September 1921, three months before the Gun Alley murder, Northcliffe had visited Melbourne, and been accorded royal treatment. When he stepped off the train at Spencer Street station, Murdoch welcomed his mentor and proudly introduced him to Fink, Baillieu and other HWT board members.[63] During his stay, Northcliffe was wined, dined and hosted by newspaper leaders and politicians. Baillieu played golf and socialised with him, but also lured Northcliffe to Risdon to view the Electrolytic Zinc works, hoping the press baron would publicise the venture.[64] The Baillieus also took the opportunity to ask Northcliffe how they could make more money in newspapers. He told them to back Murdoch.[65] Although he was now starting to show signs of the mental illness that would soon overcome him, Northcliffe was still the greatest publisher of his age. His papers were selling to 25 million readers a week.[66] His visit made a big impression on the

Baillieus, encouraging them to think more seriously about inter-state expansion, and strengthening their faith in Murdoch.

Interstate expansion was already front of mind because Denison's plan to launch in Melbourne was advancing. Murdoch decided that the best defence for the *Herald* was 'attack'.[67] Three months after Northcliffe's visit, Murdoch obtained the approval of the HWT board to head north and buy shares in Sydney's *Evening News*. The plan was to work the tired paper up to be a more effective and distracting rival to Denison's *Sun* so that he might delay, or even abort, his Melbourne foray. Murdoch had only been editor of the *Herald* for four months but he was already involved in concocting this takeover scheme, and was telling Northcliffe that he wanted to think of 'big things and big movements' not 'small issues and tuppeny things'.[68] Northcliffe gave Murdoch every encouragement to pursue his already strong dream to 'have a paper of your own'.[69] Murdoch coaxed £5000 for the *Evening News* venture from Northcliffe, which had encouraged other investors, including the HWT, and likely the Baillieus. When Northcliffe sent Murdoch the £5000 cheque in January 1922, he said 'I don't understand project but I trust you'.[70] Murdoch repeatedly assured Northcliffe that his money would not be lost, but the wealthy press baron told Murdoch, 'lose it if you like',[71] and 'Use it any wa[y] you choose. I have no desire for more money.'[72]

The most extraordinary aspect of the financing of the *Evening News* venture was Murdoch's statement to Northcliffe that he was putting in £75000 'of my own' money and had another £4000 in reserve savings.[73] Murdoch had only just started earning £2000 per year as editor of the *Herald*, a salary increase from his role as head of UCS.[74] Although famously frugal during his early career, Murdoch could not possibly have saved £79000 (equivalent to more than $5 million in today's money) just from his salary and payments for syndication of his articles. We can only speculate that he must

have made a great deal of money from investments in shares, probably on the basis of Baillieu advice, and even Baillieu financial support.[75] (In another letter to Northcliffe, Murdoch claimed that he
could 'retire' on his savings – he was only thirty-six years old!)[76]

Murdoch bought shares in the *Evening News* and obtained
undertakings from the Bennett family that they would vote 'as I
wish'. At this point, Murdoch told Northcliffe that 'Denison has
written to me that we should not fight but get together as one company. This appeals to some *Herald* directors. It would not suit me
– I would get some shares but would be overweighted, with the
Sydney influence [Denison and Campbell Jones] always against
me.'[77]

Murdoch was eager to achieve 'big things' and wanted to have
control not just of the *Herald* and the *Evening News* but also 'other
papers' in the future.[78] His impatience was palpable. Although
Murdoch was making great strides with the *Herald*, he wondered if
his career lay at the paper, and said 'the tininess of this place and its
people seem to choke me', 'often I feel that I am wasting my days
here, for people are so smug and conservative, and reforms do not
come quickly'.[79] (But Murdoch would stay at the HWT for another
thirty years, until his death.)

Between late 1921 and November 1922, Murdoch offered the
Evening News the benefit of his editorial advice. He wanted to go
further in remodelling the fifty-five-year-old paper, including taking
ads off its front page, but did not hold enough shares to exercise such
authority.[80] In March 1922, before he could build up a larger stake
in the paper, a group of Sydney drapers ruined Murdoch's plans.
Infuriated that the *Sun* had increased its advertising rates, they
decided to invest in its competitor as a way of making sure the *Sun*
would think twice about taking its advertisers for granted in the
future. The drapers injected £100 000 into the *Evening News*, giving
them nearly half its shares.[81]

Murdoch blamed Fink for this calamity, which eventually scuttled the project, because Fink had held out giving Murdoch the HWT's £25 000 contribution while he negotiated with Denison over an amalgamation ('which we afterwards refused to countenance').[82] Denison and Fink had already discussed a potential amalgamation in December 1921, when the missing extension to their cable service agreement was located and it frustrated Denison's Melbourne plans. Northcliffe had suggested to Murdoch that he partner with Denison (who Northcliffe liked). But Murdoch viewed his former boss as a rival, not a partner. It had not helped that Denison, who held shares in the HWT between 1921 and 1923,[83] seems to have backed the *Herald*'s general manager, Arthur Wise, over Murdoch during their internal 'fight'. Murdoch told Northcliffe that, 'I cannot help liking Denison but he is not a man of his word and when in January [1922] he turned tail on an agreement he had made with me I finally decided that he is better in opposition than a colleague'.[84] Nonetheless, Murdoch was going to have to countenance an alliance with Denison because Northcliffe was insisting on it, setting off a fresh round of merger talks in May–June 1922.

THE RIVAL, THE 'MADMAN' AND THE POTENTIAL MERGER

Murdoch was planning to bring the *Evening News* into the HWT organisation when the *Sun-Herald* UCS contract (with its territoriality provision) expired in June 1923. But in preparing for the expiry of that contract, Denison and his *Sun* managing editor, Campbell Jones, had the opportunity to try to negotiate exclusive rights to content from Northcliffe's newspaper publishing empire. That foreign news was crucial to both the *Sun* and the *Herald* groups and, despite his friendship with Northcliffe, Murdoch was very

concerned that he might be cut out of any new deal. In April and
May, both sides began making their appeals to an increasingly
erratic Northcliffe. 'The Chief's' mental health was declining
dramatically, but Murdoch's letters and telegrams to Northcliffe
suggest he was quite oblivious. Even when Northcliffe sent back
increasingly odd responses, Murdoch kept outlining his business
plans in minute detail.

One of the issues that Murdoch badgered Northcliffe about
was his anxiety about Campbell Jones (who was going to be the
major competitor to Murdoch's *Evening News* project). At this time,
Campbell Jones was a brightly burning star and Murdoch was trail-
ing in his wake. The 'suave and debonair' Campbell Jones was
about eleven years older than Murdoch.[85] He had previously worked
as a private secretary to an MP before he began as a journalist, but
he and Murdoch had started their metropolitan newspaper careers
at the same time, around 1903. They had both been smart, energetic,
under-paid freelancers who were paid by the line, but the *Argus* had
recognised Campbell Jones' ability and quickly promoted him to a
political reporter, and then in 1907, to its chief of staff (with the role
of news editor added in 1909), whereas *The Age* did not appreciate
what it had in Murdoch.

The two journalists were friendly when they both reported politics in Melbourne, and it was reportedly Campbell Jones who recommended that Murdoch should take his place as the *Sun*'s Melbourne
correspondent in 1912 (when Campbell Jones went to London to
inaugurate the UCS).[86] Thereafter, Murdoch had continued following in Campbell Jones' footsteps, by stepping into his shoes as the
next head of UCS. Murdoch was about five years behind Campbell
Jones in obtaining the position of editor of a major metropolitan
newspaper. During that time, Campbell Jones had gained a formidable reputation. *Truth* later called him a 'newspaper genius' who
'made the *Sun*' with his 'shrewd far-seeing brain'.[87]

Campbell Jones had his own connections to Northcliffe and *The Times* staff from his stint heading UCS, and Murdoch warned Northcliffe that Campbell Jones was coming to London in March 1922, and said, 'Chief, don't let him … attempt to put anything over me'. Murdoch then added a rather desperate postscript; 'Please watch Campbell Jones'.[88] Twelve days later, he asked Northcliffe to 'do please warn all your people to be careful of Campbell Jones'.[89] A few weeks later, Murdoch sent Northcliffe a telegram saying: 'Campbell Jones arrives England fortnight. Regard his visit most sinister. Please prevent him doing us harm.'[90]

Campbell Jones obviously had an impact though, because Northcliffe began to push for the HWT and Sun Newspapers to work together rather than against each other over the cable negotiations. In June 1922, because of this desire on Northcliffe's part that his 'friends' should cooperate, the two companies again started talking about a potential merger, this time into a massive £1 500 000 company.[91] Northcliffe's stance was hurtful to Murdoch because it would thwart Murdoch's desire to keep apart from Denison and Campbell Jones, and to gain control of his own paper – ambitions that Northcliffe was well aware of. But such was Northcliffe's power that Murdoch fell into line and telegrammed him to say that he was 'personally quite willing and endeavouring [to] find [a] basis [to] bring companies together. Please cable views and don't leave me in lurch chief.' But Murdoch also added, 'I can do better for you than can Jones … Please treat this confidentially.'[92]

The next day, Murdoch again telegrammed Northcliffe that it was looking likely that the *Sun* and *Herald* would 'come together … Wish you would cable what is going on.' Murdoch said he would have insisted on keeping the *Evening News* separate from the merger talks 'had it not been for your cables and letters to Denison showing anxiety that he and I should work together'. Murdoch said he would 'naturally be disappointed if [I had to] abandon *Evening News* project but [I] appreciate undesirability of dividing your friends here'.[93] Murdoch's pleas for Northcliffe to respond reflected how his mentor had become an unreliable correspondent. Northcliffe had also taken to accusingly telling Murdoch that there were 'curious rumours here in London'.[94] One of Northcliffe's last replies to Murdoch had an aggressive and paranoid tone. Murdoch had been desperately sending telegrams saying that the HWT would pay more for rights to his papers, but Northcliffe had merely replied by saying, '[We] must have further particulars instantly or we must in interests of our shareholders conclude news arrangement elsewhere. Many rumours in London.'[95]

Murdoch and the others had been trying to appease a man who was suffering delusions and hallucinations. Northcliffe had been ranting, waving a loaded gun around and issuing bizarre orders. Only a few weeks after Northcliffe's last telegrams to Murdoch, he was removed from control of his papers. Murdoch finally became aware of Northcliffe's 'illness' and telegrammed his best wishes for a 'speedy recovery'.[96] That was not to be. When Northcliffe died in August 1922, unsubstantiated rumours were circulating that he had syphilis, and had been certified insane.

LORD SOUTHCLIFFE OF MELBOURNE

With Northcliffe no longer able to insist upon it, the *Sun*–HWT merger again went cold, probably due again to Murdoch's strong opposition. With that off the table, and the Sydney project thwarted, Murdoch turned back to Melbourne to buttress the *Herald* against the coming competition from Denison. He expanded its advertising department, and offered attractive advertising rates to win more ads from drapers, car dealers and cinemas. It helped significantly that, in 1920, Baillieu's niece had married Sidney Myer, owner of the famous eight-storey Myer Emporium department store in Bourke Street (which had opened six years earlier). It had become a retail giant, famous for its 'Friday specials' and Monday 'star bargains' advertised in the *Herald*. When the Myer Emporium's business expanded 'threefold between 1922 and 1925', its advertising grew accordingly.[97] So many full-page ads started appearing that wags quipped the *Herald* was simply what was printed on the back of Myer's ads.

Murdoch also bolstered the paper's populist appeal by running a beauty competition in 1922 – Northcliffe had advised that the *Herald* needed more 'stockings in the paper'[98] – as well as baby photo competitions, and placing more emphasis on crosswords, comic strips, and general interest articles, including on cinema, motoring and radio. Murdoch engaged celebrity columnists, including his friend Dame Nellie Melba (who was also a friend of Northcliffe's).

In February 1923, the *Herald* moved from its gloomy, gaol-like bluestone building on the corner of Flinders and Russell streets, into a new five-storey building that dominated Flinders and Exhibition streets (Figure 7.3). Fink had been planning the building for some time, and Baillieu had provided finance for it, and researched new printing technology.[99] Murdoch's critics, for he had already attracted some, dubbed the HWT's new home the 'Colin Ross Memorial'. Inside, copy zoomed around the building by pneumatic tube, and five enormous printing presses occupied the machine-room. Keith Murdoch's oak-lined office was on the third floor, halfway down a corridor that the staff jovially referred to as 'Toorak Road'.[100] He sat behind a large desk beneath a framed photograph of himself with Northcliffe and other luminaries in London.

The new building was a commanding base from which to win a circulation war with Denison. He had launched the morning *Sun News-Pictorial* on 11 September 1922, and then the afternoon *Evening Sun* in April 1923. For three decades, the *Herald* had reaped the benefits of its monopoly in the afternoon market. As Northcliffe enviously pointed out to Murdoch, the *Herald*'s position was 'unique in English speaking journalism – one paper for eight hundred thousand people'.[101] Now, the *Evening Sun* was shattering that unusual dominance. It was the *Herald*'s first direct competitor since the *Evening Standard*, which Baillieu and Fink had taken over and absorbed into the *Herald* in 1894. With Murdoch preoccupied in fighting this important battle for the still Melbourne-focused HWT, but perhaps also because he had a strike against him for failing to pull off the Sydney takeover, when Collins House decided to move into Adelaide, it backed Davidson to start up the *News* and News Limited in 1922–23.

Murdoch's enemies had taken to calling him 'Lord Southcliffe' for his almost slavish devotion to Northcliffe's methods, but his

FIGURE 7.3 The 'Colin Ross Memorial'; the *Herald*'s grand new building, corner of Flinders and Exhibition streets, Melbourne, 1925
SOURCE Newspix (NP1264254).

techniques were having an impact. Advertising revenue had boosted the *Herald*'s profits and, by early April 1925, its daily sales had hit a record high of 145 812.[102] By the end of 1925, its sales were up to 180 000, making it the largest circulation newspaper in Victoria.[103] As Chapter 4 explained, the *Herald* successfully ground down the pink-papered *Evening Sun*, which Denison closed in 1925 before selling its stablemate, the *Sun News-Pictorial*, to the HWT.

The *Sun News-Pictorial* was a classic example of how success has many parents while failure is an orphan. One camp of newspaper watchers credits its founding editor, Monty Grover, for the paper's stunning success. Grover was widely considered one of Australia's most brilliant journalists and editors, and had already successfully re-launched the Sydney *Sun* for Denison. He was the one who created the *Sun News-Pictorial*'s unique design and winning formula of 'striking pictures and tightly written copy'.[104] In this view, Murdoch merely built upon Grover's original blueprint.

But Murdoch's admirers, including his biographer, RM Younger, claim the paper was making only 'faltering' sales under Denison and Grover and had gained only limited advertising, and it took Murdoch's deft touch to make it into a huge success.[105] According to this view, Murdoch skilfully retained elements of the paper's original flair but added a sense of the big issues and serious news so that it evolved from being a paper for frivolous flappers – lightweight reading only suitable for a train ride home and then thrown away – into a family newspaper that had 'just the right appeal for sober, domesticated Melbourne'.[106] Meanwhile, Lloyd Dumas, who was the paper's editor under Grover, credited himself for this transformation before the HWT even took over the paper. Dumas claimed he was the one who took the paper beyond Grover's 'bright flippant stuff' and gave it depth and stronger news coverage.[107] Dumas continued as editor after the HWT took over the *Sun News-Pictorial*, and Murdoch gave him significant credit for the paper achieving a

50 per cent increase in circulation in its first eighteen months in the HWT stable.[108]

Whoever deserves the most credit, the HWT now had two daily papers in its stable. The more serious broadsheet *Herald* was influential. It was the paper of which Murdoch was most proud, and which commanded his main interest. But the lighter, entertainment-driven tabloid *Sun News-Pictorial* was leaping ahead in circulation, growing an average of 20 per cent each year between 1926 and 1928, compared to the *Herald*'s modest 2 per cent.[109] By repelling the Sydney invader and acquiring such a valuable asset, Murdoch's place in the newspaper industry had been established and his authority enhanced. The HWT board had already made Murdoch managing editor in March 1924, a role that raised his status and gave him the combined powers of editor-in-chief and general manager. Because Fink intended that his youngest son Thorold would become HWT chairman when he retired, Fink had insisted that the board also approve Thorold's appointment as a director. His determination to secure the chairmanship for his son would pit Fink against Murdoch in an internal power struggle that would last for another eighteen years.[110]

Aside from Murdoch's power within the HWT, his small shareholding in the company and Baillieu's support on its board, Murdoch also shared Baillieu's vision of an interstate newspaper chain for the HWT, of the type that Northcliffe had established in the United Kingdom, and Hearst was building in the United States. Because Fink had not shared that ambition, Baillieu had been pursuing it separately from the HWT, through Davidson and News Limited, since 1922. But after Murdoch had proved himself in battle against Denison, Baillieu's confidence in him was growing.

In his first five years at the HWT, Murdoch had overseen its expansion from a company that centred around two newspapers, the *Herald* and the *Weekly Times*, to a stable of publications that also included the valuable *Sun News-Pictorial*, the popular bi-weekly pink-papered *Sporting Globe*, the weekly radio publication *Listener In*, the home decorating magazine *Australian Home Beautiful*, and *Table Talk*, which the HWT had turned into a vapid social magazine. (*Table Talk* closed in 1939. Murdoch's magic touch was less reliable when it came to magazines.) Murdoch had also eliminated newspaper competitors by killing off Denison's *Evening Sun* in 1925, and he would soon defeat the two-year-old, in-debt *Morning Post*, which would be absorbed into the *Sun News-Pictorial* in 1927. Baillieu was ready to give Murdoch another chance – not in Sydney, where the market was tough and there was no longer a defensive need, but in Perth, where there were golden opportunities.

UNWELCOME INVADERS IN PERTH

In 1926, WS Robinson was in London when he heard through his impeccable business sources that a paper which claimed to be Australia's second oldest newspaper, the *West Australian*, would soon be up for sale.[111] Baillieu and Robinson engaged Murdoch to lead a syndicate to purchase the influential paper from the Hackett estate. Baillieu had offered Fink, who was warming to the idea of interstate expansion, a chance for the HWT to be part of the syndicate. Fink even travelled to Perth in late June 1926 to investigate and make a valuation of the paper, but he decided against involving the HWT.[112]

The remaining syndicate members – Baillieu, Robinson and Murdoch – formed a public company called West Australian Newspapers Limited (WAN). Baillieu and Robinson put up all of the funds, as Murdoch did not have enough money to contribute financially. Murdoch was instead given 'a substantial number of shares' in the new company in return for organising and managing it.[113] (This is the same deal that Davidson seems to have been given for 'founding' News Limited.) WAN took over the *West Australian* on 1 July 1926, paying a premium price for the valuable asset of ten times its net annual earnings.[114] BHAS' managing director, Colin Fraser, one of the key figures at Collins House, also bought up shares.[115] Fraser had seen a confidential report on the *West Australian* prepared for Collins House executives. The report noted that the newspaper was 'the only morning paper' in metropolitan Perth, and reportedly had the highest circulation, in ratio to population, 'in the British empire'.[116]

The report's conclusion was that, because the *West Australian* was 'the leading press organ of the State ... *the paper may shape, and bring to fruition, practically any reasonable public policy desired by its directors*' (italics added).[117] This statement neatly gets to the crux of what newspaper ownership was about for an industrial complex like Collins House; using a monopoly newspaper to manipulate public and political debate in order to achieve public policies that its directors desired. As Western Australia was a state rich with mining opportunities, there were many public policies that Collins House wanted to 'bring to fruition', including mining leases, state subsidies and concessions, industrial support and access to cheap government infrastructure. The syndicate now had the most powerful voice in the state.

Baillieu and Robinson were aware that there would be local concern when Melbourne businessmen swooped in to take over such an important Perth cultural institution. The *West Australian* had been a vital part of the city's history and development, and its editor and owner, Sir John Winthrop Hackett, had been one of the state's most important figures. Baillieu suggested that any of the new shares in WAN that were not taken up by interests in London should be allocated to applicants from Western Australia in order to 'water down the impression of eastern Australia control' of the company.[118] And Murdoch duly arranged for locals to act as the directors of WAN while he managed its business side, and the syndicate pulled strings in the background.[119]

The respected Perth locals who were signed up as directors included knights and double-barrelled surnames with prestige in Perth. Sir Alfred Langler was a *West Australian* journalist who had loyally served Winthrop Hackett. General Sir Joseph Talbot Hobbs was an architect and well-respected military leader who had served at Gallipoli. Horace Benson Jackson was a lawyer who became a King's Counsel in 1930, and was on many corporate boards. Henry Percy Downing was a Perth solicitor. By 1927, Robinson was also officially on the board of directors, Langler retired, and HB Jackson became WAN's chairman. Jackson had the standard credentials required of a Collins House director – he was the director of companies that were allied to, or reliant upon, Collins House; including shipping, transport, financial services and investment funds. Jackson later became the founding chairman of a coal mining company that supplied coal to the state's gold mining industry, which, by then, was led by Robinson.

Despite the syndicate's best efforts, at a board meeting in February 1927, a shareholder asked whether it was true that 'the controlling interests in the company have been transferred to Eastern States financiers?'.[120] The chair evaded the question but the issue of non-local control continued to bubble away. Probably to mollify such concerns, in 1930, Robinson formally resigned from WAN's board after he had founded Gold Mines of Australia in Western Australia. But this was purely for appearance. Robinson was still listed as a director but offered his services 'for free'.[121] The paper's dynamic managing editor, Charles Patrick (CP) Smith, was appointed as Robinson's official replacement. Smith had shaken up the 'stuffy', 'club-like' atmosphere of the *West Australian* and made changes to the paper's layout and content while still preserving its 'sober appearance' and conservative reputation.[122] Smith and Murdoch had been political reporters covering federal parliament in Melbourne at the same time. Both had been friends of Hughes', and the two had crossed paths at Gallipoli when Smith was a war correspondent and Murdoch visited.

Robinson remained an unpaid, but highly influential, director of the paper for another seven years as his interests in WA expanded. In 1933, he formed the gold mining company Western Mining Corporation (WMC), with Colin Fraser as its founding chairman, then the Gold Exploration and Finance Company of Australia in 1934. These companies were based in Collins House but backed by substantial foreign capital from the United States, the United Kingdom and South Africa. WMC became the dominant player in the gold mining industry in Western Australia and, in its seventy-two years, mined more gold than any other company in Australia.

In 1931, questions about non-local control re-emerged when WAN tried to impose some Victorian HWT-style industrial techniques on its operations. Under Winthrop Hackett, the *West Australian* had recognised union labour and was said to have been the first company in Perth to introduce the eight-hour day. The paper's staff included active members of the PIEU who, in 1927, had undertaken a week-long strike timed for maximum effect during the Duke and Duchess of York's visit to Perth. When an industrial agreement expired in July 1931, WAN and News Limited (owner of Perth's afternoon *Daily News*, another Collins House–allied paper) gave notice that they would be cutting wages by 15 per cent to accord with lower wages in the Eastern states.[123] This led to another strike and renewed claims of Eastern state interference. The *Westralian Worker* claimed that both papers were controlled by Victorian interests intent on wage reduction in the state, and that local directors made 'frequent journeys ... to Melbourne ... to receive instructions'.[124]

In response, a straight-faced Jackson argued that he had 'never' seen any interference from outside the state, and claimed that WAN's share register showed that 75 per cent of its shares were held in Western Australia.[125] Anyone who knew the corporate creativity of Collins House, and the vital difference between share ownership and control, would have taken this claim with a grain of salt. The claim does seem to have been met with some scepticism, because in 1933 the company was still on the defensive. Murdoch and the Melbourne interests behind the *West Australian* were criticised, including in the independent *Sunday Times*.[126] But WAN now claimed that 89 per cent of its 1220 shareholders were resident in Western Australia, and that 65 per cent of the shares' values belonged to WA residents.[127]

Several of Murdoch's biographers have accepted that, at around this time, the syndicate left Western Australia. Geoffrey Serle wrote that 'Murdoch abandoned direct control [of the *West Australian*] by the early 1930s and disposed of the syndicate's interest'.[128] However, there is good reason to suspect that Collins House – if not Murdoch – continued to control, or at least heavily influence, WAN for years to come. Robinson stayed on the WAN board (gratis) until August 1937.[129] And the directors appointed by the original syndicate to represent Collins House's interests remained on the board for decades. HB Jackson remained chair until 1952, and CP Smith remained managing editor/director until 1951.

Western Australian gold mining was more a Robinson project than a Baillieu one, and it is possible that Murdoch departed in the early 1930s to focus on Baillieu-led projects in other states, while Robinson remained involved at the *West Australian*. Robinson preferred to do things quietly, and he was extremely good at staying out of the public eye. Aside from being a titan of the financial and mining worlds, for nearly forty years Robinson worked behind the scenes as a grey eminence, adviser and confidant to Australian and British political leaders, including Billy Hughes, Lloyd George, Menzies, Chamberlain, Churchill, Curtin, Chifley and Evatt. He was often behind the news, but rarely in it. So important was

Robinson during World War II, he was almost 'a secret service man, for whom no barrier or visa or permit existed'.[130]

Humphrey McQueen described Robinson as 'the most important individual in Australian political and economic life for 30 years after 1915 and possibly for the entire century'.[131] But he was not at all well known publicly because Robinson refused all offers of honours and accolades, and avoided on-the-record interviews. Reporters called him a 'silent colossus' and 'the sphinx of zinc'.[132] By contrast, Robinson's friend Murdoch was becoming a public figure and drawing unwanted attention by 1932. Murdoch's role in Joe Lyons' defection from Labor and ascension to prime minister (described in Chapters 10 and 11) had attracted attention. So had Murdoch's involvement in a series of newspaper takeovers across the country. Labour newspapers had begun to talk about 'the Murdoch press', and Robinson may well have judged it best to avoid such associations in the crucial state of Western Australia.[133]

One case study that seems to confirm that WAN *was* no longer under Murdoch's control by 1933, is the *West Australian*'s reporting of the Lyons government's Budget that year. Lyons had awarded Murdoch a knighthood in 1933, of which he was immensely proud. During parliamentary debate on the Budget, Labor MPs had made disparaging remarks characterising Murdoch's knighthood as a 'quid pro quo' for installing Lyons in power. Those remarks were *not* reported in the Murdoch-controlled newspapers, but they *were* reported in the *West Australian* even though Murdoch's friend Robinson was still a board member and a major influence at the paper.[134] It therefore seems the mining magnate, in this case, had more respect for editorial independence than the celebrated journalist who so often spoke about the need for a newspaper to report all sides of an issue without fear or favour.

Once both of Perth's daily papers were controlled by Collins House from 1926 (the *Daily News* through News Limited, and the

West Australian through WAN), they jointly campaigned for a gold bounty. For years, the gold mining interests had been lobbying the federal government to pay a subsidy to mines to stimulate the search for gold. In December 1930, the Scullin Labor government agreed to pay a subsidy of £1 per ounce of gold (close to a 25 per cent bonus). This was a 'windfall' for Western Australian mining, especially in Kalgoorlie.[135] When it was announced, the other major figure in the region's gold mining, Claude de Bernales – a flamboyant man who lacked Robinson's cautious approach to publicity – made a big show of publicly thanking the newspapers. He declared 'the Press, as a whole, deserves the thanks of the gold industry' but particularly the 'foundation support accorded' by the *West Australian* 'backed up wholeheartedly' by the *Daily News*.[136]

Murdoch had learned a great deal from the poor reception his takeover received in Perth, and in future he would be far more careful about the appearance of local control. But he seemed quite happy to cede the troublesome territory of WA to the Robinson gold interests. In 1935, only a few years after he took control of News Limited, Murdoch sold its economically sluggish Perth *Daily News* to WAN.[137] WAN appointed Robinson's close friend, James Macartney, as its editor. Macartney quickly 'lifted the paper's standing and almost doubled its sales'.[138] In 1951, he was promoted to managing editor of WAN. Robinson had remained influential within WAN, and kept up his friendship with Macartney into the 1950s.[139]

THROUGH A SIDE DOOR IN ADELAIDE

With Baillieu's support, Murdoch was appointed to fill a vacancy on the HWT board in December 1928, and given the status of managing director, giving Fink additional reason to fear and resent Murdoch's growing power within the organisation. But after the Perth venture, Murdoch had some of his own money to invest, and was keen to strike out more independently of the HWT. He set off for Brisbane in 1928, where John Wren sold him a share of his *Daily Mail*. Wren was a notorious Victorian millionaire and reputed former gangster. The target of Protestant moralisers had made his fortune through illicit dealings, including illegal bookmaking.

In the aftermath of the land boom bust, Wren had founded the Collingwood Tote in Melbourne, in 1893. At a time when off-course gambling was prohibited, the Tote was a well-fortified yard behind a shopfront where workers could illegally place shilling bets with hooded cashiers. Wren turned it into a gambling empire before the state government forced its closure in 1907. He was a very unlikely partner for Murdoch, a man who was so strait-laced and committed to Presbyterian morals that he was considered a prude. This surprising investment was left to one side for several years while Murdoch turned his attention to South Australia on another mission for the much more respectable Baillieu (whose own scandals during the land boom period had been so well concealed).

Baillieu and Murdoch established another syndicate in 1928, and this time Fink and the HWT participated as well. Fink had come to accept that the HWT, with its large cash reserve, needed to expand or it would be left behind. Collins House had already ventured into four states via News Limited (New South Wales, South Australia, Western Australia and, unsuccessfully, Tasmania). It was also in Western Australia through WAN. Even Murdoch was forging his own small holding in Queensland. But Fink was probably also encouraged by a separate, non-newspaper, corporate expansion. Myer's department store was making its first interstate move, taking over the Adelaide department store Marshalls in Rundle Street, which it renovated and re-opened as the Myer Emporium in October 1928.

The HWT was not far behind its largest advertiser, arriving in Adelaide only two months after Myer opened. In December 1928, the HWT-allied syndicate, headed by Murdoch, bought South Australia's oldest paper, the antiquated and moribund *Register*. Murdoch's strategy was to purchase the weakest point in the market, in order to get to the syndicate's real target – the healthy and influential *Advertiser*. When he became a co-director of the *Register* in 1928, its circulation was down to a sickly 14 000, and it was in financial difficulties.[140] Murdoch and Fink installed one of the HWT's brightest journalists, Sydney Deamer, to overhaul the ailing paper and lift its circulation. They turned it into a pictorial, put in larger advertisements, and began reporting more sensational topics, including divorces and abortion cases (previously the domain of *Truth*). Then they slashed its cover price to one penny. As intended, all of this activity scared the *Advertiser*'s ageing owner, the octogenarian Sir Langdon Bonython (who had also been its editor for forty-four years), into quickly selling a controlling interest to the HWT syndicate only a few weeks later, in January 1929, for the princely sum of £1 million.

The newly formed company that took over the *Advertiser* had four main shareholders: the HWT (40 per cent), Baillieu (36 per cent), and Fink and Murdoch (who both had 12 per cent).[141] As with the *West Australian* syndicate, Murdoch had no cash to invest and was granted his stake for his role in managing the venture.[142] Murdoch appointed the talented Lloyd Dumas (who claimed credit for the *Sun News-Pictorial*'s success) to be the managing editor of the *Advertiser*. Parroting the advice that Northcliffe had given him as a new editor, Murdoch told Dumas to inject 'romance, mystery [and] crime', as well as 'excitement and sensation … suited to the popular taste' in order to build up circulation.[143]

Dumas had followed a career path that was uncannily close to Murdoch's. He had been a federal politics reporter, a former Hughes publicist (a paid position in Dumas' case), and head of the UCS. After Murdoch appointed him at the *Advertiser* in 1929, Dumas remained there as the paper's editor, then managing director, and finally, chairman of its board, until his retirement in 1967. He exercised a strong influence over South Australian politics and, especially in his early years at the paper, Murdoch watched over Dumas' shoulder and gave directions and advice. We know a good deal about this because Dumas' personal papers (including letters to and from Murdoch) were donated to the National Library. Dumas was one of several former editors who left behind important documents, presumably so that history could document what they could not record through their journalism.

When Dumas took up his post at the *Advertiser* in August 1929, the future was looking extremely bright for the HWT. Murdoch had extended its reach and influence, and also made it a great deal of money. Its profits had increased nearly tenfold in ten years, and it had more than £200 000 in reserves.[144] In June 1929, it had confidently leapt into radio and became the first newspaper company to buy its own fully owned radio station, 3DB in Melbourne. But, in October 1929, just months after Dumas took charge in Adelaide, the American stock market collapsed. During the ensuing Depression, circulation for the HWT papers, including the *Herald* and the *Sun News-Pictorial*, began to stall and they faced a severe advertising downturn.[145] At one stage, the *Herald* was halved in size as a way of dealing with the financial crisis.[146]

Rather than being discouraged, Baillieu, Murdoch and the rest of the HWT board viewed the depressed business conditions as an opportunity. Firstly, they could do some housekeeping. With the *Advertiser* safely in the HWT stable, the *Register* was no longer needed. During 1930, it was reduced to a thin, sensationalist pictorial, then, citing the effects of the Depression, Murdoch closed it in February 1931. (One older journalist who lost his job at such a desperate time committed suicide.)[147] With the *Register* gone, the *Advertiser* was now in a monopoly position as the only morning paper in Adelaide. Its circulation, profits and influence were immediately boosted.[148]

The Depression also provided an opportunity to profit from the misfortune of other papers. As *Truth* had quipped in 1927, the *Herald* was an 'abnormally rich' newspaper.[149] As Melbourne's only evening newspaper, by 1928, the *Herald* was carrying two-thirds of all the display advertising published in Melbourne newspapers.[150] Its parent company had large reserves and immensely wealthy backers, and it quickly rebounded from its size cut and advertising woes. Other papers were not so fortunate. Rising costs, declining advertising revenue, and Depression-era effects that lingered for years, made them vulnerable prey. By picking off the best targets, the HWT would emerge from this period, in Fink's words, 'a gigantic corporation'.[151]

CHAPTER 8

KEITH MURDOCH: NEWSPAPER OWNER

While Keith Murdoch was building up an empire for Collins House and the HWT, he also had another plan. To achieve true 'independence in the use of power', he wanted to be a major newspaper owner in his own right.[1] Two newspapers were crucial to this personal project. The first was the Adelaide *News*. Murdoch had his eye on Davidson's paper for years before he was able to bring it within the HWT fold, and this would prove to be only a first step. Later, in the late 1940s, Murdoch would claim News Limited for himself.

The second crucial paper was the *Courier-Mail*, which Murdoch created in 1933 by merging two existing Brisbane papers. This was as close as Murdoch would get to starting a daily paper, and this was something of a sore point. Although he was the preeminent newspaper empire builder in Australia, Murdoch's critics liked to point out that he never took the risk of starting a paper from scratch (as Northcliffe, Davidson, Denison and Grover had done). Murdoch's business strategy was to buy existing newspapers, reduce their staff numbers and overhead costs, and carry them on (the *Sun News-Pictorial* and the *Advertiser*); or he closed papers (the *Register* and the *Morning Post*); or, in the case of the *Courier-Mail*, amalgamated them. *Smith's Weekly*, one of Murdoch's harshest critics, described him as a 'newspaper cuckoo ... he has perched always in a nest already well-feathered'.[2]

Originality was not Murdoch's priority. His grand plan was to create a newspaper chain that was separate from the HWT, and could be left as a legacy to his son, Rupert. In the 1930s, even as he continued to consolidate his power at the HWT, Murdoch pursued this separate, personal goal, with the help of the Baillieus, WS Robinson, and a new partner, John Wren. As mentioned in Chapter 7, Wren was a notorious reputed gangster whose 'dirty' money and underworld connections had to be kept hidden from the newspaper-reading public.

TAKING OVER NEWS LIMITED FOR THE HWT

Once Murdoch had control of the *Advertiser* in 1929, Collins House had a stranglehold on Adelaide's daily press through two different vehicles. News Limited (under Davidson) had the *News*, while Murdoch and the HWT had the *Register* (until its closure in 1931) and the *Advertiser*. But Murdoch wanted to be in complete control of Collins House's Adelaide project. As noted in Chapter 6, he had taken a step closer to the *News* in 1929 when he organised a share swap between the *Advertiser* and News Limited, supposedly as a mutual protection pact against any potential invaders from Sydney. Then, after Davidson's death in June 1930, Murdoch quickly began negotiating to buy the shares that Davidson had left to his heirs. But his biggest coup came at the end of 1930. Telling Dumas to 'keep this under your hat', Murdoch confided that he was negotiating with the Baillieus over their shares in News Limited and was confident that 'We [the HWT group] will emerge, I am sure, with complete control'.[3]

Murdoch told Dumas on 2 January 1931 that: 'We have reached a verbal agreement with the Baillieus to take over their 31,000 shares of News Limited at 11/6[d]'.[4] This was a bargain price, only a quarter of the market value of the shares a year earlier.[5] Murdoch said: '[The Baillieu shares] give us absolute control of the *News*, if everything goes through'. But he had one worry: 'I am not quite confident yet that [AE] Clarkson [chairman of News Limited, and associated with Collins House's BALM] will toe the line. If I were he, I would make every effort to avoid doing so.'[6] Dumas reassured Murdoch that Clarkson would not make trouble and, in fact, 'it will be a real relief to him if you take control'.[7] Clarkson must indeed have cheerfully acquiesced to the takeover because Murdoch retained him as News Limited's chairman until Clarkson's (presumed) death in 1936, when he disappeared at sea.[8]

But even with Clarkson's cooperation, Murdoch still had another obstacle to overcome. The *Advertiser*'s 150 000 ordinary shares in News Limited, provided as part of the share swap in mid-1929, did not have voting rights attached. Now the Depression gave Murdoch the leverage he needed to change that. News Limited was in financial trouble and was unable to meet mortgage debentures or pay preference dividends to its shareholders. Murdoch allowed the *Advertiser* and the HWT to step in and pay News Limited's commitments, but in return he successfully demanded voting rights for the *Advertiser*'s shares. With the help of David Gilbert (News Limited's general manager), News Limited's articles were quietly amended at a shareholder meeting in January 1931. They did not anticipate any trouble from greedy, unobservant shareholders. Or, as Dumas put it to Murdoch, 'As you know, most shareholders are apathetic when it comes to … matters … unaffecting dividends'.[9]

As expected, Dumas reported that the chair made a 'carefully worded [statement that] disclosed nothing … [and] passed over the [conferring of full voting rights to the shares] as though it were a routine reciprocal arrangement'.[10] The *Advertiser*'s shareholder meeting was equally uneventful. Only one shareholder turned up.

He 'said nothing' and 'the whole thing was over in two minutes'. Dumas had no intention of informing the public about the news-worthy event. He told Murdoch, 'We [the *Advertiser*] do not propose to publish any reference to the meetings'.[11]

Once the articles were changed, the HWT group held more than half the shares (and voting power) in News Limited. This meant that Murdoch had won actual control of the *News*, and with that, now had monopoly control of the daily press in Adelaide. He had also picked up News Limited's other papers: the weekly *Mail* in Adelaide, the *Daily News* in Perth, the *Barrier Miner* in Broken Hill, New South Wales, and the Port Pirie *Recorder* in South Australia. In addition, because News Limited held 114 000 shares in the *Advertiser*, the HWT had tightened its grip on the *Advertiser* and now held nearly two-thirds of its shares.[12] The takeover was important news with significant implications for Australia's corporate and political affairs. But four newspaper editors conspired to censor the news.

News Limited's general manager, Gilbert, was also managing director of its *Daily News* in Perth, where locals were so touchy about 'foreign' ownership, and where Collins House had already tried to hide Melbourne control of the *West Australian*. Dumas told Murdoch that:

> Gilbert is rather anxious that nothing should be published in West Australia. He says that news of the pending change of control has reached Perth. He thinks that we should take special steps to prevent any publication there. He is passing full information on to 'The Daily News' with instructions to publish nothing, and he asks that we do the same to 'The West Australian'. I thought perhaps you would prefer to write the note to Charlie Smith [editor of the *West Australian*] yourself. A letter written after you return from Sydney would reach Perth on Friday morning, in time to prevent any publication the following day.[13]

So much for impartial, independent reporting. Between them, Murdoch, Dumas, Gilbert and Smith censored five daily Australian newspapers. But industry insiders still noticed that the HWT had a new grip on Adelaide. In March 1931, the PIEU federal advocate G McGrath made a statement in the Arbitration Court saying that the HWT had taken control of Adelaide's newspapers and would have closed the *Register* whether there was a Depression or not. Murdoch was incensed and told Dumas that 'these statements do us incalculable harm'. He reported that he had a 'stormy scene' with McGrath.[14]

Murdoch could exercise a fascinating double-think about such matters. He was actively suppressing knowledge of the HWT take-over of the *Advertiser* and the *News*, but he was furious that anyone would suggest he was doing so. Murdoch wrote to his friend, the *Advertiser*'s chairman, Fred Downer, that: 'What I resent and feel damaging and most reprehensible is his statement that the Mel-bourne *Herald* and the Adelaide *Advertiser* are owned by a "money group" whose ramifications extend throughout the commercial world, and who use their newspapers to support their commercial interests'.[15] But it was an entirely accurate characterisation. Murdoch had promoted many Collins House ventures in the papers he controlled, but considered himself a patriot, and probably viewed his promotion of mining activities, aircraft manufacturing, banking, paper manufacturing and other ventures, to be in the national interest. The suggestion that his activities might really have been about commercial gain, or that he was acting on behalf of self-interested industrialists, seems to have deeply offended him.

Murdoch and Dumas kept tabs on Labor politicians' 'attacks' on the HWT's dominance.[16] Murdoch wanted any negative comments to be nipped in the bud immediately. In May 1931, he told Dumas to forward any criticism of 'our enterprises in Adelaide' that appeared in *Smith's Weekly* or anywhere else, including any 'public expressions of hostility'.[17] In April, Dumas, Downer and the *Advertiser* had put out a statement to 'place on [the public] record our complete independence from all outside interference'.[18] In Dumas' private papers, this is ironically tucked in between multiple letters from Murdoch directing Dumas about how to revamp the *Advertiser*, and how it should cover politics and other news. Murdoch reminded Dumas in 1932 that, politically, their respective papers needed to 'step in line', and when he felt Dumas had shown too much independence, tartly reprimanded him by saying that 'I hope our Adelaide paper has not been committed to any policy without consultation with Melbourne'.[19]

Although, on paper, Murdoch had the numbers to control News Limited as well, he was finding it more difficult in practice and that needed to change. In October 1931, he wrote to Dumas that he would soon be in Adelaide, and 'My main purpose in coming across … is to get hold of the *News*'. Murdoch asked Dumas to arrange a meeting for him with 'Jimmy Goss[e]' (James Hay Gosse, a News Limited director), as 'I don't want to chatter to him at a Club or hotel, but to have a straight talk'.[20] Only weeks later, Murdoch joined the board of News Limited. One of his first orders of business was to get rid of the *News*' editor, Horace Yelland, who had been a friend of Davidson's.

News Limited 'sold' Yelland the Port Pirie *Recorder*. The *Recorder* had not been making money for some time, as the Depression years had hit Port Pirie hard.[21] Low demand for metals had seen the BHAS smelter retrench hundreds of workers and slash the hours of most of those remaining. Politically, the paper was still valuable though, and Collins House needed it to be in the hands of someone sympathetic to BHAS' position. Like Davidson, Yelland was a journalist with a background in mining (the son of a mining engineer), who was somehow able to afford to purchase a newspaper from the company he worked for. Yelland was described as running the *Recorder* as a 'private person' and its 'sole director', but it is possible that he received a similar deal to Davidson and Murdoch (that shares were provided to him as payment for managing the paper and, in his case, for keeping quiet and out of Murdoch's way). It is not known if this is the case, but it is clear that Murdoch kept a close eye on the town that was so important to Collins House. Six months after selling the *Recorder* to Yelland, Murdoch was investigating buying Port Pirie's radio station (5PI), and in 1933, Murdoch and Dumas did arrange for the *Advertiser* to purchase the station (Chapter 13).

CONSOLIDATING POWER

Once the HWT was in control of News Limited, Murdoch had forged the largest national media empire in Australian history, and unlike Denison's fleeting empire – which had closed five newspapers during 1931, and was falling apart – the one Murdoch had built for the HWT had stability despite the biting impact of the Depression.

When Murdoch had arrived at the *Herald* ten years earlier, the HWT had just one daily newspaper. It now had six across four states. Aside from the *Herald* and *Sun News-Pictorial* in Melbourne, it controlled the only morning and afternoon dailies in Adelaide (the *Advertiser* and the *News*), the only afternoon paper in Perth (the *Daily News*), and the *Barrier Miner* (in New South Wales). Murdoch was still influencing the *West Australian* at this stage, and also had a personal stake in the *Daily Mail* in Queensland. The HWT stable also included magazines, weekly newspapers and other publications, plus the increasingly important medium of radio. It controlled 5AD in Adelaide (through the *Advertiser*), as well as 3DB in Melbourne. In Perth, the *West Australian* was broadcasting the only news bulletins on 6ML (one of the two Perth radio stations, soon to be owned by the *West Australian*). By the end of 1931, Murdoch was the most powerful newspaper executive in the country, and he used that power to help install Joe Lyons as prime minister (Chapters 10 and 11).

With Yelland removed, Murdoch was able to appoint his chief of staff, EG Bonney, as the editor-in-chief of the *News*. The independently minded Bonney found Adelaide dull and stiflingly conservative. It was, 'he complained, ruled from the Adelaide Club'[22] (Dumas was a member, and so was Gosse). Bonney only lasted about five years in Adelaide.

Murdoch appointed the former financial editor of the *Herald*, Harold Burston, general manager of News Limited. An expert on finance, Burston was extremely well connected. A golfer, member of the Athenaeum Club, and honorary treasurer of the Savage Club, he was 'the confidant of bankers and business leaders in every Australian capital', and a friend to Cabinet ministers and other political leaders.[23] In 1934, Burston privately asked Dumas for the *Advertiser*/HWT to place some of its News Limited shares into his name because he couldn't afford to buy shares himself but thought it would 'look well on the register' to 'the eyes of ordinary shareholders'. Dumas told Murdoch it was a good idea as 'it would be another small thread tying him to us'.[24]

News Limited's strong interest in the town where the company had been conceived continued. In 1933, Murdoch sent one of his most promising 'young men', John (Jack) Williams, out to the *Barrier Miner* in Broken Hill. Working on the 'boss' paper' in a union-stronghold town was an excellent testing ground for a budding newspaper executive, and Williams relished the challenge before being recalled to Melbourne two years later for promotion. He later said that Broken Hill had been the happiest and most satisfying period of his career.[25] Another promising young reporter, Colin Bednall, began as a first-year cadet at the *News* in 1932.

Williams and Bednall would both become important executives working under Murdoch, rivalling each other – and Dumas – for Murdoch's favour. Bednall later wrote in his unpublished autobiography that Murdoch 'protected his own position by keeping his lieutenants fearful and even in loathing of one another'.[26]

While distributing his talented staff around the country, Murdoch had also paid attention to the new national capital of Canberra. He wanted to build the *Herald*'s credibility in political matters, but also boost his own knowledge and influence over what was going on in federal politics. When federal parliament opened in 1927, he sent AH O'Connor, Neville Smith, and the talented future *Herald* editor, RC (Cecil) Edwards. In early 1929, Murdoch appointed the ambitious Joe Alexander to head the *Herald* bureau in the parliamentary press gallery. Alexander acted as Murdoch's 'eyes and ears' at parliament, but also as his lobbyist and 'occasional assassin'.[27] Alexander not only reported politics, he played it, and was instrumental in helping Murdoch gain influence over Joe Lyons.

By 1933, Murdoch's influence as the head of the spreading HWT empire was attracting criticism, and not just from the Labor side of politics. With Murdoch's support, Dumas had been backing Lionel Hill's economically conservative Parliamentary Labor Party in South Australia, which consisted of members who had been expelled from the Australian Labor Party. Dumas was trying to form a National Party by uniting Hill's members with the Liberal Federation. Murdoch told Dumas, 'It would be a merciful relief to us all if [Hill] could be soundly linked up with the other side',[28] but the Liberals had refused and united instead with the Country Party. Campaigning for the Liberal and Country League in March 1933, Archie Cameron (who wrote the marvellously rude letter to Dumas described in Chapter 5), told a crowd at Morgan that 'The *Advertiser* and the *News* have the same shareholders … the *Advertiser* is one of a chain of 11 or 12 newspapers in nearly every state which carry out the same policy … the *Advertiser* is out to smash the Liberal and Country League … [It wants] a weak-kneed Government which will do what the *Advertiser* wants.'[29]

Murdoch and the HWT papers were throwing their weight around politically but Murdoch still had less control than he wanted at News Limited. Fed up with what he described as 'the daily nuisance of listening to and wheedling [News Limited's] minority directors', Murdoch wanted 'an absolute and undisputed control' rather than just 'a control based on minority interests'.[30] He wanted enough shares to have 'decisive', 'unquestioned' control, to be able to 'change the Board' and so 'prevent fighting'.[31] Murdoch was hunting to buy 'a large parcel' of shares in News Limited in order to obtain that 'clear majority' for the HWT, but he was also building up a personal stake in the company. He held 3100 News Limited shares in his own name in 1933–34.[32] The Baillieus were still large shareholders in the company and one of WL Baillieu's brothers, sharebroker Maurice Howard Lawrence ('Jac'), helped Murdoch acquire News Limited shares and offered to 'carry' Murdoch so he could purchase more. Murdoch confided to Dumas that 'I have not the cash and do not want to owe money again' but he kept a close eye on the *News* and kept building up his stake throughout the 1930s and 1940s, including by selling HWT shares to pay for more News Limited shares.[33] Building up a legacy for his son, Rupert, became so important to Murdoch that he overcame his aversion to debt. As he worked towards building up a controlling stake in two major daily newspapers, Murdoch ended up owing substantial sums of money by the time of his death.

GANGSTERS, GAMBLING AND
GOLD IN QUEENSLAND

In 1933, two very different men, Murdoch and John Wren, amalgamated two very different Brisbane newspapers: the sports-focused, Labor-oriented *Daily Mail* (which Wren had owned since 1915, and Murdoch had been an investor in since 1928), and the older, more conservative *Brisbane Courier* (which Murdoch had recently prised from its owners). The two papers were fierce rivals and had been battling it out in the morning market for thirty years. Exhausted by their competition, both were still suffering the effects of the Depression loss of advertising revenue, but the *Daily Mail* was doing better financially because it was propped up by profits from Wren's racecourses. Without the benefit of such largesse, the *Courier* had become attractive prey for Murdoch, who had been trying to acquire it ever since he had bought into Wren's *Daily Mail*.

The opportunity to gain control of the *Courier* had begun in 1930, with the death in London of its largest shareholder, a sixty-nine-year-old widow named Eugenia Marion Withers. Withers had inherited the principal interest in the *Courier* from her father, EIC Browne, a Queensland politician and founder of the Brisbane Newspaper Company Ltd. She had been an absentee owner for over two decades, and the subject of high society gossip and scandalous press attention herself back in 1895, when she was named in divorce proceedings for having committed adultery.[34] It took more than two years from the time of Withers' death, but Murdoch finally convinced the trustee company representing her heirs to sell him her controlling interest in the *Courier* for a cheap price.[35] Murdoch and Wren then formed a new company, Queensland Newspapers Pty Ltd, incorporated in August 1933, to merge the two papers into one, named the *Courier-Mail*.

Murdoch's scandalous partner was well hidden in all of these transactions. Wren's name never appeared in company records for Queensland Newspapers,[36] and definitely not in public announcements or publicity. His shares were held in the name of his investment company, CWL Pty Ltd. This was how Wren commonly ran his businesses: by using his investment company or his associates' names. His ownership of the *Daily Mail* had already been concealed for more than a decade behind his friend, the *Daily Mail*'s manager, Norman White, who acted as Wren's nominee.[37] White had been promised £1000 simply for holding Wren's shares in his name, an effective way of guaranteeing his loyalty.[38]

Wren knew that he lacked the moral stature to be an acceptable owner for a respectable daily newspaper. Back in Victoria in the late 1890s to early 1900s, he had grown rich by facilitating illegal off-course betting through the Collingwood Tote. Because Wren had opened up gambling to those who could not afford to go to the races, he was popular among sections of the working class. He was also known for his generosity to the Catholic church, strikers and the needy. But Wren also had a sleazy reputation, with accusations of bribery of police and politicians, corruption, horserace–fixing and standover tactics. He was very influential within the Labor Party, where he allegedly financed Labor politicians, and where his involvement was accompanied by accusations of branch stacking, ballot rigging and intimidation. Wren had a long history of back-room dealings with authorities and had developed a reputation for being a master of political influence and an astute political 'fixer'. He was a man who could make political events happen – or not happen – simply by placing a phone call.[39]

Wren's reputation as an alleged gangster is more difficult to assess. He was a kingpin in industries that were closely linked with criminal activity, including gambling, horseracing, hotels and the liquor industry, but he was not prosecuted for any major crimes (critics suggested that bribery and his political influence protected him). His supporters claimed he was a victim of sectarian prejudice. As a Catholic and a champion of gambling, Wren was the enemy of puritans, wowsers and moral reformers who were apt to exaggerate his evil influence. Then, Frank Hardy's novel, *Power Without Glory*, published in 1950, made it difficult to separate fact from fiction because its main character, John West, was based on Wren, and was characterised as being involved in underworld activities that included cheating his gambling customers, rigging sporting events, violence, and even murder.[40]

Wren strenuously avoided publicity for himself, but he was an avid newspaper reader. Whenever he travelled, all of the major capital city newspapers were sent to him, and would be found strewn across his hotel room after he had finished reading. He had wanted to own a newspaper for years before he purchased the *Daily Mail* in 1915, in conjunction with his friend and business partner, the wealthy retailer, Benjamin Nathan.[41] Nathan was a founder of the Maple's chain of furniture and piano warehouses, which had fifteen branches across Australia. He was also a major financier of the motor car industry, a racehorse owner, and part owner (with Wren) in the Ascot racecourse in Melbourne. With the Tote closed eight years earlier, Wren was trying to shake off his unsavoury reputation and devoting himself to being an entrepreneur. He had interests in cattle stations, liquor, hotels, theatres, boxing, gold mines, cafés, cake shops and sporting venues. He and Nathan purchased the *Daily Mail* principally as a way of promoting their sporting interests in Queensland, including their racetracks and sports grounds.

Wren had become involved in Queensland four years earlier, in 1911, when he bought the Albion Park racecourse in Brisbane, sight unseen, after a conversation in Melbourne. Aiming for monopoly, he and Nathan then quietly acquired control of five other racecourses in the Brisbane and Ipswich area, including through some suspicious transactions. Wren had judged Queensland to have the same appeal as Western Australia (where he also owned a race-course) – the combination of 'a growing economy with lax government controls on racing'.[42] By 1922, Wren and Nathan had acquired all of the racetracks in the area, except one. They had been particularly active in Queensland during the period when Labor's EG Theodore was deputy premier (1915–19) and premier (1919–25). Wren had influence in the inner circles of the Queensland Labor Party at the time. He had developed friendships with several Queensland Labor politicians, but was particularly close to Theodore, whom he considered a future prime minister (and who became a newspaper owner himself, Chapters 4 and 9).

Horseracing and newspapers were natural bedfellows. Wren's friend and fellow newspaper owner, Joynton Smith, also owned race-courses. Denison and Packer both owned racehorses, and Denison bred thoroughbred horses, while Packer was a committee member of the Australian Jockey Club for twelve years. Wren recognised the cross-promotional opportunities at a time when horseracing was a national obsession, and a major topic of news in Australian newspapers. (This went back a long way. In the 1820s, William Wentworth had exploited the synergies. He had started the first racing club, the Sydney Turf Club, in 1825, and used his paper, the *Australian*, to lobby the governor to allow official race meetings, and then to promote them.)[43]

Aside from horseracing, Wren was also the power behind Stadiums Ltd, the body that ruled professional boxing in Brisbane, Melbourne and Sydney, and also staged wrestling, dancing, music and other events at its venues. Wren and Nathan had plenty of commercial ventures to promote through their newspaper, but they also had political goals. As a staunch Labor supporter, Wren ran the *Daily Mail* as a 'pseudo-Labor journal'.[44] But making a labour newspaper popular *and* profitable was a tricky business about which the inexperienced Wren knew little. He imported some expertise by poaching newspaper executive Norman White from the *Daily Standard*, a Labor-affiliated newspaper that had been launched in 1912 by JB Sharpe, Labor Member for Oxley. The *Daily Standard* played an influential role in Queensland politics. Before it was published, Labor had never won a state election. After it began in December 1912, Labor won seven of the next eight elections before the *Daily Standard* closed in 1936. Wren's pro-Labor *Daily Mail* had provided back-up support for Labor from 1915. Sharpe was another reputed former bookmaker and owner of two Brisbane racecourses that he sold to Wren. Sharpe briefly became a partner in the *Daily Mail* (and its managing director), but his involvement from November 1915 to January 1919 was punctuated with combative run-ins with Wren.

Aside from commercial promotion, Wren and Nathan also wanted to influence political debate around proprietary race tracks (the type they owned, controlled by private individuals rather than the registered racing clubs). After World War I, some Queensland politicians had complained about the enormous private profits being made by individuals (especially Wren) in proprietary racing, and the way money was flowing out of Brisbane. For over a decade, Wren's influence, the advocacy of the *Daily Mail* and Theodore's leadership had helped stall moves to legislate a ban on proprietary racing, but by 1928 a non-Labor government was looming. Aside from wanting Murdoch's expertise to reinvigorate the paper, this may be one of the reasons Wren wanted the conservatively connected and politically astute Murdoch to invest in the *Daily Mail* that year – to help navigate the coming shift in Queensland state politics. (At the federal level, Wren had his own connections. Many members of the Scullin Labor government (1929–32) reportedly had close ties to him.)[45]

At the 1929 Queensland state election, the Country and Progressive National Party, led by Arthur Edward Moore, was elected to office. It was the first non-Labor Queensland state government since Wren had bought the paper. The Moore government ordered a Royal Commission on Racing and it found in 1930 that proprietary racing in Queensland (which essentially meant Wren) was 'inherently corrupt'.[46] It recommended abolishing it, and this occurred in 1932. Wren was less affected by this than might be imagined because, as usual, he had been one step ahead of the legislation. He and Nathan had 'sold' or leased their racecourses to a mysterious organisation called the Brisbane Amateur Turf Club relinquishing day-to-day control of the courses but reportedly with almost all of the profits still flowing to them 'as more or less permanent interest repayments'.[47]

Wren's political and commercial fixing skills were legendary, but his newspaper management skills were poor. Soon after he had taken over the *Daily Mail*, his over-enthusiasm had resulted in two defamation actions, including one from the paper's rival, the *Courier* (Wren's paper had alleged the *Courier* was cheating the public through mismanagement of patriotic funds intended to help the war needy). Amusingly, Wren's biographers say the tough man, who had ruled the worlds of illegal gambling, horseracing and boxing, found himself out of his depth in the newspaper industry, which he found 'hazardous and costly'.[48] By 1928, Wren must have welcomed the arrival of Murdoch, a man who knew how to use newspapers to wield political influence *and* make money. By 1933, it was the latter that Wren principally wanted from Murdoch when they teamed up to form Queensland Newspapers.

The two haggled over the terms of their deal. Wren's CWL Pty Ltd was by far the largest investor in Queensland Newspapers. Murdoch had much less money in the venture, but at least his was 'clean' Protestant money: he could be the respectable face of the venture.[49] Wren wanted a minimum, guaranteed dividend of 5.5 per cent per annum as well as assured coverage of his sporting

promotions. Murdoch wanted editorial control and the right to nominate the company's directors. Both got what they wanted. Queensland Newspapers was set up to consist of A, B and C preference shares
as well as ordinary shares. Through the *Brisbane Courier*, Murdoch
got the A preference shares which gave him control so long as he
delivered the agreed dividend to Wren.[50]

Wren thought Murdoch was the loser in this deal. Who cared about
a trifling thing like editorial control when money was at stake? But
Murdoch understood that political influence was a profit unto itself
and that his first personal controlling interest over a daily newspaper
gave him that. Under the terms of the deal, Murdoch had the right
to nominate the entire board of directors during his lifetime and to
spend up to £50 000 without consulting a general meeting of all classes
of shareholders.[51] Wren stayed close through his friend and nominee,
Norman White, who was appointed managing director of the *Courier-Mail* after the merger, but reportedly kept his word, and did not
interfere. Murdoch also kept his, and delivered Wren the promised
financial benefits. According to Colin Bednall, these were significant
because Queensland Newspapers 'devised a method by which it could
pay untaxable dividends to its shareholders [and] the government took
no action against this enormous benefit' until later when other companies, like Fairfax & Sons, tried to take advantage of it.[52]

Just as the HWT had its own in-house commercial lawyer on
its board (Theodore Fink), Queensland Newspapers had a powerful source of internal legal advice. The trustee company that had
sold Withers' heirs' *Courier* shares to Murdoch, reportedly for a bargain price, was Queensland Trustees Limited. Its lawyer was (Sir)
Edward Henry Macartney, and his law firm, Thynne and Macartney,
had represented Queensland Trustees Ltd for over twenty years. With
more than £9 million of other people's money to manage and invest,
Queensland Trustees was a powerful commercial force in the state,
and a major investor in CSR, BHP and the National Bank.[53]

FIGURE 8.1 A rare photograph of the publicity-shy John Wren, showing a photographer pursuing him outside the City Court, Melbourne, 1950
SOURCE Newspix (NPX1076949).

Macartney had been the trustee of Withers' father's estate and helped her manage it for decades (including occupying a seat on the board of the Brisbane Newspaper Company Ltd, which owned the *Courier*). After Macartney arranged the sale of her heirs' controlling shares to Murdoch, and at such favourable terms, Murdoch made Macartney a director (and chairman) of Queensland Newspapers, a handsome reward. Macartney remained in that position for the rest of his life.

Wren was also familiar with the firm of Thynne and Macartney. Macartney's partner, AJ Thynne, was another lawyer-politician-trust fund manager. When Wren had arrived in Queensland in 1911, it was Thynne, as trustee of the estate to which the Deagon race-course belonged, who had sold it to Wren and Nathan.[54]

Once all the haggling between Wren and Murdoch was complete, and local directors, including Macartney, had been enlisted, the formation of Queensland Newspapers and the planned merger of the *Courier* and the *Daily Mail* were announced in August 1933. There was no mention of Wren, of course, and Murdoch's control from Melbourne was downplayed. But the public announcement did note that Murdoch was an investor in Queensland Newspapers. In a case of protesting too much, it insisted that 'it is a Queensland company, registered in Queensland, and managed and controlled by Queenslanders ... as proof of its thoroughly Queensland character ... the directors will be [Queenslanders]'.[55]

Like Perth, Brisbane was a proud, pioneering city. Any sense that its most important local paper would be taking dictation from Melbourne would be very unwelcome. Having learned from the Perth venture, Murdoch made sure to give the company the outward appearance of being locally owned and run. But, by now, Murdoch's reputation preceded him. Even before the first edition of the *Courier-Mail* had rolled off the presses, a Labor MP, FJ Waters, had risen in the Queensland parliament to draw attention to Murdoch's 'associations with the Baillieu group'. Waters claimed that Murdoch was now 'extending the group's tentacles to Brisbane'.[56] The Brisbane *Telegraph* gleefully placed these claims about its new rival on page one.[57] The *Worker* claimed the new paper would be 'directed from the South', and 'the interests of Queensland will be subverted to those of the southern States'.[58] But a perception of Melbourne invasion did not take hold in Brisbane in the way it had in Perth.

ROBINSON AND COLLINS HOUSE IN QUEENSLAND

Aside from promising to be locally run, the *Courier-Mail* made the standard promise to be thoroughly 'independent' and not 'attached to any political party'.[59] But Macartney, its new chairman, was an ultra-conservative retired Liberal and Nationalist politician. He had been Queensland's minister for lands in 1911–12, when Collins House was already involved in copper mining in western Queensland, through Hampden-Cloncurry Copper Mines Pty Ltd and the Mount Elliott mines.[60] In 1906, Baillieu had convinced the Queensland state government to extend the railway to the Hampden and Mount Elliott mines, a crucial decision for the mines' profitability, which Macartney had strongly supported in parliament.[61]

In 1914, Lionel Robinson and WS Robinson, along with WL Baillieu, and the British stockbroker and mining company director, Francis Govett, formed the Nagrom Syndicate (Nagrom is Morgan backwards) to buy a large parcel of shares in Mount Morgan in central Queensland. Robinson had already travelled in Queensland to survey mining opportunities, and at one stage when Mount Morgan looked to be failing, he was sent back to try to protect the syndicate's investment.[62] Around this time, Macartney was again involved in decisions that benefitted the Mount Morgan Gold Mining Company and was accused by the Labor Opposition of being 'at the beck and call' of mining syndicates.[63] Macartney also had other links to Collins House. He was a director of the Mount Cuthbert Company, in which EL and C Baillieu were involved.[64] His law firm appeared for Collins House's Hampden-Cloncurry mine and its Mount Elliott mine (including in an appeal to the Arbitration Court seeking to reduce its workers' wages).[65] Macartney was involved in syndicates searching for oil, a personal passion of WS Robinson's, and the two shared an antipathy towards the Ryan Labor government (1915–19).

Macartney despised Premier TJ Ryan,[66] while Robinson felt it would be 'dangerous' if the Ryan Labor government influenced federal politics.[67] In one of the many stoushes between Macartney and Ryan, in 1916, Ryan had accused his Thynne and Macartney law firm of operating like the big American politico-legal firms. He said its two principals used their parliamentary positions to obtain legal business, to push through legislation on behalf of their clients, and their methods included 'political blackmail' over legislators.[68]

The pro–private enterprise Macartney was fiercely anti-Labor and was considered 'the Hercules of toryism in [Queensland]'.[69] He was a director on the local boards of blue-chip companies, including AMP, and the Collins House–connected National Bank and Union Trustee Company. Labor MPs called Macartney 'the representative of monopolies and the money power', 'the emissary of [CSR]', and a front for 'the commercial magnates of the State'.[70] Wren was no longer insistent upon running a pro-Labor journal. He must have known, and accepted, that the *Courier-Mail* under Murdoch and Macartney would direct its thunder in support of the conservative side of politics. In later years, Wren would reportedly show up at its office annually and ask only two questions: what was the paper's circulation and its profits?

The *Courier-Mail* has been portrayed as an example of Murdoch striking out independently in an unexpected partnership with Wren, but both Collins House and the HWT were still there in the background behind Murdoch. This time, Robinson was the central figure rather than Baillieu (whose active involvement in business was winding down from 1930). Robinson was the link between all of the key players. He and Murdoch had been friends for approximately thirty years (and also business partners in the *West Australian* syndicate). Robinson was also friends with Wren and Patrick Cody (Wren's business partner and close friend). Cody was a Victorian hotel and racehorse owner. He was the 'C' in CWL Pty Ltd. (Wren was the 'W', while the 'L' was originally Frank Leith, another licensee of Melbourne hotels, who was charged with running an illegal gaming house and tax fraud in the 1950s.) Originally, CWL Pty Ltd was a firm that handled their establishment of a whisky monopoly, but CWL became an investment company for their many interests across various industries, including mining and Queensland Newspapers.

Perhaps Robinson befriended Wren and Cody at the racetrack, for Robinson was a horse owner as well, but the friendship developed into a business partnership. Robinson was involved with Wren and Cody in gold mining in Fiji, along with another mutual friend of both Robinson's and Wren's – EG Theodore, the former Queensland premier. Over the years, Theodore had found that his friendship with Wren was financially profitable but politically damaging. There had been allegations that Theodore had accepted £10 000 from Wren in 1915 in return for agreeing not to interfere with hotel licences and trading hours. There had been other allegations about Theodore's involvement with Wren in New Guinea mining leases, and claims that, during Theodore's stint as Labor federal treasurer, he had performed many favours for Wren. Then, in 1928, came a widely publicised allegation that Wren and Theodore had bribed a sitting Labor member in the federal seat of Dalley (in Sydney) to vacate the seat so that Theodore could shift to federal politics. This claim was the subject of a Commonwealth Royal Commission. Theodore 'emerged formally unscathed' from its inquiries, but his association with Wren had tarnished his reputation, as had the examination of the Mungana affair which involved the sale to the Queensland government, for a grossly inflated price, of a North Queensland mine in which, it later emerged, Theodore may have had a secret financial interest.[71] When Theodore lost the seat of Dalley in December 1931, following bitter attacks on him by the Lang faction of the Labor Party, he retired from politics for good and focused on business, including mining.

Although it had already caused him much trouble, Theodore obviously enjoyed the company of tough and colourful characters because he was not only friends with John Wren, but also with a young Frank Packer, who he brought into his lucrative Fijian gold mining business (see Chapter 9). When Theodore had read in the *Sydney Morning Herald* about an old prospector's gold find in Fiji, he went there and took over the site.[72] It proved to be the gold strike of the century, and Theodore's biographer, Ross Fitzgerald, believed that the exploratory capital for it came from Collins House, likely through Theodore's friendship with Robinson.[73]

The Emperor Gold Mining Company Ltd held a 500 acre (200 hectare) mining lease in Fiji, and its shares were concentrated among a small group of business associates – Theodore, Wren, Cody and Packer. After its amazing potential was promoted (connections with newspapers always help with this), a frenzy of share buying by international financiers pushed the price of £1 shares up to £30 even before any major development had taken place on the sites.[74] Money was 'poured in' to the venture and, in August 1935, a new public company called Emperor Mines was floated.[75] It acquired all of the shares of the original Emperor Gold Mining Company Ltd and paid its shareholders (Theodore, Wren, Cody and Packer) an enormous windfall of £1 000 000 plus shares and rights worth £893 000.[76] The *Argus* suggested that Theodore's syndicate was actually behind this new company as well, and the arrangement was aimed at overcoming a 'taxation difficulty'.[77] The Acting Commissioner of Stamp Duties also suspected a tax-minimisation scheme, saying it appeared 'Theodore and Company have sold to themselves their own shares … and bought them back' in a complicated transaction involving a Singapore-based 'dummy company'.[78] Not for nothing was Theodore considered a 'financial genius'.

When Emperor Mines was floated, Collins House was again involved. Robinson was reputed to be either an investor or an organiser of British finance for the new public company.[79] Colin Fraser was a shareholder. And Emperor Mines' accountant was located in Collins House. In the twenty years after the public flotation, Emperor Mines yielded more than £12 million worth of gold.[80]

Aside from the Fijian mines, Robinson was also involved with Cody and Wren in Great Boulder Proprietary Gold Mines Ltd, 'one of the oldest and richest mines' of the 'Golden Mile' area around Kalgoorlie and Boulder in Western Australia.[81] Great Boulder was a phenomenally rich mine. There is no clear picture of when Cody and Wren became involved in it, but Cody became its chairman of directors (he took over from Theodore, who had acquired the Great Boulder shareholdings of the flamboyant and financially ruined Claude de Bernales in 1948).[82] By the 1950s, Cody was one of Australia's wealthiest men, along with Wren (whose mining interests and racetrack in Perth had also made him 'a power' in the state).[83] Among his many investments, Wren had a large stake in Robinson's Western Mining Corporation (WMC). (In 1955, his widow, Ellen Wren, was still the eleventh biggest shareholder in WMC.[84])

Wren was more involved with Robinson and Collins House than has previously been recognised. The money trail from Wren's

Brisbane Daily Mail Pty Ltd also ended up back at Collins House. Its accountant, the firm of Buckley and Hughes, was located strangely far from Brisbane, at 360 Collins Street, Melbourne.[85] One of the partners of the firm, the busy accountant Harry Wilfred Buckley, also did the books for Emperor Mines Ltd, Broken Hill South, and the Zinc Corporation. The latter two companies were strongly associated with Robinson (especially the Zinc Corporation; he was its managing director from 1926 to 1947). Buckley was such a trusted figure for Collins House that he later became a director of Broken Hill South.

Behind Murdoch was another Collins House business, the HWT. Although Murdoch was a full-time executive at the HWT, he had persuaded the company to back his Brisbane venture. Fink declined a proposal for the HWT to purchase the *Brisbane Courier*, but he did give his approval for Murdoch to buy it and to merge it with the *Daily Mail*, on the condition that the HWT had the right to take up shares in the new company, and held first option to purchase Murdoch's holding if his shares ever became available.[86] (After Murdoch's death, this would prove to be significant as it allowed the HWT to acquire the *Courier-Mail* from Rupert Murdoch's debt-ridden inheritance, leaving him with 'only' the *News*.)

Fink even took up shares in Queensland Newspapers personally. He had a substantial shareholding in the *Courier-Mail* 'though at what stage [it was acquired] is unclear'.[87] And another figure associated with the HWT was also involved. When Queensland Newspapers registered a branch office in Melbourne in October 1933, it was at the office of HWT director Harry Douglas Giddy's accountancy firm (Wilson, Danby and Giddy). Giddy had joined the HWT board in 1932, reflecting the company's tradition of recruiting top businessmen as directors. Giddy was considered one of Melbourne's brightest and best connected. His firm handled the business of important manufacturers and retailers, including John Snow and

Co., a major draper and newspaper advertiser in Melbourne. But at a time when Sydney and steel were both becoming more important, probably Giddy's more valuable connection was through his brother, who was the secretary and assistant general manager of Howard Smith. It had diversified from a Melbourne-based shipping company into a Sydney-based major investor in Australian Iron and Steel Ltd (AIS). AIS became a subsidiary of BHP, and a major investor in the steel and mining giant, in 1935.

The *Courier-Mail* was a paper with fascinating connections that stretched from Collins House and blue-chip companies, to industries known for their criminal associations. It is not known what Murdoch's strict Presbyterian father made of the unholy alliance between Keith Murdoch and John Wren. Murdoch's sympathetic biographers barely mention Wren. Desmond Zwar evasively described Wren as simply 'a wealthy Melbourne investor'. Zwar emphasised that Murdoch and Wren 'never became close', and claimed that Murdoch insisted he and Wren communicate via letter.[88] This suggests Murdoch's distaste for Wren, or his distrust of him. But Wren also found Murdoch to be untrustworthy, and 'later described Murdoch as a rogue'.[89]

These two friends of Robinson did not warm to each other, but Murdoch and Wren were nonetheless in business together for nearly twenty-five years, putting aside their mutual distrust in pursuit of a shared interest in obtaining power and profits through the *Courier-Mail*. After the merger, it was the only morning paper in Brisbane and was able to charge advertisers higher rates, one of the key commercial advantages of monopoly. After sacking some staff and blending the warring elements of the two rival papers together, Murdoch applied his by now well-honed Northcliffe techniques. The *Courier-Mail* focused on concisely written news, magazine-style features, entertainment and human interest stories. It had women's news across two pages, a page of photographs (especially of photogenic women), sections on broadcasting and film, motoring, sport, and of course, horseracing. As per their agreement, the *Courier-Mail* contained plenty of horseracing news as well as publicity for boxing, wrestling and other events at Wren's Brisbane Stadium. The paper also included comic strips, including ones that later became very well-known such as the famous flapper Blondie and her boyfriend Dagwood, plus 'Ben Bowyang', an Australian bush character, and 'Wally and the Major', two Australian diggers.

BACK IN MELBOURNE: POWER STRUGGLES AND MISSING MENTORS

Although Fink had sanctioned Murdoch's move to Queensland, and even invested in the *Courier-Mail*, all was not well between the two HWT directors. The year 1933 turned out to be a big year for Murdoch. He was overseeing the launch of the *Courier-Mail*, was still locked in the ongoing internal power struggle with Fink at the HWT, and was fighting a public battle in Melbourne to defend its flagship paper, which was also the apple of his eye. On top of all this, he was also having heart trouble.

For thirty-nine years (with the exception of Denison's *Evening Sun* between 1923 and 1925), the *Herald* had enjoyed the advantages of its monopoly status. It pitched itself to advertisers by boasting that 'Melbourne by night … [was] a one-paper city', meaning 'an unequalled opportunity to reach the pocket-books of Melbourne's million [citizens]'.[90] But in 1933, the *Argus* launched an afternoon paper, the *Melbourne Evening Star*. The *Argus* wanted to pick up afternoon circulation and advertising to boost its Depression-depleted coffers, but the move was also a defensive one. The *Herald* had been trying to gain classified advertising, and the *Argus* viewed this as an ungentlemanly incursion into its territory.

This was the *Argus'* second attempt to disrupt the dominance of the *Herald*. At its first attempt, in 1881, the *Argus* had launched a cheap (halfpenny) afternoon paper, the *Evening Mail*. But it failed to thrive and the *Herald* bought it out after only a year.[91] Fifty-two years later, the *Argus'* second attempt got off to a messy and embarrassing start. The first edition of the *Evening Star* was littered with typographical errors and even contained upside-down photographs.[92] Matters improved significantly, but despite the valiant efforts of its staff, the paper was beset by a lack of funding, plus managerial inflexibility and incompetence. It was no match for the well-entrenched *Herald* and in 1936, with the *Evening Star*'s financial losses beginning to drag down the *Argus* and put it at risk, the *Argus* closed the *Star* in order to save itself.

Some of the bright young journalists who had joined the *Star* were Murdoch protégés who had defected from the *Herald*. Despite Murdoch's public vow that they should never darken his doorway again, some did return to the *Herald* after the *Star* closed, including Jack Waters and Cecil Edwards (both went on to senior positions in the HWT). Because the HWT was not known for its charitable attitude towards disloyal staff members, this led to suspicion and rumours that Murdoch had sabotaged the venture from the inside by planting trusted agents. These claims were vehemently denied by the journalists, but they indicate how Murdoch was viewed within the industry by this stage – as a formidable competitor with Machiavellian-like cunning who had again vanquished an adversary.

Despite these perceptions of his power, Murdoch was more vulnerable than outsiders knew. In 1929, he had taken another step towards the chairman's position when the HWT board agreed to pay him a director's fee. Fink had again tried to hold him off, arguing that it was inappropriate for Murdoch, as an employee of the company, to be treated as an ordinary director and paid a director's fee, and perhaps even against the company articles. But in 1929,

Baillieu was chairing the board when Fink was overseas. Baillieu wrote and told Fink that the board had agreed to pay Murdoch a director's fee.[93]

For decades, back to the dizzy days of the land boom, Fink and Baillieu had been close friends, but they now fell out because Baillieu had again helped entrench Murdoch's position on the HWT board. Fink believed that Murdoch was intent on making the HWT 'entirely a Baillieu-Keith Murdoch concern'.[94] Fink, his son Thorold, and his son-in-law, RD Elliott (a provincial newspaper owner, Senator, and mentee of Lord Beaverbrook), came to view Murdoch as a treacherous 'fiend'.[95] Murdoch told his wife, Elisabeth, that he felt secure at the HWT so long as he had Baillieu's support.[96] But he would not have it for much longer.

After thirty-seven years on the HWT board, the seventy-two-year-old Baillieu resigned in 1931. His mental health had begun to decline years earlier after his wife's death in 1925, then deteriorated sharply after the Wall Street crash of 1929 (which he and Murdoch had witnessed firsthand when they were travelling together in the United States). Previously known for exuding confidence and calm, Baillieu had become indecisive, anxious and depressed. Michael Cannon speculated that the crash may have 'subconsciously' recalled the dark days of the 1890s Melbourne land boom crash.[97] Unpleasant memories had also been stirred by the 1929 publication of a book by George Meudell that revived scandalous tales of Baillieu's financial deals in the 1880s. (Meudell's book was supressed, and later censored – reportedly at Fink's urging.)[98]

After Baillieu's retirement, his youngest son, James Latham Baillieu, was elected as an HWT director to replace him in November 1931. The selection of James represented a significant loosening of the Baillieu family's previously strong interest in the HWT. James had been a 'continual disappointment to his father', was in poor health (due to his alcoholism and a heart condition), and lacked interest and ability in business.[99] Although WL Baillieu continued providing support for Murdoch from afar (for example, in 1932, he backed Murdoch's push for the HWT to become involved in newsprint), his health was declining. Murdoch was losing his most important supporter, his financial backer and his mentor.

By 1932, Baillieu had begun to express anger in ways that shocked his friends and family. On his way home from a meeting, Baillieu attacked his chauffeur, and he had to be restrained. He was then sent quietly to London to live under the supervision of his son Clive. Ironically, Australia's 'money king', began harbouring an obsessive and irrational belief that his fortune had been lost and he was destitute. Despite all the evidence and his family's constant reassurance, Baillieu 'thought that all he had built up was collapsing in ruins'.[100] He sank into a deep depression accompanied by delusions of poverty and terminal illness.

Around 1932–33, Murdoch had begun to assert that his appointment as managing director afforded him the same status as an ordinary member of the HWT board. For years, Fink had disputed this, arguing that Murdoch was an employee, not an ordinary director. If Murdoch's claim was accepted, it would allow him to succeed Fink as chairman. Although the Fink camp on the board bitterly disputed Murdoch's interpretation, the directors allied with Murdoch accepted it.[101] But the feud was not over yet. Without Baillieu to protect him, Murdoch was newly vulnerable. In 1934, he only narrowly withstood an attempt by the Fink interests to overturn him on the board.

Murdoch had been unwell throughout 1933–34. He had suffered two heart attacks, was under significant stress, and was overworking himself, as he always did. Ordered to take rest, Murdoch was away from the office for about a year. While he was absent, Theodore Fink made secret moves to force his retirement, 'strip him of his executive powers' and install Thorold to replace him.[102]

Murdoch was aware of the plotting, and when he returned to work in May 1934, he found the board divided into two factions about whether his role should be reduced or removed. The board had actually been split into two camps ever since the late 1920s (one associated with Baillieu/Murdoch, and one with the Finks), but in 1934 there were two relatively new directors on the board: Giddy and George Caro.

Giddy had been appointed in 1932, but Caro had been on the board for less than six months. RM Younger, one of Murdoch's biographers, said that Caro's allegiance was unclear. But Caro had connections to Collins House, of which Robinson was now the major figure. Caro was a co-director with Collins House accountant, Harry Wilfred Buckley, in Zig Zag Paper Pty Ltd, a company that made cigarette papers. Caro was also the managing director of Gollin and Co, a proud old trading house that had been founded in Adelaide in the 1880s. From importing sugar, tea and other groceries, Gollin and Co had expanded to be a highly successful general merchant and importing company. Its head office was in Melbourne, but it had branches in every state in Australia, as well as in the United Kingdom and New Zealand. It handled everything from Shell kerosene to Michelin tyres, Woodrow's hats, steel sheets, tinned food and Mildura fruit. One of Caro's fellow directors at Gollin and Co was Garnet L Clark of London, the son of William Clark, WS Robinson's London partner (Garnet Clark was also Clive Baillieu's brother-in-law). The Gollin family mixed in the same social circles as the Baillieus and the Cohens (another Collins House family), especially at Sorrento and Portsea, the holiday spots for Melbourne's rich and famous.

When Giddy and Caro sided with Murdoch in 1934, the Finks were again beaten. Bednall said that Murdoch had been forced to fight 'tooth and nail to save himself against the Fink family'.[103] Once Murdoch's position was secure, he used it to get 'the upper hand over the Finks during the 1930s'.[104] From 1934, he was fighting without the support of a Baillieu on the board. James L Baillieu had resigned earlier that year to enter a private hospital, where he died soon after, aged only thirty-four. In London, WL Baillieu's health was very poor by 1935, and he died of pneumonia there in February 1936. In the decade before his death, Baillieu had transferred the bulk of his fortune to his family in order to avoid federal and state death duties.[105] He did not leave any money to charity (a previous codicil in his will that would have left money to charities selected by his children had been revoked).[106]

Without WL Baillieu as lynchpin, the tight-knit bonds that had held Collins House together slowly began to loosen. Baillieu had accepted in the 1930s 'that none of his sons would follow him in leading the Collins House companies in Australia'.[107] The selection of the unreliable James for the HWT board was an indicator of that. WL's most promising son was Murdoch's childhood friend, the barrister and financier Clive, but Clive had chosen to live in London, and had less interest in newspapers and Melbourne than his father had.[108] Clive worked with WS Robinson in the 1930s, focusing on zinc, but by the 1940s, Robinson's Zinc Corporation (one of the main ancestors of world mining giant Rio Tinto) began drifting apart from the original Collins House (Baillieu) group.

The other key director of the HWT since 1889, Theodore Fink, was also a declining figure. After Murdoch's victory in 1934, the seventy-nine-year-old Fink and his son were increasingly marginalised on the board.

When the long aftermath of the Depression began to recede, economic activity started to revive and this drove growth in newspaper circulations, sizes and revenues. In April 1935, the *Sun News-Pictorial* became Australia's largest selling daily paper, a title it would hold for decades.[109] The *Herald*'s increased sales in 1936 put it second only to the *Sun News-Pictorial* nationally.[110] With such successes, Murdoch's position was more secure. Giddy and Caro were becoming more influential on the board, and Giddy in particular was proving to be a 'staunch supporter' of Murdoch's.[111] In 1936, Murdoch successfully had himself appointed as an ordinary director of the HWT while concurrently acting as managing director. This made it almost certain that he would take over as chairman on Fink's resignation or death.

CHAPTER 9

'NEVER TRUST SYDNEY NEWSPAPER PROPRIETORS'

Even as the HWT was expanding its media empire across Australia, there was one city that it resolutely avoided – Sydney, the biggest market of all. Not until 1987, sixty years after it began its program of national expansion, did the HWT finally become linked with a daily Sydney newspaper, and this was not by choice but only because the HWT had, itself, been taken over by Rupert Murdoch's News Corporation (which then owned two Sydney papers). The glaring gap in the HWT's empire was not for lack of opportunity. In 1910, when Hugh Denison had been wondering what to do with the *Australian Star*, he had contacted Theodore Fink and WL Baillieu and tried to convince them that the HWT should participate in a joint venture. They declined. In 1921–22, Murdoch had ventured to Sydney and made overtures to gain control of the *Evening News*, but these were tentative and defensive, mainly designed to dissuade Denison from coming to Melbourne.

The HWT and Denison were, in today's vernacular, 'frenemies'. Although they battled in Melbourne in the early to mid-1920s, the two companies were linked. They were partners in UCS, Denison held shares in the HWT, and the HWT held a 'considerable' number of shares in Associated Newspapers under an alias.[1] Denison worked with Baillieu on BACAL and also had shares in another Collins House company, the Electrolytic Refining and Smelting Company.[2] When he left Melbourne, it was to the HWT that Denison sold the *Sun News-Pictorial*, and on generous terms, despite the seeming intensity of their competition. On several occasions, including in 1921, 1922 and 1929, Denison discussed with Fink and/or Murdoch a potential amalgamation of their interests.[3] Left-wing newspapers often lumped the two companies together, suspecting that they were really one entity.[4]

Collins House was also linked with Sydney's Fairfax family, owners of the *Sydney Morning Herald*, through investments of AMP's capital in various Collins House projects, and also through board directorships and old school tie links.[5] There may have been an informal 'gentleman's agreement' between interconnected board directors to keep off each other's turf in newspapers as they were cooperating together in other enterprises. This might not even have needed to be made explicit as there was a high degree of mutual respect between John Fairfax & Sons and the HWT. The directors of the two proud old companies were bastions in their respective commercial worlds. Respect firmed into cooperation in the 1930s, as the two groups worked to secure control over cable news and newsprint, and the high regard continued for decades. (When Rupert Murdoch made his first (failed) bid to take over the HWT in 1979, John Fairfax Ltd (as the company had become known) bought a 15 per cent stake in the HWT to protect it, for which the HWT's executives were very grateful.[6])

There were legal reasons why the HWT would be avoiding Sydney during some years; specifically, the territorial agreements between the HWT and Denison that restricted them from entering the other's home turf. But aside from business links and legal impediments, there might have been larger factors at play as well, because it was not just the HWT that avoided New South Wales. After Federation, when national business opportunities started to beckon, Victorian firms that had developed in more genteel and protectionist surrounds tended to avoid the wilder, former free-trade state of New South Wales. Myer, for example, ventured into Adelaide in 1928, but 'leapfrogged' New South Wales on its way up to Brisbane in the 1950s, and did not open in Sydney until 1960.[7]

Sydney was a more competitive newspaper market than Melbourne, making it less appealing for the HWT. Where Denison's *Sun News-Pictorial* had been Melbourne's first new daily newspaper in nearly thirty years,[8] Sydney in that time had seen the *Sun* (relaunched from the *Star*), the new *Labor Daily*, and would soon see the *Daily Guardian* (1923) and the *World* (1931). Sydney was the birthplace of brazen and scandalous weeklies, *Truth* and *Smith's Weekly*. It even had *six* competing Sunday newspapers in January 1930,[9] where God-fearing Melbourne had none (state law prevented the publication and sale of newspapers on Sunday in Victoria until 1969).

In the 1920s and 1930s, the HWT may reasonably have judged that the major owners had Sydney well covered and there was little to gain in such a tough market. The HWT's chief empire builder, Keith Murdoch, personally found Sydney to be fatiguing, and the Sydney owners a tough set of men to deal with. Murdoch's colleagues noted he always returned from Sydney 'mentally and morally exhausted'.[10] Rupert Murdoch claimed that his father only ever gave him one specific piece of advice about the newspaper business, and that was to 'never trust Sydney newspaper proprietors'.[11] Was Keith Murdoch thinking of the overstretched Denison and his impudent excursion to Melbourne, or the imperious, super-wealthy Fairfaxes with their tough-as-nails business brain, Rupert Henderson? Or perhaps he was thinking of the wild Nortons and cunning Packers.

NEWSPAPER ROYALTY: THE FAIRFAXES

If a newspaper industry observer of the 1920s was told that only two major newspaper groups would survive the 20th century, they would have been unlikely to nominate the Fairfax company as one of the two. In the 1920s, John Fairfax & Sons was a relatively small family company publishing one morning newspaper, the *Sydney Morning Herald*, and one weekly illustrated magazine, the *Sydney Mail*. The *Sydney Morning Herald* was an important newspaper, the oldest in the country, influential, and with a reputation for journalistic quality, but it was no media empire, and the Fairfaxes seemed content to keep it that way. From the 1920s through to the 1940s, while Associated Newspapers ravenously collected newspapers for a time, and then the HWT spread around the country in a frenzy of takeovers and acquisitions, Fairfax & Sons single-mindedly focused upon its crown jewel, the *Sydney Morning Herald*.[12] The Fairfax family saw themselves as the guardians of a sacred trust, 'Australia's Greatest Newspaper'.[13]

When the *Sydney Morning Herald* celebrated its centenary in 1931, the paper proudly published accolades from around the Empire. Lord Riddell of the Newspaper Proprietors Association in the United Kingdom described the *Sydney Morning Herald* as 'one of the outstanding newspapers of the world'. Theodore Fink commended the paper as 'fair', 'dignified', 'serious', 'accurate', 'sober' and a 'wholesome influence'. LV Biggs, editor of *The Age*, noted the *Sydney Morning Herald*'s 'power ... [as] a fearless organ of public opinion'. Keith Murdoch said it was a 'splendidly honest newspaper'. Other newspaper industry figures praised the *Sydney Morning Herald*'s commitment to the 'highest ideals', its 'loyalty to the Crown' and its unfailing commitment to 'journalistic excellence'. Horace Yelland, still editor of the Adelaide *News*, went to town, dubbing the *Sydney Morning Herald* the 'Gibraltar of the Australian press – sagacious counsellor, public educator and leader, and daunt-less defender of the people's rights'.[14]

So if the *Sydney Morning Herald*'s proprietors were somewhat pompously proud of their newspaper, it was not without encouragement. A long line of tradition lay behind the paper and the family's connection to it. John Fairfax, an English-born journalist and newspaper owner, had become a partner in the *Sydney Herald* in 1841 (it became the *Sydney Morning Herald* on 1 August 1842), and taken full ownership in 1853. Like many of the other early newspaper owners, he crossed over between politics and newspapers. He was a religious man, tending towards the puritanical, and was considered 'cautious, responsible, devout, [and to have] embodied the most respectable traditions of his class and time'.[15] But, like WL Baillieu, John Fairfax was a former bankrupt. As a publisher in England, legal expenses he had incurred defending a libel suit (probably on top of other business matters) had bankrupted him.[16] Unlike Baillieu though, John Fairfax made a point of repaying his creditors. He reportedly returned to England once he had rebuilt his fortune, and although 'under no legal obligation to do so, he repaid all debts still standing in his name from the days of his bankruptcy'.[17]

Fairfax & Sons was a family business. It took until 1927 for a non-member of the Fairfax family, the general manager WG Conley, to be appointed as a director. John's second son, James Reading Fairfax, had taken control of the paper in 1877, after his father's death, and was associated with it for sixty-seven years. He died on 28 March 1919, just before John Fairfax & Sons sustained what was likely its first ever trading loss, in 1918–19. The wartime hunger for news had made the Melbourne *Herald* profits that Fink described as 'enormous',[18] but John Fairfax & Sons had suffered a loss because it had failed to adapt to the severe rise in the cost of newsprint during the war, and then waited too long to increase the *Sydney Morning Herald*'s cover price to compensate. But the company was steered back into prosperity and 10 per cent dividends by Conley. In the 1920s, he managed to capture 'almost the whole of Sydney's classified advertising' for the *Sydney Morning Herald*.[19] The 'rivers of gold' were flowing for the paper, putting it in a strong position for the future, and further enriching the Fairfaxes.

In 1925, James Reading's twenty-three-year-old grandson, Warwick Oswald Fairfax, joined the company. He was appointed a director in 1927, but his elevation as the man with prime responsibility for the company happened much faster than anyone had foreseen after the deaths, in rapid succession, of his father in 1928, Conley in 1929, and his uncle in 1930. Warwick Fairfax's inheritance gave him 35 per cent of shares in the group.[20] He was appointed managing director in 1930, aged twenty-eight, and remained in senior management at the company, including as its chairman, for forty-seven years with only a two-month break in 1961 (to avoid a scandal over his second marriage).

In the 1920s and 1930s, Warwick Fairfax was still finding his feet. Tall, thin, and somewhat dreamy, Fairfax had been a shy boy and only child whose parents invested high hopes in him. Fairfax had received an education in the classics, including Latin, Greek and literature. As was the family tradition, he spent time in English schools, eventually studying at Balliol, Oxford, his father's college. Not surprisingly, given his background and that of the family newspaper, Warwick Fairfax was steadfastly conservative in his politics from a young age.[21]

When Warwick Fairfax became steward of the *Sydney Morning Herald* in 1930, it had been a conservative paper for over eighty years. Also sober and traditionalist, its more liberal opponents awarded it the nickname of 'Granny *Herald*'. The *Sydney Morning Herald* aimed for gravity, respectability and prudence. It was known for its Protestant Christianity, reverence for the British monarchy, support for traditional values and morals, strong advocacy of

FIGURE 9.1 The dreamy aristocrat and custodian of the *Sydney Morning Herald*, Warwick Oswald Fairfax, circa 1941

SOURCE *Newspaper News*, 1 March 1941, p. 13.

private property and free-enterprise capitalism, and its opposition to government interference and socialism.[22] Deeply suspicious of the Labor Party, the *Sydney Morning Herald* was 'nearly always critical of trade unions and the labour movement', but still reported extensively on Labor, and often in ways that were calmer, deeper, more reasoned and neutral than other papers.[23]

The *Sydney Morning Herald* believed that government was, as it argued in a 1920 editorial, 'essentially a matter of business. The State is a huge concern in which every single one of us is a shareholder ... in choosing our legislators, we should apply the same tests as we do in appointing a manager or electing a board of directors.'[24] On the issue of whether women should be awarded the vote so that they too could be 'shareholders' in the state, the *Sydney Morning Herald* had editorialised in 1900 that: 'The weakness of women, and their susceptibility to influence, would be one of the principal risks ... and until these disabilities [are] modified or removed they might cause a certain amount of mischief'. (Other conservative papers had argued similarly, with the *Argus* trying to couch its opposition as gallantry, asking 'why cast the trouble of voting upon the women?'.[25])

Weighty with lucrative classified ads, the *Sydney Morning Herald*'s 'rivers of gold' brought in huge revenue and were the envy of other proprietors. When the *Sydney Morning Herald* finally moved those ads off the front page in April 1944 to make way for news, it was the last Sydney daily paper to make the shift. The *Tribune* described it as 'Granny shyly [coming] out in flapper skirts after a century in crinolines'.[26] As RB Walker noted, the *Sydney Morning Herald* was also slow to adopt photographs, and it resisted large type, bold headlines and other frivolity or reader attractions, including circulation gimmicks that other papers used, such as crosswords, comic strips, competitions and stunts.[27]

The *Sydney Morning Herald* considered its audience to be the educated and middle classes, and prided itself on its large subscriber base rather than relying on street or casual sales.[28] It was written in a prim, serious style with long reports. It proudly considered itself a 'journal of record' and solemn custodian of history, so it reported in detail on parliament, shipping, commerce, law courts, finance and churches and featured reviews of music, literature, art and drama. What to some was a paper of record with authority and literary and educational values, to others was pretentious and fussy. Richard Twopenny wrote in 1883 that the paper had 'a fatal odour of respectable dullness'.[29] But the *Sydney Morning Herald* did not die in either the 19th or the 20th centuries. In the 2000s, the *Sydney Morning*

Herald website was consistently ranked among the top news websites accessed by Australians.[30]

During World War I, like the rest of the daily commercial press, the *Sydney Morning Herald* was virulently pro-conscription. It was so supportive of Hughes' campaign that it suspended its usual desire for balance. In the week before the 1916 referendum, the *Sydney Morning Herald* published fifty-seven letters to the editor that supported conscription, and only three for the 'no' case.[31] Behind the scenes, the associate editor of the *Sydney Morning Herald* even struck a deal, voluntarily, with Hughes that the *Sydney Morning Herald* would 'edit with special care' any references to anti-conscription meetings 'which may harm the referendum campaign'.[32] On the day of the referendum, the headlines on the main news stories included 'YES!' and 'OUR NATIONAL DUTY'. The editorial page showed a how-to-vote card marked with a cross in the 'yes' square, and on the facing page, reproduced an eye-catching handwritten note from Hughes telling Australians to 'do their duty and vote Yes!!'.[33]

Warwick Fairfax's relative youth and inexperience helps to explain why the 1920s and 1930s were such a quiet time for his company, but it was also because the key person who would be the driving force behind the expansion of the Fairfax group was also just starting out. Rupert Albert Geary (RAG) Henderson – called 'Rags', but never to his face – became the dominant figure at the *Sydney Morning Herald*. He was as important to the expansion of the Fairfax company as Keith Murdoch was to the HWT, and was also an influential leader of the Australian newspaper industry. But unlike Murdoch, Henderson stayed in the background. He was intensely private and kept to himself. It was claimed there were Fairfax employees of twenty years plus who never saw him because Henderson had a habit of arriving very early at work each day and going straight up to his panelled executive office in a private lift, and then not leaving until 11 pm.

The son of a wealthy but unhappy man, Henderson had left home at thirteen, with little formal education, and pursued a range of jobs before he began at the *Sydney Morning Herald* as a nineteen-year-old cadet in 1915. He never left, serving his whole journalistic career at Fairfax & Sons. Eleven years younger than Keith Murdoch, Henderson was similarly driven and hardworking. Henderson worked such long hours that when his son enlisted for World War II and registered his father as his next-of-kin, he gave Henderson's address as: 'the *Sydney Morning Herald*'.[34] Henderson had a very similar career trajectory to Murdoch, from political reporter to overseas management position, then back to Australia, working up the internal executive structures. Also like Murdoch, he 'assiduously courted his superiors'.[35]

Henderson was short and wore oversized clothes. He had a beak-like nose and jutting chin. He was intense and spoke with a characteristic urgency, as if someone's life depended upon it. Tough, creative and energetic, in 1920 he became the *Sydney Morning Herald*'s chief state political reporter, aged only twenty-four years, just five years after his cadetship began. Henderson was considered a brilliant journalist who could see a story where no one else could. He had 'an instinct for the jugular' that would serve him well in the cut-throat world of newspaper management.[36] As Keith Murdoch and Herbert Campbell Jones had also discovered, the connections and observations from political reporting made it an excellent training ground.

Henderson remained chief state political reporter until 1923, when he was sent to England to establish Fairfax's Fleet Street office. After he returned to Australia in 1926, Henderson started moving up the corporate ladder and occupied senior roles in the advertising and circulation departments before becoming secretary to the general manager, Athol Hugh (AH) Stuart, in 1934. Stuart had risen even faster than his friend Henderson (and especially fast by

Sydney Morning Herald standards). He had begun as a cadet reporter at the paper in 1916, became the youngest subeditor the *Sydney Morning Herald* had ever had, and by 1933, was the company's general manager when he was only forty years old. Stuart headed Fairfax's London office after Henderson (from 1926 to 1928). He was known for his amazing memory and for being a gifted writer. During the general strike of 1926, Stuart tramped around London's East End shabbily dressed, and attended strike meetings, so that he could send back vivid descriptions of what was going on.

As Stuart's understudy, Henderson was able to observe a general manager who was considered to be a very competent and innovative newspaper administrator. Stuart brought the *Sydney Morning Herald* into the modern era and played a large role in securing its future by connecting the company with Keith Murdoch's HWT in two important initiatives, the Australian Associated Press (AAP) and Australian Newsprint Mills (ANM) (Chapter 14). But Stuart's term as chief executive lasted only five years. In August 1938, he was asked to resign on medical grounds. The once 'thoroughly dependable' Stuart had experienced a mental health breakdown.[37] In 1942, he was declared insane and incarcerated in a psychiatric hospital for nine months until the minister for health ordered his release. It was later suggested (including under parliamentary privilege) that Henderson and/or Warwick Fairfax had been responsible for Stuart's confinement but this was strongly denied by the company and the allegation was not repeated outside parliament. Stuart had been confined at his brother's request.[38]

When Stuart resigned, Henderson succeeded to the role of general manager in 1938, and became the managing director in 1949. His management style was to 'rule by fear'. Maxwell Newton, also a brilliant (and colourful) journalist, called Henderson 'truly amazing', and 'the most dynamic and exciting man I've ever met'. Newton described him as 'a little man in a baggy suit hunched up behind his desk … ranting and raving over something or other … He told me once: "You'd break my heart if I had one"'.[39]

Colin Bednall viewed Henderson quite differently, describing him as a 'vulgar' 'squirt of a man' who never accepted business engagements on Thursday nights because, Henderson allegedly told him, 'that's my whoring night'.[40] Henderson moderated his earthy personality in the office, where his strategic ability balanced out the dreamy, aristocratic Warwick Fairfax, who was six years his junior. Aside from having to discourage Fairfax from occasional over-the-top contributions to the paper, especially on Christian themes, the two worked together in ways that were largely productive. Inside observers said one of Henderson's greatest skills was his ability to manage the Fairfaxes. That task was made easier during the periods when Warwick Fairfax was preoccupied with travel, renovating and the ballet. Other times, Fairfax began to involve himself more closely in the daily running of the paper.

In 1931, the *Sydney Morning Herald* was glad to see the back of the irreverent and circulation-affecting *Daily Guardian* when it closed.[41] But in the second half of the 1930s, it suddenly faced a resurgent *Daily Telegraph*, which, under Frank Packer's hand, was as enthusiastic about gimmicks and reader attractions as Fairfax was disdainful of them. The *Daily Telegraph* had comics, serials and a cartoon, where the *Sydney Morning Herald* had none of those popular devices. (Only in the mid-1940s did the paper employ its first in-house cartoonist, John Firth.[42]) As a result of the new competition, Bridget Griffen-Foley says that Warwick Fairfax allowed Henderson to modernise the company, renew its management and compete 'more energetically for scoops and racing news'.[43]

Some of its ageing and entrenched staff were moved on. Chief of staff, George J Reeve, who had spent forty-six years at the paper – twenty-seven of them as news editor – was retired, and Angus McLachlan, a former subeditor at the *Melbourne Herald* took up the

FIGURE 9.2 The 'brains' behind Fairfax & Sons, RAG Henderson, in his early seventies, outside his home in Point Piper, Sydney

SOURCE Photograph by Mark Strizic, 1968, National Library of Australia (PIC Box PIC/3167).

post.⁴⁴ In 1938, Hugh Alexander McClure Smith, who had been at Balliol, Oxford with Warwick Fairfax, became editor, taking over from the seventy-seven-year-old Charles Brunsdon Fletcher, who had been at his post for nineteen years. (A *Smith's Weekly*'s cartoon lampooned the *Sydney Morning Herald*'s elderly staff profile by depicting its copy boys as bald, with long beards, and in wheelchairs.)

While retaining its tradition of 'serious' news, the *Sydney Morning Herald* was being pulled by competition into a more modern look and content. It had introduced more photographs, and more articles on popular topics such as motoring, radio and films. Staff were reorganised. New presses were installed. Processes were streamlined, and newsprint was stockpiled by forward buying of supplies. In 1933, the *Sydney Morning Herald* even began a tabloid

Women's Supplement, published weekly, to try to compete with the Packers' *Women's Weekly*.

In matters of broader organisation, its custodians considered the *Sydney Morning Herald* so sacred and special that the company had a tendency to make its own decisions on matters such as industrial relations and to stay apart from the combined groupings and co-operative endeavours of other press groups. (Denison referred to this as the company making one of its 'usual beautiful breaks' from the rest of the papers,[45] while Murdoch lamented the *Sydney Morning Herald*'s 'arrogance' and sense of 'superiority'.[46]) The *Sydney Morning Herald* refused to join other papers in the Audit Bureau of Circulations in 1932, and pulled out of the newspaper proprietor group, the Australian Newspapers' Conference (ANC), over the issue in 1938. Even when the Australian Press Council (APC) was formed in July 1976, to make newspapers more accountable for what they published, Fairfax opposed its formation and refused to join until 1982.

But, in the 1930s, Fairfax & Sons was persuaded to join forces with the HWT and Keith Murdoch in cable news and paper production (Chapter 14). The two groups did not always see eye-to-eye. Murdoch complained about 'how contemptibly mean and selfish *Sydney Morning Herald* people can become'.[47] (What Henderson thought of Murdoch is not known.) The joint ventures helped both companies entrench their corporate power, but Fairfax & Sons was not following the HWT's expansionist path. It did not go into radio in the 1920s, 1930s or 1940s. Nor did it buy, or start up, any other newspaper during those decades. Its small attempt at expansion during this period amounted to the purchase of two magazines in 1934 that reflected the patrician Warwick Fairfax's interests. *Home* was a magazine that showed how to be tasteful in matters of home, garden and dress, and *Art in Australia* was a pioneering art journal. The more pragmatic Henderson did not approve of these purchases and, these small steps into high culture aside, Fairfax &

Sons remained content to simply protect and build up the *Sydney Morning Herald*.

Once Rupert Henderson attained the position of general manager in 1938, the closure of the loss-making weekly, the *Sydney Mail* (which had been founded by James Reading's brother, Charles Fairfax, in 1860) was a sign that the group was now making decisions based on finances rather than nostalgia. The *Sydney Mail* had been known for its high-quality illustrations from the 1880s, and become an entirely pictorial journal from World War I, but by the 1930s, this was no longer such a selling point, as the *Sydney Morning Herald* and other papers were all incorporating more photographs, supplements and magazine sections.

Like Murdoch, Henderson had ambitions to be more than just a salaried employee-executive. He too dreamed of owning an independent newspaper empire. With the support of Warwick Fairfax, and (at first) in partnership with Fairfax's second wife, Hanne Anderson, Henderson built up a business in regional newspapers from the mid-1940s that included Wagga Wagga's *Daily Advertiser* and Wollongong's *Illawarra Mercury*, and later newspapers in the Riverina and at Goulburn. When questions were raised about metropolitan newspapers taking over country papers, Henderson denied that the purchases were conducted on behalf of the *Sydney Morning Herald*, arguing they were personal transactions.[48]

The Fairfax family's old money

At the end of the 1930s, with the dynamic and intimidating Henderson at the helm, Fairfax & Sons' most active days were ahead of it. But what lay behind was just as significant to its future. For nearly a century, the Fairfax family had been reaping the benefits of prudent investments. The early Fairfaxes had invested profits from the *Sydney Morning Herald* into some of the most powerful industries of their day – sugar, banking, gas, trustee companies, breweries, shipping and life insurance. Some of these investments turned out to be wildly profitable and the Fairfaxes had grown parallel fortunes from these companies as well as from the *Sydney Morning Herald*.

Sugar was a near universal commodity in John Fairfax's time, and one of his most significant early investments was in the commercial growing of sugar in Queensland. The Colonial Sugar Refining Company (CSR) was founded in Sydney in 1855 by Sir Edward Knox. It descended from the Australasian Sugar Company, established in 1842. By 1910, CSR was one of the three largest companies in Australia, and by 1930, the richest in the nation.[49] The precise date when the Fairfax family became investors is not known, but the family was certainly involved by 1855, when John Fairfax's daughter, Emily, married the general manager of CSR. CSR expanded into milling cane in Queensland and Fiji from the 1870s. It controversially used what was effectively slave labour through the abduction and importation of tens of thousands of South Sea Islanders (disparagingly called 'Kanakas') to work in appalling conditions on Queensland sugar plantations.

Although normally a strong supporter of the White Australia policy, the *Sydney Morning Herald* wanted it suspended in the case of the canefields. It argued there was a special need for 'black' labour in the sugar fields of Queensland because the task was not suitable for white men. Campaigning against the abolition of 'Kanaka' labour, the paper argued that it was wrong to deprive the sugar planter of the 'cheap labour' he relied upon. The *Sydney Morning Herald* claimed: 'The sun, so deadly to the white man, is to [the 'kanaka'] only the source of a genial warmth ... these islanders are [like] the Australian aborigine [sic] ... just sufficiently intelligent for work in the canefield ... cheap, and ... inured to outdoor labour in a tropical climate'. Arguing that 'white men' were still getting 'all the work calling for intelligence', and would be wasted toiling in the fields, the *Sydney Morning Herald* said if the 'kanakas' had to go, then the sugar planter should be given some other form of help such as a duty on sugar.[50] At no stage did the paper declare its owners' interest in the issue.

Like other companies that became monopolies, CSR was helped along by the power of the press to put its case. Protected by an embargo on competing imports, it made enormous profits. After it took over, or forced out, other mills and refineries, a 1911 Royal Commission into the sugar industry found that CSR was so dominant that it was effectively able to fix the price of refined sugar in Australia. From 1923, when the Queensland state government signed an agreement with CSR, the company effectively had a monopoly on sugar production that would last until 1989.[51]

Another of the Fairfaxes' far-sighted investments was in life insurance. John Fairfax was a founder of the Australian Mutual Provident Society (AMP), a non-profit life insurance company and mutual society formed in 1849. He was a director of AMP, on and off, between 1849 and 1877. It reflected his Christian ethos of helping the poor because, as Geoffrey Blainey has noted, AMP 'offered social security before the governments entered that province'.[52] But AMP's proactive board of directors also took the liberty of drafting a new law that encouraged people to take out a deferred annuity pension, and then convinced state politicians to enact the law in 1850.[53] The *Sydney Morning Herald* gave AMP advance publicity when it was being established, trying to stir up interest in this 'most important and interesting' venture.[54] It also wrote glowing articles about AMP's growth, and defended it against criticism.[55]

AMP grew significantly during World War I because it was willing to insure men who were going to the front, so long as they paid a premium, whereas other life insurance companies would not. AMP was by far the largest player in the life insurance industry in

Australia, sometimes four times the size of its nearest rival.[56] It became a powerful financial institution because it controlled an immense block of capital consisting of its members' funds. Crucial to this was its status as a non-profit mutual fund which invested income for members and policyholders rather than paying dividends to shareholders. This meant AMP directors were responsible for making decisions about where to invest vast sums of its members' money. There was intense competition among wealthy Sydney businessmen to be a member of the AMP board because of the power that its directors had to direct finance towards helping or hindering other businesses. AMP became 'a major long-term investor' in other businesses (including Collins House's BHAS and CUB), and a dominant shareholder in important companies. It came to occupy a 'crucially important position in the Australian capital market as a whole'.[57]

While others might hunger for a seat on the board, the Fairfax family occupied an almost ongoing spot. A Fairfax was on the AMP board for sixty-six of the 133 years between 1849 and 1982, with an unbroken stint of thirty-three years (between 1956 and 1989). After John Fairfax, James Reading Fairfax was an AMP director between 1884 and 1887. Then came James' son, James Oswald (Warwick's father) (1907–09), as well as John Hubert Fairfax (Warwick's uncle) (1932–48), and Vincent Fairfax (Warwick's cousin) who was an AMP director for twenty-six years (1956–82). The Fairfaxes sat with captains of industry on the AMP board, including Cecil Hoskins of Australian Iron and Steel (AIS) (AMP director, 1929–60). AMP invested heavily in Hoskins' steel company, and when BHP acquired AIS in 1935, that gave the Fairfaxes a link to BHP. Several Fairfax family members also personally held BHP shares (Chapter 15). Those blue-chip shares added to the Fairfaxes' wealth.

In 1886, Warwick's grandfather, the extremely busy James Reading Fairfax, had helped found the Perpetual Trustee Company, and became its first chairman. Edmund Barton, Australia's future first prime minister and WS Robinson's uncle, was on the committee that had recommended the establishment of the trustee fund. Barton was then Speaker of the New South Wales Assembly, a sailing buddy of James Reading's, and fellow member of the Athenaeum Club. (At the Melbourne Athenaeum Club, the Baillieus and Symes socialised with their own political advocate, Deakin.)

The Perpetual Trustee Company administered the estates of the deceased. Because trustee companies held millions in assets on behalf of thousands of deceased estates, they were also an important source of investment funds for large companies (Collins House had its own allied trustee companies, including Trustees Executors & Agency Co., Union Trustee, Executor Trustee and Agency Company, and National Trustee). For obvious reasons, war is highly profitable for trustee companies, and the Perpetual Trustee Company increased its capital substantially during World War I when over 60 000 Australians were killed. By 1917, it held over £12 million in trusts.[58] By 1938, that exceeded £50 million.[59] James Oswald (Warwick's father) was a director of Perpetual Trustees. Edward Ritchie Knox (the third Edward Knox to run CSR, he was a director (1923–69) and its chairman (1933–59)) was also a Perpetual Trustee director.

Directors who control trustee companies invest assets on behalf of the deceased estates and can therefore accumulate large blocks of voting shares in other companies in the name of the trustee company. Perpetual Trustee Company invested in businesses connected to the Fairfaxes, especially CSR and BHP, but also companies allied with the Baillieus and Collins House, including APPM (paper), ICI (chemicals) and the National Bank.[60]

Bank support was also vital for the success of businesses. Collins House and the Baillieus had their own allied banks (including the National Bank, ES&A, Bank of Adelaide and Commercial Bank of Australia). But the Fairfaxes were closely connected with two others: the Bank of New South Wales, and the Commercial Banking Company of Sydney. The Bank of New South Wales (today known as Westpac) was Australia's first bank. It was the largest commercial bank in the country and, in the late 1930s, was twice the size of its nearest competitor (the Collins House–allied National Bank). It had 789 branches, and was still growing rapidly.[61]

As noted in Chapter 1, the Bank of New South Wales had been associated with the press from its earliest days, with several newspaper owners among its proprietors and directors in the late 1810s and 1820s (Howe, Wentworth, Wardell and Hall). John Fairfax became a shareholder in 1850, along with his friend, David Jones, who was also a fellow foundation director of AMP, and a fellow deacon of Fairfax's Congregational Church in Sydney. Jones' eponymous retail business would become Australia's first department store, and a crucial advertiser for Sydney newspapers, especially after it moved to grand new premises in 1927.

When James Reading Fairfax was appointed to the Bank of New South Wales board in 1896, he was described as 'an old shareholder' of the bank.[62] This was accurate: his family had been shareholders for nearly half a century. His *Sydney Morning Herald* had shown its loyalty and demonstrated its value to the bank three years earlier, during the period of depression that followed the collapse of banks in Melbourne (including the Federal Bank, to which Baillieu owed massive unpaid debts). At the height of anxiety about bank security in New South Wales, the *Sydney Morning Herald* had reassured a nervous public that the Bank of New South Wales was 'one of the soundest in the world'.[63] James Reading's highly prized Bank of New South Wales board seat was another that would be handed down through generations of Fairfaxes, including to John H Fairfax (Warwick's uncle) and Vincent Fairfax (Warwick's cousin).

The other Fairfax-allied bank, the Commercial Banking Company of Sydney (today known as the National Australia Bank (NAB) after its merger with the National Bank of Australasia), opened in 1834. It was second in size to the Bank of New South Wales, but for forty years paid the highest dividends of any bank in Australia.[64] James Reading Fairfax added a directorship in this bank to his busy schedule in 1887. CSR's founder, (the first) Edward Knox, was a fellow director (1845–1901).

When James Reading Fairfax died in 1919, the Fairfaxes were a wealthy and powerful family, and the *Sydney Morning Herald* was but one source of this. Just as significant were the profits and power that accrued from the family's involvement in some of Australia's most lucrative businesses – sugar, life insurance and banking. The Fairfaxes sat on boards with politicians and business leaders. They controlled capital and financial decisions. They used their prestigious newspaper to promote and defend companies and industries in which they had an interest. On the surface, Fairfax & Sons looked quiet during the 1920s and 1930s. But underneath, the company was paddling vigorously in a range of lucrative businesses, accumulating capital, connections and financial power that it would be able to mobilise when the time came to turn its hand to media empire building.

THE WILD MEN OF SYDNEY: THE PACKERS AND THE NORTONS

The family that built a rival to the *Sydney Morning Herald* – the Packers – were not blue-bloods or old money like the Fairfaxes. The Packers did not have the prestige that came from owning 'Granny *Herald*', nor the money that came from its firm grip on Sydney's classified advertising market. But they were tough, ruthless and unconventional. Their populist touch and forceful style in matters of business saw them usher in a new period of competition.

The Packers pushed their way into the Sydney newspaper industry with the backing of wealthy patrons and through a series of controversial business transactions that left behind a trail of victims, including dismissed staff, duped opponents and empty-handed shareholders. With his health failing in the first years of the 1930s, RC Packer had worked hard to set up his son Frank (whose full name was Douglas Frank Hewson Packer) in newspapers. He had tried to use Associated Newspapers as a base for him, but that was thwarted. The Packers then exploited Denison's fear of competition to enrich themselves and gain a large amount of capital, which they used to start the phenomenally successful *Australian Women's Weekly* in 1933 (Chapter 4).

When Frank's father died on 12 April 1934, he left behind an estate of £54 306 for his family (equivalent to about $5 million in today's money).[65] RC left his shareholdings to Frank, who married Gretel Bullmore three months later, after years of pursuing her. Some sections of Sydney society would always look down on the Packer clan because of their reputation for unethical business deals and Frank's sometimes boorish behaviour, but Gretel gave Frank admittance to the high-society life that he craved, complete with black-tie dinners, and cocktail and bridge parties. He took with enthusiasm to the elite hobbies of the Sydney rich – polo, yachting, horseracing and golf.

Gretel was the glamorous sister of Mary Hordern of the Hordern retailing empire. The Horderns' famous department store had been sold to public investors in 1926, but they were still major shareholders, and also a well-connected family of wealthy graziers and stockbrokers. Frank's brother-in-law, Anthony Hordern, was president of the New South Wales Polo Association. Through the Horderns, Packer was also linked to other newspaper owners because Anthony's brother, Samuel, was a director of AMP and Perpetual Trustee Company, while Samuel's son had recently married WL Baillieu's niece, an alliance that united two of the country's wealthiest families. The inheritance that Frank derived from RC was large, but not large enough to buy a daily newspaper in the 1930s. For a working journalist to achieve that level of ownership, a rich backer was essential. Keith Murdoch and JE Davidson had the Baillieus. RC Packer had Sir Joynton Smith (who gifted him a one-third share in *Smith's Weekly*). RC's son, Frank, secured his own patron.

Gold diggers: 'Red Ted' and the Packers' new money

EG Theodore was tall and solidly built, with thick, prominent lips. A seasoned political fighter, Theodore was nicknamed 'Red Ted' by his conservative opponents. He had founded a militant miners' union when he was twenty-one years old.

Frank and Theodore shared an interest in newspapers, and in mining. Frank had dreamed of striking it rich by finding precious metals, had dabbled in investments in tin mining in Malaya, and had some outdoor adventures trying to find gold in the Northern Territory. But Theodore had actually worked in the unrelentingly harsh conditions of mines, including at Broken Hill in 1903–06 (he would have been there when WL Baillieu arrived in 1904 to begin investing in the north and south ends of the lode).

Theodore did not prosper in mining in those early years, but he did thrive in the labour politics that he learned at Broken Hill and then applied in Queensland. In 1906, he moved to Cairns, where he started organising the district's workers and helped form the Amalgamated Workers Association (AWA) of North Queensland. He went up against CSR, whose sugar workers toiled for long hours under harsh conditions that were a legacy of CSR's exploitation of South Sea Islander labour. One of the AWA's major achievements was a victory in the sugar strike of 1911. (The *Sydney Morning*

Herald had condemned the strikers as 'callous to the welfare of their country'.[66])

After Theodore won a Queensland Legislative Assembly seat for Labor in 1909, his rise up the political ladder was rapid. He became deputy leader in 1912, and when Labor took office in June 1915, became deputy premier, treasurer and secretary for public works. In October 1919, TJ Ryan resigned to enter federal politics, and Theodore became premier aged thirty-four years old. He was still interested in mining, but now as a mine owner, not a mine labourer. After he resigned as premier in 1925, Theodore camped out with his friend, WS Robinson, and they inspected the Mount Isa silver-lead strike in north-west Queensland. Theodore was also involved in mining ventures with another mutual friend of theirs, John Wren.

In 1927, Theodore entered federal politics, and became treasurer in 1929. A determined self-improver, he worked on improving his speech and debating skills. He read voraciously and was highly knowledgeable across economic and industrial matters. Theodore's economic skills were eagerly sought by the government during the Depression but business leaders and commercial newspapers despaired of his approach (Chapters 10 and 11). Theodore's association with Wren had tarnished his reputation, and he had been caught up in a series of scandals, including the Mungana affair. He had also made enemies, particularly Lang, who helped end Theodore's political career. It was a Langite Labor candidate who defeated Theodore in the seat of Dalley in the 1931 election. In a bitter contest, Lang's supporters converged on the electorate, sang 'Yes, we have no Munganas' at Theodore's campaign rallies and threw eggs, flour and tomatoes.[67] Theodore's share of the formal vote dropped from 78 per cent in 1929, to 20 per cent.[68] It was a sudden and dramatic end to one of the most promising careers in Labor history, with Theodore now considered possibly the most talented politician never to be prime minister of Australia.

By the time forty-seven-year-old Theodore joined forces with twenty-five-year-old Frank Packer, he was out of politics and focused on making his way in business. In January 1932, only weeks after his electoral defeat, Theodore met with RC Packer on Packer's yacht at Jervis Bay. After that meeting, the events described in Chapter 4 ensued. Theodore had long wanted to own a newspaper, and had personally seen and felt the political influence of the press. The conservative press had been long-time critics, while Lang's *Labor Daily* also regularly, and bitterly, attacked him. This had all sharpened Theodore's desire to be a newspaper owner who could influence public opinion.

RC Packer had the relevant contacts and experience in the industry. But Theodore also saw something in the robust and restless Frank that made him willing to team up with the young man. Theodore became a mentor and father figure to Frank. He supplied the capital in their partnership, while Frank supplied the audacity. As explained in Chapter 4, they bluffed Hugh Denison into paying them £86 500 to abandon their much hyped, but probably fictitious, plan to turn the *World* into a penny competitor to the *Sun*. That capital allowed them to launch the *Australian Women's Weekly* in 1933.

In 1936, to stop Packer and Theodore from launching another seemingly imminent afternoon newspaper off the back of the *Women's Weekly*'s success, Denison joined forces with them. The two companies formed Consolidated Press Limited. Associated Newspapers meekly contributed its underperforming *Telegraph* (as the *Daily Telegraph* was then known during one of its many name changes), while Sydney Newspapers contributed the *Women's Weekly*. Packer then took charge of the flat-lining *Telegraph* and set about revamping it.[69]

Frank's fortunes had taken a dramatic turn for the better by this time because Theodore had struck it rich in the gold mines of Fiji, and had made Packer a minor, silent partner in a venture that also involved John Wren and Patrick Cody, and probably Robinson as financier. Theodore, the former leader of a militant miners' union, was now the owner of a Fiji gold mine that used cheap labour under a 'pliant colonial administration'.[70] The 1935 flotation of Emperor Mines made Theodore, Wren, Cody and Packer 'filthy rich'.[71] The hint of impropriety that followed Theodore from the Royal Commission and his association with Wren were now mixed in with Frank's reputation for unethical business deals.

Theodore and Packer both despised Lang and felt they had suffered enormous losses at his hand. Lang had ended Theodore's career in federal politics and tried to financially ruin the Packers. A long-time target of RC Packer's strident political coverage, in 1932, Lang had initiated a bill that would prevent ordinary shareholders from disposing of their assets without the assent of preference shareholders. Lang was going to make the law retrospective to 1 July 1929, so that it would capture Associated Newspapers' payment to Smith's Newspapers for the *Guardian*s. That 'sordid' transaction had seen the Packers pocket their share of the cash (and Associated Newspapers' shares), while Smith's preference shareholders had been given nothing.[72] The Packers had even been indemnified from any claims that might arise from this unorthodox distribution. After disquiet in business circles about the immorality of the deal, Smith had been persuaded to voluntarily return 80 000 preference shares in Associated Newspapers and £20 000 cash to Smith's Newspapers. But the Packers refused to do the same. Without the Packers' money, Smith's Newspapers was financially imperilled and never did recover. Lang insisted that the Packers were 'thieves', and if his bill, with its retrospective clause, was imposed, it likely would have bankrupted them.

Like a scene out of Chicago-style machine politics, the Packers frantically lobbied behind the scenes to stop the bill when it went to the Upper House by drawing on a network of Labor Party contacts through Theodore, the Australian Workers' Union (AWU) and Warnecke.[73] The bill did lapse when parliament was adjourned, and was then shelved permanently after Lang was dismissed as New South Wales premier on 13 May 1932, by the governor, Sir Philip Game. The confronting episode had highlighted how closely the tough worlds of newspapers and politics intersected and made a strong impression on Frank.

Frank Packer: The man and boss

The *Sydney Morning Herald* started the 1930s well ahead of its main rival, selling twice as many copies as the once innovative, but now staid, *Telegraph*. In 1936, Frank Packer and his talented editor, Syd Deamer, set out to change that. They revitalised the paper, which was once again called the *Daily Telegraph* from 23 March, when it reappeared as a new, brighter and improved paper. It had more pages, an enlarged comic section, a turf supplement that expanded into a twelve-page turf guide, and a popular section of pithy readers' letters which provoked vigorous debate.[74] Over the next two years, the *Daily Telegraph*'s circulation grew by 60 000, while the *Sydney Morning Herald*'s grew by only 9000.[75] By the mid-1940s, the *Daily Telegraph* was selling more copies than its august rival.[76]

Frank Packer remained chairman of ACP from 1936 until his death in 1974. In an embarrassingly sycophantic biography written by an employee while Frank was still alive, RS Whitington described his boss as having an 'underlying journalistic genius'.[77] But it was widely known that Frank's journalism skills were limited. His strengths were his quick intuition and strategic mind, along with his financial management skill, and his business brutality. Frank lacked his father's journalistic flair, but he inherited RC's head-kicking people management techniques and took them even further. His biographer, Griffen-Foley, observed that he was 'an interventionist, imperious and fiery proprietor'.[78]

Frank wanted the financial benefits, political power and social status that came from owning a daily newspaper, but he resented the huge expense involved in publishing newspapers. Infamously frugal, he drove his staff hard and made them work in austere conditions. He berated photographers for using more than one roll of film, and as Griffen-Foley noted, generally 'counted the paper clips at work'.[79]

Frank had a notorious temper that was exacerbated by his regular gambling losses. Journalist Claire Harvey described how, if he lost heavily at the racetrack on a Saturday afternoon, Packer was known to stride into the *Sunday Telegraph*'s office that evening and bark: 'You're all useless leeches. You're a pack of bloodsuckers. Get out. You're all sacked.' At this, the staff would get up from the battered desk they all shared to save costs, and troop downstairs to a nearby pub, where they would wait it out until Packer's mood improved. Eventually, 'the editor would rush in to the pub and tell his workers … to come back upstairs and finish producing the paper'. Not surprisingly, it was 'frequently late getting to the streets'.[80] It is impossible to imagine Keith Murdoch indulging in such unprofessional behaviour, or such deadline-affecting tantrums occurring at the *Sydney Morning Herald* office.

Although there have been valiant attempts to highlight Packer's good qualities – his kindness to his mother and occasional acts of surprising generosity seem to be the main ones – it is difficult to escape the conclusion that he was a nasty piece of work. A bully who was boastful and immature, homophobic, sexist and brutish. He was the sort of man who had no qualms about lying to competitors, going through a rival's briefcase if he happened to leave the room during sensitive business negotiations, or sacking staff if he was in a bad mood. Packer's obituary said that 'So ritualistic were

Frank's firings in the lift at work that staff had a saying: "The stairway is the safe way".'[81] Packer once said in an ABC interview that, with the exception of his friend David McNicoll, he considered his employees 'slaves'.[82] And Bednall observed that 'Frank Packer visibly relished taking money or privileges away from some employee'.[83]

Packer was an equally intimidating force at home. He relentlessly picked on his sons, including his younger son, Kerry, who recalled 'a lot' of beatings and humiliation.[84] Phillip Adams, who was a close friend of Kerry Packer's, said that 'The myths and allegations that swirl around Sir Frank Packer understate the reality ... He was a monster.'[85] Kerry would later be accused of being a harsh father himself; and RC, Frank and Kerry were all pursuers of women, and serially unfaithful husbands. Whispers of alleged sexual assault or intimidation swirled around RC and Frank, while Kerry was associated with brothels and alleged to be involved in criminal activities, but was exonerated of the most sensational claims following a Royal Commission.[86] All three Packers owned guns.[87] Frank and Kerry were amateur boxers. The seediness and undertones of violence made the Melbourne newspaper culture seem prim by comparison.

With Theodore's help, Frank Packer became a disruptive force shaking up the Sydney market. Enjoying the money and power that came from being head of a publishing business, by the mid-1930s, he would not be bought off. Murdoch made an offer to Packer and Theodore to buy into the *Women's Weekly* in June 1935, but they rejected it. In 1938, Murdoch tried again. He was still concerned about the *Women's Weekly* 'sucking' advertising away from his papers, so made another offer to buy a half interest in Consolidated Press Limited. When Frank and Theodore demanded more money, Murdoch offered to buy the whole business outright for £800 000 but they again refused. Frank told Warnecke, 'If it's worth that to him, it's good enough to keep'.[88]

An important year for Packer

By 1939, Packer had been in partnership with Associated News-papers in Consolidated Press for three years. He was in charge of the high circulation *Women's Weekly*, which had shifted to glamorous colour in December 1936, courtesy of a highly advanced printing press purchased from the United States. Through the invigorated *Daily Telegraph*, Packer was also enjoying the influence that came with being able to have a daily say on news and politics. But the paper still remained a difficult one to make money from because the *Sydney Morning Herald* had such a strong grip on the classified advertising market. In an attempt to make its own classifieds more enticing, the *Daily Telegraph* had started a competition where read-ers had to find false ads embedded in its classified section. When this did not help matters much, Frank went to Fairfax & Sons and again bluffed a rival into helping him. Packer told Fairfax that Consoli-dated Press was in serious financial trouble and he was thinking of selling the *Daily Telegraph* to the HWT. Frank wanted to increase the cover price of the *Daily Telegraph* and he needed the *Sydney Morning Herald* to raise their price as well. Not wanting the HWT to gain a foothold in the Sydney market, Henderson and Fairfax agreed.[89] This price-fixing deal seems to be yet another example of Packer's cunning as it seems unlikely that Consolidated was ever really in serious talks with the HWT.[90]

At the end of the 1930s, Packer was securing his grip on his assets. As part of this, he drove out a potential ownership rival by get-ting rid of Warnecke, the talented journalist and driving force behind the *Women's Weekly*. Packer was still mixing with high society, and wining and dining with political and commercial heavy-weights. A sign of his growing influence in the newspaper industry came in November 1939, when he was elected president of the ANC. He was only thirty-three years old, the youngest proprietor of importance at the table. He was not liked by other newspaper owners and executives, including Keith Murdoch, Lloyd Dumas, and Geoffrey Syme of *The Age*.[91] Packer's presidency did not last long. He resigned in May 1940, in protest at what he felt was a lack of support from other proprietors when the Menzies government planned to allow a newsprint licence for a new Sydney afternoon newspaper (Chapter 15).[92] Packer was difficult, unpredictable and isolationist, but the other proprietors could no longer ignore him.

Only a few days after Packer was elected to the industry leadership post, he boldly launched a new paper, at a time when most owners would no longer take the risk. The cosy deal Packer had struck with Associated Newspapers in 1936 had required that he wait three years before starting a Sunday paper. That had now expired. Packer had used the time to consolidate his finances. He wanted a Sunday edition in order to minimise his idle printing capacity. This was becoming crucial to economic viability. Packer also wanted a slice of the lucrative Sunday advertising market, and one advertiser in particular. It was a cause of great annoyance to Frank that David Jones gave more business to Associated Newspapers and the *Sydney Morning Herald*.

Packer was also partly motivated by revenge. He was still deeply resentful of Associated Newspapers' treatment, and Denison had recently rubbed salt in the wound by making scathing comments about RC Packer. Frank had responded with an article in the *Daily Telegraph* defending his father. It was headed 'SIR HUGH DENISON LIBELS DEAD MAN'.[93] Taking readers and advertisers from the *Sunday Sun* would hurt Denison, but there was another rival newspaper owner Packer also wanted to wound – a man with a temper to rival Frank's own.

The even wilder men of Sydney: The Nortons

Ezra Norton was also from a newspaper family, but one that was far more radical and dysfunctional than Frank's. Ezra's father, John Norton, was a newspaper owner and politician who, at the time of his death in 1916, owned the weekly *Truth* (published on Sundays in Sydney), plus local editions of *Truth* in Brisbane, Melbourne and Perth, as well as the *Sportsman*.[94] *Truth* was a paper with a racy writing style and detailed reporting of salacious court cases. A mixture of radical politics, scandal and muckraking, it was aimed at blue-collar workers who were willing to spend their scarce pennies on a paper that styled itself as the voice of the Australian larrikin.

Michael Cannon argued that *Truth* focused on social issues that mattered to the daily lives of its readers rather than the grand political questions tackled by the *Sydney Morning Herald*. *Truth* campaigned for protection of 'the weak and oppressed', including exploited workers, slum dwellers, women and children.[95] It campaigned against corporal and capital punishment, and exposed police corruption and mismanagement at public hospitals. It talked about poverty and it exposed 'quack remedies, massage parlours, tied public houses, rackrenting, the "sweating" of labour, Tattersall's sweeps, frauds by astrologers and confidence tricksters, and the ill-treatment of Aborigines and of prisoners of the Crown'.[96] It was also sexist and racist, displaying what one author called 'an obsessive fear and dislike of coloured people'.[97]

Shrill scandalous *Truth* was suspicious of authority, relished exposing hypocrisy and boldly took on powerful people. It made many enemies, and Norton appeared regularly in court defending himself against defamation actions. He was charged with sedition after writing that Queen Victoria was 'flabby and flatulent' and her son, the Prince of Wales, a 'card sharping, wife-debauching rascal'.[98] John Norton was an earlier breed of gun-toting Sydney newspaper proprietor. After a barrister tried to horsewhip him in the street following Norton's continued attacks on him in *Truth*, Norton fired his gun, but missed. Norton also assaulted a fellow member of parliament.

Although the dedicated working-class audience of *Truth* 'idolized' the bold, talented writer, Norton was publicly accused of being a dishonest wife beater and obscene drunk.[99] He was sometimes too drunk to stand up to deliver political speeches, and once urinated before other MPs in the parliamentary chamber. He was accused of blackmailing advertisers into paying for ads by showing them copy he would otherwise run, and even of murdering a man. The murder accusation was on flimsy evidence, but the blackmail allegation was repeated regularly enough for his biographer to wonder if there may have been some truth to it.[100] Although allegations of Norton's domestic violence and alcoholism were publicly known, he was still elected to parliament four times.

When John Norton died in 1916, he cut out of his will both his wife and their nineteen-year-old son, Ezra, whose paternity John had questioned. (Others believed the disinheritance to be a result of Ezra having defended his mother from his father's violence.) Ezra and his mother contested the will and the Equity Court agreed to redraft it in 1920. When Ezra reached the age of twenty-five, he became chief executive and obtained full control over the newspapers. He was an erratic man, psychologically damaged by a harsh and miserable childhood, and his father's terrible treatment of him and his mother.

Once in charge of *Truth*, Ezra Norton continued with its formula of 'pumping out a mixture of sex, scandal and hysteria'.[101] He fashioned himself, in the manner of his father, as a crusading journalist who rallied against monopolists, corrupt politicians and powerful men. This included rival newspaper owners. Ever since the closure of the *World*, Norton had been publishing critical and unflattering stories about the Packers' questionable business deals. Packer and Norton had temporarily found a common cause in opposing the HWT–Fairfax newsprint bounty in 1938 (Chapter 14), but then fiercely fell out over the issue in 1939.[102] They used their newspapers to carry on their personal feud.

The week after World War II was declared, the *Daily Telegraph* criticised a report in Ezra Norton's *Truth* about dealings between Germany and Britain. The next day, *Truth* published an unflattering photograph of Frank Packer and, lampooning his vanity, reported that Packer had complained when the photograph had been published on a previous occasion. In retaliation, the *Daily Telegraph* published a report about a court case in which Norton was appearing as a witness. Headlined 'NEWSPAPER PROPRIETOR BUYS ALLEGEDLY STOLEN BROOCH', it was accompanied by a photograph of Norton (who hated having his photograph taken) leaving the court with a raincoat held against his face. The next day, Packer and Norton came across each other at a Derby race meeting at Randwick, and punches were thrown. Norton was another Sydney owner with burly bodyguards, and it appears one of them stepped in to hit Packer, who fell to the ground and came away bleeding and bruised. While Norton's *Truth* and Packer's *Daily Telegraph* studiously ignored the incident, *Smith's Weekly* gleefully reported that Packer had come off second-best.[103] The incident strengthened Packer's resolve to start up a Sunday newspaper that would take on Norton's Sunday *Truth* as well as Denison's *Sunday Sun*.[104]

The *Sunday Telegraph*

Ahead of its November 1939 launch, Packer pumped money into a lavish press and radio advertising campaign to herald the arrival of the *Sunday Telegraph*. The paper's editor, until 1950, was the sharp and canny Cyril Pearl, who had honed his journalism skills to 'legendary standards' at the *Argus*' defunct Melbourne *Star*.[105] When the new *Sunday Telegraph* hit the streets on 19 November, it was a bold and lively threepenny broadsheet of sixty-four pages, with a page-one David Jones ad that pleased Packer enormously. Packer even hired a society matron, Nola Dekyvere, to write a diary column for the paper's women's section, reportedly not because of her literary ability, but because of her valuable connections to David Jones.[106]

The *Sunday Telegraph* was full of war news, fashion, society, sport (especially boxing and horseracing), investigations and crime, plus the paper's most distinctive 'sales weapon', its comics.[107] It boasted Australia's largest comic section, a cutting-edge sixteen-page tabloid lift-out in dazzling colour. The idea was that children 'would encourage their parents to buy the paper, so they could read the comics and listen along on Radio 2UW, where the comics were read aloud on Sunday mornings'.[108] The comic supplement had been created and printed in the United States, and then imported from California. This had caused complaints from the printing unions, the AJA and the Australian Black and White Artists' Club who argued that cheap, syndicated American comics were a 'menace to the livelihood' of Australian artists.[109] But after cannily exploiting divisions within the union movement, Packer was able to secure assent from the PIEUA in New South Wales for the comic supplement to be printed in the United States for twelve months, until the new paper was established.[110]

Colour printing would continue to be a distinctive feature of the *Sunday Telegraph*. In July 1940, the paper published a colorgravure supplement showing photographs of New York winter fashion and interior design. The issue was sold out. No other newspaper in Australia could produce a supplement like that at the time. (Around 1948, the *Sunday Telegraph* acquired its own four-colour Rotogravure press which was 'the paper's proudest asset'.[111]) The Sunday paper battle would go on for years. The *Sunday Sun* had a

BIRTH OF THE SUNDAY TELEGRAPH

Mrs. R. C. Packer and Hon. E. G. Theodore, Chairman of Directors, inspect
first copy of new Sunday paper. The ceremony is not a novelty to Mrs.
Packer, as she has been directly associated with the launching of six
newspapers. With her husband, the late Mr. R. C. Packer, she took part
in the ceremonies connected with the births of "Smith's Weekly," "Daily
Guardian" and "Sunday Guardian"; with her son she has seen the births
of the "Australian Women's Weekly," the newly reconstructed "Daily
Telegraph," under Consolidated Press management and the "Sunday
Telegraph."

FIGURE 9.3 Frank Packer's beloved mother, Ethel Maud Packer, and his
mentor and partner, EG Theodore, start the presses for the launch of the
Sunday Telegraph in 1939

SOURCE *Newspaper News*, 1 December 1939, p. 1.

large circulation lead, but Packer's *Sunday Telegraph* had made a big
splash. In seven months, it was selling up to 200 000 copies a week,
and snatching display advertising from its rivals.[112] In an advertisement for the paper that stressed to advertisers its capacity to print
their ads in 'rich, lifelike' colour, the tough newcomer *Sunday Telegraph* was shown to have knocked out *Truth* and to have an elderly
and worried *Sunday Sun* on the ropes (Figure 9.4).

Packers' politics

Frank had learned from his father a style of populist journalism that used brash, aggressive, politically biased reporting, and attacked politicians and causes the Packers disapproved of. RC Packer was opportunistic about his political alliances though. He was virulently anti-Lang but he had links with the UAP, the federal ALP, and two extremist right-wing groups – Charles Hardy's Riverina Movement and the fascist-leaning New Guard (one of the paramilitary organisations that was formed to mobilise against Lang in New South Wales). Frank Packer similarly saw nothing wrong with crusading political reporting that expressed his political views. He would go on to use his newspapers to campaign hard on issues that he cared about, including his passionate support for conservative leaders Robert Menzies and William McMahon, and his vehement dread of communism.

Later in his life, as Griffen-Foley noted, Frank 'crudely manipulated his own outlets'.[113] He used them to promote his increasingly conservative views and to settle scores with enemies. (These were not always political enemies. Bednall claimed that Packer once ran a vindictive campaign against British Overseas Airways Corporation (BOAC) because the airline had moved him from a window seat.[114]) But in the 1930s, Frank's interventionist tendencies were diluted by his trust in his talented editors, Syd Deamer and Cyril Pearl, and his focus on the business side of his company. Walker argued that 'the *Telegraph*'s domestic politics were quite low key ... [and Deamer and Pearl] were each allowed their independence and received no instructions about politics ... While the paper gave general support to the UAP, it did not always follow the party line.'[115]

Deamer resigned in 1939, and the bold and talented Brian Penton became editor of the *Daily Telegraph* in 1941. Penton had a passionate and irreverent style that suited the paper. He had

FIGURE 9.4 Advertisement for the 'young feller' *Sunday Telegraph* in the industry publication *Newspaper News*, 1940

SOURCE *Newspaper News*, 1 August 1940, p. 7.

previously been a Canberra press gallery reporter and columnist for the *Sydney Morning Herald* (1926–28), where his innovative, 'forceful' and 'stylish' notes stood out on its otherwise sedate pages. Billy Hughes memorably described Penton's contributions to the *Sydney Morning Herald* as 'like finding a new-born babe in a graveyard'.[116] (Penton was yet another journalist friend of the wily Hughes.) Politically, Penton shared some of Packer's views, including a disdain for 'red tape' and censorship, and he was another editor to whom Packer granted significant independence. Some observers even suggested that Packer was somewhat intimidated by his fiery editor.

But Packer's paper had already demonstrated signs of what was to come. During the 1940 federal election, the *Daily Telegraph* had taken an active stance. It called for new blood to be brought into the Menzies government, including ALP candidates, and especially Dr HV Evatt, who Packer supported at the time (Chapter 16). But the paper also intervened in one specific contest – for the seat of Wentworth. It strongly backed Norman Cowper, an independent, against the UAP candidate, Eric Harrison. Harrison had earned Packer's ire in 1939 when, as postmaster-general, he had refused a demand by Packer and other Sydney newspaper owners that the government pay them £90 000 per year to publish lists of ABC radio programs.[117]

Harrison had then compounded their resentment by agreeing to the publication of the *ABC Weekly*, a publication the ABC initiated after Sydney's daily newspapers decided to stop printing details of its broadcasts for free. The Sydney owners were incensed at its publication, viewing it as unfair government-funded competition. They put pressure on advertisers not to advertise in the *ABC Weekly*, and on newsagents not to stock it. Denison even wanted to mount a High Court challenge to stop it garnering a share of national advertising and scarce newsprint.[118] Packer was reportedly especially infuriated when Syd Deamer left to be its editor.

Packer vigorously promoted Cowper in 1940, and the candidate was widely thought to be a Packer stooge. Cowper later admitted that he was a friend of Theodore's and that he 'was pitchforked into [running]. I was very much a Packer protégé in the election.'[119] This 1940 intervention was a taste of things to come. Like his father, Frank Packer would go on to be the model of an interventionist proprietor unburdened by any commitment to fair or impartial journalism.

The Sydney scene at the end of the 1930s

Packer had a top-selling women's magazine, a daily Sydney news-paper and an accompanying Sunday paper, but he was still a small player by the standards of the HWT, and Associated Newspapers at its peak. Unlike the Baillieus and the Fairfaxes, with their wide business interests, Packer's ACP would remain a small and largely independent outfit. It was dedicated to newspapers and publishing until it entered television in the 1950s. There, it would prove to be the most dynamic of the old print owners in the new medium, and the Packers would build significant political influence through their ownership of the country's most watched television station.

In the 1930s, Packer was a comparatively small player, but he gave the *Sydney Morning Herald* a brash new competitor and Fairfax & Sons ended the 1930s on the defensive, thinking about how to protect its sacred trust. Outwardly, Fairfax & Sons was also a small publishing company, consisting of only the *Sydney Morning Herald* and some niche interest magazines. But the company had for-midable wealth and deep-rooted business connections behind it. In the 1950s and 1960s, Fairfax & Sons would start expanding in order to protect itself, and would emerge as a late-blooming media empire.

Until then, it was other New South Wales owners who showed more interest in national markets. Packer's *Women's Weekly* gave advertisers a national platform for the first time, and built an impressive national audience. John Norton had exhibited an early vision beyond state borders by expanding *Truth* from Sydney to start up subsidiaries in Brisbane (1900), Melbourne (1902) and Perth (1903). On the larger scale of a daily newspaper, Denison had tried to conquer Melbourne in the 1920s, but failed. In the 1930s and 1940s, all of the Sydney players were dwarfed by the empire-building might of the HWT. It was driving the key developments affecting the newspaper industry, including in radio broadcasting, newsprint manufacture and political influence.

PART THREE

· ·

THE BATTLES

CHAPTER 10

THE PRESS, JOE LYONS AND THE DEPRESSION

In 1931, the chaos and misery of the Depression sparked another period of political intrigue. As with Hughes in 1916, the 1931 turmoil ended with a Labor MP defecting from his party and switching to head a new conservative coalition that, strongly backed by the press, won the next election. In 1931, it was Joseph Aloysius (Joe) Lyons; and Hughes' World War I confidant, Keith Murdoch, played an even more central role. Murdoch was one of several figures associated with a secretive business cabal known as 'the Group'. Its members persuaded Lyons to leave the Labor Party, and anointed themselves his 'bodyguard' as he transferred into the leadership of the new United Australia Party (UAP). Lyons transformed from being 'a Labor minister disgraced within his own party [to a] leader of resurgent national liberalism and then prime minister of Australia in little more than six months'.[1]

Historian Humphrey McQueen argued that the activities of 'the Group' 'must be described as a conspiracy if the English language is to retain meaning'.[2] Murdoch's part in that 'conspiracy' attained an almost mythical status within political circles, and the episode is still viewed as one of the strongest examples of the power of the press in Australia.

Murdoch's involvement in events was suspected even in 1931, and he made no real attempt to hide it. In the weeks before Lyons left Labor, he was seen lunching frequently with Murdoch in his private dining room at the *Herald*, and occasionally visiting Murdoch's home. After Lyons joined with the Nationalist Party to form the UAP, he rose in the House of Representatives on 7 May 1931, and moved a motion to condemn the Scullin Labor government (of which he had been a minister only ten weeks earlier). Labor MP, John (Jack) Beasley, shouted: 'Did Keith Murdoch write that out for you?'[3]

Privately, Murdoch seemed to genuinely believe that he had created a government. In a letter he wrote to Lloyd Dumas, the managing editor of the *Advertiser*, nearly three years after Lyons had become prime minister, Murdoch described Lyons as the man 'whom we chose and made'.[4] And Murdoch wanted his influence recognised. Lyons continued to visit Murdoch at the *Herald* building in Flinders Street. His staff were concerned that this did not look suitable for a prime minister, but Lyons had replied, 'Oh, I like Murdoch. It pleases him to see me in his office and it does me no harm to go there.'[5] But Lyons' relationship with Murdoch was causing harm to his reputation and, in political and media circles, Murdoch was encouraging a perception that he was influencing the government. This annoyed senior ministers in Lyons' Cabinet who did not see Murdoch's boasting as an accurate reflection of how political decisions were made.

Lyons' wife, Enid Lyons, recalled that Murdoch maliciously said at a 1938 dinner party – in front of Lyons – 'I put him there, and I'll put him out'.[6] By then, Murdoch's relationship with Lyons had soured. Back in May 1931, Beasley had predicted it would. He said that Lyons' 'new masters' would dispose of him once he had 'done the job', just as Murdoch and Collins House had turned on Hughes after World War I.[7] Murdoch's nemesis, Labor's Arthur Calwell, said the reason that Murdoch abandoned Lyons 'a few years after [Lyons] became Prime Minister' was because 'the man [Murdoch] had made ... tried to escape from his toils by showing some independence'.[8] Once again, it was suspected that Murdoch was not acting solely of his own initiative in all of this. One of Menzies' biographers, Kevin Perkins, claimed that Lyons was the 'prisoner' of the 'Collins House group' until they threw him aside for Robert Menzies.[9] Beasley too had claimed in 1931 that Lyons' policies were 'framed … in the office of the Melbourne *Herald* … dictated by the Baillieu press'.[10]

'YES, SIR': PERCEPTIONS OF POWER

A perception of Murdoch as a puppeteer pulling the strings of the Lyons' Cabinet took hold (Figure 10.1). Duncan Clarke, a former copy boy at the *Herald* who was a Murdoch favourite until he left to join the Communist Party of Australia, added to that perception. Clarke described a scene he said he had witnessed in the 1930s when he took Murdoch his tea:

> Murdoch was still shouting and JA Lyons was standing before the desk. I put the tea down on the big desk and went out through the door. As I went through it I turned and there, with his hat in his hand, like a man seeking a job, stood the Prime Minister before Murdoch's desk.
>
> As I shut the door, I heard the leader of the nation say: 'Yes, sir.' Many years later I was to learn that the 'Herald' had played a big part in paving the way for Lyons to rat on the Labor Party and become leader of the [UAP] … (My own father, who was one of Sir Keith's confidants, was drawn into this job) … [Afterwards] Murdoch assumed personal control of the turncoat.[11]

Sir Keith Murdoch, Managing Director of the Melbourne "Herald," plays with his marionettes.

FIGURE 10.1 *Smith's Weekly* cartoonist, Stan Cross, shows Keith Murdoch manipulating Lyons and other ministers over radio station ownership limits in 1935

SOURCE *Smith's Weekly*, 23 November 1935, p. 12.

Although Murdoch's personal papers, held by the National Library, seem to have been heavily edited so that only fairly innocuous material remains, one politically sensitive letter from Lyons was left in so that historians could record Lyons' gratitude. Lyons wrote to Murdoch saying 'I should like to express … my very great appreciation of the generous assistance which was rendered to the [UAP], and to me, by your paper … I recognise that the influence of the "Herald" had an immeasurable bearing upon the [1934 election] verdict rendered by the people'.[12]

Some political insiders – including Staniforth Ricketson, the leader of 'the Group' – believed that Murdoch's ambition to be a powerful kingmaker stemmed from his desire to emulate his idol, Northcliffe.[13] Jack Lang (no stranger to political ambition himself), claimed Murdoch had 'one very simple idea. He wanted to be the most powerful man in the Commonwealth ... It was as simple as that.'[14] But Murdoch was not the only newspaper figure involved in the events of 1931, and there were much bigger issues at stake than one man's lust for power.

THE PRESS AND LYONS

Lyons' defection was one outcome of a serious contest of ideas about economic policy during the Depression. Business leaders and the mainstream press waged an all-out campaign to win a debate that struck at the heart of their finances and beliefs. While the HWT newspapers played the leading role in paving the way for Lyons' party switch and election victory, all of the major commercial daily newspapers backed the economic policies that Lyons was espousing.[15] In their reporting, newspapers focused on individuals – especially Lyons, but also Labor leader James Scullin, and his treasurer, EG Theodore – but did a poor job of covering the complicated economic policy debates. When journalists who worked during the 1930s looked back decades later, they said the Depression was 'appallingly covered' by newspapers. Journalist John Loughlin said that issues such as unemployment, evictions and hunger marches were covered 'inadequately', and 'we did little to help the people understand why it was happening to them, or whether the government was right or wrong in the policies it was following'.[16] Another journalist recalled that the mode of reporting was just 'straight' reporting of what politicians said and did, with no depth, analysis, or independent scrutiny.[17]

Partly, this reflected certain limitations at the time. The Canberra press gallery was still small. It had only about six or seven permanent members, always domiciled in Canberra.[18] Although it used to swell to about four times the size when parliament was in session, it was still isolated in an undeveloped city, and its journalists were trying to cover a frenzied and chaotic period. Dramatic political stories were happening almost daily – leadership challenges, party splits, defections, leaks, a new party, and an election. Never had politics been so prominent in Australian newspapers, and never had its reporters worked such long hours. Journalist Warren Denning wrote that twenty-hour shifts in the press gallery became common, and 'on one occasion we went for 56 hours without sleep or a break'.[19]

Financial journalism and economic reporting were also limited because the discipline of economics was only in its infancy.[20] But there was another overarching restraint on political reporting. Although the press gallery journalists in Canberra tended to have very good relations with Scullin (who gave them regular briefings and was a former journalist and editor himself), they felt caught up in their employers' 'remorseless hostility' to his economic policies.[21] There was little room for journalists to write balanced, let alone sympathetic, reports because newspaper proprietors were deeply invested in Depression-era politics and economics.

THE DEPRESSION HITS

When Murdoch and the HWT turned on Hughes in 1922, they had backed SM Bruce to succeed him as prime minister and leader of the Nationalists. Bruce was a wealthy man who openly represented business interests, and moved in the insular social circles of Melbourne's ultra-rich. (Baillieu had bought Bruce's childhood home, one of Melbourne's largest mansions, from Bruce's father.[22]) The HWT offered significant support to Bruce, and Murdoch even 'loaned' him one of its best reporters, Cecil Edwards, to act as Bruce's press officer for the 1925 election campaign. But, by 1927 to 1928, business leaders were losing faith in Bruce. He had been unable to solve the industrial disputes that were frustrating business and economic development. Since 1927, there had also been signs of difficult times ahead, with lower prices for Australian exports, including wool, sugar and meat, but Bruce's government had no answers.[23] Australia was worryingly vulnerable to any downturn in the international economy because it was so reliant on selling commodities, and because it had a very large deficit. Bruce's government, and state governments around the country, had borrowed enormous sums of money from London to finance public works, including transport, irrigation and electrification projects.

In October 1929, a snap federal election was called after Hughes, still as contrary and ambitious as ever, crossed the floor with other rebel backbenchers to bring down Bruce's government. The once electorally dominant Nationalist Party campaigned like a tired and spent force during the campaign. The newspapers chastised Bruce for his many missteps, but most still advocated a vote for the Nationalists above Labor (Table 3.1, pages 118–19). Many voters must have ignored their advice though, because the Bruce government was rejected so emphatically that Labor won office in a landslide result. (Bruce even lost his own seat, the first prime minister to do so – and the only one until John Howard lost his in 2007.) The Nationalists were reduced to just eighteen seats in the House but still had a large majority in the Senate because the 1929 election was only for the House, not the Senate. The system for electing the Senate at the time was also producing a distorted 'windscreen-wiper effect' (with Senate seats being delivered disproportionately to whichever political party was in favour at the time of the last election) so although Scullin had 'the largest one-party majority ever achieved in the House of Representatives', in the Senate, his government had 'only seven votes compared to the Nationalist Party's twenty-four and the Country Party's five'.[24] Scullin faced an implacably hostile Senate from the beginning and this would be a major obstacle for the incoming Labor government.

On arrival in Canberra, Scullin's government faced immediate economic problems. Low commodity prices had led to wage cuts, then strikes and lockouts in the New South Wales coal fields. Unemployment was already at 10 per cent. Only one week after the government had been sworn into office, there was a sudden and dramatic collapse of the world's stock markets after the Wall Street stock market crashed in New York on 29 October 1929. A worldwide depression followed. Falling world prices for primary products hit Australia hard. The 'value of Australia's wool and wheat exports halved', national income 'declined by one third', and staggeringly high unemployment followed.[25] By mid-1930, unemployment was at 21 per cent.[26] The scale of poverty and suffering scarred a generation who saw beggars, soup kitchens, shanty towns and malnourished children. Factories were idle. Houses sat empty because no one could afford the rent. Thousands roamed the country looking for work.

The newspapers were affected in various ways. The heavy fall in prices hurt exporters of wool, wheat, lead and zinc, including the pastoral interests and mining companies behind key newspaper groups. Newspapers tended to have large overdrafts with their banks so lost advertising revenue and sales started biting; they needed credit and the return of economic stability. In Melbourne, the *Argus* was finding things especially difficult. In Sydney, Lang commissioned a report on the finances of his enemies – Sydney's commercial newspapers. It concluded that the *Sydney Morning Herald*, the *Sun* and the *Daily Telegraph* 'were in financial difficulties', 'under pressure from their banks', and the 'bottom was falling out of their Stock Exchange values'.[27] Associated Newspapers was especially overstretched.

FINANCIAL WIZARDRY

After twelve years out of office, Labor, through the Scullin government, immediately had to face extremely challenging problems, but there was no consensus within the party about how to manage the economy. Terry Irving pointed out that, even before the economic crash, there were internal lines of tension between the federal Labor party and its state branches, especially over the power of Jack Lang in New South Wales. There were also differences of opinion, between Labor parliamentarians who had been union officials and those who had not, about whether the priority in formulating economic remedies should be to represent the interests of the labour movement or individual electorates and the nation. There were also differences between factions and trade unions.[28] All of these lines of political division now began to open up.

One of the biggest points of contention between the federal Labor Party and Jack Lang was what to do about the interest due on Australia's enormous foreign loans. Australian governments had borrowed heavily on the London loan market through one London firm that had obtained an exclusive mandate to represent Australian governments' financial interests in London. Since 1895, practically every Australian government loan had been written and floated by R Nivison and Co. Run by the British financier, Robert Nivison (Lord Glendyne), a 'financial genius' who was considered ruthless in business,[29] Nivison's company received a percentage of all loans as a fee for issuing them. It wielded great power over Australia's finances. It determined the fees, rates of interest, and other conditions on Australia's loans. Although these were often unfavourable, Australian governments had little choice but to take or leave them. But now that export prices for Australian goods had collapsed, Australia could not afford to pay the interest on its loans.

Scullin's treasurer, EG Theodore, had some experience of the British loan system. As Queensland premier, Theodore had faced off with Nivison in 1920, when Nivison had tried to make loans conditional on Theodore stopping policies that affected pastoral interests. Theodore had denounced the money lenders of London and tried to take them on by borrowing money from New York instead, but ultimately, he had been forced to back down. Lang also condemned the unfairness of the British loans system, but this was about all he and Theodore agreed upon. Having crossed swords in New South Wales factional politics, the two Labor politicians despised each other and proposed different economic policies to remedy the effects of the Depression.

Theodore, who had devoted years to self-directed study of economics and politics, was considered a financial whiz. To soften the impact of the Depression, he began to champion bold policies along the lines promoted by the British economist John Maynard Keynes, which advocated reflating the economy through government spending as a way of rejuvenating the economy. This was very different from traditional policy responses to recession and depression, which were spending cuts, belt-tightening and wage-cutting (manufacturers especially called for lower wages). Theodore's proposals advocated instead for 'policies of public works, with budget deficits, and "cheap credit"'.[30] In time, his methods would become conventional, a standard part of the economic toolkit available to governments, and adopted by many Western nations. Even Theodore's former opponents would come to adopt his policies, in part or in whole; and today, his plans are viewed by economists as representing only moderate expansion. But in 1930–31, Theodore's proposals were considered radical, and they were bitterly opposed by business leaders, the Opposition-dominated Senate, and the conservative-dominated board of the Commonwealth Bank, which repeatedly blocked them.

By March 1930, other federal Labor members had taken up Theodore's call for credit expansion and for the government to require the Commonwealth Bank to issue credit in order to stimulate production and employment. The Commonwealth Bank board, conservative politicians and commercial newspapers 'reacted with horror'.[31] Citing the prospect of hyperinflation, they pointed to the German economic collapse, raising the spectre of Australians having to push a wheelbarrow full of devalued notes to the corner shop in order to buy a loaf of bread.

The mainstream press strongly 'reflected the pervasive conservatism of academic economists, bankers, businessmen and senior public servants'.[32] The most vehement newspapers were the HWT papers, as well as the *Argus*, the *Sydney Morning Herald*, the *Daily Telegraph*, the *Mercury*, the *Telegraph* (Brisbane) and *Brisbane Courier*. Their attacks on the Scullin government 'reached hysterical levels'.[33] Scullin's and Theodore's plans to reflate the economy through government stimulus were described as 'economic insanity', 'weird', 'a dangerous experiment' and 'grotesque and menacing'.[34] Theodore was accused of financial 'wizardry'.[35] Although Scullin was widely considered decent and honest (even by Murdoch, whose papers attacked his government relentlessly),[36] he was dubbed 'weak', 'shifty' and 'vacillating'.[37] The press represented Theodore's policies as a giant white elephant and as financial trickery (Figure 10.2). Scullin found the coverage so disheartening that, after six months in office, he stopped reading most newspaper editorials. Otherwise, he said, he would have 'broken down'.[38]

Unexpectedly, Theodore did have one powerful business leader in his corner – his friend, WS Robinson, the mining magnate and

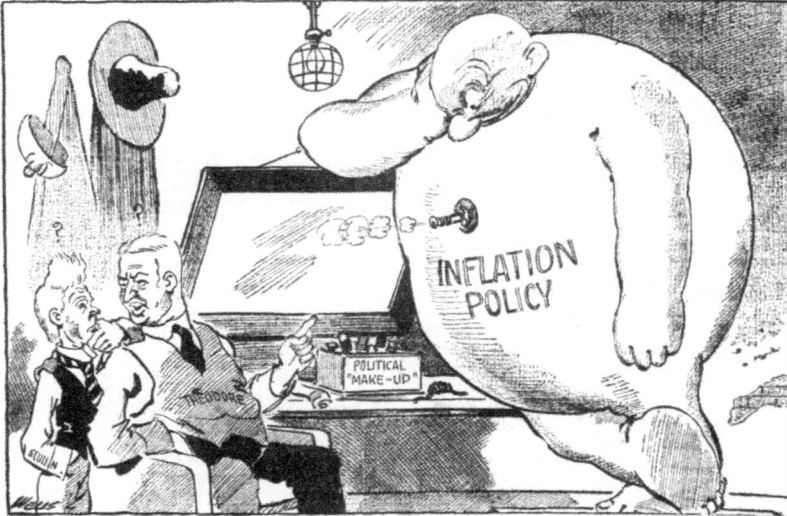

The Frankenstein Monster

Neither Mr. Scullin nor Mr. Theodore knows what to do with the white elephant of inflation which their party created.

MILLIONS AND MILLIONS

Mr. Theodore's mysterious financial scheme still has Australia guessing.

The Warning

FIGURE 10.2 How the commercial dailies represented EG Theodore's economic policies, 1931

SOURCES 'The Frankenstein monster', *News* (Adelaide), 1 December 1931, p. 6; 'Millions and millions', *Sun*, 9 February 1931, p. 7; 'The warning', *Herald*, 28 February 1931, p. 6.

Collins House leader, who was a director of West Australian Newspapers (WAN) during the Depression. It was Robinson who had arranged for a copy of Keynes' *A Treatise on Money* to be flown to Theodore as soon as it was published in 1930, ensuring Theodore had the first copy in Australia. Robinson (and Clive Baillieu) were friends with Keynes and in regular contact with him in London.[39] For a powerful industrialist, Robinson was quite a maverick and free thinker. Although it cost him significant amounts of money, he refused to hold shares in companies that he was a director of, or an adviser to (except the small parcels of shares required for qualification on the board). Nor did he allow his family to. Robinson also made his own judgements about people. He worked closely with politicians from both sides of politics. He remained friendly with Hughes when other Collins House figures had turned on him. And although he was a good friend of Murdoch's, he retained a healthy scepticism about the press magnate.

PEOPLE BEFORE BONDHOLDERS?

Unlike Robinson, other business leaders remained wedded to the rather simplistic notion that governments should be run like businesses – so when profits were low, they believed costs should simply be cut. They felt traditional deflationary responses and fiscal austerity were the best means to get the Australian economy back on track, not some untested prescription for government spending and credit expansion. If Theodore was to have any chance of gaining support for his newfangled ideas, he needed to explain and defend them. But at a crucial moment, in July 1930, he stepped down from Cabinet after the controversial (and, critics alleged, partisan) Royal Commission examining the sale of Mungana Mines to the Queensland government found him guilty of fraud and dishonesty.

Theodore resigned as federal treasurer on 5 July and Scullin added the position to his already heavy responsibilities. Theodore would spend the next vital seven months on the backbench, and when he returned, would not have the reputation he needed to carry such a radical (for the times) economic plan.

Meanwhile, the case made by conservative businessmen, politicians and the press for orthodox remedies received a boost when senior British banker, Sir Otto Niemeyer, acting as an emissary of the Bank of England, arrived in Australia in July 1930 for a four-month tour. Niemeyer had been invited by the Scullin government to give advice on economic policy. One of the industrialists Niemeyer met was WL Baillieu. The haughty Niemeyer recorded in his diary that Baillieu had come 'to lunch: hum'.[40] Baillieu also organised a 'private discussion' for Niemeyer with 'many of Australia's newspaper editors and financial writers',[41] but Murdoch needed no introduction. When Niemeyer and an accompanying economist had arrived in Australia, Murdoch had 'immediately' invited them to dinner at his home.[42]

As Niemeyer made his way around the country, he was appalled by Australia's high standard of living. He declared that Australia had lived beyond its means in the 1920s and must now pay the price through harsh cuts to living standards. Niemeyer addressed a special premiers' conference in Melbourne in August 1930. James Fenton, minister for customs, chaired the conference, and Lyons, the postmaster-general, acted as treasurer, because Scullin was absent (he was ill and scheduled to depart for the Imperial Conference in London). Addressing his Commonwealth hosts and the state premiers, Niemeyer recommended a traditional deflationary response, and told them Australia needed to savagely cut welfare, wages and public works in order to balance its budgets and pay its debts in full. Based largely on his advice, all of the premiers agreed to a heavily deflationary package of measures known as the Melbourne

Agreement, which would cut government expenditure, salaries for public servants, social services and private wages.

Having accepted this harsh deflationary prescription (via Fenton and Lyons), Scullin unwisely sailed away to London. He stayed away for four and a half months, until 6 January 1931. In his absence, Scullin appointed Fenton (a former compositor and newspaper editor) to act as prime minister, and Joe Lyons (a former Tasmanian premier), as acting treasurer. Both were conservative members of the Labor Party. They faced a federal Labor Caucus that was deeply divided over Niemeyer's recommendations. In New South Wales especially, there was growing resistance to the Melbourne Agreement, fuelled by Lang.

Before Scullin had even boarded his London-bound ship at Fremantle, Lang was arguing that if wages were going to be cut, then interest rates on all federal and state loans should be reduced by the same proportion. This would mean that lenders (bondholders) would not receive the interest they expected. There was also talk of 'repudiation'; refusing to honour the contract conditions of Australia's huge war loan debt to the United Kingdom. Scullin had already rejected repudiation, calling it 'default', and predicting that it would be 'calamitous'.[43] But Lang argued that interest payments on Australia's war loan should be stopped until repayment terms were renegotiated to match the lower rates paid by the United States. He said Australia's 'indebtedness was caused by our efforts to help England in her dark days. The least she can do is extend a helping hand to Australia.'[44]

The financial world was appalled. It viewed repudiation as 'heresy', and Lang as a dangerous extremist – especially after he began to talk about partial repudiation or renegotiation of domestic loans as well.[45] Australian companies, including Collins House businesses, were large bondholders who had lent governments money (Figure 5.3, page 191, showed Collins House promoting World

War I loan bonds). But the bulk had been lent by banks, trustee and life insurance companies, several of which were allied with newspaper owners. The Baillieus and Collins House were connected with the English-based ES&A Bank (now ANZ), the National Bank of Australasia (now NAB), and the Commercial Bank of Australasia (now Westpac), as well as several trustee companies, including Trustees Executors & Agency Co., and Union Trustee Co. The Fairfaxes were closely aligned with the Bank of New South Wales (now Westpac), the Commercial Banking Company of Sydney (now part of NAB), and also AMP and Perpetual Trustee Company. To give an example of how much some of these institutions had at stake, AMP had lent Commonwealth and state governments £22 million ($1.5 billion today).[46]

If Lang's rhetoric was acted upon, these domestic bondholders would lose millions in interest payments. Lang argued they could afford it, and it was more important to make sure the unemployed did not starve. But his conservative opponents, including the *Sydney Morning Herald*, argued that, because banks, life insurance and trustee companies distributed the money they received from loan interest payments to hundreds of thousands of bank depositors, life insurance policy holders and trustee members, bondholders were not the rich speculators that Lang implied, but were mostly small holders, including workers, widows and children, who lived off the interest from investments made on their behalf. In other words, 'the people' and bondholders were one and the same.[47]

Lyons' brief was to carry out the Melbourne Agreement while Scullin was overseas, but he and Fenton faced two opposing groups within Caucus. The press dubbed one group the 'inflationists' (those supporting Theodore's policies), and the other 'Langites' (or 'extremists'). Caucus rejected Lyons' plan in favour of the more radical, inflationary plan proposed by Theodore to create credit and expand the deficit, and then went a step further than even

Theodore wanted, and suggested deferring repayment of an overseas loan due in December. Fenton and Lyons refused, and enlisted Scullin's support via cable and radio telephone from London.

In New South Wales, a state election was scheduled for 25 October, and Lang was making rejection of Niemeyer's proposals a key plank of his campaign. He argued Niemeyer represented the interests of wealthy overseas bankers at the expense of the Australian people who were struggling to cope with the Depression. Lang's public meetings drew crowds of an estimated 20 000 to 50 000 people.[48] To get his message across, Lang also had the advantage of being an owner and director of the *Labor Daily* newspaper. After he won the election, and again became New South Wales premier, Lang continued to argue that the British loans were unfair, that circumstances had changed, and people were more important than lenders' profits. His rhetoric ramped up. He told a mass meeting in Sydney that he was not going to take 'the bread from the mouths of your sons and daughters to satisfy the insatiable greed of the financial interests'.[49]

The large amount of money that Australia owed to British financiers was an emotive issue. The mainstream press argued that paying those debts was a matter of honour and patriotism, and a marker of Australia's status within the Empire (the same lines of argument used during the World War I conscription debates). Default would mean disgrace. Newspapers stressed the 'sanctity of contracts' and called for 'sound finance'. Their rallying cry was 'balanced budgets', 'rigid economy' and 'living within our means'. Lang told a large crowd that: 'According to the newspapers and many of the leaders of Governments in Australia, it is honourable to take the pension from the war widow and give it to the London financier … That is what the bankers said we must do.'[50]

Lang said 'overseas interests', the 'same people who conscripted our sons and laid them in Flanders' fields … now demand more blood, the interest on their lives'.[51] He declared he would not cut wages or public services in New South Wales nor pay the principal or interest payments to British bankers until Australia's workers were provided for. One of Lang's open-air meetings in July 1931 drew a crowd of between 60 000 and 90 000 people.[52] There was now growing internal division within Labor about whether Lang represented the 'true Labor position', but even if his plans had popular support, Scullin and Theodore were powerless to enforce them.[53] There was no chance of getting them through a hostile Senate.

'THE GROUP'

Lang's fiery rhetoric and Theodore's strange inflationary policies caused genuine fear among the business and banking communities. The leader of 'the Group', Staniforth Ricketson, was head of JB Were & Son. It was Australia's largest stockbroker in the interwar period, a major underwriter of Australian government loans, and the Australian connection for Nivison's.[54] During 1930–31, Ricketson was regularly sending cables to Nivison's. In one, he practically begged for help to 'save Australia from the calamities that threaten us'.[55]

The other members of 'the Group' that set itself the task of bringing down the Scullin government included Ricketson's close friend, Robert Menzies. Menzies was Australia's youngest King's Counsel (KC), head of the Young Nationalist Organisation, and a Nationalist member for Nunawading in the Victorian Legislative Assembly, but he had his eye on federal politics. Ricketson's and Menzies' friend, Kingsley Henderson, was an architect whose firm designed major corporate buildings. Henderson was never an MP, but behind the scenes he was a 'force in Australian politics'.[56]

Henderson was also a friend of Lyons', and the only one of 'the Group' to remain close to Lyons in his final years.

Ambrose Pratt was a journalist, novelist and mining company director. He had connections with Collins House and was also a co-director with John Wren in two Western Australian mining companies.[57] Pratt had been a Northcliffe protégé who had worked at the *Daily Mail* as well as Australian newspapers (including *The Age* when Murdoch was there), and as editor/co-owner of a mining investors' periodical. According to Sybil Nolan, Pratt had also 'worked for the National Union's secret propaganda unit during and after the First World War'.[58] He was also a director of twelve tin-dredging companies. Tin prices had dropped disastrously, and Pratt was trying to ensure they remained profitable. Another 'Group' member, John Higgins, was a metallurgist who had become a powerful wool broker. Wool was one of the most negatively affected commodities during the Depression. The final member of 'the Group' was Charles Norris, the long-standing secretary of the National Mutual Life Association of Australasia (NMLA).

While these six have been considered the core members of 'the Group', Murdoch was also involved, and allied with its members and their cause. Some historians consider Murdoch part of 'the Group', while others view him as operating more independently. (Ricketson and Murdoch were both strong personalities and somewhat jealous of each other's access to Lyons.) Another who worked in tandem with 'the Group' was Robert Knox, a Collins House–allied businessman, and president of the National Union. The National Union was the main financial power that controlled Nationalist Party (and then UAP) funds. Collins House was a major donor to the National Union. It was a 'small, secretive clique', 'often seen as a front for a coterie of Melbourne businessmen seeking to control the party'.[59]

Menzies' biographer, AW Martin, suggested that 'the Group's' 'plot' was probably hatched at the bar of the Savage Club, a private 'gentlemen's club' just off Collins Street. Three members of 'the Group' – Henderson, Menzies and Pratt – were Savages, while Murdoch was a former member. (Lyons joined in 1933.) Martin described Ricketson as a 'major – and sometimes thought sinister – power in Melbourne's tight financial world'.[60] Ricketson was the great-grandson of JB Were's founder, and before joining the family firm, had briefly been a reporter in Tasmania where he had met and befriended Joe Lyons, then MP for Wilmot. Ricketson had a great deal at stake in 1931. His stockbroking business was 'almost at a standstill', because of Scullin's economic policies, particularly its 'Special Property Tax'.[61] More crucially, his firm had concentrated on organising domestic loans, including government loans, of up to £20 or £30 million a year in the late 1920s, and was connected to Nivison and Co.[62] Nivison's had by far the most to lose if Australia reneged on paying its foreign debts, or insisted on renegotiating them at lower interest rates. Ricketson was later accused of having acted as Nivison's Australian 'puppet'.[63]

Collins House had been linked with British finance since the late 1890s, especially through WS Baillieu's brother's London stockbroking firm, Lionel Robinson, Clark and Co. But it also had longstanding links with Nivison's. When WL Baillieu was Victoria's agent general in London in 1913–14, it was alleged in the Victorian parliament that he personally profited from negotiating state loans through Nivison's. However, Baillieu's accuser could provide no evidence, and Baillieu denied any wrongdoing.[64] When Fenton was still a Labor MP, he had claimed in 1929 that both 'the Baillieu interests' and 'the Robinson interests ... are combined with the house of Nivison' and they acted together to thwart competition in the money market for Australian loans.[65] Collins House also had links to Ricketson, including that JB Were and EL and C Baillieu regularly acted as joint share brokers and underwriters in the 1920s.[66]

Ricketson and Menzies were not only close friends and fellow Savages, but also neighbours with retreats at Mount Macedon, and co-investors in various financial projects. One venture had been launched in March 1930, about five months before Lang began proclaiming his repudiation stance. It was an investment trust called 'National Reliance Investment Trust' with Ricketson, Menzies and Kingsley Henderson as directors, and it was specifically created to take advantage of depressed conditions by buying government securities at bargain prices. (Government securities are bonds or other types of debt obligation issued by a government to finance its borrowings. If someone buys government bonds they are, in effect, lending the government money.) National Reliance had £2 million ($143 million in today's money) invested in Commonwealth and state government loans. It would be wiped out if repudiation became a reality.[67]

Not surprisingly, 'the Group's' members believed repudiation was 'repugnant' and 'a national disgrace to be fought against at all costs'.[68] Another 'Group' member for whom it was a critical issue was Charles Norris of the life insurance company NMLA. Through JB Were, NMLA had invested 40 per cent of its members' funds in government securities.[69] They were usually considered secure, low-risk investments, but now Lang's repudiation talk was putting NMLA's nearly £11 million of investments ($791 million today) at risk.[70] Several other players involved in the shadows of Lyons' defection were also connected to NMLA. SM Bruce was a former director (and would later be again), while Robert Gibson, the powerful Commonwealth Bank chairman, was a director. Throughout the period in which he was making decisions affecting government economic policy, Gibson was representing the interests of the NMLA, and also the Union Trustee Co which was associated with Collins House and BHP (Union Trustee also had millions invested in government loans). As head of what was then Australia's central bank, Gibson applied his responsibilities in a way that gave him 'an iron grip on national monetary policy'.[71] Deeply financially orthodox, he applied that influence during the Depression in a way that cheered business and conservative figures (who 'saw him as a figure of reason and responsibility in a world that seemed to be falling apart'), but that Scullin and Theodore viewed as obstructionist and unconstitutional.[72]

THE LOAN CONVERSION CAMPAIGN

At the end of 1930, a £28 million Commonwealth loan was due. Fenton and Lyons defied the Caucus decision to renew the loan for twelve months, and instead insisted that it be voluntarily converted on the market (by renegotiating its credit and terms).[73] In November and December, Lyons joined with leading figures from the Opposition, and powerful corporations and financial houses, including banks, insurance companies and stockbrokers (including JB Were). Lyons became the figurehead of a patriotic and emotional campaign that appealed to Australians to reinvest their money in a converted, new loan with a lower interest rate, in order to rehabilitate Australia's credit and restore its reputation overseas.

Murdoch's papers gave the loan conversion campaign saturation coverage including articles, advertising, and running competitions. Lyons called for subscribers to reinvest their money in the loan 'as a patriotic duty'.[74] Newspapers emphasised how many small subscribers took up that call, but Collins House companies – including BHAS, Broken Hill South, Zinc Corporation and CUB – jointly renewed the largest amount – over £85 000 ($6 million). Other large private bondholders included BHP (£35 400), Harold Darling (chairman of BHP) (£55 110), plus the Fairfax-allied CSR (£15 000) and the draper Sydney Snow Ltd (£10 000).[75]

The conversion was oversubscribed, and viewed as a stunning success. The commercial press promoted Lyons as a national hero who had stirred enthusiasm at a time of despair, and put his country before his fractured party.[76] Lyons had demonstrated his excellent campaigning skills, including as a public speaker and media performer. Lyons had spoken so often on radio during the campaign that it was said that his voice had become 'as well known as those of radio announcers'.[77] The HWT had helped through its radio stations: the important 3DB Melbourne and 5AD Adelaide (which Lyons, as postmaster-general, had approved the HWT's licence for the year before (Chapter 13)).

The press, but especially the Murdoch press, had promoted Lyons as an 'honest' man with a 'simple message' that he expressed in a folksy, down-to-earth way. Australia, he said, needed to get back to 'the good old British practice of paying your way'.[78] Lyons' genial, straightforward manner had proven appealing to Australians who were 'craving reassurance and certainty'.[79] The loan conversion campaign had demonstrated his electoral appeal, but it had also put him into closer contact with 'the Group'. Ricketson and Menzies had 'worked in the background as organizers and facilitators' and were 'deeply impressed' by Lyons.[80] As Lyons continued to face ongoing battles with Labor Caucus during December 1930 and January 1931, 'the Group' was encouraging him to hold firm to economic orthodoxy.

When Scullin returned to Australia in January, he affirmed Lyons' policies but overlooked his desire to remain treasurer, and instead reappointed Theodore. A taint still clung to Theodore, but there was also a sense that he was being persecuted by political opponents. He had not been charged with any crime in six months (a judge and jury in a subsequent civil case in August 1931 acquitted Theodore on all charges), and Scullin felt the country needed his brain.

The announcement was not made until 26 January, after a close Caucus vote, but Murdoch knew it was imminent. On 21 January 1931, he wrote to Dumas: 'With you, I cannot feel supreme faith in Scullin and Theodore. I am afraid they will proceed with their balancing and half measures. But it would be madness to be irreconcilable with [them]'. Murdoch continued:

> I feel that provided Lyons, *who must be stuck to*, is given security and is not handed over to the left wing [of Labor] as a sacrifice, we must give Scullin his full chance. We must, of course ... regret the re-introduction of Theodore whilst there is this cloud hanging over him. But I feel that a mere expression of regret is sufficient and that we should not badger him with the Mungana story ... If we created a hostile atmosphere [Scullin and Theodore] would simply swing nearer and nearer to the Reds. Scullin, in private, gives every assurance of his determination to do the right thing' [italics added].[81]

Dumas dutifully had the *Advertiser* publish an editorial that gently expressed regret at Theodore's reappointment as treasurer but, as directed, did not 'badger' him over Mungana.[82]

Lyons' biographer, Philip Hart, argued that Theodore's reappointment was the final straw that led 'the Group' to believe the Scullin government 'had to be destroyed' because the policies that Lyons had been supporting were now blocked.[83] For Lyons, it was also a personal blow. He had been encouraged by Murdoch to believe that he would be kept on as treasurer. After the loan conversion campaign, Lyons was aware of his potential outside the Labor Party. On 29 January, Lyons and Fenton resigned from Cabinet. Six weeks later, they were joined by three other Labor MPs who crossed the floor on a censure motion. Although the Scullin government would limp on for another ten months, the resignations were the beginning of the end for it.

Scullin held a second premiers' conference between 6 and 26 February. This time, Theodore proposed the reduction of interest rates so that 'there would be no repudiation of obligation, but we should bring about equality of sacrifice'.[84] He also argued for bank credit to be mobilised for national purposes, and Scullin backed his plan for credit expansion via the Commonwealth Bank. But Lang proposed an alternative plan of deferring interest payments to British bondholders until they agreed to treat Australian debt the same as American debt, plus interest reductions on all government loans, whether in London or Australia, to 3 per cent. 'Call it repudiation or partial default' he said, but there is no alternative. 'We can assure bond-holders that their money is safe', Lang continued, 'but it is impossible to pay existing rates, because they are not being earned'.[85] Scullin and Theodore were now in open conflict with Lang over policy.

The mainstream press rallied strongly against the 'Lang Plan' but also against what they characterised as moves by Scullin and Theodore to 'print money' and 'control the banks'.[86] The economic debate was becoming increasingly bitter and now being fought on street corners and in town halls. Businessmen unhappy with the Nationalist Party's performance were trying to rally public support for 'sound finance'.[87] The All for Australia League was launched at a meeting in Sydney on 12 February to 'make governments balance their budgets and restore national credit'.[88] Although presented as a grassroots, 'non-political', community-based movement, the All for Australia League in New South Wales was a 'roll call of top managerial and commercial men'.[89]

Six days later, the right-wing New Guard was also formed in Sydney as a quasi-military, fascist-leaning, anti-Lang organisation, with up to 50 000 members. (RC Packer was a member.) There were plans from within the New Guard to remove Lang by force, and later, rumours were rife that it was plotting a coup or his kidnapping. Even the normally supremely calm *Sydney Morning Herald*, poised to celebrate its centenary in April, was losing its head over Lang. The paper admitted that it was trying to 'make Mr Lang's continued tenure in office impossible', and even issued a call to arms encouraging civil war. It editorialised that if Lang persisted 'There is no other way than by violence'.[90]

On 2 March, federal Labor began the final act of tearing itself apart, when Scullin re-formed his Cabinet and dropped Beasley and other New South Wales members who were allied with Lang. On 7 March, a by-election in New South Wales saw EJ (Eddie) Ward, a Lang protégé, elected to parliament, but Scullin barred him from Caucus on the grounds that he did not represent the Labor Party. The excluded New South Wales Langites quit Labor and sat on the crossbenches with Ward. Labor had begun with a majority of forty-seven to twenty-eight but that had been split off into fragments as Labor had split three ways between Scullin loyalists, Lyons' defectors and Lang supporters. The Lang Labor group now held the balance of power. Scullin was prime minister of a minority government whose days were numbered.

CHAPTER 11

A FRIEND IN OFFICE
AND A FALLING OUT

When the excluded New South Wales Langites moved to the cross-benches in March 1931, Murdoch had already been trying various tactics over the past six months to influence federal politics. Back in August 1930, he had been directing his papers to back the Nationalists and build up its leader, John Latham (Bruce's replacement). On 12 August 1930, Murdoch had written to Dumas: 'We have to make [Latham] into a big man. We have to get him accepted as a true national leader.'[1] But this had proven difficult. Latham and the Nationalists still bore 'the odium of [their] ignominious defeat in 1929', and Latham was considered cold and aloof, with a weak, lisping voice that party hardheads considered unsuitable for the new medium of radio.[2]

Murdoch then tried sending Scullin blunt messages through his newspapers, trying to make sure that Scullin stuck to deflationary policies. He told Dumas: 'I hope that for the day Scullin is in Adelaide you will print not just a leader, but a special article as well setting out ... the choice that is before him of going down in history as a resolute leader ... or as a betrayer of the whole existing organisation of the country'.[3] Dumas duly complied so that when Scullin arrived in Adelaide on 9 January 1931, he was greeted by a long article in the *Advertiser* that called on him to be resolute in reducing staff, salaries, and social services for the good of the country.[4] But rousing editorials were not achieving the desired results. 'The

Group' was mobilising towards Lyons, and Murdoch became allied with its efforts.

MURDOCH AND LYONS SWITCH SIDES

Significantly, Murdoch was not present at 'any of the secret meetings in [early] 1931 during which Lyons' political transformation was arranged' by 'the Group'.[5] Between 4 and 7 February, Lyons had met with Ricketson and other members of 'the Group' at JB Were's offices. Menzies acted as spokesperson and asked Lyons to leave Labor with as many colleagues as he could and form a temporary government. Lyons went back to Tasmania to consult with his politically savvy wife and consider the possibility. He met again with 'the Group' on 16 February. In the meantime, its members had consulted Robert Knox, president of the National Union, and Knox began persuading Latham to step aside and let Lyons lead the anti-Labor forces.

On 2 March, Ricketson cabled Nivison in London with the happy news that Lyons 'has decided to leave the Labor Party and awaits a fitting opportunity to make a public announcement'.[6] On 12 March, Lyons agreed to form a new party with support from the Nationalist and Country parties. The details would be hammered out in April.

Murdoch (whose son, Rupert, had been born amid the intrigue, on 11 March), had been meeting with Lyons separately, and now tried to connect more with members of 'the Group'. On 25 March, Ricketson met with Murdoch at his *Herald* office. On 31 March, Murdoch sent a telegram to his secretary asking her to arrange for Ricketson, Menzies, Henry Gullett (a former *Herald* journalist and now Nationalist MP), and Richard Casey (who was connected with Collins House and SM Bruce),[7] to dine with him at the 'Thursday

men's party' (both Gullett and Casey would become UAP ministers).[8] By April, Murdoch was fully on board, and 'was enlisting support, arranging publicity, and suggesting that meetings be held at his
house'.[9] When 'the Group' provided Lyons with a private secretary
in April, former Murdoch journalist Martyn Threlfall was hired at
Murdoch's suggestion. Threlfall's appointment was an effective way
to keep a close eye on Lyons and influence his activities.

Murdoch had also been grooming Dumas to switch to Lyons
(South Australia would be an important electoral arena if Lyons was
to obtain office). Dumas was understandably wary. It was a radical
move – both for Lyons, who would be forever dubbed a 'rat' by his
Labor colleagues, and for the Murdoch press, which had strongly
supported the conservatives. Murdoch reassured Dumas that Lyons
was not a socialist and 'would put private enterprise first'.[10] Where
Frank Packer would bully and issue direct orders, Murdoch could
deftly lead his editors without ever having to be so coarse. 'I hope …
you will print', and 'we must, of course' were usually enough to get
the desired result.

Journalists like Dumas who last a long time in the profession
and rise to high ranks need to have a knack for 'sniffing the breeze'
and discerning the views of their employer, or even better, internal-
ising those views as their own. Murdoch helped the process along
by writing long, persuasive letters in high journalistic style. On
23 March, he sent Dumas an important letter that made Murdoch's
now solid support for Lyons clear, and effectively gave Dumas his
'riding orders'. Murdoch told Dumas that Lyons was:

> an experienced far-seeing and ruggedly honest legislator
> [who] has come forward and been acclaimed throughout the
> length and breadth of the land as the man for the occasion.
> His policies are sound as a bell … He has such an immense
> personal prestige already that the nation is demanding that

he should lead it. *Whether he breaks political parties or not in the course of saving the country is a minor consideration* ... Now it seems to me to be *a duty of men to get behind Lyons*, but of course each man has a perfect right to decide for himself. *Our newspapers are, however, not as free in this matter as outside individuals,* because we have stood by him and encouraged him for about nine months [so since July 1930], and at times when his decisions were extremely difficult *we told him what to do* ... It is most important I think that during the next few days we should *continue to beat the Lyons drum*. Our policy should be to demand the coming together of all classes of people of whatever party or political predilection under Lyons as the national leader [italics added].[11]

Support for Lyons was 'a duty' for newspapers and, by extension, their editors! A smart man, Dumas immediately responded: 'Your letter ... was splendid. Nothing, I think, could have put the position more clearly or more impressively.'[12]

On 9 April 1931, Lyons, Enid, and his ex-Labor parliamentary colleagues, began their campaign against the Scullin government by addressing large crowds and an interstate conference of citizens' organisations. Dumas made sure the *Advertiser* and 5AD gave Lyons a warm welcome in Adelaide. Lyons' speech at a 'monster rally' was transmitted via 5AD to stations around the country, and reached a national audience estimated at 750 000 – one-third of the adult national population.[13] The *Advertiser* reported that 'HUGE CROWDS THUNDER APPROVAL OF MR LYONS', and gushed that, with Lyons' visit, 'Adelaide had become the cradle of the most striking event in Australia's political history, the rousing of a nation by one small honest man'.[14]

For newspapers, the best way to promote deflationary policies that were going to hurt so many of their readers who were reliant upon wages was by avoiding the painful details and instead building a 'personality cult' around 'Honest Joe' Lyons, the affable, plain-speaking, family man (Lyons and his wife had ten children at the time).[15] Murdoch specifically warned Dumas to avoid the open elitism of the *Argus* 'both in policy and style ... we do not want "Argus" policies. They are reactionary and inspired of class feeling.'[16] The *Argus'* radical origins had long ago been thoroughly erased. When journalist Alan Carmichael joined the paper in 1930, he found it 'solid Establishment, the Bible of the Melbourne Club, Collins House and the honest burghers of Toorak'.[17] Two weeks before Murdoch's warning to avoid imitating the *Argus*, it had published an editorial saying that reductions in the basic wage were only 'a trifling loss to workers' and it was really employers who needed relief.[18]

During April and May, Lyons became the principal figure for burgeoning citizens' movements, especially the South Australian Citizens' League, and the All for Australia League in New South Wales and Victoria (where the League's founding officers included 'Group' members Ricketson and Henderson). These movements had the potential to become a real political force. In South Australia, academic Archibald Grenfell Price, who became leader of the 'Emergency Committee' supporting the UAP, said the Liberals planned to keep the Citizens' League 'under control until after the crisis [and then let it] collapse through lack of funds'.[19] Privately, Lyons also feared that the citizens groups could become a menace.

On 13 April, Lyons appeared in Victoria at an All for Australia League meeting, then attended a secret meeting with members of 'the Group' and the National Union. Ricketson was meeting 'every other day, and sometimes daily' with 'Group' members, and they were sometimes joined by Murdoch, Casey, Knox and EH Willis (also of the National Union).[20] Knox had talked a reluctant Latham into stepping down for Lyons, and on 17 April, Latham announced his resignation as party leader and nominated Lyons as his successor. At meetings on 18 and 19 April, Lyons was the only federal politician present when 'the Group', the National Union and other party organisers 'decided to reconstruct the different political groups on the Right into the United Australia Movement' (soon changed to United Australia Party).[21] Ricketson cabled Nivison on 18 April to advise him that the merger negotiations had been successful. 'The Group' told Lyons they considered themselves his 'special bodyguard ... constantly prepared to do anything and everything that lies within our power to help and serve you'.[22] During these crucial two weeks of negotiations, Lyons was reportedly a guest in Menzies' home in Kew.[23]

MURDOCH'S PRESS GALLERY PRINCE

Murdoch had a personal line of connection to Lyons through Joseph Aloysius (Joe) Alexander, the head of the *Herald*'s press gallery corps in Canberra. Since Alexander had arrived in the new capital in 1929, he had 'quickly established a supremacy and an influence unrivalled in Australian political journalism'. Another influential journalist, Alan Reid, said Alexander was a 'powerful and feared figure around Parliament'.[24] Alexander knew Lyons well. They shared the same first names, were both Catholics from Devonport in northern Tasmania, and had been friends since their teenage years. They had remained friends when Lyons was Tasmanian premier and Alexander covered state politics.

Like Murdoch, Alexander privately believed that he had played a key role in Lyons' defection. The month the Lyons government was sworn in, Alexander boasted in his diary that 'Everyone is saying at Canberra that I have put Lyons in as Prime Minister. It is more than half true.'[25] Alexander's role had included setting up an early meeting between Murdoch and Lyons at Murdoch's home, Cruden Farm. That meeting went so well that WL Baillieu's brother, MH 'Jac' Baillieu, was present at the next one – an indication of the Baillieu family's ongoing role in Murdoch's political decisions, even as WL Baillieu's health was declining.

Murdoch was enjoying being at the centre of the plotting and, around October 1930, told confidants that: 'My job has been to stiffen them [conservative Labor MPs who supported orthodox deflationary policies], and organise outside help so that there will be support for men who are excommunicated by their Labor people'.[26] One of those who needed support was South Australian Labor premier, Lionel Hill. The member for Port Pirie was, according to a biographer, 'a slow thinker' with a poor grasp of economics; he had become premier in April 1930.[27]

Steered by Dumas and other Adelaide business leaders, Hill had chosen to support deflationary policies. (Dumas even chaperoned Hill to the premiers' conferences of 1930 and 1931.) In August 1931, the Labor state council expelled Hill and his Cabinet from the party for opposing Labor policy. Hill remained premier and leader of an unofficial Parliamentary Labor Party minority government. Murdoch's help was entirely conditional upon Hill toeing the line. Murdoch told Dumas in September: 'We would certainly have to part company with Hill if he became a Theodore inflationist or even a Theodore semi-inflationist'.[28] Murdoch could also be condescending about his political charges, writing to Dumas about another Labor defector in South Australia: 'I hope you are making a great deal of the break away from Labour [sic] and helping poor little [John Lloyd] Price all you can'.[29]

Back in Canberra, on 13 March, the day after Lyons agreed to form a new political party, he, Fenton, and three other Labor members voted against the government in a no-confidence motion, thereby publicly placing themselves outside the Labor Party. Lyons also made an impassioned speech explaining why he had left the Cabinet back in January. The same day, Joe Alexander came into possession of confidential cables that had been sent by Scullin when he was in London (in late 1930) to Lyons and Fenton. In the cables, Scullin criticised the unruly Labor Caucus. They were sensational evidence of how divided the Caucus was, and the timing suggested the leak was designed to back up Lyons' speech, and cast his defection as a principled stand against a divided and inefficient government.

Alexander refused to disclose his source for the confidential cables. A subsequent police investigation saw Alexander, Lyons and Fenton interviewed, but no charges were laid and no culprit ever identified. However, the investigation did reveal that the cables definitely came from Lyons' files, as they were distinctive copies and the file showed evidence of being tampered with. Either Lyons leaked the copies directly, or via an intermediary, to his friend Alexander (which Lyons denied), or someone took the file from Lyons' office in a clandestine manner, or Lyons had rather carelessly lent it to some other minister and the disclosure emanated from there.[30]

The police report also revealed that, in a remarkable coincidence, Lyons was in Murdoch's office in Melbourne the day after the leak and his powerful speech, a Saturday, just as the cables story was about to go to print. According to Lyons, Murdoch informed him that he had possession of the cables from Alexander and was going to publish them, and Lyons responded that the cables were 'secret and confidential documents' and the press had no right to publish them.[31] Uncharacteristically meek in this telling of events, Murdoch reportedly agreed not to publish them, but advised Lyons that Alexander had already passed them on to a reporter at the Sydney *Sun* as part of a standard agreement between the *Herald* and the *Sun* to exchange pre-publication stories. Lyons said he urged Murdoch to call the *Sun* and ask them not to run the story but Murdoch was too late to stop the Sydney presses. According to the *Sun* journalist who received the material from Alexander, it was not a matter of timing though. By his account, the *Sun*'s formidable managing editor, Herbert Campbell Jones, simply refused Murdoch's request.[32]

A sceptical reading suggests that it was all contrived to ensure that the *Sun* published the cables. Alexander had taken the cables around to the *Sun* reporter's house on the Saturday morning.[33] Murdoch would have known the *Sun*'s publication deadlines, and also that his long-standing rival, the tough Campbell Jones, would not give up an opportunity to scoop him. When the *Sun* splashed the cables story across its Saturday afternoon edition, and prominently in its Sunday edition as well,[34] it neatly deflected attention away from Murdoch and Alexander because the *Herald*, like all Melbourne dailies, had no Sunday edition. It could not publish until Monday afternoon. The *Herald* was one of the last major papers to publish a sensational story that its own star journalist had procured.

The Speaker barred Alexander from the House of Representatives for five months for failing to explain or justify how he came into possession of confidential material. Alexander was not barred from the Opposition-controlled Senate though, and he revelled in calling politicians across an imaginary line to that half of the parliamentary precinct in order to gather information. But his work was so impeded that Murdoch recalled him to Melbourne until the matter was resolved. The cable leaks story attained a special place in press gallery folklore where rumour abounded that Lyons had passed the material to Alexander in a toilet stall near the Ministry offices at Parliament House.

SACRIFICE AND THE PREMIERS' PLAN

At some point, when Robinson had suggested that Murdoch back his friend Theodore as a unifying figure who could move the country forward, Murdoch had summoned Joe Alexander from Canberra to try to convince Robinson that, despite Theodore's undoubted gifts, the treasurer had no base of political support.[35] This was demonstrated three days after the leaked cables were published. Theodore introduced a measure for the printing of £18 million of 'fiduciary notes' to enable an issue of credit to be used for public works to employ thousands of unemployed. In his Second Reading speech, Theodore quoted Keynes. The treasurer was 'assailed hysterically' from the right, who believed his policies were too radical and would circulate 'bogus money',[36] and from the left, who felt they were nowhere near radical enough. The Senate blocked the bill.

Robinson's opposition to Niemeyer's deflationary policies, and his support for Theodore, put him at odds with the vast majority of the Australian business community, including his own brothers, conservative politician Arthur, and businessman Gerald. The *Argus* had been publishing articles written by Gerald arguing that old age, invalid and war pensions had become a 'burden' on the taxpayer and needed to be reduced.[37] The *Argus* was also promoting Menzies' forceful arguments about the 'sanctity' of contracts.[38] Australia's highest paid King's Counsel had proven the most eloquent speaker on the topic, and he insisted the principle should be applied not just to loan repayments, but also to rental contracts. On that basis, he opposed rental reductions for unemployed tenants and farmers. On one occasion, however, Menzies' usual eloquence slipped, and he made an infamously poor choice of words. He said: 'If Australia were going to get through her troubles by abating or abandoning traditional British standards of honesty, of justice, of fair play, of resolute endeavour, it would be far better for Australia that every citizen within her boundaries should die of starvation during the next six months'.[39]

Robinson later wrote in his memoirs:

> I had much sympathy for the steps taken by the [Scullin] Government … to alleviate Australia's economic crisis … there were too many leaders of business in both England and Australia who had no hesitation in reducing the wages or eliminating the jobs of their employees and yet who were most reluctant to cut fixed interest rates and rents and other items of income of the wealthier people. Income from rent, they argued, was sacred. Wages however, were fit for the guillotine.[40]

The major newspapers did not share Robinson's sympathy for the Scullin government and wage earners. The *Herald*'s anti-Scullin stance had become so vicious that, in May 1931, the Melbourne Trades Hall Council called for a union boycott against HWT publications. This lasted for six months, and reportedly led to a significant sales drop in working-class areas.

With Theodore's fiduciary notes blocked, and the Commonwealth Bank's Robert Gibson refusing further credit unless Scullin cut pensions (which he refused to do), Scullin called yet another premiers' conference from 25 May to 10 June. This one resulted in the Premiers' Plan, another deflationary economic policy based largely on Niemeyer's prescription, but with a new emphasis on equality of sacrifice, so that bondholders and the wealthy would share some of the pain. The Premiers' Plan combined major cuts in government spending, including cuts to wages and pensions, with the reduction of interest rates on bank deposits, and the interest the government paid on internal loans. Murdoch claimed to have played a leading role in its adoption. The *Advertiser* in 1933 boasted that this 'was not known to the public … [but Murdoch] had an immense influence on the final outcome ... The importance of the part he played ... cannot be exaggerated.'[41]

The Premiers' Plan went against both Labor policy and Scullin's personal ideals, but his government was in a minority in the Senate, 'had no power over credit, no power over the banks, and no way of increasing tax revenue'.[42] Under pressure to relieve the cruel effects of the Depression, Scullin accepted and began to advance the Premiers' Plan. This represented a complete reversal. Within only three months, his government 'had turned full circle' in its search for a viable economic policy.[43] Murdoch wrote to Dumas on the last day of the conference that the outcome was:

> almost too good to be true ... the conversion of Scullin and
> Theodore has been complete. If they can really get [the
> Premiers' Plan] through the caucus, it will be better for
> Australia than any other possible development ... for we
> shall achieve the economies without nearly the same public
> upheaval as would have been associated with a similar action
> by Lyons.[44]

Murdoch may have gotten cold feet on the 'upheaval' that using Lyons would unleash because, just weeks before the conference had begun, there had been a taste of it when the parliamentary National-ist Party had merged with the Lyons group to form the UAP, and Lyons had become the Opposition leader. When Lyons announced these new arrangements in parliament on 7 May 1931, he had been met with an 'outburst of rage and fury', including 'thunder-ous "boos" and hoots' from his former Labor comrades. Beasley had made his comments about Murdoch and the 'Baillieu press'. John Curtin had shouted out that Lyons was 'leader of the rats', and Frank Brennan said Lyons had treacherously 'betrayed' his constitu-ents and the government.[45]

For five and a half months, the Scullin government pushed through with the Premiers' Plan, but although Scullin and Theodore had been reluctantly 'converted' to economic orthodoxy, their party had not. The Premiers' Plan was viewed in the labour movement as an assault on workers' living conditions, and half the parliamentary Labor Party voted against it. Pushing it through, with its severe cutbacks that affected pensioners and other core Labor constituencies, hastened the destruction of the Scullin government. AC Davidson, chairman of the Bank of New South Wales, had predicted (and hoped) this would occur. He said that Scullin enacting the Premiers' Plan would 'naturally be unsavoury to [Labor's] extreme supporters' so that a split would hasten, and 'a Nationalist government will follow and obtain the credit for pulling Australia out of the mud'.[46] This is precisely what happened.

THE 1931 ELECTION AND LYONS' FIRST YEARS IN OFFICE

On 25 November, the Scullin government lost a confidence motion when the Lang faction crossed the floor to vote with the UAP against their own Labor leader. The Lang faction's votes brought down Scullin's government only two years and one month after it was sworn into office. Parliament was dissolved and an election called for 19 December.

Although Murdoch had sometimes hedged his bets, hoping that Scullin and Theodore would come through, ever since the loan conversion campaign, his newspapers had been preparing the public to accept Lyons as an alternative leader. When the unions and workers' papers had characterised him as a Labor 'rat', Murdoch's papers had promoted Lyons' honesty and integrity. They had contrasted his plain, sound policies with the financial wizardry of the shady 'Red Ted'. Now, an overwhelming effort was made to deliver Lyons to office. Enid Lyons later described her husband's ascension by saying that 'Outside Parliament there was Keith Murdoch with a newspaper empire behind him'.[47] But the HWT was no longer just a newspaper empire. Its radio stations gave Lyons ample airtime during the first 'radio election'.[48] Lyons also embraced films and newsreels, including 'talkies' organised by Murdoch's new newsreel company.

During the three-week campaign, Lyons criss-crossed the country at a frenzied pace, even using aeroplanes, still perceived as a cutting-edge technology. Murdoch installed Joe Alexander as part of Lyons' travelling campaign, giving the HWT papers inside knowledge, and giving Murdoch a direct conduit to Lyons. The Murdoch papers were notoriously one-sided during the campaign, trumpeting Lyons' 'triumphal tour', publishing glowing profiles of Lyons, and front-page photographs of him tenderly greeting his wife.[49] In Adelaide, where the HWT controlled both the morning and afternoon dailies, Grenfell Price of the UAP-linked 'Emergency Committee' noted that, 'Owing to the splendid service of the press, it has been unnecessary for us to do a great deal of publicity work'.[50]

In Sydney, the *Sydney Morning Herald* told readers that every vote for the UAP and Country Party was 'a vote for better times'.[51] The *Daily Telegraph* (the paper that Theodore would co-own five years later) damned him as a 'Red' in 1931, and spoke darkly, and bizarrely, about the police turning a blind eye to Communists who wanted to 'kill the priests' in Australia.[52] The Brisbane *Telegraph* told its readers the Scullin government needed to be 'hurled from office'. Going much further than most papers, it attacked Scullin personally, saying he was 'a political worm, without courage or character'.[53] (The Brisbane *Telegraph* was still so pro-Lyons at the next election (in 1934) that its general manager wrote to Lyons: 'We are, of course, doing our utmost to create a favourable atmosphere for your party and I think our newspaper will play no small part in the forthcoming elections. In any case we shall do our best.'[54])

The Age was the only major daily paper that did not advocate a vote for Lyons in 1931 (Table 3.1, pages 118–19). But it supported economic orthodoxy, wanted government expenditure reduced, and strongly backed the Melbourne Agreement and the Premiers' Plan.[55] *The Age*'s main objections to the UAP instead reflected the paper's idiosyncratic fixation on what had become side issues from the past, namely, tariff protection and federal industrial arbitration.[56] By the 1934 election, *The Age* had joined with all of the other major papers and backed Lyons.

In Tasmania, the *Mercury* actively helped Lyons with political organising in its state in 1931, and the paper's associate editor, Leopold Broinowski (who had previously stood as a Nationalist Party candidate), oversaw editorials declaring it a 'duty of all Tasmanians' to end the 'Theodore-Scullin-Lang menace'.[57] An electorate battered by the Depression and tired of Labor disunity duly delivered an election verdict that was a disaster for Labor. Its primary vote plunged from 49 per cent in 1929, to just 27 per cent. Six Labor ministers lost their seats in the crushing defeat. Journalists watching the election results flow in to the Melbourne GPO were 'amazed' when news arrived that Theodore was one of them.[58] The new UAP won thirty-nine of seventy-two seats, and was able to form government without having to rely on a coalition with the Country Party. Labor would not be back in government for another decade.

Dumas cabled Murdoch his 'Warmest personal congratulations', and said he considered the 'Victorian landslide [a] great personal triumph for yourself' as if Murdoch was the victor, not Lyons.[59] Dumas followed up with a letter the next day saying that Murdoch:

> must have been delighted to find the influence of 'the Herald' and 'The Sun Pictorial' in the industrial suburbs so strong

… Looking back a few months, one can realise the part the
Melbourne 'Herald' and you personally have played in the
success of the new Government. Your strong backing of Lyons
was the decisive factor in his election to the leadership of the
[UAP], and everything that has happened since has hinged on
that.[60]

Murdoch might have believed this, but did Lyons?

Lyons was grateful to those who had put him in power, and
was most influenced by Murdoch, 'the Group' and the National
Union in the early stages of his prime ministership. They tried to
dictate UAP election policy, advised Lyons on the composition of
his Cabinet, sought jobs for friends, and gave Lyons financial and
other advice. An unnamed Country Party member in a later Lyons
government wrote that: 'Lyons had a bad time from the Melbourne
king-makers. I saw how the poor man was drawn on the rack many
times in Cabinet. I have seen Cabinet decisions made a few days
later rescinded because Melbourne had disagreed with them.'[61] But
Lyons was not as pliable as his backers wanted him to be. Lyons'
biographer, Philip Hart, argued that the view of Lyons as a puppet
of either Murdoch, or the broader financial forces that led him to
defect, 'is far too simplistic'.[62]

Judged against Murdoch's boasting, George Pearce (a friend
of Murdoch's, and a defence minister for Lyons), concluded that
'Murdoch gave the impression of greater influence than he in fact
had'.[63] However, if judged by a different standard — that of the press
as a 'fourth estate' (a concept Murdoch himself professed to hold
dear) — then Murdoch was more influential than any newspaper
owner/executive had any right to be in a democracy. Murdoch influenced Lyons over the establishment of a newsprint mill in Lyons'
home state (Chapter 13), on limitations imposed on the development of the fledgling ABC, and the watering down of restrictions on

newspaper ownership of commercial radio stations (Chapter 12). Murdoch also sought special hearings on other policy issues that affected the commercial interests of his newspapers, including seeking tax exemptions.[64]

Lyons rewarded several of those involved in his defection. In mid-1933, Murdoch, Walter Massy-Greene and Archibald Grenfell Price were knighted. (The *Labor Daily* taunted the *Sydney Morning Herald* with an article headlined: 'MELB "HERALD" NOW ONE UP ON "SM HERALD"'.[65] Warwick Fairfax would not receive his knighthood until 1967.) Robert Knox, Colin Fraser and Sydney Snow received knighthoods in 1934, 1935 and 1936 respectively. Colin Fraser's was awarded at Robinson's urging. Martyn Threlfall received an OBE, while CA Norris was made a Companion of the Most Excellent Order of the British Empire.

Lyons put several old Nationalist figures and Collins House friends back into senior government positions. One was SM Bruce, who was re-elected in 1931. Bruce laid the foundations of economic policy for the UAP until he went off to be 'Australian Minister' in London. The even more closely Collins House–aligned Walter Massy-Greene replaced Bruce as assistant treasurer in July 1932. And from 1935 to 1939, Richard Casey, who was also affiliated with Collins House, was treasurer. (Even the elderly and more contrite Hughes was brought back into Cabinet. Hughes had practically begged Murdoch in a confidential letter to use his influence with Lyons to secure him a Cabinet position.)

Lyons' financial backers, especially the National Union, were particularly pleased with the 1933 Budget that Massy-Greene helped devise.[66] Labor dubbed it a budget for 'bankers, brewers and companies' and said it proved the Baillieu group 'controlled the policy of the [Lyons] government'.[67] The Budget reduced the company tax rate, which helped newspaper groups as well as other businesses. It offered financial relief to brewers and distillers like CUB, and removed the tax on gross interest for insurance companies like NMLA and AMP. Before the Budget, Lyons had asked his friend Dumas if the *Advertiser* could refrain from publishing any speculation about, or leaks from, his Budget speech. Dumas responded that it would be 'impossible' to avoid any references, but they would 'do our best to minimise the unavoidable embarrassment' to Lyons.[68]

Less than two weeks after the Budget, MPs also decided to loosen the purse strings for themselves. Their salaries had been reduced during the Depression, but at the close of an all-night sitting of Parliament on the same day that the Arbitration Commission had cut two shillings a week from the basic wage, the House voted to increase MP's salaries by £75 ($6000 in today's money). The Sydney press was scathing. The *Sydney Morning Herald* called the MP salary raise a 'raid' on the Treasury, the *Daily Telegraph* a 'Disgraceful Midnight Grab', and the *Sunday Sun* a 'salary grab in the furtive fashion of sneaks'.[69] But Murdoch had urgently cabled Dumas on the night of the vote to tell him to go easy on the government: 'Hope you will not be vitriolic on parliamentary salary question it seems to us that at least fifty pounds increase was justified in view of expenses'.[70]

Collins House's role in Lyons' defection may have been less centrally coordinated than it had been for Hughes' because of WL Baillieu's declining health, and the differing views among its remaining leaders about economic policy. But Collins House supported Lyons.[71] Clive Baillieu described him to Ricketson as 'the man Australia had been waiting for'.[72] And once Lyons was in office, his links with Collins House grew stronger. Lyons became friendly with WS Robinson, who played the 'grey eminence' role for Lyons that he had played for Hughes and other Australian and British politicians (and would also play for Labor leaders in future years). Lyons was also on good terms with Colin Fraser, and would dine at Fraser's house with mutual friends. In January 1933, Lyons attended a dinner at MH Baillieu's house with a who's who of

Collins House – Robinson, Fraser, ML Baillieu, Murdoch and Knox. Knox had become a 'firm friend' of Lyons', and was reputed to have 'significant influence' over him on behalf of National Union donors, including Collins House.[73] Knox became a director of Collins House's Dunlop-Perdriau in 1936, and later, a director (and chairman) of NMLA, the insurance company at the heart of the intrigue in 1930–31. Ricketson's JB Were went on to promote and underwrite companies associated with Collins House, including Felt and Textiles of Australia Ltd, and ICI.

THE BREAKUP

It was not just politicians on the left who felt the UAP had been cobbled together by business interests. When the conservative forces had aligned around Lyons in April 1931, the Country Party had refused to amalgamate with them. The Country Party's leader, Earl Page, had written privately to Country Party MP, Archie Cameron, that 'the mob behind the Lyons-Nationalist Coalition are all big Melbourne manufacturers and stockbrokers, and would have no more mercy on us than on Latham, whom they have buried alive'.[74]

At the 1934 federal election, when the Country Party won the balance of power, Murdoch proposed that he act as an intermediary in the complex negotiations about whether the Country Party would now form a coalition with the UAP, but Lyons rejected Murdoch's offer. Stung, Murdoch used his newspapers to press for a composite ministry,[75] and Dumas even sent the prime minister a letter warning that Lyons' 'friends' in South Australia were very disappointed that the two parties 'have not yet come together'.[76] Less than three years after Lyons had become prime minister, Murdoch was turning on him. He privately described Lyons' attitude as 'pathetic',[77] and wrote to Dumas that they 'may as well accept' that Lyons 'is an unrepentant socialist'.[78]

Murdoch's frustration boiled over into anger in 1935, when Lyons' Cabinet introduced regulations that sought to prevent newspaper companies from owning a chain of radio stations. Murdoch saw it as a personal attack (Chapter 13). By 1936, Murdoch was writing frequent letters to Clive Baillieu and WS Robinson expressing his impatience with Lyons. The *Herald* reflected Murdoch's displeasure. It published exasperated and hostile coverage in 1936 and 1937, criticising the Lyons government for inactivity, secretiveness and complacency. As CJ Lloyd noted, wider disillusionment with Lyons was tempered by 'press fears of a Lang revival and Labor instability', so '[o]ther newspapers did not rush to emulate Murdoch's lead, but there was a perceptible drift from Lyons' after 1937.[79]

Signs of this had been evident earlier though. Back in 1935, *Smith's Weekly* noted that some doubts were being expressed in the *Sydney Morning Herald* about whether 'dozy' Lyons was a fair-weather prime minister who was unsuitable when storms approached.[80] Disillusionment was more openly expressed by 1937. Newspapers complained that Lyons' government was characterised by drift, and its policy formation was sporadic and lethargic, but most continued to offer tepid support even as Lyons' political abilities (and his health) were failing towards the end of his tenure. Murdoch however, had thrown Lyons aside by 1938 and shifted his support to Menzies who, after Latham stood down from politics in 1934, had replaced him in the blue-ribbon federal seat of Kooyong and succeeded him as attorney-general (Chapter 15).

'SPLIT INTO FRAGMENTS'

The *Sydney Morning Herald* characterised the Labor splits caused by Hughes' and Lyons' defections by saying that Labor 'blew out its brains' in 1916, and 'stabbed itself in the back' in 1931.[81] But the press was no innocent bystander in either case. In 1931, the major daily newspapers were deeply invested in the economic debate, and made sure that pressure for 'sound finance' was intense. Some actors went further and tried to play an active role in breaking the Labor Party. In a letter Murdoch wrote to the chairman of Reuters, Roderick Jones, in June 1931, he gloated: 'We have won this fight entirely as regards opinion in the country ... We have, however, failed to get [the Scullin government] to the country [to face an election]' but 'we have got their party split into fragments'.[82]

Among newspaper figures, Murdoch played a prominent role in the events of 1931, but the *Argus* was also involved in the background. Lyons knew the paper's former editor, Edward Cunningham, who was still an editorial adviser. Cunningham gave Lyons tip-offs about what the paper would publish. This may have been unnecessary though, because the editor of the *Argus*, Roy Curthoys, was another member of the Savage Club who identified closely with Lyons.

Ricketson was friends with Allan Spowers, one of the partners in the firm of Wilson and Mackinnon, owners of the *Argus*, and his close relationship with the *Argus* became more apparent once the Lyons government was in office. In 1933, Ricketson's JB Were scouted for information to help the *Argus* launch its new afternoon paper (the *Evening Star*) up against Murdoch's *Herald*. Murdoch warned Dumas that JB Were was connected to the *Argus* and had been since before the Depression.[83] When the *Star* only drained the company's Depression-depleted coffers further, the *Argus*' owners had to raise a large mortgage. By 1936, the company was in trouble.

Its debts were £407000, and its assets only £587000. In 1924–25, it had made a net profit of £203000, but in mid-1936, had made only £19000 profit in nine months.[84]

In July 1936, JB Were underwrote the floating of the *Argus* as a new public company – the Argus and Australasian Ltd – after ninety years of private ownership. Ricketson became chairman of its board of directors. This raised eyebrows in corporate circles where it was felt that a stockbroker who put capital into a venture on behalf of clients should not become a director on its board.[85] Just weeks after Ricketson took charge of the *Argus*, his friend Menzies began writing special articles for the paper. When Ricketson stepped down as chairman in January 1939, another 'Group' member, Kingsley Henderson, took up the role. Henderson had also joined the *Argus'* board in 1936.

The *Argus* was connected with the men behind Lyons' defection. While the Savage Club was the venue for young and ambitious men who considered themselves bohemian, the more powerful 'old money' business and political elites congregated at Australia's most exclusive 'gentlemen's club', the Melbourne Club. The *Argus'* owners and trustees had been members since the 1890s. John Higgins of 'the Group' was a senior member, and he mingled there with the two principal owner-managers of the *Argus*, Spowers and Lauchlan Mackinnon.[86] In 1935, Ricketson and Henderson joined the Melbourne Club, having been nominated by Higgins.[87] The Melbourne Club and the *Argus* would continue to try to influence UAP leadership matters (Chapter 15).

As Lyons' defection was firmly engineered from Melbourne, Sydney interests were not as involved. But the Sydney businessman who Lyons was closest to was Sydney Snow. He was a draper, loan bondholder and director of Associated Newspapers. Lyons therefore had a friend at Sydney's largest newspaper company, until Snow resigned in May 1931. Even afterwards, Associated Newspapers' board continued to be considered highly pro-Lyons until the late 1930s. Snow was another figure who moved closer to Collins House after Lyons' ascension. He was appointed a director of Broken Hill South in 1932.

The *Sydney Morning Herald* seems to have been quite out of the loop in terms of all the political intrigue in 1931. The twenty-nine-year-old Warwick Fairfax had only been appointed managing director the year before, and he did not yet have his politically savvy general manager, RAG Henderson, by his side.[88] Although a strong advocate for financial orthodoxy, it seems the *Sydney Morning Herald* approached Murdoch's plotting with characteristic aloofness. In April 1932, Murdoch organised for the major newspapers to come to Melbourne for several days of luncheons and banquets in order to hear from Lyons, Bruce and Pearce (who wanted the newspapers' help to combat Lang). The *Sydney Morning Herald* shared the goal but it did not attend. (Not long after, the New South Wales Governor controversially dismissed Lang on 13 May 1932, on the grounds that he had directed state public servants to break federal law. The *Sydney Morning Herald* had editorialised eleven months earlier: 'Are we to be driven to absolute desperation … before the Governor dismisses him?'.[89])

During the Depression, the major Australian newspapers were run by millionaires Warwick Fairfax and Hugh Denison; along with Murdoch, who had his butler, chauffeur and country house; and RC Packer, who purchased a majestic yacht just after the Depression hit. Their papers told the unemployed and low- and middle-income readers to bear the brunt of wage cuts and reduced social services. But even as he was dispensing such medicine, Murdoch was making use of his contacts and inside knowledge to obtain financial benefits for the HWT that helped it sail through the Depression in unexpectedly good shape.

In January 1931, Australia's banks recognised that trying to maintain parity between the Australian pound and the British pound sterling was a lost cause and decided to increase the exchange rate to A£130 for £100 Sterling – the highest rate on record in Australia. Gibson appealed to Australians not to send their money overseas as that would only 'increase the difficulties facing the country'.[90] But, for weeks, Murdoch had been doing just that. He had known the policy change was coming, and had been sending 'lumps'[91] of HWT money to London (he had sent the equivalent of $2.2 million in today's money).[92] Three weeks before the exchange rate decision was announced, he was also encouraging Dumas to send across 'whatever money you can put your hands on'.[93] This proved to be a highly profitable, if unpatriotic, act. By September 1932, although unemployment was peaking with 30 per cent of Australians out of work, Dumas told Murdoch that the *Advertiser*'s overdraft had 'been wiped out'.[94] Murdoch, who was also bringing money back from London at a profit, said 'The bank position is almost embarrassing'.[95]

THEODORE'S LEGACY

Newspapers represented the interests of their owners, not their readers, during the Depression, and they did a great disservice to their readers as a result. Although the press applauded deflationary policies like the Premiers' Plan for pulling Australia out of economic catastrophe, that verdict has not stood the test of time. Later analysis by economists and a Royal Commission found that deflationary policies and bank obstructionism prolonged the effects of the Depression in Australia.[96] The Premiers' Plan caused greater unemployment in 1932–33, leading Australia to record one of the highest unemployment rates in the world during the Depression.[97]

Compared to the United States and United Kingdom, Australia's resistance to Keynesian responses such as government expenditure and relief programs, is now considered to have made the impact of the Depression harsher and longer than it needed to be. Queensland Treasury official and world-renowned economist Colin Clark later evaluated the Premiers' Plan as 'certainly harmful. This action prolonged the depression and made unemployment very much worse than it would otherwise have been.'[98] In the end, the main policy response that began the economic turnaround for Australia was, as in the United States, the elimination of ties to the gold standard.[99] The devaluation of the Australian pound (that Murdoch took advantage of) is now judged to have been the single most effective step in economic recovery. The banks' reluctance to touch the 'sacred cow' of parity with sterling for so long, and their delays in reducing interest rates in 1931–32 produced 'a devastating effect' and 'hamper[ed] recovery'.[100]

Once Lyons was in office, and Theodore and Lang had been ousted, the victors could afford to approach matters more calmly. By mid-1932, even Murdoch's *Herald* was declaring Keynes a 'brilliant economist', and Murdoch was trying to woo him to come to Australia.[101] Murdoch also 'collared' newspaper editors to try to enlist their support on behalf of the economist LF Giblin, who wanted Lyons to use bolder, more Keynesian methods to stimulate the economy through government spending.[102]

It took significantly longer for Theodore to be re-evaluated, but senior public servants, Treasury officials and economists later proclaimed him the greatest treasurer in Australian history.[103] Even political opponents went on to praise him. Bruce was reportedly among those who considered Theodore Australia's greatest treasurer.[104] The conservative New South Wales Premier Bertram Stevens described him as 'the coolest, best and most experienced financial brain in the southern hemisphere'.[105] But back in 1931, all of Theodore's financial skill and carefully reasoned arguments counted for little up against the ability of the press and their allied radio stations to mould opinion. This searing lesson must have made a big impression on Theodore, because only weeks after his shock election loss, he joined forces with RC and Frank Packer to try his hand at newspaper and magazine publishing, after meeting Packer on that majestic yacht.

CHAPTER 12

CAPTURING THE AIRWAVES: NEWSPAPERS, RADIO AND THE ABC

When the Scullin government was brought down on 25 November 1931, some newspaper groups had reason to be especially relieved. The government had intended introducing a bill that day to determine the future of radio broadcasting in Australia, but the parliament erupted and was dissolved before it could be introduced. Newspapers saw radio as a potential threat to their audiences and advertising revenue because it was becoming extremely popular, and part of people's everyday lives. Between 1925 and 1929, the number of radio listeners had increased by more than 80 per cent.[1] During the dark days of the Depression, even more Australians had turned to radio as a form of cheap entertainment and light relief. For those who could not afford to buy a valve radio set outright, retailers had begun to offer time payment plans, but many more people were accessing radio through inexpensive crystal sets, including homemade versions. The boom in listening had seen fourteen radio stations come on air in 1930, then another nineteen stations in 1931.[2]

Always acquisitive, the HWT had the largest stake in radio among the newspaper groups. It owned 3DB Melbourne (since 1929) and the *Advertiser*'s 5AD Adelaide (it was one of the stations that came on air in 1930). The other invested group was also in Victoria, where radio had proven especially popular. David Syme and Co, owner of *The Age*, was a part-owner of 3HA Hamilton, which had come on air in October 1931; and a second *Age* station, 3AW

Melbourne, would begin broadcasting in February 1932. Other newspapers had loose affiliations with local radio stations, rather than ownership of them, although in Sydney, Denison's Sun Newspapers had been an investor in Australia's first radio station, 2SB (subsequently 2BL), between 1925 and 1929, and was interested in getting back into the medium once it had overcome its financial troubles.

The Scullin government's thwarted broadcasting bill was going to create a government-established national broadcaster, modelled on the British Broadcasting Corporation (BBC). The BBC had started life as the British Broadcasting Company in 1922, but had become a public company in 1927 and operated as an independent, statutory body with sole responsibility for broadcasting in the United Kingdom. *The Age* had been calling for a BBC-style national broadcaster for Australia to be run alongside commercial broadcasters, but anti-Labor newspaper groups were anxious about a Labor government controlling such a powerful means of communication. When the press found out the broad details of the government's plan in November 1931, the *Argus* had claimed state-controlled radio would be used for Labor propaganda, while the *Mercury* called on the conservative-dominated Senate to 'throw out' the bill if it passed the House of Representatives.[3] The downfall of Scullin's government made that call redundant.

When the Lyons government took office in January 1932, there were more pressing matters to deal with, but broadcasting also required immediate attention. In 1929, the Bruce government had partly nationalised broadcasting by taking over eight stations around Australia. It had contracted a private company, the Australian Broadcasting Company (not to be confused with its successor, the similarly named Australian Broadcasting Commission (the ABC)), to provide programs for these stations for three years. The contract was going to expire on 30 June, and so it became one of the first acts of the new Lyons government to introduce its own bill on broadcasting. This bill also became the Lyons government's first major crisis. It faced a fierce press backlash that demonstrated just how quickly Lyons' supporters, especially Murdoch, could turn on him when their interests were threatened. The government hastily re-wrote its broadcasting policy, not the last time it changed course on broadcasting under pressure from the press.

When Lyons died in office in April 1939, his requiem mass was broadcast on radio, a fitting tribute to a man who had been so associated with radio, and whose government had determined the shape of broadcasting in Australia. By then, Australia had a commercial radio sector dominated by the press, and a hamstrung public broadcaster that had been so reliant upon newspapers – both their content and their permission – that it could not collect its own news or decide when to broadcast its news bulletins.

THE EARLY ADOPTERS, 1920-27

In 1920, the first demonstration of wireless transmission occurred in Australia. In an uncanny portent of how radio broadcasting would develop, the sounds were transmitted from Collins House and included a voice reading items aloud from newspapers. The novelty of hearing voices and music over the air fascinated people. Some feared that 'wireless' (as radio was then called) would cause strokes, sterility, thunderstorms or drought. Others believed it could be used to communicate with the dead, or would cure hangovers and cancer. Less mystically, it obviously had enormous potential to improve communication in a country the size of Australia.

At first, Australian newspaper owners and executives tended to view radio and its tiny sounds as an enthusiast's hobby with an uncertain future. It was a novelty that was newsworthy. 'MUSIC

THROUGH SPACE', the *Argus* rapturously reported in 1922.[4] The *Argus* asked the pioneering wireless company, Amalgamated Wireless (Australasia) Ltd (AWA) for a demonstration in its offices. *Argus* executives were fascinated by the new technology but also determined to protect their content from it.

In 1923, the postmaster-general, WG Gibson, held a conference for all parties interested in radio to help devise a policy framework for a broadcasting system. ACC Holtz, general manager of the *Argus*, exposed the newspapers' anxiety. Holtz aggressively argued for the 'rights of the press' against radio stations 'stealing' their news.[5] The newspapers made it clear they would impose strict conditions on the use of news, and Gibson accepted their claim that press news was copyright. Quashing the early hope that radio would be a news and information medium, the newspapers had begun to mark out a limited, press-controlled role for radio in news provision, and this would not be seriously questioned for another ten years.

The conference unanimously decided upon a 'closed set' system of radio broadcasting, that officially began in late 1923. Under this system, listeners paid a government licence fee plus a subscription to have their radio sets 'sealed' to a particular station or stations. Many of the early stations were run by retailers who wanted to sell radio sets, so were mindful that people needed something to listen to, or they were musical and theatrical interests who had content to broadcast. Murdoch later claimed that the 'Melbourne *Herald* was one of the first newspapers in the world to develop the theory that newspaper work and broadcasting could be joined'.[6] But Smith's Newspapers was the first to put the theory into practice in Australia.

In November 1923, 2SB became the first station on air in Australia. It was built on the roof of Smith's Newspapers building in Phillip Street, a partnership between Joynton Smith's company and Broadcasters (Sydney) Ltd (a group of enthusiasts who sold early radio equipment from a small shop in a Sydney laneway). At the time, the *Daily Guardian* was taking on the established Sydney morning dailies, and 2SB broadcast news from the *Daily Guardian* in the morning, talks to women during the day, sporting news in the afternoon, then children's bedtime stories, and an evening concert. Joynton Smith said the *Daily Guardian* would make no profit from the station, it was 'purely for the joy of delighting that the station has been installed'.[7] He was as good as his word. It made no money at all.

The 'sealed set' system was a failure. It was being widely rorted as even school children could adapt their sets to evade the sealed set restrictions. Only 1400 listeners bought licences.[8] In 1924, it was replaced by a system of 'A' and 'B' class stations. A-class stations were sustained by revenue from listeners' licence fees and limited advertising, while B-class (commercial) stations were entirely reliant upon advertising revenue. This system sparked much greater interest. When people started holding 'listening in' parties at their homes, it was clear that radio had come into vogue.[9] The HWT responded. In January 1924, the *Herald* began publishing a two-page feature on radio in its Thursday edition. In March, the HWT became a minor partner in the Broadcasting Company of Australia, which gained the licence for 3LO, Melbourne's second station to air. The HWT's partners were a powerful group of retailers, including the Sydney department store Farmer and Co, and theatrical companies JC Williamson and J and N Tait.

Manager of 3LO, Major Walter Tasman Conder, was a colourful character. A former AIF officer wounded at Gallipoli, Conder had also been governor of Pentridge Gaol. He was something of a showman, and was known to Lyons from their boyhood days in Tasmania. Under Conder's direction, 3LO began broadcasting in October 1924, with a sensational scoop, an outside broadcast of Dame Nellie Melba's farewell performance of *La Boheme*. For weeks, the *Herald* had been telling readers how to tune in to 3LO for the 'BIG EVENT'.[10]

Back in 1920, Melba had starred in the world's first broadcast concert in London at the behest of her friend Northcliffe, who milked the event's publicity value for his *Daily Mail*. Murdoch, also a friend of Melba's, may have helped persuade her to appear for 3LO, but he was quite preoccupied with newspaper matters, including fighting off Denison's *Evening Sun*. It was Theodore Fink who became a director of the Broadcasting Company of Australia. Fink was interested in music and the arts, and already had a ten-year association with the Tait company in the theatre and moving picture company, Amalgamated Pictures.

Radio station 3LO broadcast popular music, snippets of news, and weather bulletins that were said to be the first of their kind in Australia. It began regular horseracing broadcasts in 1925, which proved popular. Sporting fans enjoyed listening to descriptions of races broadcast from the course as events were in action – especially punters who had money on them. The station also became famous for its vivid ringside descriptions of wrestling matches from the Melbourne Stadium, causing a boom in ticket sales that must have delighted its owner, John Wren.

The *Herald* used various Northcliffe-like stunts to heighten popular interest in 3LO, including a 'prettiest bride' competition, radio voice contests, and a competition to find 'the perfect girl': the '3LO girl'.[11] At the height of his battle with Denison, Murdoch was especially pleased with some well-publicised test broadcasts between Australia and the United States, declaring to his staff that the HWT's venture into radio 'puts us on a little wave to unquestionable superiority'.[12]

By comparison, Denison *was* proving surprisingly slow to embrace broadcasting, especially for a radio pioneer. (In 1910, Denison had been a director of one of the two companies that introduced wireless to Australia. When it was taken over by AWA in 1913, Denison served as AWA's managing director until 1917.) In the first year of broadcasting in Sydney, Sun Newspapers even refused to print radio program lists, while the HWT took the opposite approach. In January 1925, it launched *Listener In*, a threepenny weekly that published radio program lists a week ahead, and gave radio hints and tips. It was a 'sellout' success.[13] It took until February 1928 for Sun Newspapers to follow suit and obtain its own radio publication when it purchased *Wireless Weekly*.

Denison's involvement in broadcasting was finally stirred by competition back in Sydney, where he retreated in 1925. Since the *Sun*'s rival, the *Evening News*, was supplying news to 2FC Sydney, Denison bought a share of 2BL (formerly 2SB). 2BL was no longer associated with Smith's Newspapers. Unaware of its commercial potential, Smith's staff had not given the station much attention, and let it 'go without a pang' in September 1925 because they were so busy with the *Daily Guardian*.[14] The unprofitable station was purchased by two Sydney retail giants with a shared interest in selling radio sets: Anthony Hordern and Sons, and David Jones. Charles Lloyd Jones, chairman of David Jones and grandson of its founder, became a director of 2BL for several years, but even with his resources and connections, the station continued to lose money.

Although the A- and B-class stations had proven far more successful in attracting listeners, the only one making any money was the HWT's 3LO. Other problems also remained. Radio service was still patchy, stations were not broadcasting for many hours, and New South Wales was experiencing an unexplained slump in interest (Victoria had twice as many listener licences).[15] The less populous states felt even more neglected, and reception in country areas remained limited. Many people in the country had still not even heard a radio broadcast. The government decided to hold a Royal Commission in 1927 to settle important matters of regulation, control and funding.

THE ROYAL COMMISSION AND THE RADIO OCTOPUS, 1927-28

The daily newspapers banded together to make a big impression at the Royal Commission on Wireless. As chair of the ANC, Holtz now represented the commercial metropolitan dailies and he continued to aggressively push the newspapers' case. Radio announcers 'stealing' their copyright content was less of an issue now. Australian stations had proved timid in that regard compared to American stations, but the metropolitan newspapers had also teamed up with local stations and were providing them with what one press executive admitted was 'very scrappy' news designed to encourage listeners to buy a newspaper.[16] Now, the papers were more concerned about being scooped with their own expensive cable news.

In early 1926, the world's most powerful wireless station, the British Post Office's short-wave station at Rugby, England, had begun transmitting news in Morse code. Rugby's news messages could be received in Australia, and they were based upon the same British cable news services that Australian newspapers subscribed to at great cost. Any enterprising Australian radio station could now receive and broadcast overseas news faster than the newspapers could print it, and at no cost to the radio station, thereby cutting the press out of the information flow. This prospect horrified the newspapers. They wanted material from Rugby to be restricted, and also sought to discredit it by calling it British 'propaganda' (even though it was the same agency news they used themselves, albeit it supplemented by texts of official British announcements).

Holtz and representatives from the Melbourne *Herald*, Sydney *Sun*, Hobart *Mercury*, *Brisbane Courier* and JE Davidson from News Limited, also focused on discrediting the notion that governments should operate radio stations. They were aware of the impact of the

BBC on their British counterparts, and were also concerned about Labor state governments. In Queensland, Theodore's government had secured a licence for a government-run station, 4QG, in 1925. It was profitable, and had a strong signal that made it unexpectedly popular in country areas in New South Wales, Victoria and South Australia. The newspaper representatives strongly attacked 4QG. They accused the Queensland government of using it for propaganda purposes, despite the denials of its manager.[17]

The newspapers sensed a commercial threat as well as a political one. The A-class stations were allowed to accept restricted advertising. Most were not interested, but 4QG had been broadcasting five-minute ad breaks, and demand for those slots was so great there was an eighteen-month waiting list. Newspaper executives admitted they were concerned that government could become 'an undisputed competitor to the newspapers'.[18] The *Herald* said government-run radio could 'sound the death-knell of a free press'.[19] The *Mercury* was concerned because it feared that Lyons, then Labor premier of Tasmania, intended to start a government-run broadcasting station. Newspapers in New South Wales were very worried because, in early 1927, the Lang ministry had approved a scheme to create a network of six state-owned broadcasting stations. The newspapers presented Lang's plan as part of an international plot by communists to use radio to incite revolution, and pointed to the Soviets' use of state-owned media for propaganda and government business, including police matters.[20]

Another strong conservative voice at the Royal Commission expressed a very different view of government-run broadcasting. Robert Menzies was then a thirty-two-year-old barrister with an intimidating record of legal victories. He was representing radio traders who wanted to sell more radio sets. Menzies said the concept of government-run broadcasting was essentially the same as governments running the postal and telegraphic service in order to

provide cheap and efficient facilities for the public. He argued the
Commonwealth should take over the stations of the partly government owned AWA and run them as a public utility rather than a
profit-making concern.

The *Herald*'s voice carried a lot of weight at the Royal Commission because of its involvement in the popular 3LO, the only
radio station out of the seventeen on air that was profitable in
1926. Conder believed that too much information bored listeners,
and he ran the station accordingly. In other countries, radio was
developing with more of a focus on news and information, but
the Royal Commission commended 3LO in a way that seemed to
endorse Conder's view that Australian radio should be focused on
entertainment.

Overall, the commissioners' final report was indecisive. They
concluded that 'very little change in the existing system is advisable at the present time'.[21] Their recommendations, and even their
language, suggested they had been heavily influenced by press representatives' attacks on Lang, 4QG, and government-run radio
generally. As radio broadcaster and historian Philip Geeves noted,
the commissioners 'rejected the concept of direct control of broadcasting stations by the Government and hedged about establishing
a corporation similar to the BBC'.[22] Instead, they vaguely advocated
cooperation among existing players.

Although this was vague, the postmaster-general and Prime
Minister Bruce took up the theme of cooperation and encouraged the
larger players to work together. Several stations took this as an invita-
tion (or a command, they later argued) to start organising themselves
into one large commercial group. In March 1928, 2FC and 2BL
amalgamated. In May, 3LO acquired 3AR, and both were subsumed
into a new company, Dominion Broadcasting Company, which then
set out on a buying spree. It connected up with the Sydney combine
by taking up large holdings in 2FC and 2BL. It purchased a large

interest in 5CL Adelaide, and bought 7ZL Hobart outright. It now controlled all of the A-class stations except 4QG and 6WF.

Behind this radio combine were three of Sydney's largest retailers (Farmer and Co, Hordern and Sons, and David Jones), plus Australia's dominant theatrical and entertainment companies (JC Williamson, and J and N Tait), with the 'frenemy' newspaper groups, the HWT and Sun Newspapers, the 'tentacles' of this 'broadcasting octopus'.[23] At the New South Wales end, the *Sun*'s managing director, H Campbell Jones, had a seat on the board of New South Wales Broadcasting Company Ltd, owner of 2FC and 2BL. At the Victorian end, Fink was not on Dominion Broadcasting's board, but *Smith's Weekly* believed he was the secret buyer of 3AR, and speculated that he was the 'older and wiser head' directing Conder (who became managing director of Dominion Broadcasting Co).[24]

For a brief moment, it looked as though Australia was destined to have a commercially oriented national broadcaster, but the radio combine overplayed its hand. Although the *Herald* self-servingly reported the amalgamations as 'RADIO MERGERS MAY REDUCE FEES … Better Programs … AUSTRALIA WILL HAVE BEST SERVICE IN WORLD',[25] once the combine had control of the stations, and started pocketing the government-collected licence fees, it lowered the quality of programming. It cut broadcasting hours, skimped on paying artists, and used cheaper content, including playing gramophone records instead of live performances. Up to 80 per cent of profits were instead going into directors' pockets as exorbitant directors' fees.[26] The group that *Smith's Weekly* took to calling the 'air pocketeers', also greedily overdid the advertising, apparently accepting more than the rules allowed for A-class stations. Listeners' complaints began to mount up about the decrease in quality programming, and non-aligned newspapers reported widespread discontent with the stations, especially in April–June 1928.

In July 1928, the Bruce government announced its partial nationalisation approach: when the licences granted to the A-class stations expired in 1929–30, 'they would be offered by tender for three years to a single nationwide company which would be responsible for programs while the PMG provided all technical services'.[27] In other words, the government would take over the physical assets of the A-class stations but, undoubtedly influenced by the Royal Commission report and press opposition to government control of broadcasting, it did not want to produce the content itself.[28] The combine must have felt it was the obvious choice to win the tender for providing content but Bruce had gone cold on it because of its poor service and the public backlash.

The joint tender submitted by the radio combine was unsuccessful. The contract was instead awarded to the Australian Broadcasting Company, established in Sydney by theatre owner Sir Benjamin Fuller, cinema owner Stuart Doyle, and music publisher and seller Frank Albert.[29] Dominion Broadcasting's directors were furious. They launched a compensation claim, arguing that Bruce had told the A-class stations in October 1927 that, if they amalgamated, they would receive a five-year licence renewal. Conder alleged that Bruce instead told the directors in February 1929: 'I am sorry, but the government has changed its policy. Governments are unsatisfactory to deal with. They have no business morals … I am very sorry but I cannot do anything for you.'[30]

Dominion Broadcasting sought compensation from the Commonwealth for broken promises and revenue it had spent on amalgamation. The case became even more interesting when Country Party MP Roland Green, who was on the committee investigating the claim for compensation, alleged that Conder tried to bribe him. Dominion Broadcasting (whose attorney was Fink's law firm) hired the best legal representation money could buy. Menzies successfully defended Conder at the 1930 Royal Commission into the bribery allegations. The Commission found the allegation of bribery could not be sustained, but this was not the last time that Conder's integrity was questioned.

Bruce made some powerful enemies when he put the public interest ahead of the radio combine's. The *Sun* under Campbell Jones savagely turned on him and 'adopted' Hughes as its political leader instead, championing him over Bruce during the 1929 election (when Hughes was not even a contender as a party leader). Bruce said this was part of a 'vendetta' against him for his decisions on radio.[31] *Smith's Weekly* wanted the credit for changing the course of radio, and claimed that its campaign against the combine had stopped it from taking over the airways.[32] But even the pro-business *Sydney Morning Herald* had been against it, saying the public 'was not in favour of [commercial] monopolies in such an important industry'.[33] The *Sydney Morning Herald* had instead joined in *The Age*'s calls for a BBC-style national broadcaster in Australia. This was not only because the *Sydney Morning Herald* had been deeply impressed by the high culture BBC. There was a view among newspaper executives, as revealed in internal memos from Associated Newspapers, that they would be able to 'more easily ... control' the 'news invasion by radio' through a national broadcasting service than through many separate commercial stations.[34]

THE FIRST ABC AND ITS COMMERCIAL COMPETITORS, 1929-32

When the government took over the A-class stations (including the combine's) in 1929–30, Denison was pushed out of radio broadcasting, and he stayed out for the next four years. But the HWT was determined to stay involved. When the Australian Broadcasting Company took over supplying 3LO's programs in July 1929, and

3AR's in August 1929, Conder delivered a bitter farewell, telling listeners it was taking the fruits of his company's success.[35] It was now also a competitor because, in April, the HWT had purchased a B-class station, 3DB, from the Druleigh Business and Technical College. This made the HWT the first Australian newspaper company to fully own a radio station. And this time, Murdoch was put in charge as chairman of 3DB's board, with Thorold Fink a director.

When Lyons, who was then Labor's postmaster-general, came to open 3DB's new studios in December 1929, Murdoch found him to be very friendly. Only five months later, Murdoch and Dumas were lobbying Lyons and the head of the PMG's department, Harry Percy (HP) Brown, to approve the *Advertiser*'s application for a new licence for 5AD. Brown presumably needed little convincing because he was the one who had encouraged Dumas to apply for the licence. The two were friends from years earlier, when they had both lived in London. When Dumas had told Brown that they were looking to buy an existing Adelaide radio station, Brown had looked into the matter for him and told Dumas that there was still one Adelaide station licence unallocated. According to Dumas, Brown said 'if I liked to apply for that, *I could have it* without having to [go to the expense of] buy[ing] one of the existing licences out ... This was great news.' (italics added).[36] In approving the *Advertiser*'s application, the PMG's department overlooked its own policy that 'granting more than one licence to the same company is not advisable'.[37]

The HWT's move into full ownership confirmed that radio was no longer a fad. Other newspapers were also starting to take the medium seriously. It had become obvious that newspapers could not compete with radio on speed. Radio stations were providing quick news reports on high-profile events, including the Melbourne Cup, election results, and ongoing sports coverage, including horseracing, football and cricket. In 1930, radio scooped the press for the first time in reporting Test cricket. The *Herald*'s 3DB gave ball-by-

FIGURE 12.1 A family in their living room listen to a radio broadcast in New South Wales circa 1930; note that the newspaper is still prominent and has not been usurped

source National Library of Australia (PIC/15611/11865).

ball descriptions that reconstructed the matches based on cables sent from observers in England. These broadcasts were heard as far away as Townsville and were considered a huge success, with many listeners staying up all night to listen.[38]

Cricket played a large part in radio's early popularity. Reports of Don Bradman's feats and the controversial 'bodyline' Australian Test of 1932–33 captivated audiences. By 1934, 3DB's coverage of Test matches in England had the delay in receiving cables from England down to sixty seconds.[39] The ABC in Sydney famously broadcast its popular 'synthetic' ball-by-ball descriptions, also based on cables, by adding sound effects, including a pencil striking the desk to imitate the sound of bat on ball, and crowd sound effects.

Radio offered an intimacy and immediacy that newspapers could not match. It was proving effective for targeted advertising, such as sponsored daytime programs aimed at women in charge of family budgets. And radio had an enormous advantage over newspapers because it did not have the expense of big print runs. Its costs 'were the same, whether [its] programs and advertisements were heard by two people, or two hundred thousand'.[40]

With radio becoming more of a menace to the press, and the Australian Broadcasting Company poised to take over the A-class stations when newspapers were becoming involved in B-class competitors, the ANC told its members in June 1929 to restrict the news bulletins they supplied to radio to fifteen minutes per day.[41] (Newspapers had previously been supplying fairly unlimited news to local radio stations so long as the announcer acknowledged the source.) This meant the Australian Broadcasting Company would start off with less news than the previous A-class stations. Newspapers were also starting to insist that morning news was broadcast after 8 am and evening news after 7 pm so it would not interfere with sales of morning and afternoon papers. The Company gently complained that news was much more of a feature of radio in the United States and in the United Kingdom, but its concerns were not picked up by MPs during parliamentary debates on broadcasting policy.[42]

'IN THE *HERALD*'S POCKET': THE BROADCASTING BILL, 1932

The Australian Broadcasting Company did not prosper during its three years and decided not to seek renewal of its contract when it expired in June 1932. As ABC historian, KS Inglis noted, this suited the Scullin government because Labor's official policy was to have public control of broadcasting.[43] It also suited the powerful head of the PMG's Department, the bowler hat–wearing HP Brown. Brown had worked for the British Post Office for twenty-five years and knew the British BBC system better than anyone in Australia. He was determined there should be a similar national broadcaster in Australia. Scullin was also under pressure from 'his own party members to stop 2FC and 3LO broadcasting blatant anti-Labor propaganda', and from Labor MPs who had felt the sting of one-sided press coverage during 1931, and hoped an independent, non-commercial system of radio could act as a counter balance to the commercial press.[44] The Scullin government's bill was going to create a new public broadcaster called the Australian Broadcasting Commission (ABC).

When the new Lyons government took office, it was visited by a procession of lobbyists seeking to influence the shape of its replacement broadcasting bill. Fenton, the new postmaster-general, and Latham, the attorney-general, were visited by the Australian Federation of Broadcasting Stations, which represented thirty-five B-class stations. Thorold Fink was its vice-president. Lyons, Fenton and Latham were also visited by a large delegation of Melbourne's business and cultural elite who had been assembled by the Victorian Radio Association, retailers of wireless equipment. Still representing radio retailers, Menzies was among these visitors. They called on the Lyons government not to drop the Scullin bill. They wanted a BBC-style broadcaster to improve service and educate and culturally enlighten Australians. With the focus still on entertainment, *The Age* called for a national broadcaster that would uplift 'the masses' and make them appreciate 'good music'.[45] It warned the Lyons government that 'there will be great public displeasure if, at this late stage', the government dropped plans for a national system like the BBC.[46] The *Sydney Morning Herald* was also commending 'BRITAIN'S WONDERFUL SYSTEM' as a 'model' for Australia and looking forward to BBC-style music, including the diversity of 'grand opera, classical opera and light opera'.[47]

The UAP's conservative constituents were also calling for a more efficient national broadcasting system because country, pastoral and farming interests were poorly served by radio, and Empire loyalists wanted Australia to link up with the United Kingdom in an Empire broadcasting system. There was a broad consensus, including bipartisan consensus, that Australia should have a fully nationalised system of radio broadcasting for the A-class stations so long as the commission responsible for it was non-commercial, politically independent and focused on high culture. In other words, it would have to leave popular fare (and profitable advertising) to the B-class/ commercial stations.

Fenton's re-drafted bill was therefore almost a verbatim copy of the Scullin bill. It had the backing of Lyons, the PMG's Department, influential educational organisations, a large number of citizens, and both major political parties. When the bill was introduced into parliament on 9 March it was initially treated 'quite favourably' during debate.[48] But Murdoch was horrified. The bill allowed the new ABC (for the Lyons government had even retained the same name) to have sponsored programs, to publish newspapers and magazines, and to establish newsagencies.[49] If it chose to, it could compete with the press in every major field – advertising, radio, print and cable news.

Although the BBC was not permitted to carry advertising or sponsorship, at this time, Labor wanted the ABC to be able to, so the sponsorship provision had been in the original Scullin government bill. The clause said the [ABC] 'may not publish advertisements in general', but with ministerial approval it could broadcast announcements that related to matters in the broadcast. This left the door open for the ABC to take 'sponsored programs'.[50] This was the most vigorously attacked part of the bill. The *Herald*'s Canberra press gallery bureau chief, Joe Alexander, wrote in his diary that 'KM is very concerned at provision for Sponsored [sic] programs and strong effort will be made to have it deleted'.[51] The *Herald* published strongly worded articles and editorials saying that, until now, advertising had 'been the province of private enterprise' but this bill would bring 'the Government into the advertising business', and with a £400 000 subsidy from 'the public pocket', none of the B-class stations 'would have the slightest chance of surviving' against such a competitor.[52]

The *Herald* called the sponsorship provision 'a great surprise', and 'an unwarranted encroachment' upon the B-class stations' 'sole source of revenue'.[53] It accused the government of breaking its election commitments to private enterprise, and promised a 'strong attack' on the bill.[54] The Federation of Broadcasting Stations denounced the bill as an 'invasion ... of the advertising field'.[55] On 10 March, the ANC sent a telegram to Lyons also protesting the sponsorship provision, and other newspaper proprietor associations sent similar telegrams. On 11 March, the *Herald* told the government to 'RUB IT OUT AND START AGAIN!'.[56]

Joe Alexander wrote in his diary that the UAP's Minister for Customs, Henry Gullett, was 'peeved' with Alexander's reporting on the broadcasting bill.[57] Gullett knew exactly what the *Herald* was up to because he had been one of the paper's top journalists. Like Murdoch, Gullett was a former Hughes publicist who fell out bitterly with Hughes. When Gullett joined the *Herald* in 1922, he helped it wage its publicity war on Hughes. Gullett was a friend of Murdoch's and had been a co-participant in the intrigue around Lyons' defection in 1931. He pulled Alexander aside over the *Herald*'s reporting on the broadcasting bill and, according to Alexander, 'unfair[ly] ... accused me of lobbying and said the newspapers were asking for their own selfish interests'.[58]

Although a strong supporter of national broadcasting, the other B-class licence holder, *The Age*, was also unhappy with the first draft of the bill. It wanted the sponsorship provisions removed, and also shared the *Herald*'s concern that the bill gave the minister and PMG bureaucrats too much 'political control' over the national broadcaster. What the newspapers were really worried about is also revealed in internal memos from Associated Newspapers. The newspapers feared that Brown and his public servants would act 'very adversely to newspaper interests', including by bringing about 'public distrust of the policies supported by newspapers'.[59]

For several days, the government was met with a firestorm of articles and headlines – 'SOCIALISING RADIO: BILL ATTACKED', 'THIS BROADCAST BLUNDER BILL', 'BROADCAST BILL ATTACKED', 'a sorry farce', a 'fiasco'.[60] On 14 March, there was a long Cabinet meeting to discuss the bill. That day, the *Herald* had blamed Fenton and Brown for it, reporting that Fenton had introduced the bill to parliament before the UAP's ministerial party had seen it. On the broadcasting bill, Fenton was speaking and acting more like the Labor MP he had been than the UAP one he had become, highlighting the teething problems of a governing party composed of remnants.[61] The *Herald* also quoted Brown as unconvincingly saying that the clause about the postmaster-general having the power to direct the ABC was 'an unfortunate accident' that was not supposed to be in the bill, and Fenton and the postmaster-general had no idea how it got there.[62]

Murdoch despatched Lloyd Dumas (head of the *Advertiser* and 5AD) to Canberra to pull government MPs into line. Dumas arrived on 15 March, and met with ministers and MPs ahead of a special 6 pm meeting of the UAP. Alexander wrote in his diary that '[WM] Hughes and [Fred H] Stewart strongly attacked [the] Bill' at that meeting.[63] They were both personally involved in commercial radio. Hughes had been fascinated by wireless since its earliest days in Australia, and as prime minister, had been heavily involved in making AWA a joint Commonwealth–private enterprise. He was one of its directors (and had been since 1922). AWA owned radio stations, and also installed and operated stations on behalf of other B-class licence holders. Stewart was a wealthy industrialist who had just become governing director of 2CH. He had financed this new B-class station so the united churches could run it. Just days before the broadcasting bill was introduced, Stewart had agreed to lease 2CH to Hughes' AWA.

Hughes and Murdoch now found some common ground – their interest in commercial radio. Hughes attacked the bill fiercely, and sometimes in the same words as the *Herald*, which must have gone some way towards putting him back in Murdoch's good books. Gullett was not impressed though. Alexander recorded in his diary that: 'Gullett has been very angry today at efforts made to defeat the Bill and accused me of lobbying. [He said:] "You have nearly bust up this show". I told him I owed my allegiance to my office. He said "You owe allegiance too to this Government which you did so much to create".'[64] (Notably, Alexander did not say anything about owing allegiance to his readers.)

The day after Dumas arrived, the bill was hastily re-written in ministerial party meetings. Alexander wrote in his diary that it was the most 'exciting day since the new Government took office [because] Fenton [was] furious at Party decision to drop [the] Bill saying he has been humiliated. He threatened to resign.'[65] Fenton only agreed to stay after Lyons promised not to delay passage of the bill, but it was amended to remove ministerial control over the ABC and sponsored programs.

On 17 March, the amended bill was introduced to the House of Representatives. Although Gullett had been just as appalled by the press' lobbying and self-interest, he (not Fenton) rose to explain the government's backpedalling. Putting the best possible spin on events, Gullett said 'the changes [in the revised bill] had arisen as a result of helpful and constructive criticism during the debate'.[66] But Labor MPs said the government had caved in to pressure from powerful newspaper interests. Labor's former postmaster-general Albert Green said 'Cabinet has accepted dictation from the press'.[67] Labor's David Riordan said Fenton was 'hanging his head' during the debate because he had supported the nationalisation policy for a long time, and knew the re-written bill was 'designed to bolster up private enterprise' and 'protect the interests of those who have their money invested in B class stations'.[68]

The embarrassing backdown had at least mollified the press. *The Age* called it 'A BETTER BROADCASTING BILL'.[69] The *Herald*'s tone was also conciliatory.[70] On 20 March, Murdoch arrived in Canberra to smooth matters over. UAP MPs met with him privately but knew better than to be seen with him in public. Alexander wrote in his diary that 'SMB' (Stanley Melbourne Bruce) politely declined to have lunch with Murdoch, saying that it would be unwise because 'people were saying it was the *Herald*'s government; that *Herald* people attended Cabinet meetings and that the Government was in the *Herald*'s pocket'. According to the diary notes, Murdoch instead dined privately with Bruce and 'McL' (very likely Senator McLachlan).[71]

THE NEW ABC AND ITS OLD NEWS

In all the commotion about sponsorship, what had been overlooked was the way in which the legislation that established the ABC had, at the urging of the press, severely limited its freedom, status and news role. Murdoch was determined not to let radio usurp Australian newspapers' role as the dominant provider of news and information.

The Australian newspapers knew from their British counter-parts how the BBC had developed and was affecting the British press. When the BBC's predecessor had begun daily broadcasts in November 1922, it broadcast news at 6 pm and 9 pm for its first five weeks, before newspapers and newsagencies applied pressure and made it agree not to broadcast news before 7 pm. 'We want to work smoothly with the newspapers', said the BBC's Sir William Noble.[72] At the time, it was willing to leave the expensive business of news collection to the agencies. But by 1932, the BBC had carved out a major role in news provision in the United Kingdom with a 6 pm news bulletin, its own subeditors, and a Royal Charter in 1927 that brought it a new freedom and an expanded news service, including a doubling of the amount of airtime the BBC devoted to news bul-letins. Australian newspaper owners would also have been aware that, in the United States, demand for radio news was outstripping the capacity of American newspapers to provide it, and some radio stations had hired their own editors and reporters.

In the House of Representatives, another Labor-defector-turned-Nationalist MP had made a minor amendment to the bill establishing the ABC. Based on the BBC charter, the clause read that the ABC could: 'collect, in such manner as it thinks fit, news and information relating to current events in any part of the world, and may establish and subscribe to news agencies'. When the bill arrived in the Senate in May 1932, Senator HSW Lawson represented the views of the freshly alarmed newspaper owners. He argued this pro-vision gave much wider powers to the ABC than were necessary. Getting to the nub of the press proprietors' concerns, he said that, if the ABC was permitted to collect and distribute 'news in such manner as it thinks fit, it may be empowered to publish a newspaper, or to do anything else'.[73]

Lawson successfully moved an amendment that removed the ABC's right to establish a news agency, returning it to a state of dependence on the press and the established news agencies controlled by the press (firstly, the APA, and then from 1935, the AAP under Murdoch's direction). There was no debate on this issue. (After his retirement from politics, Lawson became a director of the *Argus* in 1937.)

As historian Alan Thomas noted, just as the BBC was forging ahead with building up a news service that would be the envy of broadcasters around the world, 'the ABC was just embarking on what would be fifteen years of negotiations with the Australian press for the right to broadcast news'.[74] This 'was unique to Australia'.[75] In the United States and the United Kingdom, broadcasters were dealing with news agencies which supplied them directly with a special news service. In Australia, the Lyons government was insisting that the ABC form an agreement with newspaper owners to only take its news from newspapers. The ANC appointed Dumas and four other ANC members to take charge of these negotiations with the ABC and make sure that any news provided to the ABC would not 'seriously affect [the newspapers'] own interests'.[76] The ANC was not a corporate body, so this agreement was only a 'gentleman's agreement', but it was regarded as legally binding by both parties.

On 23 May 1932, the names of the ABC's five commissioners were announced. Charles Lloyd Jones, chairman of David Jones, was a close friend of the UAP's SM Bruce, and also a friend of Warwick Fairfax. Jones was a former director of the *Sun*-aligned 2BL. Businessman Herbert Brookes was Alfred Deakin's son-in-law, a friend of Menzies and Ricketson, and had helped found two anti-Labor parties. He was a director of the NMLA, the life insurance company that had been deeply involved in Lyons' defection, and was also prominent in the UAP's fundraising arm, the National Union. Brookes' family business, the Australian Paper Mills, was linking up with Denison and Collins House to work out

how to manufacture newsprint in Australia (Chapter 14). This pro-
vided a strong motivation to make sure newspapers kept growing.
RS Wallace was Sydney University vice-chancellor, and considered a
UAP supporter. EM Couchman was Australian Women's National
League president and a UAP supporter. RB Orchard was an ex-
Nationalist Party member of Parliament.

Thomas noted: 'In appointing people known to be active in
anti-Labor politics, the government exposed itself to charges of political favouritism'.[77] But the *Labor Daily* was the only metropolitan
daily to criticise the selection of ABC's foundation commissioners
for their partisan backgrounds. Other papers, including the *Herald*,
praised the choice of appointees.

On 1 July 1932, the ABC was inaugurated by Prime Minister
Joseph Lyons and began broadcasting as a national network consisting of twelve former A-class stations. At its first meeting with the
ANC, in October 1932, the ABC's request to be allowed to gather
news in addition to that supplied by the press was rejected. Instead,
the ABC signed an agreement forbidding it to collect its own local
news (except market reports, shipping movements and weather
forecasts). It had to take local news from the metropolitan daily
papers, at a cost of £200 per year (which the ANC set aside as funds
to be used to 'police' the ABC's compliance with the agreement).[78]
The ABC could broadcast only two news bulletins per day. The first
had to be between 10 am and 11 am (after even the most leisurely
reader would have finished the morning paper), and the second was
to be an evening bulletin of five minutes duration to be broadcast
after 7.50 pm (when people would have finished reading the *Herald*
and other afternoon papers).

In total, the ABC was allowed to broadcast only fifteen minutes of 'new' local news per day, all taken from the press after publication, which reduced its value to the listener significantly. As for
overseas news, for £1250 per year, the ABC was allowed 200 words

of cabled news per day that could not be broadcast until one hour after publication.

The ABC would have to begin with less news than the Australian Broadcasting Company, and less than the Company's predecessor, the *Sun Herald*–linked radio combine. As media historian Neville Petersen noted, this, 'as far as can be determined, was not the subject of any political or public comment'.[79] The ABC's news would consist essentially of announcers reading out the headlines and introductory sentences from hours-old press stories pasted onto a piece of paper. Because listeners were unaware of the reason why the ABC's news service was so inadequate, they blamed the broadcaster.

CHAPTER 13
EMPERORS OF AIR

Several newspaper groups expanded enthusiastically into commercial radio when Lyons was in office. Led by Keith Murdoch, they tried to ensure that the new ABC would not pose a threat either to the viability of newspapers, or their new interests in radio. This set the stage for years of negotiations and political battles over whether the ABC would have to remain reliant upon newspapers, or could instead collect its own news. As part of this contest over the authority of the ABC, an attempt was made to rein in the dominance of the press over radio. When this failed, it provided an indication of just how powerful the major press groups had become.

THE RISE OF NEWSPAPERS ON COMMERCIAL RADIO

Once the ABC had taken over the A-class stations, as a former postmaster-general noted, there was a 'danger of somebody getting crushed in the rush for' B-class licences.[1] But with a grateful Lyons government in office, the HWT was front of the queue. It had two licences when Lyons came to power. Four years later, it had eleven.

In South Australia, Lyons' 1931 promoter and friend, Dumas, looked after the HWT's interests, and was particularly blessed. In 1933, the *Advertiser* was allowed to take over station 5PI in Port Pirie, a town of long-standing significance to the HWT and its owners. When the new 5PI opened in 1933, it was the first commercial regional relay station in Australia, transmitting programs from 5AD. It had low power, just 50 watts, but in February 1934, the PMG gave permission for 5PI to be moved to Crystal Brook where it received a boost that made it the most powerful station in Australia. Six times more powerful than any of its commercial competitors in South Australia, 5PI now had an enormous advantage in gaining audiences and advertisers. In early 1935, the PMG approved of the *Advertiser* taking a controlling interest in a third station, 5MU Murray Bridge.

In Western Australia, the still HWT-connected West Australian Newspapers (WAN) joined up with Musgrove's Ltd, sellers of musical instruments and radio sets, to form WA Broadcasters Ltd. This company took over the existing station that Musgrove's owned (6ML), and the licence that WAN had been given for a new station called 6IX in Perth. In 1935, the PMG offered WA Broadcasters a third B-class licence that became 6WB Katanning.

In Queensland, five months after Murdoch forged the *Courier-Mail* in 1933, it purchased 4BK Brisbane, which featured coverage of Wren's boxing and wrestling events, and was then granted a second licence for a new station on the Darling Downs, 4AK Oakey. 4AK opened in August 1935, and was soon permitted to double its aerial output power to 2000 watts.

Denison knew that he was being left behind, and once the pro-business Premiers' Plan helped a downsized Associated Newspapers pull itself back from the brink of economic ruin, the company turned back to radio. In 1933, it bought a half share in 2UE Sydney. Denison said his board had wanted to get back into radio for 'a long time' because broadcasting would become 'either a great help or possibly a serious menace to newspapers' in terms of news and advertising.[2]

The PMG head, Brown, privately believed advertising on Australian radio had already reached 'nauseating' levels.[3] But it was only increasing as advertisers who traditionally relied upon newspapers began to sample radio advertising. In May 1933, 3DB's managers finally persuaded Sidney Myer to use radio for Myer advertisements. Myer made a deal to buy a two-and-a-half-hour slot on 3DB from Monday to Saturday for twelve months. The Depression had also seen the rise of bargain chain store competitors such as GJ Coles and Co, and Woolworths. In 1937, Woolworths tried radio, sponsoring a popular evening program on 2GB. Other companies, such as the Australian arm of the US multinational soap company, Colgate-Palmolive, also turned to radio that year. The commercial stations were moving towards round-the-clock programming and cheaper, sponsored formats such as US soap operas and quiz shows.

'WHAT SORT OF MEAT DO THEY EAT?': ABC NEWS AND RADIO OWNERSHIP LIMITS, 1935

Two related battles broke out over broadcasting in 1935. The first was over the ABC's heavily restricted news programming. In the United States, most early evening radio news bulletins in the 1930s were fifteen minutes long, and broadcast at either 6 pm, 6.15 pm or 6.30 pm. In the United Kingdom, the BBC was broadcasting news at 6 pm and 9 pm. Although the BBC still relied on raw material from news agencies such as Reuters, it was using its own editorial staff to select and craft that material. In Australia, due to the ABC's agreement with newspapers, ABC listeners had to wait until 7.50 pm for just five minutes of local news, read straight out of published newspapers.

As press historian RB Walker observed, the newspapers were walking a tightrope, trying to restrict 'the supply [of news] as much as they could without forcing the ABC in despair to start

its own service'.[4] But as the ABC grew, it did start to despair. ABC
executives felt the news supplied by metropolitan newspapers was
neither impartial nor national, both of which the ABC desired to be.
They also observed that commercial radio stations were sometimes
broadcasting their own news bulletins earlier than 7.50 pm, and at
twice the length allowed for the ABC's.

In 1935, the ABC, under WJ Cleary as chairman, began to push
back against the restrictions. Cleary was taking on the ANC, a powerful body, and one he noted was well-equipped to obtain 'publicity for
its point of view'.[5] In October, the ABC announced it would begin
relaying its five minutes of Australian news at 7.30 pm, twenty minutes earlier than the ANC–ABC 'gentleman's agreement' permitted.
Provocatively, the ABC began broadcasting at this earlier time the
day before its 3 October meeting with the ANC.

The B-class-owning *Age* argued, on 14 October 1935, that
listeners found too much news on the ABC 'tedious'.[6] Murdoch also
kept up this self-interested argument, insisting that the public 'does
not want to hear much talking over the air' (a claim that was amply
disproven when talk radio began in the 1960s and was still popular
into the 2010s).[7] Fairfax's RAG Henderson believed that Murdoch
had an 'exaggerated fear' of news broadcasting on the radio and saw
the ABC as 'a very real rival'.[8] Murdoch would not budge on the
timing of ABC news. He was, as political scientist Rodney Tiffen
noted, trying 'to protect his evening newspaper sales but [also] to
advantage his commercial radio stations'.[9]

During negotiations, the ABC put its news back to 7.50 pm,
but on 12 November, Cleary told the government and the ANC
that if the newspapers did not agree to the earlier time, the ABC
would have to start collecting its own news, which it had always
been entitled to do under the 1932 Act. The ANC members discussed Cleary's threat at their 13–15 November meeting. A copy
of the minutes shows that Murdoch reminded his fellow executives

and owners that the newspapers had 'carefully chosen' the later broadcast time of 7.50 pm because it was 'the time at which people were on their way to theatres or their attention was being distracted in other ways'. He said of Cleary and the ABC executives pushing for an earlier time, that 'these men [are] very dangerous'.[10]

Murdoch also conceded two things among his fellow owners and executives that he would never admit publicly. The first was that 'there was no copyright in news – only in the form of expression used'. There was legally nothing to stop the ABC – or any broadcaster – obtaining early copies of the newspapers, re-writing the news articles in their own words, and broadcasting that content. Murdoch also admitted that newspapers 'were up against an inevitable contest with broadcasting' and he believed 'most firmly' that 'the broadcasting of news in any large way did affect sales; it affected the surprise value of newspapers and had limited their progress'.[11]

Murdoch canvassed several ways of 'fight[ing]' the ABC, including going through Cabinet and 'making it quite a fighting point with Ministers', as well as using 'the editorial columns of [our] newspapers'.[12] To take action using the first tactic, he wrote a letter to Lyons, complaining about Cleary's 'attitude' and describing the ABC's actions as 'unfair' and 'uncouth'.[13] But when Lyons personally asked Murdoch to accept the new timing of 7.30 pm, Murdoch agreed, probably because he recognised an earlier time was less threatening than the ABC starting its own news service.

While these tense negotiations were going on, the PMG's Department suddenly issued a new set of regulations on 23 October 1935, limiting the number of B-class stations that one body could own or control. The regulations limited owners to one metropolitan radio station in a state, two metropolitan stations across Australia, and a maximum of three stations in a state and five in the Commonwealth. Murdoch, already frustrated with Lyons, was furious. He not only oversaw the HWT's stations, but also had a personal stake in three of the metropolitan stations. Murdoch saw the regulations as a personal attack. He complained privately to Lyons. Publicly, the government was again met with intense lobbying. The Federation of Australian Commercial Broadcasting Stations attacked the restrictions. The *Herald* reported 'NEW RADIO RULES CONDEMNED'.[14] The *Daily Telegraph* slammed the 'radio dictatorship' of the PMG.[15] The *Sun* said: 'RADIO INDUSTRY IS ALARMED', and dramatically claimed that private enterprise in broadcasting might not survive.[16]

On 25 November, Murdoch wrote an angry letter to Lyons claiming he had heard that the postmaster-general and 'another Minister' designed the regulation 'to corner Murdoch and his crowd'. Murdoch told Lyons that it was 'such a pity' to the see the government do 'such a dreadful thing as this regulation'.[17] Lyons wrote back to reassure Murdoch that no one in Cabinet wanted to 'inflict some injury upon you through the Radio regulations'. Lyons said that although his ministers 'like myself, might sometimes complain of criticism by the papers of your group they all realise only too well what the government and party owe to those papers'. Lyons noted the regulations were already being modified and asked plaintively, and apparently in frustration, 'what more can we do?'.[18]

Two days after Murdoch's letter, revised regulations were announced that watered down the ownership restrictions, allowing the chain groups to own a much larger number of stations (Table 13.1).

TABLE 13.1 Regulations for B-class radio station ownership limits, 1935

	Metropolitan		Total licences	
	In one state	In Australia	In one state	In Australia
23 October 1935	1	2	3	5
29 November 1935	1	4	4	8

SOURCE Walker, *Yesterday's News*, p. 119.

The new rules allowed four metropolitan stations across Australia, instead of two; and eight stations in total, instead of five.

The new restrictions appeased the press interests because they did not have to divest stations. Parliament continued to debate the matter. William McCall, a twenty-seven-year-old novice UAP MP and 'crony of Billy Hughes', represented the views of the newspaper chains and Hughes, who had an interest in protecting AWA, the other main target of the restrictions.[19] McCall argued the original restrictions were too harsh and an imposition on commercial freedom. The UAP's defence minister, Robert Archdale Parkhill, who had previously been the postmaster-general (from October 1932 to October 1934), rose to put his junior colleague in his place, and launched a stinging attack on the newspaper combines, especially the HWT group. Parkhill was very likely the 'other Minister' Murdoch had referred to. It seems he was the one making the case for restrictions on ownership, and that Parkhill was motivated, at least partly, by the restrictions the newspapers were forcing on the ABC.

Parkhill seems to have fallen out with Murdoch, perhaps not only over the ABC restrictions, but also due to internal jostling within the UAP for the deputy leader's job. Parkhill was Menzies' rival for that position, and the Murdoch press was increasingly supporting Menzies. A tough and experienced political organiser, Parkhill had been the 'man behind the throne of Nationalism' before he entered Parliament himself.[20] (He was also a friend of Hughes' and had organised the infamous £25 000 cheque.)

Although Parkhill was no longer postmaster-general, he represented the postmaster-general (Senator AJ McLachlan) in the House of Representatives, and he was well informed. Parkhill provided a list showing the HWT group had holdings in eleven of the sixty-five B-class stations (3DB, 4BK, 4AK, 4GY, 5AD, 5MU, 5PI, 6ML, 6KA, 6MD, 6IX).[21] Significantly, Parkhill counted WAN's stations as part of the HWT group. The HWT responded by claiming it only owned one station, 3DB, plus a minority interest in 5AD and its two relay stations, and a 'few non-voting shares in 4BK Brisbane and its relay station' (so six stations).[22] Parkhill pointed out that there were different ways of exercising control, and he could have added, of masking it. He stood by his claim.

Parkhill said it was not 'right or proper' that there should be 'a monopoly of this kind'. Although Parkhill had signed off on transactions that had brought the HWT more firmly into radio broadcasting, he told the parliament that, in his two years as postmaster-general, 'I did not at any time feel comfortable in regard to the commercial broadcasting stations. I foresaw what has arisen today.' He described how the ABC was being 'attacked in every way' and not getting a 'fair run'. Parkhill said: 'We have growing up in this country a monopoly of newspapers and broadcasting which, in combination, constitute a danger that this Parliament cannot view with equanimity, and steps should be taken to deal with it'.[23]

Parkhill said the original ownership restrictions were generous enough and, referring to the watered-down restrictions, said:

> What sort of meat do these newspaper proprietaries eat,
> which gives them the courage to propound these proposals?
> This is a piece of the sheerest effrontery that I have ever
> experienced in my public life. Having these concessions,
> building up these monopolies, they yet attempt to blackmail
> this Parliament into giving them further concessions. They
> utilize the inexperience of the youngest member of this
> House [McCall] in order to achieve their ends. He ought to
> know better than to be used by them.[24]

The newspaper owners did not forget McCall's help though, and years later, when he was in a 'tough [election] fight', they showed their gratitude by making cash donations to his campaign funds. Denison seems to have known him personally.[25]

Labor leader John Curtin commended Parkhill's stance, and so too did the tempestuous Country Party MP Archie Cameron, who had his own history of run-ins with the HWT. Cameron said the power of the press over Australian politics was too great, and if broadcasting was not controlled it would control the parliament.[26] But Parkhill's stance won him no bouquets from within his own party. The day after his forceful speech, he lost the party ballot for the UAP's deputy leader position to Menzies on the second count of votes. The most prominent New South Wales MP in the Lyons government had tried to stake his claim to the position by standing up to the Victorian-based Murdoch press, but this had backfired. The *Herald* rubbed salt in Parkhill's wound with the headline: 'A FUTURE PRIME MINISTER: The Rise of RG Menzies'.[27] Murdoch's support helped ensure Menzies' continued ascendancy over Parkhill.

By the end of 1935, the government had achieved radio ownership limits, but they were weak and would never be properly enforced. The ABC had also made only small gains in its battles with the newspapers – an earlier timeslot for its evening news bulletins, an additional three minutes of news from the morning papers, and an additional two minutes from the afternoon papers at 1 pm (when many people were at work). The ANC had insisted that the ABC could only retain access to press news if it abandoned its own news-gathering plans. Lyons knew that Murdoch's loyalty to him was already much diminished, but he also knew that he would need press support for the 1937 election. Several government ministers had tried to help the ABC and stop the radio chains from spreading even further, but as Menzies (who had stayed out of the issue and thus avoided baiting the HWT) later told Sir John Reith, the Director-General of the BBC, 'everybody got cold feet about the next election'.[28]

CALLING THE TUNE: PRESS-RADIO CHAINS

Newspaper groups interpreted the Lyons government's backdown on ownership restrictions as a green light. In 1936, Denison's family company, Denison Estates, acquired control of 2GB, formerly owned by the theosophists, and in partnership with two other companies was awarded a licence to broadcast in the Hunter Valley (2HR Singleton). An internal memo to Associated Newspapers' chairman, had said that 'we should, by means *which will keep the matter out of the PMG's regulation*, obtain an interest in Canberra, Wollongong, Singleton, and possibly Taree' (italics added).[29] They were already plotting how to get around the regulations.

The combined coverage of 2GB and 2UE gave Associated Newspapers 'complete physical coverage' of Sydney without being 'antagonistic to the Murdoch group'.[30] Associated Newspapers had come to the conclusion that they needed to build their own radio chain quickly because the new medium was affecting circulation, not only due to broadcasts of news flashes but also of sporting events, especially horseracing. An internal memo had recommended to Denison that 'the only way of limiting the news broadcasting activities of radio stations is to control them directly', and this would also allow the company to gain a share of advertising revenue that 'we may lose from our newspapers'.[31]

One of the Lyons government's most committed press supporters, the *Argus*, also surged into broadcasting. In 1935, it had only a loose affiliation with 3UZ, but by the end of 1936 it owned three stations, after Staniforth Ricketson had become chairman of the *Argus*' board in July. Ricketson had been instrumental in putting Lyons in office, and was also a close friend (and business partner) of the attorney-general, Menzies. With Ricketson in charge, the *Argus* took over 3WR Shepparton (Ricketson had its call sign changed to 3SR – his initials). In December, 3SR received approval to boost its power to 2000 watts so it could broadcast to the whole state. By then, the *Argus* had also purchased two smaller stations at Warrnambool (3YB) and Warragul (3UL). In January 1937, it formalised its loose arrangement with 3UZ by taking up an interest in that station, and then linked it with its three country stations. Two months later, this 'Argus group' of four stations signed an agreement to link up with another eight stations in New South Wales and Queensland. The *Argus* had gone from having no holdings in radio to having a radio chain in about six months.

The Age was also allowed to expand further in radio. It took over 3SH Swan Hill in April 1937. By then it also controlled 3TR Sale/ Gippsland, as well as 3AW and 3HA, allowing it to cover the whole of Victoria, and some of New South Wales. In June 1937, *The Age*'s 3HA station received a much sought-after power boost (although not enough to match the *Argus*' 3SR).

The HWT was not left out. In 1936, 3DB obtained PMG per-mission to transfer a licence it had purchased for a small 50 watt station at Horsham to Lubeck, and turn it into a high-powered station running at 2500 watts, greater power than was technically allowed at the time. The Lubeck station now had the strongest power in the Commonwealth. In July 1937, the *Advertiser* added a fourth South Australian radio station, 5SE, to its network (this one was in the postmaster-general's home town of Mount Gambier).

But the most interesting HWT acquisition was in the politically and industrially important mining town of Broken Hill, where the HWT and its owners had long-standing links. Private correspon-dence held in the papers of Sir Colin Fraser, managing director of Broken Hill Associated Smelters (BHAS), sheds some light on this acquisition.

In July 1934, a new B-class station had opened at Broken Hill, 2BH, owned by a small company named Radio Silver City. By February 1935, Fraser was concerned the station was about to fall 'into the hands of the "Red men" [union leaders] at Broken Hill'.[32] He had been alerted to this possibility by a letter that Harold Burston, the general manager of News Limited (owner of Broken Hill's *Barrier Miner*), had written to Menzies warning him that 2BH was in financial difficulties and the unions might take it over.

Menzies passed Burston's note on to the postmaster-general, Senator Alexander McLachlan, who took it upon himself to cast about for a new owner for 2BH. McLachlan approached Harold Darling of BHP, but BHP were 'very little interested in Broken Hill now', so McLachlan called for Fraser.[33] Fraser investigated and confirmed that the WIU (Workers Industrial Union) was going to try to acquire the station 'through some intermediary party'. McLachlan told Fraser that the PMG could not refuse a transfer of the station to new owners, but the government did not want it to 'get into the wrong hands' so urged BHAS 'to do something'.[34]

BHAS sought advice from William Queale, who had previously been general manager of the Broken Hill Junction Lead Mining Co, and was now chairman of Hume Broadcasters (and managing director of the mechanical supplies company that became Kelvinator). Queale had UAP links, and also links to McLachlan through Hume Pipe Enterprises (McLachlan was a director of Hume Pipes, and would resign as postmaster-general in 1938 after being accused of misusing his position to help Hume Pipes obtain contracts). Fraser wanted Queale to 'acquire this Broken Hill Station, [with] the mining companies, in the background, of course, guaranteeing them against loss' and perhaps even putting up the money 'through some other party' and leasing it to Queale's radio company.[35] Nearly twenty years after they had installed JE Davidson in the town and secretly set him up to buy the local paper, BHAS was still trying to covertly control Broken Hill's media.

BHAS also sought advice from WT Conder. In April 1933, the HWT had gained an inside contact at the ABC when 3LO's old manager was appointed the ABC's general manager. Conder encouraged the covert approach, telling Fraser that BHAS should 'take this Station while you have the chance ... There would be no need for you to take it in your own name, but you could have the controlling interest and get somebody else to run it.' Conder suggested AWA might put it 'in their name'.[36] The letters suggest that Conder may have been using his position as ABC manager to obtain information on the current owners of the Broken Hill radio station and about the station itself, which he passed on to Fraser.[37] Such ethical flexibility would be Conder's undoing. Only four months later, he was dismissed from the ABC, apparently because of financial irregularities. (Conder was then involved in a failed circus venture, and was declared bankrupt. After failing to comply with a court order, he was briefly held as a prisoner at Pentridge, the gaol he used to run.)

WS Robinson also encouraged Fraser to covertly buy 2BH because it could be used for 'indirect' 'propaganda' that 'stifles the other side'.[38] One of the important shareholders of News Limited, MH Baillieu, began sounding out Harold Burston and offering £700 if News Limited would buy 2BH.[39] Burston told Colin Fraser that they would also need an ongoing subsidy to 'limit our loss'.[40] In October 1936, News Limited purchased Radio Silver City. Burston had asked John Butters, chairman of Associated Newspapers, to stop its negotiations with 2BH's owners and allow News Limited to buy it. Burston told Butters that News Limited 'urgently require station [to] combat union efforts [designed to] force our newspaper [to] cease publication'.[41]

Burston became 2BH's managing director and it became the *Barrier Miner*'s station. Burston reported to Colin Fraser in December 1936 that the station was at 'full power' and running its best programs which have 'completely captured the whole of Broken Hill, and this naturally has caused consternation in the WIU camp'. Burston triumphantly told Fraser that 'Week by week we are gaining popularity, particularly since last Saturday when the Town Hall was crowded out with hundreds for a special Christmas meeting of 2BH's "Smilers" Club. An ice-cream and a packet of lollies apiece sent many exceedingly happy kiddies home to tell their WIU fathers what a wonderful institution 2BH is!'[42]

THE NETWORKS

By 1937, there were complaints that the newspaper–radio combines were so large they were driving independent, local stations 'to the wall'.[43] Labor papers alleged that Murdoch had been given favourable treatment, and Curtin began asking questions in parliament. In the Senate, the postmaster-general, McLachlan, said the story of press monopoly in radio was an old one, and 'There is nothing in it'.[44] He listed nine stations the HWT was involved with (one more than the regulations allowed). It was only because WAN was counted as separate from the HWT that the total was not twelve, and this helps explain why, after the ownership limits came into effect, the HWT would have been especially keen to create the appearance of WAN as a distinct company (whether it actually was is difficult to determine).

In the House of Representatives, Parkhill still represented the postmaster-general, but he was far more subdued than two years earlier. Parkhill reported that newspaper proprietors wholly controlled twenty out of ninety stations, and partly controlled a further eleven. He argued the ownership restrictions had not been infringed, although the ownership lists suggested otherwise, and he no longer complained about a dangerous press monopoly in radio.

Radio had become so popular by 1938 that two out of every three homes had a set, and in some capital cities, it was nine out of ten.[45] Large advertising agencies had integrated themselves so thoroughly into radio that they were increasingly determining program content. Back in the late 1920s, the HWT had recognised that advertisers were willing to spend money on producing expensive programs as long as they were broadcast over a large area to a wide audience. In 1930, its first attempt to establish a national broadcasting network, called the Federal Network, linked up six stations. It had made a second attempt in 1933, but the HWT's third version, formed in 1938, was the most enduring. Called the Major Network, at first it consisted of 2CH Sydney, 3DB Melbourne, 4BK Brisbane, 5AD Adelaide, 6IX Perth and 7HT Hobart. By 1942, it had fourteen member stations.

Not to be outdone, Denison built a larger network to provide advertisers with 'maximum listener coverage'.[46] Sun Newspapers still held half the shares of 2UE, and Denison Estates had an interest in 2GB Sydney, 2CA Canberra, 2HR Singleton/Lochinvar and 2WL Wollongong; and through 2GB, in 3AW and 5DN Adelaide. Denison organised these stations into the Macquarie Network. It linked up nineteen radio stations by July 1938, and fifty-four stations by 1943. By 1941, the Macquarie Network claimed it could reach 94 per cent of Australian listeners. Its buying power was vast, and it became an organisation 'of size and power to rival the ABC'.[47]

THE ABC STRIKES BACK

In 1936, negotiations between the ABC and the newspapers were still testy. An exchange recorded in the minutes of a meeting between Murdoch and the ABC's general manager, Charles Moses, records Murdoch asking Moses: 'Is 7 pm the best hour for the evening?' When Moses replied: 'Yes, that is the best time', Murdoch said: 'You have taken the best time for yourselves. There must be room for bargaining … It amounts to this: If you can't alter the hour, the question that concerns us is how much you should pay us. The damages to us are very considerable.'[48]

In 1937, the ABC was making more concrete moves to establish its own independent news service, and was again trying to broadcast news at an earlier time. In response, Murdoch's papers started a campaign calling for listeners' licence fees (then the main source of the ABC's funding) to be cut, thus depriving the ABC of the funding it would need to set up its own news service. Herbert Brookes, vice-chairman of the ABC, responded by publicly saying that the metropolitan press' treatment of the ABC was 'unmerciful and misleading ... they are frightened their purse might be injured'.[49] This would become something of a pattern, that pro-business, conservative appointments to the ABC board would become unexpectedly committed to it, a type of executive 'Stockholm syndrome' that conservative critics of the ABC would despair of. (This would also not be the last time the Murdoch family called for public funding to the ABC or BBC to be cut.)

In 1939, the ABC was finally able to start establishing an independent news service. As the target of press-enabled plots to depose him, Lyons had become fed up with misleading media coverage. He gave a five-minute speech on the ABC, trying to correct press speculation about government policy. Always averse to criticism, the press slammed Lyons for using the public broadcaster for 'propaganda'. This helped convince Lyons that an independent source of news was really needed. With the support of the HWT's old adversary, Archie Cameron (now postmaster-general), Lyons' Cabinet invited the ABC to appoint a representative to the Canberra press gallery.

Cameron suggested his close friend Warren Denning for the job. Denning had worked in the press gallery for nine years and had the unusual mix on his CV of having worked for both the *Labor Daily* and the *Argus*. Petersen said that 'Denning's appointment was greeted with absolute total dismay by the newspapers because it broke the barrier that they had set up against the ABC [establishing] its own newsgathering service'.[50] The newspapers demanded that the ABC not appoint any other newsgatherers elsewhere in Australia.

Worried that Denning would broadcast the news before they could print it, his former press colleagues did not want him to attend news conferences. They appealed to Menzies and the (now) new prime minister agreed to give two press conferences – the first for newspaper journalists, and then a separate conference with Denning. Menzies soon grew weary of this time-consuming arrangement, and moved back to holding just one press conference for all per day. The tactic had backfired on the newspapers anyway because Denning's private daily conversations with Menzies had gained him some exclusive stories. Print journalists were so worried about radio that Denning was physically attacked by two Canberra journalists on a train trip from Sydney to Canberra. Journalist Jack Commins said the thinking at the time was 'that radio and radio news would eventually kill newspapers. That's [why] all the newspaper boys were very jumpy'.[51]

The ABC finally secured agreement to broadcast local news at 7.10 pm in 1939, just weeks after Australia had entered World War II.[52] Public demand for up-to-the-minute overseas news, which had so boosted the newspapers during World War I, now boosted radio, which was the superior medium for providing breaking news. In the United Kingdom, the BBC moved from two bulletins per day to six. In Australia, the ABC gained better access to BBC news (which the papers had controversially, and in defiance of BBC statements, claimed they held copyright over). Charles Moses, still the general manager of the ABC, told Menzies that, despite their vehement public statements, the newspapers 'know perfectly well that there is no copyright in news'.[53]

In 1946, a Standing Committee on Broadcasting divided along party lines on the issue of independent newsgathering for the ABC.

The Labor majority recommended the ABC should establish a fully independent news service, while Liberal and Country Party members (including Menzies) urged the ABC to continue to take its news from the newspapers. As it was now a Labor government, headed by Ben Chifley, an amendment to the ABC's Act was introduced requiring the broadcaster to set up its own news service. After an all-night debate in August 1946, the bill passed. The ABC's independent news service began at 7 pm on 1 June 1947. For fourteen years and eleven months, the ABC had been at the mercy of the press. It is an interesting side note that Murdoch, the man who had led the campaign against the national broadcaster having its own news, would listen to the ABC when he wanted radio news.[54]

LYONS' LICENCE WINNERS

In seven years, the Lyons government gave out more than seventy radio licences (more than half were allocated when McLachlan was postmaster-general). Newspaper groups gained more than their fair share of these, and because they got in during the Lyons era, they had a major advantage when new licences dried up in the 1940s. (In the 1930s, ninety-two commercial stations came on air, but only nine in the 1940s, and then just six in the 1950s.) The sought-after metropolitan licences became especially scarce. Most were allocated before the mid-1930s, and no new metropolitan station came on air between 1947 and 1976. Meanwhile, the HWT's original commercial metropolitan station, 3DB, which had been cross-promoted in HWT papers since 1929, was so dominant that it held more than 35 per cent of the Melbourne audience into the 1940s.[55]

The newspaper industry had so successfully colonised Australian radio broadcasting in the 1930s that, by 1943, fifty-two of

TABLE 13.2 Newspaper ownership of radio stations under the Lyons government, 1932–39

	January 1932 (when Lyons took office)	1939 (the year Lyons died)
Herald and Weekly Times	3DB Melbourne 5AD Adelaide	3DB Melbourne 3LK Lubeck 2BH Broken Hill 4AK Oakey 4BK Brisbane 5AD Adelaide 5MU Murray Bridge 5PI Crystal Brook 5SE Mount Gambier
West Australian Newspapers Ltd		6IX Perth 6ML Perth 6WB Katanning
Associated Newspapers		2UE Sydney 2GB Sydney 2CA Canberra 2HR Singleton 2WL Wollongong 3AW Melbourne 5DN Adelaide
The Argus and Australasian Ltd		3UZ Melbourne 3SR Shepparton 3YB Warrnambool 3UL Warragul
David Syme and Co. Ltd (*The Age*)	3HA Hamilton	3AW Melbourne 3HA Hamilton 3SH Swan Hill 3TR Sale
Davies Brothers Ltd (the *Mercury*)		7HO Hobart

NOTE Ownership includes outright ownership and control of stations and minor shareholdings.

the ninety-eight commercial stations were owned, controlled or strongly influenced by newspapers.[56] At more than half, this was a much higher proportion than in the United States where newspapers in the 1940s owned about a third of stations.[57] The daily metropolitan papers in Australia owned or controlled twenty-nine of the ninety-eight licences (30 per cent). And the groups closest to Lyons during his 1931 defection – the HWT, the *Argus* and Associated Newspapers – had been the most successful in the stampede for licences during his terms in office (Table 13.2).

Newspaper groups that did not move into radio ownership in the 1930s found they had waited too long. In the early 1940s, the Packers' Consolidated Press offered to pay £1000 annually for a licence for a Sydney radio station, but in the end, the Packers received a television licence in the 1950s before they obtained a radio licence. It was not until 1960 that they gained control of a radio station, 3AK. Within ten years, Consolidated Press controlled eight stations. The *Sydney Morning Herald* was also a late bloomer in radio. Fairfax acquired its first shareholding in a station – 2GB Sydney – in 1953. After its own spurt of empire building, by 1970, Fairfax had a majority holding or a controlling interest in nine stations.[58] With nine stations, including six in one state, and four metropolitan licences, Fairfax was seemingly in clear breach of the ownership restrictions, but the newspaper groups' slippery legal manoeuvres around the definition of 'control', and governments' tolerance of their exploitation of that loophole, meant the restrictions were easily evaded.

THE LEGACY OF THE PRESS IN RADIO

Newspaper groups in Australia were determined that radio should not be a serious news outlet. They encouraged the perception that radio was an entertainment medium by taking control of as many commercial stations as they could, and by limiting news on those stations, and on the ABC. They wanted Australians to think that newspapers *were* the news. Judging by newspaper circulation figures, they were fairly successful in this project. The circulation of most of the major daily papers doubled between 1933 and 1949,[59] and Australian proprietors seem to have been more successful at stemming the flow away from newspapers than those in the United States and the United Kingdom, where radio focused more on news and information.[60]

With the acquisition of radio stations, the major newspaper groups had an even greater ability to influence public opinion, making them more powerful entities. By 1970, the HWT had an interest in fourteen broadcasting licences 'instead of the fixed maximum of 8', Fairfax had its nine, Consolidated Press had five, and Rupert Murdoch's News Limited controlled four.[61] By then, the major newspaper groups had also taken control of television. Because they had learned from the experience of radio in the 1930s, they made sure they were first in line when television licences were handed out in the 1950s.

CHAPTER 14

PAPER AND CABLE CARTELS

Paper was the lifeblood of a newspaper in pre-digital times, and Australia's newspaper publishers lived in fear of running out of it. Paper that was suitable for high-speed printing presses – newsprint – could not be commercially manufactured in Australia before 1941.[1] Newsprint had to be imported – usually from Canada, the United States or Scandinavia – at significant cost to the newspaper companies for freight and importation charges, and supply was always vulnerable to trade and transport disruptions – especially during war. The situation became so critical during World War I that some owners began searching for a way to make newsprint locally from Australian hardwood – a feat then considered technically impossible.

After two decades of experimentation, high hopes, disappointments and delays, the HWT and Fairfax & Sons joined forces in the mid-1930s to make Australian-made newsprint a reality. When ten daily newspapers were printed on locally produced newsprint in 1941, the press proclaimed it the greatest 'romance' of the newspaper industry, and testament to a leap of 'faith and courage' as much as technical 'genius'.[2]

The HWT and Fairfax & Sons were also cooperating in another important venture. In 1935, they had put aside more than sixty years of rivalry in gathering overseas news to form a cooperative cable news service, the Australian Associated Press (AAP). Paper and cable news were the two most expensive and essential raw materials for newspapers. By creating twin monopolies in these industry staples, the HWT and Fairfax & Sons strengthened their positions. Keith Murdoch was the driving force behind both projects, and the HWT was already a giant, but the joint enterprises elevated Fairfax's standing, and moved it closer to the displays of industrial and political strength it exhibited in the 1940s, before setting out on its own round of empire building in the 1950s.

THE GREAT PAPER CHASE BEGINS

Australian newspaper owners had dreamed of locally made newsprint from the early 1900s, but the problem was Australia's predominantly hardwood forests. Newsprint has to be cheap – because it is purchased in large quantities – but it also has to be soft, thin, elastic, highly ink-absorbent, and strong enough to go through high-speed printing presses. The newsprint that was made in the Northern Hemisphere, which had all of these properties, was pulped from long-fibred softwoods. Overseas experts declared it impossible to make from short-fibred hardwood.

In 1908, Australia's country newspapers urged the government to offer a reward for the manufacture of newsprint in Australia, but a 1915 report by an American paper expert dashed the industry's hopes. The report found that it was technically possible to make newsprint from hardwood but the process would be too expensive to make it a viable business proposition. However, the dramatic shortage of paper during World War I created a crisis in the Australian newspaper industry and the Tasmanian and Western Australian governments sponsored further research. In 1918, chemists IH Boas and RJ Benjamin, working with the Commonwealth Bureau of Science and Industry, conducted tests in Perth that provided new hope. They concluded that it was possible to make viable newsprint from hardwood if modifications were made to the process. In 1919, the Perth *Daily News*' owner, Arthur Lovekin, provided funds for a pulp-grinding machine so the Bureau's successor could undertake further tests.

Newspaper owners were genuinely concerned about running out of paper and hoped that the end of World War I would bring relief. But by 1920, imported newsprint was still costing more than four times the pre-war price, and there was a 'paper famine'.[3] Several newspaper owners started looking more actively for a local solution. Around 1920, Hugh Denison became a large shareholder in, and director of, the Australasian Paper and Pulp Company. By far the largest of its kind in Australia, the company was an amalgamation of several mills in Melbourne, Sydney and Adelaide, and was controlled by the Brookes family. (Herbert Brookes had been its chairman before handing over to his brother Norman, a famous tennis player. Their father had founded the forerunner company. Herbert later became a foundation member of the ABC board (Chapter 12).) While Australasian Paper and Pulp Company could not make newsprint, it did import softwood pulp from overseas and make it into other types of paper, giving it the best prospects of finding some way to manufacture Australian newsprint. In August 1921, Denison declared that was one of the company's future aims.[4]

Two other newspaper owners also devoted attention to the issue. WL Baillieu was still the leader of Collins House and an owner and director of the HWT. Gerald Mussen was a Collins House consultant (*Smith's Weekly* wryly called him 'Collins House's most versatile son').[5] Along with JE Davidson, Mussen had co-founded News Limited, owner of the Adelaide *News*, for Collins House, and still had a parcel of shares in that newspaper company. Mussen was later given a great deal of credit for founding paper-making from Australian timber through his 'bulldog tenacity' over nearly twenty years.[6]

Mussen had been to Burnie in the north-west of Tasmania in 1908 and seen its vast forests. His interest in making paper there

FIGURE 14.1 Imported newsprint reels are loaded onto the presses at the Sydney *Sun*, circa 1930

SOURCE National Library of Australia (PIC/15611/17716).

was piqued by new reports from scientists. By 1921, the body which would become the Council for Scientific and Industrial Research (CSIR, the predecessor of CSIRO), had proven that it was technically feasible to make paper from hardwoods, and even delivered their report on paper made from hardwood pulp. Another of its reports in 1923 encouraged hope that it could be done on a large scale as a viable industry. A key breakthrough was the finding that it was not the timber that was unsuitable, but the process for making it into pulp. Hardwood was not suitable for grinding, it had to be broken down by chemical means instead.

Years later, Mussen gave an account of his role in founding the industry that suggested he was acting independently of Collins House at first, although this is difficult to believe. Mussen claimed he was walking along Collins Street one day in the early 1920s when he bumped into WL Baillieu. When Baillieu asked what he was working on, Mussen told him he was investigating paper production, and Baillieu suggested the project might suit Collins House's Amalgamated Zinc (De Bavay's) Ltd (AZ). According to Mussen's account, he was reluctant to involve AZ 'because I had the idea of bringing in some of the big newspapers', but realising the project would need 'big money', he agreed for AZ to look into it.[7] AZ was in an unusual situation. It had a 'hoard of cash' but a disappearing business model because North Broken Hill and Broken Hill South had decided to treat their own output and tailings.[8] AZ's 'raw material' would be gone after 1924, when those contracts expired, so it needed to diversify quickly or else be liquidated.[9]

Collins House had its own chemist, David Avery, report on the possibilities of hardwood paper-making. Baillieu's biographer, Peter Yule, said that when the reports were encouraging, Baillieu convinced AZ's shareholders ('of whom he was a significant one'), that rather than receiving a cheque in the mail upon the winding up of the company, they should invest AZ's cash into this new, and rather speculative, venture.[10] Avery was appointed to the AZ board in 1923 to oversee the move into paper-making. Mussen was also thoroughly convinced that the project should go ahead.

Paper was not within Collins House's technical fields of expertise, which were mining and the treatment of base metals. But the project interested Baillieu because, with the war over and mining ore a diminishing resource, he knew Collins House had to diversify into new industries. He was looking for industries where the product was 'equally important in war or peace; the raw material was available in Australia … and the product was not subject to substitution'.[11] As ML Baillieu pointed out later, timber 'regenerates its natural requirements' through replanting, whereas 'ore bodies do not'.[12] It would be one of the ironies of the project that Australian paper-making machines could not use iron, of which Collins House had plenty, because if iron came into contact with the acid in eucalyptus pulp, it stained it an unsuitable dark colour. The machines had to be made out of steel – yet another sign of the growing importance of steel and BHP as opposed to iron and Collins House.

AZ had strong links in Tasmania due to its establishment of Electrolytic Zinc, and one person who was thrilled by its interest in paper-making was then Tasmanian premier, Joe Lyons. Premier from 1923 to 1928, Lyons was pro-business, encouraged mining in the state, and received significant support from state Nationalists, and even the conservative *Mercury*. He was desperate to improve Tasmania's foundering economy and believed Tasmania's 'salvation' lay in developing secondary industries.[13] Knowing of AZ's interest in paper-making, five weeks after he became premier, Lyons made a speech laying out the welcome mat by saying there were millions of pounds of wealth in Tasmania's forests waiting to be exploited.[14]

In 1924, Mussen, Harold Cohen (son of Collins House senior figure, Montague Cohen, director of AZ and EZ) and Neil Elliott Lewis (the former conservative Tasmanian premier) went to see

Lyons about the possibility of starting the industry at Burnie. Mussen then negotiated the purchase of the whole of the assets of the Van Diemen's Land Company, which included 257 000 acres (104 000 ha) of freehold forest on the north-west coast, near Burnie. Lyons initiated a special Act of parliament which was quickly passed and provided AZ with cutting rights on 600 000 acres (243 000 ha) of Crown lands, water rights, and income tax and land tax deductions. Over the years, the Tasmanian government would continue to provide every assistance to see a secondary industry established in Tasmania that promised to be a major customer of Tasmania's hydro-electricity schemes and employ large numbers of unskilled workers.

A BOUNTY: BRUCE SIDES WITH THE PAPERS

In 1925, Collins House sent a trial shipment of 100 tons of Tasmanian eucalypt timber to the Netherlands for experiments. The tests proved that eucalypt could be used to viably produce more expensive grades of paper, such as fine writing paper used for typewriting and in magazines and books, but it was unclear whether it could viably produce cheap newsprint. In order to make sure the project would be profitable, AZ decided it would need an economic subsidy from the government and protection from cheaper imported newsprint.

In May 1925, AZ applied to the Tariff Board for a bounty of £6 per ton to be paid to AZ when it produced locally made newsprint. It suggested this should be paid for by imposing a duty of 40 per cent on imported newsprint. As all of Australia's newspapers were importers, they strongly opposed the duty-funded bounty (except *Smith's Weekly* and the *Daily Guardian*). ACC Holtz, chair of the ANC, said newspapers would have to reduce pages, raise their advertising rates and dismiss staff to pay for such a heavy duty. Theodore Fink, chairman of the HWT, said AZ had plenty of money and should conduct the enterprise on its own without asking for government help.[15] (Although the HWT and AZ were both connected to the Collins House empire, their interests were opposed on this issue.)

Heavy paper users, the *Sydney Morning Herald* and *The Age*, strongly opposed the duty-bounty. *The Age* was criticised for its hypocrisy because it was a protectionist paper. It daily advocated protection for other industries, but now that it was at its own door, opposed protection and demanded continued access to the cheapest imports. The *Mercury* said it could not support the 'bad' proposal because a 40 per cent duty would result in more job losses in the newspaper industry than a new paper-making industry would bring to its home state. The *Mercury* said it was also concerned a duty-bounty would 'exclude competition and create a monopoly'.[16]

Prime Minister SM Bruce was in a tight spot. AZ was among the largest donors to his Nationalist Party, and Collins House was an extremely powerful entity. But newspapers were also powerful, and Bruce needed their support for the imminent 1925 election. The Labor Opposition supported a bounty, and increased the pressure by supporting AZ, making for an unusual alliance between Labor and its traditional class enemy, Collins House. In his election policy speech, Labor leader Matthew Charlton said it was appalling that the Bruce government had turned its back on AZ when the company was going to spend £2 million in Tasmania, and provide employment to thousands.[17] Charlton said his party would do 'everything possible' to support the newsprint industry.[18]

Under pressure, Bruce agreed to a bounty of £4 per ton and a deferred duty, but AZ wanted £6. Bruce was concerned that such a heavy duty would hurt newspapers, and newspaper consumers (that is, voters). To Collins House, Bruce's £4 limit was a betrayal.

It caused a deep rift between Bruce and his previously close sup-porters, Baillieu and WS Robinson. Five years later, Robinson wrote to his brother Arthur, 'Personally, I never can completely trust Bruce again after his behaviour to WL [Baillieu] and myself in 1925'.[19]

AZ abandoned the project. It considered the £4 bounty insuf-ficient, but there were also other factors. Although Cohen and Avery remained keen on the venture, Baillieu had been deeply affected by his wife's illness and death in 1925, and did not wish to pursue such a large and risky project. Mussen resolved to carry on sepa-rately from AZ, albeit with the backing of several individual Collins House investors. He said he wanted to make sure they did not lose their money and thereby 'suffer for their faith' in him.[20] Mussen also had a great deal at stake personally. He was still convinced that the prospects for capturing a slice of the £3.7 million imported paper market were good, and not least because the Tasmanian govern-ment's generosity guaranteed 'one of the cheapest wood supplies for paper making in the world'.[21]

In January 1926, the federal Tariff Board reported. It recom-mended a bounty of £4 per ton to support the new industry. (Her-bert Brookes was one of the Tariff Board's members.) Bruce issued a statement from London reaffirming that his government would enact a bounty.[22]

A SPLIT IN COLLINS HOUSE

With AZ out, Mussen returned to his original idea and called a con-ference of big newspaper proprietors. They told him that they would not contribute any money to the scheme, but afterwards (Sir) James Fairfax took Mussen aside and told him that he did not agree with his fellow proprietors. Fairfax believed that the newspaper industry had no security if it did not 'have control of its own raw materials'.[23]

Mussen enlisted his support for starting a smaller scale company that would begin by making the more viable fine writing paper, and if that went well, would then investigate adapting its processes to manufacture newsprint. James Fairfax agreed to invest £10 000 and signed a contract for a twenty-five-year supply of newsprint. The *Argus* then came on board, and so did the *Brisbane Courier*, the Adelaide *Advertiser*, the *Bulletin*, *Truth* and Burnie's *Advocate*. Although he had not produced one sheet of paper, let alone the more challenging newsprint, Mussen secured contracts from newspapers for 50 000 tons of newsprint over fifteen years.

Mussen asked Lyons to transfer the concessions offered to AZ in the north-west to him. With AZ's assent, its Act was repealed and a new Act put the concessions into Mussen's name in March 1926. Mussen then left for the United Kingdom to try to raise capital there. While he was away, AZ suddenly re-entered the race without him. In August 1926, Avery got another Act through the Tasmanian parliament granting cutting rights (in Avery's name) in the Kermandie area, which was not in the north, where Mussen was focusing, but in south-east Tasmania.

Baillieu's interest in the paper project had been re-kindled, and AZ was actively pursuing it again. Avery's plan was for a small, but fully functioning, experimental mill to be erected at Kermandie. In 1927, AZ registered Tasmanian Paper Pty Ltd. Its principal shareholders were AZ, EZ, North Broken Hill, Austral Development (London), Edward Lloyd Ltd (a large mill owner in the United Kingdom), Sir Alfred Ashbolt (a Tasmanian businessman), and National Metal and Chemical Bank Ltd (London). The experimental mill was completed in early 1928. That year, WL Baillieu also negotiated a merger between Tasmanian Paper and the Brookes-Denison company, which was now called Australian Paper Manufacturers (APM). Australasian Paper and Pulp Company had merged with its greatest rival, Cumberland Paper Board Mills, so the newly named

APM now controlled five of the six paper mills in Australia. It had also been carrying out its own research into making paper from hardwood. Baillieu recognised that it was better to cooperate with the industry's largest player than try to compete with it.[24] APM took up shares in Tasmanian Paper and supplied it with technical advice, facilities and cooperation.

Meanwhile, Mussen had formed a small company in 1928, opaquely called 'Canberra Activities Pty Ltd', with Fairfax & Sons and the *Argus*. Colin Fraser, Alex Stewart, and Henry Somerset of Collins House also had interests in this company. While Mussen was away trying to solicit British capital, James Fairfax died in July 1928. Although Warwick Fairfax (James' son) continued to back the project, James Fairfax's death was a blow to its prospects. In February 1930, Mussen, Fairfax & Sons, and the *Argus* registered a new company called Paper Makers Ltd, aimed at establishing pulp and paper-making at Burnie. Paper Makers' address was Collins House, its investors included Fraser and other Collins House figures, and its auditor was Sherlock and Daniels (the Collins House accountant that helped set up News Limited).

Paper Makers in the north of Tasmania and Tasmanian Paper in the south were both connected to Collins House, but apparently running separate races. In 1928–29, both were waiting for the government to enact a bounty. Before Baillieu departed overseas, he wrote to Bruce in February 1929 asking when he would fulfil his promise.[25] Bruce re-committed publicly in March, but the bounty still had not eventuated when he lost government in October. The incoming prime minister, Scullin, had also pledged a duty-funded bounty, but the Depression changed everything. Finance dried up for private investment and from government coffers. Mussen was still intent on 'forc[ing]' the federal government 'to find the capital' for his venture, and it helped that Lyons was now in federal politics.[26] Although making a name for himself as a

FIGURE 14.2 The complicated race to make newsprint in Australia, 1920s to 1941

SOURCE The author.

AUSTRALIAN NEWSPRINT MILLS (ANM)

Formed 1938

The Herald

The Sydney Morning Herald

The Sun
NEWS-PICTORIAL

The Courier-Mail

THE SUN

The Advertiser

THE NEWS

The West Australian

The Mercury

BOYER, TAS = NEWSPRINT

ASSOCIATED PULP AND PAPER MANUFACTURERS (APPM)

Formed 1936

Collins House

BURNIE, TAS = FINE WRITING AND PRINTING PAPER

APM worked with Tasmanian Paper from 1928 but withdrew in 1935

AUSTRALIAN PAPER MANUFACTURERS (APM) LTD

Formed 1926

Brookes family and Denison

MARYVALE, VICTORIA AND OTHER MILLS = PACKAGING PAPER AND BOARD

Merges with Cumberland Paper Board Mills Ltd in 1926

fiscal conservative, Lyons wanted his Depression wracked government to commit to a £750 000 guarantee of debentures for the new
paper-making industry. Wary of picking sides though, the Scullin
government made the offer conditional upon Paper Makers and
Tasmanian Paper amalgamating, but negotiations between the
two groups failed.

As acting treasurer, Lyons agreed to a newsprint bounty of
£4 a ton and a duty of £1 per imported ton but, as Mussen later
recalled, the newspapers 'began to scream [again] and the bill was
never introduced'.[27] Mussen was about to go to Canberra to lobby
for the bill when Baillieu suggested they team up. According to
Mussen, he won the support of Scullin, Lyons and the Opposition
leader, JG Latham, but 'to my horror one of [them] said he was not
going to agree to the scheme, as he did not think the government
should assist any industry'. Mussen did not name the recalcitrant,
but he did say that 'the bill was already drafted and I had to get in
touch with Canberra and tell them not to introduce it until they
had heard from me'. This strongly suggests it was Latham. According to Mussen, 'I was on the verge of fixing the dispute up when the
[Scullin] Government was defeated. Once again an opportunity
had been lost.'[28]

It was not entirely lost though, as Lyons had switched sides and
was now the prime minister. Lyons appointed a committee consisting of IH Boas of CSIR and Herbert Gepp (a Collins House–
connected chemist and metallurgist who had previously been
general manager of AZ for seventeen years). (Denison described
Gepp to Murdoch as 'our mutual friend'.[29] Gepp soon became
APM's technical director and later its managing director.) Not surprisingly, the Gepp–Boas report, delivered in June 1931, said the
pulp and paper industry was feasible and should go ahead. But
both groups had stalled. The Depression had made raising finance
difficult, but low prices for imported newsprint had also taken the

impetus out of getting the industry started. Tasmanian Paper's experimental mill at Kermandie had ceased operations in 1930, while Mussen's group had been unable to raise enough capital, and although Baillieu had suggested they work together, Tasmanian Paper 'changed its decision' and no longer wanted to amalgamate with Mussen's group.[30]

THE HWT ENTERS THE RACE

One important newspaper group never signed up to Mussen's speculative contracts for newsprint because it had its own plans. In December 1932, the HWT entered the paper race as a new, third player – albeit, like the other two, also connected with Collins House. The HWT was racing against Mussen–Fairfax's Paper Makers (focused on Burnie) and AZ's Tasmanian Paper (with its experimental mill at Kermandie and its alliance with APM). Murdoch had secured Baillieu's blessing for the HWT to join this crowded field of would-be paper-makers. Like AZ, the HWT headed to the south of Tasmania. It formed the Derwent Valley Paper Company in December 1932, which had an option to purchase 500 acres (200 ha) at Boyer, and a timber concession of 256 000 acres (104 000 ha) along the Florentine and Styx tributaries of the Derwent River, which had been granted by yet another Act of the busy Tasmanian Parliament.

For years, the HWT, and especially Murdoch, had been keenly observing the race to make newsprint. In February 1930, Murdoch and Thorold Fink had accompanied top Collins House directors – including Baillieu, Colin Fraser, WS Robinson and EH Shackell – to inspect the Kermandie mill. At the end of 1931, a frustrated Lyons, concerned the project had stalled, personally requested that the HWT 'use its best efforts to assist in the establishment of [the paper] industry' (which indicates that the requests for favours were going both ways, not just from the HWT to the Lyons government).[31] Murdoch's interest in paper-making was well known in Canberra. He was keen to again follow in Northcliffe's footsteps (in 1906, Northcliffe had been a pioneer of newspaper control of newsprint).[32] But Murdoch and the HWT had also realised that they were at the mercy of successive governments which might want to impose duty on newsprint. Far better to be a manufacturer, and be paid any bounty, rather than merely an importer who would be paying duty for someone else's benefit.

In 1932, Murdoch secured the backing of the increasingly unwell WL Baillieu to convince the HWT board that local newsprint manufacture should be pursued. Theodore and Thorold Fink visited Tasmania and convinced the state government to grant it those timber cutting concessions in the valleys of the Florentine River, Russell Falls River, Styx River and a portion of the Derwent Valley. This land included the finest area of enormous *Eucalyptus regnans* – known as 'swamp gum' in Tasmania and 'mountain ash' in Victoria – in Australia. The land was close to a hydro-electric generating station and to fresh water (paper-making requires a great deal of power and water), as well as a river that could be used for transporting heavy machinery in, and finished paper rolls out. But the greatest attraction was the eucalypts. The HWT's tests had discovered that, of the 500-plus species of gum trees in Australia, only *Eucalyptus regnans* was suitable for making viable newsprint. The Florentine Valley's *Eucalyptus regnans* were so tall and profuse that the HWT believed they would be able to produce 100 000 tons of newsprint a year, and through re-planting, could do so indefinitely.[33]

Mussen had been backing the wrong site for newsprint – Burnie had the wrong species of eucalypt. And while Mussen had convinced Fairfax and the other newspaper investors that the best way to produce newsprint was to make fine printing paper first, the HWT was taking a more direct route. It was interested only in newsprint, and it had the superior site for producing it. It was only a matter of time before Fairfax came to the conclusion that all of its time and money were leading in the wrong direction. As Dumas wrote to Murdoch in September 1932, 'I cannot believe that Fairfax or LKS Mackinnon [of the *Argus*] would dream of going on in opposition on a less favourable site'.[34]

Murdoch had been enlisting support to make his opposition more formidable. The month before, he had written to Denison of Associated Newspapers to warn of 'an important development'. Murdoch reported that the Mussen–Fairfax group was going to issue a prospectus seeking public money for their venture. Murdoch said, 'There is just a chance that it is bluff, but I do not think it is. I feel certain that the Fairfax family has agreed to back this venture very heavily.' Playing the Sydney interests off against each other, Murdoch warned Denison that, 'This seems to me a very definite threat to newspapers outside the *Sydney Morning Herald* group. [We] must either [move or] sit still and wait to be fleeced. It would be two or three years off, but eventually the fleecing would be properly done. Or we can get together and consider what is to be done in the South [of Tasmania].'[35]

Murdoch and Denison proceeded to throw obstacles in Mussen's way, and to obtain information, sometimes surreptitiously, on the Mussen–Fairfax Paper Makers.[36] It was still short of the £450 000 it needed to build a mill, and by 1932, several of Mussen's contracted newspapers had changed hands and were now controlled by the HWT, including the *Advertiser* and, most importantly, the ones Mussen had been associated with – the *News*, and the *Daily News* (Perth). When Mussen had started the paper chase, he was the co-founder and largest shareholder of News Limited, but after Davidson's death in 1930, Murdoch had led the HWT's takeover of

News Limited in early 1931. Mussen was no longer an important newspaper owner.

The HWT had been sponsoring experiments at AZ's Tasmanian Paper Kermandie mill and, at this stage, was negotiating with AZ. In September 1932, Herbert Syme (*The Age*) and Denison met with Murdoch at the *Herald* offices. Another meeting with representatives of AZ and APM was held the following day. All agreed to keep pursuing the newsprint venture if independent experts confirmed the Florentine Valley site the 'best available'.[37] But AZ was hedging its bets. The same month, its Tasmanian Paper Company entered into a three-party agreement with Mussen–Fairfax's Paper Makers and APM. Under the agreement, they had to form a manufacturing company by 11 September 1935. But by the end of 1933, weary Tasmanian MPs had their doubts, and argued the companies did not seem seriously interested in starting the industry, had broken promises, were working against each other, and were peddling 'humbug and dishonesty'.[38]

FAIRFAX TEAMS UP WITH THE HWT

While the three parties meandered fruitlessly towards their September 1935 deadline, Murdoch and Thorold Fink continued to pursue the project separately for the HWT. Thorold performed most of the initial work. (After June 1933, Murdoch was busy helping the *Herald* fight off the *Argus*' imminent new afternoon paper, the *Evening Star*.) Attempts were made to unite all the major players – Tasmanian Paper, the APM, the HWT and Paper Makers. Thorold led the negotiations in 1933 on behalf of the HWT, but Harold Cohen (chairman of AZ) and JS Teulon (a director of AZ and Paper Makers) were concerned about the lack of progress.[39]

Although Murdoch was busy, he was still working on recruiting Associated Newspapers – which he called one of the 'Big Three' (along with the HWT and Fairfax).[40] Murdoch invited Denison to visit the HWT's forest concessions with him, and told Denison in March 1933 that he wanted Associated Newspapers 'formally ranged alongside us now'.[41] Murdoch wanted the newspaper industry to take control of newsprint manufacture, and he needed as many newspapers as possible to be 'drawn in', especially the *Sydney Morning Herald*.[42] But Thorold had not been able to unite the HWT with AZ and the Mussen–Fairfax group. Dumas reported that Teulon was 'rather upset' and found 'Thorold's assumption of control and infallibility … a little galling'. Teulon felt the project was being 'allowed to die'.[43] While Thorold was in Canada overseeing tests on a sample of 2000 tons of timber in 1934, Fairfax's general manager, AH Stuart, approached Murdoch and suggested that Paper Makers and the HWT's Derwent Valley Paper Co should merge.

Fairfax & Sons had finally had enough of the expensive technical problems associated with the northern site and wanted to join with the HWT to pursue the aim of cheap newsprint controlled by the newspapers. The majority of newspapers associated with Mussen followed Fairfax's lead. As the *Argus' Star* was being soundly beaten by early 1935, Murdoch overtly took over the paper project. Thorold Fink still worked on it, but as Don Garden noted, he 'appears to have been largely pushed aside'.[44] (Later, when Thorold asked to be appointed a director on the newsprint company board, Murdoch refused. And Thorold was written out of histories of the enterprise.)

Murdoch convinced Fairfax and the other major newspaper groups that Mussen and his investors would plunder them with high prices if they gained control of newsprint. Murdoch told an ANC meeting in 1935 that they had to stop 'the exploitation of the newspapers by interested people who could readily get a duty imposed'. He argued that the commercial investors' 'only objective

… [was] high profits and the newspapers would be quite helpless in their hands'.[45]

In September 1935, the three-party agreement was allowed to lapse, as the groups had reoriented themselves. Paper Makers had split in two. In January 1935, the newspaper interests (led by Fairfax) bought out all of the Paper Makers shares held by non-newspaper interests (Mussen and his Collins House investors). Associated Newspapers' general manager characterised this as avoiding a 'newsprint war' by the newspapers 'pa[ying] off' the Mussen–AZ investors to 'get rid' of them.[46] As part of this agreement, Mussen negotiated to keep 20 acres (8 ha) of the mill site at Burnie and the rights to cut wood on the Surrey Hills concessions. This was conditional upon his agreeing not to make newsprint. Mussen took these assets to AZ's Tasmanian Paper and joined up with them. Mussen said that Harold Cohen, Sir Walter Massy-Greene and Sir Colin Fraser now 'swung in behind us with all their power and influence', bringing North Broken Hill, Broken Hill South, AZ, EZ and Zinc Corporation with them.[47] The Tasmanian government granted them further concessions on large areas of land in the north, and in January 1936, Mussen's interests and Tasmanian Paper's were merged to form Associated Pulp and Paper Manufacturers (APPM). APPM would focus on fine writing and printing paper at Burnie,[48] while the Brookes–Denison company – APM – left Tasmania and went back to focusing on making packaging paper and cardboard on the mainland.

The paper market had been carved into three, and the largest segment – newsprint – had been snatched from far more established and formidably financed players by Murdoch and the major news-papers. This was a sign of the growing economic might of the news-paper industry, but especially the HWT. For thirty-five years, the HWT had been a 'prolific money spinner'.[49] It had been making annual profits of over £100 000 (and often over £150 000) for more than ten years. In 1937–38, it made a profit of £252 000, while Collins House's traditional money-spinners had been hit hard by low prices for zinc and lead. In 1938, North Broken Hill and Broken Hill South both saw their profits drop by 50 per cent, and AZ was wound up.[50] Collins House was by no means short of pennies, but its best days in mining were behind it. It was diversifying into new industries because it had to.

One final push was needed to cement the newspapers' position in the south. In July 1937, Murdoch hosted a conference attended by all of the big metropolitan dailies except the *Labor Daily*, and convinced them of the need to act fast. When Associated Newspapers' director, Graham Waddell, returned to Sydney he reported back to its board that there was still a serious risk of 'outside interests' gaining control of the HWT's timber reserves, and if the newsprint industry should 'fall into [their] hands … [backed] by a friendly Tariff Board' it would cost the newspapers dearly.[51] The situation appeared urgent because, as Murdoch told Denison in October 1937, the Tasmanian government was not just 'restless – it is threatening'. Ministers, he said, were 'out of sympathy for us'. Because the HWT had neither built a mill nor laid a railway in the Styx valley, 'We are now defaulters under our Act' and the government 'has full power to cancel the concession'. Murdoch said 'the Big Three' (the HWT, Fairfax & Sons and Associated Newspapers) needed to 'move quickly' and 'should march together and do this for their own advantage and for no one else … [or] We will be all held up to an unmerciful racket'.[52]

A fully convinced Denison pledged £100 000 from Associated Newspapers, on the condition that no one group ended up controlling the venture. Associated Newspapers considered this money well spent because of the risk that a federal Labor government would gain office and impose more than £5 duty on imported newsprint to help the Mussen–AZ group. Denison pledged his support to do 'everything possible to help in establishing the Newsprint industry under Newspaper control [sic]'.[53] His company's money came at a crucial time to kick-start the project.

Fairfax & Sons merged its assets from Paper Makers with the HWT's Derwent Valley Paper Co into a new company called Australian Newsprint Mills Pty Ltd (ANM). ANM was registered in March 1938 with a huge authorised capital of £4 million, and paid up capital of £1.3 million. It was promoted as a joint venture of eight separate newspaper publishers. The two biggest owners were the HWT, which had the largest shareholding, and Fairfax & Sons. The other owners were Associated Newspapers, Advertiser Newspapers, News Limited, Queensland Newspapers, WAN and Davies Bros Ltd (of course, several of these 'other' companies were associated with the HWT).

Murdoch became ANM's foundation chairman, and remained in the role until 1949. Its other foundation directors were Warwick Fairfax, Hugh Denison, Lloyd Dumas, HD Giddy (HWT director), HB Jackson (WAN) and Eric Johnson (representing the Tasmanian government). The Tasmanian government had a seat on the board because it had contributed a quarter of the capital. The newspaper groups put in only £750 000 of the required £1 million. The cash-poor *Argus* was a noticeable absentee, and *The Age* was another. Although David Syme and Co had expressed an early interest, it had backed out, saying it had discovered it could not put money into the venture due to the complicated terms of David Syme's will (which was even shown to the other newspapers). The Tasmanian government under Labor Premier Ogilvie put in the shortfall of £250 000 as preference shares, controversially using public money to invest in a private company.

Newspapers that had rallied against government intervention in the economy during the Depression, opposing stimulus spending and even old age and war pensions, were happy to accept state aid when it was for them. ANM could not have been built without the

Tasmanian government supplying a quarter of its capital, plus valuable forestry concessions, heavily subsidised hydro-electric power, cheap railway transport, concessions on wharf fees, taxation discounts, water rights, and the right to dump effluent into the sea and rivers. Later, the Tasmanian government even dredged the Derwent River so ships could reach ANM, and developed the Butler's Gorge power scheme specifically to provide ANM with more power.

After years of false starts, the newspapers had triumphed and it looked like newsprint production was finally going to happen. With World War II looming, it was not a moment too soon. In mid-December 1938, headlines such as 'EUROPE IN TURMOIL', 'FEARS OF HITLER' and 'BRITISH ARMS READY FOR WAR' boosted newspaper sales so much that the *Herald* used a record amount of newsprint – 759 tons in a week – a record that would stand for almost another seventeen years.[54]

A BOUNTY AGAIN

When ANM was being formed in 1938, the price of imported newsprint had dropped to an average of £11 per ton in the previous two years. The HWT and Fairfax & Sons knew their newsprint, made in Australia on a small scale, would exceed that price (they were expecting to sell for about £17–18 a ton).[55] Now that they were no longer merely importers, but also would-be manufacturers, they wanted a duty-funded bounty to protect them, just as AZ had in 1925. ANM applied to the Tariff Board for a bounty of £4 per ton to be financed by an import duty of 17s 6d. Murdoch represented ANM at the Tariff Board and argued the bounty was necessary for the industry to be established. Newspapers that had stridently opposed an increase in duty back in 1925 had changed their tune now that any bounty would be paid to them.

Murdoch used the papers under his control to lobby for the bounty, and the *Herald* argued the proposed duty to pay for it was 'inconsiderable'.[56] Hoping its readers did not have long memories, the *Herald* said it had always been 'obvious that in its early stages the industry would require protection'.[57] The *Sydney Morning Herald*, which had also opposed a bounty twelve and a half years earlier, lent its full support to the application now that it was a partner in the venture. This was another case of a newspaper putting self-interest ahead of longstanding policy, just as *The Age* had in 1925, because the *Sydney Morning Herald* had long been a free-trade newspaper but was now calling for protection. The *Mercury* had also changed its position. It was no longer concerned about a newsprint 'monopoly' now that it was going to be part of that monopoly.

Publications outside the ANM venture – including independent papers, workers' papers, country papers, *The Age* and the *Argus* – opposed having to pay increased duty, and again warned of job losses and the potential closure of newspapers. Consolidated Press, Ezra Norton's Truth and Sportsman Pty Ltd, and the *Labor Daily*, also opposed the application. Some of these opponents pointed out that it was not only about cost but also about control, because ANM would have a monopoly over newsprint production in Australia and would have the power to hurt independent papers that were not its shareholders. Norton and Packer both appeared at the Tariff Board inquiry to criticise the proposal. They also mounted a campaign, including union involvement, aimed at influencing members of parliament against a duty-funded bounty. Nearly 100 000 signatures were gathered on a petition, and a public rally was held at the Sydney Town Hall.[58] Murdoch countered their campaign through private lobbying and public rebuttals. His papers called bounty-opponents' concerns 'foolish' and 'propaganda'.[59]

The Lyons government decided on a compromise. If the price of imported newsprint fell below £18/11/3, it would provide a bounty to ANM on a sliding scale so, as the imported cost fell, the bounty would increase to a maximum of £4 per ton. With Labor's enthusiastic support, the parliament unanimously passed this legislation, but the bounty never materialised and the Act was never proclaimed because the price of newsprint rose sharply when World War II began and it did not drop back below £18 per ton. By 1941, when ANM started producing its first rolls of paper, the price of imported newsprint was £25 a ton.[60] By 1948, it was £46.[61] ANM was able to sell its product for high prices and without fear of being undercut by imports, so it was able to carry on without a bounty.

'TWENTY-FOUR YEARS TO ACHIEVE THE IMPOSSIBLE'

When World War II led to the return of high prices for newsprint, the Sydney dailies (the *Sydney Morning Herald*, *Sun* and *Daily Telegraph*) raised their cover price in unison to two pence in February 1940. (The Melbourne dailies held off until July 1941.) In June 1940, newsprint became not only expensive but also severely limited when the government introduced newsprint rationing in order to conserve scarce dollars for the purchase of aeroplanes and war equipment from non-sterling countries (especially the United States), as well as to free up freight space for armaments and war materials. Daily newspapers met the rations of 35 per cent of their 1938–39 usage by raising their advertising rates, limiting advertisers and condensing news. When newsprint rationing was raised to 60 per cent, effective from October 1941, the *Sydney Morning Herald* criticised the move as 'unjustified'.[62] Adding to the *Sydney Morning Herald*'s (and other Sydney papers') ire was the Menzies government's decision to allow Ezra Norton a newsprint licence in the midst of rationing so he could begin a new paper (discussed in the next chapters).

Although major newspapers had anticipated trouble and stockpiled newsprint before the war – especially the *Sydney Morning Herald* which reportedly warehoused a year's supply – rationing meant they could not necessarily use it and had to reduce their size significantly. For example, in 1939 the *Courier-Mail* had averaged twenty-four pages, but was down to only six or eight by 1945. But demand for war news was so great – and news on the radio still so limited – that its circulation nonetheless doubled between 1935 and 1945.[63] Mounting circulations were clashing with fixed newsprint quotas, but the Australian papers were better off than their British counterparts (which had to reduce to four pages).[64] In 1945, the *Sydney Morning Herald* was still ten to twelve pages in size.

Paper was always of special importance to the weighty *Sydney Morning Herald*, which is why James Fairfax had taken the lead in investing in local newsprint production. In submissions to the government on rationing, the *Sydney Morning Herald* argued that it should be considered a special case because it was a 'paper of record' that provided more comprehensive coverage of matters of public importance than other papers.[65] But it was also about fitting in classified advertising. The *Sydney Morning Herald* promoted itself as 'the Greatest Advertising Medium in the Southern Hemisphere', and claimed it had fifty times as many advertisements as the 'next best New South Wales newspaper' (Chapter 16).[66] While other papers reduced their page size to tabloid to save paper (Table 2.3, page 83), this was not an option for the highbrow *Sydney Morning Herald*. Henderson believed reducing to tabloid size would result in the 'complete destruction' of the *Sydney Morning Herald*.[67]

World War II and rationing had created a big opportunity for ANM. It had a ready market, desperate for newsprint, if only it could begin producing. But the war also created problems that delayed production. When ANM's mill was being built at Boyer on the Derwent River in late 1939, equipment ordered from Switzerland was seized by the Germans in France. Other parts were seized when Norway was invaded, and there were delays in the shipment of motors and pumps from England. ANM also faced increased costs due to wartime conditions and was having to find technical solutions to a range of issues, from its massive consumption of water, to the problem of blowflies drowning in the ground-up wood pulp and causing breaks in the paper. More capital was needed, and in August 1940, a new issue of 275 000 £1 preference shares in the HWT was floated. The HWT used the money to invest in ANM.

ANM's mill opened in early 1941, and on 12 May, ten metropolitan daily newspapers in six states were printed entirely on Australian newsprint. They proudly proclaimed the historic nature of the occasion, and the *Sydney Morning Herald* threw rationing caution to the wind and published a twelve-page supplement celebrating the creation of ANM.

ANM's owners had been concerned when its first batch of newsprint had been quite brown and crumbly. Its quality had improved by the time of the May unveiling, but the Tasmanian product was still only one-tenth the whiteness of American newsprint, and Murdoch was not particularly happy with it.[68] It was better than nothing though, especially after Japan entered the war in December 1941, and it became 'impossible' to bring newsprint into Australia.[69] Rationing had reduced newsprint consumption so much that ANM's small output from one paper-making machine produced a quarter of Australia's newsprint consumption in 1941. By 1943, after the stricter rations were imposed, ANM was providing close to 50 per cent of consumption.[70] But this was as good as its contribution would get.

ANM helped the newspaper industry get through World War II, but optimistic predictions made in the jubilation surrounding the

FIGURE 14.3 Australian Newsprint Mills, Boyer, Tasmania, circa 1950s
SOURCE Tasmanian Archive and Heritage Office (AB713-1-17-2).

'birth of an industry', that Australia's huge importation of foreign newsprint would decline and be replaced by all Australian-made paper, did not eventuate.[71] ANM could not keep up with demand. In 1948, the HWT made a further issue of shares so that it could invest more money in ANM, and a second paper machine was added in 1952, giving it a capacity of 95 000 tons per year. But demand for newsprint still outpaced ANM's capacity, especially when newsprint rationing (an artificial ceiling holding down newsprint consumption) was lifted.

After World War II ended, newsprint rationing was continued for daily and weekly newspapers (with some relaxations) until the end of 1948. This was partly because Australia was still trying to conserve dollar resources, and because of a postwar global newsprint shortage. But newspapers had also found the newsprint pool to be a blessing because every paper received its quota at the same price. It might also be suspected that the papers involved in ANM were happy to see rationing continue as a way of keeping imports down while ANM established itself. However, one aspect of rationing that newspapers had not enjoyed was having to restrict their advertising. Once rationing ended on 1 January 1949, they were free to chase the advertising revenue they had been rejecting for years due to lack of space. Unleashed, the HWT's advertising revenue nearly doubled in twelve months.[72] All of those extra ads took up extra paper, and so did the trends towards supplements, and more photographs and comics.

While newsprint demand kept increasing, ANM's production remained 'almost static'.[73] Even in 1950–51, when the Korean War caused a shortage of charter shipping that led to a global shortage of newsprint, ANM was providing only 21 per cent of Australia's consumption.[74] This fluctuated, but in 1969, was still at only 23 per cent.[75] Decades after ANM began, Australia's newspapers were still reliant upon imported foreign newsprint. The headaches of paper supply and cost had not gone away. Before World War II, newsprint had cost between £11 and £17 per ton and accounted for about 30 per cent of the major newspapers' production costs.[76] Between 1939 and 1949, the price of newsprint rose by 350 per cent.[77] By 1954, newsprint was costing more than £80 a ton and accounted for between 60 and 70 per cent of the newspapers' costs.[78] Bearing in mind that Frank Packer was not always the most reliable source on such matters, his *Daily Telegraph* claimed its newsprint costs had increased from £3000 per week in 1939 to £90 000 per week in 1949.[79] Newspaper proprietors had been able to keep a lid on wages growth, but not on newsprint costs. In 1939, Associated Newspapers was spending four times as much on newsprint as on editorial salaries for the *Sun*.[80]

High prices did help ANM's profits though, which made its newspaper owners simultaneously victims and beneficiaries of expensive newsprint. There was no competition to stimulate local production or compete on price because the major papers owned ANM, and that was a strong deterrent to any potential competitors. ANM could therefore charge high prices almost commensurate with the imported product. In 1948, it was charging £41 per ton. This was lower than the £46 charged for Canadian newsprint, but the Canadian product was superior, and it also included long-distance freight and importation costs.[81] By 1958, Ezra Norton, by then owner of the *Daily Mirror*, was attacking ANM for its 'excessive prices', which he said had resulted in 'gigantic' and 'excessive' profits.[82] In four years, ANM had made profits of £2 439 364.[83]

Back in 1935, Murdoch had told newspaper owners that 'all unnecessary profit should be avoided' from the newsprint venture so 'the benefit would come back in the way of cheaper newsprint to the publishers'.[84] But ANM was making large profits by the 1950s. In 1959 alone, it made a net profit of £1 187 637.[85] Norton argued the company could afford to charge less for newsprint to enable cheaper newspapers and advertising rates but it chose not to. Frank Packer also intermittently complained about 'exploitation' by newsprint manufacturers, and he kept the *Daily Telegraph* out of the ANM venture until 1946.[86]

As the major shareholders in ANM, the HWT and Fairfax & Sons were paying high prices for newsprint but they were paying part of this to themselves, and also making money off their fellow newspaper owners. However, paper remained such a scarce and essential commodity that it still caused the occasional spat between the partners. After leaving the ANC in 1938, Fairfax had re-joined its fellow proprietors in a new body called the Australian Newspaper Proprietors' Association (ANPA) in 1941. In 1948, the Murdoch papers and Packer–Theodore's Consolidated Press resigned from that collective and set up their own group (called the Australian Newspapers Council). The dispute was over newsprint rationing, which was still in force and being administered through the voluntary newsprint pool.

Each newspaper was still being given a quota of newsprint based on the quantity that it had used back in the base year of 1938–39 (the year before rationing was introduced). Some papers, like the *Sydney Morning Herald*, were thick with pages even then, but in the nine years since, their circulation had not grown much. (According to Dumas, this was deliberate. He believed the *Sydney Morning Herald* (and *The Age*) held back circulation on purpose during newsprint rationing 'in order to accommodate as much [classified] advertising as possible'.[87]) Since 1938, the HWT's best sellers, the *Sun News-Pictorial* and the *Herald*, had grown in circulation by more than 150 000 each, and Packer's *Daily Telegraph* had grown by 122 000, while the *Sydney Morning Herald* and the *Argus* had only grown by 52 000 and 24 000 respectively.[88] Murdoch and Packer argued the basis for sharing newsprint had become unfair, and slow-growth papers were receiving more paper than they could use and were hoarding it, while popular newspapers were not getting enough. They wanted the formula changed, but the Chifley Labor government had grown tired of trying to mediate between quarrelling proprietors when wartime conditions no longer required it, so dropped the 'hot potato' issue by announcing the end of rationing in November 1948.[89]

A 'ONE-EYED VIEW': AUSTRALIAN ASSOCIATED PRESS, 1935

The other major raw material cost that newspaper owners despaired of was foreign news cables. In 1934, when the HWT and Fairfax

& Sons were considering joining forces to make newsprint, there were two big overseas news-gathering organisations in Australia – the Australian Press Association (APA) and the *Sun-Herald* United Cable Service (UCS). The two organisations were strong competitors in the 1910s and 1920s, with the HWT and Fairfax & Sons in opposing camps.

The APA was the older service, originally centred around morning papers, and was jointly managed by the *Argus* and the *Sydney Morning Herald*. Its Australian office was in the *Argus* building in Melbourne. It also had its own office in London where, with an Australian eye, its staff selected and edited foreign news from a constant flow of material that came in day and night, before forwarding it on to APA's member newspapers in Australia via telegraph. APA had two main sources of material. It paid for 'proofs' (typeset pages of articles ready for printing) from five British newspapers, and also subscribed to news agencies, including Reuters and Central News, which sent in 'spot' news via automatic printers and 'tape' machines. APA also had an American office in the *New York Times*, where it collected that influential paper's daily proofs.

APA was once the premier news agency in Australia and its members had included the bulk of the daily newspapers and most country newspapers. But UCS – the cable service set up by Denison for the *Sun* and then gate-crashed by Fink for the *Herald* – had been the first real challenge to APA. It used the prestigious *The Times* as the main basis of its news resources; and Herbert Campbell Jones, who headed the service in London between 1912 and 1915, and his replacement, Keith Murdoch (1915–21), built the cable service up to be a strong rival to APA. The rise of the Murdoch press in the 1920s and early 1930s then seriously depleted APA's ranks. The HWT had taken over several papers, closed down some (including the *Register*, once an integral part of APA), while others – such as the *Evening News* and *Daily Guardian* – had perished separately.

By 1934, the only daily newspaper members left in the APA were the *Sydney Morning Herald*, the *Argus*, *The Age*, the Brisbane *Telegraph* and the *Mercury*. They had to cover steeply rising costs that had previously been shared between a larger number of papers. The *Sun-Herald*'s UCS had become the stronger organisation. It still had its editor in *The Times* office in London, an office in New York, its own subscriptions to international news agencies, and exclusive rights not only to *The Times* but also to the *Daily Mail* and the *Manchester Guardian* (which changed its masthead to the *Guardian* in 1959).

It was an expensive business for both cable agencies to maintain international offices and to pay news agency subscriptions and cable fees. It did not help that the two organisations sometimes bid against each other for exclusive stories in their eagerness to 'get something different, which would be of special interest to Australians'.[90] Recognising that they could reduce costs by working together, in the early 1930s the two organisations set up an 'omnibus' service where they divided up routine work, such as court cases or shipping movements, between their offices so that only one cable was sent to all members of both organisations, thereby halving their cable costs. By 1935, so much news was going through the omnibus service that an amalgamation seemed inevitable.

When the two organisations were negotiating a potential merger in the early 1930s, the *Sydney Morning Herald*'s desire for access to *The Times* had been a sticking point. Associated Newspapers' board concluded that 'in no circumstances, should the company's rights to *The Times* cables be prejudiced'.[91] However, once Murdoch began directing negotiations more closely, he found out how much the APA was paying for its news services, and told Denison that he was 'ashamed' at how much UCS was paying by comparison for *The Times*, and especially the *Daily Mail*.[92] Murdoch argued that pooling APA and UCS resources and subscriptions would bring the two organisations' costs down from £44000 each per year to around £25000 (saving both about $1.4 million annually in today's money).[93]

In January 1932, the HWT, Associated Newspapers, the *Sydney Morning Herald*, the *Argus* and *The Age* were canvassing possible models for the integration of the APA and UCS. In May 1935, Australian Associated Press (AAP) was formed from the merger of the two services. AAP was to be controlled by the HWT and John Fairfax & Sons. (Murdoch told Denison that it had been 'delicate work' to 'get the *Argus* safely outside the [leadership of the] cable Association'.[94]) AH Stuart, Fairfax's innovative general manager, had again worked with Murdoch to achieve a significant merger. Murdoch became AAP's first chairman (from 1935 to 1940).

AAP was established as a non-profit cooperative (it became a normal profit-and-loss company in the 1980s). Its costs were shared between member papers on the basis of the population in the area they covered (although Murdoch engineered a special deal for Queensland that helped his *Courier-Mail*).[95] The system was designed to allow smaller newspapers to be members in addition to the larger metropolitan dailies. As with newsprint, Murdoch knew that a monopoly over an essential raw material would have to have broad support to be accepted.

It did not have universal support though. When AAP was formed, UAP Minister Archdale Parkhill was in his phase of rallying against press monopolies and he told parliament that amalgamation had led to 'remarkably similar' news being published across all major papers. He said that country papers' subscription rates had doubled and, because AAP was a monopoly, newspapers had no choice but to accept its conditions even when they were unfair.[96] Frank Packer withdrew the *Daily Telegraph* from AAP in 1936, and instead sought his own source of foreign news through the London *Daily Express* and the Hearst-based International News Service. However, Packer was back re-applying for membership to AAP in 1939 (granted in 1940), reportedly because he was unable to maintain the cost of a separate service.[97]

Back in 1905, an unusually frank newspaper executive had admitted that one of the biggest advantages of a cable combine was that it discouraged competitors because any paper outside of the 'ring' had to finance their own overseas service and that cost was 'really prohibitive [especially] to a new venture'.[98] (This was one of the reasons the Fisher government had tried to break APA's hold in 1910 amid reports that the APA–Reuters' service was charging exorbitant rates to newspapers outside the combine 'as a form of oppression to stall off competitors'.[99])

One of the advantages of AAP in 1935 was that it provided yet another way to limit news on the radio. When commercial radio stations applied to AAP in 1935, it initially refused to supply them with news but 'raised no objections to them broadcasting [AAP] news already published in the press'.[100] Murdoch, as chairman of AAP, also objected to the amount of AAP news being used by the ABC, and he insisted that AAP held copyright over Reuters news in BBC news bulletins (a claim that the ABC's general manager knew to be legally dubious). On this basis, Murdoch denied requests (from both the ABC and the BBC) for the ABC to be allowed to re-broadcast BBC news bulletins during the war. This made Australia one of only two Empire countries in the world that were unable to re-broadcast BBC bulletins for free (the other was New Zealand). When knowledge of this spilled into the public domain, Murdoch expressed 'intense concern and anger' about the damage to AAP's image because AAP was criticised for being greedy and unpatriotic.[101] AAP then reversed its stance and 'allowed' the ABC to re-broadcast BBC bulletins for free.

AAP's newspaper members quickly came to rely upon it for overseas news, especially during the war. Empire press cable rates, which had already been reduced to four pence per word in 1935, were lowered to just a penny a word in 1941, significantly reducing AAP's transmission costs.[102] (AAP used its collective power to lobby governments for lower cable rates for the press, something newspapers had been doing since the 1870s.) Independent outlets criticised AAP's syndication model (where it gathered news for many papers at once and sent the same report to every newspaper it served) as 'chain store journalism' and news 'poured from the one mould'.[103] Publicly, Murdoch countered such accusations by saying that AAP was just a base service and its members could use the cost savings from it to pay for their own correspondents overseas. But in the original, private documents he drew up during negotiations in 1931, one of the advantages of a joint service that he promoted to other owners was that 'We would abolish our foreign correspondents [and] rely upon Reuter's men [sic]'.[104]

By 1942, all of Australia's metropolitan dailies took AAP except for Ezra Norton's *Daily Mirror*. Norton had originally sought access to AAP when he was planning for the *Daily Mirror* in 1940, but Associated Newspapers opposed his application, and Norton had also baulked at the price, then said he preferred independent sources anyway. He used the Hearst-based International News Service and United Press (Scripps-Howard). In 1945, Labor's Arthur Calwell said that AAP had so 'completely bagged and syndicated' foreign news, for both newspapers and commercial radio, that, 'with the exception of [Norton's *Daily] Mirror* and the ABC, there is not an independent news service in Australia'.[105] (Faced with the threat of Packer's service supplying news to commercial radio stations in 1938, AAP had started providing stations with a limited news service that required them to adhere to conditions on the timing and length of broadcasts.)

Norton said it infuriated the major papers that he broke their cable news monopoly. He also accused AAP of political bias, arguing its owners were 'fiercely anti-Labor'.[106] This claim was met with an immediate rebuttal from AAP's chairman, RAG Henderson. It was a serious allegation because AAP had been established with the specific goal of supplying news 'without any tendency toward or opportunity for the exercise of political partisanship or bias'.[107] It could not sell newspapers or advertising space, and had 'only its good name to trade on'.[108] Impartiality was an essential selling point to its clients. But Norton had a point. Of the thirteen newspapers that founded AAP, all had advocated a vote for the Lyons UAP government the year before its founding.[109]

As with newsprint manufacturing, because AAP was owned by the major media groups, it was pointless for any competitor to start up against it, and when AAP formed a partnership with Reuters in 1946, it became an even larger, global player. This too was Murdoch's idea.[110] AAP took up a one-seventh share in Reuters and gained a seat on its board.

CABLES AND PAPER: CANARIES IN THE COAL MINE

The cable and paper ventures had such important, long-term effects on newspapers and journalism that it is worth briefly considering them before returning to the 1940s.

Although AAP was originally created as a foreign news service, its owners appreciated its cheaper, syndicated news model so much that they tried to expand its role into domestic newsgathering from the 1940s. This too had been a secret intention all along. Minutes from the 1935 ANC meeting show that AAP was promoted as an organisation that would begin with foreign news, but hopefully, in the future, would also collect routine domestic news in the way Associated Press (AP) and United Press (UP) did in the United States.[111]

In 1942, AAP's owners drew up a wishlist of a pooled national news service that would include reporting of the federal and state parliamentary galleries, the stock exchange, and 'possibly' courts and photographers.[112]

For over two decades, the AJA fought a vigorous campaign against AAP expanding into domestic news. Some Labor federal MPs who had been journalists (and were still AJA members) supported the fight to stop AAP reporting on parliament. But, as journalist Rob Chalmers noted, the newspaper 'proprietors kept up the pressure and finally the AJA ended its resistance. In the early 1970s, AAP opened its own bureau in Canberra.'[113] By the mid-1980s, as press gallery historian CJ Lloyd observed, AAP was providing 'the only significant … account of parliamentary debates and proceedings to the Australian media'.[114] By the 2010s, it was not unusual for the AAP journalist to be the only reporter sitting in the press gallery for long periods.

After 1970, AAP grew rapidly into a major supplier of domestic news, and expanded into other new areas, such as Formguide, which provided information about horseracing – once a bread-and-butter topic for individual newspapers. By the 1980s, the ABC was the only major media organisation that was not an AAP subscriber. To the public, AAP was a fairly mysterious entity. There were no by-lines for AAP's reporters, and they were generally unknown even to other reporters. AAP had a high staff turnover because of its 'notorious' high pressure working conditions.[115] (In 1970, AAP employed forty journalists. By 1980, it employed 120. But during those ten years, it was estimated that over 1000 journalists had worked for it.[116])

AAP's newsgathering methods proved to be the model of the future though. AAP was at the forefront of using cutting-edge technology, and its staff selected news from a constant flood of material coming off teleprinters, before re-packaging it, and distributing it across multiple outlets. This was a precursor of how journalism would be practised once the internet replaced teleprinters. With twenty-four-hour newsrooms to feed, newspapers also became more reliant upon sources such as AAP. By the 2010s, AAP copy was increasingly 'churned, disseminated, [and] "put up" on [subscribers' websites] as soon as possible with little or no change'.[117]

While AAP's model was enduring, the newsprint manufacturing venture was more problematic for newspaper owners. In 1946, the newspapers bought out the Tasmanian government's shares, and then converted ANM into a public company. An expansion, including the addition of its second paper machine, was financed in 1948. The newspapers subscribed £500 000 for the expansion, while £1 million was raised through preference shares, and another million was advanced by the National Bank.[118] (The chairman of the National Bank board was HD Giddy, an HWT and ANM director.) But ANM's increased capacity still lagged behind demand, and the global newsprint shortage of the early 1950s put the Australian industry in a worse position than World War II.[119] Even so, the newspapers did not want to invest the huge capital required for another mill in the late 1950s, partly because they were now focused on investing in television. It took until 1969 for a third paper-making machine to be installed at ANM, and this was not enough to protect Australian proprietors from the effects of another worldwide shortage of newsprint that lasted for two years from 1973.

Since the 1940s, ANM's owners had known, but did not make public, that they had misjudged aspects of the venture. At a 1945 board meeting, the ANM directors conceded among themselves that the quality and colour of Tasmanian-made paper would never be as good as the Canadian product.[120] They also conceded that, once World War II ended, non-shareholders of ANM were going to be able to 'obtain supplies from overseas of better quality and at a lower price'.[121] Murdoch and Dumas wanted to *again* lobby the government to impose a duty-funded bounty so that 'rival users [should] share the burden'.[122] The directors even canvassed the idea of lobbying the government to impose a licensing system that would force newsprint consumers to take a portion of Tasmanian newsprint so its 'cost and quality issues' would be borne by all users.[123] ANM's expensive, poor-quality paper was not such an issue if every newspaper had to use it, but rivals who were standing outside the venture were exposing its shortcomings. In May 1945, ANM's directors agreed that it was 'vital at this stage of the industry to have Norton in' and especially because 'whether he comes in or not seems to determine whether the *Argus* will also join up'. (The *Argus* made a substantial investment in ANM in August 1945. Norton, Packer and the Brisbane *Telegraph* signed contracts with ANM in 1946.[124])

Henderson had been very concerned about Murdoch rushing into expanding ANM in 1947–48, not only because of quality issues, but also because it had come to light that the supply of wood was not as secure as the industry's promoters claimed. The original estimates for timber regeneration were wrong, and Henderson was worried that, in seeking new finance for expansion, this secret would be disclosed to the banks and underwriters 'and could destroy the whole financial structure' of ANM.[125] The forest concessions were only going to deliver 50 000 tons per year instead of 100 000. Henderson said, 'had we [the *Sydney Morning Herald*] suspected that … we might never have come in'.[126] While Murdoch and Dumas wanted 'a bounty or a duty', Henderson argued ANM should not have to seek such measures because of 'our own inefficiency'.[127]

The great 'romance' of the newspaper industry was less romantic than it had been portrayed. By the 1980s, the neglected ANM was uncompetitive and needed substantial reinvestment. In 1997, Fletcher Challenge, a New Zealand company, took it over, marking the end of the dream of Australian-owned, locally made newsprint controlled by the major newspapers. In 2000, ANM was taken over again, this time by a Norwegian company. By then, newspapers were painfully making the transition to digital and there was a shrinking market for newsprint. Technology had finally solved the publishers' long-standing problem of paper – but it had also taken their audiences and advertisers. While the newspaper industry struggled to adapt to that reality, the paper-making industry prepared for the decline of printed newspapers. In 2012, it was a poignant moment when ANM converted one of its machines to produce lightweight coated paper for glossy magazines and catalogues instead of newsprint.

Of course, all of this was a long way off in the early 1940s. Then, the major newspapers were desperately reliant upon paper, they had record-breaking audiences, more advertising than they could squeeze in during rationing, and two new collective ventures on newsprint and cables. They were a force to be reckoned with – as Hughes, Bruce and Lyons had already discovered. Now, it was Menzies' turn to make the painful journey from newspaper darling to newspaper target.

CHAPTER 15

'KILLING ME': MENZIES AND THE PRESS

Robert Menzies would become Australia's longest-serving prime minister, and serve a record continuous period in office of sixteen years, from December 1949 to January 1966. But that was his second term in office. Menzies' first term, from April 1939 to August 1941, was something of a false start, ending in humiliating fashion with Menzies resigning during World War II after losing the support of his party colleagues. He was the first prime minister to 'be overthrown by his own party', and it would not happen again for another thirty years.[1] Menzies blamed the press for his downfall. In his public resignation speech, he said that his colleagues had told him frankly that he was 'unpopular with large sections of the press and the people'.[2] Note that the press came first in this analysis.

Privately, Menzies recorded in his diary that the *Sydney Morning Herald* had at least been openly bent on his destruction, whereas the Murdoch press had been 'praising and killing me in the same breath, the technique being that of the skilled slaughterman who calls attention to the beauties of the beast just as he strikes it down'.[3] Menzies never deviated from his analysis, and Labor would use it against him. During the 1949 election, Ben Chifley said Menzies 'abdicated in the hours of his country's greatest need. One of the reasons he gave for his action was that he was unpopular with the press; fancy a great national leader standing down because four or five press barons did not like him.'[4] There was a commercial and political context to the press barons' hostility.

SYDNEY'S SUGAR DADDIES AND MELBOURNE'S MEN OF STEEL

World War I was the making of BHAS and Collins House, but by the late 1930s, it was the age of steel, and BHP was the company that was forging ahead. In his first few years in politics, Menzies' involvement in 'the Group' had pulled him into the world of powerful Melbourne-based business networks associated with the National Union, including Collins House and BHP. Menzies became friends with one of the most influential figures in the National Union, Harold Darling, the chairman of BHP and one of its largest shareholders. Darling was a giant of Australian industry, the Australian equivalent of a Vanderbilt or a Rockefeller, but he shunned publicity (even more thoroughly than WS Robinson), and Australian newspapers largely complied. Even his funeral in 1950 was 'strictly private'.[5]

The National Union also consisted of senior Collins House figures, including Colin Fraser and Harold Cohen. Although left-wing publications spoke of a 'BHP-Collins House group' as if they were one entity, technically, BHP and Collins House were separate, but connected.[6] Between 1915 and 1925, they were closely linked because BHP (the original leader of the Broken Hill field) partly owned Collins House's BHAS. The two groups remained linked in other ways after BHP sold its shareholdings to the other BHAS partners in 1926.

One significant connection was that the Baillieus were large shareholders in BHP. The family still held BHP shares into the 1960s (with an estimated value of $50 million in today's money).[7] Board directorships provided other links. Darling, for example, was a director of ICI – maker of chemicals, fertilisers, explosives and dyes – and also the National Bank. Both were linked with Collins House. Bowes Kelly, a director of BHP, was also a director of Metal

Manufacturers, which was connected with the Baillieus and Cohens. There were also social and family links, including that Harold Darling's daughter, Elizabeth, married John Baillieu (son of MH Baillieu) in 1938; and WS Robinson and BHP's powerful managing director, Essington Lewis, were 'good friend[s]'.[8]

BHP had moved into steel production after it exhausted its silver-lead mine at Broken Hill, opening its Newcastle steelworks in 1915. During World War I, BHP produced tens of thousands of tons of steel rails and munitions for the Western Front, which boosted its profits and funded an expansion. But the 1920s were a lean period because BHP could not compete with cheaper imported steel. Its rapid expansion in the 1930s was only made possible by tariff protection extended under successive governments, including the Lyons government when Menzies was minister for industry (from 1934 to 1939). The company was another recipient of significant state assistance, not only through a high tariff wall, but also through subsidies, a bounty system, freight concessions and capital works. During the Depression and immediately afterwards, BHP's industrial ruthlessness drove its local competitor, Australian Iron and Steel (AIS), to the wall, allowing BHP to buy it out in 1935.

Menzies moved among the BHP set. Two of the few businessmen he considered friends were BHP's chairman, Darling, and another of BHP's large shareholders, Geoffrey Syme, owner of *The Age*. In 1921, the protectionist *Age* called Australia's steel industry 'AN ASSET WORTH PROTECTING' through 'higher duties'. Ten years later, it was still arguing the 'NEED FOR INCREASED DUTIES' on imported iron and steel products.[9]

More significantly, Menzies' father was a consultant for BHP.[10] James Menzies was a paid lobbyist for tariff protection for BHP (his official title was 'statistician and tariff reviser').[11] This pertinent fact does not seem to have been disclosed in parliament, nor is it mentioned in some of the weighty but admiring biographies of

Menzies. Instead, James' occupation as a local storekeeper in Jeparit has been emphasised, but that was over by 1911. He was a Victorian MP between 1911 and 1920, and started working for BHP in 1926. When he died in 1945, obituaries noted this, and said that James had been working for BHP 'until recently'.[12] His work for BHP therefore crossed over with the first decade of Menzies' career in federal politics, including the period when he was industry minister.

Political colleagues said that Menzies, who considered himself a man of the law, tended to view business and commerce as 'slightly grubby'.[13] He had a reputation for not paying much attention to business matters, including his own (which he outsourced to Ricketson, and later to his brother). One of Menzies' ministers, Allen Fairhall, said that Menzies 'had an attitude of considerable reserve about businessmen and business affairs'.[14] But another Menzies' minister (and later prime minister), William McMahon, said there *was* one company that Menzies 'always took a strong interest in' – BHP.[15] His partiality for the company was alleged by opponents in parliament, but also publicly immortalised in the deprecating nickname 'pig-iron Bob' (applied to Menzies after he took a firm stand against waterside workers who refused to load BHP scrap iron headed for militarist Japan in 1938).

Once BHP took over AIS, it had a complete monopoly of the steel industry in Australia, and only two years later, made its largest profit to date: over £1 million.[16] The Lyons government's decision to allow the takeover had been made when Menzies was industry minister and attorney-general. In 1935, Jack Beasley, the Lang Labor Party leader, called for an inquiry into whether a steel monopoly was against Australia's economic interests. The Lyons government refused.

In parliament, Beasley read out a list of BHP shareholders that included the Baillieus, Fairfaxes, Symes and the governor-general. Menzies replied that this was 'a great entertainment because I hear so many names of my friends read out'. He cheekily added that he was 'only sorry that I [am] not a shareholder myself'.[17] Had Beasley known of Menzies' father's involvement with BHP, Menzies might not have been so brash. And Menzies' complicated financial affairs via Ricketson may also have provided fodder for more pointed questions later. Less than a month after Beasley's call for an inquiry, Menzies became a director of the Equity Trustees Executors and Agency Co, which held shares in BHP by 1939, and possibly earlier.[18] Two months after Beasley's speech, Menzies also became a director of, and shareholder in, the Capel Court Investment Trust.[19] The trust controlled four (sometimes five) lucrative investment companies operated by JB Were & Co. They held shares in BHP, ICI and other Collins House–affiliated companies, including Broken Hill South and EZ.[20]

Collins House was so large that the only rivals to its power in the interwar period were BHP and the Fairfax-allied sugar company, CSR. In 1931, CSR was the largest company in Australia. It made a profit of £734 823, compared to only £83 257 for BHP.[21] But World War II established BHP as a company to be reckoned with. In 1941, it overtook CSR to become the largest profit-making public company in Australia, and would remain so for decades to come.[22] During World War II, BHP's steel was among the cheapest and best quality in the world. It was used in gun barrels, shells, engines, armour plate and rocket tubes. It was also used to build destroyers and naval vessels, aeroplanes, tanks, steel helmets, hand grenades, tools, barbed wire, steel fence posts and drag nets.

The wealthy Fairfax family was not left behind by this development. This was not only because CSR diversified in the 1940s – into mining and into manufacturing building products – as a response to the slowing sugar market, but also because, as Beasley's shareholder list showed, the Fairfax family joined the Baillieus and Symes and became BHP shareholders. As explained in Chapter 9, Fairfaxes had sat on the AMP board with Cecil Hoskins of AIS, and AMP had invested heavily in his steel company. When BHP acquired it, that gave the Fairfaxes a strong link to BHP through AMP's investment, but by 1935, several members of the Fairfax family also personally held BHP shares.[23] By 1945, Warwick Fairfax had joined them and become a BHP shareholder, along with two other family member directors of the *Sydney Morning Herald* – JH Fairfax and Edward Fairfax.[24] Importantly, Warwick Fairfax's interest in BHP may have happened *after* the paper's 'open warfare' with Menzies in 1940–41.

Menzies' first term in office put him at the centre of rivalries between Melbourne and Sydney financial interests that were expressed in their allied newspapers. The Sydney financial powers were centred around the Fairfax and Knox (CSR) families and their allied companies – CSR, Bank of New South Wales, Commercial Bank, AMP and Perpetual Trustee Company. But Menzies was mixing in a very Melbourne-centred financial world. Collins House and BHP both had their headquarters in Melbourne, 'despite the fact that none of [BHP's] steelmaking was carried on within four hundred miles'.[25] The Harold Darlings lived in a mansion in Orrong Road, Toorak, two doors from MH Baillieu. The second generation of Baillieus and Darlings were also neighbours in Toorak's St George's Road. Menzies and his wife lived one suburb over, in the still leafy, but less well-to-do, suburb of Kew.

In Sydney, there was concern that Menzies favoured Victoria in national decisions. There was also conflict between the Melbourne-based National Union and the Consultative Council of Sydney over control and financing of the UAP (this would become more inflamed during 1943). Another source of disagreement in the late 1930s was Menzies' support for the British government's appeasement policies under Neville Chamberlain. Warwick Fairfax and his *Sydney Morning Herald* were stern critics of appeasement. But Menzies remained a supporter even after the British had abandoned the policy. For some weeks after the outbreak of World War II and the German invasion of Poland, Menzies was still urging negotiations with Hitler.[26]

Murdoch had given consideration to appeasers' views after he visited Europe in 1936, but later became convinced of the proximity of war and the need for a more active stance. Within Collins House, WS Robinson was an early believer that war was inevitable. After a trip to the United Kingdom and North America in 1934, he became convinced that 'Australia had to make her own aircraft if she was to survive the [imminent] war'.[27] This led Collins House to join with BHP in another joint project, Commonwealth Aircraft Corporation, formed in October 1936. The partners involved in the project to manufacture military aircraft and engines in Australia were BHP (which supplied the steel), two Collins House companies – BHAS and Electrolytic Zinc – plus General Motors Holden, ICI and Orient Steam Navigation Co Ltd (P&O). As part of taking up a major role in the defence industry, BHP also began building ships at the South Australian port of Whyalla in 1940.

When Menzies first ascended to office, the Fairfaxes' *Sydney Morning Herald* was growing in confidence. It had been on the sidelines when Murdoch was exercising influence during the early Lyons era, but by the late 1930s was ready to become more active in political and industrial matters. Industrially, AH Stuart had paved the way by setting Fairfax & Sons up in partnership with the HWT in ANM and AAP. Upon taking over from Stuart, RAG Henderson had undertaken a major reorganisation of the company that included cutting costs, investing in new printing presses and focusing on classified advertisements. This drove a boom in Fairfax & Sons' advertising profits, putting it in a position of financial strength by the time World War II began.

The once industrially aloof *Sydney Morning Herald* joined with the other metropolitan daily papers in 1941, in a new body called the Australian Newspaper Proprietors' Association (ANPA). Significantly, its first meeting was held at the *Sydney Morning Herald* office. Henderson was elected president, and ANPA's headquarters moved to Sydney. (This rapprochement between the major newspaper companies lasted seven years before they split over postwar newsprint rationing.)

MENZIES, THE PRESS PROPRIETORS AND THEIR REPORTERS

The Depression had brought together strange political bedfellows to fight 'radical' economic policies. Once that emergency was over, a lack of shared purpose brought out political strife within the UAP, a 'party of spare parts'.[28] Lyons found it difficult to be definitive in policy-making not only because of internal party conflict, but also because of pressure from external forces, especially those who had put him in power. He made heavy compromises, and his government appeared unenergetic, stagnant and indecisive.

A revitalised Labor Party under John Curtin increased its share of the vote at the 1937 election. Murdoch was already critical of Lyons. So were top executives at BHP. In July 1936, Essington Lewis had written to Darling that: 'The federal government at present is leaderless, brainless and gutless ... we are drifting'.[29] By early 1939, Murdoch was privately expressing 'disgust' at Lyons' passivity in the face of the deteriorating international situation.[30] Murdoch wrote to Clive Baillieu that the government needed a new leader, as Lyons had 'lost his usefulness'.[31]

Menzies had also fallen out with the prime minister. In 1934, Menzies had switched from his thriving career in state politics to become a federal MP and minister on the understanding that Lyons would stand down after a suitable period, making Menzies prime minister. In 1936, Lyons explicitly promised to resign shortly, but the commitment was never honoured. Lyons' health was poor, he wanted to leave politics and made repeated requests to do so, but as Philip Hart revealed, the financial and political leaders who had shepherded him into office (especially within the National Union) convinced Lyons to stay because of their concerns about Menzies' electoral popularity. Menzies was considered aloof and arrogant, whereas Lyons was friendly, down-to-earth and popular. As Menzies himself admitted, he was suspicious of showing emotion and preferred to be in the realm of cold logic, hence his affinity with the law.

Murdoch was one of those who had his doubts about Menzies. Originally, he had been impressed, writing to Menzies in 1933, 'You are a much greater man than I', 'Great distinction, honours and achievement will be yours and I will be content indeed to doff my hat to you'.[32] In 1934, Murdoch told Dumas that 'Menzies undoubtedly is first-class in political brain'.[33] But it was not a smooth relationship. Menzies was independently minded and forthright. In late 1936, he took offence when the *Herald* criticised him for rudely cutting down an MP who had asked a question. Menzies described the article as 'contemptuous and certainly defamatory', and asked Murdoch for an apology.[34] Murdoch arranged for a conciliatory piece to be published, but also wrote back to Menzies that 'Surely criticism, when backed as ours is by proven friendly desire, is not to be ranked as hostility'.[35]

Menzies was not so sure there was no hostility. The *Herald*'s Joe Alexander had been the top political journalist during the Depression, partly because he was close to Lyons, but Alexander had a frosty relationship with Menzies. According to Alexander, Menzies complained in 1936 that 'the *Herald* has clearly shown that it is opposed to the present Commonwealth Government – was indeed its worst enemy'.[36]

For his part, Murdoch was not convinced that Menzies was a suitable replacement for Lyons, but by late 1938, he was so dissatisfied with Lyons that he helped with what CJ Lloyd described as Menzies' 'sustained, and largely subterranean, campaign to ease Lyons out of the Prime Ministership'.[37] Even so, Murdoch's newspapers expressed their support for Menzies in lukewarm terms, especially compared with the glowing tributes that had paved the path to office for Lyons. An October 1938 *Herald* article pointed out Menzies' virtues as a future prime minister, but then said his political rise had come too easily, he needed to work harder, connect more with the electorate, and stay home more rather than making so many overseas trips.[38]

Menzies' relationship with Murdoch was mutually ambivalent, and it would remain so until Murdoch's death in 1952. But Menzies did have a warmer relationship in the 1930s with two other press proprietors whom he considered friends. As already noted, one was Geoffrey Syme. His *Age* was reportedly Menzies' favourite newspaper, and the paper was 'an early supporter' of Menzies, particularly under HAM Campbell, editor from 1939 to 1959.[39] Campbell had been considered one of the best federal politics reporters in Australia in the 1920s, and the friendly, decorated World War I veteran built a good relationship with Menzies.

Menzies was also friends with Warwick Fairfax. As *Sydney Morning Herald* historian Gavin Souter noted, the *Sydney Morning Herald* had 'spoken well of Menzies from as early as 1936', and Menzies became a 'frequent visitor' to the Fairfaxes' Bellevue Hill home and, during summer, to their holiday home at Palm Beach.[40] Menzies also lunched occasionally at the *Sydney Morning Herald*'s office with Fairfax, RAG Henderson and Hugh McClure Smith (editor from 1938 to 1952). In April 1939, Warwick Fairfax, writing under his pen name ('A Political Observer'), called Menzies a 'BRILLIANT INTELLECT'. Addressing Menzies' renowned bluntness,

Fairfax said perhaps 'we are on the dawn of a new era in Australia
… when forthrightness will count more than politics', but he also
admitted that even Menzies' 'best friends' would acknowledge that
he sometimes came across as arrogant.[41]

Some of the advice the *Herald* and the *Sydney Morning Herald*
were giving Menzies was good advice, and he should have listened.
His lack of connection with the public, his absence overseas for
long stretches, and his arrogance and impatience with those he considered intellectually inferior, would all be factors in his downfall.
Menzies' lightning fast wit could sometimes be cruel. Since his university days, his 'cutting tongue' had been much remarked upon.[42]

Journalists were among those who regularly felt the sting of
Menzies' sharp tongue and this diminished the good will he should
have been able to draw upon from journalists because, as an industrial arbitrator in 1927, Menzies had brought in a grading system that
gave journalists access to industrial awards (albeit at lower pay rates
than the AJA had asked for). He had also developed a reputation as a
useful Cabinet leak during his time as a Lyons government minister.
But Menzies was generally not well liked among journalists because
he treated many with 'thinly-veiled disdain'.[43] (In his diary, Menzies
wrote in 1935, 'Why are newspaper reporters so frequently crude,
illiterate and lazy!'[44]) Conversely, there were 'frequent complaints'
from journalists about Menzies' rudeness.[45] Press gallery reporter,
and the ABC's first Canberra political correspondent, Warren
Denning, recalled that Menzies' approach was disarmingly inconsistent. One minute he was 'genial, friendly, warm' and charming.
The next, he was 'cold, aloof, remote … disdainful, contemptuous
… petulant'.[46]

The journalist who developed the best relationship with
Menzies was the *Sydney Morning Herald*'s Canberra correspondent,
Eric McLoughlin, the most authoritative press gallery reporter of
his day. Allan Fraser was one of McLoughlin's contemporaries in

the press gallery, and later became a Labor MP. Fraser said McLoughlin's Monday commentary 'was required reading' for journalists, politicians and politics-watchers. 'And this was only partly because McLoughlin had a private chat with Menzies every Saturday morning.'[47]

MENZIES' CAMPAIGN TO BECOME PRIME MINISTER

By early 1939, Lyons was sick and exhausted. In March, the *Herald* called on him 'to make way gracefully' for a new leader, but even then, Murdoch's flagship paper described Menzies as just one among 'four possible successors'.[48] Two months earlier, Murdoch had written to Clive Baillieu that:

> Bob [Menzies] has a curiously disconcerting way of
> discouraging adherence, whilst in fact eagerly seeking it. He
> is a most difficult man to work for. I do not know whether
> it is utter laziness or pride ... he never invites confidence.
> The public is beginning to actually dislike him, which is a
> great pity. Each week now he is becoming less likely as Prime
> Minister.[49]

Menzies, who had been unsuccessfully angling to drive Lyons out for months, finally made a definitive move in March 1939. He dramatically resigned from Lyons' Cabinet and his position as deputy leader of the UAP over the government's failure to fulfil a promise to bring in a comprehensive national insurance scheme (a policy backflip said to have been caused by opposition from some of the UAP's Melbourne financiers).[50] Menzies' stance seemed to be driven more by political ambition than conscience, and Lyons

and his supporters saw it as a deliberate attempt to destabilise his
leadership.

The *Sydney Morning Herald* applauded Menzies' resignation.
So too did the *Herald*, which said 'Admiration for Mr Menzies will
run high today'. It hoped his stand would mean 'at last an end ...
to the drifting career of [this] Government'.[51] *The Age* said Menzies'
'action does him honor', while the *Sun* admired Menzies' courage
and his principles.[52] The only UAP-supporting paper that did not
applaud was the *Argus*. Menzies' friend, Staniforth Ricketson, had
resigned as chairman of the *Argus* board in January 1939, and then
resigned as a director two weeks before Menzies' resignation. A
determined pocket of resistance to Menzies had been forming there.

The new chair of the *Argus* board was Kingsley Henderson.
Like Ricketson and Menzies, he had been a member of 'the Group',
but Henderson had become very close to Lyons and disapproved of
Menzies' disloyalty to the ill prime minister. Ricketson later wrote to
Menzies that he felt the paper's anti-Menzies turn was also due to
its managing editor, Errol Knox. According to Ricketson, Knox was
'on record as saying he would "get Menzies"'.[53]

Knox, who had once been a strong Menzies supporter, was a
dynamic force in the newspaper world, with a reputation for being
able to resuscitate dying newspapers. He had revitalised the *Evening
News* in 1922, and was lured to the *Argus* in 1937 to pull it back into
prosperity, without any stunts or 'jazz methods' that might startle
its conservative, affluent audience.[54] Knox had managed to replace
advertisements with news on its front page.

But the opposition to Menzies went even higher than its editor
and board chairman. The *Argus'* main owner-managers were
Lauchlan Mackinnon and Allan Spowers. Historian Sybil Nolan
has described how both were strongly opposed to Menzies and
actively worked to keep him out of the exclusive Melbourne Club,
where they were prominent and had long family links.[55] Menzies'

failure to enlist during World War I was counting very heavily against him at the *Argus*. Mackinnon, Spowers and Knox were all veterans. Knox, in particular, had seen extended active service. But Menzies' independence was also a factor.

Cameron Hazlehurst argued that 'the money men of the UAP [and Murdoch] had lost their confidence in Menzies' by the start of 1939. They had 'come to believe that [he] was too independent for their taste'.[56] *Smith's Weekly* said similarly that the chieftains of Collins House preferred 'the pliant politician who can be Press made and unmade'.[57]

The *Argus* had been closely involved with 'the Group' (Chapters 10 and 11), and therefore the National Union and Collins House, but it also had ties of its own to Collins House. JB Aitken, a trustee of the Mackinnon estate and an *Argus* director, was appointed a director of North Broken Hill in 1944. Another *Argus* director, George Dalziel Kelly (appointed in 1936), resigned in January 1940, only to become a director of the HWT ten months later. Kelly was associated with the pastoral and wool industries, but had also replaced Menzies as a director of the Capel Court Investment Trust in 1938. Menzies had stepped down from company directorates that year to avoid perceptions of conflicts of interest, but it seems he, and his wife, remained shareholders in Capel Court Investment Trust into at least the 1950s, and that the trust companies held shares in Collins House and BHP subsidiaries.[58]

On 7 April, Lyons died, in the midst of the *Herald*'s campaign to remove him from office. This set off a scramble at the *Argus* because they did not want Menzies to succeed Lyons. The 'squattocracy' at the paper preferred Casey, who was even more closely connected to Collins House and had served in staff positions in Gallipoli and France. When Casey's numbers in the party room looked insufficient, the *Argus* backed an improbable plan to lure Bruce back from his position as Australian High Commissioner in London.

The *Argus* even spread a rumour that if Bruce returned, Menzies would become High Commissioner, presumably to make the prospect appealing for Menzies. But Bruce did not even want the job.

As Hart pointed out, the National Union had been able to convince Latham to stand aside for Lyons in 1931, but it was not able to repeat that degree of influence and make either Bruce or Casey Lyons' successor in 1939.[59] Menzies became UAP leader and prime minister – but he only scraped in. During his four years as Lyons' likely successor, Menzies had failed to build a strong base of supporters around him. He had alienated colleagues through his tactlessness and contempt, especially within the Country Party. In the leadership ballot, Menzies defeated the grizzled, near-deaf, seventy-six-year-old Billy Hughes by only four votes after four ballots. This was one sign of the lack of confidence in him. Another was that Page refused to serve under Menzies, and the Country Party declined to enter into a coalition with him. Without Lyons' personal influence and his conciliatory approach, political and personal conflict was immediately boiling over.

Just days after Menzies narrowly defeated Hughes, Page made an extraordinary statement in the House of Representatives. He said Menzies' failure to serve during World War I meant that, with another war looming, he was ill-equipped to lead the nation. Page claimed Menzies resigned from the Australian military in 1915 to avoid overseas service.[60] Menzies responded that he had not resigned; his term of compulsory service had expired, and he had not renewed it. (Menzies had undertaken four years' compulsory military training, serving part time in the Melbourne University Rifles from 1915 to 1919.) Like Murdoch, Menzies had been an advocate of conscription who did not enlist for overseas service himself. Page not only implied Menzies was a coward but also accused him of disloyalty to Lyons. As a medical doctor, Page personally believed that Menzies' sniping had hastened Lyons' death.

Roy Curthoys was a previous editor of the *Argus* who had resigned in 1935 over conflict relating to the paper's editorial stance. He wrote to his friend, JR Darling, headmaster of Geelong Grammar, that 'Your Melbourne Club friends in the National Union and their opposite numbers in the Union Club in Sydney, aided and abetted by Page ... and by Casey ... made a dead set on Menzies'. Curthoys believed the National Union 'felt that Menzies [would] not be sufficiently amenable to its orders. Hence the first move was to try to get Bruce back'.[61] Curthoys had formed this view after speaking with Kingsley Henderson.

The Fairfaxes were prominent members of Sydney's Union Club but Curthoys cannot have meant them because, whereas the Melbourne Club stalwarts at the *Argus* had not wanted Menzies, the *Sydney Morning Herald* 'welcomed' him to the leadership, and 'defended him' when Page mounted his attack.[62] Murdoch's *Herald* also supported Menzies, expressing the prediction (perhaps it was a hope) that being a national leader would bring out the best in him.[63]

Four months after Menzies became prime minister, World War II broke out when Britain and France declared war on Germany. On 3 September 1939, Menzies announced on radio that it was his 'melancholy duty' to officially inform Australians that, 'Great Britain has declared war upon her [Germany] and that, as a result, Australia is also at war'.[64] On 18 October 1939, Menzies wrote to Bruce in London: 'though I honestly believe we have been doing very well under difficult circumstances, we have some newspaper critics – notably Murdoch – while Page and [Archie] Cameron [of the Country Party] are conducting specially poisonous public campaigns'.[65]

Perhaps because he had witnessed Murdoch's overbearing relationship with Lyons, Menzies seemed determined to hold Murdoch at arm's length. Menzies was reportedly one of those who felt Lyons' prime ministerial visits to the HWT office had been

FIGURE 15.1 RG Menzies with Otto Olsen, the Canberra representative for the *Sun*, 1939

SOURCE Associated Newspapers' *Staff News*, vol. 1, no. 13, August 1939, p. 1, Fairfax Media Business Archive, MS 9894, box 147, State Library of New South Wales.

undignified. When Menzies became prime minister, Murdoch went to him at parliament house. One account of the meeting reported that it took place just before lunch, so Menzies felt obliged to ask Murdoch to stay for lunch, but throughout, tried to steer the conversation away from politics and on to cricket, and other safe topics. Afterwards, Menzies headed towards his office and Murdoch followed. When they got there, Menzies told him it was a pleasure to see him, said 'goodbye', and closed the door. Murdoch was left standing outside in the corridor.[66]

NORTON'S NEWSPRINT LICENCE

Ezra Norton controlled Truth and Sportsman Ltd, the company whose papers were founded by his volatile father, John. It published the sensational Sunday newspaper, *Truth*, in Sydney, Melbourne and Brisbane, which both shocked and thrilled its audience with stories of personal scandal and social injustice.[67] The company's other newspaper, the *Sydney Sportsman*, was a bi-weekly focused on horseracing and sports. One critic begrudgingly noted that the papers reflected 'the peculiar Norton recipe for ranting rags [that could only come from] the peculiar, twisted genius of a John or an Ezra'.[68]

Some of the other, smaller shareholders in Norton's company were advertisers of products aimed at its working-class audience: Penfold's Wines, Bushell's tea, the cigarette manufacturer WD & HO Wills, and various public bars. In 1943, Norton's mortal enemy, Frank Packer, also bought a small parcel of shares in Truth and Sportsman Ltd (this was not uncommon as a way of keeping an eye on opponents).

Packer and Norton were both big horseracing fans, stingy in their business operations, and partial to abusing and sacking their staff. But where Packer was loud, showy and brash, Norton was enigmatic and introverted, a lone wolf. They both considered themselves outsiders up against establishment newspaper figures like Murdoch and Fairfax, and the two had banded together over the newsprint bounty in 1938. But they had then fallen out in 1939 and used their outlets to wage war on each other, resulting in their notorious brawl at Randwick racecourse, and an assault by one of Norton's bodyguards on a *Daily Telegraph* photographer. An Adelaide journalist quipped that the feud between Norton and Packer was 'the kind of press feud which Sydney alone of all Australian cities could produce'.[69]

Packer's *Sunday Telegraph* had been hurting *Truth*'s sales and revenue since the *Sunday Telegraph* began in 1939, sharpening Norton's long-standing desire to publish a daily paper. Intermittently between 1932 and 1935, Norton had sought the benefit of the inside knowledge of Herbert Campbell Jones (the *Sun*'s former managing editor). When Campbell Jones resigned, Norton kept going, making plans and ordering new printing plant in 1937. He wanted to create a new afternoon daily that would compete directly with Associated Newspapers' *Sun*, but would also snatch readers and advertisers from Packer's morning *Daily Telegraph*.

Norton had a friend in Menzies' Cabinet. Eric Harrison was the local MP for Wentworth, the electorate in which both Norton and Packer lived. Harrison had already shown he was an unusually brave politician in terms of standing up to Sydney's daily paper owners. He had angered them in 1939 when he was postmaster-general because he had refused their demands that the government pay them £90 000 a year to publish ABC programs, and then allowed the ABC to start its own publication, the *ABC Weekly*. It was said that Harrison was elevated to Cabinet in 1934, at the insistence of Sydney Snow, the former Associated Newspapers director who, along with Campbell Jones, had resigned in 1931, after they had taken on Denison and lost. Snow was very influential in New South Wales UAP circles, and in 1932, had become a director of Broken Hill South.

On 1 March 1940, Truth and Sportsman Ltd applied to the Menzies government for a licence to import newsprint, a crucial prerequisite for starting a paper. Cabinet gave its approval, and on 29 March, Truth and Sportsman Ltd was granted the all-important licence. Harrison had stood down from the Cabinet two weeks earlier because another coalition between the UAP and the Country Party had been negotiated (despite lingering hostility towards Menzies within that party), and this had required him to make way for a Country Party minister. But Harrison's influence was still evident in Cabinet's decision.

Norton's new afternoon paper was to be called the *Daily Mirror* and he immediately ordered newsprint stock for it, hired 120 staff, signed contracts for overseas news services, organised delivery mechanisms, and began remodelling *Truth*'s Kippax Street premises, spending tens of thousands of pounds in preparation for the launch.

Associated Newspapers was appalled by Cabinet's decision. Since the closure of the *Evening News* in March 1931, the *Sun* had enjoyed the advantages of monopoly as Sydney's only afternoon paper. But the *Sydney Morning Herald*'s executives were also concerned because any new daily, even an afternoon one, would result in loss of advertising revenue, circulation and scarce newsprint. While Cabinet was considering Norton's application, executives from Sydney's major papers had met in the *Sydney Morning Herald* offices and agreed to offer to voluntarily restrict their newsprint consumption by 35 per cent. They were hoping to head off any greater restrictions, but this also had the advantage of making it more difficult for the government to justify giving Norton a licence when newsprint was being rationed.

Packer had additional reasons to despair of the decision: his personal hatred of Norton, and also the financial position of his company. Unlike the *Sydney Morning Herald*, Consolidated Press was not financially robust, making it vulnerable to new competition. The *Australian Women's Weekly* was still selling extremely well, but it was not necessarily making money, and the launch of the *Sunday Telegraph* had dragged Consolidated Press into financial difficulties.[70] Even before its launch, the company was carrying a large amount of debt. In 1938, its after-tax profit was £57 016, but its debts were £226 118.[71] By March 1941, the company's debts had jumped to £376 425 and the cost of its newsprint stocks had skyrocketed from £17 260 to £185 240.[72] Even into 1942, the *Sunday*

Telegraph was losing £6000 per month, cancelling out profits from the *Daily Telegraph*.[73] Frank Packer's notorious penny-pinching had a basis in real concerns after all.

Packer and Associated Newspapers wanted the help of the ANC, especially the powerful Murdoch, to lobby the government to reverse its decision. But Murdoch refused. Norton's paper would have no impact on any of his papers so he could afford to take a detached, philosophical position about it. When Hugh Denison's son, Reg Denison, reacted angrily to Murdoch's indifference, Murdoch wrote to him saying that, in his opinion, protesting to the government 'was a mistake. All, or nearly all, of the Federal Cabinet are against you, the leading Canberra officials are against you, and the protest cannot succeed ... the newspapers will rightly be thought by the public to have sought a bad ruling to meet their own special interests.'[74]

Murdoch also told Reg Denison that 'If the power of the Customs Department is to be invoked to limit newspapers, then we are at the beginning of the destruction of the freedom of the Press. I believe this sincerely and surely have a right to this opinion.'[75]Denison was unmoved by this freedom-of-the-press lecture and again expressed his regret that 'your attitude towards us ... was not more friendly'.[76] Norton gleefully rubbed salt in the wound by publicly thanking Murdoch for his support in the columns of *Truth*. Packer's Consolidated Press and Associated Newspapers resigned from the ANC in protest at Murdoch's 'attitude' in late April 1940.[77]

Hugh Denison and Associated Newspaper executives were fiercely lobbying the government to reverse its decision. Norton and three of his executives headed to Canberra to defend the licence. They saw the minister for trade and customs, Senator McLeay, on 27 and 28 May. McLeay assured them of his support, so Norton and his group returned to Sydney. But Denison and Graham Waddell of Associated Newspapers had also made their way to Canberra and were seeing a higher authority – Menzies – and lunching with ministers. They were accompanied by RD Field, who had previously worked for Norton but had switched sides. Denison, Waddell and Field reportedly waited outside while Cabinet reconsidered its position and decided to revoke Norton's licence. Warwick Fairfax had also made his own protest, writing to Menzies to say that his company would resist the licence approval 'by every legitimate means'.[78]

Norton heard that something was going on. Extremely flustered, he hotfooted it back to Canberra and enlisted Curtin's help to gain a meeting with Menzies. Norton explained that he had made extensive financial commitments and his new employees would be put out of work if the government revoked his licence. But the decision had already been made.

Murdoch had been wrong when he said that protest was futile. On 31 May, McLeay wrote and told Norton the licence had been revoked. Norton was outraged and *Truth* published a series of articles about the: 'CONCERTED PLAN TO SABOTAGE THE "DAILY MIRROR"', 'MONOPOLY INTERESTS AGAIN TAKE CHARGE OF FEDERAL CABINET' and 'MENZIES GOVT REPUDIATES ITS PLEDGED WORD'.[79] *Truth* said Associated Newspapers was a 'MONOPOLY THAT LIVES ON THE KILL-ING OF ALL OPPOSITION' and the 'PM [had] rescued news-paper knights from virile competition'.[80] In a front-page 'OPEN LETTER TO SIR HUGH DENISON', Norton gave full vent to his fury and ended with a warning that 'the time will come, Sir Hugh, when the *Sun* will have to face up to virile competition'. He signed off 'with bitter regards'.[81]

Norton filed a compensation claim of nearly £138 000 from the government. Harrison helped promote it by asking a question about the claim in parliament. Although the government had legal advice that it was not liable for Norton's wasted costs, there was an element of moral force to his argument so the solicitor-general advised paying him £38 000.

In the feud over Norton's newsprint licence, Murdoch had ranged himself against the major Sydney owners. Unwittingly, he was also about to be the cause of the Menzies government's next offence against the press.

CHAPTER 16

MENZIES' DOWNFALL

With the Sydney papers becoming increasingly critical of him, Menzies started drawing Murdoch closer. The prime minister told his colleagues at a meeting of the War Cabinet on 21 May 1940, that wartime public morale was about to be tested, and 'they should get the best publicist and journalist in Australia' to fortify it and build support for the government's war effort.[1] Menzies offered Murdoch a new, honorary position as director-general of the Department of Information. Before he accepted, Murdoch consulted his fellow newspaper proprietors and received their support. When he took up the post on 10 June, the *Daily Telegraph* said Murdoch was a man 'whom not only [Menzies], but all of Australia can trust'.[2]

Menzies was in need of a good publicist because his government was being regularly criticised for its administration of the war. Historian Stuart Macintyre reflected that the Menzies government seemed 'reluctant to make decisions and incapable of implementing the decisions it did make', and 'little was done to mobilise the country's resources or curtail consumption'.[3] Menzies attempted to put his government onto a firmer war footing by appointing businessmen into senior government roles. Murdoch's appointment was one of two that Menzies announced on 9 June. The other was Essington Lewis, chief general manager of BHP, who became director-general of munitions (giving him unlimited authority over Australian industry). Despite his reputation as a master publicist, it was Murdoch's appointment that proved to be the more controversial and short-lived of the two. It was another strike against Menzies, and the proprietors' hostility towards him was mounting.

MURDOCH'S GREATEST BLUNDER

When Murdoch took up the position of director-general of information, it gave him power and prestige. Northcliffe had played a similar role in the United Kingdom during World War I. Murdoch now had wide control over Australian media, access to the War Cabinet and to confidential military material. Only the prime minister had the power to override Murdoch's authority (reportedly at Murdoch's insistence). He was in charge of disseminating positive publicity, but also censorship to stop the Australian media reporting information that could be of value to the nation's enemies.

Murdoch had been encouraged to take the role by his friend Henry Gullett, who had been the minister for information. Gullett was a skilled journalist himself, but he had found the position tough, and had been criticised for bungling the formation of the Department, and being too heavy-handed in censoring radical publications. Gullett's difficulties should have been a warning to Murdoch, and perhaps they were. When he said goodbye to his staff, Murdoch said it was one of the risks of the job that his reputation, 'a lifetime career, could vanish in half-an-hour'.[4]

Murdoch stepped aside from leading the HWT and all of his other business commitments except one. He remained chairman of the ANM – an all-important project for him. Dumas filled in as the acting managing director of the HWT, taking up the position as its flagship paper, the *Herald*, was celebrating its centenary.

Revealingly, Murdoch's first act as director-general was to take control of evening radio news broadcasts, that pesky 7 pm time slot he had opposed for the ABC because it provided competition to his afternoon papers. Murdoch appointed three senior journalists to write news scripts on behalf of the Department of Information and made it mandatory for all stations (ABC and commercial) to broadcast these sessions at the same time every day. This was implemented on 26 June 1940, and from Monday to Saturday, the department's 'News Survey' was broadcast on all radio stations between 7 pm and 7.23 pm so listeners could not listen to anything else. The sessions consisted of ten minutes of patriotically presented overseas news, five minutes of interviews with people connected with the war industry, and eight minutes of commentaries and local news. On Sunday, the department provided a mandatory 9 pm–9.30 pm musical session instead, which contained a ten-minute 'inspirational talk on the war'.[5]

Somehow, despite his appointment of excellent journalists, and his own finely tuned news instincts, the news sessions Murdoch forced on all radio stations were considered 'dull', 'stale', and below the standard of the ABC's previous news bulletins.[6] However, the ABC staff resisted an outright fight with him, 'lest they stir Murdoch into assuming control over the whole of its activities'.[7] Instead, the ABC forwarded complaints from its unhappy listeners to Murdoch. The commercial radio stations were also displeased at having to give up popular programs and their most valuable advertising time slot. In one swoop, Murdoch had made 7 pm radio news less appealing to audiences *and* advertisers, and also interrupted the ABC's newsgathering advances. This was all to the advantage of the press, and helps explain why his fellow newspaper owners may have so strongly supported Murdoch's appointment.

Murdoch's next act was not so well received though. Back on 19 June, the same day that he had commandeered radio airtime, Murdoch had also sought an increase to his censorship powers. His new regulations, gazetted on 17 July, gave him the right to insist upon a correction if a media outlet made a misleading or incorrect statement. Murdoch was to be the arbiter of what was 'true', and able to insist that the government's version – the 'correct' version – be reported with the same prominence as the original 'falsehood'. Murdoch now had the power to compel corrections in the form of words he wanted, and in the case of newspapers, on the date and within the space he specified, whether the front page or some other prominent space. In his own words, Murdoch said that he wanted power on behalf of the government to say: 'That statement has been harmful. Here is the truth. Print it and print it where we tell you.'[8]

The War Cabinet had endorsed this plan, and Murdoch took it to a conference of newspaper editors and executives on 1 July. He tried to convince them that this method of corrections allowed for greater freedom of expression than some elaborate censorship regime of pre-vetting material. But they were not convinced. They accepted the need for censorship during wartime, and that the government could direct them about what they should *not* publish in order to prevent important information falling into enemy hands or to maintain public morale. But Murdoch's plan was different. It allowed the government to tell them *what to publish*, and even where in the paper they had to put it.

When the government's chief law officer saw the draft regulations, he sounded a warning too, telling Murdoch they were 'going a long way' and would likely be criticised.[9] But Murdoch still ploughed ahead. On 17 July 1940, the new regulations were gazetted. Newspapers were outraged that Murdoch had such a sweeping power to 'control' their content. He argued again that corrections were better than 'suppression by censorship', and added that the new regulations would be little used because 'reputable' newspapers took care to avoid mistakes and corrected them when they became aware. But his fellow owners were unanimous that their independence to decide what they published should never be breached.

(The regulations also applied to cinema and radio, but only the newspapers protested.)

Murdoch had written plenty of scathing attacks over the years, but he was not used to being on the receiving end of them. The *Sydney Morning Herald* thundered that the regulations were a violation of its property rights because Murdoch's 'drastic powers' gave the government authority to 'commandeer space'.[10] Space was at a premium due to newsprint rationing and the *Sydney Morning Herald*'s argument revealed the issue was not just about press freedom. Owners were worried about losing advertising space.

The *Daily Telegraph* expressed its opposition in characteristically sensational and combative terms. It declared 18 June 'the last day of a free Press', and 'NEW REGULATIONS LIKENED TO A DICTATORSHIP'.[11] The *Daily Telegraph* also took aim at Murdoch in a very personal way that would have deeply unsettled him. Packer's newspaper claimed Murdoch's regulations were aimed at Sydney:

> because in New South Wales Sir Keith has no control over the newspapers. He needs no special regulations to help him force his views on the people of South Australia, Victoria or Queensland. There he is already overlord of the Press ... The three big Sydney papers, who generally do not agree ... agree on [their opposition to Murdoch's regulations], and have refused to be bamboozled and silenced by Sir Keith.[12]

The *Daily Telegraph* thundered on that: 'Sir Keith is surprised at this public reaction. Because he is utterly out of touch with public opinion. He is so used to getting a docile "Yes, Sir Keith" from those who trot at his beck and call in Melbourne ... that he expected the whole Australian people to bow down humbly and submit in the same way.'[13] Presumably, Packer's co-owner, EG Theodore (who had been a target of the Murdoch press in the early 1930s), enjoyed seeing Murdoch get a taste of his own medicine.

The *Canberra Times* said Murdoch had taken out 'dictatorial powers'.[14] In an editorial headed 'THE GOEBBELS TOUCH', the Sydney *Sun* said 'the regulation is a crime against the very ideals of freedom for which Australia entered the war'.[15] Hugh Denison said the powers given to Murdoch were 'almost totalitarian'.[16] *The Age* said they were 'unnecessary, intolerable and highly dangerous'.[17] Only the papers that Murdoch controlled defended him and repeated his assurances that there was no sinister intent behind the regulations.

This was not good enough for Theodore Fink, still chairman of the HWT board, who took the opportunity to sink the boot into Murdoch as part of their internal power struggle. Dumas described in his autobiography how he wrote a carefully worded editorial for the *Herald*. It argued that the regulations had been 'unfortunately worded' so this had made them 'an unnecessary piece of interference with the freedom of the press', but this must have been because they 'had been drawn up hurriedly to meet some need', so the editorial simply urged that they be withdrawn and redrafted.[18]

Fink wanted the *Herald*'s editorial to go further and attack Murdoch's overstep like the non-Murdoch press, but the board backed Dumas' gentle editorial. Dumas also tried to soothe disgruntled owners and executives and even took it upon himself to redraft the regulations and read the new version over the phone to Murdoch, who accepted the changes. Dumas then advised the Sydney owners, *The Age* and the *Argus*. As a result they published more conciliatory editorials. The *Sydney Morning Herald*'s was called 'RETRIEVING A BLUNDER'.[19]

Fink was not mollified though, and wrote his own article, under his name as chairman of the Commonwealth Press Union, saying he 'wished to dissociate himself from the views expressed in the publications of the [HWT] in favour of the regulations'. Fink said he wanted instead to associate himself with the non-HWT papers and to condemn the regulations as an 'objectionable and a dangerous and unnecessary attack on the liberty of the press and public'.[20] Fink's statement was published in *The Age* and the *Argus*, but Dumas and HWT directors Harry Giddy and George Caro managed to stop it appearing in the *Sun News-Pictorial* or the *Herald*.

For days, Murdoch was attacked on the front page of newspapers around the country by peers within his own industry, but also by politicians, union leaders, the AJA, the Australian Association of National Advertisers, academics and businessmen. Labor leader John Curtin said it had long been suspected that Murdoch wished to control public opinion in Australia and now he had achieved it.[21] The Queensland premier attacked the regulations. So did the Victorian premier, who asked, 'Have they gone mad?'[22] The *Daily Telegraph* even ran public opinion surveys – still a new concept at the time – asking the public to weigh in. One found that 78 per cent of the public believed the regulations 'ended individual liberty'.[23]

At first, Menzies tried to defend Murdoch's regulations but the backlash was too intense, and on 19 July, he announced that the regulations had been withdrawn for redrafting. A much weaker version was then gazetted (and never acted upon). Two days after the back-down, the *Daily Telegraph* reported an exclusive it described as the 'real story' behind the regulations. This account exonerated Menzies and laid all the blame on Murdoch. The *Daily Telegraph* said it had learned 'from high authority' (possibly Menzies or one of his Cabinet supporters) that Murdoch had 'led Mr Menzies to believe that Australian newspapers had agreed in advance to accept them', so Menzies had been 'grossly misled' and 'misinformed by his Director-General'.[24] The *Sydney Morning Herald* also sympathised with Menzies that Murdoch's request for 'dictatorial powers over the press' had been done in such a way that Menzies was unaware of 'the implications of what he was asked to do'. The *Sydney Morning Herald* said Menzies had 'no exact knowledge of the terms of [Murdoch's proposal] until the regulations were published in the newspapers'.[25] Someone in 'high authority' had fed Murdoch to the wolves.

Just how Murdoch had come to make such an error of judgement in the first place is difficult to understand. Murdoch knew better than anyone the press' acute sensitivity to any hint of government control. As Dumas noted, if Murdoch had been in his normal job 'he would have been the first newspaperman to oppose [the regulations] bitterly'.[26] Instead, Murdoch had given little warning of the regulations, no real explanation or justification of why they were needed, and had bluntly introduced them without adequate consultation. Murdoch had long aimed his pen at overzealous bureaucrats and inept politicians, but when he was given a job with public responsibilities, he had immediately bungled it.

The vicious reaction to his misstep deeply hurt Murdoch. He had failed in the post and his credibility was severely damaged. In August, Murdoch's staunchest supporter in Cabinet, Gullett, was killed in a plane crash. Murdoch's biographer, RM Younger, said in the 'face of increasing pressure of newspaper opinion ... Menzies withdrew his support'.[27] When Murdoch resigned as director-general, the pencilled minutes of the War Advisory Council meeting of 30 October recorded that he was resigning because he could do better service in his group of newspapers than as director-general, and also because of the 'Opposition of Sydney press'.[28]

The opposition arose not only from lingering resentment about Murdoch's refusal to join their campaign against Norton's newsprint licence, and his 'Goebbels-like' new censorship powers. There was also a suspicion that Murdoch had been 'providing the government with commercial information about the use of newsprint that the other companies had not been prepared to supply'.[29]

Labor MP Arthur Calwell gloated that Murdoch 'was hounded from office by his fellow newspaper proprietors'.[30] Younger said the event was '[p]erhaps the greatest disappointment of [Murdoch's] life'.[31] Although his own overreach had caused the crisis, Murdoch and his wife, Elisabeth, also blamed Menzies. They seemed to believe that Menzies had persuaded Murdoch to take the post against his best interests, and then deserted him when it backfired. After this 'horrid time' (as Elisabeth called it), Murdoch became a more willing participant in the anti-Menzies campaign being waged by Fairfax and Packer.[32]

THE 1940 ELECTION

On 19 May 1940, the *Daily Telegraph* began a series of front-page editorials headed 'PLEASE READ THIS, MR MENZIES'. Over three weeks, the paper gave Menzies unsolicited advice in its provocative and melodramatic style: 'Spend £100,000,000 if necessary, but get planes, and guns, and tanks – and get them as quick as you can. We have the money and we want safety.'[33] The paper also said, 'Australia needs a new Government'.[34] Less dramatically, but with essentially the same message, the *Sydney Morning Herald* told its readers that the Menzies government 'has sadly lacked vigour and inspiration. There has been wholly insufficient drive … a refusal to face the implications of total war', and Menzies lacked the 'popular and inspiring leadership so urgently required'.[35]

On 22 June 1940, Menzies wrote to Warwick Fairfax: 'I hope you will permit me to say, as a friend, that the constant allegation of complacency and leisureliness which your Editor permits himself to level against the Government, and presumably against myself, are … unfounded'.[36] The 13 August plane crash in Canberra killed not only Gullett but also two other federal ministers and seven others.

It was a huge blow to Menzies personally and politically because those ministers were three of his strongest and most loyal supporters. Menzies' position within his party had suddenly become more precarious.

For some time, there had been a push for a British-style all-party national government that put the parliament's 'best brains' together for the war effort, even if they were from different parties. But Curtin had rejected Menzies' offer to give five or six portfolios to the Labor Party. This would have postponed the election and, Curtin argued, robbed the people of an effective Opposition. With the election scheduled for 21 September, the *Sydney Morning Herald* and the *Daily Telegraph* took a remarkably, and some said suspiciously, similar position. Both papers ultimately expressed support for the conservative government, but they called for 'new men [sic]' of outstanding ability to be brought into a national government, even if they displaced sitting UAP MPs. In the case of the *Daily Telegraph*, the 'new men' included first-time Labor candidate Dr Herbert Vere (HV) Evatt. The news editor of Consolidated Press' *Australian Women's Weekly* was even ordered to caption a photo of Evatt as 'Stepping forth' and one of Menzies as 'Complacency'.[37]

With unusual candour for a newspaper proprietor, Packer signed an editorial before polling day admitting that he had provided support to particular candidates in his efforts to get new blood into parliament. He revealed that 'Evatt had received secretarial assistance and that others had been given access to facilities at 2UW, with which the *Telegraph*s were now aligned'.[38] Among those listed as having received help were Eric Spooner (UAP), Bertram Stevens (UAP), Dr LW Nott (UAP), Dr Frank Louat (UAP), William McCall (UAP) and Captain JP Abbott (Country Party). The *Sydney Morning Herald* had also singled out UAP candidates Stevens, Spooner, Cowper, Louat and Abbott as 'outstanding' men who would 'increase the Government's vigour'.[39] This was controversial because, at the time, the UAP allowed multiple candidates to run under its party name. (In the seat of Wentworth, for example, there were three endorsed UAP candidates.) In several seats the two papers were backing new UAP candidates, and calling for the sitting UAP MP to be replaced.

Neither paper went so far as to call for a Labor government, nor for Menzies to be replaced. The *Daily Telegraph* blamed the 'weak team on which Mr Menzies has had to rely' for the inadequate war effort. It called on voters to 'give him a better team – men who want to improve our slow-coach administration and have the expert administrative experience to do so'.[40] On the day of the election, the *Sydney Morning Herald*'s editorial reminded readers to beware of Labor and to stick with the Menzies government. Contrary to the criticism it had been hurling at Menzies for months, it now claimed he was 'firmly in command of the great war machine which [the government] has built up'.[41] Despite its increasing dislike of Menzies, the *Sydney Morning Herald* was still a conservative paper, and its advocacy of individual candidates against sitting UAP MPs had been heresy enough, and resulted in Fairfax being snubbed in the Union Club.

Both papers had vigorously backed solicitor Norman Cowper over Eric Harrison, the sitting UAP MP, former postmaster-general and Norton supporter. As noted in Chapter 9, Cowper was a partner in the law firm that handled Consolidated Press' legal matters, and a friend of EG Theodore's. Ezra Norton's *Truth* pointed out the commercial vendetta behind the papers' opposition to Harrison. But Norton also had his own commercial motives mixing with political advocacy. *Truth* was strongly backing Labor in the hope that a Labor government would give Norton a newsprint licence. Norton had donated £3000 to Labor's campaign.[42]

The *Sydney Morning Herald*'s and *Daily Telegraph*'s campaigning efforts were not in the league of Keith Murdoch's Joe Lyons

publicity coup of 1931. Instead, they were embarrassingly unsuccessful. Harrison received twice as many votes as Cowper and was
returned as Wentworth's local MP. In the broader contest, the loss of
UAP and Country Party seats reflected public dissatisfaction with
the government. Menzies was returned to office but was forced to
rely upon the support of two independents and had to accept Page
into his Cabinet.

Menzies made a statement saying that the New South Wales
results were out of step with other states, and that only New South
Wales 'had administered a setback to the government'. He said this
was caused not by the 'government's avowed enemies but [by] some
of its supposed friends. Important sections of the Sydney press ...
have for many months constantly decried the government's war
efforts and attacked individual Ministers. This kind of thing has
its inevitable effect, as I have frequently pointed out to my Sydney
friends.' He said he hoped they would learn 'a lesson' from the election result.[43]

Holding out an olive branch, Fairfax sent Menzies a telegram
a few days later saying 'Should be glad to assist you if possible in
stabilising position and would greatly appreciate opportunity [for]
us to see you [in] near future'.[44] Menzies replied he would be 'Very
pleased [to] see you'.[45] The rapprochement would not last, and
although Menzies was in a very 'unstable situation, with only a tenu-
ous hold on Government and the leadership' and some persistent
media critics, he unwisely decided to go to London to discuss war
matters.[46]

THE *DAILY MIRROR*

The *Sydney Morning Herald*'s and *Daily Telegraph*'s campaigns against Harrison during the election had not endeared them to him. Unfortunately for them, when Harrison retained his seat, he was appointed the minister for trade and customs with responsibility over newsprint licencing and rationing. On 24 January 1941, four days after Menzies had departed for London, leaving Country Party leader, Arthur Fadden, as acting prime minister, Harrison wrote to Norton. He advised that Cabinet had again reversed its decision and would now grant Norton a newsprint licence so long as he dropped his compensation claim against the government. Only two months earlier, Hugh Denison had died. He had been spared having to see his worst commercial nightmare come true, but without him, Associated Newspapers' influence had taken an immediate hit.

Harrison had argued that newsprint rationing should not be used to protect a monopoly, and Menzies had been present when the decision was made. Norton once more marshalled his resources to prepare for the launch. After three different Cabinet decisions, the *Daily Mirror* finally rolled off the presses on 12 May 1941. It made history as the first afternoon tabloid in Australia (the *Sun* would remain a broadsheet until 1947). A hefty forty pages long, the *Daily Mirror* was a kick in the teeth to the established newspapers fretting about their rationing-enforced slim down. At the last moment, Norton had ordered his staff to model it on the still highly successful *Sun News-Pictorial*, so the *Daily Mirror* had many half-tone photographs and other types of illustrations. Its first front page included a striking photograph of the royal family surveying the damage of the latest German bombing raid on London during the blitz (Figure 16.1). The *Sun* appeared text-heavy and cluttered by comparison, while the *Sydney Morning Herald* still had classified advertisements on its front page.

THE WEATHER

FORECAST. — Fine and mild day, with light to moderate easterly breeze in afternoon. Cool, misty to foggy night. Isolated frost in western suburbs.

DAILY ⊞ MIRROR

SYDNEY

FINAL EDITION

Telephones: Editorial {FL3041 (10 lines). / FL5041 (10 lines).

Telephones: Business—BW3741 (6 lines).

Vol. 1, No. 1.　　SYDNEY, MONDAY, MAY 12, 1941.　　PRICE, 2d.

HITLER ENRAGED BY R.A.F.

All-Night London Raid As Savage Reprisal

WESTMINSTER ABBEY HIT

From F. E. BAUME, Daily Mirror European Correspondent.

LONDON, Monday.—Authentic reports reaching here by neutral channels indicate that Hitler's alarm at the severity of R.A.F. raids on Germany was responsible for the savage Nazi attack on London on Saturday night. A high British official told me last night: "The Nazi wails when Berlin is bombed indicate this, but, believe me, the real blitz on Berlin will come later."

THIS is supported by a Moscow message which says that Colonel Zhuravlef, writing in the Red Army paper Red Star, declares that the R.A.F. is approaching parity with the Luftwaffe. He also gives a list of bombed German towns.

Saturday night's raid on the British capital, which the Londoners take in their gallant stride, is actually Hitler's method of attempting to answer the R.A.F.'s summer offensive, which is steadily growing in intensity.

Powerful forces of the British Bomber Command blasted shipyards and industrial areas at Hamburg (Germany) on Saturday night, while other units raided Berlin, Emden (Germany), and Rotterdam (Holland).

Westminster Abbey and Hall, Big Ben, the House of Commons, the House of Lords, the British Museum, a children's hospital, and a prison were among places bombed by the Germans on Saturday night.

Big Ben, although blackened and scarred, still chimes, but the roof of the Abbey has fallen in, its Deanery has been burned down, its pulpit destroyed. The debating chamber of the Commons is in ruins and the Museum has been damaged by fire bombs.

Grim Revenge Sought

CIVILIAN casualties are heavy and much damage has been done to other churches, hospitals, flats and houses. But the London crowds want a grim revenge. They are becoming as bitter as the people of Clydeside, for this is on the home front—a civilians' war.

The spirit of these Londoners is magnificent. By 9 a.m. yesterday, thousands who had not had a minute's sleep during the night of hell were on their way to church, digging their gardens, preparing the Sunday dinner, helping the homeless, or giving the dog a walk.

Practically the full available strength of the German Air Force was used in the raid; the official total of 33 raiders shot down is still regarded as the minimum.

Hitler could not send a real force anywhere else in Britain on Saturday night, so our attacks against Berlin are making him groggy. A few raiders appeared over south-east and south-west England, and East Anglia, but damage was small and casualties few.

In this greatest night battle of the war, French and Czech airmen fought alongside their British comrades. Loveliest of all the amazing scenes were the blazing Nazi bombers spiralling to earth in the brilliant moonlight.

It is almost certain that Australian and New Zealand pilots were members of one fighter force which shot down four raiders and kept three intelligence officers busy taking down notes on its success.

An alert was sounded just before midnight yesterday, when 120 raiders heading for London were driven off by our fighters. Three of them were shot down.

(See Baume in Thick of London Blitz, Page 6.)

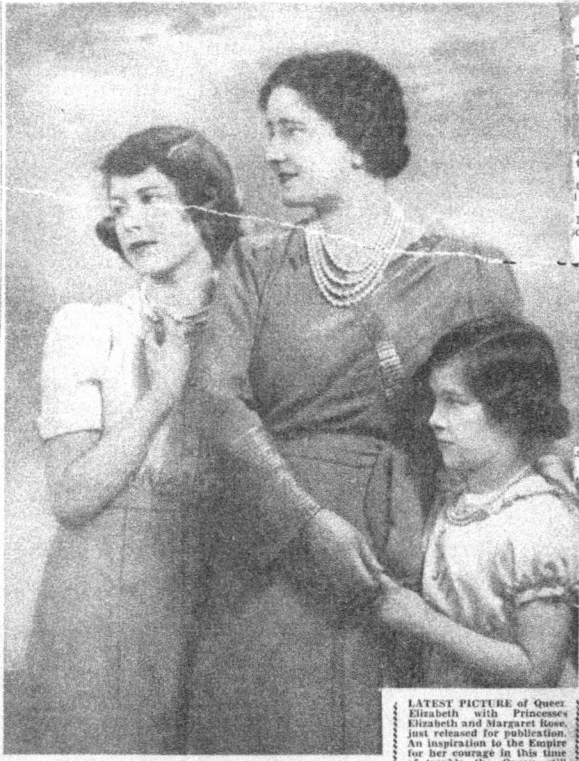

LATEST PICTURE of Queen Elizabeth with Princesses Elizabeth and Margaret Rose, just released for publication. An inspiration to the Empire for her courage in this time of trouble, the Queen still finds time to be a devoted mother.

American Food For Britain In Giant Bombers—Page 3

Inside, the *Daily Mirror* was 'busting with war news'.[47] It relied upon an independent cable service, and the services of Eric Baume, once a protégé of RC Packer's and a former editor of the *Sunday Sun*. Baume was a flamboyant bon vivant and 'incorrigible showoff'.[48] His unconventional method of foreign newsgathering consisted of holing himself up in the Savoy Hotel in London where he picked up information by socialising with visitors and dignitaries (the Savoy was a base for 'international correspondents based in London, and a favourite watering hole for well-connected military and foreign-office types').[49] Baume famously scooped the *Sun* on Germany's invasion of Russia using information he received from Lady Oxford, a fellow guest at the Savoy, who had heard about German troop movements from Churchill.

Baume later said about Norton that 'Before you joined him he was all politeness. Once you had joined him it was all fear and you became his body-servant. I loathed every bit of my service with him.'[50] Norton's staff worked in 'spartan conditions', where chairs and typewriters 'were in short supply'.[51] They tried to adequately express what Norton wanted to say lest they receive a volley of abuse. When Norton was 'displeased by anything in editorial, news item or advertisement', he would ring up 'with a roar' and have the stop press button behind the editor's chair pushed. This would bring people scurrying about 'in all directions to right the wrong'.[52] As to what Norton wanted to say in terms of politics, Labor MPs and union leaders had been among those who sent their heartiest public congratulations on the new paper.

Victorian Labor leader John Cain was glad that there would be an 'independent voice' in 'these days of chain newspapers', while the

FIGURE 16.1 The first edition of the *Sun*'s worst nightmare, the *Daily Mirror*, 12 May 1941

SOURCE *Daily Mirror*, 12 May 1941, p. 1.

secretary of the Melbourne Trades Hall Council said, although it would 'not be a real Labor paper ... I hope it will supply news more informative to the Labor mind than is now available in the afternoon newspaper field'.[53] Norton's political views were pragmatic and inconsistent. Critics charged that he supported whoever he felt would be most useful to him. Although the *Daily Mirror* would come to be considered the most Labor-leaning of the daily commercial papers, it was not uniformly pro-Labor. It swung between both major parties, advocating a strong vote for one and then the other, even when elections were only one or two years apart (see Tables 3.1 and 3.2, pages 118–19 and 122–23, but note that 1958 was the last election the *Daily Mirror* covered while still owned by Norton).

Sydney's newsboys now called out '*Sun* or the *Mirror!*' to homebound commuters. The newcomer did not necessarily play by the rules. When the *Sun* published photographs of survivors from a German shipwreck off the West Australian coast, the *Daily Mirror* photographed the *Sun*'s images and included them in its own next edition. Aside from lots of photographs and war news, the populist, outspoken *Daily Mirror* also included political cartoons, jokes and sporting caricatures.

As the other Sydney owners had feared, because the government had allowed the *Daily Mirror* to begin at a time of forced paper rationing, and when there was such strong demand for news on the war, the new paper had been given almost a government-guaranteed road to early success. Walker said the *Daily Mirror* had the 'rare, if not unique, distinction of making a profit in its first year'.[54] Its circulation was over 145 000 by August 1942.[55] When it appeared, the market value of Associated Newspaper's shares dropped dramatically, its profits in 1941–42 'were the lowest for ten years', and sales of the *Sun* dropped from 229 102 in March 1941 to 189 874 a year later.[56] The *Sun* was the only major paper whose circulation

PUZZLED PUNTERS
AT RANDWICK

■ MR. FRED SMITH ("Mr. Constable") and MR. FRANK PACKER ■ snapped in pensive mood at Randwick yesterday. Mr. Packer will very shortly be leaving for overseas service.

FIGURE 16.2 *Truth* lampoons Frank Packer's military service, 1941
SOURCE *Truth* (Sydney), 14 September 1941, p. 25.

in 1941 was less than in 1933.[57] By the end of the war, the *Daily Mirror*'s circulation had overtaken the *Sun*'s. Not until the mid-1950s did the *Sun* manage to claw back the lead, and this was only by a slim margin before the *Daily Mirror* pulled out in front again in the mid-1960s.[58]

Associated Newspapers' financial position improved after the initial shock, but over the long term, the 'virile competition' that Norton had promised drained his rival. The paper had been significantly advantaged by its wartime launch. Hunger for war news, and strict rationing that meant advertisers were limited in other outlets, made it immediately viable. A disgruntled Warwick Fairfax complained to Menzies that 'in peace-time' the *Daily Mirror* 'would not have had a dog's chance'. He said that it was only because of newsprint rationing that advertisers like David Jones, General Motors and others 'who would sell their soul for the extra column or two in the [*Sydney Morning Herald*] which we have not got to give them, are flocking into the *Daily Mirror*', sending its 'share of retail advertising jump[ing] from nothing to 25%'.[59]

Although busy with the new paper, Truth and Sportsman Ltd still found time to carry on Norton's feud with Packer. After Packer was made a lieutenant in the 1st Armoured Brigade and sent for training at Puckapunyal, north of Melbourne, in 1941, *Truth* delighted in pointing out how Packer's military service did not hamper his social life or business commitments. It published photographs of Packer in uniform at the races, 'out and about' in Melbourne in his 'cute beret', and eating oyster mornay at the exclusive Menzies hotel.[60] *Truth* also sarcastically drew attention to his lack of service near any active conflict zone, captioning one photo 'Captain Packer will be leaving for the front shortly' (see also Figure 16.2).[61]

FAIRFAX'S FURY

Menzies so admired the *Sydney Morning Herald*'s political reporter, Eric McLoughlin, that, two weeks before he announced the date of the 1940 election, he asked Warwick Fairfax if he could 'borrow' McLoughlin for two months, but Fairfax refused, saying they could not 'spare' him.[62] Soon enough the company was glad to see the back of their once star political reporter because, when the *Sydney Morning Herald* started turning on Menzies before the election, McLoughlin did not. He remained steadfastly supportive of Menzies in his Monday commentary, which his *Sydney Morning Herald* superiors judged to be 'resent[ing] and resist[ing] direction'.[63] McLoughlin was allowed to stay for the election, but after a series of incidents that underlined his distress at the change in policy, McLoughlin was recalled from Canberra and banished to Moscow, via London.

McLoughin's successor was Ross Gollan, who was far more critical of Menzies and very friendly with Fadden. While Menzies was away, Gollan 'subtly buil[t] up the notion' that Fadden had proved himself during Menzies' absence 'as the coming leader of the Government', and managed to convince *Sydney Morning Herald* management that it was true.[64] Fadden was one of the many who had been wounded by Menzies' cruel wit. At a farewell function for Menzies hosted by journalists, Fadden had been called upon to say a few words. Speech making was not one of his strong suits and Menzies verbally cut him down in front of the gathered journalists. According to Fraser, 'From that day [Fadden] was ready to see the criticisms of Menzies mount in the *Sydney Morning Herald* and to provide some of the ammunition which Ross Gollan used and [his paper] published'.[65]

After an absence of four months, Menzies returned to Australia on 24 May 1941. In June, Harrison announced the more drastic newsprint restriction of 60 per cent. Fairfax & Sons was outraged and believed the cut was deeper than even Harrison's own department considered necessary. For several days in early July, the *Sydney Morning Herald* carried out a public argument with Harrison. It attacked his action, then published his defence under the heading 'MR HARRISON TRIES TO EVADE THE FACTS: ANOTHER MISLEADING STATEMENT', and put its rebuttal underneath.[66]

On 17 July 1941, an irate Warwick Fairfax wrote to Menzies, 'My dear Bob':

After the last elections you told us pretty plainly what you thought of us … The time has now come to return the compliment. You have allowed one of your Ministers to perpetuate the most outrageous series of injustices that the [Sydney Morning Herald] has suffered in 110 years. You have allowed him to sabotage the work of four generations, and to emasculate one of the greatest forces for good in the public life of Australia ... the Minister's case, from the very beginning when a licence was first granted to 'Truth', is as rotten as a worm-eaten log.[67]

Fairfax wanted Harrison to resign or be sacked, saying 'Individuals are seldom indispensable, great institutions are'.[68] Menzies reply, to 'My dear Warwick', was equally forthright. He said 'although my personal relations with yourself and [editor] Hugh McClure Smith have always been very pleasant, it has been clear for nearly two years that politically you would prefer to see me sitting in opposition'. Menzies said he would not 'abandon' Eric Harrison, whom he considered an 'honest', 'hard-working and conscientious' minister.[69] (Howard Beale, another minister who later served under Menzies, said that, despite their different personalities and backgrounds, 'Menzies loved Harrison' and Harrison was 'devoted to Menzies'.[70])

Menzies said he was 'frankly ... at a loss to understand' why the Sydney Morning Herald considered itself so special when all the papers were making 'the sacrifice' of newsprint restrictions. He said, speaking 'as an outsider', it seemed that the Sydney Morning Herald would be making more money than before the war because less newsprint meant lower costs, its circulation had increased, its advertising was still 'buoyant', and it had been allowed to increase its price.[71] Menzies was right. The Sydney Morning Herald's before-tax profits had leapt from £119 500 in 1938 to £286 500 in 1941.[72] This information was not publicly known, because Fairfax & Sons was not a public company so did not have to disclose it, but Menzies had more than an inkling.

Menzies also issued a veiled threat that he was considering holding a Royal Commission into newsprint rationing but it would have to look into the finances of the respective papers. He knew that Fairfax & Sons would not want their embarrassingly large wartime profits disclosed because it looked like war profiteering.

Two days after Menzies' robust response, the *Sydney Morning Herald* published its most critical editorial yet. For the first time, it seriously suggested that Menzies' party should be thinking of a 'better alternative to Mr Menzies ... After two years of war the political position in this country is more than ever a source of weakness and a matter for shame.' It said that 'Mr Fadden's name has been mentioned'.[73]

Warwick Fairfax then sent Menzies a private, six-page letter explaining in great detail why the *Sydney Morning Herald* was so special. But, first, he told Menzies that:

> I do not think it is fair ... to describe our attitude to you as
> one of opposition. It was intended as constructive and critical
> support ... If you had ever been in [New South Wales] at a time
> when the '[*Sydney Morning*] *Herald*' was trying to turn out a
> really bad Government you would, I can assure you, soon see
> the difference![74]

Fairfax said the *Sydney Morning Herald* was special because it was a 'paper of record' like *The Times*, and had to include material that had no commercial benefit, such as law reports, legal notices, long reports of parliamentary debates, and university examination results, because this information was needed by the community and expected by *Sydney Morning Herald* readers. Combined with this, the *Sydney Morning Herald* had what Fairfax described as 'the problem, unique within Australia, of a monopoly of classified advertising' (this was a 'problem' other papers longed to have). He said

'You cannot ration or hold over classified advertising as you can display advertising, and to attempt to do so would threaten the mass goodwill upon which it is built up'.[75]

As Fairfax noted, 'Classified advertising is the foundation of the whole of the financial structure of the [*Sydney Morning Herald*]'.[76] The problem was, and Fairfax attached figures to demonstrate, due to rationing, the *Sydney Morning Herald* had cut its news columns to the bone to fit in the all-important classifieds. More than half the paper, 62 per cent, was now advertisements. But the *Sydney Morning Herald*'s rivals – the new *Daily Mirror* and the *Daily Telegraph* – were winning audiences over because they were not stuffed with ads. Three-quarters of their content was still devoted to news. (The *Sun* was less of a threat because it was over 50 per cent ads too, retail ads being its speciality.[77])

The most revealing part of Fairfax's letter was his admission that he was not concerned about a loss of money, but a loss of 'power'. Fairfax ended his letter by saying that: 'the power of the [*Sydney Morning Herald*], for good or evil, which has been entrusted to my care, is the greatest thing in my life ... I must admit honestly that the prospect of this power being weakened ... has moved me very profoundly'.[78]

The conflict between the country's oldest newspaper and its prime minister soon became public. One of Menzies' disgruntled colleagues leaked an account of what Menzies said at the 28 July parliamentary UAP meeting. Menzies told his colleagues that a 'very influential newspaper' (which he did not name) was one of the country's biggest war profiteers, but even though it was making enormous profits even under newsprint rationing, it had pressured him to remove a minister and then attacked him when he had refused to 'bow down' before it.[79] The *Sydney Morning Herald* then outed itself as the unnamed paper and accused the Commonwealth Prices Branch of leaking confidential information about its profits (which it had supplied during negotiations over its pricing).[80]

Menzies replied that no public official had leaked any information and challenged the *Sydney Morning Herald* to prove him wrong about its finances by publicly releasing its annual profit statements. The paper did not accept this challenge but, in his long letter to Menzies, Fairfax had pointed out that the Menzies government did not mind BHP making large profits from the war so why should it begrudge Fairfax & Sons?[81]

PUSHING MENZIES OUT

While Menzies had been away, some of his UAP colleagues had been plotting against him, and Gollan had been building Fadden up. Menzies' public popularity sank even lower when he returned to Australia and delivered a tone-deaf 'hectoring, lecturing speech to the nation' that implied Australians were not doing enough for the war effort.[82] Menzies' relationship with the press gallery also deteriorated because he cancelled the practice of holding two press conferences a day, one timed for the morning papers, and one for the afternoon dailies. Menzies said that two per day was too much for a wartime leader and it was not expected in the United States or the United Kingdom. He moved to holding one per day, alternated to suit morning and evening deadlines. Eventually, some brave party operative told the prime minister that there was 'pointed criticism of you ... In my time here, Mr Bruce, Mr Scullin and Mr Lyons held two Press Conferences every day ... I am bound to say that your aloofness is not meeting this problem effectively. That is not being cheeky. It is merely being frank.'[83]

Menzies believed the *Sydney Morning Herald* was carrying out a vendetta over newsprint and its commercial interests, while the

Daily Telegraph was also 'helping to destabilise his leadership'.[84] The *Daily Telegraph*'s potency had been increased by its new editor from early 1941, the brilliant but ruthless Brian Penton, who 'had a gift for incisive and pungent writing'.[85] Bridget Griffen-Foley noted that Menzies 'privately complained about the "crapulous" actions of Packer's newspaper and described it as a "rag"'.[86] But Menzies was also unhappy with the Murdoch press and, in the week before he resigned, banned the *Herald*'s Joe Alexander from attending any of his interviews or press conferences.

At the 28 August Cabinet meeting, multiple ministers voiced their belief that a new leader was needed. Recognising that he had lost the support of a majority of his Cabinet, Menzies announced his resignation. (Eric Harrison, still Menzies' loyal ally, had burst in late and demanded, 'Boss, what are they doing to you?'[87])

Fadden succeeded Menzies as prime minister. Allan Fraser considered this Gollan's handiwork, that Gollan 'built [Fadden] for and into the position ... a journalistic first in Australia'.[88] But Gollan only 'enjoyed the kudos of a successful king-maker' for forty days.[89] The instability had continued under Fadden and two Victorian-based independents voted against his budget, paving the way for Labor's John Curtin to become prime minister on 7 October 1941.

Menzies was not the first politician to believe that the press had been out to 'kill' him. Nor would he be the last. One journalist and executive who knew from the inside how the press proprietors operated was Colin Bednall. He was Keith Murdoch's right-hand man, but also worked for Frank Packer, and for the *Argus*. Bednall saw all of the major owners and executives up close, including RAG Henderson and the HWT's John Williams (who succeeded Murdoch as managing director/chairman of the HWT). Bednall observed that the newspaper emperors:

were always talking of having somebody killed. The victim
might be a politician, a trades union official or an industrialist
or some former employee who had got too big for their comfort.
For them 'to kill' was not actual murder, but close to it. They
might destroy a man's public image, strip him of power or
deprive him of his living.[90]

POSTSCRIPT

When Curtin became prime minister in 1941, the newspaper owners again had to deal with a Labor government. Even worse for them, after Labor won the 1943 election, Curtin appointed the press nemesis, Arthur Calwell, as the new minister for information. Calwell's fiery clashes with press owners led all the way to the High Court.

Murdoch, to compensate for his overzealous attempts at government control of the press in 1940, became an anti-censorship warrior, but also a frustrated armchair general who was on the outer when Labor was in power. Murdoch was still convinced in 1942 that Menzies' 'gifts are very superficial and … he cannot lead this country', but he came to see Menzies as a lesser evil than dealing with Labor.[1]

The *Daily Telegraph* was also highly critical of the Labor government, and Packer became a staunch and long-term admirer of Menzies. Warwick Fairfax's relationship with Menzies recovered to be cordial, if not as warm as it once had been (but then a long rapprochement between them was again shattered in 1961).

Menzies reformed the non-Labor side of politics in 1944–45 in a way that met with the major newspaper owners' approval, and led to the end of the UAP and the formation of a new Liberal Party in 1944–45. By the time he regained prime ministerial office in 1949, Menzies had learned how to live with the newspaper proprietors, and also how to draw the confidence of the public and his colleagues. He went on to win seven consecutive elections, and ruled for that record sixteen-year term, until January 1966.

By then, Associated Newspapers was no more. Norton's 'peculiar, twisted genius' was extinguished from newspapers. And Murdoch's son, Rupert, the underestimated 'boy publisher', was taking the media world by storm – first in Australia, and then internationally. Rupert was intent on grasping the mighty HWT, the empire his father had built up, and he achieved that in 1987. He also ushered in a new phase of press baron–influenced politics with an Australian flavour that he exported to the United Kingdom, United States and other countries, and which drew upon many of the techniques his father had put into practice.

The expansion of Fairfax in the 1950s and 1960s positioned it to survive alongside Rupert Murdoch's News Limited/News Corporation in Australia as the two remaining press-centred mass media empires by the 1990s. Packer had left the daily newspaper business in 1972 to focus on television.

Television's profitability and impact took the newspaper industry to new heights of power and influence between the mid-1950s and the mid-1980s, opening the way for expansion of the small number of remaining newspaper empires. But the industry's attitude to other new technology remained fearful. In the same defensive way that owners had approached radio – with what Rodney Tiffen called a determination to 'hold back ... the march of history' – they would also approach digital television, cable television, the internet and streaming television, with dire consequences.[2]

Back when Menzies resigned in 1941, the immediate concern for newspaper owners was not technology. It was power, as Warwick Fairfax acknowledged. Newspapers had long sought to influence the biggest policy issues of their time – including conscription, industrial relations, economic policy, the Depression and wartime administration – but they had been particularly active whenever any public policy would have an impact upon their commercial success. The papers had been active players, including in lobbying for subsidies for special postage and telegraphic rates, seeking protective tariffs for industries with which they were allied, shaping the nature of radio broadcasting, and obtaining government assistance for new commercial ventures such as paper production. They had also actively lobbied for, or against, particular parties, individual politicians and leaders. Throughout this time press proprietors told newspaper readers and the general public that their papers were just neutral, impartial observers of politics. They would still be claiming this for decades to come.

APPENDIX: BIOGRAPHIES OF KEY NEWSPAPERS

These thumbnail sketches focus on the major newspapers discussed in this book, including what has happened to them since 1942 (up to 2018). Newspapers that began after 1942 are not included.

The *Advertiser* (Adelaide): Began in 1858. A morning broadsheet with a bolder format than most, a strong local identity and, as the name suggests, a large number of classified advertisements. The *Advertiser* was an influential paper in South Australia, especially after 1931, when it was in a monopoly position in the morning market after the closure of the *Register*. It was controlled by the Herald and Weekly Times (HWT) from 1929 until 1987 when Rupert Murdoch's News Corporation took over the HWT.

The Age (Melbourne): Began in 1854. A morning broadsheet with a large, lucrative share of classified advertising. Under owner David Syme, it pushed social liberal causes, was dubbed the 'worker's paper', and considered vibrant and influential. After Syme's death in 1908, *The Age* stagnated in both editorial outlook and physical design. By the 1920s, it had a reputation for being staid and for pursuing idiosyncratic causes. It underwent a period of rejuvenation in the mid- to late 1960s. Fairfax & Sons bought shares in the paper's owner in 1966, took a controlling interest from 1972, and bought the remaining shares in 1983. It changed to a 'compact' size in 2013.

The *Argus* (Melbourne): Began in 1846, closed 1957. In the late 19th and early 20th centuries, the *Argus* was a prestigious morning broadsheet. Read by the Melbourne establishment, it was the voice of conservatism, and a paper of record with long, unvarying and unemotional columns. By the 1930s and 1940s, the paper was in financial trouble. In 1949, it was purchased by London's Daily Mirror Group and dramatically altered to a chatty, pro-Labor tabloid. It was purchased and closed down by the HWT in 1957.

The *Canberra Times*: Begun in 1926 by the Shakespeare family – committed federalists who wanted the paper to take a national approach to political issues. It began as a weekly then changed to a morning broadsheet. It shifted to a tabloid size in 1956–64, reverted to broadsheet size from 1964 to 2016, and then became a tabloid again. The paper was acquired by Fairfax & Sons in 1964, but then had various owners from 1987 until 2007, when Fairfax Media became the owners again upon merging with Rural Press Ltd.

The *Courier-Mail* (Brisbane): The morning broadsheet *Courier-Mail* was formed in 1933, when Keith Murdoch and the shadowy entrepreneur John Wren amalgamated two Brisbane newspapers (the *Brisbane Courier* and the *Daily Mail*). The *Courier-Mail* was known for its political conservatism, but also for being a unique hybrid of the traditional and sensational. Keith Murdoch was one of its largest shareholders at his death in 1952 and wanted it to be part of his son Rupert's inheritance, but the HWT acquired the paper in 1953. Rupert Murdoch regained it in 1987 when his News Corporation took over the HWT. The paper did not change to a tabloid size until 2006.

The *Daily Guardian* (Sydney): Began in 1923, closed 1931. A morning tabloid pictorial that combined the witty, irreverent patriotism of

Smith's Weekly with the visual style of the *Sun News-Pictorial*. Under Robert Clyde (RC) Packer, the paper used various circulation-boosting ideas including beauty contests, competitions, free insurance and sensational crime reporting. Already struggling during the Depression, the paper was purchased by Associated Newspapers in 1930. It lost its vigour and populist touch, and in 1931, was merged with its stablemate, the *Daily Telegraph*.

The *Daily Mirror* (Sydney): Began 1941, merged 1990, expired 1996. An afternoon tabloid controversially launched by Ezra Norton in 1941 despite wartime newsprint rationing. It immediately posed a challenge to the *Sun*, setting off decades of vigorous competition between the two papers. The *Daily Mirror* was taken over, with some secrecy, by Fairfax & Sons in 1958 and then sold to Rupert Murdoch in 1960. Under Murdoch, its content became more sensational and less family-oriented. It championed the page-three girl. It was merged with the *Daily Telegraph* in 1990. In 1996 the *Daily Telegraph-Mirror* reverted to being the *Daily Telegraph*, thus removing the last trace of the *Daily Mirror*.

The *Daily News* (Perth): A broadsheet launched in 1882 with antecedents from 1840 that became an afternoon tabloid. Closed in 1990. The paper was purchased by News Limited in 1926, which sold it to West Australian Newspapers Limited (WAN) in 1935. Under James Macartney (editor from 1936 to 1951), the paper shifted to a more lively format with frequent updates, including 'stop press' sporting results. The paper's columnists, cartoonists, crime stories and women's pages were also distinctive. The HWT formally took over WAN in 1969. The paper had several owners in the corporate chaos of the late-1980s, including Alan Bond and Robert Holmes à Court, before it was closed.

The *Daily Telegraph* (Sydney): Launched in 1879. Originally a morning broadsheet, it pioneered a lighter, brighter style that saw its circulation overtake that of its rival, the *Sydney Morning Herald*, by the end of the 1880s. The paper later changed owners and took on various incarnations. In the 1920s, this included a tabloid pictorial format, then several more variations of its name and layout, including going back to a broadsheet between 1931 and 1942. Neglected and starved of funding, the paper received fresh attention in 1936 when Hugh Denison's company went into partnership with EG Theodore and Frank Packer. It moved permanently to a tabloid format in 1942 and was purchased by Rupert Murdoch in 1972.

The *Evening News* (Sydney): Founded in 1867 by Samuel Bennett Ltd. Closed 1931. An afternoon broadsheet that converted to a tabloid. Originally lively and popular, by the 1910s, it had a reputation for dull presentation. It was revitalised from 1922 under new managing editor Errol Knox, and pioneered the use of crossword puzzles in Australia. Under Knox, the paper's circulation doubled in less than a year but its owners still lacked capital for land and a new building. In 1929, Bennett merged his company with Denison's, but after Depression-era competition took its toll, the paper was closed.

The *Evening Star* (Melbourne): Began 1933. Closed 1936. The *Evening Star* was another ill-fated attempt to beat the *Herald*. An afternoon tabloid begun by the *Argus'* owners, the *Star* featured a distinctive green-tinged newsprint and art deco format. Although it had excellent news, sport and society coverage, and imitated the large striking photographs and bold headlines of the popular *Sun News-Pictorial*, in a fragile Depression-era newspaper market, the *Star* was unable to compete with the popular *Herald* and was closed after only two and a half years.

The *Evening Sun* (Melbourne): Launched in 1923. Closed in 1925. Hugh Denison launched the afternoon broadsheet in order to compete directly against the *Herald* but his pink-papered *Evening Sun* was too brash for the sedate Melbourne market. It could not match the sales of the *Herald*, and after two years, the *Evening Sun* was losing money, cancelling out profits made from Denison's more successful *Sun News-Pictorial*. Denison closed the *Evening Sun* in 1925 and exited the Melbourne market.

The *Herald* (Melbourne): Began in 1840, merged in 1990. An afternoon broadsheet sold on city street corners to afternoon shoppers and evening commuters, the *Herald* outlived several rivals and was in a dominant position in Melbourne by the 1930s. It had a bold format and snappy presentation with extensive sports coverage, prominent department store advertising and added features sections. Although politically conservative, the *Herald* was a pioneer in popular news formats but it was also known for its strong news coverage and considered a more serious afternoon paper than those in other cities. It was controlled by the HWT until 1987 when Rupert Murdoch's News Corporation took over the HWT. It was merged with the *Sun News-Pictorial* in 1990 to become the morning *Herald-Sun*.

The *Labor Daily* (Sydney): Began in 1922 as the official organ of the Australian Labor Party. Closed 1941. The *Labor Daily* was known for its popular sports coverage and was the first paper to introduce a free form guide for the horse races. Politically, the paper was a strong supporter of Jack Lang, NSW Labor premier from 1925 to 1927 and 1930 to 1932. Lang contributed financially to the paper and strongly influenced its content. The paper became a 'political football' amid bitter in-fighting in the Labor Party, and this lessened its credibility, appeal and profitability. Its name was changed to the *Daily News* in 1938. In 1941, it was taken over by Frank Packer's *Daily Telegraph* and closed.

The *Mercury* (Hobart): A morning broadsheet begun in 1854 by former convict John Davies and a partner. Davies soon became the sole owner and his family continued to be associated with the paper for more than a century. It was known for its strong local content in a news-pictorial presentation. In 1962, the HWT purchased a large shareholding in the *Mercury*'s parent company, which it increased to give it effective control of the *Mercury* from 1963. Rupert Murdoch gained that majority holding when he acquired the HWT in 1987.

The *News* (Adelaide): Launched 1923. Closed 1992. An afternoon broadsheet that became a tabloid in 1948. It was launched by Gerald Mussen and journalist James Edward Davidson, but their powerful backers are discussed in this book. The HWT under Keith Murdoch gained control of the company in 1931. Around 1948–49, Murdoch convinced the HWT to sell its shares in the paper's owning company, News Limited, to him personally. When Keith Murdoch died in 1952 his son Rupert inherited the *News* and used it as a base to found an international media empire. News Limited became a subsidiary of Rupert Murdoch's News Corporation. The *News* was the last paid afternoon newspaper in Australia when it was closed in 1992.

The *Register* (Adelaide): First published under an earlier title in 1836. Closed in 1931. The *Register* was considered a high-quality and influential newspaper by the 1880s. In 1928, a syndicate led by Keith Murdoch arranged for the takeover of the *Register*. Converting the broadsheet to a more sensational pictorial tabloid, Murdoch used it as a competitive threat to successfully pressure Sir Langdon Bonython into selling him the *Advertiser* in 1929. Once Murdoch's HWT had the *Advertiser*, it closed the *Register* in 1931.

Smith's Weekly (Sydney/national): Launched in 1919 by Sir James Joynton Smith, Claude McKay and RC Packer. Closed 1950. A weekly tabloid published in Sydney but read nationally. It flamboyantly took up the cause of the 'common man', the 'underdog' and returned World War I diggers (one of its key markets), and prided itself on being irreverent, funny and anti-authority. It was also chauvinistic, nationalistic and fiercely anti-communist. It included lively cartoons, illustrations and vivid artwork, and mixed satire, controversial opinions, and sporting and financial news. Unable to meet rising costs and with a new owner more interested in the real estate owned by the business than its journalism, *Smith's Weekly* closed in 1950.

The *Sun* (Sydney): Began 1910. Closed 1988. An afternoon broadsheet launched by Hugh Denison from the ashes of the *Australian Star* (1887–1910). Designed by talented staff including its foundation editor, Montague Grover. The *Sun* had front-page news, a striking pictorial emphasis, and sensational coverage of 'human interest' and crime news. After the closure of the *Evening News* in 1931, it became Sydney's sole afternoon paper and was known for being jam-packed with retail advertisements. In May 1941, the *Sun* lost its lucrative monopoly position when Ezra Norton launched the *Daily Mirror*. The *Sun* became a tabloid in 1947. In 1953, Fairfax & Sons took control of it. A victim of the death of afternoon papers in the late 1980s, the *Sun* closed in 1988.

The *Sun News-Pictorial* (Melbourne): Launched by Hugh Denison in 1922. Merged in 1990. A morning tabloid and Australia's first dedicated pictorial newspaper. Its design was the brainchild of Montague Grover and included bold front-page headlines, novel photographs and easy-to-digest news coverage in a tabloid format. It was instantly popular, but hampered financially by Denison's decision to launch the loss-making *Evening Sun* and was sold to the HWT in 1925. During the late 1920s and 1930s, many newspapers in Australia attempted to imitate the *Sun News-Pictorial*, but its circulation figures were never matched. It remained controlled by the HWT until 1987, when Rupert Murdoch's News Corporation took over the HWT. In 1990, it was merged with the *Herald* to form the *Herald-Sun*.

The *Sydney Morning Herald* (Sydney): Founded in 1831, and Australia's oldest continually published newspaper. A serious and earnest morning broadsheet with self-declared 'old-fashioned' values and a conservative stance, the *Sydney Morning Herald* gained a lucrative grip on classified advertising in Sydney. It was owned by the Fairfax family for five generations, and with Warwick Fairfax in charge for forty-seven years, from 1930 to 1977. The Fairfax family considered the paper a force for public good, with a moral and educative purpose. It was styled as a 'paper of record' with detailed reports on parliament and courts, and authoritative reporting on general political, international and business news. After a disastrous takeover bid by one of Sir Warwick's sons in 1987, the Fairfax family lost control of the *Sydney Morning Herald*'s parent company. It ended up in receivership in 1990, and was then re-floated. It was controlled by Canadian Conrad Black for a period but was later owned by a range of shareholders including investment groups. The *Sydney Morning Herald* changed to a 'compact' size in 2013.

The *Telegraph* (Brisbane): First published 1872. An afternoon broadsheet until 1948, then a tabloid until it closed in 1988. The *Telegraph* was considered less serious than the *Courier-Mail*. Its Saturday evening sports edition was printed on distinctive pink newsprint. In 1955, the HWT bought a majority interest in the *Telegraph*. Rupert

Murdoch gained that majority holding when he acquired the HWT in 1987. The paper was closed in 1988.

The *West Australian*: Claims to be the second oldest surviving newspaper in Australia, dating, through several changes of title, back to 1833, although that claim has not been universally accepted. A morning broadsheet, it became a tabloid in 1949. The paper was known for its strong local content and staunch conservatism. Formerly owned by Sir Winthrop Hackett, it was purchased in 1926 by WAN – a syndicate involving Keith Murdoch, WL Baillieu, WS Robinson and the *Herald* board. It has been claimed that Murdoch disposed of the syndicate's interest in the early 1930s, but the HWT seems to have remained involved for some time. The HWT took formal ownership of the paper in 1969. In the late 1980s, WAN was sold to Robert Holmes à Court and then Alan Bond. It was re-floated as a public company in 1991–92. Owned by Seven West Media, the *West Australian* in 2018 was the only metropolitan daily in Australia that was not owned by either Fairfax Media or News Corporation.

NOTES

ABBREVIATIONS

ADB	*Australian Dictionary of Biography*
AJCP	Australian Joint Copying Project
ANU	Australian National University
ASIC	Australian Securities and Investments Commission
BHAS	Broken Hill Associated Smelters
CPD	*Commonwealth Parliamentary Debates*
FMBA	Fairfax Media Business Archive (Mitchell Library)
HR	House of Representatives
HWT	Herald and Weekly Times
KM	Keith Murdoch
NAA	National Archives of Australia
NLA	National Library of Australia
PROV	Public Record Office Victoria
SMH	*Sydney Morning Herald*
SLNSW	State Library of New South Wales
SRSA	State Records of South Australia
UMA	University of Melbourne Archives

Introduction
1   Bowman, p. 4.
2   Carey, p. 235.
3   Picard, 2009.
4   Letter from John Butters to William Dunstan, 9 February 1945, FMBA, MLMSS9894, box 1230, SLNSW.

5   Kim Lockwood, 'Doing it in style', *In House* (HWT internal magazine), July–
         September 1988, p. 9.
6   Williams, 2010, p. 126.
7   Tiffen and Gittins, p. 182.
8   Griffen-Foley, 2009, p. 23.
9   Goot, p. 7.
10   Quoted in Petersen, p. 55.

1   **The first days of the Australian 'fourth estate'**
1   Asquith, p. 106; Curran, 1978; Curran, 2006, p. 76.
2   Thank you to James Curran for pointing these trends out to me.
3   Asquith, p. 107.
4   Curran, 2011, pp. 143–45.
5   *SMH*, 29 May 1852, p. 2. James Curran pointed out in an email to the author that
         the *SMH* was too hopeful as individual radical titles continued to flourish until the
         abolition of the stamp duty in 1855.
6   Curran, 2011, p. 147.
7   Curran, 2010a, p. 18; Curran, 1978, pp. 55, 56, 58; Williams, 1978, p. 46.
8   Quoted in Curran, 2010b, p. 21; see also Williams, 1978, p. 46.
9   Kirkpatrick, 2016, p. 8.
10   Walker, 1976, p. 3.
11   *SMH*, 11 April 1935, p. 10.
12   NLA, 2011.
13   *Sydney Gazette and New South Wales Advertiser*, 30 November 1816, p. 2.
14   Holder, 1970, pp. 14–15, 26.
15   Turnbull, p. 315.
16   Woodberry, p. 56.
17   Byrnes.
18   Turnbull, p. 316.
19   Slee.
20   Walker, 1976, pp. 26, 73.
21   Kirkpatrick, 2016, pp. 13–14.
22   *ibid.*, p. 14; *ADB*, 1966.
23   Holder, 1970, pp. 71, 83.
24   Woodberry, p. xxxi.
25   *ibid.*, p. 132.
26   *ibid.*, pp. xxiv, xxx.
27   *Sydney Monitor*, 26 April 1834, p. 2.
28   Ihde, p. xvi.
29   Blair, p. 23.
30   Ihde, p. 26.
31   Persse.
32   *Sydney Gazette and New South Wales Advertiser*, 28 December 1816, p. 1.
33   On the contrary, even the *Australian* induced colonists to be enterprising, to make
         profits for the colony, including from opium exporting, and to aim for 'opulence'.
         (See *Australian*, 20 June 1827, p. 3; 8 August 1827, p. 3 and 9 July 1828, p. 3).
34   Cryle, p. 37.

35   *ADB*, 1967.
36   Walker, 1976, p. 37.
37   *Daily Advertiser*, 18 April 1931, p. 2.
38   *Sydney Mail*, 2 April 1919, p. 8.
39   *Sydney Herald*, 5 September 1831, p. 2.
40   *SMH*, 5 October 1842, p. 2.
41   Walker, 1976, p. 39.
42   *SMH*, 21 March 1844, p. 2.
43   Martin, 1974; Walker, 1976, p. 67.
44   Walker, 1976, pp. 58–59.
45   *Empire*, 23 May 1859, p. 4.
46   Walker, 1976, p. 74.
47   *Herald* prospectus in Younger, 1996, see pp. 39–41.
48   Serle, 1976a.
49   A figure of 20 000 has been published in various sources (including Younger, 1996, p. 23). But the *Argus*, 26 August 1854, p. 4 gives a figure of 15 000.
50   *Argus*, 3 February 1853, p. 4.
51   Younger, 1996, p. 38; Dow.
52   Serle, 1976a.
53   Turnbull, p. 319.
54   *Empire*, 3 September 1856, p. 5.
55   Mayer, p. 18.
56   Walker, 1976, pp. 55, 196; Mayer, p. 18.
57   Walker, 1976, p. 195.
58   *Sydney Mail*, 28 December 1938, p. 6.
59   Walker, 1976, p. 197.
60   *South Australian Register*, 2 January 1850, p. 2.
61   *Bendigo Independent*, 2 September 1904, p. 2; Mayer, pp. 19–20; *Australian Star*, 28 July 1899, p. 3.
62   *South Australian Register*, 2 January 1850, p. 2.
63   See articles in *Australian Financial Review* on 17 February 2014 ('News Corp's $882m blew the budget') and 11 May 2015 ('Rupert Murdoch's News Corp is ATO's top tax risk') and the ABC online on 'Fox Sports' $30m budget funding brought into question'.
64   *Newspaper News*, 1 July 1931, p. 1.
65   *Western Argus*, 7 July 1931, p. 13.
66   *CPD* (HR), 27 October 1933, p. 4032.
67   *ibid.*, 28 August 1957, p. 92.
68   Brown, p. 36.
69   *Mercury*, 2014, p. 2.
70   *Evening Telegraph*, 16 January 1907, p. 2.
71   Conboy, pp. 114, 117; '*West Australian*, 24 August 1935, p. 6.
72   *SMH*, 8 October 2004.
73   *Mercury*, 13 November 1925, p. 6.
74   *ibid.*, 12 April 1910, page 4.
75   *Adelaide Times*, 31 May 1855, p. 2.
76   *The Age*, 17 October 1854, p. 4.

77   *Morning Chronicle*, 9 November 1844, p. 2.
78   *Truth*, 2 October 1904, p. 1; *SMH*, 3 September 1880, p. 3.
79   SA Memory, 'A short history of the *Register* newspaper'.
80   *ibid*.
81   *Daily Telegraph* (Launceston), 2 February 1921, p. 4.
82   *Advertiser*, 16 December 1903, p. 6.
83   Grover, p. 2; Bongiorno, p. 64.
84   *Argus*, 19 November 1903, p. 5.
85   Sayers.
86   Rood.
87   Kirkpatrick, 2016, pp. 34–35.
88   Forell.
89   *ibid*.
90   *Ovens and Murray Advertiser*, 23 August 1879, p. 1.
91   La Nauze quoted in Nolan, 2013, p. 36.
92   Bongiorno, pp. 25, 54, 170.
93   *ibid*, p. 110.
94   E.g. the Brisbane Newspaper Company and the Geelong Newspaper Company.
95   In the United Kingdom, it has been claimed that Northcliffe was 'the first to offer shares in a newspaper company' around 1905 (Williams, 2010, p. 139).
96   Turnbull, p. 321.
97   Johnson.
98   Lloyd, 1985, back cover.
99   *Mercury*, 8 November 1879, p. 2.
100   *SMH*, 6 October 1890, p. 4.
101   McMullin, 2006.
102   *ibid*.
103   The *Advertiser* expressed a different view, saying the Watson government deserved 'a respectful reception', (*Advertiser*, 27 April 1904, p. 4).
104   McMullin, 2006 and 2004.
105   The labour-oriented daily, the *National Advocate*, began in Bathurst in 1889 and later became a fully-fledged Labor paper.
106   Walker, 1980a, p. 72.
107   *Mercury*, 2014, p. 2.

2   **The rise of newspapers**

1   Twopenny.
2   Thank you to Rod Kirkpatrick for assisting me on these points. See also Kirkpatrick, 2016, pp. 31–32; and HRSCPM, 1992, p. 48.
3   Walker, 1976, p. 177.
4   *Lithgow Mercury*, 23 August 1928, p. 2.
5   *Bendigo Independent*, 23 October 1901, p. 2.
6   *Macleay Argus*, 18 January 1954, p. 2.
7   Wiener, p. 59.
8   Younger, 1996, pp. 43, 55–56.
9   *ibid*., 1996, p. 60.
10   Front-page headlines from the *Sun*, 1–5 July 1910.

11   *Sun*, 4 July 1910, p. 1.
12   *Sun*, 4 August 1914, p. 7; and 5 August 1914, p. 9.
13   *ibid.*
14   Roberts, 2015, p. 72.
15   Sun Newspaper annual report synopsis, Minute Book of Sun Newspapers Ltd, 1914–18, FMBA, MLMSS 9894, box 44, SLNSW.
16   *Lithgow Mercury*, 1 March 1918, p. 7.
17   *SMH*, 28 June 1858, p. 3.
18   *Age*, 26 May 1868, p. 4.
19   *Queenslander*, 4 February 1893, p. 237; Walker, 1976, p. 74.
20   Kirkpatrick, 2016, pp. 39, 41.
21   *Australasian*, 29 April 1893, p. 24.
22   *SMH*, 12 January 1893, pp. 1, 6.
23   *ibid.*, 12 July 1893, p. 6.
24   *Mercury*, 2 October 1893, p. 2.
25   Kirkpatrick, 2016, pp. 39, 52.
26   Wiener, p. 192.
27   Blair, pp. 30, 34–35.
28   *Satirist and Sporting Chronicle*, 11 March 1843, p. 3.
29   Mayer, pp. 22–23.
30   E.g. *Daily Telegraph*, 7 January 1890, p. 2; *Adelaide Observer*, 11 January 1890, p. 26.
31   Juergens, p. 41; Smith, p. 160.
32   *SMH*, 9 December 1911, p. 22.
33   Wiener, p. 170.
34   Smith, p. 160.
35   Wiener, p. 170.
36   *SMH*, 7 May 1904, p. 4.
37   Smith, p. 160.
38   *Mercury*, 19 May 1898, p. 3.
39   *Sun*, 2 January 1924, p. 8.
40   Wiener, p. 204.
41   *ibid.*, p. 200.
42   Roberts, 2015, p. 101
43   Wiener, p. 192.
44   Quoted in 'Journalism in the '30s'.
45   *ibid.*
46   Dunstan, 1990, p. 121.
47   *SMH*, 22 March 1988, p. 17.

3   **The age of press empire building**
1   Emery, pp. 459, 701.
2   Lee, 1978, p. 123.
3   Williams, 2010, p. 140.
4   Williams, 2010, p. 125
5   Murray, pp. 11, 17.
6   *ibid.*
7   Mayer, p. 21.

8   *ibid.*, p. 2.
9   Sun Newspaper Ltd Minute Book entry, 1 August 1930, FMBA, MLMSS 9894, box 1730, SLNSW.
10   Younger, 1996, pp. 95, 100.
11   *Newspaper News*, 1 October 1931, p. 11.
12   *ibid.*
13   *ibid.*
14   Tiffen, 2011, p. 35.
15   Wealth as measured by the value of companies' total assets (Ville and Merrett, pp. 33–37).
16   *Sun*, 19 May 1927, p. 13; *Examiner*, 18 November 1929, p. 9.
17   Ville and Merrett, pp. 33–37.
18   Souter, 1981, p. 126.
19   *Sunday Times*, 10 July 1904, p. 5.
20   *Sun*, 24 April 1925, p. 7.
21   Kirkpatrick, 2016, p. 54.
22   *Register*, 18 September 1924, p. 6; *News*, 4 September 1930, p. 14.
23   *Smith's Weekly*, 31 July 1926, p. 16.
24   *ibid.*
25   Corden quoted in Holden, p. 17.
26   The HWT's involvement with Perth daily newspapers is an aspect of HWT history that requires further investigation. Preliminary findings are discussed in later chapters.
27   McKercher, p. 18.
28   Curran, 2010a, p. 328.
29   Calculated using figures for 1937 from Goot, supplemented by circulation figures for the *Canberra Times*. (Associated Newspaper's total includes Consolidated Press in which it was still then a major shareholder.)
30   Goot, pp. 4–6, plus own calculations. (Note this refers to the combined circulation of metropolitan daily newspapers not ownership of individual newspaper titles.)
31   And the trend towards concentration would accelerate in later years, so that, by 2014, one owner (News Limited/News Corporation – which had taken over the HWT in 1987) controlled 63 per cent of Australia's national daily circulation (Tiffen, 2015, p. 66).
32   Lebovic, p. 69.
33   Quoted in Pickard, p. 473.
34   Pickard, p. 476.
35   Emery, p. 462.
36   Temple, p. 32.
37   Bingham, p. 22.
38   Although regional newspaper chain growth continued (Curran and Seaton, pp. 75–76).
39   The new form of press criticism instead came from the right wing of politics and declared a 'liberal' bias in the media (Lebovic, pp. 73–76).
40   Murray, p. 95.
41   *ibid.*
42   The Conference was variously called the Australian Newspaper Conference and the Australian Newspapers' Conference.

43   Souter, 1981, p. 627, note 187.
44   Associated Newspapers advertisement, *Newspaper News*, 2 November 1931, p. 7.
45   *Daily Telegraph* advertisement, *Newspaper News*, 1 July 1938, p. 9.
46   *ibid.*, 1 February 1939, p. 5.
47   Taylor, p. 32.
48   Some of the American papers noticeably increased their political coverage within only a year of commencing (Schudson, p. 21).
49   Greenwall, pp. 56–57.
50   Jewell.
51   Associated Newspapers advertisement, *Newspaper News*, 1 March 1933, p. 5.
52   *ibid.*
53   *Daily Telegraph* advertisement, *Newspaper News*, 1 June 1933, p. 7.
54   Asquith, p. 113.
55   Associated Newspapers advertisement, *Newspaper News*, 2 November 1931, p. 7.
56   *Sun*, 15 October 1929, p. 2.
57   Sun Newspapers, p. 12.
58   *ibid.*, p. 14.
59   *Sun*, 3 September 1914, p. 4.
60   Over its seventy-eight-year history, from 1910 until it was closed in 1988, the *Sun* supported Labor only three times: in 1961, 1984 and 1987. In 1961, it was owned by Fairfax and was caught up in its owner's crusade to bring down Menzies. In 1984 and 1987, its support for Labor was in step with other newspapers which also felt they could support Bob Hawke's pro-business Labor.
61   *Herald*, 29 December 1984, p. 1.
62   *Daily Guardian*, 14 November 1928, p. 8.
63   *Labor Daily* article reproduced in the *Windsor and Richmond Gazette*, 14 May 1926, p. 12.
64   *News*, 13 November 1925, p. 6.
65   See *News*, 1 February 1924, p. 6; and 29 July 1929, p. 6.
66   Murray, p. 93.
67   *SMH*, 12 December 1919, p. 8.
68   Mott, p. 357.
69   Seymour-Ure, pp. 166–67.
70   *Daily Telegraph*, 18 September 1940, p. 1.
71   In 1969, the *Sun* did not publish an election editorial.
72   Nolan, 2013, p. 42.
73   Fitzhardinge, 1983.
74   McNicoll, 1997, p. 36.
75   Gardner, 1932, p. 222.
76   Twopenny (no page number available on this ebook copy of the original).

4   **Hugh Denison: Australia's first newspaper emperor**
1   In 1910, as measured by total assets (Ville and Merrett, p. 33).
2   Denison, p. 29; Walker, 1981.
3   Given, p. 165.
4   Sun Newspapers, pp. 11–12.
5   Presumably these were some of the businessmen board members that the *Star*'s

critics said had captured the paper, making it less progressive than in the past (Walker, 1976, p. 88, 108, 140).

6   *Sun*, 15 October 1929, p. 2.
7   Share registers of Sun Newspaper Company Ltd, 1911-18, FMBA, MLMSS 9894, box 2003x, SLNSW.
8   Sun Newspapers, p. 14; Cannon, 1993, pp. 20–22.
9   Sun Newspapers, p. 15.
10 *ibid.*, p. 16.
11 *West Australian*, 24 August 1935, p. 6.
12 Sun Newspapers, p. 19.
13 *ibid.*, pp. 20–21.
14 Younger, 1999, p. 345.
15 Garden, p. 144. Note that Younger (1996, p. 345) says that JE Davidson played a crucial role in securing early cooperation between the two papers.
16 Garden, p. 144.
17 After a year's service, staff were able to take up employees' shares and the company paid twice the rate of dividend for these shares as it declared for ordinary shares (Sun Newspapers, p. 35).
18 Zwar, p. 52.
19 Verbatim report of extraordinary meeting of shareholders, King's Hall, 12 June 1931, FMBA, MLMSS 9894, box 101, SLNSW.
20 Sun Newspapers, p. 26.
21 *ibid.*
22 *ibid.*, p. 48.
23 Sun Newspaper annual report synopsis, Minute Book of Sun Newspapers Ltd, 1914–18, box 44; and Sun Newspapers Ltd balance sheet, 26 March 1922, FMBA, MLMSS 9894, box 45, SLNSW.
24 Letter from KM to Northcliffe, 30 December 1921, Northcliffe Papers, M 1641, AJCP.
25 'Report of third annual general meeting of Sun Newspapers Ltd, 21 May 1923' in Minute Book, 1922–24, FMBA, MLMSS 9894, box 45, SLNSW.
26 Cannon, 1993, p. 27.
27 *ibid.*
28 *ibid.*, p. 28.
29 Denison, p. 67; Cannon, 1993, p. 28; Younger, 2003, p. 133.
30 *House News*, September 1944 (shown in Younger, c1996, between pp. 167 and 168); and *Weekly Times*, 2 May 1925, p. 9.
31 Denison, p. 69.
32 *House News*, September 1944 (shown in Younger, c1996, between pp. 167 and 168).
33 'Annual meeting of the shareholders [Sun Newspapers Ltd], 21 May 1925' in Minute Book, 1924–26, FMBA, MLMSS 9894, box 45, SLNSW.
34 *ibid.*
35 Balance sheets for Denison Estates Pty Ltd, 30 April 1923 and 30 April 1924, Denison family Papers, MLMSS 6364, box 1, SLNSW.
36 Griffen-Foley, 1999, p. 5.
37 *Truth*, 30 August 1931, p. 1.
38 Connell and Irving, p. 213; *Smith's Weekly*, 5 March 1927, p. 14.
39 Walker, 1980b, p. 9.

40   Fitzhardinge, 1979, p. 583.
41   *Australian*, 28 December 2005, p. 2.
42   *Smith's Weekly*, 31 July 1926, p. 16.
43   *Australian*, 28 December 2005, p. 2; Griffen-Foley, 2000, pp. 44–45.
44   Walker, 1980b, p. 20.
45   Murray, p. 108; Denison, p. 77.
46   *SMH*, 16 December 1929, p. 10.
47   Sun Newspapers, p. 50.
48   *ibid.*, p. 53. Associated Newspapers subsequently bought out the *Daily Telegraph* shareholders.
49   Sun Newspapers, p. 48.
50   Walker, 1980b, p. 16.
51   'Associated Newspapers Ltd balance sheet as at 27 September 1931', FMBA, MLMSS 9894, box 54, SLNSW.
52   Walker, 1980b, p. 18.
53   Whitington, p. 76
54   *Truth*, 5 January 1930, p. 13.
55   Letter from Sydney Snow to Hugh Denison, 15 April 1930, FMBA, MLMSS 9894, box 102, SLNSW.
56   Letter from Hugh Denison to Sydney Snow, 8 May 1930, FMBA, MLMSS 9894, box 102, SLNSW.
57   *ibid.*
58   Verbatim report of extraordinary meeting of shareholders, King's Hall, 12 June 1931, FMBA, MLMSS 9894, box 101, SLNSW.
59   *Labor Daily*, 10 February 1933, p. 10.
60   Letter from Hugh Denison to Sydney Snow, 30 July 1930, FMBA, MLMSS 9894, box 102, SLNSW.
61   Letter from Sydney Snow to Hugh Denison, 29 July 1930, FMBA, MLMSS 9894, box 102, SLNSW.
62   Cable from Hugh Denison to Sydney Snow, 15 July 1930; letter from Hugh Denison to Sydney Snow, 15 July 1930, FMBA, MLMSS 9894, box 102, SLNSW.
63   Letter from Hugh Denison to Sydney Snow, 30 July 1930, FMBA, MLMSS 9894, box 102, SLNSW.
64   *ibid.*
65   Letter from Sydney Snow to Hugh Denison, 29 July 1930, FMBA, MLMSS 9894, box 102, SLNSW.
66   *ibid.*, 27 August 1930, FMBA, MLMSS 9894, box 102, SLNSW.
67   *ibid.*, FMBA, MLMSS 9894, box 102, SLNSW.
68   Sun Newspaper Ltd Minute Book entry, 12 September 1930, p. 12, FMBA, MLMSS 9894, box 1730, SLNSW.
69   Verbatim report of extraordinary meeting of shareholders, King's Hall, 12 June 1931, FMBA, MLMSS 9894, box 101, SLNSW.
70   *ibid.*, p. 46.
71   Griffen-Foley, 2000, p. 59.
72   *National Advocate*, 13 June 1931, p. 5.
73   Letter from Sydney Snow to Hugh Denison, 2 July 1930, FMBA, MLMSS 9894, box 102, SLNSW.

74   Griffen-Foley, 1999, p. 15; *Newspaper News*, 1 October 1931, p. 1.
75   Letter from Sydney Snow to Hugh Denison, 29 July 1930, FMBA, MLMSS 9894, box 102, SLNSW.
76   Letter from RC Packer to Hugh Denison, 31 July 1931, FMBA, MLMSS 9894, box 102, SLNSW.
77   *ibid.*
78   *Smith's Weekly*, 13 June 1931, p. 10; Murray, p. 108. The six papers were the *Sunday News*, the *Daily Guardian* (which was merged with the *Daily Telegraph*), the *Daily Pictorial*, the *Sunday Pictorial*, the *Evening News* and the *Sunday Guardian* (which was merged with the *Sunday Sun*).
79   Denison, p. 79.
80   Griffen-Foley, 2000, p. 72.
81   Dyrenfurth, p. 128.
82   *Australian*, 28 December 2005, p. 2; and Griffen-Foley, 2000, p. 77.
83   Souter, 1981, p. 626. See also Griffen-Foley, 2000, p. 79.
84   Whitington, p. 131.
85   *Australian Women's Weekly*, 21 April 1934, p. 14.
86   Whitington, p. 100; Griffen-Foley, 2000, p. 27.
87   Walker, 1980b, p. 53.
88   Griffen-Foley, 2000, p. 97.
89   *Sun*, 3 December 1935, p. 13.
90   Whitington, p. 136.
91   *Sun*, 18 March 1936, p. 9; *Truth*, 2 February 1936, p. 21; and 29 March 1936, p. 17.
92   Whitington, pp. 138–40; Griffen-Foley, 2000, p. 102.
93   Whitington, p. 141. Note: the figures in Goot, suggest the *Daily Telegraph*'s circulation was 110 000 in 1935, rising to 166 000 in 1937, and 196 000 in 1938.
94   *Tweed Daily*, 22 May 1941, p. 2.
95   Author conversation with Bill Denison, 15 February 2017. When Lady Denison died in 1949 she left one-third of her own estate to charity.
96   Memo from Hugh Denison to RC Packer, 22 November 1932, FMBA, MLMSS 9894, box 102, SLNSW.
97   Letter from Keith Murdoch to Hugh Denison, 7 November 1932, FMBA, MLMSS 9894, box 933, SLNSW.
98   He refused to take direction from Packer (when Packer was in charge at Associated Newspapers), his cables were too 'sensational' and 'general' for Murdoch's liking, and he told other staff that he did not plan to stay in London long (letters from Hugh Denison to Keith Murdoch, 27 April 1933 and 23 November 1933; and from Keith Murdoch to Hugh Denison, 24 April 1933, FMBA, MLMSS 9894, box 933, SLNSW).
99   Including Thomas Bavin, the former NSW premier (letter from John Butters to Hugh Denison, 19 July 1934, FMBA, MLMSS 9894, box 102, SLNSW).
100   Letter from John Butters to Hugh Denison, 19 July 1934, FMBA, MLMSS 9894, box 102, SLNSW; and document headed 'Prospect', undated, FMBA, MLMSS 9894, box 101, SLNSW.
101   *Smith's Weekly*, 27 June 1942, p. 11.
102   *Punch* (Melbourne), 11 March 1915, p. 32.
103   *Smith's Weekly*, 27 June 1942, p. 11.

104 Denison, p. 99.
105 'Associated Newspapers Ltd balance sheet as at 30 September 1934' and 'Balance sheet as at 24 September 1944', FMBA, MLMSS 9894, box 54, SLNSW.
106 Chairman's report to shareholders, Associated Newspapers annual general meeting, 2 December 1953, pp. 1–2, FMBA, MLMSS 9894, box 923, SLNSW.
107 Whitington, p. 100.

5   'Who owns the owners of the *Herald*?': The kingdom of Collins House
1   Younger, 1996, p. 109.
2   *Taralga Echo*, 2 May 1925, p. 1; Goot, p. 5.
3   McFarland, p. 5; Younger, 1996, unnumbered loose page between pp. 167 and 168; Goot, pp. 55–56.
4   Yule, 2013, p. 65.
5   Letter from AG Cameron to Dumas, 29 March 1933, Dumas Papers, MS 4849, NLA.
6   Yule, 2012, pp. 19–20; *Smith's Weekly*, 26 November 1932, p. 1.
7   Yule, 2012, p. 20.
8   *Table Talk*, 16 June 1893, p. 8.
9   *Age*, 26 February 1889, p. 9; *Argus*, 8 July 1889, p. 10.
10   Cannon, 1986, p. 271.
11   *ibid.*; *Table Talk*, 16 June 1893, p. 9; see also Kennett, 1980, p. 41.
12   Cannon, 1986, p. 273.
13   *ibid.*, p. 1.
14   Yule, 2012, pp. 34, 46.
15   Although Peter Gardner's paper, undated (b), is the most comprehensive attempt to account for this.
16   Yule disputes this, see Yule, 2012, p. 36; but see also Garden; and Gardner, undated (a), p. 4.
17   Cannon, 1986, p. 130.
18   *ibid.*, pp. 131–32.
19   E.g. compare *Table Talk*, June 1893 and April 1894 coverage with *The Age*, 10 October 1893, p. 7.
20   Garden, pp. 78–82, 136–37. Note: due to the complexities around this period of time, the transaction has sometimes been viewed as the *Herald* buying out the *Daily Telegraph* (e.g. Younger, 1996, p. 328).
21   *Table Talk*, 25 November 1892, p. 8.
22   *Argus*, 22 July 1893, p. 15.
23   Garden, p. 79.
24   *ibid.*, p. 81.
25   *ibid.*
26   *ibid.*, pp. 136–37.
27   *Age*, 2 November 1894, p. 7.
28   Kirkpatrick, 2016, pp. 42–43.
29   Garden, pp. 136–37.
30   Gardner, undated (c), p. 9.
31   *Weekly Times*, 17 August 1895, p. 36.
32   Yule, 2012, p. 78.

33 Note that the date of Fink's ascension to chairman has sometimes been recorded incorrectly (e.g. Garden gives the date as 1913 (Garden, pp. 141, 175)). Fink ascended to chairman upon Massina's retirement in 1906 (*Herald*, 2 July 1925, p. 8).

34 Garden, p. 139.

35 Rawling, p. 69; Cannon, 1986, pp. 262, 288; *Smith's Weekly*, 30 December 1933, p. 5; *Argus*, 16 October 1943, p. 2.

36 E.g. HWT board member James Moloney was Collins House's solicitor.

37 E.g. Fink was part of a syndicate with Baillieu to take over the Duke mines in Maryborough, a venture that helped Baillieu's financial recovery after the land boom crash (Yule, 2012, p. 36). Baillieu was also involved with Fink in Wunderlich Ltd, a metal pressing company (Richardson, 1988b, p. 230).

38 Kennett, 1980, p. 104.

39 Robinson in Blainey, 1970, pp. 37–38.

40 Yule, 2012, p. 78.

41 Macintyre, 2004.

42 Garden, pp. 54, 77.

43 *ibid*., p. 138.

44 At the Athenaeum, the Baillieus rubbed shoulders with David Syme, who had been a founding member, plus his sons, and other influential Deakinite liberals. Other key figures from the Collins House group were also members including Watt, Robinson, BHAS manager Colin Fraser and Baillieu's brother-in-law Edward Shackell.

45 *Herald* on 10 October 1900, p. 4; 17 October 1900, p. 4; 23 October 1900, p. 4.

46 *ibid*., 17 October 1900, p. 4.

47 But the paper was also concerned about Baillieu having been involved as shareholder in a company that marketed a 'birth control' product (*Bendigo Independent*, 2 August 1901, p. 2).

48 Yule, 2012, pp. 98–99.

49 *Bendigo Independent*, 5 August 1901, p. 3.

50 *Age*, 6 August 1901, p. 6.

51 *Smith's Weekly*, 30 December 1933, p. 4.

52 *CPD* (HR), 19 November 1920, p. 6751.

53 Yule, 2012, p. 235.

54 Yule, 2013, p. 63; Yule, 2012, p. 68.

55 Hoover, p. 88.

56 WS Robinson quoted in Blainey, 1993a, p. 272.

57 Blainey, 1993a, p. 272.

58 *ibid*., p. 267.

59 *Australian Financial Review*, 28 November 1961, p. 6.

60 Kennedy, 1984, p. 108.

61 Robinson in Blainey, 1970, p. 87.

62 Fitzhardinge, 1983.

63 Kennedy, 1984, p. 109.

64 Yule, 2012, p. 205.

65 *ibid*.

66 *Barrier Miner*, 13 January 1926, p. 6.

67 BHAS executives believed that BHP lied to them about the state of its Port Pirie

smelter, and BHAS executives like Robinson considered BHP's harsh treatment of its workers to be counter-productive.

68   Fitzhardinge, 1964, p. 212.
69   Yule, 2012, p. 229.
70   *CPD* (HR), 16 November 1934, p. 392.
71   *Sun*, 13 December 1915, p. 6.
72   Richardson, 1988a.
73   Yule, 2013, p. 62.
74   Horne, p. 76.
75   Undated notes on KM in Robinson Papers, 2001.0070, box 4, file 74, UMA.
76   Whyte, p. 340.
77   Garden, p. 180.
78   Yule, 2012, p. 214.
79   Garden, pp. 200–03.
80   McMullin, 2001, p. 47.
81   Yule, 2012, p. 229.
82   Connell and Irving, pp. 212–13.
83   Lee, 1997, pp. 82–83.
84   Bolton, 2001, p. 122.
85   *ibid*.
86   Hughes Papers, MS 1538, series 2, NLA.
87   Yule, 2012, p. 229.
88   *ibid*., p. 205.
89   Iremonger, p. 265.
90   Roberts, 2015, p. 95.
91   Garden, p. 198.
92   Roberts, 2015, p. 95.
93   *ibid*., p. 97; see also pp. 64–66.
94   *Herald*, 3 October 1922, p. 4.
95   *ibid*., 30 October 1922, p. 8.
96   *Age*, 26 October 1922, p. 8.
97   *ibid*., 11 December 1922, p. 8.
98   *Herald*, 15 December 1922, p. 4.
99   E.g. *Advocate*, 22 November 1920, p. 2 and *Western Argus*, 30 November 1920, p. 29.
100 Robinson Papers, 2001.0070, box 4, file 74, UMA.
101 *Sun*, 21 November 1920, p. 1.
102 *Herald*, 3 October 1922, p. 5.
103 Letter from Colin Fraser to Owen Cox, 28 November 1922, BHAS Papers, 1969.0006, box 1, folder 26, UMA.
104 Letters from Owen Cox to Colin Fraser, 16 January 1922 and 20 November 1922, BHAS papers, 1969.0006, box 1, folder 26, UMA.
105 Letter from Owen Cox to Colin Fraser, 29 November 1922, BHAS papers, 1969.0006, box 1, folder 26, UMA.
106 *Westralian Worker*, 10 November 1922, p. 4; *Daily Herald*, 28 October 1922, p. 6. See also statement made by Eddie Ward, *CPD* (HR), 24 September 1941.
107 *Sunday Times*, 26 March 1922, p. 4; *Recorder*, 12 August 1922, p. 1; *Daily News*, 30 April 1926, p. 4.

108 *Herald*, 9 October 1922, p. 1.
109 Hughes, 1922.
110 *Daily Mercury*, 1 June 1922, p. 7.
111 Ville and Merrett, pp. 30–33.
112 Howard Smith also had a large stake in the separate Australian Sugar Company Ltd (*Register*, 23 March 1922, p. 3; *Daily Commercial News and Shipping List*, 29 September 1922, p. 4).
113 *SMH*, 15 December 1922, p. 10.
114 Howard Smith formally moved its headquarters to Sydney in 1928 (*SMH*, 24 April 1928, p. 13).
115 Fitzhardinge, 1979, p. 509.
116 *ibid.*, p. 523.
117 And the two men stayed in friendly contact (letter from WS Robinson to WM Hughes, 22 December 1948 in Robinson Papers, box 4, file 80, UMA).
118 *Barrier Daily Truth*, 22 November 1931, p. ; *Advertiser*, 1 September 1917, p. 11; *Daily Telegraph* (Tasmania), 15 February 1917, p. 2; *Register*, 22 February 1912, p. 7; *Examiner*, 26 August 1912, p. 2; *Daily Commercial News and Shipping List*, 10 September 1919, p. 8.
119 Yule, 2012, p. 245.
120 *Australian Financial Review*, 30 November 1961, p. 6.
121 Blainey, 1993a, p. 152.
122 Fox, p. 12.
123 Yule, 2012, pp. 76–77.
124 Gibson, p. 12; Blainey, 1993a, p. 275.
125 Rawling, p. 31.
126 Yule, 2012, p. 352.

6   The real story of the birth of News Limited
1   *Daily Telegraph*, 7 June 1997, p. 34.
2   *News*, 24 July 1973, pp. 24–25.
3   Fink's description (Garden, p. 141).
4   *News,* 2 June 1930, p. 6.
5   Grover, p. 2.
6   *ibid.*
7   *Australasian Journalist*, 18 April 1927, p. 54 (in AJA Victorian branch records (1993.0133), UMA).
8   *ibid.*
9   Page, p. 27.
10 *News*, 4 June 1930, p. 11.
11 Bridge.
12 Garden, p. 175.
13 *ibid.*, p. 141.
14 *Argus*, 29 November 1918, p. 5; Blainey, 1970.
15 Gregson, p. 208.
16 *ibid.*, p. 209.
17 *Bathurst Times*, 21 January 1918, p. 2.
18 Kirkpatrick, 2000, p. 205; Kennedy, 1984, p. 101.

19   Gregson, p. 211. See also Kearns, p. 6.

20   *ibid.*

21   Kennedy, 1984, p. 101.

22   Colin Fraser, 'What is Wrong With Broken Hill?', 29 June 1918, pp. 5–6, in BHAS Papers, 1969.0006, UMA.

23   *ibid.*

24   *ibid.*, entry on 8 March 1918, p. 7.

25   *ibid.*, WE Wainwright entry, 29 June 1918, pp. 10–11.

26   *ibid.*

27   *ibid.*

28   Garden, p. 176 and endnotes.

29   Fraser's original letter to Robinson is missing but Robinson's reply indicates this is what was suggested (letter from WS Robinson to Colin Fraser, 12 December 1918, p. 2, BHAS Papers, 1969.0006, UMA).

30   *ibid.*

31   *ibid.*

32   *Daily Commercial and Shipping List*, 11 February 1919, p. 15. While Fraser and Robinson's letters were criss-crossing the globe in December 1918, Davidson had been in Broken Hill with a newspaper auditor from Melbourne, examining the books of the *Barrier Miner* (*Barrier Miner*, 15 February 1919, p. 3).

33   Yule, 2013, p. 63.

34   Kennedy, 1986.

35   *Daily Commercial News and Shipping List*, 11 February 1919, p. 15. But only 5000 shares were taken up and paid for when the company was registered (Port Pirie *Recorder*, 932–355, PROV).

36   *ibid.*

37   *Age*, 27 February 1908, p. 7; 28 February 1908, p. 7.

38   E.g. Dumas Papers, MS 4849/3/14, 'Sherlock & Daniels' is auditor for a Collins House draft prospectus for Paper Makers Ltd.

39   *Recorder* (Port Pirie), 21 February 1919, p. 1.

40   *Barrier Miner*, 15 February 1919, p. 3.

41   Yule, 2012, p. 252.

42   Kennedy, 1986.

43   Inglis and Brazier, p. 213.

44   *Barrier Miner*, 30 September 1919, p. 2; 9 August 1919, p. 3; 31 May 1919, pp. 1, 4.

45   Letter from Colin Fraser to WS Robinson, 20 March 1919, BHAS Papers, 1969.0006, UMA.

46   Yule, 2012, p. 253.

47   *ibid.*

48   *Barrier Miner*, 29 May 1919, p. 2; 3 November 1919, p. 3; 29 September 1919, p. 2; 3 July 1919, p. 4; 11 September 1919, p. 2; 24 September 1919, p. 2.

49   *Barrier Miner*, Friday 13 May 1921, p. 1.

50   *ibid.*, 29 May 1919, p. 2; 3 November 1919, p. 3; 29 September 1919, p. 2; 3 July 1919, p. 4; 11 September 1919, p. 2; 24 September 1919, p. 2.

51   Letter from John Smethurst to Colin Fraser, 4 March 1935, BHAS Papers, 1969.0006, UMA.

52   *ibid.*, 17 December 1934, p. 4.

53   Letter from Colin Fraser to John Smethurst, 21 December 1934 and letter from
     Colin Fraser to WS Robinson, 8 March 1935, BHAS Papers, 1969.0006, UMA.
54   Letter from WS Robinson to Colin Fraser, 25 April 1917, BHAS Papers, 1969.0006,
     UMA.
55   *Barrier Miner*, 16 December 1921, p. 2.
56   *ibid.*, 12 May 1921, p. 2.
57   *ibid.*, 15 December 1921, p. 1.
58   *ibid.*, 16 December 1921, p. 2.
59   *ibid.*
60   *West Australian*, 20 April 1922, p. 8.
61   *Albury Banner and Wodonga Express*, 21 April 1922, p. 4.
62   *Barrier Miner*, 11 May 1921, p. 1.
63   News Limited shareholder list, 31 March 1924, News Limited (GRS/513/11,
     file 74/1922), SRSA.
64   Regan, p. 42.
65   It seems that Mussen was provided with 10 500 shares as payment. Correspondence
     between KM and Dumas shows that Murdoch wanted to buy these shares from
     Mussen in 1933 (letter from Dumas to KM, 24 August 1933, Dumas Papers, MS
     4849, NLA). Mussen's name no longer appears on the shareholder list by 1941.
66   *Recorder* (Port Pirie), 7 October 1922, p. 2.
67   *Register* board minutes of 31 July 1923 quoted in SA Memory, 'The *News*'.
68   *News*, 29 September 1923, p. 8.
69   *News.*, 24 July 1923, p. 7.
70   E.g. see *News*, 6 December 1923, p. 4; 31 October 1923, p. 2; 3 November 1927,
     p. 18; 27 October 1925, p. 11; 25 October 1927, p. 17.
71   *News*, 13 December 1923, p. 4.
72   *News*, 29 September 1923, p. 8. Davidson must have had only around 4550 ordinary
     shares before he took up the 10 000 extra.
73   When Dumas wanted to hide shares in News Limited, he put them in the name of
     the Executor Trustee Company (letter from Dumas to KM, 5 July 1934 in Dumas
     Papers, MS 4849, NLA). Shareholder lists show the Executor Trustee and Agency
     Co of South Australia's shareholding then leapt from 16 shares to 41 778.
74   *News*, 29 September 1923, p. 8; *Advertiser*, 27 April 1936, p. 15.
75   The other directors were: AEH Evans, an Adelaide accountant and auditor,
     later connected with Collins House companies through aviation and flying, and
     dredging and mining equipment; David John Gilbert, secretary and later general
     manager of News Limited, also a journalist and member of the National Party; and
     G Mostyn Evan, a lawyer and sportsman who was prominent in Adelaide.
76   *Mail*, 9 June 1923, p. 1.
77   News Limited shareholder list, 31 March 1924, News Limited (GRS/513/11,
     file 74/1922), SRSA.
78   Alexander, p. 48.
79   *News*, 29 September 1923, p. 8.
80   *ibid.*, 30 September 1924, p. 9.
81   *ibid.*, 25 September 1925, p. 11.
82   Alexander, pp. 22, 23, 38.
83   E.g. see *Mercury* (Hobart), 21 December 1921, p. 7; 27 March 1922, p. 2; 26 March

1927 p. 8; 13 January 1926, p. 7.

84   Garden, p. 176 and endnotes.

85   Page, p. 59.

86   *News*, 12 December 1923, p. 5. See also Roberts, 2015, p. 168.

87   McNicoll, 1997, p. 8.

88   Zwar, p. 84.

89   *News*, 22 March 1929, p. 16.

90   *ibid.*, 28 September 1929, p. 7.

91   *West Australian*, 9 September, 1930, p. 5.

92   *Recorder* (Port Pirie), 3 June 1930, p. 1.

93   Page, p. 27.

94   *News*, 29 September 1923, p. 8; *Recorder*, 22 July 1922, p. 2.

7 Keith Murdoch: Journalist, kingmaker, empire builder, puppet?

1   Particularly Tom Roberts' *Before Rupert*, but see also Mark Baker's 'The myth of Keith Murdoch's Gallipoli letter', and earlier, sections in George Munster's *Rupert Murdoch: A Paper Prince*.

2   Letter from KM to his father, 21 June 1908, quoted in Roberts, 2015, p. 2.

3   Letter from KM to Theodore Fink, 31 July 1919, quoted in Putnis, 2011, p. 72.

4   Letter from KM to his father, 26 March 1909, quoted in Ward, p. 6.

5   Roberts, 2015, p. 93.

6   Putnis, 2011, p. 83.

7   Hetherington, p. 100.

8   The prominent Scots (or Scottish descent) figures in newspapers included not only Syme and Murdoch, but also Lauchlan Mackinnon, John Blair, Donald Campbell, JE Davidson (whose mother was Scottish), James Swan, Andrew Dunn, James McAlpine Tait, James MacCallum Smith, RD Elliott (Fink's son-in-law) and several other important owners, printers and journalists.

9   WS Robinson's undated notes on KM, Robinson Papers, 2001.0070, box 4, file 74, UMA.

10   Colin Bednall's typed unpublished autobiography, p. 211, Bednall Papers, MS 5546/3, NLA.

11   Hetherington, p. 104.

12   Roberts, 2015, p. 48.

13   Ward, p. 9.

14   *ibid.*, p. 233.

15   *ibid.*, p. 104; see also Sun Newspapers, p. 20.

16   *ibid.*, pp. 40–47; Baker.

17   *Canberra Times*, 29 September 1985, p. 25. Arthur Calwell, years later, accused Murdoch of having gone to Gallipoli as a 'spy' for Northcliffe (Telegram outlining Calwell's comments, contained in Dumas Papers, MS 4849/10/66; *Advocate* (Tasmania), 26 March 1941, p. 2.

18   Serle, 1986.

19   Brendon, p. 117.

20   Ward, p. 21.

21   Zwar, p. 50

22   *Smith's Weekly*, 25 March 1922, p. 2.

23 Roberts, 2015, p. 41.
24 *ibid*., p. 65. One piece of information that Murdoch and Hughes sought to suppress was the result of the overseas AIF vote because they knew that it would be a bad look at home if the AIF soldiers voted against conscription (Fitzhardinge, 1979, pp. 206–07 and 209).
25 Ward, p. 24.
26 *ibid*., p. 22.
27 *ibid*.
28 *ibid*, p. 22.
29 WS Robinson's undated notes on KM, Robinson Papers, 2001.0070, box 4, file 74, UMA.
30 *Smith's Weekly*, 25 March 1922, p. 2.
31 Letter from KM to Northcliffe, 13 March 1921, Northcliffe Papers, M 1641, AJCP.
32 *ibid*., 9 April 1921, Northcliffe Papers, M 1641, AJCP.
33 Roberts, 2015, p. 177; Younger, 2003, p. 123.
34 Yule, 2012, p. 322.
35 *ibid*., pp. 136, 147; *Smith's Weekly* (Sydney), 11 November 1922, p. 10; Younger, 2003, pp. 123–24.
36 Younger, 2003, p. 124.
37 *ibid*., p. 124.
38 Garden, pp. 230–31.
39 Calwell, 1978, p. 89.
40 WS Robinson's undated notes on KM, Robinson Papers, 2001.0070, box 4, file 74, UMA.
41 *Smith's Weekly*, 15 October 1927, p. 14.
42 Roberts, 2015, pp. 178–79; *Mercury* (Hobart), 1 January 1930, p. 8; *Register News-Pictorial* (Adelaide), 6 January 1930, p. 5.
43 *Smith's Weekly*, 30 April 1932, p. 8.
44 E.g. Zwar, pp. 64, 62, 66.
45 *Canberra Times*, 29 September 1985, p. 25.
46 Putnis, 2011, p. 78.
47 Cannon, 2015.
48 See letters from KM to Dumas in the Dumas Papers, MS 4849, NLA.
49 Ralph Simmonds, quoted in Younger, 2003, p. 120.
50 Author interview with John Dahlsen, 22 February 2017.
51 Hetherington, p. 113.
52 JA Alexander interview with Mel Pratt, 1971, NLA.
53 Roberts, 2015, p. 251.
54 Handwritten version of Colin Bednall's unpublished autobiography, [no page numbers], Bednall Papers, MS 5546, NLA.
55 WS Robinson's undated notes on KM, Robinson Papers, 2001.0070, box 4, file 74, UMA.
56 Younger, 2003, p. 125; Putnis, 2011, p. 77.
57 Roberts, 2015, p. 145.
58 *ibid*.
59 Putnis, 2011, p. 79.
60 *ibid*., p. 79.

61   Roberts, 2015, p. 145.

62   *ibid.*

63   *Weekly Times*, 17 September 1921, p. 5.

64   Letter from WL Baillieu to WS Robinson, 26 September 1921, in Robinson Papers, 2001.0070, file 62, box 3, UMA.

65   According to Rupert Murdoch, 'They took his word for it. They bought shares in the *Herald* and supported him in his takeover of the Adelaide *Advertiser*.' But WL Baillieu had already been an HWT shareholder for over twenty years (Zwar, p. 70).

66   Younger, 1999, p. 364.

67   Roberts, 2015, p. 127.

68   Letter from KM to Northcliffe, 30 December 1921, Northcliffe Papers, M 1641, AJCP.

69   Letter from Northcliffe to KM, undated but circa March 1922, p. 2, Northcliffe Papers, M 1641, AJCP.

70   Roberts, 2015, p. 325 endnote 111.

71   Letter from Northcliffe to KM, 25 January 1922, Northcliffe Papers, M 1641, AJCP.

72   *ibid.*, 18 April 1922, p. 2, Northcliffe Papers, M 1641, AJCP.

73   Letter from KM to Northcliffe, 12 March 1922, pp. 4–5, Northcliffe Papers, M 1641, AJCP.

74   *ibid.*

75   The author gratefully acknowledges Tom Roberts for his thoughts on Murdoch's mysterious cash flow.

76   Letter from KM to Northcliffe, 25 June 1922, p. 2, Northcliffe Papers, M 1641, AJCP.

77   *ibid.*, 30 December 1921, Northcliffe Papers, M 1641, AJCP.

78   *ibid.*, 12 March 1922, p. 4, Northcliffe Papers, M 1641, AJCP.

79   *ibid.*

80   *ibid.*, p. 147.

81   *Daily Commercial News and Shipping List* (Sydney), 13 December 1922, p. 11; *Smith's Weekly* (Sydney), 25 March 1922, p. 2.

82   Letter from KM to Northcliffe, 12 March 1922, pp. 4–5, Northcliffe Papers, M 1641, AJCP.

83   Denison had 1866 shares in the HWT during those years, but by 1924, no longer had HWT shares in his own name (balance sheets for Denison Estates Pty Ltd, 30 April 1921, 1922 and 1923, Denison family Papers, MLMSS 6364, box 1, SLNSW).

84   Letter from KM to Northcliffe, 12 March 1922, p. 4, Northcliffe Papers, M 1641, AJCP.

85   *Mail* (Adelaide), Saturday 7 June 1930, p. 2; Death certificate of Herbert Campbell Jones (certificate 14345/1942).

86   *Australasian Journalist*, 18 April 1927, p. 54 in AJA Victorian Branch Records, 1993.0133, UMA.

87   *Truth* (Sydney), 13 April 1930, p. 1.

88   Letter from KM to Northcliffe, 12 March 1922, p. 4, 6, Northcliffe Papers, M 1641, AJCP.

89   *ibid.*, 24 March 1922, p. 2, Northcliffe Papers, M 1641, AJCP.

90   Telegram from KM to Northcliffe, 17 April 1922, p. 2, Northcliffe Papers, M 1641, AJCP.

91 *ibid.*, 25 June 1922, p. 2, Northcliffe Papers, M 1641, AJCP.
92 *ibid.*, 25 May 1922, p. 2, Northcliffe Papers, M 1641, AJCP.
93 *ibid.*, 26 May 1922, Northcliffe Papers, M 1641, AJCP.
94 Telegram from Northcliffe to KM, 18 May 1922, Northcliffe Papers, M 1641, AJCP.
95 *ibid.*, 24 May 1922, p. 2, Northcliffe Papers, M 1641, AJCP.
96 Telegram from KM to Northcliffe, 18 June 1922, Northcliffe Papers, M 1641, AJCP.
97 Hyslop.
98 Letter from Northcliffe to KM, containing undated notes (circa February 1922), p. 14, Northcliffe Papers, M 1641, AJCP.
99 Yule, 2013, pp. 64–65.
100 Thank you to Joan Newman for this recollection.
101 Letter from Northcliffe to KM, undated notes (circa February 1922), p. 14, Northcliffe Papers, M 1641, AJCP.
102 Younger, 2003, pp. 136, 142.
103 *ibid.*, p. 154.
104 Macklin, p. 19. See also Cannon, 1993.
105 Younger, 2003, pp. 145, 154.
106 Younger, 1996, p. 109; Murray, p. 102.
107 Dumas claimed that Grover was a very 'likeable' man and a 'brilliant' writer, but 'a calamity' as an editor and he (Dumas) had 'complete control' over the paper, and had widened its audience appeal so that its circulation increased by 50 per cent in 12 months (Dumas, pp. 36–37).
108 *Australasian Journalist*, 18 April 1927, p. 58 in AJA Victorian Branch Records, 1993.0133, UMA.
109 Younger, 2003, p. 155.
110 *ibid.*, p. 136.
111 See Kirkpatrick, 2016 for a dissenting view about the paper's true age.
112 Garden, p. 220; *Sunday Times* (Perth), 1 August 1926, p. 1; and 27 June 1926, p. 1.
113 Yule, 2013, p. 66; and Garden, p. 220.
114 Letter from WS Robinson to JE Macartney, 19 October 1959, in Robinson Papers, 2001.0070, box 2, file 47, UMA.
115 Fraser cabled WS Robinson on 4 September asking Robinson to secure 24 000 shares in WAN for 'Ted, Stewart, Hamer Somerset, Woodward [and] myself … Clive [Baillieu] states you are our only hope' ('Copy of Cable to WS Robinson', 4 September 1926, in Colin Fraser Papers, BHAS archive, 1969.0006, UMA).
116 Undated document (but circa 1926) titled 'Confidential: Particulars of the "West Australian" Newspaper Co. Limited, Perth' in folder 'Westralian Newspapers' in Colin Fraser papers.
117 *ibid.*
118 Roberts, 2015, p. 184.
119 Younger, 2003, p. 156.
120 *West Australian* (Perth), 10 February 1927, p. 10. The *West Australian* emphasised the chair's response that the paper was being run in the interests of Western Australia – a noticeably vague response.
121 *ibid.*, 28 August 1930, p. 7; and *Mercury* (Hobart), 29 August 1930, p. 6.
122 Hurst; *Telegraph* (Brisbane), 1 June 1939, p. 16.
123 *Western Mail* (Perth), 3 September 1931, p. 18.

124   *Westralian Worker*, 14 August 1931, p. 3; *Western Mail*, 3 September 1931, p. 18.

125   *Western Mail*, 3 September 1931, p. 18.

126   *Sunday Times* (Perth), 26 March 1933, p. 1.

127   As many of the shareholder records lodged with the WA government are missing, this claim could not be assessed against the records (*West Australian*, 24 August 1933, p. 14).

128   Serle, 1986.

129   When Robinson resigned from the board in 1937, it was the year a royal commission was held into charges made by former Labor MP, TJ Hughes, against members of the state Labor ministry. Hughes told the inquiry that it was 'common knowledge' that the Labor government had become 'the puppets' of the *West Australian* newspaper, and the inquiry drew attention to the paper, its operations and ownership (*West Australian*, 23 January 1937, p. 20; Bolton, 1996). When Robinson resigned from the board, his brother (and lawyer) Arthur Robinson said he hoped the resignation would 'have the desired effect' (perhaps of minimising appearances of WS Robinson's influence on the paper) (letter from Arthur Robinson to WS Robinson, 10 August 1937, in Robinson Papers, 2001.0070, box 2, file 50, UMA).

130   *Courier-Mail*, 6 February 1952, p. 2.

131   Quoted in Tsokhas, p. 19.

132   *Advertiser*, 2 February 1952, p. 2.

133   E.g. *Labor Daily* (Sydney), 9 June 1932, p. 7; *Australian Worker* (Sydney), 12 October 1932, p. 15; *Sunday Times* (Perth), 26 March 1933, p. 1.

134   *West Australian*, 19 October 1933, p. 13.

135   Blainey, 1993b, p. 128. It was also beneficial for Queensland, where Robinson's friends and business partners, Wren (who had many friends in the Scullin Cabinet) and Murdoch, ran the *Daily Mail*. The devaluation of the Australian pound by the federal government in 1931 was also valuable. It caused the price of Australian gold to jump up by 25 per cent, the only commodity which saw a price rise during the Depression (Blainey, 1993b, p. 128).

136   *West Australian*, 29 December 1930, p. 5.

137   Letter from KM to Dumas, 16 February 1934, Dumas Papers, MS 4849/3/18, NLA.

138   Austen.

139   Letters to and from Robinson and Macartney in Robinson Papers, 2001.0070, box 2, file 47, UMA.

140   Munster, p. 22; Zwar, p. 81.

141   *ibid*.; Yule, 2013, p. 66.

142   Garden, p. 220.

143   Roberts, 2015, p. 183.

144   Younger, 1996, pp. 115, 109; *Truth* (Brisbane), 4 August 1929, p. 12; *News* (Adelaide), 6 November 1929, p. 13.

145   Younger, 2003, pp. 165, 192.

146   *ibid*.

147   Dumas, p. 55.

148   'Advertiser Newspapers Limited directors' report and balance sheet', 31 December 1939 and 31 December 1940, the *Advertiser* (GRS513/11/102), file 9), SRSA. By 1933, it was reporting a net profit of £66 000 (*News*, 21 February 1933, p. 7).

149 *Truth* (Sydney), 4 September 1927, p. 13.
150 Advertisement for the *Herald* in *Newspaper News*, 1 June 1931, p. 20.
151 Roberts, 2015, p. 185.

8   Keith Murdoch: Newspaper owner
1   KM to Theodore Fink, 31 July 1919, quoted in Putnis, 2011, p. 72.
2   *Smith's Weekly*, 7 October 1944, p. 3.
3   Roberts, 2015, p. 184.
4   Letter from KM to Dumas, 2 January [1931], Dumas Papers, MS 4849/2/7, NLA.
5   Zwar, p. 196.
6   Letter from KM to Dumas, 2 January [1931], Dumas Papers, MS 4849/2/7, NLA.
7   Letter from Dumas to KM, 5 January 1931, Dumas Papers, MS 4849/2/7, NLA.
8   The sixty-year-old was last seen wandering the deck of a passenger ship in the early hours of the night in his pyjamas and dressing gown. When his dressing gown was found near the saloon, it was presumed that Clarkson, who had been ill, had jumped overboard.
9   Letter from Dumas to KM, 28 January 1931, Dumas Papers, MS 4849/2/7, NLA.
10 *ibid.*, 6 February 1931, Dumas Papers, MS 4849/2/7, NLA.
11 *ibid.*
12 Zwar, p. 84.
13 Letter from Dumas to KM, 28 January 1931, Dumas Papers, MS 4849/2/7, NLA. This letter shows that Murdoch was still in control at the *West Australian* in January 1931 (although for how long afterwards is unclear).
14 Letter from KM to Dumas, 12 March 1931, Dumas Papers, MS 4849/2/7, NLA.
15 Letter from KM to J Fred Downer, 23 March 1931, Dumas Papers, MS 4849/2/7; letter from KM to Dumas, 12 March 1931, Dumas Papers, MS 4849/2/7, NLA.
16 Letter from KM to Dumas, 17 April 1931, Dumas Papers, MS 4849/2/7, NLA.
17 *ibid.*, 13 May 1931, Dumas Papers, MS 4849/2/8, NLA.
18 Letter from Dumas to KM, 17 April 1931, Dumas Papers, MS 4849/2/8, NLA.
19 Letter from KM to Dumas, 23 February 1932, Dumas Papers, MS 4849/2/11, NLA.
20 *ibid.*, 16 October 1931, Dumas Papers, MS 4849/2/10, NLA.
21 *News*, 30 September 1932, p. 9.
22 Myers, p. 83.
23 *Recorder* (Port Pirie), 16 March 1939, p. 1; *Newcastle Sun*, 15 March 1939, p. 7.
24 Letter from Dumas to KM, 5 July 1934, Dumas Papers, MS 4849/3/21, NLA.
25 Younger, 1999, p. 434.
26 Colin Bednall's unpublished typed autobiography, p. 208, in Bednall Papers, MS 5546, NLA.
27 Lloyd, 2001a, p. 198.
28 Letter from KM to Dumas, 23 January 1933, Dumas Papers, MS 4849/3/15, NLA.
29 Transcript of Cameron's remarks at Morgan on 29 March 1933, sent by Dumas to KM, 13 March 1933, Dumas Papers, MS 4849/3/15, NLA.
30 Letter from KM to Fred Downer, 27 January 1934, Dumas Papers, MS 4849/3/18, NLA.
31 *ibid.*, 26 January 1934, Dumas Papers, MS 4849/3/18, NLA.
32 Letters from KM to Dumas, 25 August 1933 and 26 January 1934, Dumas Papers, MS 4849/3/18, NLA; News Limited shareholder lists for 1933 and 1934, News

Limited (GRS/513/11, file 74/1922), SRSA.

33   Letter from KM to Dumas, 16 February 1934; letters to and from Jac Baillieu and KM, including one dated 26 January 1934, Dumas Papers, MS 4849/3/18, NLA.

34   She was then known as Lady Gore (*Evening News* (Sydney), 27 February 1895, p. 4).

35   It has not been entirely clear in some sources whether only Murdoch bought the *Courier*, or if it was Murdoch and Wren together. However, it seems from the share arrangement in Queensland Newspapers and the research by Dorothy Gollner, that it was principally, if not solely, Murdoch (Gollner 1995; Colin Bednall's handwritten version of unpublished autobiography [no page numbers]; Bednall Papers, MS 5546, NLA; Zwar, p. 81).

36   Colin Bednall's handwritten version of unpublished autobiography [no page numbers], Bednall Papers, MS 5546, NLA.

37   White was listed as the Daily Mail Pty Ltd's principal shareholder from 1920 until 1934 (joint principal shareholder from 1926 with Lorna Hannan (Benjamin Nathan's daughter)). White's shares were transferred back to Wren in 1934 (Gollner, 1995).

38   Griffin, 2004, p. 202.

39   Colin Bednall's handwritten version of unpublished autobiography [no page numbers], Bednall Papers, MS 5546, NLA.

40   Hardy.

41   In 1906 there had been an attempt in Victoria, and even rumours that he would take over the respectable *Argus* (*Gadfly* (Adelaide), 13 June 1906, p. 8; *Punch* (Melbourne), 22 February 1906, p. 20).

42   AE Cockram quoted in Griffin, 2004, p. 169.

43   *Australian*, 17 June 1826, p. 2.

44   Griffin, 2004, p. 198; *Labor Call* (Melbourne), 11 May 1916, p. 11.

45   Brennan.

46   Griffin, 1990.

47   'Brian Mc'.

48   Buggy, p. 228.

49   Munster, p. 23; Page, p. 62.

50   Gollner.

51   Zwar, p. 81. But see also Griffin, 2004, p. 204.

52   Colin Bednall's handwritten version of unpublished autobiography [no page numbers], Bednall Papers, MS 5546, NLA.

53   *Sunday Mail* (Brisbane), 28 August 1932, p. 5; Campbell, p. 82.

54   Royal Commission on Racing and Racecourses, p. 18; *Daily Standard* (Brisbane), 11 October 1929, p. 7; *Truth* (Brisbane), 15 May 1910, p. 5; *Daily Standard* (Brisbane), 11 October 1929, p. 7; *Telegraph* (Brisbane), 11 October 1929, p. 2.

55   *Brisbane Courier*, 15 August 1933, p. 11.

56   Younger, 2003, p. 198.

57   *Telegraph* (Brisbane), 17 August 1933, p. 1.

58   *Worker* (Brisbane), 3 August 1933, p. 6.

59   *Brisbane Courier*, 15 August 1933, p. 11.

60   Since 1905–06 (Yule, 2012, p. 136).

61   Yule, 2012, p. 136; Kennedy, 1978, p. 7.

62   *Queenslander* (Brisbane), 24 February 1912, p. 9; Yule, 2012, p. 147–48; Richardson, 1988a. Robinson advised RG Casey Senior, chairman of directors of Mount Morgan Gold Mining Co., to take out fire insurance for Mount Morgan. When there was a subsequent fire, Lloyd's insurance agent suspected it 'was a swindle' before eventually paying the claim out (Robinson Papers, 2001.0070/4/83, UMA.

63   *Daily Standard* (Brisbane), 3 September 1913, p. 7.

64   *Brisbane Courier*, 11 July 1911, p. 6.

65   *Townsville Daily Bulletin*, 18 October 1913, p. 4; *Daily Standard* (Brisbane), 15 January 1919, p. 5. Even in the 1940s, Macartney's law firm was Marshall Lawrence Baillieu's lawyer (*Courier-Mail*, 7 November 1942, p. 7).

66   Johnston, 1986.

67   Fitzgerald, p. 127.

68   *Parliamentary Debates* (*Hansard*), Queensland Legislative Assembly, 8 December 1916.

69   Johnston, 1986.

70   *ibid*.

71   Cain, 1990.

72   Buggy, p. 258; Fitzgerald, p. 344.

73   Fitzgerald speculates the money was 'borrowed from Collins House' but it may just as easily have been provided in return for a silent stake in the venture (Fitzgerald, pp. 360–61).

74   Buggy, p. 259;

75   *Australasian* (Melbourne), 17 August 1935, p. 43

76   *Daily Examiner*, 9 August 1935, p. 5; *SMH*, 9 August 1935, p. 12; *West Australian*, 10 August 1935, p. 15.

77   *Argus*, 19 July 1935, p. 4.

78   Emberson-Bain, p. 38.

79   *West Australian*, 10 August 1935, p. 15; *Argus*, 10 August 1935, p. 21. See also *Advertiser*, 30 April 1938, p. 26, regarding Haddon A Smith, of the chartered accountancy firm, Cook, Tomlins and Mirams, who was also involved in Great Boulder.

80   *Courier-Mail*, 27 October 1953, p. 3; Fitzgerald, p. 363.

81   Laurence.

82   *West Australian*, 23 June 1948, p. 9.

83   *Truth*, 20 May 1954, p. 34.

84   Griffin, 2004, p. 372.

85   'List of Amounts Paid or Payable to Contributors (Brisbane Daily Mail Pty Ltd)', 7 January 1938, obtained from the Queensland State Archives, appendix to Gollner, 1995.

86   Younger, 1996, p. 136.

87   Garden, p. 221. Eight years after Fink's death, his daughter, Hilda Elliott, and his son, Hugh Roland Fink, still held a small number of shares in Queensland Newspapers ('Form no .1', hand dated '1950', appendix to Gollner, 1995).

88   Zwar, p. 81. Other sources found evidence the two did meet, at least in the early years of their partnership.

89   Colin Bednall's handwritten version of unpublished autobiography [no page numbers], Bednall Papers, MS 5546, NLA. Wren and Murdoch fought about

who was responsible for paying a land tax bill in a case that ended up in the High Court in 1940 (see *Telegraph* (Brisbane), 13 March 1940, p. 8; and Griffin, 2004, pp. 204–05 (which includes a recollection from John Williams about the case but has some errors regarding the details)).

90   *Herald* advertisement, *Newspaper News*, 1 July 1933, p. 9.
91   Younger, 1996, p. 56.
92   Griffen-Foley, 2001a, p. 97.
93   Garden, p. 227.
94   Roberts, 2015, p. 185.
95   Garden, p. 226.
96   Yule, 2012, p. 324.
97   Cannon, 1986, p. 266.
98   Langmore, 1986; Griffin, 2004, p. 43.
99   Yule, 2012, p. 280.
100   Yule, 2012, p. 357.
101   Garden, p. 228.
102   *ibid.*, p. 229; Younger, 2003, p. 199.
103   Colin Bednall's typed unpublished autobiography, p. 209, Bednall Papers, MS 5546/3, NLA.
104   Yule, 2012, p. 324.
105   *ibid.*, pp. 361–62; Cannon, 1986, p. 266.
106   *Barrier Miner*, 2 October 1936, p. 3.
107   Yule, 2012, p. 355.
108   *ibid.*, p. 365. Clive's main interests were in zinc, Dunlop Rubber, insurance and banking.
109   Younger, 1996, p. 139.
110   *ibid.*, p. 148.
111   Cockburn; Younger, 1999, p. 442.

9   **'Never trust Sydney newspaper proprietors'**
1   Denison held HWT shares in the early 1920s in his own name. In 1945 KM was trying to sell some of the HWT's shares – part of what he said was the HWT's 'considerable holding in Associated Newspapers' that it had held for 'some time' but in another name – to Associated Newspapers' board members (letter from KM to John Butters, 23 March 1945, FMBA, MLMSS 9894/1230, SLNSW.
2   Balance sheets for Denison Estates Pty Ltd, 30 April 1928, 30 April 1923, 30 April 1927, Denison family papers, MLMSS 6364, SLNSW.
3   *Smith's Weekly* (Sydney), 11 November 1922, p. 10; see also letter from KM to Hugh Denison, 14 February 1924, reproduced in Denison, 2004, p. x; and letter from KM to Hugh Denison, 26 March 1929, reproduced in Denison, 2004, pp. 112–15.
4   E.g. *Sunday Times* (Perth), 26 March 1933, p. 1; and *Smith's Weekly*, 9 July 1932, p. 4.
5   Including ANM (with which Associated Newspapers was also involved), and through AMP's investments in Collins House companies, including BHAS and CUB, plus multiple directorships (Crough, p. 7).
6   *Canberra Times*, 14 December 1979, p. 10; Memo from John Dahlsen to Sir Keith

MacPherson, 7 March 1980, John Dahlsen papers, provided to the author.

7   Carroll, 2001.

8   Putnis, 2011, p. 81 says it was thirty-one years earlier, but Rod Kirkpatrick believes the previous daily introduced was twenty-eight years earlier – the *Daily Shipping Gazette* – in June 1894.

9   *Labor Daily* (Sydney), 27 January 1930, p. 5. Rod Kirkpatrick kindly confirmed that the six Sunday newspapers being published in Sydney at the beginning of 1930 were: *Truth*, *Sunday Sun*, *Sunday Guardian*, *Sunday Times*, *Sunday News* and the *Sunday Pictorial*. The *Sunday Pictorial* closed on 15 February 1931.

10 Zwar, p. 121.

11 *ibid.*

12 The company was called John Fairfax & Sons from 1856 until 1916. In 1916 it became John Fairfax & Sons Ltd. In 1937 it became John Fairfax & Sons Pty Ltd. In 1963 it reverted back to John Fairfax & Sons Ltd. Throughout this book it is therefore referred to as 'Fairfax & Sons' to cover the minor variations in name.

13 *Newspaper News*, 1 May 1931, p. 6.

14 *SMH*, 18 April 1931, p. 22.

15 Turnbull, p. 318.

16 Souter, 1981, p. 12; *SMH*, 18 April 1931, p. 2.

17 Souter, 1981, p. 42.

18 Letter from Theodore Fink to KM, 10 February 1919, quoted in Ward, p. 50.

19 Souter, 1981, p. 42.

20 Griffen-Foley, 2007.

21 Souter, 1981, pp. 134–35.

22 See Warwick Fairfax's summation of the company's values quoted in Wiltshire and Stokes, p. 102.

23 Walker, 1980b, p. 11.

24 *SMH*, 19 March 1920, p. 8.

25 *Argus*, 10 April 1902, p. 4.

26 *Tribune* (Sydney), 27 April 1944, p. 4.

27 Walker, 1980b, p. 192.

28 *ibid.*

29 Twopenny.

30 Young, p. 80.

31 Souter, 1981, p. 118.

32 *ibid.*

33 *ibid.*, pp. 118–19; *SMH*, 28 October 1916, pp. 12–15.

34 Attestation Form, 25 October 1939, Rupert William Geary military records, B883, NX5366, NAA.

35 Souter, 1981, p. 151.

36 Farrelly.

37 *Wimbles Reminder*, April 1933, p. 9.

38 Souter, 1990.

39 Farrelly.

40 Colin Bednall's handwritten version of unpublished autobiography [no page numbers], Bednall Papers, MS 5546, NLA. Note: the handwritten version does not use Henderson's name but he is named in the typed version.

41   The *Daily Guardian* claimed circulation of 182 000 in 1929 (*Smith's Weekly*, 28 September 1929).
42   Souter, 1981, pp. 160, 256; *Tribune* (Sydney), 27 March 1945, p. 3.
43   Griffen-Foley, 2000, p. 108.
44   Unusually, Fairfax had separate posts for the news editor and the editor. The editor controlled editorials and leader columns, feature articles on the leader page and letters to the editor, while the news editor controlled news – a division designed to keep fact and opinion separate (Souter, 1981, p. 170).
45   Letter from Hugh Denison to KM, 4 September 1931, FMBA, MLMSS 9894/933, SLNSW.
46   Letter from KM to Hugh Denison, 7 September 1931, FMBA, MLMSS 9894/933, SLNSW.
47   Souter, 1981, p. 156.
48   *Daily Advertiser* (Wagga Wagga), 24 October 1946, p. 1; *Tumut and Adelong Times* (NSW), 29 October 1946, p. 1.
49   Fleming et al., pp. 15, 31; and Connell and Irving, p. 271.
50   *SMH*, 17 August 1901, p. 5.
51   Dyster and Meredith, p. 241.
52   Blainey, 1999, p. vii.
53   *ibid.*, pp. 17–18.
54   *ibid.*, pp. 7, 9–10.
55   E.g. *SMH*, 14 May 1910, p. 12.
56   Fleming et al., p. 63.
57   Crough, p. 6.
58   *Adelong and Tumut Express and Tumbarumba Post* (NSW), 13 April 1917, p. 8.
59   *SMH*, 20 August 1938, p. 8.
60   Campbell, p. 91.
61   Fleming et al., p. 33, 87.
62   *SMH*, 18 November 1896, p. 4.
63   *SMH*, 15 May 1893, quoted in Holder, 1970, p. 462.
64   *Mercury* (Hobart), 14 August 1940, p. 8; *Farmer and Settler* (Sydney), 26 May 1932, p. 3.
65   Dean.
66   *SMH*, 21 July 1911, p. 8.
67   Hawkins; *SMH*, 5 September 1945, p. 7.
68   Cain, 1990.
69   Its circulation rose rapidly, although perhaps not quite as rapidly as Whitington suggests (contrast Whitington, p. 141 with Goot, p. 5).
70   Iremonger, p. 275.
71   Fitzgerald, p. 362.
72   Barry, 1993, p. 16
73   Griffen-Foley, 2000, p. 69.
74   Walker, 1980b, p. 84.
75   Goot, p. 5.
76   *ibid.*, pp. 5–6.
77   Whitington, p. 122.
78   Griffen-Foley, 2000, p. 92.

79   *ibid.*, p. xv.
80   Harvey, 2009a.
81   Lawson, 2005.
82   Colin Bednall's typed unpublished autobiography, Bednall Papers, MS 5546/3, NLA.
83   *ibid.*
84   *Daily Telegraph*, 29 July 2008, p. 17.
85   ABC, 2014.
86   Barry, 2008; Parnell; Fowler.
87   Barry, 2008, p. 21; Colin Bednall's typed unpublished autobiography, Bednall Papers, MS 5546/3, NLA.
88   Whitington, p. 145; Griffen-Foley, 2000, p. 110.
89   Denison, 2004, p. 81; Souter, 1981, p. 179.
90   Griffen-Foley, 2000, p. 117.
91   *ibid.*, pp. 116–17.
92   *Newspaper News*, 1 June 1940, p. 13; Griffen-Foley, 2000, p. 118.
93   Whitington, p. 146.
94   Cannon, 1981, pp. 8–10.
95   *ibid.*, p. 11
96   Walker, 1976, p. 123.
97   Murray, p. 97.
98   Cannon, 1981, p. 10.
99   *ibid.*, p. 11
100   *ibid.*, pp. 27, 49.
101   Denis O'Brien quoted in Fitzgerald, p. 324.
102   Hall, p. 173.
103   *ibid.*, p. 178.
104   Griffen-Foley, 2000, p. 115.
105   Buckridge, 2012; Harvey 2009a.
106   *Australian*, 16 November 2009, p. 2.
107   *ibid.*
108   Harvey, 2009b.
109   *Tribune* (Sydney), 28 November 1939, p. 3.
110   Griffen-Foley, 2000, p. 115; Walker, 1980b, p. 86.
111   *Australian*, 16 November 2009, p. 2.
112   Harvey, 2009b.
113   Griffen-Foley, 2000, p. xv.
114   Colin Bednall's typed unpublished autobiography, Bednall Papers, MS 5546/3, NLA.
115   Walker, 1980b, p. 84. See also Griffen-Foley, 2000, p. 108.
116   Lloyd, 1988, p. 80.
117   *Truth* (Sydney), 15 September 1940, p. 13.
118   Letter from Hugh Denison to KM, 12 December 1939, FMBA, MLMSS 9894/1230, SLNSW.
119   Walker, 1980b, p. 193. See also Griffen-Foley, 1999, pp. 76–78, 120.

10   The press, Joe Lyons and the Depression

1   Lloyd, 2001b, p. 154.
2   McQueen, p. 24.

3   *CPD* (HR), 7 May 1931, p. 1714.
4   KM to Dumas, 14 September 1934, quoted in Roberts, 2015, p. 205.
5   Zwar, p. 89.
6   Hart, 1979, p. 115.
7   *CPD* (HR), 7 May 1931, p. 1699.
8   Calwell, p. 93.
9   Quoted in Hart, 1979, p. 113.
10   *CPD* (HR), 7 May 1931, p. 1699.
11   Clarke, 1962, p. 8. Clarke claimed that 'bribes' were part of the negotiations, including 'a pension of 500 pounds for Dame Enid'. He was not the only one to make such a claim, but no sound evidence of bribery has yet been uncovered.
12   Letter from Joe Lyons to KM, 2 October 1934, Murdoch Papers, MS 2823/1/4, NLA.
13   Roberts, 2015, p. 198.
14   *Truth* (Sydney), 4 August 1957, quoted in Hetherington, p. 112.
15   After he became Opposition Leader, the Australian Newspapers' Conference (ANC) publicly expressed its hope that the 'end of a vacillating [Scullin] Federal Government' was in sight due to the elevation of Lyons, 'a man around whom the bulk of the people would rally with confidence' (*Telegraph* (Brisbane), 18 March 1931, p. 9).
16   'Journalism in the '30s'. (Note: Lloyd, 1988, p. 90 incorrectly said this quote was from Geoff Sparrow.)
17   *Canberra Times*, 2 September 1986, p. 5.
18   Lloyd, 1988, p. 83.
19   Haggarty.
20   Markwell, p. 29. (Note: Newspapers did employ some economists to provide expert commentary, such as Douglas Copland, who wrote 'profusely for the newspapers' (Lloyd, 1988, p. 90).)
21   Lloyd, 1988, p. 89.
22   Yule, 2012, p. 111.
23   Brett.
24   Souter, 1988, p. 257.
25   Eklund.
26   Treasury of Australia, p. 57.
27   Lang.
28   Irving, pp. 60–64.
29   *Morning Bulletin* (Rockhampton Qld), 4 August 1922, p. 10.
30   Markwell, p. 29.
31   Irving, p. 63.
32   Lloyd, 1988, p. 90.
33   Fitzgerald, p. 323.
34   *Argus*, 9 July 1934, p. 8; 28 February 1931, p. 21; and 3 November 1930, p. 8.
35   *Argus*, 3 November 1930, p. 8
36   Roberts, 2015, p. 194.
37   *News*, 18 December 1931, p. 6; *Sun* (Sydney), 18 December 1931, p. 12; *Brisbane Courier*, 18 December 1931, p. 12; *Canberra Times*, 15 December 1931, p. 2.
38   Lloyd, 1988, p. 89.

39   Millmow, p. 133; Yule, 2012, p. 353.
40   Henderson, 2011, p. 225.
41   Yule, 2012, p. 353.
42   Younger, 2003, p. 183.
43   *Goulburn Evening Penny Post* (NSW), 27 August 1930, p. 3.
44   *Labor Daily*, 24 February 1931, pp. 1, 6.
45   *SMH*, 4 March 1931, p. 13; Yule, 2012, p. 354.
46   *Telegraph* (Brisbane), 8 August 1931, p. 3.
47   *SMH*, 14 June 1932, p. 10.
48   *Western Age* (Dubbo, NSW), 22 October 1930, p. 2; *Labor Daily* (Sydney),
     25 October 1930, p. 9. The *Labor Daily* figures may have been exaggerated given
     the paper's connection to Lang, but the mainstream daily press did not provide
     estimates and only said 'large crowds' or 'thousands'.
49   *Labor Daily*, 24 February 1931, pp. 1, 6.
50   *ibid.*
51   *ibid.*
52   *Queensland Times*, 27 July 1931, p. 7; *Tweed Daily*, 27 July 1931, p. 3.
53   Irving, p. 64.
54   'The Group' was sometimes called 'the Capel Court Group' after JB Were's address
     (across the road from Collins House).
55   Quoted in *National Times*, 22–27 May 1978, p. 7.
56   *Argus*, 7 April 1942, p. 2.
57   *Western Argus* (Kalgoorlie), 16 August 1932, p. 3; *Sunday Times* (Perth),
     15 December 1935, p. 16. Pratt had worked with Massy-Greene on tariff policy, and
     with WA Watt on industrial negotiating (*Smith's Weekly* (Sydney), 24 November
     1923, p. 11). He had promoted Electrolytic Zinc (*Examiner* (Launceston), 25 March
     1927, p. 2). One of the mining companies he was involved with was purchased by
     WS Robinson's company (*Western Argus* (Kalgoorlie), 25 October 1932, p. 3).
58   Nolan, 2010, p. 169.
59   Martin, 1993, p. 60; Sloan.
60   Martin, 1993, p. 73.
61   Hart, 1979, p. 134.
62   *Smith's Weekly*, 9 June 1928, p. 10.
63   Lloyd, 2001b, p. 140. When Robert Nivison died in June 1930, aged eighty, his son,
     John Nivison, inherited his title and took over running Nivison and Co.
64   *Age*, 20 October 1914, p. 9.
65   *CPD* (HR), 14 March 1929, p. 1234.
66   *Sun*, 11 July 1928, p. 4; *Herald* (Melbourne), 11 July 1928, p. 20; *Age*, 30 April 1924,
     p. 17. And Ricketson was an early investor in the *Advertiser* when it was taken over
     by the HWT in 1929 (the *Advertiser*, GRS513/11/102, SRSA). Ricketson knew both
     Clive Baillieu and WS Robinson.
67   As would Ricketson's other million pound investment company, Were's Investment
     Trust (of which Menzies soon became a director too). *News*, 20 February 1930,
     p. 18; *Sun,* 14 July 1928, p. 2; *Age*, 22 September 1934, p. 18; *Argus*, 22 September
     1932.
68   Martin, 1993, p. 84.
69   NMLA board Minute Books for 1926, 1929, NMLA Board Minute Books,

2012.0049, UMA. See also *Telegraph* (Brisbane), 23 September 1926, p. 9; *Age*, 18 December 1929, p. 17.
70   NMLA report of the directors for year ending 30 September 1930, NMLA Board Minute Books, 2012.0049, UMA. It is an interesting sidenote that, in the United Kingdom, Keynes too was involved in life insurance, and was chairman of the British National Mutual Insurance Company. (It is unclear whether his company had purchased Australian government securities.)
71   Lloyd, 2001b, p. 141.
72   Schedvin, 1981.
73   Martin, 1993, pp. 82–83.
74   *Age*, 10 November 1930, p. 7.
75   *Advocate* (Burnie), 18 December 1930, p. 7; *SMH*, 18 December 1930, p. 11; and *Telegraph* (Brisbane), 12 December 1930, p. 9.
76   Lloyd, 2001b, p. 140.
77   Roberts, 2015, p. 195.
78   *Advertiser*, 18 December 1931, p. 26.
79   Lloyd, 2001b, p. 147.
80   Martin, 1993, p. 85.
81   Letter from KM to Dumas, 21 January 1931, in Dumas Papers, MS 4849, NLA.
82   *Advertiser*, 28 January 1931, p. 6.
83   Hart, 1969, p. 44.
84   Quoted in Cain, 2001.
85   *ibid*.
86   E.g. see *SMH*, 17 December 1931, p. 8.
87   Hart, 1969, p. 46.
88   *Sun*, 13 February 1931, p. 7; *SMH*, 12 February 1931, p. 10.
89   *Argus*, 11 February 1931, p. 6; Martin, 1993, p. 87.
90   *SMH*, 20 February 1931, p. 10; 19 February 1931, p. 8.

11   A friend in office and a falling out
1   Roberts, 2015, p. 194.
2   JA Alexander interview with Mel Pratt.
3   Letter from KM to Dumas, 6 January 1931, [misdated 1930], Dumas Papers, MS 4849/2/7, NLA.
4   *Advertiser* (Adelaide), 9 January 1931, p. 15.
5   Hart, 1979, p. 126.
6   Quoted in *National Times*, 22–27 May 1978, p. 7.
7   His father, also named Richard Casey, was chairman of the Mount Morgan Gold Mining Co. and the Electrolytic Refining and Smelting Company at Port Kembla.
8   Telegram from KM to 'Miss Munro', *Herald* office, 31 March 1931, Dumas Papers, MS 4849/2/7, NLA.
9   Hart, 1979, p. 126.
10   Roberts, 2015, p. 198.
11   Letter from KM to Dumas, 23 March 1931, Dumas Papers, MS 4849/2/7, NLA.
12   Letter from Dumas to KM, 24 March 1931, *ibid*.
13   *Advertiser and Register* (Adelaide), 10 April 1931, p. 21; *News* (Adelaide), 8 April 1931, p. 1.

14 *Advertiser and Register* (Adelaide), 10 April 1931, p. 19.
15 Roberts, 2015, p. 194; *Mercury* (Hobart), 11 February 1931, p. 9.
16 Letter from KM to Dumas, 21 January 1931, Dumas Papers, MS 4849/2/7, NLA. Dumas had previously worked at the *Argus* and knew the paper well.
17 'Journalism in the '30s'.
18 *Argus*, 8 January 1931, p. 6.
19 Grenfell Price quoted in Connell and Irving, p. 328.
20 Henderson, 2011, p. 268.
21 Hart, 1979, p. 116.
22 Lloyd, 2001b, p. 116.
23 *National Times*, 22–27 May 1978, p. 7.
24 Lloyd, 1988, p. 95.
25 Quoted in Lloyd, 2001b, p. 141.
26 Roberts, 2015, p. 195.
27 Broomhill.
28 Letter from KM to Dumas, 21 September 1931, Dumas Papers, MS 4849/2/9, NLA.
29 *ibid.*, 12 March 1931, p. 2, in Dumas Papers, MS 4849/2/7, NLA. A Labor MP, Price had just crossed the floor in March 1931, and soon became parliamentary secretary of the UAP.
30 Richardson, 2006.
31 Lloyd, 1988, p. 100.
32 Fraser, p. 42.
33 Even if the house was only three doors away. Fraser.
34 *Sun*, 14 March 1931, p. 1; 15 March, p. 1.
35 Lloyd, 1988, p. 95; plus JA Alexander interview with Mel Pratt, NLA.
36 *Argus*, 5 May 1931, p. 7.
37 *ibid.*, 9 February 1931, p. 9.
38 *ibid.*, 21 May 1931, p. 7.
39 Martin, 1993, p. 92.
40 Blainey, 1970, p. 148.
41 *Advertiser*, 3 June 1933, p. 15.
42 Fraser.
43 Hart, 1969, p. 51.
44 Letter from KM to Dumas, 10 June 1931, Dumas Papers, MS 4849/2/8.
45 *Queensland Times*, 8 May 1931, p. 7; *Examiner* (Launceston), 8 May 1931, p. 10.
46 Lloyd, 2001b, p. 151.
47 Younger, 2003, p. 187.
48 *News*, 2 December 1931, p. 7.
49 *Advertiser and Register*, 10 April 1931, p. 19; *Herald*, 4 December 1931, p. 1; 18 December 1931, p. 4; 21 December 1931, p. 22; and 10 December 1931, p. 5.
50 Lloyd, 2001b, p. 153.
51 *SMH*, 18 December 1931, p. 6.
52 *Daily Telegraph*, 18 December 1931, p. 6.
53 *Telegraph* (Brisbane), 18 December 1931, p. 10.
54 Quoted in Lloyd, 1988, pp. 108–09.
55 *Age*, 16 March 1931, p. 6; and 26 June 1931, p. 6.
56 *ibid.*, 11 December 1931, p. 8; and 18 December, p. 10.

57   *Mercury* (Hobart), 18 December 1931, p. 8. The *Mercury* helped Lyons and the National Union form a branch of the All for Australia League, along with the Nationalist Premier and leading businessmen (Hart, 1979, pp. 118–19).

58   Warren Denning quoted in Lloyd, 1988, p. 104.

59   Telegram from Dumas to KM, 20 December 1931, Dumas Papers, MS 4849/2/10, NLA.

60   Letter from Dumas to KM, 21 December 1931, *ibid.*

61   Hart, 1979, p. 111.

62   *ibid.*, p. 113.

63   Quoted in Serle, 1986.

64   Roberts, 2015, p. 209.

65   *Labor Daily*, 3 June 1933, p. 5.

66   The National Union's president sent Lyons his congratulations on the Budget. Lyons replied, with some accuracy, that his achievements had 'been made possible only by the splendid support and encouragement given to me by yourself and others associated with the National Union' (Hart, 1979, p. 130).

67   *West Australian*, 19 October 1933, p. 13; 'Nationalist Press', *Maryborough Chronicle, Wide Bay and Burnett Advertiser*, 18 August 1933, p. 7.

68   Letter from Dumas to Joe Lyons, 23 August 1937, Dumas Papers, MS 4849/10/6, NLA.

69   Walker, 1980b, p. 129; *Sun*, 16 November 1933, p. 19.

70   Cable from KM to Dumas, 20 October 1933, Dumas Papers, MS 48493/17, NLA. Lyons occasionally asked the HWT papers to cover events in a particular way, or to withhold information from the public, including information that might affect his negotiations with Nivison over loan terms, or his negotiations for assistance to the wheat industry (Dumas Papers, MS 4849, NLA).

71   Several Baillieus were sharing power (especially WL's brother 'Jac', son Clive, and nephew Marshall 'ML') with Colin Fraser, managing director of BHAS. WS Robinson's unconventional support for Theodore had to be taken into account along with more conventional business circle views. Clive Baillieu was also very interested in Keynes' prescriptions. Murdoch's role was complicated by the different opinions evident in Collins House, and Ricketson's diary showed that MH Baillieu and Ricketson opposed Murdoch over loan conversion (Hart, 1979, p. 136).

72   Quoted from Staniforth Ricketson's diary extract, 17 March 1932, in Millmow, p. 122.

73   Hart, 1979, p. 113.

74   Hart, 1969, p. 49.

75   Telegram from KM to Dumas, 9 October 1934, Dumas Papers, MS 4849, NLA.

76   Letter from Dumas to Joe Lyons, 11 October 1934, Dumas Papers, MS 4849, NLA.

77   Letter from KM to Dumas, 15 October 1934, Dumas Papers, MS 4849/3/19, NLA.

78   Quoted in Roberts, 2015, p. 219.

79   Lloyd, 1988, pp. 108, 111.

80   *Smith's Weekly*, 22 June 1935, p. 12.

81   *SMH*, 6 December 1949, p. 2.

82   Dated 8 June 1931, quoted in Roberts, 2015, p. 201.

83   Letter from KM to Dumas, 10 April 1933, Dumas Papers, MS 4849/3/15, NLA.

84   *SMH*, 10 July 1936, p. 12 (assets not including 'good will').

85   *Argus*, 19 September 1936, p. 17; *Telegraph* (Brisbane), 2 July 1936, p. 15.
86   Spowers was not only friends with Ricketson, but also with Richard Casey. Casey
      was the godfather of Spowers' son (Collins Persse).
87   Nolan, 2017, pp. 9–10.
88   Fairfax & Sons did have a line of influence on economic debates via its allied
      businesses, especially the Bank of New South Wales. Its general manager, AC
      Davidson, played a leading role in banking and monetary policies (Holder, 1981).
89   *SMH*, 15 June 1931, p. 8.
90   *Queenslander*, 22 January 1931, p. 42.
91   Letter from KM to Dumas, 7 September 1932, Dumas papers, MS 4849/3/14, NLA.
92   Letter from KM to Dumas, 6 January 1931 [but misdated 1930], Dumas Papers, MS
      4849/2/7, NLA.
93   *ibid*.
94   Letter from Dumas to KM, 6 September 1932, Dumas Papers, MS 4849/3/14, NLA.
95   Letter from KM to Dumas, 7 September 1932, Dumas Papers, MS 4849/3/14, NLA.
      Note: The HWT had cash to send across because, a few months before the New
      York stock market crash, its board had approved a share issue (Younger, 2003, p.
      192).
96   Royal Commission into the Monetary and Banking Systems 1937; Millmow.
97   Schedvin, 1970; Eklund.
98   Quoted in Gruen and Clark, p. 28.
99   Fishback.
100 Holder, 1981; Gruen and Clark, p. 37. Theodore had called parity a 'conservative
      fetish' (*Register News-Pictorial* (Adelaide), 20 January 1931, p. 23).
101 Clive Baillieu, WS Robinson and Murdoch offered Keynes the generous fee of
      £2500 plus all expenses if the economist would tour Australia and write exclusively
      for Murdoch's newspapers. He declined but did write a piece for the *Herald* which
      included the line 'I am sure that the Premiers' Plan last year saved the economic
      structure of Australia' (*Herald*, 25 June 1932, p. 1). Murdoch's papers made much
      of this line although Keynes' full piece showed his support was qualified. He went
      on in the article to counsel against continuing with austerity measures of wage
      reductions and currency deflation (Markwell, p. 23; Millmow, p. 133).
102 Coleman, Cornish and Hagger, pp. 122–23.
103 *Sun*, 15 December 1935, p. 16; *SMH*, 5 September 1945, p. 7; Hawkins.
104 Calwell, 1978, p. 63.
105 *SMH*, 5 September 1945, p. 7.

12   **Capturing the airwaves: Newspapers, radio and the ABC**
1   *West Australian*, 8 May 1931, p. 3.
2   Jones, p. 25.
3   *Argus*, 16 November and 25 November 1931; *Mercury* (Hobart), 6 November 1931,
      p. 6.
4   Walker, 1973, p. 9.
5   Petersen, p. 20; *SMH*, 26 May 1923, p. 14.
6   Transcript of KM speaking at the opening of a new radio station in Victoria, 1937,
      ABC archival material kindly provided by Stan Correy.
7   *Daily Guardian*, 14 December 1923, p. 7.

8   *West Australian*, 8 May 1931, p. 3.
9   *Herald*, 27 August 1924, p. 1.
10 *ibid.*, 4 October 1924, p. 6; and 13 October 1924, p. 6.
11 *ibid.*, 3 September 1926, p. 1; 30 January 1925, p. 6; and 25 October 1926, p. 4; Roberts, 2015, pp. 164–65.
12 Roberts, 2015, p. 165.
13 *ibid.*, p. 163.
14 *Smith's Weekly*, 19 December 1942, p. 12; *Sunday Times* (Sydney), 13 September 1925, p. 1.
15 *SMH*, 18 April 1931, p. 27.
16 JJ Knight, Brisbane Newspaper Company, quoted in Petersen, p. 48.
17 Petersen, p. 29.
18 Leopold Broinowski, associate editor of the *Mercury*, quoted in *The Age*, 4 April 1927, p. 11.
19 *Herald*, 24 March 1927, p. 2.
20 Petersen, p. 30.
21 Geeves, pp. 52–53.
22 *ibid.*, p. 53.
23 *Smith's Weekly*, 4 August 1928, p. 4.
24 *ibid.*, 24 July 1926, p. 11; and 30 June 1928, p. 12.
25 *Herald*, 3 May 1928, p. 1.
26 *Age*, 23 January 1930, p. 9; *Smith's Weekly*, 30 June 1928, p. 1; and 4 August 1928, p. 4.
27 Inglis, p. 11.
28 Petersen, p. 30.
29 Fink stayed close to the winners. Four months after Doyle's success, he became a co-director (with Fink and Tait) of Amalgamated Pictures.
30 *West Australian*, 21 January 1930, p. 8.
31 *Smith's Weekly*, 29 August 1931, p. 10; *Sun*, 11 October 1929, p. 12; and 2 September 1929, p. 9.
32 *Smith's Weekly*, 15 June 1929, p. 7.
33 *SMH*, 11 May 1928, p. 8; Petersen, p. 28.
34 Memo from Frederick Daniell to chairman of Sun Newspapers Ltd, 14 June 1935, FMBA, MLMSS 9894/931, SLNSW.
35 *Herald*, 8 August 1929, p. 6; *Register News-Pictorial*, 9 August 1929, p. 3.
36 Dumas, pp. 56–57.
37 *ibid.*
38 *Herald,* 16 June 1930, p. 10.
39 Younger, 1996, p. 129.
40 Jones, p. 36.
41 Walkerb, 1980b, p. 119.
42 Petersen, p. 49.
43 Inglis, p. 17.
44 Thomas, 1980, p. 12.
45 *Age*, 11 February 1932, p. 6.
46 *ibid.*, 20 January 1932, p. 6.
47 *SMH*, 16 November 1931, p. 8.
48 Roberts, 1972, pp. 150–51.

49   Alexander Papers, diary entry 9 March 1932, MS 2389, NLA.
50   *Herald*, 10 March 1932, p. 6.
51   Alexander Papers, diary entry 10 March 1932, MS 2389, NLA.
52   *Herald*, 14 March 1932, p. 4.
53   *ibid.*, 9 March 1932, p. 8; and 10 March 1932, pp. 6–7.
54   *ibid.*, 10 March 1932, p. 6; and 11 March 1932, p. 8.
55   *ibid.*, 14 March 1932, p. 2.
56   *ibid.*, 11 March 1932, p. 8.
57   Alexander Papers, diary entry 11 March 1932, MS 2389, NLA.
58   Alexander Papers, diary entry 17 March 1932, MS 2389, NLA.
59   Memo from Frederick Daniell to chairman of Sun Newspapers Ltd, 14 June 1935,
     FMBA, MLMSS 9894/931, SLNSW.
60   *Herald*, 14 March 1932, p. 4; 10 March 1932, p. 7; 15 March 1932, p. 10; 16 March
     1932, p. 5; *Age*, 11 March 1932, p. 5.
61   Roberts, 1972, p. 150.
62   *Herald*, 14 March 1932, pp. 2, 4.
63   Alexander Papers, diary entry 15 March 1932, MS 2389, NLA.
64   *ibid.*
65   *ibid.*, diary entry 16 March 1932.
66   *CPD* (HR), 17 March 1932, p. 1257.
67   *ibid.*, 3 May 1932, p. 259.
68   *ibid.*, p. 261.
69   *Age*, 16 March 1932, p. 8.
70   *Herald*, 17 March 1932, p. 1.
71   Alexander Papers, diary entry 21 March 1932, MS 2389, NLA.
72   BBC, 'About BBC News'.
73   *CPD* (Senate), 12 May 1932, p. 632.
74   Thomas, 1980, pp. 37–38.
75   *ibid.*, p. 38.
76   'Managing director's report, 6 September 1932', p. 1, Dumas Papers, MS 4849/3/14,
     NLA.
77   Thomas, 1980, p. 18.
78   'Managing director's report, 6 September 1932', p. 1, in Dumas Papers,
     MS 4849/3/14, NLA.
79   Petersen, p. 51.

13   Emperors of air
1   *CPD* (HR), 3 December 1935, p. 2364.
2   *Sun*, 30 November 1933, p. 21.
3   Petersen, p. 24.
4   Walkerb, 1980b, p. 121.
5   Cleary quoted in Petersen, p. 56.
6   Quoted in Petersen, p. 56.
7   *Telegraph* (Brisbane), 7 July 1936, p. 9.
8   Roberts, 2015, p. 213.
9   Tiffen, 2006, pp. 99–100.
10   Australian Newspapers' Conference minutes of 22nd half-yearly meeting,

Melbourne, 13–15 November 1935, p. 9, FMBA, MLMSS 9894/934, SLNSW.

11 *ibid.*, p. 10.

12 *ibid.*, p. 11.

13 Letter from KM to Joe Lyons, 25 November 1935, p. 4, Murdoch Papers, MS 2823, NLA.

14 *Herald*, 3 December 1935, p. 3; 29 October 1935, p. 9.

15 Quoted in Walker, 1980, p. 119.

16 *Sun*, 3 November 1935, p. 11.

17 Letter from KM to Joe Lyons, 25 November 1935, Murdoch Papers, MS 2823, NLA.

18 Letter from Joe Lyons to KM, 29 November 1935, Murdoch Papers, MS 2823, NLA.

19 Percy Spender (minister for the army, Menzies' once close colleague) from his diary quoted in Hazlehurst, 1979, p. 242.

20 *Mudgee Guardian and North-Western Representative* (NSW), 23 October 1924, p. 15.

21 *CPD* (HR), 3 December 1935, p. 2366.

22 *Herald*, 4 December 1935, p. 3.

23 *CPD* (HR), 3 December 1935, pp. 2367–68.

24 *ibid.*, p. 2368.

25 Letter from KM to Hugh Denison, 19 October 1937, FMBA, MLMSS 9894/1230, SLNSW.

26 *CPD* (HR), 3 December 1935, p. 2371.

27 *Herald*, 5 December 1935, p. 6.

28 Quoted in Petersen, pp. 58–59.

29 Memo to chairman, author not named, 15 October 1936, FMBA, MLMSS 9894/931, SLNSW.

30 Memos from Frederick Daniell to chairman of Sun Newspapers Ltd, 22 June 1935 and 14 June 1935, FMBA, MLMSS 9894/931, SLNSW.

31 Memo from John Butters to Hugh Denison, 6 October 1936, FMBA, MLMSS 9894/931, SLNSW.

32 Letter from Colin Fraser to MB Hamer, 8 February 1935, BHAS Papers, 1969.0006, UMA.

33 Memo from Colin Fraser to WS Robinson, ML Baillieu, MH Baillieu and WM Wainwright, 6 February 1935, BHAS Papers, 1969.0006, UMA.

34 Letter from Colin Fraser to Harold Burston, 15 February 1935, BHAS Papers, 1969.0006, UMA.

35 Letter from Colin Fraser to MB Hamer, 8 February 1935, BHAS Papers, 1969.0006, UMA.

36 Letter from WT Conder to Colin Fraser, 14 February 1935, BHAS Papers, 1969.0006, UMA.

37 *ibid.*, 16 February 1935, BHAS Papers, 1969.0006, UMA.

38 Memo from WS Robinson to Colin Fraser, 12 March 1935, BHAS Papers, 1969.0006, UMA.

39 Text of telegram from MH Baillieu to Gilbert, 23 February 1935, BHAS Papers, 1969.0006, UMA.

40 Telegram from Harold Burston to MH Baillieu, 24 February 1935, BHAS Papers, 1969.0006, UMA.

41 Telegram from Harold Burston to John Butters, 3 [month unclear] 1936, FMBA, MLMSS 9894/923, SLNSW.

42   Letter from Harold Burston to Colin Fraser, 17 December 1936, BHAS Papers, 1969.0006, UMA.

43   *Labor Daily*, 26 August 1937, p. 6; *Truth* (Sydney), 21 February 1937, p. 26.

44   *CPD* (Senate), 8 September 1937, p. 712.

45   Griffen-Foley, 2006, p. 135; *News*, 6 December 1938, p. 11; *West Australian*, 13 October 1938, p. 20.

46   *Sun*, 10 July 1938, p. 15.

47   Jones, p. 58.

48   Correy.

49   *Horsham Times*, 26 February 1937, p. 3.

50   Quoted in Correy.

51   Quoted in Petersen, p. 109.

52   Petersen, p. 102.

53   Letter from Charles Moses to RG Menzies, 27 May 1939, Menzies Papers, MS 4936/36/2/1, NLA.

54   Zwar, p. 118.

55   Jones, pp. 49, 130.

56   *CPD* (HR), 27 September 1944, pp. 1633–44.

57   Stamm, p. 5, 195; Lebovic, p. 69.

58   2GB, 2WL, 2CA, 2NM, 2NX, 2LF, 3AW, 5DN and 4BH.

59   Goot, p. 5.

60   Comparing circulation figures with precision is difficult, but the figures do broadly suggest circulation growth in Australia of 45 per cent in the 1940s, compared to around 31 per cent in the United Kingdom, and 30–32 per cent in the United States (Stamm, p. 4; Noam, p. 137; Pew Research Center).

61   *CPD* (HR), 25 August 1970, pp. 452–55.

14   Paper and cable cartels

1   The Liverpool Mill in New South Wales had produced 'news printing paper' in reels from around 1866. It was used in local newspapers and, on occasion, in the *Echo* and *The Age*, but its newsprint business was wiped out when a duty on imported paper was repealed in 1884, and it closed around 1905.

2   *Newspaper News*, 2 June 1941, supplement, p. 1; *West Australian*, 12 May 1941, p. 6; *Courier-Mail*, 12 May 1941, p. 6.

3   *The Week* (Brisbane), 2 January 1920, p. 19.

4   *Argus*, 30 August 1921, p. 3.

5   *Smith's Weekly*, 6 September 1924, p. 3.

6   *Advocate* (Burnie, Tasmania), 10 September 1937, p. 7 (includes text from a speech Mussen gave to the Burnie Chamber of Commerce on 9 September 1937).

7   Speech by Gerald Mussen, reproduced in the *Advocate*, 22 February 1939, supplement, p. 6.

8   Yule, 2012, p. 300.

9   Richardson, 1987, pp. 12–13.

10   Yule, 2012, p. 299.

11   Poynter.

12   ML Baillieu quoted in Jamieson, p. 173.

13   *Age*, 6 December 1923, p. 8; *World* (Hobart), 6 December 1923, p. 4.

14   *ibid.*
15   *Age*, 18 July 1925, p. 17.
16   *Mercury* (Hobart), 22 August 1925, p. 8.
17   Charlton.
18   *Advocate*, 13 October 1925, p. 2.
19   Quoted in Yule, 2012, p. 300.
20   *Advocate*, 10 September 1937, p. 7.
21   'Draft prospectus: Paper Makers Ltd', September 1932, p. 6, Dumas Papers, MS 4849/3/14, NLA.
22   *Advocate*, 8 April 1929, p. 2.
23   Warwick Fairfax quoted in *Newspaper News*, 2 June 1941, supplement, p. 2.
24   Yule, 2012, p. 301.
25   *ibid.*
26   Joe Lyons, 'Australia welcomes the birth of the new industry', *Advocate*, 22 February 1939, p. 7.
27   *Advocate*, 22 February 1939, p. 6.
28   *ibid.*
29   Letter from Hugh Denison to KM, 27 September 1932, FMBA, MLMSS 9894/933, SLNSW.
30   *Advocate*, 22 February 1939, p. 6.
31   Richardson, 2006, p. 8.
32   Younger, 2003, p. 217.
33   *Herald*, 25 August 1938, p. 6.
34   Letter from Dumas to KM, 8 September 1932, Dumas Papers, MS 4849/3/14, NLA.
35   Letter from KM to Hugh Denison, 22 August 1932, FMBA, MLMSS 9894/933, SLNSW.
36   Telegram from Hugh Denison to KM, undated (but likely September 1932), FMBA, MLMSS 9894/933, SLNSW; and letter from Hugh Denison to KM, 27 September 1932, FMBA, MLMSS 9894/933, SLNSW.
37   'Managing director's report, 6 September 1932', p. 1, Dumas Papers, MS 4849/3/14, NLA.
38   *Advocate*, 14 December 1933, p. 7.
39   Letter from Dumas to KM, 27 July 1933, Dumas Papers, MS 4849/3/16, NLA.
40   Letter from KM to Hugh Denison, 22 October 1937, FMBA, MLMSS 9894/1230, SLNSW.
41   *ibid.*, 28 March 1933, FMBA, MLMSS 9894/933, SLNSW.
42   Letter from Dumas to Thorold Fink, 31 July 1933, Dumas Papers, MS 4849/3/16, NLA.
43   Letter from Dumas to KM, 27 July 1933, Dumas Papers, MS 4849/3/16, NLA.
44   Garden, p. 230.
45   Minutes of ANC 22nd half-yearly meeting in Melbourne, 13–15 November 1935, p. 33, FMBA, MLMSS 9894/934, SLNSW.
46   Memo from Associated Newspapers' general manager to John Butters, 30 August 1934, FMBA, MLMSS 9894/934, SLNSW.
47   *Advocate*, 22 February 1939, p. 6.
48   Mussen became one of APPM's directors, along with Colin Fraser, Walter Massy-Greene, ML Baillieu and Harold Cohen. Although still a UAP senator, Massy-

Greene was also an active executive for Collins House by now and he became APPM's first chairman. Mussen went to England and did not come back until May 1937 when the works for the Burnie mill were underway. In August 1938, APPM started manufacturing writing paper and fine printing paper. Mussen remained a major shareholder of APPM, and was knighted in 1939.

49   *Sunday Times* (Sydney), 15 January 1928, p. 16.
50   *Telegraph* (Brisbane), 28 September 1938, p. 11; *Argus*, 7 October 1938, p. 11. Electrolytic Zinc's profits had also declined but were still healthy (*SMH*, 21 December 1938, p. 12).
51   Report to the board of directors of Associated Newspapers by Graham Waddell, 12 July 1937, FMBA, MLMSS 9894/1731, SLNSW.
52   Letter from KM to Hugh Denison, 22 October 1937, FMBA, MLMSS 9894/1230, SLNSW.
53   Letter from Hugh Denison to KM, 25 October 1937, FMBA, MLMSS 9894/1230, SLNSW.
54   *Herald*, 1 December 1938, p. 1; 10 December 1938, p. 5; 14 December 1938, p. 11; and Younger, 1996, p. 148.
55   *Herald*, 25 August 1938, p. 6.
56   *ibid*.
57   *ibid*.
58   *Truth* (Sydney), 21 August 1938, p. 20.
59   *Courier-Mail*, 1 September 1938, p. 2.
60   *Newspaper News*, 2 June 1941, supplement, p. 3.
61   *Argus*, 31 August 1948, p. 6.
62   *SMH*, 30 June 1941, p. 8.
63   Butler, p. 20.
64   Parliament of Great Britain, 1949, p. 134.
65   Notes of conference, dated 7 September 1942, 'Newsprint rationing', A11751-13-part 3, NAA.
66   *SMH* advertisements in *Newspaper News*, 1 May 1931, p. 19; and 1 July 1938, p. 7.
67   Griffen-Foley, 2000, p. 155.
68   *Newspaper News*, 2 June 1941, p. 7; Roberts, 2015, p. 259.
69   Keith Murdoch quoted in *Mercury* (Hobart), 16 February 1943, p. 4.
70   *Newspaper News*, 2 June 1941, supplement, pp. 2, 7; Younger, 1996, p. 166.
71   *SMH*, 12 May 1941, supplement; *Daily Examiner* (Grafton), 19 March 1941, p. 5; *Smith's Weekly*, 9 August 1941, p. 14.
72   Younger, 1996, p. 182
73   Greenslade, p. 63.
74   Souter, 1981, p. 291.
75   *Canberra Times*, 18 March 1969, p. 15.
76   HWT, *Annual Report*, 1947, pp. 6–7.
77   *Sun*, 10 May 1949, p. 7.
78   *SMH*, 27 May 1954, p. 4; Mayer, pp. 62–63.
79   *Tumut and Adelong Times*, 16 August 1949, p. 4.
80   'Associated Newspapers Ltd production account, 24 September 1939', FMBA, MLMSS 9894/54, SLNSW.
81   *Herald*, 30 November 1948, p. 5.

82   Quoted in Mayer, p. 64.
83   *Tribune* (Sydney), 30 April 1958, p. 9.
84   Minutes of the ANC 22nd half-yearly meeting, Melbourne, 13–15 November 1935, p. 33, FMBA, MLMSS 9894/934, SLNSW.
85   Australian Newsprint Mills Holdings Ltd, *Annual Report 1959*, FMBA, MLMSS 9894/72, SLNSW.
86   Quoted in Mayer, p. 63; Greenslade, pp. 66–67; Griffen-Foley, 2000, p. 160.
87   Dumas, pp. 58–59.
88   Goot, p. 5.
89   *Herald*, 30 November 1948, p. 5. The ANPA papers, led by RAG Henderson, had been urging the government to do so (letter from RA Henderson to JB Chifley, 10 November 1948, FMBA, MLMSS 9894/511, SLNSW).
90   Dumas, p. 42.
91   Minutes of Sun Newspapers Ltd board meeting, 15 June 1931, FMBA, MLMSS 9894/46, SLNSW.
92   Letter from KM to Hugh Denison, 5 October 1931, FMBA, MLMSS 9894/933, SLNSW.
93   Document attached to letter from KM to Hugh Denison, titled 'Rough notes on reconstruction of cable services', 6 October 1931, FMBA, MLMSS 9894/933, SLNSW.
94   Letter from KM to Hugh Denison, 22 October 1937, FMBA, MLMSS 9894/1230, SLNSW.
95   Minutes of ANC's 21st half-yearly meeting, Brisbane, 29–30 May 1935, p. 26, FMBA, MLMSS 9894/934, SLNSW.
96   *CPD* (HR), 6 December 1935, pp. 2802–03.
97   *Smith's Weekly* (Sydney), 6 April 1940, p. 5; Griffen-Foley, 2000, p. 116; *Newspaper News*, 1 June 1940, p. 1.
98   Quoted in Mayer, p. 28.
99   *The Worker* (Wagga), 2 June 1910, p. 13; Putnis, 1999, p. 139.
100   Walker, 1980b, pp. 120–21.
101   Petersen, p. 104.
102   Putnis, 2014, p. 81.
103   *Tribune* (Sydney), 11 January 1946, p. 8.
104   Document attached to letter from KM to Hugh Denison, titled 'Rough notes on reconstruction of cable services', 6 October 1931, FMBA, MLMSS 9894/933, SLNSW.
105   *Tribune* (Sydney), 8 May 1945, p. 7.
106   *Australian Worker* (Sydney), 18 April 1945, p. 7.
107   AAP, 2010, p. 13.
108   *ibid.*, p. 13.
109   The thirteen foundation newspapers of AAP were the *Herald, Sun News-Pictorial, Courier-Mail, Advertiser, News, West Australian, SMH, Argus, Sun, Daily Telegraph, Daily News, Age* and *Mercury*.
110   When in the United Kingdom, Murdoch raised the idea of a partnership with Reuters' directors (*Advertiser*, 23 December 1946, p. 6).
111   Minutes of the ANC 21st half-yearly meeting, Brisbane, 29–30 May 1935, p. 26, FMBA, MLMSS 9894/934, SLNSW.

112 'The *Sun*: House memo', 4 June 1942, FMBA, MLMSS 9894/933, SLNSW.
113 Chalmers, p. 23.
114 Lloyd, 1988, p. 243.
115 Bonney and Wilson, p. 118.
116 *New Journalist*, June 1981, pp. 15, 18.
117 Johnston and Forde, pp. 207–08.
118 *Herald*, 21 January 1948, p. 1.
119 Memo from WT Turner, Comptroller-General, 16 April 1951, 'Reopening of news control branch', A117571-1-50, NAA.
120 Minutes of ANM board of directors' meeting, 10 October 1945, FMBA, MLMSS 9894/794, SLNSW.
121 *ibid.*, 31 July–1 August 1945, p. 5, FMBA, MLMSS 9894/794, SLNSW.
122 *ibid.*, p. 7.
123 *ibid.*, p. 5.
124 Letter from RA Henderson to HD Giddy, 6 June 1945, FMBA, MLMSS 9894/789, SLNSW; Letter from HD Giddy to RA Henderson, 23 May 1945, FMBA, MLMSS 9894/789, SLNSW. (The *Argus* had made a small investment in ANM by 1943 but its substantial investment came in 1945.) Griffen-Foley, 2000, p. 160.
125 Cable from RAG Henderson to 'Palmer' at *SMH*, 21 June 1947, FMBA, MLMSS 9894/1612, SLNSW.
126 Letter from RA Henderson to KM, 3 April 1945, FMBA, MLMSS 9894/789, SLNSW.
127 *ibid.*

15 'Killing me': Menzies and the press
1   Tiffen, 2017, p. 2.
2   *Argus*, 29 August 1941, p. 1.
3   RG Menzies, 'A record of my resignation', 1 September 1941, Menzies Papers, MS4936/583/44, NLA.
4   *Westralian Worker* (Perth), 9 December 1949, p. 8.
5   *Daily News*, 26 January 1950, p. 2.
6   *Tribune* (Sydney), 26 February 1949, p. 5.
7   Gibson, p. 16; Aarons, pp. 12–13.
8   Blainey, 1970, p. 174.
9   *Age*, 3 June 1921, p. 7; and 11 June 1931, p. 9.
10 Although cited as brand new information in Thompson and Macklin, it had been known since at least the 1940s (e.g. *Tribune*, 12 March 1940, p. 3; and *Age*, 2 November 1945, p. 3; *Argus*, 2 November 1945, p. 3).
11 *Herald*, 1 November 1945, p. 10.
12 *Age*, 2 November 1945, p. 3; *Argus*, 2 November 1945, p. 3.
13 *National Times*, 22–27 May 1978, p. 11.
14 *ibid.*, p. 11. See also the views of CD Kemp quoted in Henderson, 1994, p. 87.
15 William McMahon, paraphrased in *National Times*, 22–27 May 1978, p. 11.
16 Wheeler, 1981.
17 *CPD* (HR), 2 October 1935, p. 428.
18 *Argus*, 30 October 1935, p. 6.
19 *SMH*, 16 December 1936, p. 17; *Tribune* (Sydney), 13 March 1957, p. 6.

20   *Herald*, 21 September 1942, p. 8; *Tribune* (Sydney), 5 April 1946, p. 5. Menzies' brother, Frank, later became a director of Capel Court investment trust (*Newcastle Sun*, 21 December 1954, p. 12).

21   *Sun*, 15 May 1932, p. 10; *Weekly Times*, 6 August 1932, p. 13.

22   Fleming, Merrett and Ville, p. 15.

23   *Telegraph* (Brisbane), 3 October 1935, p. 9.

24   *Tribune*, 14 December 1945, p. 3.

25   Connell and Irving, p. 276.

26   The significance of a Menzies' letter to SM Bruce was discussed in ABC, 2001.

27   Blainey, 1970, p. 174.

28   *Daily Telegraph* (Sydney), 26 May 1931, p. 1.

29   This letter was quoted by historian Kosmas Tsokhas, and in Such.

30   Letter from KM to Clive Baillieu, 4 January 1939, quoted in Martin, 1993, p. 258.

31   *ibid.*, p. 247.

32   Letter from KM to RG Menzies, 6 June 1933, Menzies Papers, MS 4936/1/1, NLA.

33   Letter from KM to Dumas, 17 October 1934, Dumas Papers, MS 4849/3/19, NLA.

34   Younger, 2003, p. 209.

35   Letter from KM to RG Menzies, 17 November 1936, Murdoch Papers, MS 2823/1/6, NLA.

36   Holt.

37   Lloyd, 1988, p. 111.

38   *Herald*, 7 October 1938, p. 7.

39   Nolan, 2010, p. 2; Nolan, 2014, p. 13.

40   Souter, 1981, p. 184.

41   *SMH*, 19 April 1939, p. 14.

42   Percy Joske quoted in Martin, 2001, p. 178.

43   Lloyd, 1988, p. 125.

44   RG Menzies' diary entry, 21 February 1935, quoted in Lloyd, 1988, p. 6.

45   Lloyd, 1988, p. 127.

46   Denning quoted in Lloyd, 1988, p. 129.

47   Fraser

48   *Herald*, 7 March 1939, p. 3.

49   Letter from KM to Clive Baillieu, dated 4 January 1939, quoted in Martin, 1993, pp. 247–48.

50   The scheme had gone through Cabinet and been passed by both houses of parliament but it was then suddenly withdrawn, reportedly because the UAP's Melbourne financiers did not approve of how much it would cost them (Hart, 1979, pp. 111–12).

51   *Herald*, 15 March 1939, p. 6.

52   *Age*, 15 March 1939, p. 12; *Sun*, 15 March 1939, p. 4.

53   Henderson, 2014, p. 84 (but note that Anne Henderson confuses Kingsley Henderson for RAG Henderson and erroneously refers to JB Aitken as the *Argus'* editor).

54   *Argus*, 11 September 1937, p. 22.

55   Nolan, 2017, pp. 8–9.

56   Hazlehurst, 2013, pp. 262, 263.

57   *Smith's Weekly* (Sydney), 30 September 1933, p. 2.

58 *Tribune*, 4 September 1957, p. 9. Menzies' involvement with the Capel Court Investment Trust is another gap in otherwise comprehensive biographies of him. The mainstream media also shied away from the topic. The Communist party's *Tribune* intermittently reported share register lists. One former member of JB Were's, Arthur Goode, claimed in 1978 to remember (from forty years earlier) that Menzies 'sold all his ordinary shares when he became Prime Minister' (*National Times*, 22–27 May 1978, p. 10). But *Tribune* reported that share registers from 1944 showed Menzies and his wife held 20 000 shares in Capel Court companies (*Tribune*, 5 April 1946, p. 5). In 1939, Labor's EJ Ward said the Menzies were Capel Court company shareholders. Menzies replied that he had resigned from all directorships but he did not deny that he was still a shareholder (*Recorder* (Port Pirie), 23 October 1939, p. 2). Menzies also held shares in Equity Trustees (which invested in Howard Smith, one of the largest BHP shareholders) (*Age*, 14 October 1938, p. 9; *Recorder* (Port Pirie), 23 October 1939, p. 2; *Courier-Mail*, 1 October 1938, p. 4).
59 Hart, 1979, p. 130.
60 *CPD* (HR), 20 April 1939, pp. 16–17.
61 Letter from RL Curthoys to JR Darling, 24 April 1939, quoted in Martin, 1993, p. 269.
62 Souter, 1981, p. 185.
63 *Herald*, 14 April 1939, p. 9.
64 *Age*, 4 September 1939, p. 11.
65 Quoted in Marchant, p. 39.
66 *Daily Telegraph*, 21 July 1940, p. 10.
67 A Perth edition had closed in 1931.
68 'Standover man' (no author or date listed), McNicoll Papers, MLMSS 7419/19, SLNSW.
69 *Mail* (Adelaide), 26 December 1942, p. 2.
70 'Profit and loss statement', 6 March 1942, McNicoll Papers, MLMSS 7419/19, SLNSW.
71 'Consolidated Press', author not indicated, 1953, p. 3, McNicoll Papers, MLMSS 7419/19, SLNSW.
72 *ibid.*, p. 4.
73 'Profit and loss statement', 6 March 1942, McNicoll Papers, MLMSS 7419/19, SLNSW.
74 Letter from KM to RE Denison, 27 April 1940, Murdoch Papers, MS 2823/3/6/15, NLA.
75 *ibid.*
76 Extract of letter from RE Denison to KM, 3 May 1940, Murdoch Papers, MS 2823/3/6/15, NLA.
77 They would reconcile with the other major papers (except Norton's), in the replacement body, ANPA, in 1941.
78 Letter from Warwick Fairfax to RG Menzies, 29 May 1940, FMBA, MS 9894/511, SLNSW.
79 *Truth* (Sydney), 19 May 1940, p. 20; 16 June 1940, p. 20.
80 *ibid.*, 23 June 1940, pp. 25, 17.
81 *ibid.*, 7 July 1940, p. 1.

16   Menzies' downfall
1   Hasluck, p. 238.
2   Quoted in Hilvert, 1984, p. 56.
3   Macintyre, 2015, p. 38.
4   Quoted in Roberts, 2015, p. 226.
5   Hilvert, 1984, p. 57.
6   *ibid.*, p. 58.
7   *ibid.*
8   *Age*, 19 July 1940, p. 8.
9   George Knowles quoted in Younger, 2003, p. 241.
10   Quoted in Younger, 2003, p. 243.
11   *Daily Telegraph*, 18 July 1940, pp. 1, 5; 19 July 1940, p. 1.
12   *ibid.*, 19 July 1940, p. 1.
13   *ibid.*
14   *Canberra Times*, 19 July 1940, p. 2.
15   *Sun*, 18 July 1940, p. 1.
16   Denison quoted in *Daily Telegraph*, 18 July 1940, p. 5.
17   *Age*, 18 July 1940, p. 6.
18   Dumas, p. 68.
19   *SMH*, 22 July 1940, p. 8.
20   *Age*, 22 July 1940, p. 6.
21   *Canberra Times*, 19 July 1940, p. 2.
22   *ibid.*; *Daily Telegraph*, 19 July 1940, p. 1.
23   *Daily Telegraph*, 12 July 1940, p. 9.
24   *ibid.*, 21 July 1940, p. 1.
25   *SMH*, 22 July 1940, p. 8.
26   Dumas, p. 67.
27   Younger, 2003, p. 245.
28   Quoted in Younger 2003, p. 245.
29   Vickery, pp. 199–200.
30   Quoted in Vickery, p. 201.
31   Younger, 2003, p. 238.
32   Elisabeth Murdoch quoted in Roberts, 2015, p. 230; Younger, 2003, p. 246.
33   *Daily Telegraph*, 7 June 1940, quoted in Henderson, 2014, p. 79.
34   *Daily Telegraph*, 19 May 1940, p. 1.
35   *SMH*, 4 June 1940, p. 8 and *SMH*, quoted in Younger, 2003, p. 238.
36   Letter from RG Menzies to Warwick Fairfax, 22 June 1940, FMBA, MS 9894/511, SLNSW.
37   Griffen-Foley, 2000, p. 120.
38   Griffen-Foley, 1999, p. 95; *Daily Telegraph*, 20 September 1940, p. 8.
39   Unlike the *Daily Telegraph*, the *SMH* in its seat-by-seat how-to-vote guide endorsed the UAP's candidate above Evatt in the seat of Barton (*SMH*, 21 September 1940, p. 16).
40   *Daily Telegraph*, 18 September 1940, p. 1.
41   *SMH*, 21 September 1940, p. 14.
42   Walker, 1980b, p. 197.
43   *Age*, 23 September 1940, p. 7.

44 Telegram from Warwick Fairfax to RG Menzies, 26 September 1940, FMBA, MS 9894/511, SLNSW.
45 Telegram from RG Menzies to Warwick Fairfax, 27 September 1940, FMBA, MS 9894/511, SLNSW.
46 Marchant, p. 40.
47 Hall, p. 207.
48 *ibid.*, p. 176.
49 *ibid.*, p. 189.
50 Lawson, 2000.
51 Hall, p. 209.
52 'Standover man', McNicoll Papers, MLMSS 7419/19, SLNSW.
53 *Truth* (Sydney), 5 May 1940, p. 24.
54 *ibid.*, p. 197.
55 *ibid.*, p. 197.
56 *ibid.*, p. 198.
57 Goot, p. 5.
58 *ibid.* See also Tiffen, 1989, pp. 16–19.
59 Letter from Warwick Fairfax to RG Menzies, 29 July 1941, FMBA, MS 9894/511, SLNSW.
60 *Truth* (Sydney), 16 March 1941, p. 16; 13 April 1941, p. 23; 16 February 1941, p. 16.
61 Quoted in Lawson, 2000.
62 Telegrams between Warwick Fairfax and RG Menzies, 8 August 1940, FMBA, MS 9894/511, SLNSW.
63 Souter, 1981, p. 190.
64 Martin, 1993, p. 374; Souter, 1981, p. 191.
65 Fraser.
66 *SMH*, 3 July 1941, p. 6.
67 Letter from Warwick Fairfax to RG Menzies, 17 July 1941, FMBA, MS 9894/511, SLNSW.
68 *ibid.*
69 Letter from RG Menzies to Warwick Fairfax, 24 July 1941, FMBA, MS 9894/511, SLNSW.
70 Beale.
71 Letter from RG Menzies to Warwick Fairfax, 24 July 1941, FMBA, MS 9894/511, SLNSW.
72 Souter, 1981, p. 199.
73 *SMH*, 26 July 1941, p. 10.
74 Letter from Warwick Fairfax to RG Menzies, 29 July 1941, FMBA, MS 9894/511, SLNSW.
75 *ibid.*
76 *ibid.*
77 Letter from RA Henderson to Secretary, Commonwealth Prices Branch, 23 July 1941, FMBA, MS 9894/511, SLNSW.
78 Letter from Warwick Fairfax to RG Menzies, 29 July 1941, FMBA, MS 9894/511, SLNSW.
79 Souter, 1981, p. 197.
80 *SMH*, 29 July 1941, p. 6.

81 Letter from Warwick Fairfax to RG Menzies, 29 July 1941, FMBA, MS 9894/511, SLNSW.
82 *Canberra Times*, 20 September 1976, p. 42.
83 When the unnamed official ventured this advice is not known ('Government Public Relations', anonymous and undated, pp. 5–6, Menzies Papers, MS 4936, NLA).
84 Griffen-Foley, 2000, p. 128.
85 *West Australian*, 25 August 1951, p. 3.
86 Griffen-Foley, 2000, p. 128.
87 Quoted in Macintyre, 1996.
88 Fraser, p. 42.
89 Souter, 1981, p. 200.
90 Colin Bednall's typed unpublished autobiography, p. 21, Bednall Papers, MS 5546/3, NLA.

Postscript
1 Letter from KM to Dumas, 15 July 1942, quoted in Roberts, 2015, p. 233.
2 Tiffen, 2006, pp. 99–100.

BIBLIOGRAPHY

ARCHIVES AND MANUSCRIPT MATERIAL

Australian Joint Copying Project (AJCP)
Northcliffe (Sir Alfred Harmsworth) Papers, correspondence with Keith Murdoch, 1915–1922, M 1641.

John Dahlsen papers
John Dahlsen papers relating to the HWT, provided to the author.

Mitchell Library, State Library of New South Wales
David McNicoll Papers, MLMSS 7419.
Denison family Papers, MLMSS 6364.
Fairfax Media Limited Business Archive, MLMSS 9894.

National Archives of Australia (NAA)
'Newsprint – rationing of stocks and supplies', (A11751-13-part 3).
'Reopening of news control branch', (A117571-1-50).
Rupert William Geary military records, (B883, NX5366).

National Library of Australia (NLA)
Arthur Augustus Calwell Papers, MS 4738.
Colin Blore Bednall Papers, MS 5546.
Joseph Aloysius (JA) Alexander Papers, MS 2389.
Keith Arthur Murdoch (Sir) Papers, MS 2823.
Lloyd Dumas Papers, MS 4849.
Robert Menzies (Sir) Papers, MS 4936.
William Morris Hughes Papers, MS 1538.

Probate Registry of South Australia
James Edward Davidson probate packet (48947).

Public Record Office Victoria
Port Pirie *Recorder*, 932-355.

Queensland State Archives
Corporate documents related to Queensland Newspapers Pty Ltd, the Brisbane
  Newspaper Company Ltd and the Brisbane Daily Mail Pty Ltd. Research performed
  by Dorothy Gollner kindly provided to the author via Gollner and Rodney
  Kirkpatrick.

State Records of South Australia (SRSA)
The *Advertiser* (GRS513/11/102).
The Port Pirie Recorder Pty Ltd (GRS/513/3, file 4/1919).
News Limited (GRS/513/11, file 74/1922).

University of Melbourne Archives (UMA)
Australian Journalists' Association (AJA), Victorian branch records (1993.0133).
Broken Hill Associated Smelters (BHAS), including Sir Colin Fraser Papers (1969.0006).
National Mutual Life Associated Limited (NMLA) Board Minute Books (2012.0049).
William Sydney (WS) Robinson Papers, (2001.0070).

INTERVIEWS AND TRANSCRIPTS

Alexander, Joseph Aloysius, interviewed by Mel Pratt, 1971, ORAL TRC 121/10, NLA.
Charlton, Matthew, election speech delivered at Sydney, 9 October 1925, <https://
  electionspeeches.moadoph.gov.au/speeches/1925-matthew-charlton>.
Dahlsen, John, interview with the author, Melbourne, 22 February 2017.
Dean, Sarah, 'The last will of Australia's pioneers', *Mail Online*, 9 February 2015.
Gruen, David and Clark, Colin, 'What have we learnt? The Great Depression in
  Australia from the perspective of today', 19th Annual Colin Clark Memorial Lecture,
  Brisbane, 11 November 2009.
Hughes, William Morris, 1922 election campaign launch speech, delivered at North
  Sydney, New South Wales, 20 October 1922, <https://electionspeeches.moadoph.gov.
  au/speeches/1922-billy-hughes>.
'Journalism in the '30s', 1976, ORAL TRC 121-85, NLA.
McNicoll, David, interviewed by John Farquharson, 1997, ORAL TRC 3591, NLA.

OFFICIAL RECORDS
Australian Securities and Investments Commission (ASIC)
WAN incorporation document (025053339).

New South Wales Registry of Births, Deaths and Marriages
Herbert Campbell Jones, death certificate (4345/1942).

Parliament of Australia
Commonwealth Parliamentary Debates (*CPD*) (*Hansard*).
House of Representatives Select Committee on the Print Media (HRSCPM), *News & Fair*

Facts: The Australian Print Media Industry, the Parliament of the Commonwealth of
Australia, Australian Government Publishing Service, Canberra, March 1992.
Jolly, Rhonda, 'Media ownership and regulation: A chronology', Parliamentary Library
Research Paper, Parliament of Australia, Canberra, 1 February 2016.
Royal Commission into the Monetary and Banking Systems 1937.
Royal Commission on Wireless, 1927.

Parliament of Great Britain
Royal Commission on the Press 1947–1949, *Report*, London, HMSO, 1949.

Public Record Office Victoria
Port Pirie *Recorder*, 932-355.
The Herald and Sportsman Newspaper Company, 932-101.
The Herald and Standard Newspaper Company, 932-142.
The Herald and Weekly Times, 932-172.
The Herald and Weekly Times, 932-324.

Queensland Parliament
Parliamentary Debates (*Hansard*), Queensland Legislative Assembly.
The Royal Commission on Racing and Racecourses, *Report*, Brisbane, 1930.
'Macartney, Sir Edward Henry', <http://www.parliament.qld.gov.au/members/former/
bio?id=2416794024>.

Victorian Registry of Births, Deaths and Marriages
Norman Thorne Davidson, also known as Norman Gilbert Davidson, death certificate
no.15045/68.
James Edward Davidson, birth certificate, entry 496, District of Harrow, 1871.

PUBLISHED WORKS, THESES AND
UNPUBLISHED MANUSCRIPTS

AAP (Australian Associated Press), *On the Wire: The Story of Australian Associated Press*,
AAP, Sydney, 2010.
Aarons, Eric, *The Steel Octopus: The Story of the BHP*, Current Book Distributors,
Sydney, 1961.
Abbott, GJ, 'Kemp, Charles (1813–1864)', *Australian Dictionary of Biography (ADB)*,
vol. 2, 1967, <http://adb.anu.edu.au/biography/kemp-charles-2295>.
ABC (Australian Broadcasting Corporation), *AM* program, 19 April 2001,
<http://www.abc.net.au/am/stories/s279548.htm>.
——, *Packer's Road*, April 2014, <http://www.abc.net.au/interactives/kerry-packers-
road/>.
ACTU (Australian Council of Trade Unions), 'History of unions',
<https://www.actu.org.au/about-the-actu/history>.

ADB (*Australian Dictionary of Biography*), 'Hindmarsh, Sir John (1785–1860)', vol. 1, 1966, <http://adb.anu.edu.au/biography/hindmarsh-sir-john-1315>.

ADB, 'Stevenson, George (1799–1856)', vol. 2, 1967, <http://adb.anu.edu.au/biography/stevenson-george-2699>.

AEC (Australian Electoral Commission), 'Events in Australian electoral history', <http://aec.gov.au/Elections/Australian_Electoral_History/reform.htm>.

Alexander, Alison, *The Zinc Works: Producing Zinc at Risdon 1916–1991*, Pasminco Metals–EZ, Hobart, 1992.

Amos, Keith, 'Campbell, Eric (1893–1970)', *ADB*, vol. 7, 1979, <http://adb.anu.edu.au/biography/campbell-eric-5487>.

Anderson, Fay and Sally Young, *Shooting the Picture: Press Photography in Australia*, Melbourne University Publishing, Melbourne, 2016.

Anderson, Hugh, 'Fawkner, John Pascoe (1792–1869)', *ADB*, vol. 1, 1966, <http://adb.anu.edu.au/biography/fawkner-john-pascoe-2037>.

Anderson, John and Geoffrey Serle, 'Watt, William Alexander (1871–1946)', *ADB*, vol. 12, 1990, <http://adb.anu.edu.au/biography/watt-william-alexander-9011>.

Asquith, Ivan, '1780–1855' in George Boyce, James Curran and Pauline Wingate (eds), *Newspaper History: From the 17th Century to the Present Day*, Constable and Company, London, 1978, pp. 98–116.

Auchmuty, James J, 'Wentworth, D'Arcy (1762–1827)', *ADB*, vol. 2, 1966, <http://adb.anu.edu.au/biography/wentworth-darcy-1545>.

Austen, TE, 'Macartney, James Edward (Jim) (1911–1977)', *ADB*, vol. 15, 2000, <http://adb.anu.edu.au/biography/macartney-james-edward-jim-10893>.

Bain, Jim, *A Financial Tale of Two Cities: Sydney and Melbourne's Remarkable Contest for Commercial Supremacy*, UNSW Press, Sydney, 2007.

Baker, Mark, 'The myth of Keith Murdoch's Gallipoli letter', *Inside Story*, 26 July 2016, <http://insidestory.org.au/the-myth-of-keith-Murdochs-gallipoli-letter/>.

Baker, Nicholson and Margaret Brentano, *World on Sunday: Graphic Art in Joseph Pulitzer's Newspaper (1898–1911)*, Bulfinch Press, New York, 2005.

Baldasty, Gerald J, *EW Scripps and the Business of Newspapers*, University of Illinois Press, Urbana, 1999.

Barnett, Stephen R, 'The FCC's non-battle against media monopoly', *Columbia Journalism Review*, vol. 11, no. 5, 1973, pp. 43–50.

Barry, Paul, *The Rise and Rise of Kerry Packer*, Bantam, Sydney, 1993.

——, *The Rise and Rise of Kerry Packer Uncut*, Bantam, Sydney, 2008.

BBC (British Broadcasting Corporation), 'About BBC News', undated <http://news.bbc.co.uk/aboutbbcnews/spl/hi/history/noflash/html/1920s.stm>.

Beale, Howard, 'The man whom Menzies called "Boss"', *Sydney Morning Herald*, 27 September 1974, p. 9.

Bednall, Colin, unpublished autobiography, two versions contained in the Colin Blore Bednall Papers, MS 5546, NLA, undated.

Bingham, Adrian, *Family Newspapers?: Sex, Private Life, and the British Popular Press 1918–1978*, Oxford University Press, Oxford, 2009.

Blaikie, George, *Remember Smith's Weekly?*, Rigby, Adelaide, 1966.

Blainey, Geoffrey (ed.), *If I Remember Rightly: The Memoirs of WS Robinson, 1876–1963*, Cheshire, Melbourne, 1970.

——, *The Rush that Never Ended: A History of Australian Mining*, Melbourne University Press, Melbourne, 1993a.

——, *The Golden Mile*, Allen & Unwin, Sydney, 1993b.

——, *A History of the AMP, 1848–1998*, Allen & Unwin, Sydney, 1999.

Blair, Sandra, 'The convict press: Edward Smith-Hall and the Sydney Monitor', in Dennis Cryle (ed.) *Disreputable Profession: Journalists and Journalism in Colonial Australia*, Central Queensland University Press, Rockhampton, 1997, pp. 21–40.

Boland, Ronald R, 'Introduction', in Adrian Savvas and Andrew Becker, *Sixty Nine Years of Events from the Pages of the News*, A. Savvas, Adelaide, 1992, p. 3.

Bolton, GC, 'Hughes, Thomas John (1892–1980)', *ADB*, vol. 14, 1996, <http://adb.anu. edu.au/biography/hughes-thomas-john-10566>.

Bolton, Geoffrey, 'William Morris Hughes' in Michelle Grattan (ed.) *Australian Prime Ministers*, New Holland, Sydney, 2001, pp. 100–25.

Bongiorno, Frank, *The People's Party: Victorian Labor and the Radical Tradition, 1875–1914*, Melbourne University Press, Melbourne, 1996.

Bonney, Bill and Helen Wilson, *Australia's Commercial Media*, Macmillan, Melbourne, 1983.

Bonnin, Margriet R and Nancy Bonnin, 'Hill, Mary Ernestine (1899–1972)', *ADB*, vol. 14, 1996, <http://adb.anu.edu.au/biography/hill-mary-ernestine-10503>.

Borchardt, DH, 'Knox, Sir Robert Wilson (1890–1973)', *ADB*, vol. 9, 1983, <http://adb.anu.edu.au/biography/knox-sir-robert-wilson-6993>.

Bowman, David, *The Captive Press*, Penguin Books, Melbourne, 1988.

Brendon, Piers, *The Life and Death of the Press Barons*, Atheneum, New York, 1983.

Brennan, Niall, *John Wren, Gambler: His Life and Times*, Hill of Content, Melbourne, 1971.

Brett, Judith, 'Stanley Melbourne Bruce' in Michelle Grattan (ed.), *Australian Prime Ministers*, New Holland, Sydney, 2001, pp. 126–39.

'Brian Mc', 'Part 8 Queensland', 2 August 2014, <http://www.racehorsetalk.com.au/racing-talk/race-records-of-champion-racehorses/msg519204/>.

Brice, Chris, 'Seventy one years later the lights go out', in Adrian Savvas and Andrew Becker, *Sixty Nine Years of Events from the Pages of the News*, A. Savvas, Adelaide, 1992, p. 5.

Bridge, Carl, 'Davidson, James Edward (1870–1930)', *ADB*, vol. 8, 1981, <http://adb.anu.edu.au/biography/davidson-james-edward-5901>.

Broomhill, Ray, 'Hill, Lionel Laughton (1881–1963)', *ADB*, vol. 9, 1983, <http://adb.anu.edu.au/biography/hill-lionel-laughton-6671>.

Brown, Allan, *Commercial Media in Australia: Economics, Ownership, Technology and Regulation*, University of Queensland Press, Brisbane, 1986.

Bryce, Merilyn J, 'Bennett, Samuel (1815–1878)', *ADB*, vol. 3, 1969, <http://adb.anu.edu.au/biography/bennett-samuel-2975>.

Buckridge, Patrick, 'Penton, Brian Con (1904–1951)', *ADB*, vol. 15, 2000, <http://adb.anu.edu.au/biography/penton-brian-con-11367>.

——, 'Pearl, Cyril Altson (1904–1987)', *ADB*, vol. 18, 2012, <http://adb.anu.edu.au/biography/pearl-cyril-altson-15048>.

Buggy, Hugh, *The Real John Wren*, Angus and Robertson, Sydney, 1986.

Burgmann, Verity, *In Our Time: Socialism and the Rise of Labor, 1885–1905*, George Allen & Unwin, Sydney, 1985.

Butler, Genevieve, 'War brings sombre tone in an era of restrictions', *Courier-Mail*, 20 June 1996, p. 20.

Byrnes, JV, 'Howe, George (1769–1821)', *ADB*, vol. 1, 1969, <http://adb.anu.edu.au/biography/howe-george-1600>.

Cain, Frank, 'Jack Lang's 1930s government: The first 150 days', Australian Society for the Study of Labour History Conference, 2001, <https://labourhistorycanberra.org/2014/10/2001-conference-jack-langs-1930s-government-the-first-150-days/>.

——, *Jack Lang and the Great Depression*, Australian Scholarly Press, Melbourne, 2005.

Cain, Neville, 'Theodore, Edward Granville (1884–1950)', *ADB*, vol. 12, 1990, <http://adb.anu.edu.au/biography/theodore-edward-granville-8776>.

Calwell, Arthur, *Be Just and Fear Not*, Lloyd O'Neil in association with Rigby, Melbourne, 1978.

Cameron, Clyde R, 'When incompetence and corruption merge: The AWU and the *World* newspaper', *Labour History*, no. 70, May, 1996, pp. 169–81.

Campbell, Ernest W, *The 60 Rich Families Who Own Australia*, Current Book Distributors, Sydney, 1963.

Cannon, Michael, *That Damned Democrat: John Norton, An Australian Populist, 1858–1916*, Melbourne University Press, Melbourne, 1981.

——, *The Land Boomers*, Lloyd O'Neil, Melbourne, 1986.

—— (ed.), *Hold Page One: Memoirs of Monty Grover, Editor*, Loch Haven Books, Melbourne, 1993.

——, 'The enigma of Keith Murdoch', *Inside Story*, 18 November 2015, <http://insidestory.org.au/the-enigma-of-keith-Murdoch/>.

Carey, James, 'Journalism and criticism', *The Review of Politics*, vol. 36, no. 2, 1974, pp. 227–49.

Carroll, VJ, 'Taking care of business', *Sydney Morning Herald*, 18 January 2001, p .13.

——, 'Henderson, Rupert Albert Geary (1896–1986)', *ADB*, vol. 17, 2007, <http://adb.anu.edu.au/biography/henderson-rupert-albert-geary-12621>.

Chalmers, Rob, *Inside the Canberra Press Gallery: Life in the Wedding Cake of Old Parliament House*, ANU Press, Canberra, 2011.

Clark, Krissy and Geoff McGhee, 'Did the West make newspapers, or did newspapers make the West?', *Stanford Rural West Initiative*, 2015, <http://web.stanford.edu/group/ruralwest/cgi-bin/drupal/content/rural-newspapers-history>.

Clarke, Duncan, *Meet the Press*, Coronation Press, Melbourne, 1962.

Clarke, Patricia, 'The "Prince of the press gallery": The extraordinary life of Joe Alexander, CDHS's greatest benefactor', *Canberra Historical Journal*, no. 79, September 2017, pp. 1–10.

Cochran, Negley D, *EW Scripps*, Harcourt, Brace and Company, New York, 1933.

Cochrane, Tom, *Blockade: The Queensland Loans Affair 1920 to 1924*, University of Queensland Press, Brisbane, 1989.

Cockburn, S, 'Dumas, Sir Frederick Lloyd (1891–1973)', *ADB*, vol. 14, 1996, <http://adb.anu.edu.au/biography/dumas-sir-frederick-lloyd-10058>.

Cole, Barry George, 'The Australian Broadcasting Control Board and the regulation of commercial radio in Australia since 1948', PhD thesis, Northwestern University, Illinois, 1966.

Coleman, William, Selwyn Cornish and Alf Hagger, *Giblin's Platoon: The Trials and Triumphs of the Economist in Australian Public Life*, ANU E-Press, Canberra, 2006.

Collins Persse, Michael, 'More English than the English, but really dinky-di', *Sydney Morning Herald*, 18 July 2009.

Conboy, Martin, *The Press and Popular Culture*, Sage, London, 2002.

Connell, RW and TH Irving, *Class Structure in Australian History: Documents, Narrative and Argument*, Longman Cheshire, Melbourne, 1980.

Correy, Stan, 'How the newspapers tried to kill an independent ABC news before it even began', ABC website, 1 June 2017, <http://www.abc.net.au/news/2017-06-01/how-the-newspapers-tried-to-kill-abc-news-before-it-even-began/8568482>.

Courier-Mail, *Courier Mail 50th Anniversary Souvenir: 1933–1983*, Queensland Newspapers, Brisbane, 1983.

Cowling, Maurice, *The Impact of Labour 1920–1924: The Beginning of Modern British Politics*, Cambridge University Press, Cambridge, 1971.

Crough, Greg, 'Small is beautiful but disappearing: A study of share ownership in Australia', *Journal of Australian Political Economy*, no. 8, July 1980, pp. 3–14.

Cryle, Denis (ed.), *Disreputable Profession: Journalists and Journalism in Colonial Australia*, Central Queensland University Press, Rockhampton, 1997.

Cunneen, Chris, 'Smith, Sir James John Joynton (1858–1943)', *ADB*, vol. 11, 1988, <http://adb.anu.edu.au/biography/smith-sir-james-john-joynton-8475>.

Curran, James, 'The press as an agency of social control' in George Boyce, James Curran and Pauline Wingate (eds), *Newspaper History: From the 17th Century to the Present Day*, Constable and Company, London, 1978, pp. 51–75.

——, *Media and Power*, Routledge, London, 2006.

——, 'The liberal theory of press freedom', in James Curran and Jean Seaton, *Power Without Responsibility: Press, Broadcasting and the Internet in Britain*, 7th edn, Routledge, New York, 2010a, pp. 326–40.

——, 'The ugly face of reform', in James Curran and Jean Seaton, *Power Without Responsibility: Press, Broadcasting and the Internet in Britain*, 7th edn, Routledge, London, 2010b, pp. 17–23.

——, *Media and Democracy*, Routledge, London, 2011.

——, and Jean Seaton, *Power Without Responsibility: Press, Broadcasting and the Internet in Britain*, 5th edn, Routledge, London, 1997.

David Jones, 'The story of David Jones', undated, <https://www.davidjones.com.au/About-David-Jones/The-Story-of-David-Jones>.

Dean, J, 'The last will of Australia's pioneers', *Mail Online*, 9 February 2015.

Denison, James L, *Building a Nation: Hugh Robert Denison KBE: Patron and Patriot*, James L Denison, Sydney, 2004.

Dilley, Andrew, *Finance, Politics and Imperialism*, Palgrave Macmillan, London, 2011.

Dow, Gwyneth, 'Higinbotham, George (1826–1892)', *ADB*, vol. 4, 1972, <http://adb.anu.edu.au/biography/higinbotham-george-3766>.

Dumas, Lloyd, *A Full Life*, Sun Books, Melbourne, 1969.

Dunning, John, *On the Air: The Encyclopaedia of Old-Time Radio*, Oxford University Press, Oxford, 1998.

Dunstan, David, 'Myer, Sir Norman (1897–1956)', *ADB*, vol. 15, 2000, <http://adb.anu.edu.au/biography/myer-sir-norman-11216>.

——, 'Williams, Sir John Francis (1901–1982)', *ADB*, vol. 18, 2012, <http://adb.anu.edu.au/biography/williams-sir-john-francis-15864>.

Dunstan, Keith, *No Brains At All: An Autobiography*, Viking, Melbourne, 1990.

Dyrenfurth, Nick, *A Powerful Influence on Australian Affairs: A New History of the AWU*, Melbourne University Press, Melbourne, 2017.

Dyster, Barrie and David Meredith, *Australia in the International Economy in the Twentieth Century*, Cambridge University Press, Melbourne, 1990.

Eklund, Erik, '10 June 1931', *Inside Story*, 20 October 2008, <http://insidestory.org.au/10-june-1931/>.

Ellis, Gavin, *Trust Ownership and the Future of News*, Palgrave Macmillan, Basingstoke, 2014.

Emberson-Bain, Atu, *Labour and Gold in Fiji*, Cambridge University Press, Cambridge, 1994.

Emery, Edwin, *The Press and America: An Interpretative History of the Mass Media*, Prentice-Hall, Englewood Cliffs, 1972.

Fairfax, James O, 'Fairfax, John (1804–1877)', *ADB*, vol. 4, 1972, <http://adb.anu.edu.au/biography/fairfax-john-3493>.

Fairfax Media, *Fairfax Media Annual Report*, Fairfax Media, Sydney, 2015.

Farrelly, Alan, 'Fairfax dynamo calls it a day', *Australian*, 12 October 1978, p. 7.

Faulkner, John and Stuart Macintyre (eds), *True Believers: The Story of the Federal Parliamentary Labor Party*, Allen & Unwin, Sydney, 2001.

Fishback, Price V, 'Relief during the Great Depression in Australia and America', Noel G Butlin lecture for the *Australian Economic History Review*, ANU Centre for Economic History, Discussion Paper, July 2012.

Fitzgerald, Ross, *'Red Ted': The Life of EG Theodore*, University of Queensland Press, Brisbane, 1994.

Fitzhardinge, Laurence F, *William Morris Hughes: That Fiery Particle, 1862–1914*, Angus & Robertson, Sydney, 1964.

——, *The Little Digger: 1914–1952*, Angus & Robertson, Sydney, 1979.

——, 'Hughes, William Morris (Billy) (1862–1952)', *ADB*, vol. 9, 1983, <http://adb.anu.edu.au/biography/hughes-william-morris-billy-6761>.

Fleming, Grant, David Merrett and Simon Ville, *The Big End of Town: Big Business and Corporate Leadership in Twentieth-Century Australia*, Cambridge University Press, Melbourne, 2004.

Forell, Claude, 'The Age – a century-and-a-half of reporting', *The Age*, 26 January 2004.

Fowler, Andrew, 'The Turnbull files', *The Monthly*, 2015, <https://www.themonthly.com.au/blog/andrew-fowler/2015/07/2015/1444169203/turnbull-files>.

Fox, Len, *Wealthy Men*, Current Book Distributors, Sydney, 1946.

Fraser, Allan, 'An old gallery hand looks back', *Canberra Times*, 20 September 1976, p. 42.

Freeman, RD, 'Davies, Sir Matthew Henry (1850–1912)', *ADB*, vol. 4, 1972, <http://adb.anu.edu.au/biography/davies-sir-matthew-henry-3879>.

Fry, Eric, 'Barker, Tom (1887–1970)', *ADB*, vol. 7, 1979, <http://adb.anu.edu.au/biography/barker-tom-5131>.

Garden, Don, *Theodore Fink: A Talent for Ubiquity*, Melbourne University Press, Melbourne, 1998.

Gardiner, Lyndsay, 'Kerr, William (1812–1859)', *ADB*, vol. 2, 1967, <http://adb.anu.edu.au/biography/kerr-william-2304>.

Gardner, Gilson, *Lusty Scripps: The Life of EW Scripps*, The Vanguard Press, New York, 1932.

Gardner, Peter D, 'Brief notes on some fraudulent aspects of the secret compositions of William Lawrence Baillieu and friends 1892', *Victorian Historical Journal*, vol. 80, no. 1, June 2009, pp. 61–75.

——, 'Notes on the early chapters of Peter Yule's William Lawrence Baillieu', undated (a), <http://petergardner.info/wp-content/uploads/2012/11/Notes-on-Peter-Yules-William-Lawrence-Baillieu.pdf>, accessed 20 July 2016.

——, 'How WL Baillieu recovered from his secret Composition of 1892', undated (b), <http://petergardner.info/wp-content/uploads/2012/11/How-W.L.Baillieu-Recovered-from-his-Secret-Composition-rev.ed_..pdf>, accessed 20 July 2016.

——, 'Moguls and the media: The Baillieu/Fink group and the Herald Saga', undated (c), <http://petergardner.info/wp-content/uploads/2013/03/Moguls-and-the-Media-the-Baillieu-Fink-group-and-the-Herald.pdf>, accessed 9 October 2017.

Gaylard, Geoff, *One Hundred and Fifty Years of News from the Herald*, Portside Editions, Melbourne, 1990.

Geeves, Philip, *The Dawn of Australia's Radio Broadcasting*, Federal Publishing Company, Sydney, 1993.

Gibson, Ralph, *Who Owns Tasmania?*, R. Gibson, Melbourne, 1958.

Given, Jock, 'Not being Ernest: Uncovering competitors in the foundation of Australian wireless', *Historical Records of Australian Science*, vol. 18, no. 2, 2007, pp. 159–76.

Gollner, Dorothy, 'A history of the *Courier-Mail*: The men behind the *Brisbane Courier* and the *Daily Mail*, and the beginning of a media monopoly', essay and accompanying resources, Department of Journalism, Faculty of Arts, University of Queensland, Brisbane, 1995.

Goot, Murray, 'Newspaper circulation in Australia, 1932–1977', Media Centre Paper no. 11, Centre for the Study of Educational Communication and Media, La Trobe University, Melbourne, 1979.

Gorman, Lyn and David McLean, *Media and Society into the 21st Century: A Historical Introduction*, Wiley-Blackwell, Chichester, 2009.

Green, FC, 'Davies, John (1813–1872)', *ADB*, vol. 4, 1972, <http://adb.anu.edu.au/biography/davies-john-3374>.

——, 'Casey, Richard Gardiner (1846–1919)', *ADB*, vol. 3, 1969, <http://adb.anu.edu.au/biography/casey-richard-gardiner-207>.

Greenslade, NW, *A Study of the Origins and Achievements of Australian Newsprint Mills Ltd From its Inception Until the Present*, Tasmanian College of Advanced Education, Hobart, 1971.

Greenwall, Harry J, *Northcliffe: Napoleon of Fleet Street*, Wingate, London, 1957.

Gregson, Sarah, 'Foot soldiers for capital: The influence of RSL racism on interwar industrial relations in Kalgoorlie and Broken Hill', PhD thesis, UNSW, Sydney, 2003.

Griffen-Foley, Bridget, *The House of Packer: The Making of a Media Empire*, Allen & Unwin, Sydney, 1999.

——, *Sir Frank Packer: The Young Master*, Harper Collins, Sydney, 2000.

——, 'The battle of Melbourne: The rise and fall of the *Star*', *Journal of Australian Studies*, vol. 25, no. 69, 2001a, pp. 89–102.

——, 'The press proprietor and the politician: Sir Frank Packer and Sir Robert Menzies', *Media International Australia*, no. 99, May 2001b, pp. 23–34.

——, 'Radio' in Stuart Cunningham and Graeme Turner (eds), *The Media and Communications in Australia*, 2nd edn, Allen & Unwin, Sydney, 2006, pp. 133–53.

——, 'Fairfax, Sir Warwick Oswald (1901–1987)', *ADB*, vol. 17, 2007, <http://adb.anu.edu.au/biography/fairfax-sir-warwick-oswald-1247>.

——, *Changing Stations: The Story of Australian Commercial Radio*, UNSW Press, Sydney, 2009.

Griffin, Helga M, 'Higgins, Sir John Michael (1862–1937)', *ADB*, vol. 9, 1983,

<http://adb.anu.edu.au/biography/higgins-sir-john-michael-6663>.

Griffin, James, 'Wren, John (1871–1953)', *ADB*, vol. 12, 1990, <http://adb.anu.edu.au/biography/wren-john-9198>.

——, *John Wren: A Life Reconsidered*, Scribe Publications, Melbourne, 2004.

Grover, Montague, 'Jack Davidson: His work was his life', (Port Pirie) *Recorder*, 10 June 1930, p. 2.

Haggarty, Nick, 'Federal Parliamentary Press Gallery', undated, <http://pressgallery.net.au/history-2/>.

Hall, Sandra, *Tabloid Man: The Life and Times of Ezra Norton*, Fourth Estate, Sydney, 2008.

Hancock, IR, 'Cook, James Newton Haxton Hume (1866–1942)', *ADB*, vol. 8, 1981, <http://adb.anu.edu.au/biography/cook-james-newton-haxton-hume-5762>.

——, 'Denning, Warren Edwin (1906–1975)', *ADB*, vol. 13, 1993, <http://adb.anu.edu.au/biography/denning-warren-edwin-9950>.

Hannah, William, 'Fink, Theodore (1855–1942)', *ADB*, vol. 8, 1981, <http://adb.anu.edu.au/biography/fink-theodore-6171>.

Hardy, Frank J, *Power Without Glory: A Novel*, Lloyd O'Neil, Melbourne, 1972.

Harris, Paul, 'The story of the *Daily Mail*', *Associated Newspapers*, 2013, <http://gale.cengage.co.uk/images/The%20Story%20of%20the%20Daily%20Mail.pdf>.

Hart, Philip, 'JA Lyons Labor Minister – leader of the UAP', *Labour History*, no. 17, October 1969, pp. 37–51.

——, 'The piper and the tune' in Cameron Hazlehurst (ed.), *Australian Conservatism: Essays in Twentieth Century Political History*, ANU Press, Canberra, 1979, pp. 111–48.

—— and CJ Lloyd, 'Lyons, Joseph Aloysius', *ADB*, vol. 10, 1986, <http://adb.anu.edu.au/biography/lyons-joseph-aloysius-joe-7278>.

Harvey, Claire, 'Looking back over 70 years at the *Sunday Telegraph*', *Sunday Telegraph*, 20 November 2009a, <http://www.dailytelegraph.com.au/looking-back-over-70-years-at-the-sunday-telegraph/story-fn4hieht-1225800182102>.

——, 'An eye on Sydney and Australia since 1939', *Sunday Telegraph*, 22 November 2009b, p. 1.

Hasluck, Paul, *The Government and the People, 1939–41*, Australian War Memorial, Canberra, 1952.

Hawkins, John, 'Ted Theodore: The proto-Keynesian', *Economic Roundup*, iss. 1, The Treasury, Canberra, 2010.

Hazlehurst, Cameron, *Menzies Observed*, Allen & Unwin, Sydney, 1979.

——, *Ten Journeys to Cameron's Farm: An Australian Tragedy*, ANU E Press, Canberra, 2013.

Henderson, Anne, *Joseph Lyons: The People's Prime Minister*, UNSW Press, Sydney, 2011.

——, *Menzies at War*, NewSouth Publishing, Sydney, 2014.

Henderson, Gerard, *Menzies' Child: The Liberal Party of Australia, 1944–1994*, Allen & Unwin, Sydney, 1994.

Herald and Weekly Times (HWT), *Annual Report*, HWT, Melbourne, 1947.

Heren, Louis, *The Power of the Press*, Orbis, London, 1985.

Hetherington, John, 'Keith Murdoch: The man in the paper mask', in Matthew Ricketson (ed.), *The Best Australian Profiles*, Black Inc., Melbourne, 2004, pp. 99–124.

Heyward, Philip, 'Boyer mill Norske Skog keeps turning fresh pages in constant reinvention to stay ahead', *Mercury* (Hobart), 7 December 2013.

Hill, AJ, 'Gullett, Sir Henry Somer (Harry) (1878–1940)', *ADB*, vol. 9, 1983a, <http://adb.anu.edu.au/biography/gullett-sir-henry-somer-harry-448>.

——, 'Hobbs, Sir Joseph John Talbot (1864–1938)', *ADB*, vol. 9, 1983b, <http://adb.anu.edu.au/biography/hobbs-sir-joseph-john-talbot-6690>.

Hills, Ben, *Breaking News: The Golden Age of Graham Perkin*, Scribe Publications, Melbourne, 2010.

Hilvert, John, *Blue Pencil Warriors: Censorship and Propaganda in World War II*, University of Queensland Press, Brisbane, 1984.

——, 'Edmund Garnet (1883–1959)', *ADB*, vol. 13, 1993, <http://adb.anu.edu.au/biography/bonney-edmund-garnet-9538 Bonney>.

Holden, W Sprague, *Australia Goes to Press*, Melbourne University Press, Melbourne, 1962.

Holder, Reginald F, *Bank of New South Wales: A History: Volume One: 1817–1893*, Angus and Robertson, Sydney, 1970.

——, 'Davidson, Sir Alfred Charles (1882–1952)', *ADB*, vol. 8, 1981, <http://adb.anu.edu.au/biography/davidson-sir-alfred-charles-5895>.

Holt, Stephen, 'Alexander, Joseph Aloysius (Joe) (1892–1983)', *ADB*, vol. 17, 2007, <http://adb.anu.edu.au/biography/alexander-joseph-aloysius-joe-12128>.

Hoover, Herbert C, *The Memoirs of Herbert Hoover: Years of Adventure 1874–1920*, Hollis & Carter, London, 1952.

Horne, Donald, *The Little Digger: A Biography of Billy Hughes*, Macmillan, Melbourne, 1983.

Hudson, WJ, 'Casey, Richard Gavin Gardiner (1890–1976)', *ADB*, vol. 13, 1993, <http://adb.anu.edu.au/biography/casey-richard-gavin-gardiner-9706>.

Hunt, Lyall, 'Hackett, Sir John Winthrop (1848–1916)', *ADB*, vol. 9, 1983 <http://adb.anu.edu.au/biography/hackett-sir-john-winthrop-6514>.

Hurst, John, 'Smith, Charles Patrick (1877–1963)', *ADB*, vol. 11, 1988, <http://adb.anu.edu.au/biography/smith-charles-patrick-8464>.

Hyslop, Anthea, 'Myer, Simcha (Sidney) (1878–1934)', *ADB*, vol. 10, 1986, <http://adb.anu.edu.au/biography/myer-simcha-sidney-7721>.

Ihde, Erin, *Edward Smith Hall and the Sydney Monitor*, Australian Scholarly Press, Melbourne, 2004.

Inglis, Kenneth S, *This is the ABC: The Australian Broadcasting Commission, 1932–1983*, Melbourne University Press, Melbourne, 1983.

—— and Jan Brazier, *Sacred Places: War Memorials in the Australian Landscape*, Melbourne University Press, Melbourne, 2008.

Iremonger, John, 'Rats' in John Faulkner and Stuart Macintyre (eds), *True Believers: The Story of the Federal Parliamentary Labor Party*, Allen & Unwin, Sydney, 2001, pp. 265–86.

Irving, Terry, 'The growth of federal authority: 1929–40' in John Faulkner and Stuart Macintyre (eds), *True Believers: The Story of the Federal Parliamentary Labor Party*, Allen & Unwin, Sydney, 2001, pp. 60–75.

Isaacs, Victor, 'Front page news', *Australian Newspaper History Group Newsletter*, no. 3, January 2000, pp. 4–5.

——, 'Labour dailies', May 2015, <https://labourhistorycanberra.org/2015/05/labour-dailies/>.

—— and Rod Kirkpatrick, *Two Hundred Years of Sydney Newspapers: A Short History*, Rural Press, North Richmond, NSW, 2003.

Jamieson, Allan, *The Pulp: The Rise and Fall of an Industry*, Forty Degrees South, Hobart, 2011.

Jewell, John, 'Press baron and propagandist who led charge into World War I', *The Conversation*, 31 July 2014, <https://theconversation.com/press-baron-and-propagandist-who-led-charge-into-world-war-i-29855>.

Johnson, Robert A, 'Halfey, John (1825–89)', *ADB*, vol. 4, 1972, <http://adb.anu.edu.au/biography/halfey-john-3692>.

Johnston, Jane and Susan Forde, '"Not wrong for long": The role and penetration of news wire agencies in the 24/7 news landscape', *Global Media Journal*, vol. 3, no. 2, 2011, pp. 1–16.

Johnston, W Ross, 'Macartney, Sir Edward Henry (1863–1956)', *ADB*, vol. 10, 1986, <http://adb.anu.edu.au/biography/macartney-sir-edward-henry-7290>.

Johnstone, Carolyne, 'A history of the origins, formation and development of the Broken Hill Associated Smelters Pty Ltd at Port Pirie, South Australia', PhD thesis, University of Melbourne, 1982.

Jones, Colin, *Something in the Air: A History of Radio in Australia*, Kangaroo Press, Sydney, 1995.

Joynton Smith, James, *My Life Story*, Cornstalk Publishing, Sydney, 1927.

Juergens, George, *Joseph Pulitzer and the New York World*, Princeton University Press, Princeton, NJ, 1966.

Kearns, RHB, *Broken Hill 1915–1939*, The Broken Hill Historical Society, Broken Hill, New South Wales, 1975.

Kennedy, BE, 'Mussen, Sir Gerald (1872–1960)', *ADB*, vol. 10, 1986, <http://adb.anu.edu.au/biography/mussen-sir-gerald-7718>.

Kennedy, Brian, *A Tale of Two Mining Cities: Johannesburg and Broken Hill 1885–1925*, Melbourne University Press, Melbourne, 1984.

Kennedy, Kett H, 'The profits of boom: A short history of the Cloncurry Copper Field' in Lectures on North Queensland History, 3rd series, History Department, James Cook University of North Queensland, Townsville, 1978.

Kennett, John, 'The Collins House group', PhD thesis, Monash University, Melbourne, 1980.

——, 'Fraser, Sir Colin (1875–1944)', *ADB*, vol. 8, 1981, <http://adb.anu.edu.au/biography/fraser-sir-colin-6236>.

Kenny, MJB, 'Hall, Edward Smith (1786–1860)', *ADB*, vol. 1, 1966, <http://adb.anu.edu.au/biography/hall-edward-smith-2143>.

Kirkpatrick, Rod, *Country Conscience: A History of the New South Wales Provincial Press, 1841–1995*, Infinite Harvest Publishing, Canberra, 2000.

——, 'Press timeline: Select chronology of significant Australian press events to 2011', *Australian Newspaper History Group*, National Library of Australia, 2012, <https://www.nla.gov.au/australian-newspaper-plan/for-researchers/newspaper-chronology>.

——, *Dailies in the Colonial Capitals: A Short History*, Rod Kirkpatrick, Brisbane, 2016.

Lang, JT, 'The night the press nabob wept', *Truth* (Sydney), 24 January 1954, p. 23.

Langhans, Ron, 'The first twelve months of radio broadcasting in Australia 1923–1924', Historical Radio Society of Australia, Sydney, 2013.

Langmore, Diane, 'Meudell, George Dick (1860–1936)', *ADB*, vol. 10, 1986,
  <http://adb.anu.edu.au/biography/meudell-george-dick-7564>.
——, 'Reay, William Thomas (1858–1929)', *ADB*, vol. 11, 1988, <http://adb.anu.edu.au/
  biography/reay-william-thomas-8170>.
Laurence, John H, 'de Bernales, Claude Albo (1876–1963)', *ADB*, vol. 8, 1981,
  <http://adb.anu.edu.au/biography/de-bernales-claude-albo-5935>.
Lawson, Sylvia, 'Archibald, Jules François (1856–1919)', *ADB*, vol. 3, 1969,
  <http://adb.anu.edu.au/biography/archibald-jules-francois-2896>.
Lawson, Valerie, 'Norton, Ezra (1897–1967)', *ADB*, vol. 15, 2000, <http://adb.anu.edu.
  au/biography/norton-ezra-11260>.
——, 'Obituary: Packer, Kerry Francis (1937–2005)', *Sydney Morning Herald*,
  28 December 2005, reproduced at <http://oa.anu.edu.au/obituary/packer-kerry-
  francis-17045>.
Lebovic, Sam, 'When the "mainstream media" was conservative: Media criticism in
  the age of reform' in Bruce J Schulman and Julian E Zelizer (eds), *Media Nation:
  The Political History of News in Modern America*, University of Pennsylvania Press,
  Philadelphia, 2017, pp. 63–76.
Lee, Alan, 'The structure, ownership and control of the press, 1855–1914' in George
  Boyce, James Curran and Pauline Wingate (eds), *Newspaper History: From the 17th
  Century to the Present Day*, Constable and Company, London, 1978.
Lee, Andrew, 'Nothing to offer but fear? Non-Labor federal electioneering in Australia,
  1914–1954', PhD thesis, Australian National University, Canberra, 1997.
Lloyd, CJ, *Profession – Journalist: A History of the Australian Journalists' Association*, Hale
  & Iremonger, Sydney, 1985.
——, *Parliament and the Press: The Federal Parliamentary Press Gallery 1901–88*,
  Melbourne University Press, Melbourne, 1988.
——, 'Reporting Caucus' in John Faulkner and Stuart Macintyre (eds), *True Believers:
  The Story of the Federal Parliamentary Labor Party*, Allen & Unwin, Sydney, 2001a,
  pp. 184–202.
——, 'Rise and fall of the United Australia Party' in JR Nethercote (ed.), *Liberalism and
  the Australian Federation*, Federation Press, Sydney, 2001b, pp. 134–62.
Lowndes, AG, 'Knox, Sir Edward (1819–1901)', *ADB*, vol. 5, 1974, <http://adb.anu.edu.
  au/biography/knox-sir-edward-573>.
——, 'Ross, Joseph Grafton (1834–1906)', *ADB*, vol. 6, 1976, <http://adb.anu.edu.au/
  biography/ross-joseph-grafton-4509>.
McChesney, Robert W and John Nichols, *The Death and Life of American Journalism*,
  Nation Books, Philadelphia, 2010.
McClelland, D, 'The press in Australia', *Australian Quarterly*, vol. 34, no. 4, 1962,
  pp. 22–28.
McClung Lee, Alfred, *The Daily Newspaper in America*, Macmillan, New York, 1937.
McFarland, John S (compiler), *66 Years of The Sun News-Pictorial*, Herald and Weekly
  Times, Melbourne, 1988.
Macintyre, Stuart, 'Latham, Sir John Greig (1877–1964)', *ADB*, vol. 10, 1986, <http://
  adb.anu.edu.au/biography/latham-sir-john-greig-7104>.
——, 'Harrison, Sir Eric John (1892–1974)', *ADB*, vol. 14, 1996, <http://adb.anu.edu.au/
  biography/harrison-sir-eric-john-10441>.

——, 'Alfred Deakin: A centenary tribute', *Papers on Parliament*, no. 42, December 2004, <http://www.aph.gov.au/About_Parliament/Senate/Research_and_Education/pops/~/link.aspx?_id=9F3C3A2F530E4DA7AF107CB32AE5C7E4&_z=z>.

——, 'Alfred Deakin' in Michelle Grattan (ed.), *Australian Prime Ministers*, New Holland, Sydney, 2010, pp. 36–53.

——, *Australia's Boldest Experiment: War and Reconstruction in the 1940s*, NewSouth Publishing, Sydney, 2015.

McKercher, Catherine, *Newsworkers Unite: Labor, Convergence, and North American Newspapers*, Rowman & Littlefield Publishers, Lanham, MD, 2002.

Macklin, Robert, 'The gun of the *Sun*', *Canberra Times*, 31 December 1995, p. 19.

McLaren, Ian F. 'Ham, Thomas (1821–1870)', *ADB*, vol. 4, 1972, <http://adb.anu.edu.au/biography/ham-thomas-3700>.

McMullin, Ross, 'Leading the world: 1901–16' in John Faulkner and Stuart Macintyre (eds), *True Believers: The Story of the Federal Parliamentary Labor Party*, Allen & Unwin, Sydney, 2001, pp. 30–46.

——, *So Monstrous a Travesty: Chris Watson and the World's First National Labour Government*, Scribe Publications, Melbourne, 2004.

——, 'First in the world: Australia's Watson Labor Government', *Papers on Parliament*, no. 44, January 2006, <https://www.aph.gov.au/binaries/senate/pubs/pops/pop44/mcmullin.pdf>.

McNicoll, DD, 'News empire that knows no limit', *Australian*, 7 June 1997, p. 8.

McQueen, Humphrey, 'None dare call it conspiracy', *Politics*, vol. 11, no. 1, 1976, pp. 23–27.

Marchant, Sylvia, 'Things fall apart: The end of the United Australia Party 1939 to 1943', Master of Letters thesis, Australian National University, Canberra, 1998.

Markwell, Donald J, 'Keynes and Australia', Research discussion paper 2000–04, Research Department, Reserve Bank of Australia, June 2000.

Martin, AW, 'Parkes, Sir Henry (1815–1896)', *ADB*, vol. 5, 1974, <http://adb.anu.edu.au/biography/parkes-sir-henry-4366>.

——, *Robert Menzies: A Life, vol. 1, 1894–1943*, Melbourne University Press, Melbourne, 1993.

——, 'Sir Robert Gordon Menzies' in Michelle Grattan (ed.) *Australian Prime Ministers*, New Holland, Sydney, 2001, pp. 175–205.

Mayer, Henry, *The Press in Australia*, Lansdowne Press, Melbourne, 1968.

Media Entertainment Arts Alliance (MEAA), 'A proud history at the forefront of Australian journalism', 8 December 2017, <https://www.meaa.org/news/meaa-media-aja-history/>.

Media Museum of Northern California, 'Edward W. Scripps', undated, <http://www.norcalmediamuseum.org/?page_id=475>.

Mercury, '160 years of the *Mercury*, 1854–2014', 23 June 2014, <http://www.themercury.com.au/news/tasmania/years-of-the-mercury-1854-2014/news-story/e9deb23eada671a0ed1f7daf8c242fbe>.

Middleman, Raoul F, 'Pinschof, Carl Ludwig (1855–1926)', *ADB*, vol. 11, 1988, <http://adb.anu.edu.au/biography/pinschof-carl-ludwig-8052>.

Millmow, Alex, *The Power of Economic Ideas: The Origins of Keynesian Macroeconomic Management in Interwar Australia 1929–39*, ANU Press, Canberra, 2010.

Mitchell, Ann M, 'Munro, James (1832–1908)', *ADB*, vol. 5, 1974,

<http://adb.anu.edu.au/biography/munro-james-4271>.

Moran, James, *Printing Presses: History and Development from the Fifteenth Century to Modern Times*, University of California Press, Berkeley, 1974.

Morrison, Elizabeth, *David Syme: Man of The Age*, Monash University Publishing, Melbourne, 2014.

Mott, Frank Luther, 'Newspapers in presidential campaigns', *The Public Opinion Quarterly*, vol. 8, no. 3, 1944, pp. 348–67.

Munster, George, *Rupert Murdoch: A Paper Prince*, Penguin, Melbourne, 1987.

Murray, Robert, *The Confident Years: Australia in the Twenties*, Allen Lane, Melbourne, 1978.

Myers, Hal, *The Whispering Gallery*, Kangaroo Press, Sydney, 1999.

Nairn, Bede, 'Lang, John Thomas (Jack) (1876–1975)', *ADB*, vol. 9, 1983, <http://adb.anu.edu.au/biography/lang-john-thomas-jack-7027>.

——, *The 'Big Fella': Jack Lang and the Australian Labor Party 1891–1949*, Melbourne University Press, Melbourne, 1986.

National Archives of Australia (NAA), 'William Morris Hughes', <http://primeministers. naa.gov.au/primeministers/hughes/>.

National Library of Australia (NLA), 'History of Australian newspapers', 2011, <https://www.nla.gov.au/anplan/heritage/history.html>.

Noam, Eli M, *Media Ownership and Concentration in America*, Oxford University Press, Oxford, 2009.

Nolan, Sybil, 'The *Age* and the young Menzies: A chapter in Victorian liberalism', PhD thesis, University of Melbourne, 2010.

——, 'The second generation: Geoffrey Syme, managing editor of *The Age*, 1908–42', *Victorian Historical Journal*, vol. 84, no. 1, June 2013, pp. 34–52.

——, '*Age*' in Bridget Griffen-Foley (ed.), *A Companion to the Australian Media*, Australian Scholarly Publishing, Melbourne, 2014, pp. 12–14.

——, 'The snub: Robert Menzies and the Melbourne Club', *Australian Historical Studies*, vol. 48, no. 1, 2017, pp. 3–18.

Oldfield, Audrey, *Woman Suffrage in Australia*, Cambridge University Press, Melbourne, 1992.

Osborne, Graeme and Glen Lewis, *Communication Traditions in 20th-Century Australia*, Oxford University Press, Melbourne, 1995.

Page, Bruce, *The Murdoch Archipelago*, Simon & Schuster, London, 2003.

Parnell, Sean, 'Even FBI doubted Goanna story about Kerry Packer', *Australian*, 25 August 2012.

Parsons, George, 'Hoskins, Sir Cecil Harold (1889–1971)', *ADB*, vol. 9, 1983, <http://adb.anu.edu.au/biography/hoskins-sir-cecil-harold-7072>.

Parsons, Vivienne, 'Mansfield, Ralph (1799–1880)', *ADB*, vol. 2, 1967, <http://adb.anu. edu.au/biography/mansfield-ralph-2429>.

Peak, Wayne, 'Unregistered proprietary horse racing in Sydney 1888–1942', PhD thesis, University of Western Sydney, 2004.

Pearl, Cyril, *Wild Men of Sydney*, Angus & Robertson, Sydney, 1977.

Perpetual, 'Our history', undated, <https://www.perpetual.com.au/about/our-history>.

Persse, Michael, 'Wentworth, William Charles (1790–1872)', *ADB*, vol. 2, 1967, <http://adb.anu.edu.au/biography/wentworth-william-charles-2782>.

Petersen, Neville, *News not Views: The ABC, the Press and Politics 1932–1947*, Hale and Iremonger, Sydney, 1993.

Pew Research Center, 'US daily newspaper circulation, 5-year increments', 12 March 2007, <http://www.journalism.org/numbers/u-s-daily-newspaper-circulation-5-year-increments/>.

Phillips, Nan, 'Browne, Eyles Irwin Caulfield (1819–1886)', *ADB*, vol. 3, 1969, <http://adb.anu.edu.au/biography/browne-eyles-irwin-caulfield-3083>.

Picard, Robert G, 'OMG! Newspapers may not be dead!', *The Media Business*, 10 August 2009.

Pickard, Victor, 'Laying low the shibboleth of a free press', *Journalism Studies*, vol. 15, no. 4, 2014, pp. 464–80.

Pike, AF, 'Gibson, William Alfred (1869–1929)', *ADB*, vol. 8, 1981, <http://adb.anu.edu.au/biography/gibson-william-alfred-6312>.

Pitcher, WB, 'Bonython, Sir John Langdon (1848–1939)', *ADB*, vol. 7, 1979, <http://adb.anu.edu.au/biography/bonython-sir-john-langdon-5286>.

Porter, Ann, 'Langler, Sir Alfred (1865–1928)', *ADB*, vol. 9, 1983, <http://adb.anu.edu.au/biography/langler-sir-alfred-7029>.

Porter, Muriel (ed.), *The Argus: The Life and Death of a Great Melbourne Newspaper 1846–1957*, RMIT University, Melbourne, 2001.

Poynter, JR, 'Baillieu, William Lawrence (Willie) (1859–1936)', *ADB*, vol. 7, 1979, <http://adb.anu.edu.au/biography/baillieu-william-lawrence-willie-5099>.

Pretyman, ER, 'Bent, Andrew (1790–1851)', *ADB*, vol. 1, 1966, <http://adb.anu.edu.au/biography/bent-andrew-1771>.

Procter, Ben, *William Randolph Hearst: The Early Years, 1863–1910*, Oxford University Press, Oxford, 1998.

Putnis, Peter, 'The press cable monopoly, 1895–1909: A case study of Australian media policy development', *Media International Australia*, iss. 90, 1999, pp. 139–55.

——, 'Lord Northcliffe, Keith Murdoch and the development of the Melbourne *Herald* in the 1920s', *Australian Journal of Communication*, vol. 38, no. 2, 2011, pp. 71–86.

——, 'Cable news', in Bridget Griffen-Foley (ed.), *A Companion to the Australian Media*, Australian Scholarly Publishing, Melbourne, 2014, p. 81.

Queensland Government Statistician's Office, 'Life expectancy at birth (years) by sex, Queensland and Australia, 1881–1890 to 2013–2015', <http://www.qgso.qld.gov.au/products/tables/life-expectancy-birth-years-sex-qld/index.php>.

Quirk, Victor, 'London's silken cords and the Depression we had to have', paper presented at the 12th Path to Full Employment/17th National Unemployment Conference, 3 December 2010, Centre of Full Employment and Equity, University of Newcastle, New South Wales.

Ralph, Gilbert M, 'The Broken Hill-Collins House connection: Mining personalities', *Journal of Australasian Mining History*, vol. 2, September 2004, pp. 198–221.

—— and Michael D Softley, 'Brief illustrated history of Western Mining Corporation', undated, <https://www.ipenz.org.nz/heritage/conference2007/papers/Ralph_Final_Paper.pdf>.

Rawling, James N, *Who Owns Australia?*, Modern Publishers, Sydney, 1939.

Regan, Simon, *Rupert Murdoch: A Business Biography*, Angus and Robertson, Melbourne, 1976.

Richardson, Nick, 'Sir Keith Murdoch's relationship with Prime Minister Joseph Lyons: Public lecture for the National Archives of Australia', Canberra, 5 May 2006.

Richardson, Peter, 'The origins and development of the Collins House group 1915–1951', *Australian Economic History Review*, vol. 27, no. 1, 1987, pp. 3–29.

——, 'Robinson, William Sydney (1876–1963)', *ADB*, vol. 11, 1988a, <http://adb.anu. edu.au/biography/robinson-william-sydney-8247>.

——, 'Collins House financiers WL Baillieu, Lionel Robinson and Francis Govett' in RT Appleyard and CB Schedvin (eds), *Australian Financiers: Biographical Essays*, Macmillan, Melbourne, 1988b.

Ricketson, Matthew, 'Staniforth Ricketson and the rejuvenation of the *Argus*', in Muriel Porter (ed.), *Argus: The Life and Death of a Great Melbourne Newspaper (1846–1957)*, RMIT Publishing, Melbourne, 2003, pp. 62–67.

Roberts, GA, 'Business interests and the formation of the ABC', *Politics*, vol. 7, no. 2, 1972, pp. 149–54.

Roberts, Tom DC, *Before Rupert: Keith Murdoch and the Birth of a Dynasty*, University of Queensland Press, Brisbane, 2015.

Robertson, JR, 1988, 'Scullin, James Henry (1876–1953)', *ADB*, vol. 11, 1988, <http://adb.anu.edu.au/biography/scullin-james-henry-8375>.

Rood, David, 'Out of the gold rush, a radical voice is born', *The Age*, 24 January 2004.

Rutledge, Martha, 'Barton, Sir Edmund (Toby) (1849–1920)', *ADB*, vol. 7, 1979, <http://adb.anu.edu.au/biography/barton-sir-edmund-toby-71>.

SA Memory, 'A short history of the *Register* newspaper 1836–1931', <http://www.samemory.sa.gov.au/site/page.cfm?c=2564>.

——, 'The *Advertiser*', <http://www.samemory.sa.gov.au/site/page.cfm?c=2531>.

——, 'The *News*', <www.samemory.sa.gov.au/site/page.cfm?c=2627>.

——, 'South Australian shipping lines: Adelaide Steamship Company – expansion', <http://www.samemory.sa.gov.au/site/page.cfm?u=640>.

Sayers, CE, 'Syme, David (1827–1908)', *ADB*, vol. 6, 1976, <http://adb.anu.edu.au/ biography/syme-david-4679>.

Schedvin, CB, *Australia and the Great Depression: A Study of Economic Development and Policy in the 1920s and 1930s*, Sydney University Press, Sydney, 1970.

——, 'Gibson, Sir Robert (1863–1934')', *ADB*, vol. 8, 1981, <http://adb.anu.edu.au/ biography/gibson-sir-robert-6310>.

Schudson, Michael, *Discovering the News: A Social History of American Newspapers*, Basic Books, New York, 1978.

Serle, Geoffrey, 'Wilson, Edward (1813–1878)', *ADB*, vol. 6, 1976a, <http://adb.anu.edu. au/biography/wilson-edward-4866>.

——, 'Winter, Samuel Vincent (1843–1904)', *ADB*, vol. 6, 1976b, <http://adb.anu.edu. au/biography/winter-samuel-vincent-4875>.

——, 'Murdoch, Sir Keith Arthur (1885–1952)', *ADB*, vol. 10, 1986, <http://adb.anu. edu.au/biography/murdoch-sir-keith-arthur-7693>.

Seymour-Ure, Colin, *The Political Impact of Mass Media*, Constable, London, 1974.

Shafer, Jack, 'The lost world of Joseph Pulitzer', *Slate*, 16 September 2005, <http://www. slate.com/articles/news_and_politics/press_box/2005/09/the_lost_world_of_joseph_ pulitzer.html>.

Shakespeare, Arthur T, *A Brief History of the Australian Provincial Press Association, 1906–1956*, Federal Capital Press, Canberra, 1956.

Simpson, Caroline, 'Hordern, Sir Anthony (Tony) (1889–1970)', *ADB*, vol. 9, 1983, <http://adb.anu.edu.au/biography/hordern-sir-anthony-tony-7071>.

——, 'Hordern, Samuel (1909–1960)', *ADB*, vol. 14, 1996, <http://adb.anu.edu.au/biography/hordern-samuel-10544>.

Sinclair, CM, 'Barrow, John Henry (1817–1874)', *ADB*, vol. 3, 1969, <http://adb.anu.edu.au/biography/barrow-john-henry-2943>.

Slee, John, 'Sydney as world libel capital', *Australian Press Council News*, vol. 2, no. 1, 1990.

Sloan, Andrew, 'Willis, Ernest Horatio (1867–1947)', vol. 12, 1990, <http://adb.anu.edu.au/biography/willis-ernest-horatio-9123>.

Smith, Anthony, *The Newspaper: An International History*, Thames and Hudson, London, 1979.

The Smithsonian's National Postal Museum, 'Newspaper publishers', <https://postalmuseum.si.edu/americasmailingindustry/newspapers.html>.

Souter, Gavin, *Company of Heralds: A Century and a Half of Australian Publishing*, Melbourne University Press, Melbourne, 1981.

——, *Acts of Parliament: A Narrative History of the Senate and House of Representatives, Commonwealth of Australia*, Melbourne University Press, Melbourne, 1988.

——, 'Stuart, Athol Hugh (1893–1954)', *ADB*, vol. 12, 1990, <http://adb.anu.edu.au/biography/stuart-athol-hugh-8703>.

——, *Heralds and Angels: The House of Fairfax 1841–1990*, Melbourne University Press, Melbourne, 1991.

——, 'Deamer, Sydney Harold (1891–1962)', *ADB*, vol. 13, 1993, <http://adb.anu.edu.au/biography/deamer-sydney-harold-9932>.

Spearritt, Peter, 'Snow, Sir Sydney (1887–1958)', *ADB*, vol. 12, 1990, <http://adb.anu.edu.au/biography/snow-sir-sydney-8570>.

Stamm, Michael, *Sound Business: Newspapers, Radio, and the Politics of New Media*, University of Pennsylvania Press, Philadelphia, 2011.

Strahan, Frank, 'Ricketson, Staniforth (1891–1967)', *ADB*, vol. 16, 2002, <http://adb.anu.edu.au/biography/ricketson-staniforth-11521>.

Suich, Max, '1930s couldn't happen again – could they?', *Australian*, 30 June 2012.

Sun Newspapers, *Sun Newspapers Ltd 1920–1929*, Sun Newspapers, Sydney, 1929.

Taplin, Harry, 'Spowers, Allan (1892–1968)', *ADB*, vol. 16, 2002, <http://adb.anu.edu.au/biography/spowers-allan-11747>.

Taylor, SJ, *The Great Outsiders: Northcliffe, Rothermere and the Daily Mail*, Weidenfeld & Nicolson, London, 1996.

Temple, Mick, *The British Press*, Open University Press, Maidenhead, 2008.

Templeton, Jacqueline, 'Mackinnon, Lauchlan (1817–1888)', *ADB*, vol. 5, 1974, <http://adb.anu.edu.au/biography/mackinnon-lauchlan-4116>.

Thomas, Alan, *Broadcast and Be Damned: The ABC's First Two Decades*, Melbourne University Press, Melbourne, 1980.

——, 'Conder, Walter Tasman (1888–1974)', *ADB*, vol. 8, 1981, <http://adb.anu.edu.au/biography/conder-walter-tasman-5747>.

Thompson, John Lee, *Northcliffe: Press Baron in Politics 1865–1922*, John Murray, London, 2000.

Thompson, Peter and Robert Macklin, *The Big Fella: The Rise and Rise of BHP Billiton*, Random House, Sydney, 2010.

Tiffen, Rodney, 'The *Sun* also sets: *Mirror* monopoly shock', *Media Information Australia*, vol. 52, May 1989, pp. 16–20.

——, 'The press', in Stuart Cunningham and Graeme Turner (eds), *The Media and Communications in Australia*, 2nd edn, Allen & Unwin, Sydney, 2006, pp. 97–112.

——, 'Has the gap between qualities and tabloids increased? Changes in Australian newspapers 1956–2006', *Australian Journal of Communication*, vol. 38, no. 2, 2011, pp. 33–52.

——, 'From punctuated equilibrium to threatened species: The evolution of Australian newspaper circulation and ownership', *Australian Journalism Review*, vol. 37, iss. 1, July 2015, pp. 63–80.

——, *Disposable Leaders: Media and Leadership Coups from Menzies to Abbott*, NewSouth Publishing, Sydney, 2017.

—— and Ross Gittins, *How Australia Compares*, Cambridge University Press, Melbourne, 2004.

Treasury of Australia, 'Australia's century since Federation at a glance', Economic Roundup, The Treasury, Australian Government, iss. 1, 2001, pp. 53–63.

Tsokhas, Kosmas, '"I believe in Australia": The last years of WS Robinson, 1956–63', *Australian Journal of Politics & History*, vol. 30, iss. 1, pp. 19–30.

Turnbull, Clive, 'Journalism' in Clinton H Grattan (ed.), *Australia*, University of California Press, Berkeley, 1947, pp. 314–25.

Twopenny, Richard, *Town Life in Australia*, Penguin Books, Melbourne, [1883] Project Gutenberg ebook version, 2005, <http://www.gutenberg.org/files/16664/16664-h/16664-h.htm>.

United Press International (UPI), 'On this day', 15 July 2017, <https://www.upi.com/Top_News/2017/07/15/On-This-Day-110-years-ago-United-Press-is-formed-by-EW-Scripps/8301499903644/>.

Van Heekeren, Margaret, 'Stop the presses: Strikes in the Australian news media', *Media International Australia*, no. 150, 2014, pp. 41–46.

Vickery, Edward, 'Telling Australia's story to the world: The Department of Information 1939–1950', PhD thesis, Australian National University, Canberra, 2003.

Ville, Simon and David Merrett, 'The development of large scale enterprise in Australia, 1910–64', *Business History*, vol. 42, no. 3, 2000, pp. 13–46.

Walker, Robin B, *The Newspaper Press in New South Wales, 1803–1920*, Sydney University Press, Sydney, 1976.

——, 'The fall of the *Labor Daily*', *Labour History*, no. 38, May 1980a, pp. 67–75.

——, *Yesterday's News: A History of the Newspaper Press in New South Wales from 1920 to 1945*, Sydney University Press, Sydney, 1980b.

——, 'Denison, Sir Hugh Robert (1865–1940)', *ADB*, vol. 8, 1981, <http://adb.anu.edu.au/biography/denison-sir-hugh-robert-5955>.

Walker, RR, *The Magic Spark: 50 Years of Radio in Australia*, The Hawthorn Press, Melbourne, 1973.

Walsh, GP, 'Jones, David (1793–1873)', *ADB*, vol. 2, 1967, <http://adb.anu.edu.au/biography/jones-david-2279>.

——, 'Nichols, George Robert (Bob) (1809–1857)', *ADB*, vol. 5, 1974, <http://adb.anu.edu.au/biography/nichols-george-robert-bob-4296>.

Ward, Michael, 'Sir Keith Murdoch: The Flinders Street broker', BLitt thesis, Australian National University, Canberra, 1981.

Warren, AP, *The Kingdom of Collins House*, AP Warren, Sydney, 1939.

Waterhouse, Jill, 'Brient, Lachlan John (1856–1940)', *ADB*, vol. 7, 1979, <http://adb.anu.edu.au/biography/brient-lachlan-john-5356>.

Wheeler, Doreen, 'Darling, Harold Gordon (1885–1950)', *ADB*, vol. 8, 1981, <http://adb.anu.edu.au/biography/darling-harold-gordon-5884>.

——, 'Kelly, Anthony Edwin (1852–1930)', *ADB*, vol. 9, 1983, <http://adb.anu.edu.au/biography/kelly-anthony-edwin-6916>.

White, Richard, 'Packer, Robert Clyde (1879–1934)', *ADB*, vol. 11, 1988, <http://adb.anu.edu.au/biography/packer-robert-clyde-7940>.

Whitington, R.S, *Sir Frank: The Frank Packer Story*, Cassel Australia, Melbourne, 1971.

Whyte, William F, *William Morris Hughes: His Life and Times*, Angus and Robertson, Melbourne, 1957.

Wiener, Joel H, *The Americanization of the British Press, 1830s–1914*, Palgrave Macmillan, Basingstoke, 2011.

Williams, Kevin, *Read All About It!: A History of the British Newspaper*, Taylor and Francis, New York, 2010.

Williams, Raymond, 'The press and popular culture: An historical perspective', in George Boyce, James Curran and Pauline Wingate (eds), *Newspaper History: From the 17th Century to the Present Day*, Constable and Company, London, 1978, pp. 41–50.

Wiltshire, Kenneth W and Charles H Stokes, 'Government regulation and the printed media industry', CEDA (Committee for Economic Development of Australia), July 1977.

Witwer, David Scott, *Shadow of the Racketeer: Scandal in Organized Labor*, University of Illinois Press, Urbana, 2009.

Woodberry, Joan, *Andrew Bent and the Freedom of the Press in Van Diemen's Land*, Fullers Bookshop Publishing Division, Hobart, 1972.

Young, Sally, *How Australia Decides: Election Reporting and the Media*, Cambridge University Press, Melbourne, 2011.

Younger, Ronald Michel, 'Let's Go to Press: The Saga of Melbourne's Longest Running Newspaper and its Place in the Community', unpublished manuscript, undated (circa 1996).

——, 'Profiles', unpublished document detailing profiles of HWT personnel, (circa 1999).

——, *Keith Murdoch: Founder of a Media Empire*, Harper Collins, Sydney, 2003.

Yule, Peter, *William Lawrence Baillieu: Founder of Australia's Greatest Business Empire*, Hardie Grant Books, Melbourne, 2012.

——, 'WL Baillieu and the Growth of the Herald & Weekly Times, 1889–1931', *Victorian Historical Journal*, vol. 84, no. 1, June 2013, pp. 53–71.

Zwar, Desmond, *In Search of Keith Murdoch*, Macmillan, Sydney, 1980.

INDEX

Page numbers referring to images are
in *italics*. Page numbers referring to
tables are in **bold**.

2BH Broken Hill 442–45
2BL Sydney (formerly 2SB) 407,
409–10, 415–16, 429
2CA Canberra 446
2CH Sydney 426, 446
2FC Sydney 412, 415–16, 422
2GB Sydney 434, 441, 446, 451
2HR Singleton/Lochinvar 441, 446
2UE Sydney 169, 433, 441, 446
2UW Sydney 345, 526
2WL Wollongong 446
3AK Melbourne 451
3AR Melbourne 415–16, 419
3AW Melbourne 406–7, 442, 446
3DB Melbourne
    advertising 434
    dominance 449
    HWT ownership of 276, 419, 439
    Joe Lyons and 376, 419
    Lubeck station 442
    in the Major Network 446
3GG (formerly 3UL Warragul) 442
3HA Hamilton 442
3LO Melbourne
    acquisitions and takeovers 410,
    415, 418
    link to ABC 443
    popularity of 412, 415
    subject matter 410–11, 422
3SH Swan Hill 442
3SR (formerly 3WR Shepparton) 441
3TR Sale/Gippsland 442
3UL Warragul 442
3UZ Melbourne 441–42
3YB Warrnambool 441
4AK Oakey 433

4BK Brisbane 433, 439, 446
4QG Brisbane 414
5AD Adelaide
    5PI transmits from 433
    HWT ownership of 284, 376, 439
    Joe Lyons and 376, 383, 419
    in the Major Network 446
5CL Adelaide 416
5DN Adelaide 446
5MU Murray Bridge 433
5PI Port Pirie 432–33
5SE Mount Gambier 442
6IX Perth 433, 446
6ML 284, 433
6WB Katanning 433
7HT Hobart 446
7ZL Hobart 416

AAP *see* Australian Associated Press
Abbott, JP 526
ABC radio
    AAP and 487, 490
    creation of 422–31
    fights restrictions 432, 434–36,
    439–40, 446–49
    HWT's insider at 443–44
    Keith Murdoch and 449, 519
    publication of program lists 349
    restrictions on 395
    sports coverage 420
ABC Weekly 349
ACP *see* Australian Consolidated Press
Adams, Phillip 339
Adelaide, SA 19, 23, 206–8, 226
Adelaide Club 285
Adelaide Examiner 40
Adelaide Express 71
Adelaide Steamship Company Ltd
    230

Adelaide Times 37
Advertiser
    Archie Cameron on 286–87
    biography of 545
    on the Budget 397
    finances of 277
    under the HWT 235–36, 275–77,
        469
    Keith Murdoch and 280–85, 390
    launch of 39
    launches *Adelaide Express* 71
    News Limited and 236, 280–85
    paper production 462
    politics 377, 380, 383–84
    profiting from the Depression 403
    radio broadcasting 432–33, 442 *see
        also* 5AD Adelaide
    staff 275–76
Advertiser Newspapers' paper
    production *see* Australian
    Newsprint Mills Pty Ltd
advertising *see also* Australian
    Association of National Advertisers
    (AANA); *names of specific
    newspapers*
    companies chosen 93–94
    control of advertisers 111, 147
    'display' advertising 131–32
    focus on 15, 89, 93–94, 108
    promotions to advertisers 108, 110
    radio 433–34, 445–46
    during WWI 60–61
Advocate 462
Afternoon Telegram 75
The Age
    Ambrose Pratt at 372
    bias 178, 185
    biography of 545
    competition with other papers
        71–72, 139
    Fairfax buys 545
    forms AAP 486
    on the fourth estate concept 38
    on Keith Murdoch 522–23
    Keith Murdoch at 133, 196, 215,
        242, 244–45
    newspaper trains 33

    on paper production 460, 476
    photography in 57
    politics 41–42, 45, 120, 124, 196,
        202, 394
    pricing of 73, 92–93
    printing 68–69
    radio and 406–7, 418, 422, 425,
        427, 435, 442
    Robert Menzies and 503, 506
    size 84
    on the steel industry 496
    WS Robinson at 184, 214
AGL (Australian Gas Light Company)
    38
AIS (Australian Iron and Steel Ltd)
    203–4, 303, 328, 496, 497
Aitken, JB 507
AJA *see* Australian Journalists'
    Association
Albert, Frank 417
Albion Park racecourse 290
Alexander, Joseph Aloysius 'Joe'
    at the *Herald* 253, 286, 385, 387–
        88, 424–27, 502, 540
    political interventions 385–89, 393
All for Australia League 378, 384
Allen, James 39, 44
Allnutt, E 229–30
ALP *see* Labor Party
Amalgamated Miners' Association of
    Broken Hill 226
Amalgamated Pictures Ltd 222, 411
Amalgamated Wireless (Australasia)
    Ltd 130, 409, 412, 415, 426, 438
Amalgamated Workers Association
    (AWA) 333
Amalgamated Zinc
    paper production 457–60, 461–62,
        466, 470–72
    winds up 473
American 103
Anderson, Hanne 325
Anthony Hordern and Sons 412, 416
ANZ (formerly ES&A) 329, 369
APA *see* Australian Press Association
APPM *see* Australian Pulp and Paper
    Mills Ltd

Argus
  advertising 304
  APA and 484–86
  Bert Cook at 106
  biography of 546
  cable system 132
  circulation 29, 483
  Collins House and 507
  competition with other papers 72,
    139
  in debt 400–401
  effect of the Depression on 361
  elitism of 384
  'the Group' writes for 401
  Herbert Campbell Jones at 260
  HSW Lawson as director of 429
  HWT buys and closes 546
  JE Davidson at 214
  on Keith Murdoch 522–23
  launches other papers 304–5
  links to Staniforth Ricketson
    400–401
  on mining 301
  newspaper trains 33
  paper production 462, 463, 476,
    492
  politics 28–29, 41, 46, 364, 389,
    400, 506–9, 546
  pricing of 73, 92–93
  radio and 407, 409, 441–42, 451
  tone of 95
Argus and Australasian Ltd 401
Arnold, Thurman 104
Art in Australia 324
Arthur, George 14, 16–18, 20
Ascot racecourse 290
Ashbolt, Alfred 462
Ashton, L Latham 232
Associated Newspapers Ltd (Aus)
  see also Australian Consolidated
    Press; *Evening Sun*; *Sun*; *Sun News-
    Pictorial*
  advertising 108, 110–11, 341
  after Hugh Denison's death 165
  competition with other papers
    167–68, 532–33
  vs the *Daily Mirror* 513–15

deal with Sydney Newspapers
    159–60
  develops from the *Sun* 90
  dominance 102–3
  effect of the Depression on 362
  end of 150–63, 164–66, 543
  Fairfax buys 168
  finances of 158, 168, 532–33
  formation of 98, 146–47
  formation of AAP 485–86
  formation of Consolidated Press
    163–64, 340–41
  Hugh Denison's impact on 168–69
  HWT shares in 311
  newspaper chain expansion
    150–52, 159–60, 336, 547
  Packers and 155, 157–62, 341
  paper production 471–73, 481 *see
    also* Australian Newsprint Mills
    Pty Ltd
  pricing 92, 151
  radio and 418, 425, 433, 441, 444,
    451
  role in creation of the *Women's
    Weekly* 160–62
  staffing strategy 153–54
  supports Joe Lyons 401
Associated Newspapers Ltd (UK) 89
Associated Press (AP) 88
Associated Pulp and Paper Mills
  (APPM) 207, 472
Athenaeum Club 329
Atlas 23
Audit Bureau of Circulations 108, 324
Austral Development 462
Australasian Paper and Pulp Company
  455, 462
*Australasian Sketcher with Pen and
  Pencil* 24
Australasian Sugar Company 326
Australian
  advertising 15–16
  changes in ownership 21–23
  end of 26
  horseracing in 291
  launch of 15
  on libel laws 17–18

size 84
Australian Associated Press (AAP)
  321, 429, 453, 486–91
Australian Association of National
  Advertisers (AANA) 108, 523
Australian Black and White Artists'
  Club 345
Australian Broadcasting Commission
  see ABC
Australian Broadcasting Company
  407, 417–18, 421–22
Australian Consolidated Press (ACP)
  vs the *Daily Mirror* 514
  David McNicoll on 121
  finances of 513
  formation of 163–64
  Frank Packer and EG Theodore
    at 168, 337–41, 350, 451–52, 476,
    482–83, 514
  move from ANPA to Australian
    Newspapers Council 482–83
  on paper production 476
  radio broadcasting 451–52
  in TV 350, 451
Australian Federation of Broadcasting
  Stations 422, 424
Australian Home Beautiful 267
Australian Iron and Steel Ltd (AIS)
  203–4, 303, 328, 496, 497
Australian Jockey Club 291
Australian Journalists' Association
  (AJA)
  vs the AAP 490
  complains about imported comics
    345
  formation of 106, 214–15
  JE Davidson at 214–15
  Keith Murdoch and 215, 245, 523
  meekness of 45, 106
Australian Labor Party *see* Labor Party
Australian Mutual Provident Society
  (AMP)
  EH Macartney and 298
  Fairfaxes and 156, 312, 327–28, 499
  links to Collins House 312, 369
  links to the Packers 332
  role of 327–28

Australian Natives' Association (ANA)
  185, 197
Australian Newspaper History Group
  53
Australian Newspaper Proprietors'
  Association (ANPA) 482, 500
Australian Newspapers Cable Service
  see United Cable Service (UCS)
Australian Newspapers' Conference
  (ANC) *107*
  on the AAP 489
  Audit Bureau of Circulations 108,
    324
  formation of 107
  Frank Packer at 340
  on paper duties 459
  radio and 413, 421, 424, 429–30,
    435, 440
Australian Newspapers Council
  482–83
Australian Newsprint Mills Pty Ltd
  (ANM)
  applies for paper bounty 475–77
  becomes a public company 491
  building *480*
  expansion of 491
  first Australian newsprint papers
    479
  formation of 474–75
  increased demand for paper 477–
    78, 481–82
  problems with 478–82, 491–92
  takeovers 492–93
Australian Paper Manufacturers
  (APM) 462–63, 466, 470, 472
Australian Paper Mills 429
Australian Party 153
Australian Press Association (APA)
  429, 484–87
Australian Press Council (APC) 324
Australian Pulp and Paper Mills Ltd
  329
Australian Star see *Sun*
Australian Test of 1932-33 420
Australian Typographical Union 106
Australian Women's National League
  430

Australian Women's Weekly
  advertising 350
  circulation 162, 513
  colour printing of 340
  contribution to Consolidated Press 163
  George Warnecke fired from 340
  Keith Murdoch attempts to buy 339
  launch of 108, 161–62
  politics 526
Australian Worker 48
Australian Worker's Union (AWU) 48–49, 159, 160, 337
Avery, David 457–58, 462
AWA Ltd 130, 409, 412, 415, 426, 438

Baillieu, Arthur 180
Baillieu, Baillieu 197–98
Baillieu, Clive 'Joe' *see also* EL & C Baillieu
  cares for WL Baillieu 307
  financial activity 373
  friendship with EG Theodore 366
  on Joe Lyons 397
  Keith Murdoch and 197, 250
  mining interests 298, 309
  racism of 229
Baillieu, Edward Lloyd 298, 373 *see also* EL & C Baillieu
Baillieu, Elizabeth 496
Baillieu, George Francis 183
Baillieu, Harry 190
Baillieu, James Latham 306, 309
Baillieu, John 496
Baillieu, Margaret (born Robinson) 190
Baillieu, Maurice Howard Lawrence 'Jac' 250, 287, 386, 444, 499
Baillieu, ML 207, 458
Baillieu, William Lawrence *174 see also* Munro and Baillieu
  at the *Advertiser* 276
  brewing 176
  buys the *Advertiser* 275
  buys the *Herald* 175, 178–83

  buys the *Register* 235, 274–75
  buys the *West Australian* 234, 267–69
  death 309
  debts 177–77, 330
  Dulux and 230, 232
  Gerald Mussen and 217
  and the *Herald* 186–88, 263–64
  Hugh Denison and 143, 311
  at the HWT 170, 206–8, 221–23, 237, 266, 273, 306
  illness 307
  interactions with the *Sun* 311
  JE Davidson and 221–22
  Keith Murdoch and 197, 244, 249–51, 266, 267, 273, 274, 306–8, 467–68
  links to British finance 373
  Lord Northcliffe and 256
  mansions 250–51
  mining interests 175, 188–89, 192–96, 207, 232, 297
  at News Limited 231–32
  Otto Niemeyer and 367
  paper production 457–58, 461–62, 466–68
  personality 173
  politics 186–87, 190, 196–97, 199–200
  promotion in the *News* 229
  retires 306
  at WAN 267–69
  WS Robinson and 184
Baillieu family
  invests in BHP 495, 497–98
  Keith Murdoch and 197, 248–51, 279–80
  links to bondholding 369
  links to Collins House 171, 189–90
  links to the Packers 332–33
  Lord Northcliffe and 256–57
  Perpetual Trustee Company and 329
  politics 329
  sells News Limited 279–80
Balfour, James 179
Ballarat Mechanics' Institute *24*

Bank of Adelaide 230, 329
Bank of England 367
Bank of New South Wales
    concern over Robert Menzies 499
    Edward Smith Hall at 16
    Fairfaxes and 156, 330, 369
    formation of 22
    George Howe invests in 14
Barrier Daily Truth 48–49, 219–20, 224
Barrier Miner
    2BH 442–45
    JE Davidson steps back from 227
    John Williams at 285
    stance on mining companies 219–
        20, 224–26
    takeovers 209, 221–23, 232, 281
Barrow, John Henry 39
Barton, Edmund 184, 328–29
Baume, Eric 531
Bavay, AFJ de 189
BBC *see* British Broadcasting
    Corporation
Beale, Howard 536
Beasley, John 'Jack' 355–56, 379, 391,
    497–98
Bednall, Colin
    on destroying reputations 540
    on financial strategy 294
    on Frank Packer 339, 347
    on Keith Murdoch 253, 286, 308
    at the *News* 285–86
    on penny-a-liners 244
    on RAG Henderson 322
'Ben Bowyang' comic 304
Bendigo, NSW 200
Bendigo Independent 186
Benjamin, RJ 454
Bennett, Samuel 27, 44, 71, 548 *see
    also* Samuel Bennett Ltd
Bennett family 258
Bent, Andrew 14, 16, 17, 20
Bernales, Claude de 273, 301
BHP (Broken Hill Proprietary
    Company Limited) *see also*
    Australian Iron and Steel Ltd
    allied figures and companies 194,
        294, 328–29, 374, 495–98

as a bondholder 375
Commonwealth Aircraft
    Corporation 500
    finances of 498
    investors 497–99
    in Melbourne 499
    mining 188–89, 194, 203
    turns against Joe Lyons 501
    during WWI 496, 498
Big Strike 219
Biggs, LV 314
Black, Conrad 552
Blainey, Geoffrey 206, 327
Boas, IH 454, 466
La Boheme 410
Bonaparte, Napoleon 2
Bond, Alan 547, 553
Bonney, EG 285
Bonython, John Langdon 39, 275
Boulder, WA 301
Bourke, Richard 25
Bowman, David 1
Boyer, Tas 467, 479
Brack, John 189
Bradman, Don 420
Branson, WE 231
Brennan, Frank 391
Brient, LJ 120
Brisbane, QLD 290
Brisbane, Thomas 14–15
Brisbane Amateur Turf Club 293
Brisbane Courier 288, 293, 296, 364,
    413, 462 see also *Courier-Mail*
Brisbane Daily Mail Pty Ltd 302
Brisbane Newspaper Company Ltd
    288, 296
Brisbane Stadium 304
Britain *see also* England
    appeasement policy 499–500
    exchange rate changes 402–4
    mining imports 195
    newspaper chains in 81, 87–88,
        102, 103
    newspaper design in 52
    newspaper postage in 31
    newspaper printing in 19
    penny newspapers in 69–70

politics of newspapers in 115
regulation of newspapers in 104–5
stamp duty in 10–12
war debts to 368–71, 373, 374–78
British Australian Cotton Association
    Ltd (BACAL) 143, 311
British Australian Lead Manufacturers
    Pty Ltd (BALM) 230, 232
British Broadcasting Corporation
    ABC and 407, 422–23, 448, 487
    allowances and restrictions 423,
    428–29, 434
British Overseas Airways Corporation
    (BOAC) 347
British Post Office 413, 422
British Tobacco (Australia) Ltd 129
Broadcasters (Sydney) Ltd 409
Broadcasting Company of Australia
    410–11 *see also* 3LO
Broinowski, Leopold 394
Broken Hill Associated Smelters
    (BHAS) *see also* Commonwealth
    Aircraft Corporation
    as a bondholder 375
    formation of 194
    Gerald Mussen at 217–18
    influence over *Barrier Miner* 221
    linked companies 194, 328, 495
    politics and 194–95, 203, 217
    radio broadcasting 442–44
    retrenchments 283
    unrest at 223–26
Broken Hill Junction Lead Mining
    Co 443
Broken Hill, NSW *see also* Broken
    Hill South; North Broken Hill
    mining industry 192, 205, 218–20,
    223–26, 230–31, 333, 457, 496
    radio broadcasting at 442–44
    South Australia and 206
Broken Hill Proprietary Company
    Limited (BHP) *see* BHP
Broken Hill South 302, 375, 402, 473
Brookes, Herbert 429, 447, 455, 461
Brookes, Norman 455
Brookes family 455
Brown, Harry Percy 419, 422, 425, 433

Browne, EIC 288
Bruce, Stanley
    anti-Lang sentiment 402
    becomes assistant treasurer 396
    becomes Australian High
        Commissioner in London 396
    becomes PM 205
    on EG Theodore 404
    Herbert Campbell Jones on 153
    institutes paper bounty 460–61, 463
    loses 1929 election 153, 359–60
    at NLMA 374
    papers attempt to bring back 507–9
    radio policy 407, 415, 417–18, 427
Buckley, Harry Wilfred 302, 308
Buckley and Hughes (company) 302
Bulletin 49, 198, 462
Bullmore, Gretel 332
Burnie, Tas 459, 463, 468, 472
Burra mines 39
Burston, Harold 285, 443, 444
Bushell's tea 511
Butler's Gorge power scheme 475
Butters, John 1–2, 165, 168, 444
Buttrose, Ita 6

cable system 33–34, 61–62, 129–30
    see also Australian Associated Press;
    United Cable Service
Cain, John 531
Calwell, Arthur 250, 355, 488, 525, 542
Cameron, Archie 170–71, 286, 440,
    447, 509
Campbell, HAM 503
Campbell Jones, Herbert
    assisting Ezra Norton 166, 512
    on the *Daily Guardian* 152
    as director of Associated
        Newspapers 154–57
    at the HWT 258
    Keith Murdoch and 249, 258,
        260–61
    letters to the editor 167
    politics 153
    radio broadcasting 416
    role in leaking James Scullin's

cables 388
at the *Sun* 131, 133–34, 136, 152–53, 166–67, 259–61
at Truth and Sportsman Ltd 167
as UCS European correspondent 167

Canberra Activities Pty Ltd 463
Canberra press gallery 359, 447, 490, 504–5
Canberra Times 84, 120, 522, 546
Cannon, Michael 140, 176–78, 252, 306, 342
Capel Court Investment Trust 498, 507
Carey, James 1
Carlton and United Breweries (CUB) 176, 182, 189–90, 328, 375
Carmichael, Alan 384
Caro, George 308, 310, 523
Casey, Richard 384, 396, 507, 509
censorship 542 *see also* Department of Information; freedom of the press
Central News 484
Chalmers, Rob 490
Chamberlain, Neville 499
Charlton, Matthew 460
Chifley, Ben 483, 494
Christiansen, Arthur 76
Citizens' League 384
City Newspaper Company Limited 179–80
Clark, Colin 404
Clark, Garnet L 308
Clark, William 189
Clarke, Duncan 356
Clarkson, AE 229–30, 236–37, 280
Clarkson Ltd 230
Cleary, WJ 435–36
Cliveden 250
Cody, Patrick 299, 300–301, 336
Cohen, Harold 458, 470, 472, 495
Cohen, Montague 189, 458
Cohens 496
Coles 434
Colgate-Palmolive 434
Collingwood Tote 274, 290

Collins House *see also* Broken Hill Associated Smelters; Broken Hill South; Carlton and United Breweries; Commonwealth Aircraft Corporation; Dulux; Electrolytic Refining and Smelting Company; Herald and Weekly Times; News Corporation; North Broken Hill; Zinc Corporation Limited
allied companies 269, 270–73, 312, 329, 372–74, 398, 495, 498
Argus and 507
as a bondholder 368–69, 375
building 189, *191*
connections to 'the Group' 372
Courier-Mail and 299
Daily Mail and 302
dynasty 190
finances of 222
first radio transmission 408
George Caro's links to 308
hiding control of papers 281–83
interwar diversification 206–7, 208
Keith Murdoch promotes 251
in Melbourne 499
mining interests 193–96, 199, 205–7, 270, 272–73, 297–98, 300–301
News Limited and 208, 217–18, 222–27, 229–32, 236–39, 272
paper production 457–60, 463, 467
political influence 186–87, 200–203, 204, 356, 397, 398, 495
reach of 274
rivalry 234
subsidiaries drift from 309
support for conscription 196–97
'What is wrong with Broken Hill?' 219–20
WL Baillieu's running of 183
'Collins St, 5 pm' (artwork) 189
Colonial Bank 44
Colonial Office 21, 28
colonialism in Australia 12–23
colour printing 80, 340, 345–46
comic strips 92, 304, 322, 345
Commercial Bank of Australia 329, 369, 499

Commercial Banking Company of
Sydney 330–31, 369
Commins, Jack 448
Commonwealth Aircraft Corporation
500
Commonwealth Bank 364, 374
Commonwealth Bureau of Science
and Industry 454–55
Commonwealth Prices Branch 538
Commonwealth Royal Commissions
300
Commonwealth Scientific and
Industrial Research Organisation
457, 466
Conder, Walter Tasman
at ABC 443–44
in commercial radio 410, 415–19
dismissal and jailing 444
Congregational Church 330
Conley, WG 315–16
conscription
The Age on 43
Barrier Miner on 220
Collins House's support for 196–
98, 200, 216, 247–48
politicians on 135–37, 196–97,
200, 508
Sydney Morning Herald on 319
conservatism *see also* Liberal Party;
names of specific newspapers;
Nationalist Party; United Australia
Party
"apolitical" 35–38, 50, 112–17
consolidation increasing 50, 103–4
corporate ownership increasing
44–46, 103–4
impact of papers on politics 125
tendency towards 25, 30–31, 115–
17, **118–19**, 120, **122–23**, 124
Consolidated Press *see* Australian
Consolidated Press
Consolidated Zinc (formerly Zinc
Corporation Limited) 189, 195,
302, 375
Consultative Council of Sydney 499
Cook, Bert 106, 235
Cook, James Hume 199

Cook, Joseph 190
Cooke, John and Henry 42, 44
Coolgardie, WA 217
Couchman, EM 430
Council for Scientific and Industrial
Research 457, 466
Country and Progressive National
Party 292
Country Party *see also* Cameron,
Archie; Green, Roland
forms Liberal and Country League
286
newspapers supporting 201,
393–94
radio and 449
reconciles with the UAP 512–13
refusal to work with Joe Lyons 398
refusal to work with Robert
Menzies 508
replaces Billy Hughes with Stanley
Bruce 205
replaces parliamentary members
526
wins balance of power in 1934
election 398
Courier-Mail see also 4AK Oakey; 4BK
Brisbane
biography of 546
circulation 478
finances of 486
formation of 278, 293–94, 296, 302
HWT buys 546
length of 478
News Limited buys 546
politics 297–98
structure of 299
subject matter 303–4
Cowper, Norman 349–50, 526–27
Cox, Harry 164
Cox, Owen 203
crime *see also* libel; The Gun Alley
Mystery
in *The Currency Lad* 77
in the *Daily Guardian* 146
in the *Daily Mail* 81–82
in the *Evening News* 77
in the *Herald* 77, 252

in Joseph Pulitzer's papers 78
in penny newspapers 69
popularity of 85
Cross, Stan 357
Crystal Brook, SA 433
CSIRO 457, 466
CSR (Colonial Sugar Refining
    Company)
    as a bondholder 375
    concern over Robert Menzies 499
    dominance 204, 327
    EH Macartney's support for 298
    finances of 498
    formation of 326
    Knoxes at 326, 329
    sugar strike against 333
    trustee companies and 294, 329
Cumberland Paper Board Mills 462
Cunningham, Edward 400
Cunningham, JC 220
Curran, James 11–12
The Currency Lad 77
Curthoys, Roy 400, 509
Curtin, John 391, 440, 501, 523, 526,
    540
CWL Pty Ltd 289, 293, 299

Daily Advertiser 325
Daily Express 52, 76, 164, 486
Daily Free Press 214
Daily Guardian
    biography of 546–47
    broadcasting of 410
    circulation 101, 154
    closes 322, 484
    fall of 152–55
    finances of 101
    launch of 91–92, 101, 145
    merges with the *Daily Pictorial* 154
    merges with the *Daily Telegraph* 547
    on paper production 459
    politics 113, 153
    sale to Hugh Denison 150–51
    'yellow journalism' 95–97, 145–46
Daily Mail (Aus) see also *Courier-Mail*
    defamation 293

John Wren and Benjamin Nathan
    buy 290
    Keith Murdoch invests in 274
    politics 291–92
Daily Mail (UK)
    Ambrose Pratt at 372
    design of 52
    incorporation 89
    launch of 52, 78, 81
    politics 109
    size 84
    subject matter 81–82, 411
    tone of 98
    UCS subscribes to 485
Daily Mirror Group 546
Daily Mirror (Sydney)
    advertising 538
    biography of 547
    circulation 532
    competition with other papers 167,
        532–33, 538
    design of 529
    Fairfax buys 547
    finances of 532
    launch of 513–15, 529
    merges with the *Daily Telegraph* 547
    news source 488
    politics 531–32
    Rupert Murdoch buys 547
    subject matter 529–32
Daily Mirror (UK) 82
Daily News (formerly *Labor Daily*)
    biography of 549
    critiques ABC's foundation
        commissioners 430
    Daily Telegraph buys and closes 49
    financial policy 370
    on knighthoods 396
    launch of 48
    on paper production 476
    politics 48, 335, 549
    pricing of 92, 152
    subject matter 49
Daily News (Perth)
    Arthur Lovekin at 455
    biography of 547
    closes 547

HWT buys 281, 469
News Limited buys 233, 272
WAN buys 272–73
Daily Pictorial
circulation 154
merges with the *Daily Guardian* 154
Daily Standard 292
Daily Telegraph Sunday News Pictorial 146
Daily Telegraph (Sydney)
1883 takeover 179
1892 shutdown 179
advertising 108, 110–11, 152, 340, 538
Billy Hughes at 194, 205
biography of 548
Brian Penton at 347, 349
buys and closes the *Daily News* 48
circulation 164–65, 337, 483
comic strips 322
competition with other papers 72, 73, 538
Consolidated Press takes over 163–64
design of 146–47, 158, 164
effect of the Depression on 361
on Ezra Norton 344
finances of 101, 151, 163, 514
Gerald Mussen at 193, 214
on Hugh Denison 341
Hugh Denison buys 146
on Keith Murdoch 517, 521, 523
launch of 154
merges with the *Daily Guardian* 547
merges with the *Daily Mirror* 547
on MP wage increase 397
paper production and 481–82
politics 48, 117, 120–21, 347, 349–50, 364, 393, 525–27, 540, 542
pricing of 92, 477
on radio 437
rotogravure pictorial supplement 162
Rupert Murdoch buys 548
Smith's Weekly on 95

subject matter 77
withdraws from AAP 486
Daily Telegraph (UK) 69
Dale, George 226
Daniell, Esmond Tuckett 222
Darling, Harold 375, 495–96, 499
Darling, Ralph 16–18
Darling Downs, QLD 433
David Jones 330, 341, 345, 412, 416
David Syme and Co see also *The Age* 406, 474
Davidson, Alan 237
Davidson, Allan 211, 214, 237
Davidson, James Edward *212–13*
critiques of 226, 234
death 237–38
early life 214
fights nationalisation of radio 413
formation of AJA 214–16
at the *Herald* 54, 198, 249
at the HWT 206, 214–17, 221–22, 234
Keith Murdoch and 234–35, 249
News Limited and 101, 113–14, 209–10, 217, 222–29, 235, 236–38, 550
personality 210–11, 234
role in UCS 134
Davidson, James Johnstone 211, 214
Davidson, Norman 209, 238
Davies, Charles 40
Davies, John 40, 550
Davies, Matthew 179
Davies Bros Ltd see also the *Mercury* 474
Dawson, Geoffrey 247–48
de Bavay, AFJ 189
De Bavay's *see* Amalgamated Zinc
de Bernales, Claude 273, 301
Deagon racecourse 296
Deakin, Alfred
The Age on 120, 184–85
becomes PM 42
defeat of 190
invests in the *Herald* 185
Keith Murdoch and 244
networking 185, 197, 329

Deamer, Sydney 'Syd' 164, 275, 337,
   347, 349
defamation *see* libel
Dekyvere, Nola 345
Denison, Hugh *131*
   altruism 168–69
   at BACAL 143
   buys the *Guardians* 150–51
   as Commissioner for Australia in the
      US 143
   conflict with Frank Packer 341
   with Consolidated Press 163–64
   vs the *Daily Mirror* 514–15
   deal with Sydney Newspapers
      159–60
   death and will 165–66
   dominance of papers 102
   early life 129
   at the *Evening Sun* 140, 142–43, 263
   formation of Associated Newspapers
      98
   horse breeding 291
   horse racing 129
   hurdles for Associated Newspapers
      151, 167–68
   HWT and 137–40, 170, 258, 259,
      311–12
   Keith Murdoch and 245–46, 248–
      49, 258–59, 266, 311–12, 469, 522
   knighthood 143
   merger with the *Daily Telegraph* 146
   paper production 429, 455, 470, 471,
      473, 474
   personality 133–34
   politics 40, 136
   pricing of papers 150–51
   radio broadcasting 411–12, 418,
      433, 441, 446
   response to *ABC Weekly* 349
   rise and fall of 128
   sets up UCS 484
   staff lose confidence in 155
   staffing strategy 153–54, 157
   at the *Sun* 54, 112, 130–31, 132–33,
      134, 137–39, 140, 142–43, 245–46,
      249, 311
   at the *Sun News-Pictorial* 82, 92–93,

      139–40, 142, 263, 265, 312
   Sydney Morning Herald and 152,
      324
Denison, Leslie 165–66
Denison, Reginald 165–66, 169, 514
Denison, Sara Rachel 165–66
Denison, William Leslie 'Bill' 166
Denison Estates 166, 441, 446
Denison family 162
Denning, Warren 359, 447–48, 504
Department of Information 517–25
depressions 25 *see also* Great
   Depression
Derwent River, Tas 195, 467–68, 475,
   479
Derwent Valley Paper Company
   467–71, 474
Detroit, US 214
Detroit Free Press 53
Detroit News 214
Dixson, Hugh 129
Dixson, Robert 129
Dominion Broadcasting Company
   415–17
Downer, Alexander 230
Downer, Fred 282–83
Downing, Henry Percy 269
Doyle, Stuart 417
Druleigh Business and Technical
   College 419
Dulux 230, 232
Dumas, Lloyd
   in the Adelaide Club 285
   at the *Advertiser* 275–76, 280–84,
      377, 380, 383–84, 397, 403
   at ANM 491–92
   dislike for Frank Packer 341
   HP Brown and 419
   at the HWT 171, 432, 518
   impact on broadcasting 419, 425,
      429, 432
   on JS Teulon 471
   paper production and 469, 474
   politics 286, 382–83, 386, 394, 398
   response to Department of
      Information 522–24
   at the *Sun News-Pictorial* 265

on the *Sydney Morning Herald* 483
Dunlop Rubber Company 186
Dunlop-Perdriau 398
Dunstan, Keith 85

Echo 75
editorials 116, 216
education 42
Edward Lloyd Ltd 462
Edwards, Cecil 305, 360
Egypt 246
EL & C Baillieu 183, 199
Electrolytic Refining and Smelting
    Company 311
Electrolytic Zinc (EZ) 195,
    207, 232–33, 256, 458, 462 *see
    also* Commonwealth Aircraft
    Corporation
Elliott, RD 306
Emperor Gold Mining Company Ltd
    300
Emperor Mines Ltd 300–302, 336
Empire 26–27, 45
England 18, 64, 196, 320, 420
English, Scottish & Australia Bank Ltd
    (ES&A) 329, 369
Equity Trustees Executors and Agency
    Co 498
Eureka Stockade 29, 42
Evatt, Herbert Vere 349, 526
Evening Journal 103
Evening Mail 305
Evening News
    biography of 548
    broadcasting of 412
    circulation 147, 154
    closes 155, 484
    comic strips 92
    design of 147
    finances of 151–52
    incorporation 89
    investment in 257–59
    Keith Murdoch and 311
    launch of 27
    plant and premises 163
    pricing of 71, 92

subject matter 77
Evening Standard 179–81, 264
Evening Standard Company 180
Evening Star 400, 548
Evening Sun 140, 142, 170, 263–65,
    549
Evening Telegraph 36
Executor Trustee and Agency
    Company 229, 329
Express and Telegraph 228

Fadden, Arthur 529, 535, 537, 539–40
Fairfax, Charles 325
Fairfax, Edward 499
Fairfax, Emily 326
Fairfax, James Oswald 328–29, 461–63
Fairfax, James Reading 39, 315,
    328–31
Fairfax, John
    buys Associated Newspapers 168
    invests in the Bank of New South
        Wales 330
    politics 40
    at the *Sydney Morning Herald* 26,
        38, 65, 68, 315
Fairfax, John Hubert 328, 330, 499
Fairfax, Vincent 328, 330
Fairfax, Warwick Oswald *317*
    childhood of 316
    Daily Mirror and 515, 533–34
    inexperience 319
    invests in BHP 499
    knighthood 396
    paper production 463, 474
    personality and interests 322, 324
    position at Fairfax 316
    Robert Menzies and 503–4, 515,
        528, 535–38, 542
    at the *Sydney Morning Herald* 402,
        534–39
Fairfax family
    concern over Robert Menzies
        499
    linked companies 156, 204, 328–
        31, 369, 497–99
Fairfax & Sons (later Fairfax Media)

see also Australian Associated Press;
Sydney Mail; Sydney Morning Herald
AH Stuart at 320–21
building 320
buys The Age 545
buys the Canberra Times 546
buys the Daily Mirror 547
Collins House and 312
dominance 543, 553
finances of 315–16, 500
focus on the Sydney Morning Herald
314, 325
investments 325–26
isolation from other papers 324
launches Art in Australia 324
launches Home 324
links to the HWT 312, 321, 324
loses the Sydney Morning Herald
552
paper production 453–54, 463,
468–71 see also Australian
Newsprint Mills Pty Ltd
price-fixing 340
radio broadcasting 451–52
RAG Henderson at 319–22,
324–25
response to paper rationing 535–37
untaxable dividends 294
Fairhall, Allen 497
Farmer and Co 410, 416
Fatty Finn 92
Fawkner, John Pascoe 40, 44
Federal Bank 176, 330
Federal Communications Commission
(FCC) 105
Federal Finance Council 200
Federal Network 446
Federal Trade Commission (FTC)
103
Federation 32
Federation of Australian Commercial
Broadcasting Stations 437
Felt and Textiles of Australia Ltd 398
Fenton, James
deflationary strategy 367–70, 375
impact on broadcasting 422–23,
425, 426–27

on monopolies 373
no-confidence motion 386
resignation from Cabinet 377
role in leaking James Scullin's
cables 387
Field, RD 515
Fiji 299–302, 326, 335
Financial Review 190
Fink, Benjamin 175–76, 182
Fink, Catherine 182
Fink, Theodore 174
at the Advertiser 276
at the Broadcasting Company of
Australia 411
buys the Advertiser 275
buys the Register 274–75
considers buying the West
Australian 267
at the Herald 60, 113, 134, 175,
178–83, 185, 198, 209, 216,
249–50, 263–64, 315
hidden assets 232
at the HWT 138, 182, 206, 208,
216, 220–22, 227, 234, 259, 273,
277, 304–9, 522
interactions with Hugh Denison
311–12
invests in Queensland Newspapers
302
joining UCS 484
Keith Murdoch and 248–50, 259,
266, 273, 274, 302, 304–9, 522–23
legal work 176–78
mining interests 175
paper production and 460, 468
politics 186, 196, 198, 200–201
real estate firm 172
on the Sydney Morning Herald 314
Fink, Thorold
broadcasting 419, 422
at the HWT 266, 307
on Keith Murdoch 306
paper production 467–68, 470–71
at war 198
Fink, Wolfe 175
Fink family 173, 182
Firth, John 322

Fisher, Andrew
  1910 election win 190
  Keith Murdoch and 244–46
  policy on cable systems 132, 487
  resigns as PM 193
  on WL Baillieu 190
Fitzgerald, Ross 300
Fletcher, Charles Brundson 323
Fletcher Challenge 492
Florentine River, Tas 467–68
Forest, Lord 214
Formguide 490
Fosters Brewery 189
'fourth estate' concept 35–39, 50
Fox, Len 207
Fraser, Allan 504–5, 540
Fraser, Colin
  on Arthur Fadden 535
  at BHAS 203, 218–21, 224–25
  invests in Emperor Mines 301
  invests in the West Australian 268
  Joe Lyons and 396–97
  knighthood 396
  in the National Union 495
  at News Limited 231–32
  paper production 463, 472
  radio broadcasting 442–44
  at WMC 207, 270
freedom of the press 10–23, 542 see
  also censorship; 'fourth estate'
  concept
Freemasons' Hotel 226
Freney Kimberley Oil Company 230
Fuller, Benjamin 417

Gallipoli letter 246–47
Garden, Don
  on Alfred Deakin 185
  on Theodore Fink 180, 182, 185,
    198
  on Thorold Fink 471
  on the UCS 134
  on WL Baillieu's debt erasure 177
Gardner, PD 177
Geeves, Philip 415
gender see sexism

General Motors Holden 500
George, Lloyd 247–48
George Wills & Co 230
Gepp, Herbert 466
Germany 192–93
Giblin, LF 404
Gibson, Robert 374–75, 390, 403
Gibson, WG 409
Giddy, Harry Douglas
  at the HWT 302, 308, 310, 523
  paper production 474, 491
  Wilson, Danby and Giddy 302–3
Gilbert, David 280–81
Ginger Meggs 92
Glendyne, Lord see Nivison, Robert
Gold Exploration and Finance
  Company of Australia 270
Gold Mines of Australia 269
Gollan, Ross 535, 539–40
Gollin and Co 308
Gosse, James Hay 230, 283, 285
Govett, Francis 189, 297
Great Boulder Proprietary Gold Mines
  Ltd 301
Great Depression
  affects Port Pirie 283
  dealing with war debts during
    368–71, 373–78
  deflation exacerbates 403–4
  effect on newspapers 101, 151, 154,
    168, 236, 280, 288, 361–62
  effect on paper production 466–67
  exchange rate increase due to
    402–3
  James Scullin's response to 362–
    64, 365, 366–70
  JT Lang's response to 368–71
  lifting of 309
  newspaper coverage of 154, 358–
    59, 402
  start of 361
Green, Albert 427
Green, Roland 417
Gregson, Sarah 218
Griffen-Foley, Bridget
  on Frank Packer 347
  on George Warnecke 159

on RC Packer 144, 155, 338
on Robert Menzies 540
on Warwick Fairfax 322
'the Group'
    connections with the *Argus* 401
    financial policy 374–78
    Joe Lyons repays 395
    members of 371–74
    separates Joe Lyons from the ALP
        381–88
Grover, Montague
    on JE Davidson 210–11
    politics 137
    at the *Sun* 131–32, 153, 551
    at the *Sun News-Pictorial* 138–39,
        265, 551
    at the *World* 49
Guardian 52, 84, 485
Gullett, Henry 424, 426–27, 518, 524
The Gun Alley Mystery 254, *255*, 256
Hackett, John Winthrop 268–69, 270
Hackett family 267
Halfey, John 44, 175
Hall, Edward Smith 16–18, 20–23
Hampden-Cloncurry Copper Mines
    Pty Ltd 297–98
Hardy, Charles 347
Hardy, Frank 290
Harmsworth, Alfred *see* Northcliffe,
    Lord
Harmsworth, Harold 89
Harrison, Eric
    ABC and 512–13
    campaigns against 527–29
    elected as Wentworth's MP 527–28
    helps publish the *Daily Mirror* 515
    loyalty to Robert Menzies 536, 540
    as minister for trade and customs
        529
    paper rationing 535
Harrow, Vic 211
Hart, Philip 377, 395, 502, 508
Harvey, Claire 338
Hay, Alexander 39, 230
Hazlehurst, Cameron 507
Hearst, William Randolph
    on crime and scandal coverage 85

newspaper chain 78–80, 88, 103
    politics 79–80, 103, 109–10, 121
Heathfield 251
Henderson, Kingsley
    in the All for Australia League 384
    at the *Argus* 401, 506
    in 'the Group' 371–74
    at the Melbourne Club 401
    on Robert Menzies 509
Henderson, Rupert Albert Geary
    'Rags' *323*
    at AAP 489
    on ANM 492
    at the ANPA 501
    personality 321–22
    price-fixing 340
    on radio 435
    regional papers 325
    at the *Sydney Morning Herald* 319–
        22, 324–25, 478, 500–501
Herald
    1871 takeover 44
    1890 takeover 179
    adoption of 'new journalism' 76
    advertising 94, 173, 262–63, 265,
        277, 304
    The Age and 72
    Alfred Deakin's shares in 185
    attempted merger with the *Sun*
        261–62
    Baillieus and 171, 175, 178–83
    Bert Cook at 106
    bias 1–2, 181–87
    building 99, 245, 263, *264*
    buys the *Evening Mail* 305
    circulation 82, 309, 475, 483
    competition with other papers 137,
        170, 181, 263–64
    David Syme buys and sells 71–73
    delivery vehicles *62*
    design of 52–53, 56
    dominance 207, 304
    fights nationalisation of radio
        413–14
    finances of 181, 188, 206, 236,
        265–66, 315
    grab for exclusive content rights

259–62
Guy Innes appointed editor at 220
helps the *News* 227
HWT develops from 90
illustrations and photography in
  56–57
JE Davidson at 113, 209, 215–16
on John Maynard Keynes 404
on Keith Murdoch 522
Keith Murdoch at 140, 234, 246,
  248–66, 305
merges with *Sun News-Pictorial*
  549
paper production 89, 476
politics 113, 120, 124, 183–87, 192,
  195, 197–98, 200–204, 216, 286,
  355–57, 390, 394–95, 399, 424,
  505
press gallery corps staff 286, 385
pricing of 71, 72–73, 93
printing of 65
radio and 409–11, 416, 424–27,
  430, 437
on Robert Menzies 440, 502–6, 509
Robert Menzies bans from press
  conferences 540
role in leaking James Scullin's
  cables 387–88
subject matter 27, 53, 77, 85, 98,
  252, 263
The Sun and 133–34
Theodore Fink at 175, 178–83,
  185, 198, 216–17
tone of 95, 265
UCS and 259, 484
William Thomas Reay at 215
during WWI 57, 60
Herald and Sportsman Newspapers
  Co. Ltd 175, 179
Herald and Weekly Times *see also*
  3DB Melbourne; 5AD Adelaide;
  Advertiser; Australian Associated
  Press; *Herald*; *Weekly Times*
  advertising 481
  Alfred Deakin's shares in 185
  attempted merger with Sun
    Newspapers 261–62

Baillieus and 182, 206, 221–23
bias 1–2
boycott of 390
building 62, 66, 263, 264
buys 3DB 276
buys and closes the *Argus* 546
buys and closes the *Evening Sun*
  140
buys the *Advertiser* 235–38, 275,
  469
buys the *Courier-Mail* 546
buys the *Daily News* 469
buys the *Mercury* 550
buys the *Register* 235, 274–75
buys the *Telegraph* 552
Collins House and 171
competition with other papers
  312–12
develops from the *Herald* 90
dominance 102, 103, 114, 284, 351
finances of 98, 276, 479–80
Finks at 182, 206, 216–17, 220–22,
  522
formation of the *Courier-Mail* 299,
  302
forms AAP 486
impact on rivals 484
interactions with Hugh Denison
  140, 142–43, 311–12
invests in the *Evening News* 257–61
JE Davidson at 214–15, 220–22
Keith Murdoch at 138–39, 249–50,
  258–59, 266–67, 276, 285, 287,
  302, 305–10, 467–74
Keith Murdoch steps away from
  518
links to Fairfax 312, 321, 324
Lloyd Dumas as managing director
  518
News and 114, 227, 469, 550
News Limited/News Corporation
  and 235–38, 279–83, 285, 287,
  545–46, 549–50, 552–53
opinion of readers 85
paper production 453–54, 460,
  467–75 *see also* Australian
  Newsprint Mills Pty Ltd

politics 196–97, 216, 358–60, 364,
   392–93
profiting from the Depression
   402–3
radio broadcasting 376, 406, 410–
   12, 415–16, 418–19, 432, 436–39,
   442–43, 445–46, 449, 451–52 *see
   also* 3DB Melbourne
staff appointments 305–6
The Sun and 133–34
Sun Newspapers and 138–39
Sun News-Pictorial and 140, 142,
   169–70, 265–67, 312
takes over WAN 547
West Australian and 267, 553
Herald-Sun 549
Hetherington, John 253
Higgins, John 372, 401
Hill, Alfred 77
Hill, Lionel 286, 386
Hill's Life 77
Hobart, Tasmania 232–33
Hobart Town Gazette 14
Hobbs, Joseph Talbot 269
Hoe, Richard 68
Holmes à Court, Robert 553
Holtz, ACC 409, 413, 459
Home 324
Hoover, Herbert 188–89
Hordern, Anthony 332 *see also*
   Anthony Hordern and Sons
Hordern, Mary 332
Hordern, Samuel 332
Hordern family 190
Hoskins, Cecil 328
Hoskins family 203–4
Howard Smith Ltd 203–4, 303
Howe, George 13–15
Howe, Robert 15–16, 22
Hughes, William Morris 'Billy'
   1917 election win 200
   1939 defeat 508
   on Brian Penton 349
   at the *Daily Telegraph* 205
   departure from ALP 192, 199
   expulsion from the Nationalists
      153

formation of the Nationalists
   199–200
friendship with WS Robinson 366
Gerald Mussen and 214, 217
impact on broadcasting 425–26,
   438
Joe Lyons procures position for 396
Keith Murdoch and 196–97, 200–
   202, 245, 247–48, 426
loses prime ministership 205
newspaper support for 120–21,
   135–37, 145, 153, 200, 319, 400
response to the mining industry
   192–96
sentiment against 201–4, 217, 424,
   426
against Stanley Bruce 360
support for conscription 135–37,
   196–97, 200
Hume Broadcasters 443
Hume Pipe Enterprises 443
Hummer 48
Hunter Valley, NSW 441
HWT *see* Herald and Weekly Times

ICI (Imperial Chemical Industries of
   Australia Ltd) 329, 398, 495, 500
Illawara Mercury 325
Independent Cable Service 132
Inglis, KS 422
Innes, Guy 206, 220, 251
International News Service 486, 488
Ipswich, QLD 290
Irving, Terry 362
Isaacs, Victor 53

J and N Tait 410–11, 416
Jackson, Horace Benson 269–71, 474
JB Were & Co
   Argus and 400–401
   Collins House and 373, 398, 498
   Joe Lyons and 375
   Nivison's and 371
   NMLA and 374
JC Williamson 410, 416
John Fairfax & Sons *see* Fairfax Media

John Snow and Co. 302–3
Johnson, Eric 474
Jones, Alan Campbell 169
Jones, Charles Lloyd 412, 429
Jones, David 330, 341
Journal 228

Kalgoorlie, WA 301
Kavanagh, George 44
Kelly, Bowes 495
Kelly, George Daziel 507
Kelvinator 443
Kemp, Charles 38, 40
Kermandie, Tas 462, 467, 470
Kerr, George 226
Kerr, William 28
Kew, Vic 499
Keynes, John Maynard 363, 366, 389,
    403–4
King, Philip Gidley 13
King, Thomas 39
Kirkpatrick, Rod 19, 53
Klug, George 231
Knox, Edward 326, 331
Knox, Edward Ritchie 329
Knox, Errol 147, 506–7, 548
Knox, Robert 372, 381, 384, 396, 398
Knox family 499
Korean War 481

La Boheme 410
La Nauze, Andrew John 42
La Trobe, Charles 28
Labor Daily see *Daily News*
Labor Papers Ltd 48
Labor Party *see also* Beasley, John
    'Jack'; Curtin, John; Evatt, Herbert
    Vere; Fisher, Andrew; Lang, John
    Thomas 'Jack'; Scullin, James;
    Theodore, Edward Granville;
    Watson, Chris
    AAP and 488–90
    The Age on 43, 120, 124
    anti-conscription sentiment 197
    Argus on 546
    Ben Chifley in 483, 494

    Billy Hughes and 135–36, 192–99,
        400
    Canberra Times on 120
    Collins House and 200
    Daily Guardian on 113
    Daily Mail on 291–92
    Daily Mirror on 531–32
    Daily Standard on 292
    Daily Telegraph on 120–21, 349
    EH Macartney and 298
    encourages paper production 477
    on EZ 233
    formation of the *Daily News* 48–50
    George Warnecke and 159
    Herald on 113
    JE Davidson's support for 215
    on Joe Lyons 396
    Joe Lyons defects from 354–58, 400
    John Wren's support for 289,
        291–92
    on Keith Murdoch 272
    Keith Murdoch and 245–46,
        296–97, 445
    Labor Papers Ltd 48
    Mercury on 37
    radio and 427, 449
    RC Packer's links to 347
    response to formation of UAP 391
    splits 378–81
    Sun on 137
    supports paper bounty 460
    Sydney Morning Herald on 36–37,
        317
    Truth supports 527
Lang, John Thomas 'Jack'
    anti-Lang sentiment 49, 347,
        362–63, 378–79
    attacks EG Theodore 300
    commissions report on newspapers
        361
    Daily News supports 334–36, 549
    dismissal 337, 402
    financial policy 363, 368–71, 378
    at the *Labor Daily* 48–49, 92
    nationalisation of radio 414
    opinion of Keith Murdoch 358
    separation from the ALP 379

shareholding bill 336–37
Voltaire Molesworth and 113
Langler, Alfred 269
Latham, Edward 176
Latham, John 380–81, 384, 422, 466
Launceston Advertiser 44
Law, Bonar 247–48
Lawson, HSW 428–29
Leith, Frank 299
Lewis, Essington 496, 501, 517
Lewis, Neil Elliott 458
libel 16–18, 20, 28, 39, 342
Liberal Federation 286
Liberal Party
    formation of new Liberal party 542
    formation of the Nationalist Party
        135
    Joseph Cook in 190
    newspaper support for **118–20,
        122–23**
    radio and 449
    revival of 201
    support for Billy Hughes 199
    support for conscription 197
    WL Baillieu in 187
Lionel Robinson, Clark and Co. 373
Listener In 267, 412
Lloyd, CJ 399, 490, 503
London, UK
    Keith Murdoch in 136, 246–51
    Lord Northcliffe in 89
    money lenders in 362–63
    partisanship of newspapers in 36
    printing of Australian newspapers
        in 19
Louat, Frank 526
Loughlin, John 358
Lovekin, Arthur 455
Lyons, Enid 355, 393
Lyons, Joseph Aloysius 'Joe' 357
    1931 election win 394–95
    as acting treasurer 367–70, 375–77
    anti-Lang sentiment 402
    broadcasting bill 407–8
    contacts 372–73
    death 408, 507
    encourages paper production 458–

59, 462–63, 466–68, 476
    financial policy 396–97
    problems with leadership 501
    radio and 419, 422–23, 426,
        429–30, 432, 436–37, 440–41, 447,
        449–51
    radio station ownership under **450**
    repays supporters 272, 395–96,
        432, 451
    response to BHP buying AIS 497
    response to formation of UAP 391
    Robert Menzies and 501–2
    role in leaking James Scullin's
        cables 387–88
    separation from the ALP 354,
        378–79, 381–83, 386–87
    support for 114, 355–57, 381–85,
        392–95, 396–97, 400, 401–2, 489
    turn against 355–56, 397–400, 503

Macartney, Edward Henry 294,
    296–98
Macartney, James 273, 547
Macdonell House 48, 160
Macfaull, Charles 19
Macintyre, Stuart 517
Mackinnon, Lauchlan 29, 401, 506–7
Macquarie Network 446
Mail 232–33, 281
Major Network 446
Malvern, Vic 244–45
Mansfield, Ralph 38
Maple's 290
Marconi Wireless Telegraph Company
    130
Marshalls store 274
Martin, AW 372–73
Massina, Alfred Henry 175, 180
Massy-Greene, Walter 217, 396, 472
Mayer, Henry 77, 92
McCall, William 438–40, 526
McCay, Adam 153
McGrath, G 282
McKay, Claude 101, 144–45, 150
McKinley, James 179
McLachlan, Alexander 167, 322, 438,

443, 445
McLeay, George 514–15
McLoughlin, Eric 504, 534–35
McMahon, William 40, 347, 497
McMullin, Ross 46
McNicoll, David 121, 339
McQueen, Humphrey 272, 354
Mechanics' Institutes 24, *24*, 42
Melba, Nellie 263, 410–11
Melbourne, Vic *see also* The Gun
  Alley Mystery
  Baillieus' mansions in 250–51
  JE Davidson in 214
  land boom 172–73, 175–77
  News Limited/News Corporation
    run from 231
  newspaper market 313
  price fixing in 92–93
  Robert Menzies' focus on 499
  suburbs 251
Melbourne Advertiser 44
Melbourne Agreement 367–69, 394
Melbourne Club 401, 506, 509
Melbourne Evening Star 304–5
Melbourne Press Bond 214–15
Melbourne Stadium 411
Melbourne Trades Hall Council 390
Menzies, James 496–97
Menzies, Robert *510*
  The Age on 43
  becomes PM 508, 542
  becomes UAP's deputy 440
  Daily Telegraph on 349
  on Eric Harrison 536
  Eric McLoughlin and 534–35
  financial policy 389
  focus on Victoria 499
  formation of Liberal Party 542
  Frank Packer's support for 347
  friendships with journalists 503–5
  in 'the Group' 371–74, 376, 495
  institutes industrial awards for
    journalists 504
  Joe Alexander and 502
  Joe Lyons and 501–2
  on journalists 504
  Keith Murdoch and 399, 438, 440,

494, 502–10, 517–18, 523–25, 542
  licence-granting 166, 512
  links to BHP 495–98
  in the National Reliance
    Investment Trust 374
  on the press 3, 504
  press criticism of 120, 494, 525–27,
    534–40
  radio and 414–15, 417, 422, 441,
    448–49
  reduces press conferences 539
  resignation 494, 505–6, 540
  returns as PM 528
  revokes the *Daily Mirror*'s licence
    515
  Warwick Fairfax and 542
  writes for the *Argus* 401
  during WWII 517
Mercantile Bank 179
Mercury
  adherence to fourth estate concept
    35, 50
  anti-ABC sentiment 407
  in the APA 485
  biography of 550
  on colour printing 80
  fights nationalisation of radio
    413–14
  HWT buys 550
  owner 40
  paper production and 460, 476
  politics 37, 50, 364, 394, 458
  pricing of 73, 75
  strike 45
  support for EZ 233
Metal Manufacturers 495–96
Meudell, George 306
Mills, Beryl 146
Mills, Peggy 235
Milner, Alfred 248
Miners' Federation 48
Miss Australia contest 146
Molesworth, Voltaire 113, 155
Moloney, James 185
Monitor 16, 20–21, 26
Monopolies and Mergers Commission
  104–5

Moodie, John 179
Moore, Thompson 181
Morning Journal 78–80
Morning Post 267
Moses, Charles 446, 448
Mount Cuthbert Company 298
Mount Elliott mines 297–98
Mount Isa 334
Mount Lyell 207
Mount Morgan 297–98
Mount Morgan Gold Mining
   Company 297–98
Mungana affair 300, 334, 366
Munro, Donald 172–73, 175, 177
Munro, James 173, 176, 184
Munro and Baillieu (company) 172–
   73, 175–78
Murdoch, Elisabeth 525
Murdoch, Keith *243, 357*
   AAP and 429, 453–54, 485–87, 489
   at the *Advertiser* 276, 280–85
   at the *Age* 133, 244–45
   in the AJA 215
   ALP on 445
   at ANM 491–92
   anti-censorship crusade 542
   anti-Lang sentiment 402
   against appeasement 500
   appointment to UCS 136
   Billy Hughes and 196–97, 200–202,
      245, 247–48, 426
   buys News Limited/News
      Corporation 279–80
   buys the *Advertiser* 275
   buys the *Register* 235, 274–75
   buys the *West Australian* 234,
      267–69
   cedes control of the *West Australian*
      272–73
   closes the *Register* 276
   controls the *News* 281–83
   at the *Courier-Mail* 298–99, 303–4
   creation of the *Courier-Mail* 278,
      288–89, 292–94, 296–97, 302
   on the *Daily Mirror* 514
   at the Department of Information
      517–25

   dislike for Frank Packer 341
   early life and family 242–46
   EG Theodore and 377, 389
   in Egypt 246
   failed bids 339
   fights for subsidies 34
   financial policy 390–91
   in 'the Group' 372, 381–88
   at the *Herald* 137–38, 140, 182, 234,
      236, 241, 246, 248–66, 286, 305,
      355–56, 409, 476, 502–3
   HWT and 85, 102, 170, 206, 208,
      237, 241, 249–50, 258–62, 266–67,
      273, 276, 280–83, 285–86, 287,
      302, 304–12, 411, 467–74, 518
   illness 307
   impact on rivals 484
   invests in the *Daily Mail* 274
   invests in the *Evening News*
      257–61
   on James Scullin 377
   JE Davidson and 234–35, 238
   Joe Lyons and 376, 380–88, 392–99,
      408, 419, 436–37, 501–2, 505
   John Maynard Keynes and 404
   listens to the ABC 449
   in London 246–51
   Lord Northcliffe and 82, 242, 247,
      252–64, 275, 358, 468
   move from ANPA to Australian
      Newspapers Council 482–83
   at the *News* 278
   at News Limited/News Corporation
      235, 237, 280–83, 285, 287
   Otto Niemeyer and 367
   paper production 453–54, 467–74,
      476, 479, 482
   on paper rationing 483
   personality and motivation 6, 134,
      242–44
   politics 121, 242, 245–46, 272, 286–
      87, 298, 354–58, 360, 364, 375
   public image of 240–41
   RA Parkhill and 438
   radio and 409, 419, 423–27, 432,
      435–37, 446–47
   on readers 85

Robert Menzies and 399, 438, 440, 494, 502–10, 517–18, 523–25, 542
role in leaking James Scullin's cables 387–88
sending money overseas 403
splitting the ALP 400
strategy 278–79, 286
at the *Sun* 133, 245–46, 248–49
at the *Sun News-Pictorial* 265–66
support for conscription 196–98, 248
on the *Sydney Morning Herald* 324
on Sydney newspapers 313–14
tone of newspapers 95
UAP promotion in the *News* 114
at the UCS 246–47
at WAN 267–69, 271
wealth 402
will of 165
at the *World* 246
Murdoch, Patrick 197, 243–44
Murdoch, Rupert
acquires HWT 311, 312, 543, 545
birth of 381
buys the *Daily Mirror* 547
buys the *Daily Telegraph* 548
Keith Murdoch and 279, 287, 302, 313
at the *News* 550
politics 121, 543
public image of 240
Murphy, Frank 85
Murray, Robert 90, 115
Musgrove's Ltd 433 *see also* WA Broadcasters Ltd
Mussen, Gerald
at Collins House 455, 457–58
friendships 214
loss of newspapers 469–70
managing unrest 223–24
at News Limited 209–10, 217–18, 226, 231, 455
paper production 455, 457–58, 461–63, 466–72
reconciles Billy Hughes and Collins House 193
Myer 263, 274, 313, 434

Myer, Sidney 262, 434
Myer family 190
Nagrom Syndicate 297
Nathan, Benjamin 290–91, 292, 296
National Bank of Australasia (NAB) 294, 298, 329–31, 369, 491, 495
National Labor 199
National Library 276, 357
National Metal and Chemical Bank Ltd 462
National Mutual Life Association of Australasia (NMLA) 372, 374, 398, 429
National Reliance Investment Trust 374
National Trustee 329
National Union
companies linked to 372, 495
conflict with the Consultative Council of Sydney 499
function of 372
Joe Lyons and 381, 395–96, 398, 502
Robert Menzies and 509
with UAP 385, 429
Nationalist Party 113, 371, 380 *see also* Bruce, Stanley; Hughes, William Morris 'Billy'; National Union; United Australia Party
'New Deal' 103
New Guard 347, 378–79
New Guinea 299
'new journalism'
adoption of 91
early elements of 77
JE Davidson's adherence to 113, 215, 228
Keith Murdoch adopts 82
at the *Sun* 132
tenets of 76
in the UK 81–82
in the US 78–81
New South Wales 31–32, 203, 214, 313, 412
New South Wales Advertiser 13–14
New South Wales Broadcasting Company Ltd 416

New South Wales Polo Association 332
New South Wales Vindicator 26
New York American 78–80
New York Times 81, 484
New York, US 208
Newcastle, NSW 496
Newcastle Sun (formerly *Northern Times*) 137
News (Adelaide)
    the *Advertiser* and 236
    bias 229
    biography of 550
    closes 550
    editor-in-chief 285
    finances of 232–34
    HWT acquires 278–83, 469
    launch of 101, 210, 227–28
    'new journalism' 228
    News Corporation develops from 90
    politics 113–14
    pricing of 228
    Rupert Murdoch at 550
    self-description 239
    staff *212–13*
    subject matter 95, 228–29, 235
News (Hobart) 233
News Limited (later News Corporation) *see also* Australian Newsprint Mills Pty Ltd
    acquires the HWT 311, 545–46, 549–50
    buys the *Daily News* 233
    buys the *Mail* 232–33
    Colin Fraser invests in 232
    Collins House and 208, 222–27, 229–32, 236–39, 272–73
    develops from the *News* 90
    dominance 274, 543, 553
    fights nationalisation of radio 413
    finances of 235–37, 463
    formation of 209–10, 217–18, 235
    Harold Burston at 285
    HWT acquires 236–37, 278–83, 287, 469–70
    Keith Murdoch buys 550
    radio broadcasting 442–44, 452

    wage cuts 270
News Survey 519
Newspaper News 107, 156, 317, 346, 348
Newspaper Proprietors Association 314
newspapers *see also* advertising; freedom of the press; 'new journalism'; penny newspapers; printing
    news on the front page **53**
    penny newspapers 69–76, **72**, 92–93
    photography in 56–57, 94, 252
    politics *see* politics
    size 82, **83**, 84 *see also* paper rationing
newsprint... *see* paper...
Newton, Maxwell 321–22
Nichols, George 23, 40
Niemeyer, Otto 367, 370, 389–90
Nivison, Robert 362–63, 371
Nivison and Co. 362–63, 373
Noble, William 428
Nolan, Sybil 120, 372, 506
Norris, Charles 372, 374, 396
North Broken Hill 462, 473
Northcliffe, Lord
    agreements with other newspapers 259–62
    Ambrose Pratt and 372
    at the *Daily Mail* 52, 84, 411
    death 262
    illness 256, 260–62
    Keith Murdoch and 82, 242, 247, 252–64, 275, 358, 468
    launches *Daily Mail* 78, 81–82
    newspaper chain expansion 89
    paper production 87, 89
    personality 88
    on pictorial papers 139
    politics 109–10
    on power 2
    The Times cable system 132–33
Norton, Ezra
    AAP and 488
    conflict with Frank Packer 344, 511–14, 534
    control of Truth and Sportsman Ltd 511

end of Associated Newspapers 543
Eric Baume on 531
family 342–43
launches the *Daily Mirror* 166–67,
    513–15, 529
paper production and 476, 482, 492
personality 511, 531
politics 531–32
at the *Truth* 343–44
Norton, John 342–43, 351
Nott, LW 526

Observer 89
Ogilvie, Albert 474
Olsen, Otto *510*
Orchard, RB 430

P&O 500
Packer, Douglas Frank Hewson *see*
    Packer, Frank
Packer, Ethel Maud *346*
Packer, Frank *533*
    at the AAP 486–88
    at the ACP 337–39
    at the ANC 340–41
    at Associated Newspapers 150,
        157–59
    in the Australian Jockey Club 291
    buys and closes the *Daily News* 49
    buys the *World* 159
    conflict with Ezra Norton 344,
        511–14, 534
    conflict with Hugh Denison 341
    with Consolidated Press 163–64,
        168, 339, 340
    at the *Daily Telegraph* 49, 117,
        120–21, 322, 337, 340
    on the Denisons 169
    EG Theodore and 335–37, 339,
        405, 548
    fights shareholding bill 336–37
    inheritance 332–33
    invests in Truth and Sportsman
        Ltd 511
    launches the *Sunday Telegraph*
        344–45

marriage 332, 339
mining interests 300–301, 333, 336
move from ANPA to Australian
    Newspapers Council 482–83
on paper production 476, 481–82
on paper rationing 483
personality 6, 337–39, 511
politics 117, 120–21, 347, 349–50,
    526, 542
response to *ABC Weekly* 349
and the *Sunday Telegraph* 338
with Sydney Newspapers 158–62,
    163
TV licence 543
and *Women's Weekly* 340
work for *Daily Guardian* 145–46
Packer, Gretel 332
Packer, Kerry 339
Packer, Robert Clyde
    at Associated Newspapers 155–58
    death and will 162, 165, 332–33
    EG Theodore and 405
    formation of Consolidated Press
        335
    infidelity 339
    launches and runs *Smith's Weekly*
        144–46
    launches the *Daily Guardian*
        101
    politics 336, 347, 378
    at the *Sun* 159–60
    wealth 402
Packer family 331–33, 336
Page, Earle 205, 398, 508–9
paper bounties and tariffs 459–61,
    463, 466, 475
Paper Makers Ltd 463, 466, 468–69,
    470–72, 474
paper prices 481–82
paper production 453–55, *456,*
    457–59, 461–62, *464–65 see also*
    Canberra Activities Pty Ltd;
    Derwent Valley Paper Company;
    Paper Makers Ltd; Tasmanian Paper
    Pty Ltd
paper rationing 477–80, 481–83,
    512–13, 535–38

Parkes, Henry 26–27, 40
Parkhill, Robert Archdale 34, 438–40, 445, 486
Parliamentary Labor Party 286
Parramatta Gaol 17
Pearce, George 395, 402
Pearl, Cyril 344, 347
Pearson, Arthur 52
Penfold's Wines 511
penny newspapers 69–76, **72**, 92–93
Penton, Brian 347, 349, 540
Pentridge gaol 444
People's Advocate 26
Perkins, Kevin 356
Perpetual Trustee Company 328–29, 332, 369, 499
Perth, WA 19, 207–8, 214, 233
Perth Gazette 19
Petersen, Neville 431
photography in newspapers 56–57, 94, 252
Picard, Robert G 1
Pickard, Victor 104
Pine Hills, Vic 211
politics *see also* conservatism; *names of specific parties*
  newspaper owners as politicians 40–43
  newspapers' partisanship **118–19**, **122–23**
popularisation 84–86 *see also* 'new journalism'
Port Augusta Dispatch 214
Port Kembla, NSW 203–5
Port Phillip Herald see *Herald*
Port Phillip Patriot 44
Port Pirie, SA
  Depression affects 283
  mining at 194, 205–6, 218, 224, 231
  radio in 284, 432
Postmaster-General's Department (PMG) 417, 419, 423–24, 433, 436–37, 441
Power Without Glory 290
Pratt, Ambrose 372–73
Premiers' Plan 390–91, 394, 403–4, 433
Price, Archibald Grenfell 384, 393, 396

Price, John Lloyd 386
Prince of Wales 342
printing 62–65, *66–67*, 68–69, 99 *see also* colour printing
Printing Industry Employees Union (PIEU) 106, 270, 282, 345
propaganda *see* Department of Information
Pulitzer, Joseph 78–80, 109–10

Queale, William 443
Queensland 290–91, 296–97, 300, 326, 327 *see also* Mungana affair
Queensland Newspapers Pty Ltd 288–89, 293–94, 296, 302 *see also* Australian Newsprint Mills Pty Ltd; *Courier-Mail*
Queensland Trustees Limited 294

R Nivison and Co. 362–63, 373
racism 145, 229, 252, 326, 333, 342
radio *420 see also* 2BL; Broadcasting Company of Australia
  advertising 433–34, 445–46
  first transmission 408
  Hugh Denison and 412–13
  HWT's interest in 393, 406, 410–12
  limitations of 412
  nationalisation of 406–8, 413–15, 417–18 *see also* ABC; Australian Broadcasting Company
  policy framework regarding 409–10, 412–15, 436–39, **437**
  popularity of 445
  separation of news from 451–52
  sports coverage 419–21, 433
  station ownership under Joe Lyons **450**
  during WWII 448
Radio Silver City 442–44
reading rooms 24, *24*
Reay, William Thomas 185, 215
Recorder 209, 221–23, 232, 281, 283–84
Redmond, George 153
Reeve, George J 322
Register

biography of 550
cable system 132
closes 282, 550
finances of 275
HWT syndicate buys 235, 275
politics 39, 46
on postage 33
printing of 65
staff 275
subject matter 275
Reid, Alan 385
Reid, George 41
Reuters 484, 487, 489
Ricketson, Staniforth
  in the All for Australia League 384
  Argus and 400–401, 441
  becomes chairman of JB Were 401
  in 'the Group' 371–74, 376, 381
  on Keith Murdoch 358
  at the Melbourne Club 401
  political contacts 371–74, 376, 381,
    506
Riddell, Lord 314
Rio Tinto 195
Riordan, David 427
Risdon, Tas 195, 205, 232–33
Riverina Movement 347
Robb, John 179
Robinson, Arthur 187, 230, 389
Robinson, Gerald 389
Robinson, Lionel 297
Robinson, Margaret 190
Robinson, William Sydney
  at *The Age* 184
  buys the *West Australian* 234,
    267–69
  at Collins House 308
  at the *Courier-Mail* 299
  E Allnutt and 230
  EG Theodore and 300–301, 334,
    364, 366, 389
  establishes WMC 207
  financial policy 389–90
  Gerald Mussen and 214, 217
  Joe Lyons and 397
  Keith Murdoch and 196, 202, 244,
    248, 250, 253, 267, 279, 299, 366

links to British finance 373
mining interests 189, 194–95, 205,
  221, 297–98, 309, 334, 336
and News Limited/News
  Corporation 231
personality 366
politics 196, 200, 205, 271–72, 461,
  500
on radio 444
at WAN 267–73
Robinson's Zinc Corporation 309
Roosevelt, Franklin Delano 103–4,
  115
Ross, Colin 254, *255*, 256
Rothermere, Viscount 89
Royal Charters 428
Royal Commissions
  on corruption 300
  on deflation 403
  on Kerry Packer's alleged crimes
    339
  on the Mungana affair 366
  on the press 104–5
  on racing 293
  on radio 412–15, 417
  on the sugar industry 327
Rugby, UK 413
Rural Press Ltd 546
Russell Falls River, Tas 468
Ryan, TJ 298

Samuel Bennett Ltd 98, 147, 548
San Francisco Examiner 78
Satirist 77
Savage Club 372–73, 401
Sayers, CE 41
Scripps, Edward Willis (Wyllis) 87–
  88, 103, 110, 121, 214
Scripps, James E 214
Scullin, James
  1929 election win 360–61
  effect of the ALP splintering on
    379
  financial policy 362–64, *365*, 366–
    70, 373, 376–78, 390–91, 463, 466
  'the Group' vs 371–77

Joe Lyons condemns 355
leaked cables of 387
mining subsidy 273
press relationship with 358–59, 380
radio and 406–7, 422–23
views on Robert Gibson 375
sedition 342
Serle, Geoffrey 271
Seven West Media 553
sexism 6, 145, 318, 342
Seymour-Ure, Colin 115
Shackell, EH and HL 231
Shakespeare family 546
Sharpe, JB 292
Sherlock, Harold Herbert 222
Sherlock and Daniels (company) 463
size of newspapers 82, **83**, 84 *see also*
   paper rationing
'The Slaughter in Daisy Wood' 248
Smethurst, John 219, 225, 235
Smith, Charles Patrick 269–71
Smith, Hugh Alexander McClure 323
Smith, James Joynton
   horseracing 144, 291
   launches *Smith's Weekly* 144–45
   launches the *Daily Guardian* 101,
      145
   launches the *Sunday Guardian* 150
   radio broadcasting 409–10
   sale of *Guardians* 150, 155, 336
Smith's Newspapers 150–51, 336,
   409, 412
Smith's Weekly
   biography of 551
   closes 551
   on Ezra Norton and Frank Packer's
      conflict 344
   on Gerald Mussen 455
   on Herbert Campbell Jones 167
   on Keith Murdoch 248, 249, 278
   launch of 144–45
   launches the *Daily Guardian* 92,
      145
   on paper production 459
   politics 49, 145, 357, 507
   on radio 416, 418
   on the *Sydney Morning Herald* 323,

399
   tone of 95, 145, 551
Snow, Sydney
   at Broken Hill South 402
   Eric Harrison and 512
   Hugh Denison and 152, 154–55,
      157
   knighthood 396
   launch of the *Daily Mirror* 167
   supports Joe Lyons 401
Society of Melbourne Brewers 182
Somerset, Henry 463
Souter, Gavin 503
South Australia 31, 206–7, 214, 231
South Australian Advertiser see
   Advertiser
South Australian Brewing Company
   230
*South Australian Gazette and Colonial
   Register* 19
South Australian Register 23
South Sea Islands 326, 333
Southern Australian 23
Spooner, Eric 526
Sporting Globe 267
sports coverage
   Formguide 490
   in papers 54, 291, 549
   on the radio 411, 419–20, 433
Sportsman 342
Spowers, Allan 400–401, 506–7
Stadiums Ltd 291
Staff News 510
Stamp Duty Act 16
Standing Committee on Broadcasting
   448
Star 44
Star and Working Man's Guardian 26
Statesman (UK) 15
Stephens, JF 12
Stephens, John 39, 44
Stevens, Bertram 404, 526
Stewart, Alexander 231, 463
Stewart, Fred H 156, 425–26
strikes 45, 106, 219, 224, 333–34
Stuart, Athol Hugh 320–21, 471, 486
Styx River, Tas 467–68, 473

suffrage 19, 21, 26–27, 40, 42, 120
Sun (formerly *Australian Star*)
  advertising 111, 131–32, 154, 258,
    551
  Associated Newspapers develops
    from 90
  attempted merger with the *Herald*
    261–62
  biography of 551
  building 99, *148–49*
  cable system 132–34
  circulation 137, 147, 154, 532
  closes 551
  competition with other papers 142,
    166–67, 512, 532–33
  deal with Sydney Newspapers Ltd
    159–60
  design of 54–55, 158, 529, 551
  dominance 513
  effect of the Depression on 361
  Herbert Campbell Jones at 131,
    133–34, 136, 152–53, 166–67,
    259–61
  Hugh Denison and 128, 130–31
  HWT and 138–39, 142, 311
  Keith Murdoch at 133, 245–46,
    248–49, 260
  launch of 551
  Montague Grover at 131–32, 153,
    551
  name change 54
  'new journalism' 76
  paper production 89, *456*
  politics 111–12, 117, 135–37, 153,
    200, 418, 506
  pricing of 92, 477
  radio and 413, 437
  role in leaking James Scullin's
    cables 387–88
  size 101
  subject matter 55, 98
  tone of 54–55
  UCS and 259–62, 484
  during WWI 57–58, 60
Sun (New York) 69, 78
Sun Newspapers
  finances of 61, 98

  Herbert Campbell Jones at 259–61
  HWT and 138–39, 261–62
  launch of 130–31
  merging with the *Daily Telegraph*
    146
  politics 137
  radio broadcasting 407, 412, 416,
    446
Sun News-Pictorial
  absorbs the *Morning Post* 267
  biography of 551–52
  circulation 309, 483, 552
  competition with other papers 263,
    313
  design of 551
  finances of 276
  under the HWT 140, 142, 169–70,
    265–67, 312, 552
  inspires *Daily Mirror* 529
  inspires the *Daily Guardian* 145,
    547
  launch of 82, 91, 93, 139–40, 141
  merges with the *Herald* 549
  reports on John Butters 1
  supports Joe Lyons 394
Sunday Guardian 150–55, 157
Sunday Pictorial 155
Sunday Sun
  comic strips 92
  competition with other papers 151
  design of 158
  merges with *Sunday Guardian*
    157–58
  on the MP wage increase 397
  staff 144, 161
  Sunday Telegraph on 346
Sunday Telegraph
  advertising *348*
  colour printing 345
  comic strips 322, 345
  competition with other papers 512
  finances of 513–14
  launch of 344–45, 346, *346*
  subject matter 345
  working conditions at 338
Sunday Times 271
Surrey Hills, Tas 472

Sydney, NSW
  delivery trains 33
  libel in 18
  newspaper market 313
  politics 201, 499, 528
  price fixing in 92–93
Sydney Gazette 13–15
Sydney Mail 28, 32, 57, 314, 325
Sydney Morning Chronicle 38
Sydney Morning Herald (formerly
  Sydney Herald)
  AANA and 108
  advertising 74, 316, 341, 478,
    537–38
  AH Stuart at 320–21
  ANM and 492
  in the ANPA 500–501
  APA and 484–86
  bias 204, 326–27, 330
  biography of 552
  Brian Penton at 349
  building *28, 99, 100*
  cable system 132
  circulation 146, 165, 337, 483
  competition with other papers 538
  vs the *Daily Mirror* 513
  design of 56, 318, 323, 325
  effect of the Depression on 361
  Fairfax loses 552
  finances of 315–16, 536, 538–39
  as focus of Fairfax 314, 325
  foundation of 44
  Hugh Denison considers buying
    152
  isolation from other papers 324
  on Keith Murdoch 521–24
  launches *Women's Supplement*
    323–24
  leak regarding 538–39
  Montague Grover at 131
  opinions on 314–15, 318–19, 324,
    396
  paper production and 89, 460,
    476–79
  penny newspapers and 70–71
  photography in 57, 323
  politics 12, 25–27, 35–37, 40, 46,

    115, 117, 120, 204, 316–19, 364,
    379, 393, 397, 399–400, 402, 499
  postage of 32–33
  pricing of 70–71, 73–74, 92, 340,
    477
  printing of 63–65, 68–69
  racism of 326–27
  radio and 418, 423, 451
  RAG Henderson at 319–22
  relationship with AGL 38
  Robert Menzies and 494, 503–4,
    506, 509, 525–27, 534–37
  size 84, 478, 552
  Smith's Weekly on 323
  sports coverage 56
  strikes and 45, 334
  subject matter 63–64, 323, 537
  tone of 73–74, 95
  Warwick Fairfax at 316, 322, 402
  on William Randolph Hearst 80
  women's page 56
  during WWI 59
  on 'yellow journalism' 79
Sydney Newspapers Ltd 159–61, 163
Sydney Snow Ltd 375
Sydney Sportsman 511
Sydney Town Hall 476
Sydney Turf Club 291
Sydney University 430
Syme, David
  at *The Age* 41–42, 68, 71–72,
    184–85, 244
  buys the *Herald* 71–72
  contacts 184–85, 197
  death 545
  hires Keith Murdoch 244
  politics 41–42
Syme, Ebenezer 42
Syme, Geoffrey 43, 341, 496, 503
Syme, Herbert 470
Syme family 329, 497–98

Table Talk 173, 178–79, 267
tabloids, increase in 82, **83**, 84
Talbot, Reginald 66
Tariff Board 459, 461, 475–76

Tasmania
  censorship in 14, 16–17
  mining interests in 195, 207
  paper production in 458–60, 462–
    63, 466–68, 473–75, 491–92
  politics in 40
Tasmanian Paper Pty Ltd 462–63,
  466–67, 470–72
Telefunken company 130
Telegraph (Adelaide) 71
Telegraph (Brisbane)
  in the APA 485
  biography of 552–53
  design of 552
  on Keith Murdoch 297
  launch of 44
  politics 364, 393
telegraph and telephone use 33–34,
  61–62, 129–30 *see also* Australian
  Associated Press; United Cable
  Service
television 451–52, 543
Teulon, JS 470–71
Thackaringa Station, NSW 211
Theodore, Edward Granville *346*
  4QG 414
  buys and closes the *World* 159–60
  with Consolidated Press 163–64,
    168, 335, 339
  financial policy 363–64, *365*, 366,
    369, 389
  John Wren and 291, 292, 299–300,
    334
  JT Lang and 334–37
  legacy 404
  loses seat 394
  mining interests 300–301, 333–35
  move from ANPA to Australian
    Newspapers Council 482–83
  Norman Cowper and 350
  in the papers 358
  political career 333–34, 367,
    376–78
  teams up wth Frank Packer
    159–62, 335
  with Sydney Newspapers 159–60,
    163

views on Robert Gibson 375
WS Robinson and 334, 364, 366,
  389
Thomas, Alan 429–30
Threlfall, Martyn 382, 396
Thynne, AJ 296
Thynne and Macartney (company)
  294, 296, 298
Tiffen, Rodney 435, 543
The Times
  building 247
  cable system 57, 132–34, 484–85
  delivery of 31, 33
  design of 52
  Herbert Campbell Jones at 166
  Lord Northcliffe buys 89
  political beginnings 36
  printing of 64
  size 84
Tirtschke, Alma 254
Toorak, Vic 251, 499
Tout, Frederick 156
trade unions *see also* Australian
  Journalists' Association; Australian
  Worker's Union; Printing Industry
  Employees Union; strikes
  Amalgamated Workers Association
    333
  boycott HWT publications 390
  miners' unions 219–20, 223–26,
    270
  press as a weapon against 12
A Treatise on Money 366
trial by media 256
Trustees Executors & Agency Co. 329,
  369
Truth
  competition with other papers 512,
    515
  expansion of 351
  on Frank Packer 344, 533–34
  on the *Herald* 277
  on Herbert Campbell Jones 260
  on Keith Murdoch 514
  paper production 462
  politics 49, 527
  on the sale of the *Guardians* 151

staff 166–67
subject matter 77, 342–44, 511
    Sunday Telegraph on 346
Truth and Sportsman Pty Ltd 167,
    476, 511–12
Tudor, Frank 187
Turner, GW 203
Twopenny, Richard 51, 124, 318

UK *see* Britain
Union Club 509, 527
Union Trustee Company 298, 329,
    369, 374
unions *see* trade unions
United Australia Party (UAP) *see
    also* Bruce, Stanley; Consultative
    Council of Sydney; National Union
    1931 election win 394–95
    creation of 385
    end of 542
    funds 372
    Joe Lyons in 354–58, 392–99,
        401–2, 423–27, 489
    links to ABC 429–30
    plots against Menzies 539
    problems in 501
    radio policy 423–27, 438
    RC Packer's links to 347
    reconciles with the Country Party
        512–13
    replaces parliamentary members
        526–27
    Sydney Snow in 167
    Voltaire Molesworth in 113
    William Queale and 443
United Cable Service (UCS)
    creation of 57, 60, 133–34
    formation of AAP 484–86
    Herbert Campbell Jones at 166–67,
        259–61
    Keith Murdoch at 136, 196, 246–
        47, 259–61
    Lloyd Dumas as head 276
    members of 311
    Sun-Herald agreement 57, 133–34,
        259–61
United Kingdom *see* Britain

United Press (UP) 88, 488
United States
    comic printing in 345
    JE Davidson in 214
    'new journalism' in 78
    newspaper chains in 87–88, 102–3
    newspaper design in 52
    penny newspapers in 69
    politics of newspapers in 36, 115
    postage in 31–32
    radio in 428–29, 434
    regulation of newspapers in
        103–4

Van Diemen's Land Company 459
Versailles Conference 201
Victoria 40, 203–4, 312–13, 412
Victoria, Queen 342
The Victorian Four 41
Victorian Newspaper Company 180
Victorian Radio Association 422

WA Broadcasters Ltd 433, 438–39, 445
Waddell, Graham 156, 473, 514–15
Wainwright, WE 220
Wainwright, William 231
Walker, RB
    on the ABC 434
    on the *Daily Mirror* 532
    on Hugh Denison 155
    on left-wing papers 25
    on newspaper postage 32
    on the *Sunday Telegraph* 347
    on the *Sydney Morning Herald* 318
Wall Street crash *see* Great Depression
Wallace, RS 430
'Wally and the Major' comic 304
Walstab, George 175
Ward, Eddie 379
Wardell, Robert 14–16, 19, 23
Warnecke, George 159, 161, 164, 337,
    340
Warnecke, Nora 161
Waters, FJ 296
Waters, Jack 305
Watson, Chris 46, 48

Watt, William Alexander
  in ANA 185
  Billy Hughes and 197, 199–200,
    201, 204
  formation of the Nationalists
    199–200
  links to Collins House 186–87,
    200–01
WD & HO Wills 511
Weekly Dispatch 89
Weekly Times 179–81
Wentworth, Charles 14–16, 19, 21–22
Wentworth, William 291
West Australian
  bias 268, 272–73
  biography of 553
  political reporting 272
  radio broadcasting 284–85
  staff 214, 269–73, 281
  WAN buys 267–68
  working conditions 270
West Australian Newspapers Limited
  (WAN) *see also* Australian
  Newsprint Mills Pty Ltd; WA
  Broadcasters Ltd
  buys the *Daily News* 547
  buys the *West Australian* 267–68
  formation of 267
  HWT buys 547
  links to Collins House 269,
    272–73, 433
  mining interventions 272–73
  staff 269–73, 281
  wage cuts 270
Western Australia 207, 214, 270–71,
  273, 372
Western Australian Journal 19
Western Mining Corporation (WMC)
  207, 270, 301
Westpac *see* Bank of New South Wales
Westralian Worker 270
Wheeler, Albert Fordyce 131–32, 152,
  158
White, Norman 289, 292, 294
White Australia policy 252, 326
Whitington, RS 337
Whyalla, SA 500

Williams, John 'Jack' 85, 285–86
Willis, EH 384
Wilson, Danby and Giddy 302–3
Wilson, Edward 28–29
Wilson and Mackinnon 400
Winter, Samuel Vincent 175, 179, 185
Wireless Weekly 412
Wise, Arthur 250, 259
Withers, Eugenia Marion 288, 294,
  296
WL Baillieu & Co 176
WMC (Western Mining Corporation)
  207
women *see* sexism
Women's Supplement 324
Women's Weekly see *Australian
  Women's Weekly*
Woolworths 434
Worker 47–48, 297
Workers Industrial Union (WIU)
  443–45
World 78–81, 103, 159–60, 246
World War I *see also* conscription
  Ambrose Pratt in 372
  AMP during 327
  effect on the mining industry 192,
    223, 496
  Gallipoli letter 246–47
  impact on Perpetual Trustee
    Company 329
  newsprint production during
    453–55
  sales boom 57–62
  war debts 368–71, 373, 374–78
World War II *see also* Department of
  Information; paper rationing
  appeasement policy 499–500
  Daily Mirror and 529, *530*, 531–34
  Herald on 475
  Robert Menzies during 509, 517
  Truth on 344
  WS Robinson during 271–72
Wren, Ellen 301
Wren, John *295*
  at the *Courier-Mail* 288–89, 293–
    94, 296, 298–99, 303–4
  criminal activity 274, 290–91

at the *Daily Mail* 274, 291–94, 302
mining interests 300–301, 334,
   336, 372
politics 289, 291–92, 298–300
racecourses 290–93, 296

Yelland, Horace 283–84, 314
'yellow journalism' 79, 95
Young Nationalist Organisation 371
Younger, RM 265, 308, 524–25
Yule, Peter 177, 187, 193, 200, 224, 457

Zig Zag Paper Pty Ltd 308
Zinc Corporation Limited 189, 195,
   302, 375
Zwar, Desmond 236, 303